GOVERNMENT
IN AMERICA

People, Politics, and Policy

GOVERNMENT IN AMERICA
People, Politics, and Policy

Third Edition

Robert L. Lineberry
University of Kansas

Little, Brown and Company
Boston   Toronto

Library of Congress Cataloging in Publication Data

Lineberry, Robert L.
　　Government in America.

　　Includes bibliographies and index.
　　1. United States—Politics and government.
I. Title.
JK274.L573 1986　　　　320.973　　　　85–18143
ISBN 0–316–52674–6

Library of Congress Catalog Card No. 85–18143

ISBN 0-316-52674-6

9　　8　　7　　6　　5　　4　　3　　2

MU

Published simultaneously in Canada
by Little, Brown & Company (Canada) Limited

Printed in the United States of America

Photo Credits

Page 6: Kevin Galvin/The Picture Group. *Page 7 (top):* Paul Conklin. *Page 7 (bottom):* Uniphoto. *Page 8 (both):* Wide World. *Page 10:* Department of Defense. *Page 17:* Wide World. *Page 24:* David Conklin. *Pages 28 and 31:* Paul Conklin. *Page 36:* The Bancroft Library. *Page 38:* Cindy Charles/Gamma-Liaison. *Page 39:* Montes/Gamma-Liaison. *Page 40:* Paul Conklin. *Page 41:* Steve Harbison/Black Star. *Page 56:* Paul Conklin. *Page 57:* McCracken/Gamma-Liaison. *Page 58:* Martha Stewart/The Picture Cube. *Page 70 (left):* Jacob A. Riis Collection/The Museum of the City of New York. *Page 70 (right):* Wide World. *Page 72:* The Metropolitan Museum of Art, Bequest of William Nelson. *Page 74:* The Metropolitan Museum of Art, Bequest of Charles Allen Munn, 1924. *Page 75:* The Bettmann Archive. *Page 82 (top and bottom):* The Free Library of Philadelphia. *Page 83 (top):* The Bettmann Archive. *Page 83 (bottom):* The Franklin Institute. *Pages 84 and 97:* The Bettmann Archive. *Page 109:* UPI/Bettmann Newsphotos. *Page 110:* Kathleen Foster/Black Star. *Page 112:* Wide World. *Page 116:* Courtesy, South Carolina State Development Board. *Page 118:* Paul Conklin. *Page 121 (left):* Jean-Claude Lejeune/Stock Boston. *Page 121 (right):* Sepp Seitz/Woodfin Camp and Associates. *Page 126:* Andrew Sacks. *Page 139:* Sloan/Gamma-Liaison. *Page 141:* Bryce Flynn/The Picture Group. *Pages 144 (both) and 146:* Wide World. *Page 147:* Paul Conklin. *Page 150:* Dan Walsh/The Picture Cube. *Page 157:* Flip Schulke/Black Star. *Pages 159, 163, and 172:* Wide World. *Page 177:* Rob Nelson/The Picture Group. *Page 178:* Sarah Greenwood/Gamma-Liaison. *Page 179:* Paul Conklin. *Page 181:* Ellen Shub/The Picture Cube. *Page 182:* Bill Owens/Archive Pictures. *Page 191:* Wide World. *Page 197 (top right and bottom left):* Paul Conklin. *Page 197 (top center):* Carrie Boretz/Archive Pictures. *Page 197 (top left):* Charles Gatewood/Magnum. *Page 200:* Morry Gash. *Page 204 (left):* Dave Schaefer. *Page 204 (center):* Paul Conklin. *Page 204 (right):* Rodney E. Mims/Uniphoto. *Pages 209 and 210:* Culver Pictures. *Page 211:* UPI/Bettmann Newsphotos. *Page 213 (both):* Wide World. *Page 217 (both):* Paul Conklin. *Page 224:* Faverty/Gamma-Liaison. *Page 230 (left):* Paul Conklin. *Page 230 (right):* UPI/Bettmann Newsphotos. *Page 238:* Shepard Sherbell/The Picture Group. *Page 243:* Diana Walker/Gamma-Liaison. *Page 245:* Joan Liftin/Archive Pictures. *Page 248:* Wide World. *Pages 249, 250, and 258:* UPI/Bettmann Newsphotos. *Page 260 (top left and bottom right):* Wide World. *Page 260 (top right):* UPI/Bettmann Newsphotos. *Page 260 (bottom left):* Sygma. *Page 262:* Michael Evans/Contact Press Images. *Page 268:* Library of Congress. *Page 270 (left):* Ed Kashi/Cindy Charles/Joe Traver/Gamma-Liaison. *Page 270 (right):* Joan Liftin/Archive. *Page 272:* Paul Conklin. *Page 273:* UPI/Bettmann Newsphotos. *Page 276:* The Bettmann Archive. *Page 286:* National Broadcasting Company. *Page 289:* Jim Anderson/Woodfin Camp and Associates. *Page 306:* Paul Conklin. *Page 312:* Courtesy PRODEMCA. *Page 313:* Paul Conklin. *Page 315:* Peter Borsari/Camera 5. *Page 319:* Cliff Chiappa/The Picture Group. *Page 324 (both):* Wide World. *Page 336 (top left, bottom left and right):* Paul Conklin. *Page 336 (top right):* Pete Souza/The White House. *Page 341:* Diana Walker/Gamma-Liaison. *Pages 343 and 347:* Paul Conklin. *Page 348:* Cynthia Johnson/Contact. *Page 353:* Paul Conklin.

(continued on page 677)

Preface

This year marks a milestone for me. It represents my twentieth straight year of teaching introductory American government. First as a graduate "TA" at the University of North Carolina, and then on the faculties of the University of Texas, Northwestern University, and the University of Kansas, I have never missed a year in front of freshman and others eager (sometimes eager, anyway) to learn about American government and politics. This year is also an important milestone for *Government in America: People, Politics, and Policy*, now coming out in its third edition. I will have been laboring in the vineyard of this book for a decade.

Convictions

This edition shares much with its predecessors. Throughout my years of work on *Government in America*, I have had strong convictions about the teaching of American government, beliefs I have tried to incorporate into this book.

First, I believe that there are certain basics about American government and politics—the "nuts and bolts" in the vernacular of the textbook trade—that are indispensible. Like other texts, this one includes ample material about the constitutional system, political behavior, and policymaking institutions. But studying American government does not mean studying a string of disconnected facts. I strongly feel that political science is a theoretical discipline. Without being dogmatic, I hope, I emphasize the interplay of four basic theories of American politics: democratic theory, elite and class theory, pluralism, and hyperpluralism. No single theory of American government monopolizes these pages. Instead, I insist that students stretch their minds and their understandings by confronting these venerable perspectives.

Second, this book adopts a policy approach to American government. The study of public policy is, in my judgment, not merely fashionable, but fundamental to understanding government and politics today. *Government in America* continues to focus on key issues of American political conflict: our political economy, the issue of equality, and the problems of resources in a time of scarcity. As we enter the third American century, our issues change; the importance of debates about public policy does not.

Third, having taught several thousand American government students these past twenty years, I believe that they deserve and can handle the best that political science has to offer. Hence, I continue to incorporate, within the obvious limits of space, both new research and material from the classics of our discipline. I have never understood why many American government books, unlike books in economics or psychology, see a trade-off between timely, lively writing and serious scholarship. I do not shy away from presenting some concepts that are rigorous and complex, but important. My job is to translate complex ideas into comprehensible language. A Woodrow Wilson award-winning book is an important example of scholarship, and it is wise to pay attention to it. The reactions we have had from students and instructors suggest that this is not an impossible dream.

We have retained and, of course, substantially updated some well-received features of the first two editions. Each chapter continues to begin with a memo from the author to the reader; each contains extensive material in boxes, either to highlight a case study or to present some specific research on a question; and each includes a contemporary bibliography and a listing of key terms in the chapter. And, at the end of the book, we collect some important features: a glossary, a Data and Documents section, the Declaration of Independence (new to this edition), and the Constitution.

Changes in the Third Edition

High Technology. This edition embarks upon some new courses, while retaining the elements I have outlined above. The most important new element is the argument that American government and politics are shaped by a wave of high technology. This wave is visible in three areas: the biomedical transformation, in which government is increasingly called upon to make decisions about life and death; the computer and communications revolution, in which politics and government are more and more shaped by "technotronic" forces; and the nuclear revolution, which has shaped our mode of warfare and our energy system. As I write, we are keeping people alive with artificial hearts, while others are asking the courts to disconnect them from life, so to speak. This is but one outcropping of the technological impact on our government and policymaking system. The governor or mayor hustling new, "high tech" industry is another. Parties, elections, federalism, and other conventional topics are addressed with an eye toward these technological changes.

Media Coverage. It is important here to distinguish between our approach to, say, the telecommunications revolution as a topic throughout the book, and the efforts of some books merely to include an obligatory chapter on the media. More is argued in this book than that the media are important in American politics. Rather, we stress (particularly in Chapters 1, 2, 6, 8, 9, and 11) that the media are but a part of a larger computer and telecommunications revolution that is shaping American politics.

Four Communities. Being increasingly complex, the world of politics and government is difficult to explain. In Chapter 2 of this edition, I introduce a microscopic view of American politics, seeing it through the lenses of four American communities. One of these, San Jose, California, is a high-tech haven. Another occupies the opposite end of the economic and geographical continuum: Bethlehem, Pennsylvania, symbolizes many of the difficulties of the American political economy, buffeted by federal environmental regulations and by the challenges of Japanese trade. San Antonio, Texas, the third community, is a place where a new Hispanic majority tries to overcome a heritage of urban poverty through the economic bootstrap of technological development. Finally, Smyrna, Tennessee, home of a giant Nissan factory, symbolizes the nexus between the domestic and the world economies, what we have called the global connection. Throughout this third edition—in our treatment of elections, Congress, the courts, and elsewhere—we draw upon these cases of politics at the grassroots to show how economic and other changes shape American politics. Environmental politics, for example, is more meaningful when we talk about the connection between federal requirements for energy-efficient cars and the decline in steel production in Bethlehem. Some of the courts we describe are real courts, involving real cases, in San Antonio. Through these four communities, we try to apply the abstractions of American government to real people and real decisions.

Parties and Elections. To construct this third edition, we have relied heavily on both users and reviewers. Both have been generous with their comments, particularly in stressing the need for expanded coverage of parties and elections. Thus, this edition includes a greatly revised chapter on parties and two full chapters on nominations, campaigns, and elections. I predict neither the demise nor the resurrection of the parties, simply because the evidence is not in yet. Our coverage, though, of the contemporary party and election system is far more extensive than in earlier editions.

Coverage. In addition to the increased coverage of parties and elections, we have thoroughly updated facts, figures, and research, including of course coverage of the 1984 election. We have also strengthened the coverage of PACs, the politics of defense spending, and the global connection.

Boxes. Throughout, we have updated old boxes and added many new ones on timely and provoking issues. The graphs in the boxes have been made clearer and simpler.

Photos. We have increased the number of photographs in this edition by about twenty percent.

viii

Preface

Ancillaries

A number of excellent ancillaries are available to accompany the third edition of *Government in America*. The *Instructor's Manual*, by Morton Sipress, opens with a section on putting together an introductory survey course, including a section on using computers and lists of audio-visual and computer software sources. The manual then continues with outlines, lecture and discussion ideas, bibliographies, and student projects for each chapter of the text.

The *Test Bank*, also by Morton Sipress and available in both printed and computerized formats, contains approximately two thousand test items, along with a mid-term and a final exam.

The *Study Guide*, by Janice A. Beecher, includes learning objectives, chapter summaries, numerous review and study questions, and suggestions for research activities.

Finally, Little, Brown is offering an Educational Resources Reimbursement Program that will enable instructors to rent and/or purchase such educational aids as films and computer courseware.

Acknowledgments

A new edition can be a trying experience for many people, not the least of whom are long-suffering staff at 18 Tremont Street in Boston, the offices of Little, Brown's College Division. The fine staff at Little, Brown, including Don Palm, John Covell, Sue Warne, and Lauren Green, have been delightful and professional in every way. They continue to confirm my decade-old belief that Little, Brown is the finest house with which a political scientist could sign. I continue to be indebted to Janice A. Beecher, friend, former graduate student, sometime bureaucrat, and now mother, who has helped to update and make this edition more accurate and useful in countless ways.

Many, many colleagues have given me invaluable counsel on the second edition and the early drafts of this third edition of *GIA*. Some of these are men and women whom I know; most of them are not. I do not agree with every counsel they provide, nor can I incorporate every suggestion they make. But they have offered me the chance to partake of their knowledge at every fork of the road. I am deeply indebted, not only to those who have assisted us in user questionnaires, but also to those who have served as reviewers. They are: James Anderson, University of Houston; Charles Andrain, San Diego State University; Larry Baum, Ohio State University; Jeffrey Berry, Tufts University; John Bibby, University of Wisconsin; Janet Boles, Marquette University; John Brigham, University of Massachusetts; Seyom Brown, Brandeis University; David Cingranelli, State University of New York, Binghamton; Susan Clark, University of Colorado; William Crotty, Northwestern University; Larry Elowitz, Georgia College; Michael Grossman, Towson State University; Gary Halter, Texas A & M University; Barbara Hinckley, University of Wisconsin; G. John Ikenberry, Princeton University; Gary Jacobson, University of California, San Diego; John Kay, Santa Barbara City College; John Kingdon, University of Michigan; Sam Krislov, University of Minnesota; Michael Martinez, Texas A & M University; Warren Miller, Arizona State University; Alan Monroe, Illinois State University; Michael Nelson, Vanderbilt University; David Neubauer, University of New Orleans; Marian Palley, University of Delaware; B. Guy Peters, University of Pittsburgh; Richard Riley, Baylor University; Randall Ripley, Ohio State University; Michael Robinson, George Washington University; Stephen Rosenstone, Yale University; L. Earl Shaw, University of Minnesota; Leonard Shipman, Mount San Antonio Community College; Frank Sorauf, University of Minnesota; Harold Stanley, University of Rochester; Susette Talarico, University of Georgia; Jeffrey Tulis, Princeton University; Thomas Tyler, Northwestern University; Stephen Wasby, State University of New York, Albany; Steve Weatherford, University of California, Santa Barbara; Herb Weisberg, Ohio State University; Alan Wyner, University of California, Santa Barbara; and Betty Zisk, Boston University.

Certainly none of these reviewers should be held accountable for mistakes made despite their best efforts to steer me from the path of error. I let all these good people off the hook, but not without my thanks.

As always, my greatest debts are to those closest to me: Nita, Nikki, and Keith. College is ahead for Nikki and Keith. To Nikki, whose freshman year marks my full circle, I dedicate this edition of *Government in America*. A little more peace is ahead for Nita and me—at least until it is time for another revision.

R. L. L.
Lawrence, Kansas

Note to the Student

Every student who undertakes a course begins a long journey. Learning about American government involves a dialogue, not a monologue. I have a role in this dialogue: to give you evidence about how our politics and government work and some tools for mastering this information. Your job is equally difficult. You should master this evidence. But you should not stop there; you should use this evidence to reach your own informed conclusions about our system of government. I will ask you to reflect upon four theories of American government. None of these is completely correct; all are stated to highlight the differences among them. Your task is to assess the evidence about the way our government works and to draw upon these theories to form your own reasoned understanding of government in America.

Several features of *Government in America* should make your task easier and, I hope, more enjoyable. First, note that each chapter begins with a memo that outlines what I tried to put into the chapter and what I think you should take out of it. From time to time, you will run across a symbol like this: 4. It will refer you to a neighboring box containing useful information about a particular case study that illustrates a point or a specific piece of scholarly research. Throughout each chapter, we have tried to indicate **key words** in this kind of type. At the end of the chapter you will see them gathered together, and they are all defined in the glossary at the back of the book. Also at the end of the chapter is a bibliography of important and recent items to pursue. An appendix, which we call "Beyond the Call of Duty," lists a number of important readings about the subject of each chapter.

I hope the study guide to the text, prepared by Janice A. Beecher, will be useful to you. It includes a thorough chapter summary, a set of learning objectives, and a battery of test questions about each chapter. You should use it, and its study questions, to think about, rather than merely memorize, key information about government in America.

Do remember that you will spend the bulk of your lives in the twenty-first century. Much of the key to whether we arrive at that time in good shape depends on you. You are an important part of the democratic process Americans claim to enjoy.

Brief Contents

15   **The Courts**   **475**

16   **Budgeting: Taxing, Spending, and
     Public Policy**   **507**

V   **POLICIES**   **539**

17   **Political Economy and Public Policy**   **541**

18   **Public Policy and Equality**   **563**

19   **Energy, Environment, and Public Policy**   **585**

20   **The Global Connection**   **599**

Appendix 1   **The Declaration of Independence**   **635**

Appendix 2   **The Constitution of the United States
             of America**   **639**

Appendix 3   **Beyond the Call of Duty: Data
             and Documents**   **655**

             Glossary   **661**

             Index   **679**

Contents

16   Budgeting: Taxing, Spending, and Public Policy   507

V   POLICIES   539

17   Political Economy and Public Policy   541

18 Public Policy and Equality   563

19 Energy, Environment, and Public Policy   585

20 The Global Connection   599

GOVERNMENT IN AMERICA

People, Politics, and Policy

INTRODUCING GOVERNMENT IN AMERICA

Government in America (which we sometimes abbreviate *GIA*) requires some introduction; I try to provide that introduction in Part I. Throughout *GIA*, I will be doing two things. First, I will explain and describe how the American political system works to make policy. Second, to do more than merely describe, I will try to give you the tools to understand and evaluate our American government. To help you down those two long roads, Part I introduces some basic ideas about government in general and American government in particular.

Chapter 1 introduces three key terms: *politics, government,* and *public policy.* Politics surrounds us and arises from conflict. Despite its bad press, politics is inherently neither good nor bad, but simply inevitable in a society complex enough to have diverse opinions. Government helps to settle those conflicts arising through politics. What government decides, and how it allocates benefits and burdens, is called public policy. Our government faces countless policy choices. We focus on three, namely, those in the issue arenas of political economy, equality, and energy-environment. Each has a domestic and a global face.

In Chapter 2, I offer some tools for a deeper understanding of American government. Because politics, government, and policies show up everywhere, I illustrate them with some "local color." Specifically, I discuss four American communities, their politics and government. Each is like your own community in some ways; no doubt they are different in others.

Also in Chapter 2, I outline four theories of American politics and government. First is *democratic theory,* suggesting that the majority of the people govern (or should govern). A second, called *class and elite theory,* holds that a select few—upper-class men and women of enormous power and often wealth—have vast power to shape our society's destiny. The third is called *pluralism.* To pluralist theorists, groups dominate government and its policies. Last is *hyperpluralism,* an extreme or perverted form of pluralism in which groups become so powerful that government itself is weakened and helpless. We will use these four theories throughout the rest of *Government in America* to sharpen our understanding of how government works.

Politics and Government in the Third American Century

MEMO

In this chapter, we examine American politics and government at the beginning of the third American century. Important changes affect our political system, changes we call political "megatrends." Our technologies are changing: Transformations in communications, in biomedical sciences, and in the awesome weaponry of war pose new challenges to government in America. The growth of our government is another megatrend, one which divides Americans.

Specifically, we introduce three key concepts in this chapter:

■ *Politics* is the struggle over "who gets what, when, and how." Our images and stereotypes of politics and politicians are not comforting ones. I hope to convince you that good people should be interested in politics, because political decisions determine which paths we take into the future, who will pay the costs, and who will reap the benefits.

■ *Government* consists of those institutions and processes that make public policy. How it works and whether it works well are major concerns of this book.

■ *Public policies* are the choices government makes—and declines to make—in response to political issues. These choices affect people and policy problems.

Also in Chapter 1, we introduce three policy arenas—the economy, equality, and energy-environment—which now dominate our political debate. These three issue arenas have two faces: a domestic face and a global face. We confront policy problems about the economy, about equality, and about energy-environment both at home and abroad.

OUR GOVERNMENT IN AMERICA is now just over two centuries old. Many Americans approach the third American century with trepidation. President Ronald Reagan has recently tried to reassure us by appealing to traditional American values—that old-time religion, the family, military strength, and so on—yet the worries remain. Deficits haunt our government, but more is at stake than the size of the federal budget shortfall. Writers tell us that we are in or are headed for a "postindustrial society," a "high-tech economy," and a "global village." We are warned of a "zero-sum society," where growth will be limited and gains for some must inevitably be at a cost for others. [1] We are told of "megatrends" engulfing us, powerful forces of economic and technological change, which we can only weakly control. [2] [1]

---

[1] John Naisbitt's "Megatrends"

Not everyone will agree with John Naisbitt about what is happening in America. But his list of megatrends is one way of looking at those large, societywide changes in American life:

—We are moving to an information-based society from an industrial society.
—"High-tech" activities are becoming our dominant form of technology.
—The world economy is displacing the national economy.
—Long-term concerns are displacing short-term ones.
—Decentralized institutions are replacing centralized ones.
—Self-help is edging out institutionalized help.
—Participatory democracy is displacing representative democracy.
—Networking is displacing hierarchies.
—The south is replacing the north.
—Multiple options are displacing "either-or" thinking.

Source: John Naisbitt, Megatrends: Ten New Directions Transforming Our Lives (New York: Warner Books, 1982).

Others warn that "since the late 1960s, America's economy has been slowly unravelling." [3] So, too, has our party system and our electoral system. In recent elections a smaller proportion of Americans have bothered to vote than a generation ago.

The role of government today is larger and more pervasive than ever before. Altogether, our American governments—national, state, and local —spend about one dollar in three of our **gross national product,** which is the total dollar value of all goods and services produced in a year. Government controls a mighty nuclear arsenal that could produce what former President Jimmy Carter once called a "World War II every second." Increasingly, government makes life-and-death decisions about its citizens, slowing or hastening the very act of death itself. Government tries to control the toxicity of our water, the costs of our energy, the safety

[1] Lester C. Thurow, The Zero-Sum Society (New York: Basic Books, 1980).
[2] John Naisbitt, Megatrends: Ten New Directions Transforming Our Lives (New York: Warner Books, 1982).
[3] Robert B. Reich, The Next American Frontier: A Provocative Program for Economic Renewal (New York: New York Times Books, 1983), p. 1.

of our work place, and the security of our streets. Government and politics, as we enter the third American century, affect nearly every aspect of our lives.

Our government can seem complicated, confusing, and forbidding, but it is never irrelevant. You cannot make a bargain with government that if you will not bother it, it will not bother you. Let us begin with a look at some major changes afoot.

POLITICAL MEGATRENDS

John Naisbitt called his book about the future of American society *Megatrends* because it described nine key trends in our nation that were bound to shape our economy, our society, and our lives.[4] There are megatrends in politics, too. We will discuss two political megatrends: (1) the rise of high-tech politics, and (2) the phenomenal growth of government and the choices that growth implies for us all.

The Rise of High-Tech Politics

The American political system has rushed rapidly into a new period of **high-tech politics.** This is a politics in which the behavior of citizens and policymakers, and the political agenda itself, are increasingly shaped by technological change.

Two hundred years ago, when the American constitution was signed, times seemed to be simpler. Lacking radio, television, satellite communication, or even national newspapers, most Americans knew nothing of their new government for weeks or months. A dozen years later, when the government located its new headquarters along the swampy Potomac, the entire government moved there in the back of two conestoga wagons.

Ours is a complex time. We move things not by wagons, but by high-speed telecommunications, often beamed off satellites. Today, television, computers, death-delaying machines, satellite communications, and modern weaponry have become a part of daily life on our planet. We know more about what happened an hour ago in Cairo or Beijing today than colonial New Yorkers knew about what happened in Philadelphia the month before. The President of the United States and the Premier of the Soviet Union can communicate instantly about an imminent nuclear crisis through a "hot line" linking Washington and Moscow. Even ordinary people today have access to technology that one of the richest men in the early Republic, George Washington, could not have imagined. There are a billion telephones in the world. In the United States, each one can hook into massive computer banks, sifting through personalized news on stocks, shopping, games, or, sometimes, meddling with bank accounts or even military codes. These are not dreams of a science fiction hereafter, but realities today.

Government has had to adjust to the new technology at a time when support for American government is waning. For more than two decades,

---

[4] Naisbitt, *Megatrends.*

Television and the Candidate. *Television and high speed telecommunications have revolutionized American political life. Now, politicians can convey whatever image they want by carefully choosing the style and the graphics of their commercials. Senator Gary Hart's (D—Colo.) PR agency combined his photogenic presence with Star Wars-like graphics to convey a youthful, forward-looking image.*

the Survey Research Center at the University of Michigan has been asking samples of the American population this question: "How much of the time can you trust the government in Washington?" The choices are: "just about always, most of the time, some of the time, hardly ever, or don't know." In 1958, about 76 percent of the population could be called trusting; by 1980, the proportion of people who trusted their government dropped to 29 percent. In the 1980s, our basic trust in government began to pick up again. But it has a long way to go before it reaches its level of two decades ago.

Three new technological revolutions shape politics and our public policy choices: the computer and communications revolution; the biomedical revolution; and the revolution of the technology of warfare. The new technology is a double-edged sword. With it, we bring information more quickly to the people; but in doing so, we make it easier to manipulate political opinion. We save lives with it; but in doing so, we raise questions about the wisdom and costs of prolonging life. We enhance our national security with it; but in doing so, we escalate an arms race, adding more kilotonnage annually than all the bombs dropped in all our earlier wars.

From the Old Machines to the New Machines: The Computer-Communications Transformation. At the turn of the twentieth century, our politics was very different from what it is now. Voting turnout among eligible citizens was high. (The national election of 1896 marked the high point in American voting participation.) One reason was that the American party system was thriving. Often, parties were organized into **machines,** tightly organized local parties, which often exchanged favors for votes. Machines and their local leaders personalized politics. Friendship was the currency of the local party leader, and friendship often led to jobs, or contracts with the government, or other favors. These kinds of political machines are rare today. Party politics is often disorganized and seems incapable of holding the allegiance of most Americans. [5]

Today, politics has come to be dominated by the media or the interest groups. The technological revolution in American life made both media and interest groups possible, even inevitable. Our party system has been weakened as groups and the media grow in importance. Former President Carter's key aide, Hamilton Jordan, aptly observed that "the enormous political void left by the demise of the party was filled by television. Through its skillful use, candidates could appeal directly to the voters over the heads" of the parties. [6] What Professor Jeffrey Berry called the "interest group spiral" has produced a multitude of special interest groups, each looking to its own goals. Senator Gary Hart (D.—Colo.) grumbled that "I hate to get on the plane for Denver. For three hours, the lobbyists just line up in the aisle to get a word with me." [7] So many groups, all refusing to take no for an answer, make heavy, even unreasonable, demands on our government.

New machines have displaced the old ones. Polling and public relations are key ingredients in the new political machinery. Since their invention in the 1930s, we have been able to conduct preference surveys of the American population. Today, we test public opinion on everything from presidential popularity to the popularity of toothpastes. So accurate are public opinion polls that Pat Caddell, President Carter's pollster in the 1980 election campaign, taking last-minute soundings, could confront a president of the United States on election eve and report that "Mr. President, I'm afraid its gone." [8] A new breed of public relations specialists and political consultants have made politics their trade.

Computers are another important part of the new machinery of politics. Anticipating President Reagan's reelection, the White House Personnel Office installed a computer to keep track of governmental job applicants and their political sponsors. The old party machines relied on an army of "foot soldiers"—the precinct captains, the ward committeemen, and other party workers. Today, computers "allow a politician to speak directly to small segments of the population who the computerized polling operations have shown can provide the extra swing vote or the last few extra dollars." [9] In 1984, the Republican party spent $10 million in an effort to add 1.5 to 2 million voters to the pro-Reagan rolls. In Denver, for example, the Republicans installed a computer phone bank in the basement beneath the Women's Bank on West Colfax Street. Computers (not people) called unregistered voters, asked them questions to which they could respond by pressing a telephone digit (the computer politely terminated the interview if opposition to Reagan-Bush was indicated), and urged the unregistered to register. [10]

Exit Polls. *One of the most controversial aspects of American elections, exit polls are used by the TV networks and other media to forecast results—even before the polls have closed. Some evidence from political scientists suggests that these projections can influence last-minute, West Coast voters. Congress has debated making them illegal.*

The New Machines. *Once, the political "machine" included an army of precinct workers and doorbell ringers. Today's new machines are highly sophisticated hardware and software packages. The new machines look like this one in the Reagan-Bush headquarters in New Hampshire in 1984.*

[5] On the decline of parties, see William Crotty, *American Parties in Decline*, 2nd ed. (Boston: Little, Brown, 1984).

[6] Hamilton Jordan, *Crisis: The Last Year of the Carter Presidency* (New York: Berkley Books, 1982), p. 310.

[7] Quoted in Jeffrey M. Berry, *The Interest Group Society* (Boston: Little, Brown, 1984), p. 17.

[8] Jordan, *Crisis*, p. 348.

[9] *New York Times*, January 28, 1984, p. 9.

[10] *Washington Post Weekly Edition*, May 7, 1984, p. 9.

The news media play a key role in the new technological politics by shaping politics into drama. Politicians are their leading actors; often, they are the scriptwriters, too. Politicians do not sit idly by and wait for the media to find the "news"; they are often active generators. We shall see in Chapter 11 how the media works in Washington—and how Washington works the media.

The Politics of Life and Death: The Biotechnical Transformation. The acts of procreating, giving birth, and dying seem, at first glance, far removed from politics as we understand it. Yet, they, too, have become entangled in a political thicket. Our capacity for manipulating life itself is by now well advanced. A biomedical revolution has brought improved, but significantly more costly, health care. We Americans currently spend 11 percent of our gross national product on health care, and because we are an aging society, our health-care bills will continue to spiral. The technology of medical care raises complex political issues.

In 1980, for the first time, the Supreme Court upheld (in the case of *Diamond* v. *Chakraharty)* the right to patent a new life form. Shortly, genetic engineering in the laboratory will enable us to manipulate DNA and orchestrate life. (One wit coined the phrase "designer genes" for such experimentation.) Because medical technology can keep less developed fetuses alive, issues of medical care for the barely born are raised. Robert and Peggy Stinson, whose extremely premature baby Andrew died after six months of agony on life-support systems, observe that "a central absurdity of modern medicine is that the machinery in an intensive care unit is more sophisticated than the codes of law and ethics governing its use." [11] [2] Many Americans feel strongly that the right to manipulate

[11] Robert and Peggy Stinson, *The Long Dying of Baby Andrew* (Boston: Atlantic-Little, Brown, 1984), p. 288.

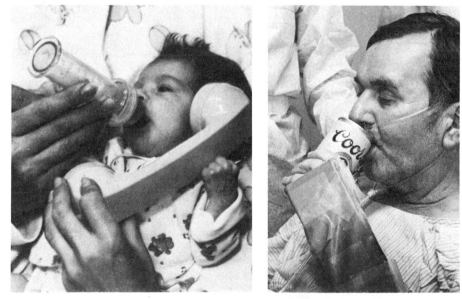

The Politics of Life and Death. *Today, government's policy choices are involved in matters as private as life and death. In 1984, a baby, called "Baby Fae" by the press, was given a baboon's heart in Loma Linda, California, without the elaborate governmental clearances required for medical experimentation on humans. On the other hand, William Schroeder, the recipient of the world's second "permanent" artificial heart in Louisville, Kentucky, knowingly entered an experiment approved by the Food and Drug Administration. The families of men and women attached to life-sustaining machines sometimes battle hospital officials for the right to die. Hospitals and physicians sometimes fear malpractice suits if they "turn off the machines" prematurely. These days, birth and death may involve the long reach of public policy.*

Decisions about life and death are among the most personal of decisions. It is hard to imagine a government intruding into such private and family matters. Yet government is more intimately involved with the beginnings and endings of life than ever before. Because of the strong moral dimensions surrounding birth and death, many Americans see a governmental obligation to enforce standards of behavior.

Consider this problem: More than 250,000 seriously ill or deformed infants are born in this country every year. In April of 1982, a baby—called "Baby Doe" by the press— was born in Indianapolis, Indiana. The baby had Down's syndrome (once called mongolism) and an undeveloped esophagus. The parents requested the hospital not to operate to correct the deformed esophagus. The hospital then went to court to seek an order enforcing surgery. When news of the incident spread via the press to Washington, President Reagan decided that Baby Doe's case constituted a "right-to-life" issue. Baby Doe died before the President could intervene, but the Reagan administration ordered every hospital receiving federal funds to post new rules concerning the care of deformed infants. It instructed hospitals to display prominently a "hot-line" number concerning newborn deformed babies.

If birth can be involved in political conflict, so also can death and its prospect. Today, we can transplant kidneys and other vital organs. Yet who gets an organ transplant and who should pay for it? Private insurance companies typically will not compensate for liver or heart transplants. Not surprisingly, many people—especially those needing transplants—think the government should pay.

In July 1983, President Reagan, in one of his weekly radio broadcasts, appealed for a liver donor for a Texas baby after her local congressman had shown the President pictures of the child. Texas welfare officials refused to pay for the staggering cost of the procedure. The speaker of the Texas House of Representatives, pestered about the case by a Dallas television reporter, rammed a bill through the state legislature guaranteeing $41,000 for the operation. (The baby died before a suitable donor could be found.) Reviewing the intense publicity surrounding life-and-death issues of transplants, Representative Henry Waxman (D.—Calif.) grimly remarked that the politics of transplants depended more and more on "whether the president or some congressman decides to give you visibility."

Source: For more information on the politics of transplants, see Howard Kurtz, "Transplants: Life and Death Political Patronage," *Washington Post National Weekly Edition,* May 7, 1984, pp. 6–7.

birth should not include the right to abort an unwanted fetus. Legislatures and courts constantly debate abortion policies.

As at birth, so at death does public policy govern life-and-death decisions. In early 1985, a California court upheld the right of a man (by then quite dead) to have himself withdrawn from life-support systems in a hospital. About $2 billion is now spent on kidney dialysis machines from medicare budgets alone. The costs of artificial hearts could easily dwarf the costs of kidney machines as technology steadily improves. The wonders of our medical technology will continue to add to the costs of life-sustaining care, and will fuel debate about the meanings and morality of life and death themselves.

Will There Be a Day After? The New Technology of War. One of the most watched television programs in history was an ABC movie called *The Day After.* It was about the days after and a few days before a nuclear war. The nuclear technology of war was revealed in 1945, just at the end of World War II. Since then, the world's nuclear arsenals have grown exponentially. American presidents always have an aide at their side, carrying around a briefcase (called "the football") containing the codes needed to begin World War III.

In March 1983, President Reagan proposed that our nation build a nuclear umbrella in space. It would consist of satellites geared to launch anti-missile missiles at any enemy missiles fired toward the United States. Critics—and there were many, including the Congressional Office

Star Wars. *President Reagan has proposed to move warpower even further toward a dependency on technology through a plan that critics call "Star Wars." This envisioned space-based sensor would provide high-orbiting surveillance of all objects travelling around the earth, distinguishing (one hopes) among missiles, decoys, and debris. Experiments with primitive prototypes of star wars technology began in the summer of 1985. Although the actual deployment of defensive anti-missile systems would violate American and Soviet agreements, President Reagan wanted to use the development of a star wars system as a bargaining chip in the Geneva arms reduction talks.*

of Technology Assessment—called the scheme far-fetched and unwork-able. It was, the critics sneered, a "star wars" proposal. Workable or not, high technology permeates all elements of our national defense system.

High technology is expensive, and certainly that is true also of the technology of war. In 1983, our nation spent $209.9 billion on its national defense. This represented about 6.4 percent of our gross national product. These expenditures may not always buy weapons that work. James Fallows has noted with grave concern that "the cost of military equipment keeps going up, the number of units in the inventory goes down, and their reliability becomes open to serious question." [12] Because each item purchased—a fighter plane, rifle, or whatever—is technologically more advanced than its predecessor, it has many more parts and therefore more likelihood that one or another of them will malfunction. The costs of any single fighter or bomber is greater than ever, but flying time is down. Indeed, Fallows reports, if the cost of a single fighter plane continues to skyrocket as it has in recent years, by the year 2054, that year's entire defense budget will be able to purchase only a single aircraft. [13] Not only defense, but government as a whole, does not come cheap.

[12] James Fallows, *National Defense* (New York: Vintage Books, 1981), p. 49.
[13] Ibid., p. 38.

Big Government, Big Choices

Our government spends a third of our gross national product, but rarely do we examine carefully where these public moneys go. The amounts spent by government are so large (the late Senator Everett Dirksen used to say "a billion dollars here, a billion dollars there, pretty soon it adds up to real money") that it is hard to assess public expenditures.

Few issues so strongly divide Americans as the role and size of government. No issue so clearly separates liberals from conservatives. Liberals have long supported an active government, one committed to advancing equality and keeping the economy stable. Conservatives see the government as a chain dragging on the operation of a free market.

Unquestionably, our government is huge. One quick way of examining public expenditures for various public policies is to look at 3 .

---

3   The Costs of Public Policy

Often, the numbers used to describe government spending are so large that they are not easily related to common experience. Every so often, stories appear to tell us how long it would take us to spend a billion dollars or how many times a billion dollars in small bills would wrap around the world. One of the most useful ways of thinking about the costs of government and its policies is to compare governmental expenditures with what we spend in the private sector. The government's food stamps program may not look so expensive when we compare it to our expenditures on furniture, liquor, or cars.

Here is a list of selected expenditures, some by government (the public sector) and some by the private sector. Look at them carefully and make your own comparisons between the costs of the government's public policies (in italics) and our private spending patterns.

Clearly, the most costly item we buy is medical care. It is largely a private cost, though a sizable portion of it is borne by our tax dollars. After that, the most expensive items we buy in the United States are our groceries and automobiles, followed by expenditures for education and the budget for the Department of Defense. The next item, social security—the expenditures government makes to older Americans—will soon become our most expensive public policy.

Beyond those "big-ticket" items, though, compare further. We match every dollar we spend for Medicare with a dollar for apparel and accessories; private sector expenditures for household appliances only slightly exceed public sector expenditures for Aid to Families with Dependent Children; a nuclear Trident submarine will cost almost as much as all of our energy assistance and more than twice as much as the College Work Study Program. Remember that although these are merely rough-and-ready approximations of some of our private and governmental expenditures, they remind us that public policies can be measured in dollars and cents and that valuing what government spends depends upon the comparisons one makes.

(box continues on next page)

WHY POLITICS?

As a nation, we will wrestle with these and many other issues through politics, asking the government to make decisions about them, decisions that we will call public policy.

Harold D. Lasswell has offered, perhaps, the briefest, but one of the most useful, definitions of **politics:** "*who gets what, when, and how.*"[14] This broad definition covers a lot of territory (office politics, sorority politics, and so on), but political scientists are interested in one kind of politics only: that related to government decision making. Politics produces authoritative decisions about public issues.

Sometimes we focus mainly on the *who* of politics: voters, groups, officials, parties. *How* people play politics is important, too. This they do through bargaining, compromising, lobbying, and so on. *What* in political language refers to policy, the substance of political conflict. We adopt

[14] Harold D. Lasswell, *Politics: Who Gets What, When and How* (New York: McGraw-Hill, 1938).

a policy approach in this book. We are interested not only in who wins and who loses, but in the substance of government's policy choices. A policy approach to American government reminds us that politics is not merely for private advantage but also for serving a larger public purpose.

How and Why Do People Play Politics?

For a handful of Americans, politics is the staff of life, vocation and avocation wrapped together. To most Americans, politics is only—as Robert A. Dahl once said—"a sideshow on the circus of life." Typically, it ranks well below work, family, and leisure activities. Still, most of us at one time or another will enter the political arena, if only sporadically (say, to vote in a presidential election).

All of the ways in which people enter the political arena are called **political participation.** The most common means of political participation in a democracy, of course, is voting. If voting turnouts are a measure of a healthy democracy, ours should have cause for concern. Turnout in presidential elections was at its highpoint in the late 1800s, not 1984. Moreover, as Wolfinger and Rosenstone have shown in their careful study of the nonvoter, "voters are not a microcosm of the entire body of citizens, but a distorted sample that exaggerates the size of some groups and minimizes that of others."[15] With our huge mass information media, citizens may be more "tuned into" politics today, simply because of the extensive coverage of government and politics; unfortunately, they are more "tuned out" when it comes time to vote.

Voting, though, is only one form of participation. Just discussing politics or paying attention to political events and personalities are other forms. Participation in political groups is increasing. These "pressure groups" or "special interest groups" have mushroomed in size and number in the past two decades.[16]

[15] Raymond E. Wolfinger and Steven J. Rosenstone, *Who Votes?* (New Haven, Conn.: Yale University Press, 1980), p. 198.

[16] On the rapid growth of interest groups in America, see Jack L. Walker, "The Origins and Maintenance of Interest Groups in America," *American Political Science Review* 77 (June 1983): 390–406.

Not everyone who participates in politics, of course, loves the game; not even all presidents enjoy the job. [17] Franklin D. Roosevelt delighted in decision-making and politics. But Warren G. Harding summed up his view of the presidency in four words: "God, what a job!" Richard Nixon carried his burdens gloomily and publicly even before he was trapped in the quicksand of Watergate. He commonly spoke of "crises," of "testing," of the "exquisite agony" of political power. Whatever Nixon sought in politics, he took little pleasure in what he found.

One may get very little joy out of politics but still cultivate power over things and people. Henry Kissinger once remarked (presumably only half-seriously) that "power is the ultimate aphrodisiac." **Power** is the capacity to get people to do something that they would not otherwise do. [18] The ability to alter a congressional vote or to move a nation is an awesome power. And the search for power is a strong motivation to political activity. One book—touted by its publisher as "America's number 1 best-seller"—proclaimed:

> All life is a game of power. The object of the game is simple enough: to know what you want and get it . . . The master players . . . seek power itself, knowing that power can be used to *obtain* money, sex, security, or fame. None of these alone constitutes power; but power can produce them all. [19]

Most political scientists would consider this perspective hard-boiled if not downright amoral. But they are realistic enough to stress that political participation often involves power seeking.

People also participate in policymaking because they see their interests affected by government. Some of these interests may be high-minded and noble, others base and greedy. Blacks and whites, women and men, the poor and not-so-poor advocate policies concerning equality in America. Corporations, unions, consumers, and workers want government to make economic decisions. Other people raise new policy issues about the environment and energy, seeking to balance environmental blessings with the need for energy. These groups all become involved in politics because the outreach of public policy is long and because they are able to see how public policies touch their interests.

GOVERNMENT

No tribe, community, or society has ever managed to get along without some means of governing itself. We can define **government** as the institutions and processes through which public policies are made for a society. In some (but not all) modern governments, a written constitution fixes the institutional form of a government. Whether or not governments are

---

[17] James David Barber, *The Presidential Character*, 2nd ed. (Englewood Cliffs, N.J., Prentice-Hall, 1977).

[18] This definition of power may be found in the classic article by Robert A. Dahl, "The Concept of Power," *Behavioral Science* 2 (July 1957): 202.

[19] Michael Korda, *Power: How to Get It, How to Use It* (New York: Ballantine Books, 1975), p. 4.

actually based on some printed document, they all perform the following necessary functions:

1. They maintain a military and supply its arsenal.
2. They provide such public services as hospitals, old-age pensions, and police protection.
3. They collect taxes. (In America, governments collect about one out of every three dollars of the gross national product.)
4. They socialize their citizens into the political and social system by providing schooling.

In recent years, governments (and the amounts spent on them) have grown in the United States and other countries. In fact, if we compare our government spending with that of other economically developed nations in western Europe, ours has one of the lesser amounts as a percentage of the gross national product.

Schoolchildren here, and in most other countries, learn quickly that governments have legislative, executive, and judicial tasks to perform. In the United States, these tasks are described in Articles I, II, and III of the Constitution. Congress is to be the main performer in the legislative role, although the president is assigned some important legislative tasks as well. The president is to be the executive, whose executive task is spelled out in just nine words of the Constitution ("take care that the laws shall be faithfully executed"). Today the executive branch includes a vast federal bureaucracy to execute the laws of the national government. Finally, every government possesses some means of settling disputes. This task belongs to the courts, which have always been powerful and often controversial elements in our governmental process.

Together, the legislative, executive, and judicial branches of government are involved in deciding what the government will do in a tremendous number of situations. How will it spend its tax revenues? How will it deal with the disputes that involve one person's rights against another's? How will it deal with the pollution of the air or water? Sometimes the branches of government agree with each other while often they do not. Sometimes they respond to public pressure and sometimes not. Nevertheless, whenever the government decides to do something, it has made public policy.

WHAT PUBLIC POLICY MEANS

Defining Public Policy

Years ago, people solved their own problems; now more and more people and groups take their problems to government. We do not expect government to say "go away and don't bother me." We expect it to listen attentively to the issues citizens put on its agenda. Government is thus faced with an agenda of decisions. A choice that government makes in response to an issue is called **public policy**.

A policy, therefore, is a course of action taken with regard to some problem. The store clerk says, "It is not our policy to make cash refunds."

The university library says, "It is our policy that overdue books are charged at a quarter a day." The employer says, "Our policy is not to hire people without experience." These and other policies are necessary because something scarce is being allocated: refunds, library books, and jobs. David Easton once defined a political system as "the authoritative allocation of values for society as a whole."[20] So public policy is the authoritative allocation of something of value for the people as a whole.

Throughout *Government in America*, we will be concerned with government's public policy choices. We believe that there are three singularly important policy arenas in which our government is called upon to make choices. These are the areas of *political economy, equality,* and *energy-environment,* and we will discuss them later in this chapter.

Policymaking as Choice-taking

All policies represent choices among courses of action. The store could permit cash refunds, but it does not; the university library could charge no fines for overdue books, but it does not; and the employer could hire someone without experience, but he or she does not.

Dealing with political issues also requires that choices be made. Public policymaking, therefore, is choice-taking. Henry Kissinger, a political scientist before he became a policymaker, once wrote a book called *The Necessity for Choice.* [21] Those four words accurately summarize a policy approach to government. Confronted with any policy problem, government faces not one but two choices:

1. Should government act at all? Doing nothing, or nothing different from what we already do is of course a choice in itself. Policymakers may hope that the problem will go away by itself or they may fear that the new policy will create worse problems than the present ones.
2. If government should make or change policy, what policy alternative should be selected? Some alternatives will be politically unpopular, others might not work, and still others might worsen rather than improve the situation. Sometimes, a government must choose a bad policy over a worse alternative.

Politicians often recount how difficult their choices were in some momentous policy decision. Lyndon Johnson wrote, "When I had an important decision to make as president, I tried to focus my power of concentration on that issue like a laser beam, shutting out all outside thoughts and distractions."[22] Richard Nixon used to retire to the presidential retreat at Camp David, Maryland, with a supply of yellow legal pads for his "exquisite agony" of decision.

Politicians probably exaggerate the agony, the loneliness, the definitiveness of their decisions, but choice-taking is not easy. Policymakers often try desperately to avoid the necessity for choice. It sometimes

[20] David Easton, *The Political System* (New York: Alfred A. Knopf, 1953), Chap. 5.
[21] Henry Kissinger, *The Necessity for Choice* (New York: Harper and Row, 1961).
[22] Lyndon B. Johnson, *The Vantage Point* (New York: Holt, Rinehart, and Winston, 1971), p. x.

Henry Kissinger's Shuttle Diplomacy. *Henry Kissinger, National Security Advisor and then Secretary of State for Presidents Nixon and Ford, was adept at "shuttle diplomacy," shuttling by plane from one side to another to negotiate conflicts, particularly in the Middle East. Here, he visits the temple of Queen Hatshepout in Luxor, Egypt, in 1974. Such flamboyant diplomacy has sometimes (but not always) helped to keep regional conflicts limited. The tightening web of the global connection keeps presidents and their leading diplomats constantly involved in other nations' conflicts.*

seems that politicians' choices are yes, no, and waffle. They may prefer nondecisions to decisions. No politician likes to risk alienating a single potential supporter. Politicians hate to say no to anyone, but the necessity of choice comes for all policymakers. Members of Congress may seem to debate interminably, but they have to vote on a policy issue eventually. Judges may pore over briefs and hear arguments for weeks, but the plaintiff or defendant will eventually get a decision. Presidents may agonize over policy choices, but they eventually make them.

Here is one example of policymaking as choice-taking. No amount of hand wringing, political rhetoric, or brilliant political leadership will put more oil under American soil. Few issues touch so many interests. People want more energy to heat homes, provide jobs, and drive cars. American Jews and others oppose policies that support oil-rich Arabs at the expense of Israel's future. Powerful oil companies seek high profits to encourage new exploration. Environmentalists favor use of more energy sources, but oppose strip-mining and nuclear plants. Automobile companies and unions oppose expensive energy-reduction equipment in cars for fear that people will buy fewer cars. Everyone favors having some policy to obtain energy, but not all agree on a single policy. What is government to do?

The choices in energy policy should convince us that all policy choices involve **trade-offs.** Making a trade-off means that we may have to sacrifice some of one goal to achieve another: "There ain't no such thing as a free lunch." If we encourage strip-mining we damage our environment. If we build nuclear plants we risk our safety. If we increase gasoline prices we squeeze everyone financially, especially the poor. Making policy choices means not only that we try to do the "right" thing, but also that we may have to sacrifice one value to get another.

THE POLITICAL SYSTEM

We have looked at politics, government, and public policy. Now it is time to link them together by describing a model of the American political system. All systems have parts, but every system constitutes a working whole, too. In this book, we define a **political system** as a set of institutions and activities that link together people, politics, and policy. [23]

Most systems can be sketched out on paper. We can draw a picture of how a nuclear power plant or an automobile works. We can also represent on paper how a political system works, and we do that in ☐4. Of course, the rest of this book is devoted to fleshing out this skeletal version of our political system, so you should not expect this sketchy model to tell you everything you need to know about that system. Still, the model will help you identify several key elements.

There are three basic messages you should glean from the political system pictured in ☐4. To understand it, you need to know (1) how policy issues get on the policy agenda, (2) how policymakers make policy, and (3) what impacts policies have on people.

[23] All political systems models are indebted to David Easton, "An Approach to the Analysis of Political Systems," *World Politics* 9 (April 1957): 379–89.

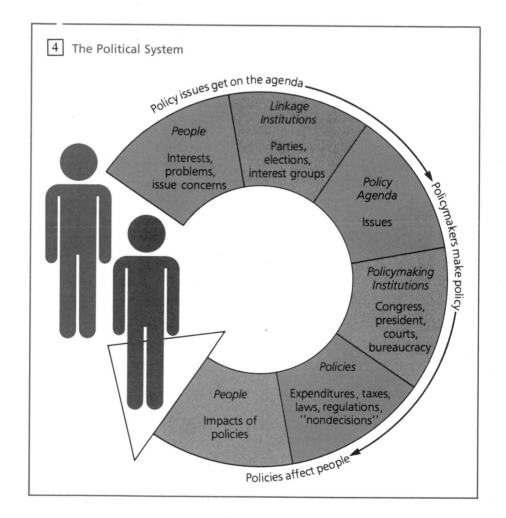

4 The Political System

Policy issues get on the agenda

People — Interests, problems, issue concerns

Linkage Institutions — Parties, elections, interest groups

Policy Agenda — Issues

Policymakers make policy

Policymaking Institutions — Congress, president, courts, bureaucracy

Policies — Expenditures, taxes, laws, regulations, "nondecisions"

People — Impacts of policies

Policies affect people

Policy Issues and the Political Agenda

Politics, of course, begins with people, and people do not always agree on the best course of action. A **political issue** arises when people disagree about a problem and a public policy choice. There is never any shortage of political issues in this country. Government will never act upon any issue, though, that does not get its attention.

Government being large and complex, you cannot get its attention by tapping it on the shoulder or yelling. But there are ways in which people can get government to pay them heed. Some write letters to their senators or representatives or to the White House, others march on Washington or form protest demonstrations elsewhere, a few take out full-page advertisements in the *New York Times*, and still others form pressure groups. In our political system, most issues catch government's eye because they are raised through three major linkage institutions: political parties, interest groups, and elections. **Linkage institutions** are the channels or access points through which issues get on the government's policy agenda.

The **policy agenda,** according to John Kingdon, is "the list of subjects or problems to which governmental officials, and people outside of government closely associated with those officials, are paying serious attention at any given time." [24] Of course, government officials could deal with any issue at any time: the problem of nuclear disarmament at 9:00, Central America at 9:30, pollution control at 10:00, and so on. In reality, government is not quite that organized. Like individuals, public officials try to prioritize their time. Some issues will be seriously considered, others will not.

In a democratic government, parties, elections, and groups should be a key link between the preferences of citizens and the policy agenda of government. When you vote, you are really looking to see whether or not Candidate A shares your agenda. If you are worried about abortion, nuclear disarmament, and high taxes, and Candidate A wants to deal with the social security crisis, Central American dictatorships, and the cost of fuel oil, then you should find another candidate. The parties should help us sort out our agendas. Party officials spend much time writing party platforms every four years. There is more than idle rhetoric in these platforms. If you do not find either of the two major parties' agendas compatible with your ideas, try joining an interest group. There is one for almost every imaginable policy interest. Wherever the agenda comes from, in a democracy a close correspondence must exist between the public's agenda and that of the government.

Making Public Policy: The Policymaking Institutions

Policymakers stand at the core of the political system. They scan the issues on the policy agenda, select some for attention, and make policy about them, working within the government's institutions. The Founding

[24] John Kingdon, *Agendas, Alternatives, and Public Policies* (Boston: Little, Brown, 1984), p. 3.

Fathers designed three policymaking institutions: Congress, the presidency, and the courts. Today the power of the bureaucracy has grown so great that we can more accurately speak of four policymaking institutions.

Very few policies are made by a single policymaking institution acting alone. In Part III these institutions are described separately, but they do not operate in watertight compartments. Environmental policy is a good example. Some presidents have used their influence with Congress to urge clean air and water policies. When Congress passed legislation to clean up the environment, bureaucracies had to implement it. Rules and regulations issued by the bureaucratic agencies fill fat volumes. Every law passed and every rule made is also fair game for a challenge in the courts. Courts make decisions about what the policies mean and whether they conflict with the Constitution. In policymaking, every political institution gets into the act.

Implementing Public Policies

Proclaiming a new policy is easy. Implementing it is much more difficult. **Implementation** means translating the goals and objectives of a policy into an operating, ongoing program. If a policy is poorly implemented, it is almost surely doomed to failure. Jeffrey Pressman and Aaron Wildavsky told the sad story of a bold government project to stimulate jobs in economically depressed Oakland, California.[25] Fancy plans in Washington yielded only failure in Oakland. Millions were spent on an elaborate scheme that resulted in only thirty-odd jobs.

All policies require implementation before they can work. In a few cases, implementation is straightforward. Building a highway is expensive, but not difficult. Putting billions of dollars into the hands of social security recipients is expensive but easy. Other policies require more elaborate implementation. Ensuring that tens of thousands of employers comply with occupational safety and health standards requires a massive bureaucratic effort. Getting schools to comply with desegregation policies has been a slow, painstaking process.

Policies Have Impacts

Policy impacts are the effects a policy has on people and problems. People advocate policies because they think the impacts will benefit them. People who raise a policy issue want more than just a new law, a fancy proclamation, a bureaucratic rule, or a court judgment. They want a policy that *works*. Environmentalists want a policy that not only claims to clean up dirty air, but does so. Consumers want a policy that actually reduces inflation. Minority groups want a policy that not only promises them more equal treatment, but helps ensure it.

Having a policy implies that we have some goals we want to achieve. Whether we want to reduce poverty, cut crime, clean up the water, or hold

[25] Jeffrey Pressman and Aaron Wildavsky, *Implementation* (Berkeley: University of California Press, 1973).

down inflation, we have a goal in mind. The analysts of policy impacts ask how well we achieved our policy goal—and at what cost. Sometimes policy analysts use a *cost-benefit ratio* to assess a policy's impact. Costs and benefits of various policy alternatives are estimated and then compared. Obviously, we could accomplish lots of worthy goals if our motto were "hang the cost—full speed ahead." If we cleaned up the dirty air over steel-making centers like Bethlehem, Pennsylvania by closing all the steel plants and putting thousands of people out of work, we might consider that a high cost to pay for the benefit received. If we created new jobs for the unemployed but the cost per job created was $500,000, we might wonder about the cost-benefit ratio. The analysis of policy impacts carries the political system back to its point of origin: people—their interests, problems, and issue concerns.

THREE POLICY ARENAS

Politics and government are *about* something. They are about policy issues. Of course, government has a crowded agenda. We could start now, list every issue that government has addressed, and keep going until the end of the book. But the rest of this book reflects the fact that American government and politics constantly confront three critical policy arenas: economics, equality, and energy-environment. While not every issue government addresses fits tidily into these three issue clusters, the most significant touch one or another of them. We will return to these policy arenas often throughout *Government in America*.

Politics and the New Political Economy

Robert Reich remarks that "ultimately, America's capacity to respond to economic change will depend upon the vitality of its political institutions." [26] To remain vital, though, political institutions have to be financially viable. Thus, our government in Washington in 1985 was borrowing money at an annual rate in excess of $210 billion. These huge sums were borrowed to pay for an equally huge federal deficit. Essentially, the government in Washington was paying out more than it was receiving in taxes, which necessitated borrowing, the biggest borrowing spree ever by a government in peacetime. This government borrowing would be added to the national debt of $1,500,000,000,000.

Economics has long been called "the dismal science," and these days, it is easy to see why. Senator Daniel Patrick Moynihan (D.—N.Y.) once remarked that "the crucial stage in solving a problem is that point where one defines what kind of problem it is." [27] Today, we define more and more of our problems as essentially economic in nature and most of these end up in the lap of government. Unemployment, inflation, foreign trade deficits, sagging industries, a sea of federal red ink, high interest rates— the list of economic problems goes on and on.

[26] Reich, *Next American Frontier*, p. 255.
[27] Daniel Patrick Moynihan, *Coping* (New York: Random House, 1973), p. 12.

Economics and Politics. The relationship between government and economics is called **political economy.** Government and the economy have always been closely linked in America—closer than most conservatives like to admit. The emergence of a new political economy made this linkage more intimate than ever. Few issues of economic policy are not grave and anguishing these days.

Americans have always tended to think of their economy as capitalistic. In **capitalism,** individuals and corporations, not the government, own the principal means of production and seek profits. (In socialism, the major means of production are owned by the government.) Americans have long held that capitalism and democracy are virtually identical. Historian Louis Hartz has spoken of our "two national impulses: the impulse toward democracy and the impulse toward capitalism."[28] Historian Richard Hofstadter remarked that to Abraham Lincoln, "the vital test of a democracy was economic—its ability to provide opportunities for social ascent to those born in the lower ranks."[29]

If capitalism requires strict noninterference by government in the affairs of business, ours has never been a purely capitalistic system. Many of the Founding Fathers favored creating a strong industrial economy and intended to use the powers of government to spur those efforts. Alexander Hamilton, the first secretary of the treasury, wrote in his "Report on Manufactures" to the House of Representatives, "Not only the wealth but the independence and security of a country appear to be materially connected with the prosperity of manufactures."[30] Hamilton stressed the many powers of the Constitution that could be used to favor industrial growth. Then, as now, government has stabilized and subsidized business. With canals, highways, railroads, defense contracts, business loans, and assistance of all kinds, government has helped American industries.

Today, government's role in the economy is far greater than Hamilton imagined. Government spends a third of our GNP; it employs one-sixth of our work force; it regulates our economy. So great is government's role that we call ours a **mixed economy,** one in which the government is deeply involved. Here is how:

— Government is a regulator. Although there have been some efforts to "deregulate" the economy, few sectors escape the long arm of price, quality, or competitive regulation.
— Government is a consumer. Our national government is the world's biggest consumer, buying jeeps, missiles, concrete, computers, food, and so forth.
— Government is a subsidizer. Aid to farmers, to workers displaced by foreign competition, to some companies confronted by bankruptcy, and to school lunch programs are but a few examples of the thousands of governmental subsidies.

[28] Louis Hartz, *The Liberal Tradition in America* (New York: Harcourt, Brace, and World, 1955), p. 89.
[29] Richard Hofstadter, *The American Political Tradition and the Men Who Made It* (New York: Knopf, 1948), p. 104.
[30] Alexander Hamilton, "Report on Manufacturers," in Alpheus Thomas Mason (ed.), *Free Government in the Making* (New York: Oxford University Press, 1949), p. 325.

— Government is a taxer. High taxes levied on one part of the economy may discourage investment in it, while low rates elsewhere may encourage investment there.
— Government is an employer. One in every six Americans works for our national, state, or local governments. The most common government jobs, as you might suspect, are police officer, teacher, and postal carrier.
— Government is a borrower. When government borrows—and it borrowed more than $200 billion in 1985—moneys that you or I could have borrowed go instead to government, and may raise interest rates to private borrowers.

So much economic activity by government galvanizes the attention of interest groups. Think of government as the largest spender in the world. Obviously, many people have many interests in directing government's spending choices. No one has ever counted the number of interest groups involved in getting or preventing particular public policies, but they number in the thousands. Unions, business groups, tobacco growers, private pilots, teachers—almost every group imaginable is moved to action. It is, as Jeffrey Berry remarks, a "bull market for interest groups." [31]

There are some intimate links between the economic performance of government and public opinion. *Voters evaluate the government and the politicians running it on the basis of economic conditions.* Politicians might well agree with the observation of Harry Truman that the pocketbook is the most sensitive part of the voter's anatomy. Consider that:

— Citizens' evaluation of how well the president is managing the economy have a significant effect on the president's popularity. [32]
— The state of the election-year economy has an important effect on the results of the election. [33]

For these reasons, smart politicians invariably put economic policy high on their agenda.

The Perilous Politics of the High-Tech Transformation. It is said that our nation is moving from an industrial to an information economy. Many of our basic industries, such as steel production, are faltering. Cities and regions with these older industries face high unemployment rates and sluggish economic growth while elsewhere, growth abounds.

As a whole, the American economy has been sluggish for more than a decade. Harvard economist Bruce R. Scott reports that "No one can dispute that the United States has been losing its margin of economic leadership for more than thirty years—and that in the last 15 years the deterioration has become more widespread and severe." [34] In the international marketplace, our place of world leadership has eroded. Even in

---

[31] Berry, *Interest Group Society*, p. 67.

[32] George C. Edwards, III, *The Public Presidency: The Pursuit of Popular Support* (New York: St. Martins, 1983), pp. 226–36.

[33] Steven J. Rosenstone, *Forecasting Presidential Elections* (New Haven, Conn.: Yale University Press, 1983), p. 142; D. R. Kinder and D. R. Kiewit, "Economic Grievances and Political Behavior," *American Journal of Political Science*, 23 (August 1979): 495–527.

[34] Bruce R. Scott, "National Strategies for Stronger U.S. Competitiveness," *Harvard Business Review* (March–April, 1984), p. 77.

The Global Economy Comes to the Neighborhoods. *Once New England's textile industry was strong; then textile firms moved south. Today, most textile products (these jeans, for example) are made abroad, particularly in "Pacific Rim" countries such as South Korea, Hong Kong, and the Philippines. In 1985, the U.S. "balance of payments"—the amount we spent for foreign goods versus the amount foreigners spent for our goods—was about $150 billion in the red, meaning that Americans spent that much more for foreign products than the foreigners spent for ours. Not only jeans, but steel, automobiles, computers, and electronics products are often more cheaply made abroad.*

"high-tech" areas—aircraft, office and computing machines, industrial chemicals, and so forth—our share of the world's market has declined since 1965.[35] Investment has shifted from factories to tax shelters, mutual funds, and simply buying out companies. Despite widespread concerns about a "capital shortage" in the United States, American firms have found plenty of cash to purchase one another. Dupont borrowed $4 billion to buy out Conoco; massive ABC was bought by middling Capital Cities Communications; Chevron spent billions buying Gulf Oil Company. Our economy has become dominated, says Robert B. Reich, by "paper entrepreneurs," where money is spent mostly by acquiring, merging, or buying our companies.[36] Little of this "paper entrepreneurialism" actually is invested in new plants or products, which create new jobs, which in turn create new sources of capital.

President Reagan thought he had the solution to our economic problems. Influenced by some deeply committed economists, he preached an economic policy called **supply-side economics.** It emphasized that the economy could be stimulated only by increasing the supply of money in investors' hands. Short-run economic manipulations of the economy were in vain, because long-run investment was more important. If government took too big a bite of economic wealth in taxes, then a tax cut was needed to return money into the hands of investors. Reagan's tax cuts favored the rich, who supposedly had more to invest. The poor lost because cuts in spending tended to hurt them more deeply.

In the Reagan economic policies, as in the economy as a whole, what one group gains, another loses. Today, we live in what economist Lester Thurow called a "zero-sum society." What you win, I must lose, and vice versa. Bluntly, Thurow put it like this: "Whenever government policies raise someone's income, they must lower someone else's income."[37] Political choices must flow from economic realities.

Some believe that our government needs to develop an industrial policy. Government might (as the Japanese do) target certain industries for growth and let others decline. Perhaps government could hand out subsidies to sunrise (growing) industries, thus enabling this country to enjoy a competitive edge in the world's markets. Others hope that government could help out "basic," but declining industries. Government has given handsome loan guarantees to the aircraft manufacturer Lockheed and the automaker Chrysler. These and other economic issues will dominate our economic debate well into the third American century.

Our economic policies help determine our wealth and our income. When government chooses one economic policy over another, groups gain or lose. Not only economic issues, but issues of equality surround wins and losses of various groups in the political arena.

Equality and Public Policy

On December 8, 1955, a black maid named Rosa Parks disobeyed a law in Montgomery, Alabama. Tired after a day's work, she refused to give up

[35]Ibid., p. 79.
[36] Reich, *Next American Frontier*, ch. 8.
[37] Thurow, *Zero-Sum Society*, p. 27.

her bus seat, as required by law, to a white man. That one episode helped spark what was to become the civil rights movement. Black groups, and then other minority groups, challenged laws that caused segregation and discrimination.

However, even after three decades of action, and of policy responses, black and white incomes remain quite unequal. As in all industrial, western nations, a substantial gap exists between the wealthiest and the poorest Americans, many (but not all) of whom are members of minority groups.

Jennifer Hochschild begins her examination of income distribution—who's rich and who's poor and why—by turning to the great fictional detective, Sherlock Holmes. He draws the attention of Watson, his ever-present companion, "to the curious incident of the dog in the night-time." Watson retorts that the dog did nothing in the night. "That," says Holmes, "was the curious incident." Sometimes, says Hochschild, what people do *not* do, what does *not* happen, is worth a close look.

Even though, she says, there is a vast gulf in our country between rich and poor, "the United States does not now have, and seldom has had, a political movement among the poor seeking greater economic equality." [38] The poor, like all Americans, have long been uncertain about equality, pulled toward it as one of our main political symbols on the one hand, but at the same time fearful of it on the other.

What, we should ask, do people really mean by equality? Surely most of us favor it. But where does it begin and where does it end?

American Ambivalence about Equality. Thomas Jefferson, who wrote the Declaration of Independence, was a master phrasemaker. The Declaration proclaimed that "all men are created equal." Since Thomas Jefferson was also a slaveholder, this was indeed a curious observation. Perhaps we should dismiss it as rhetorical exaggeration. Yet Americans often value equality in theory even while they remain ambivalent about it in practice. Jefferson typified this ambivalence. He feared that the wrath of God would be visited upon slaveholders, but he did not free his own slaves. Even the Great Emancipator, Abraham Lincoln, was less than an enthusiastic crusader for abolition. Not until 1845, at age thirty-six, did Lincoln make public his opposition to slavery.[39] Northerners were ambivalent about equality even during the Civil War. "Saving the Union" unified the North more than any abstractions about equality between blacks and whites.

After surveying the American public and its political party leaders, Herbert McClosky concluded, "Both the public and its leaders are uncertain and ambivalent about equality."[40] A clear majority of Americans agreed that "we have to teach children that all men are created equal, but almost everyone knows that some are better than others." Even though most people claimed to favor equality in the abstract, a majority also agreed that "it will always be necessary to have a few strong, able people

[38] Jennifer Hochschild, *What's Fair? American Beliefs about Distributive Justice* (Cambridge, Mass.: Harvard University Press, 1981), p. 1.

[39] Hofstadter, *American Political Tradition*, p. 109.

[40] Herbert McClosky, "Consensus and Ideology in American Politics," *American Political Science Review* 58 (June 1964): 368.

running things." People can favor one kind of equality (say, an equal right to vote), but oppose other forms (say, equal incomes). Robert Lane, after extensive interviews with several working-class men, wrote about their fear of equality. "Many members of the working classes," he wrote, "do not want equality. They are afraid of it."[41] These people had incomes below the national average, but they did not view the rich as unjustly rewarded. They thought the rich were as much entitled to the rewards of their labors as anyone else.

Political versus Economic Equality. To find out how Americans feel about equality, Hochschild interviewed twenty-eight people intensely. Some were rich, some poor, and some in-between. One factor pervaded her thoughtful interviews: Attitudes about equality were characterized by "hesitancy, contradictions, ambiguity." The people she talked to about equality "shade, modulate, deny, retract, or just grind to a halt in frustration."[42] People's views about equality became clearer when they could distinguish between *political* and *economic* equality. Hochschild found that both rich and poor "are generally egalitarian in the political domain. They want political and civil rights to be distributed equally to all citizens." In the economic realm, there was quite another story. There, "both rich and poor support differentiation in the economic domain."[43] Strong support for equality in politics is not matched by a commitment to economic equality.

Today, denying people the right to vote because they are black or female offends Americans' egalitarian impulses. The Bill of Rights is supposed to guarantee equal rights to free speech, press, and religion. Everyone is supposed to enjoy equal rights to trial by jury, to protection against cruel and unusual punishment, and to a fair trial. People are also supposed to enjoy equal access to the ballot box. Constitutional amendments forbid certain kinds of voting inequalities, particularly those based on race and sex. Congress has written other protections of equal voting rights into law while still others have been mandated by court decisions.

Political equality is not identical with social and economic equality. Giving people equal votes may or may not give them more equal incomes, schooling, or housing opportunities. How people fare in the private sector may differ from how they fare in the political arena. Yet issues of social and economic equality often enter the political arena. Most often, they take the form of

— Issues about the distribution of income and wealth.
— Issues about the relationships between blacks or other minorities, and whites.
— Issues about the relationships of males and females.

How Equal Are Americans? Even if, in theory, Americans are equal in the political arena, they are not so equal in the economic arena, as shown

---

[41] Robert E. Lane, "The Fear of Equality," *American Political Science Review,* 53 (March 1959):35.
[42] Hochschild, *What's Fair?,* p. 238.
[43] Ibid., pp. 181 and 147.

In all societies, income is unequally distributed. The top group of income recipients gets a lot; the bottom group gets very little. The Dutch economist Jan Pen suggested that we look at the distribution of income in an industrial society by imagining a parade, where people march by in order of their income, poor first, rich last. In the parade, people's heights are directly proportional to their incomes. Poor people are very, very short. Rich people are like skyscrapers.

Suppose, Pen said, that we are on the reviewing stand watching the parade go by. The parade takes one hour. Remarkably, the first thing we see is a few people of "negative height." These exceptional people are (let us say) walking with their heads in the ground. They are the few people who had negative incomes last year—principally business owners and investors whose losses required them to dip into their capital to make ends meet. But after a few seconds of these bizarre people, the smallest of people begin to appear, people barely the size of matchsticks. Their numbers seem endless. They are often very young or very old, and frequently they are females (the parade seems to follow the rule of "ladies first"), minorities, and handicapped people. After about ten or fifteen minutes, some dwarfs begin to appear. This is the working class, particularly its nonunionized element—farm workers, laborers, and the like. Even at the midpoint of the parade, thirty minutes, we are still seeing dwarfs, though now they are mostly blue-collar workers.

Surprisingly, people of normal height do not appear until forty-eight minutes through the parade. These people are the school teachers, the civil servants, the postal clerks, the unionized workers, and the like. We do not see people of normal height at the midpoint of the parade because the *mean* (or average) income is higher than the *median* income. (The mean is brought up by the handful of very rich people we shall soon see.) But the median income recipient, of course, appeared exactly at the midpoint (thirty minutes) of the parade. Only in the last five minutes of the parade do we begin to see people we might call "middle class." They are the school

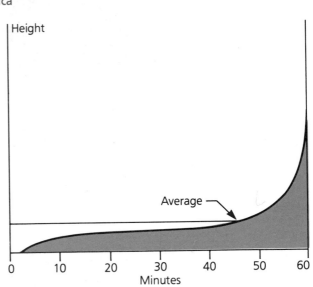

principals, the college professors, the less successful lawyers and engineers, the middle-managers, and the more successful salesmen. In the United States, of course, this group is made up almost completely of white males. Then comes a minute or two of the upper-middle class: the doctors, major lawyers, and corporate executives. But most surprising of all, at the very last seconds of the parade, we see a few real giants—people as tall as skyscrapers or as a city block. These people, who flash by in a split second, are the rich and super-rich. Their numbers are only in the thousands in a parade of 150 million adult Americans.

What lessons does the parable of the parade suggest?

1. Most people have incomes below the *mean,* and dwarfs greatly outnumber giants.
2. The racial and sex distribution of people in the parade is most noticeable. Females and minorities are much shorter than males and whites.
3. There are very, very few rich people in this country, but they are very, very rich indeed.

Source: Adapted from Jan Pen, *Income Distribution: Facts, Theories, Policies* (New York: Praeger, 1971), pp. 48–59.

in 5 . Among the economically developed nations, the United States has one of the least equal distributions of income and wealth. The presidents of some major corporations earn salaries and benefits exceeding $1 million annually. (Actually, some movie and sports celebrities do even better than the presidents of General Motors, Exxon, or other corporate giants.) Yet the *median* family income is only about $24,580, meaning that half the families get more and half get less than that. About 15 percent of the population has income below the *poverty line,* an income level the Bureau of the Census defines as separating poor people from not-poor people. If

More Women in Politics. *A few decades ago, a woman governor elected in her own right (rather than after the death or impeachment of her husband) was a rarity. Vermont's Governor Madeleine Kunin spoke to her fellow governors at the National Governor's Conference in Washington, D.C., in February, 1985. Two United States Senators (Kassebaum, R-Kan. and Hawkins, R-Fla.) are women, but the share of women officials is still far below women's share of the population.*

people are really "created equal," as the Declaration of Independence holds, they certainly do not grow up to be very equal.

Two groups—nonwhites and females—are especially likely to populate the bottom rungs of the income ladder. More than a century has passed since slavery in America was ended by the Thirteenth Amendment, but inequality between blacks and whites persists. The civil rights movement of the 1950s and 1960s, led by Nobel Peace Prize winner Martin Luther King, Jr., focused debate on the gaps between whites and blacks. School desegregation, school busing, open housing, equal employment, and other public policies were used in an attempt to end what President Lyndon Johnson called the "terrible walls that imprison men because they are different from other men." Yet it is clear that the black-white affluence gap has not ended.[44]

An affluence gap also prevails between male and female workers. In general, the male-female income gap is narrowing. In 1965, the average full-time female worker received only 30 percent of the income of the average full-time male worker. Today she gets 62 percent. Women, though, are much less likely to be full-time workers. Millions work part-time. Some are desperately trying to add to a meager family income.

[44] For one balanced assessment, see Reynolds Farley, "Trends in Racial Inequality: Have the Gains of the 1960s Disappeared in the 1970s?" *American Sociological Review* 42 (April 1977):189–208.

Others fit the more conventional stereotype of a wife's seeking part-time employment to supplement a husband's comfortable income. But almost all women workers today expect more equal incomes than they now get.

Equal Opportunity or Equal Results? Our ambivalence about equality complicates our policy choices. Most policies have been designed to promote **equal opportunity,** to try to give everyone a fair chance. Equal opportunity to get a job or buy a house or enter medical school means that we do not discriminate on the basis of sex or skin color or religion or age. But as Allan Sindler remarked, "The American version of equal opportunity ... has always involved acceptance of a large inequality of results among individuals (in income, status, and the like)."[45] Some people think that giving people an equal opportunity is enough. Others believe that bolder and farther-reaching policies are needed to promote more *equal results.* They would give compensatory treatment, using **affirmative action,** to aid traditionally disadvantaged groups (the poor, females, blacks, and other minorities). Affirmative action is intended to require special efforts to hire and promote people from these groups. Governmental policies have frequently insisted that universities, firms, and schools use affirmative action in their hiring and promotion policies.

A man named Bryan Weber worked at a Kaiser Aluminum and Chemical Company plant in Gramercy, Louisiana. He applied there for admission to an apprenticeship training program but was turned down by the company. As a part of its agreement with the union, the company had set aside half of the places in this program for minority applicants. Both the union and the company believed that there were too few skilled minority workers in Kaiser industries. Weber took Kaiser to court, and argued that this affirmative action policy discriminated against whites and favored blacks. Eventually, the United States Supreme Court ruled on this challenge to "reverse discrimination." The Court held that it was not unconstitutional for the union and the company to expand opportunities for minority groups by setting aside places for them in a job-training program. The Weber case, though, reminded us that sometimes equality can be a zero-sum game, in which your gains are my losses. Then, equality becomes a far more controversial goal.

American ambivalence toward equality has fueled policy conflict. Women and minority groups, especially, do not enjoy incomes equivalent to average American incomes. Deploring that state of affairs is one thing; doing something about it requires public policy responses.

Energy, Environment, and Public Policy

One night in March 1979, alarm lights blinked red and warning sirens screamed in a nuclear power plant at Three Mile Island in Pennsylvania. The plant's radioactive core was quickly becoming overheated. Radioactive gasses were beginning to seep into the air. Even more frightening was

[45] Allan P. Sindler, *Bakke, Defunis and Minority Admissions* (New York: Longman's, 1978), p. 11.

the awful prospect of a "meltdown," which would have had the same effect as a hydrogen bomb explosion. Officials fretted privately, but their public story was soothing. Some residents were evacuated, while others fled voluntarily. President Jimmy Carter stayed in close touch as engineers contained the potential disaster. These days, the search for energy is fraught with policy problems and governmental involvement.

The Search for Energy. Growth has produced abundance, higher standards of living, and comfortable profit margins. Even the poor in America are rich by the standards of four-fifths of the world. But growth does not come free. Economic growth requires resources, and the United States is far and away the world's heaviest consumer of nature's bounty. First in many things, the United States is also first in resource consumption.

Oil, coal, tin, nickel, and other minerals are **nonrenewable resources.** Nature does not replenish these resources when we consume them. Most of our energy is taken from nonrenewable resources. The United States contains only 5 percent of the world's population, but it accounts for more than a third of the world's annual energy use. Today our domestic supplies of oil are shrinking, and we are buying more and more from other nations. Our consumption has risen since 1970, while our production has declined. The gap is increasingly narrowed by buying foreign oil, much of it from Arab countries. Transported across the oceans in supertankers, this Arab oil is a political weapon as well as an economic resource. Many oil-exporting nations have formed a group called **OPEC,** the Organization of Petroleum Exporting Countries. Controlling so much of the world's oil—even withholding it from the United States and other countries when displeased—OPEC has tried to become a new world power.

The United States is increasingly oil-poor. This blunt fact prompted several political scientists to remark, "If the name of the game is oil, the United States cannot play."[46] If the game were *coal,* the United States could be an active player. Coal reserves are massive in the United States. But Americans use relatively little coal these days. Even though roughly 90 percent of our energy reserves are coal, only a little over a fifth of our energy consumption comes from coal. The primary reason takes us to another side of the energy/environment issue, the problem of pollution. Coal is a dirty fuel, blackening cities as surely as it blackens the lungs of coal miners.

Protecting the Environment. The cleanliness of our air and water has become a policy issue, just as energy has forced itself onto the policy agenda. Rivers and lakes (like the Mississippi, Ohio, and Potomac Rivers, and Lake Erie) have become dumping grounds for municipal and industrial waste. If George Washington were to attempt his (entirely legendary) feat of tossing a dollar across the Potomac today, it would cross one of

---

[46] Edward Friedland, Paul Seabury, and Aaron Wildavsky, "Oil and the Decline of Western Power," *Political Science Quarterly* 90 (Fall 1975): 445.

Montana's Strip-mining. *Strip-mining, like this activity in Montana, raises issues of energy scarcity and environmental protection. The United States is coal-rich. Enough coal is available to supply our energy needs for a millenium or more. But coal is our most polluting fuel, creating "acid rain" that kills life in lakes and forests in the United States and Canada. Strip-mining is now subject to close government regulation. President Reagan responded to Canadian concerns about acid rain by promising to study the problem carefully before he proposed any legislation to deal with it.*

the most polluted rivers in North America. As with the water, so too with the air: Air pollution has risen to dangerous concentrations in many cities.

Cleaning up water and air, however, can be costly, both monetarily and politically. Workers hear that enforcement of clean air policies may threaten their employer's survival and thus their own jobs. And unemployed workers are in an ugly mood on election day. Automobile drivers welcome cleaner air but resist the cost of pollution-control devices on new cars.

Keeping the environment healthy, free of toxic wastes, beautiful, and unpolluted is one of those goals that almost everyone can be enthusiastic about—at least in the abstract. A survey conducted by the group Resources for the Future asked a sample of Americans what they thought about an extremely strongly worded statement about environmental policy: "Protecting the environment is *so important* that requirements and standards cannot be too high, and continuing improvements must be made *regardless* of cost." Just about half of everyone surveyed agreed with this virtual blank check for environmental protection. [47]

Yet abstract support can easily melt into political conflict. Few people so polarized the issue of environmental protection as President Reagan's first secretary of the interior, James Watt. A conservative, born-again Christian Colorado lawyer, Watt was promoted for the job by a group of westerners sometimes called the Sagebrush Rebellion. They sought private development of federally owned western lands. Colorado brewer Joseph Coors introduced Watt to Reagan's close friend and advisor, Nevada Senator Paul Lexalt. Impressed in a twenty-minute interview, Reagan hired Watt. But the new Secretary of the Interior immediately found himself at odds with environmentalists and others on almost every issue. Outrage over a slur about minorities and the handicapped finally forced Watt to quit. Most environmentalists rejoiced.

[47] "Public Opinion on Environmental Issues," Appendix A of *Environmental Quality,* Eleventh Annual Report of the Council on Environmental Quality (Washington: Government Printing Office, 1980), p. 402.

The conflict between Watt and the environmentalists emphasizes that the choices between energy and environment are hard ones. They require trade-offs: We can open up more lands to development of energy, but more trees, mountains, and wildlife will be disturbed or destroyed in the process. We would pay less attention to this trade-off if we had ample energy resources of our own. But we do not. America now imports about a third of its oil. This draws us more tightly into the global connection.

THE GLOBAL CONNECTION

The Romans had a god named Janus, who had two faces: One faced east, the other west. Public policy issues have two faces, too. One is the domestic face, and the other we call the global connection. Once we could neatly separate domestic and foreign policy issues. Today, they are a web of interconnections. One connection is the nuclear umbrella: American and Soviet missiles can reach any spot on the globe in a matter of minutes. The world is connected by issues of the economy, equality, and energy/environment, too.

We just looked at the American domestic face of these issues. Global issues mirror domestic ones: Our economic penetration into the world economy increases the importance of international economic issues; the gap between rich and poor nations raises issues of international equality; our dependence on foreign raw materials makes us vulnerable to political decisions in other nations.

Economically, we are linked to the rest of the world by a web of financial transactions, loans, and debts. American banks are a major lender to poor nations. Latin American nations in particular have borrowed heavily to keep their economies afloat. Brazil now owes other nations $90 billion, Mexico almost $90 billion, and Argentina more than $40 billion to banks and international lending agencies. The British economist Lord Lever has written about this "time bomb of debt" that "the nine biggest banks in the United States have lent to risky countries in Latin America and elsewhere, sums amounting to more than 250 percent of their capital and reserves."[48] In other words, for every dollar on deposit, these banks have lent out two and a half to third-world, often economically shaky, countries. These governments often "renegotiate" their loans periodically just to be able to pay the accumulating interest. Although it is an explosive economic issue, debts are not the only issue on the global economic agenda.

Staggering inequalities separate rich from poor nations. The United States, for example, is an economic giant, with only 6 percent of the world's population, but a third of the world's income. India has a full 15 percent of the world's population and a small fraction of its income. The *Global 2000 Report to the President* predicts that by the year 2000 "the gap between the richest and the poorest [countries] will have increased."[49] Poor nations react to their distressed status internally and externally.

[48] Harold Lever, "The Debt Won't Be Paid," *New York Review of Books*, June 28, 1984, p. 3.
[49] *The Global 2000 Report to the President* (New York: Penguin Books, 1982), p. 39.

Revolutionary movements demand a redistribution of wealth from upper classes to the poor. In international organizations, such as the United Nations, poor nations insist that the developed nations support plans for eradicating malnutrition, poverty, and inequalities.

Energy and environmental issues are not confined to the domestic face of public policy. National boundaries divide the world and consequently control of its natural resources. Oil is but one example. Cobalt, essential for the manufacture of jet aircraft engines, comes mostly from the African nation of Zaire. More than half the world's reserves of platinum, manganese, chromium, and gold, as well as a quarter of its uranium resources, are located in the turbulent nations of southern Africa. [50]

Today, issues of the global connection go well beyond issues of war and peace. The nuclear umbrella covers another world of problems, ones which affect American lives directly.

POLITICS AND GOVERNMENT IN THE THIRD AMERICAN CENTURY SUMMARIZED

Important megatrends are at work in American politics. At the beginning of the third American century, technology is transforming our politics. Even matters of life and death often involve public policy decisions. A biomedical transformation, new technologies of computing and communications, and the frightful new technologies of war are—if nothing else—expensive. We took a quick peek in this chapter at how these trends are reshaping our government and our politics. The growth of government has been significant in the last several decades. Many people believe that we cannot do everything at once.

In Chapter 1, we defined three key terms: politics, government, and public policy. There are many reasons why people become involved in politics: some for the sheer fun of it; and some because they see that our national future is shaped by a government that spends one-third of our gross national product.

Public policy represents the choices government makes in response to some issue on its agenda. In a democratic government, political linkage institutions (parties, groups, and elections) play a key role in determining a government's agenda. Once an issue is on the government's agenda, policymaking institutions (presidents, Congress, the bureaucracy, and the courts) scan the agenda and select policies. Policies have to be implemented; few of them automatically achieve their goals.

To be sure, there are many issues on our national agenda. We have stressed three issue arenas: the economy, equality, and energy-environment. Each of these has two faces. Once, our nation could pay attention mainly to the domestic policy agenda. Now it is tangled in the skein of the global connection. On the world stage, we also deal with policy issues involving the world economy, equality among nations, and the world's environment and energy.

[50] James Coates, "Metals Speculators Boost Defense Costs," *Chicago Tribune*, June 30, 1981, p. 1f.

Key Terms

gross national product	trade-offs	capitalism
high-tech politics	political system	mixed economy
machines	political issue	supply-side economics
politics	linkage institutions	equal opportunity
political participation	policy agenda	affirmative action
power	implementation	nonrenewable
government	policy impacts	resources
public policy	political economy	

For Further Reading

Caro, Robert A. *The Power Broker: Robert Moses and the Fall of New York* (1974). A massive Pulitzer Prize winning biography about how politics and power can literally reshape the landscape of a major city.

Hochschild, Jennifer L. *What's Fair? American Beliefs about Distributive Justice* (1981). An assessment, based upon in-depth interviews, of what Americans believe about the distribution of income in our country.

Kingdon, John W. *Agendas, Alternatives, and Public Policies* (1984). One of the first major efforts to examine the rise and fall of issues on the policy agenda.

Naisbitt, John. *Megatrends* (1982). A popularized, but provocative book on some possible long-run changes in America's society, economy, and government.

Peters, B. Guy. *American Public Policy* (1982). An excellent introduction to the processes and content of American public policy.

Reich, Robert B. *The Next American Frontier: A Provocative Program for Economic Renewal* (1983). Reich criticizes our "paper entrepreneurs" and stresses the key role of our political system in any economic renewal.

Thurow, Lester C. *The Zero-Sum Society* (1980). Thurow examines an economy in which growth is minimal and emphasizes that politics will shift from issues of growth to issues of redistribution.

Understanding American Government

> **MEMO**
>
> With our rapidly changing technology, government in America today is especially complex. In this chapter, we show that government and politics take place in real places, with real people, at the grassroots. We introduce four American communities: San Jose, California; Bethlehem, Pennsylvania; San Antonio, Texas; and Smyrna, Tennessee. In each of them we see politics at work. You will find the discussions of the four communities easy to grasp, because each is like your own community in some ways.
>
> I also present four principal theories of American government and politics. Each asks: Who really has power in our government? Their assumptions are different; so are their explanations of the dynamics of the system. Thus, they cannot all be equally correct. These four theories are:
>
> - *Democratic Theory.* In a democratic government, people have power over their policymakers. Majorities rule, while respecting the rights of minorities. In the long run, at least, public policy conforms to the preferences of the majority.
> - *Elite and Class Theory.* A class-based interpretation of American government holds that upper classes—the elite—have power greatly out of proportion to their numbers. Policies are made by a handful of men, and an even smaller number of women.
> - *Pluralist Theory.* American politics can be seen as the struggle of groups to control public policy. Many groups enter the political arena, each competing for public policy advantage.
> - *Hyperpluralist Theory.* Policymaking in America is complex. Many groups are in the political arena. Government can become so complex that the effectiveness of the system is threatened. Too much hyperpluralism produces rigidification.
>
> Keep in mind these four theories as you read the rest of *Government in America.* We will meet them again and again. Do not stake your claim yet. Consider the evidence, now and later, and shape your own reasoned understanding of American government.

A FEW YEARS AGO, when the government issued the annual edition of its *Organization Manual*, which lists the locations, telephone numbers, and staff of all its agencies, it made a wise choice for its cover: a labyrinth.

Nineteenth-century Supreme Court Justice Joseph Story once remarked that "in proportion as a government is free, it must be complicated." If our government's complexity equals freedom, Americans must be a free people indeed. Washington lawyer Robert N. Kharasch aptly titled his book about government *The Institutional Imperative: How to Understand the United States Government and Other Bulky Objects.* [1] Our complicated government sometimes looks like a Rube Goldberg contraption. ☐1 Understanding this "bulky object" called American government is our task in this chapter.

Often we speak about "the government." Yes, there is "a government" in Washington, but it is composed of bits, pieces, shards, parts, elements, and fragments which do not always fit neatly together. Perhaps Justice Story would be proud of how complicated our government has become. Consider the following tidbits:

— The United States Bureau of the Census not only counts how many *people* live in the United States, but how many *governments* we have. At its latest count, there were 82,341 governments in our country. Early in this chapter, we will look at four of them in four American communities. The biggest of these many governments, of course, is the one in Washington, and fifty are state governments. A staggering 82,290 are local governments. Nearly 500,000 Americans are *elected* public officials. One, of course, is our President but hundreds of thousands are local school board members, city council members, and so forth. Justice Story would find plenty of complexity here.

[1] Robert N. Kharasch, *The Institutional Imperative* (New York: Charterhouse Books, 1973).

☐1 A Rube Goldberg Contraption. A Metaphor for American Government?

— All our laws passed by Congress are collected in what is called the *United States Code.* Its index alone comprises ten volumes. All the rules of the various bureaucratic agencies are recorded in the *Federal Register,* and it ran to 50,998 pages in 1984. President Reagan sometimes cites the declining size of the *Federal Register* as an example of how he has helped get "government off our backs."
— A reporter for the *Chicago Tribune* once interviewed one of those "faceless bureaucrats" in Washington, the woman who edits the *United States Government Organization Manual.* So massive is her job of compiling everything about the government in one book that she stoutly maintained, "If we don't have a board or commission, it isn't because it has been misplaced or forgotten. It's because we don't know about it for some reason or another. We'll find it eventually." [2] It would be comforting to Justice Story to know that the government is not likely to lose or misplace parts of itself.

Our job in this chapter is to find our way through this labyrinth. We obviously need some roadmaps. We begin where politics often begins, at the grassroots.

A TALE OF FOUR CITIES

Politics takes place everywhere. It takes place in the White House and the U.S. Capitol—in homes, schools, neighborhoods, and work places. Here we look for some lenses through which we can see in *micro*scopic detail the *macro*scopic American political system at work. We find four such lenses in four American cities. They may be like your community in some ways, different in others. Use this early chance to reflect upon how they are similar to and different from your community.

San Jose: The Politics of Silicon Valley

A popular song asks if you know the way to San Jose. [3] Indeed, it is not hard to find. It is at the southern tip of a twenty-five-mile long strip from Palo Alto, the home of Stanford University.

San Jose, California, is the nation's seventeenth largest city, with a population reported to be 625,763 in the 1980 census. (This represents a hefty boost from the city's 200,000 population only twenty years before.) Santa Clara County, in which it is located, had 1.3 million people. San Jose is one of America's high-tech capitals, a modern boomtown. Its industry—often referred to as "sunrise industry" to distinguish it from the supposedly declining "sunset industries" of the industrial northeast—was begun in the 1930s and it boomed in the 1970s. In 1938, two young scientist-entrepreneurs, William Hewlett and David Packard, formed Hewlett-Packard, now one of America's largest computer corporations. An "HP" is a standard in the computer business. (Apple Computers is just down the road in nearby Cupertino.)

[2] *Chicago Tribune,* July 4, 1976, p. 23.
[3] On San Jose politics, see Philip J. Trounstine and Terry Christensen, *Movers and Shakers: The Study of Community Power* (New York: St. Martin's, 1982).

Hewlett-Packard. *Crowning Silicon Valley is the mighty Hewlett-Packard Corporation, a major defense contractor and a principal supplier of business computing systems. Silicon Valley could not survive if it depended on the home computer market alone; major defense contracts are a key to its success. Hewlett-Packard's founder, David Packard, is a former Defense Department official, a member of San Jose's and the nation's elite, and one of the wealthiest men in America.*

Equally important, HP is one of the nation's largest defense contractors. Familiar names in the defense contracting business—Fairchild, General Electric, Lockheed, Hewlett-Packard, and National Semiconductor—have operations in or around San Jose in what is known as Silicon Valley. Although Santa Clara County comprises only about .5 percent of the nation's population, it captures about 3 percent of the nation's defense contracts.[4] Computer technology did not come about merely because families wanted personal computers. The technology that brings us home, school, and office computing is the same technology that can send missiles to Moscow.

San Jose is a small part of our most populous state. California politics is like no other; it shifts like the San Andreas fault, which cuts through the state. Politicians as diverse as Richard Nixon, Jerry Brown, and Ronald Reagan have hailed from it. Political parties in the Golden State are weak. California is the citadel of groups and group politics: Orange County's conservative and right-wing groups, women of many political persuasions, liberal activists, Mexican-American farm workers, San Francisco's gays, business and industrial leaders who advised first Richard Nixon and then Ronald Reagan, and many others. Politicians in a big state must play a different game from politicians in a smaller one. To reach so many voters, technology is important—and expensive. Christensen and Gerston report on high-cost politics in a high-tech state:[5]

> "It's funny," one advertising man said, "but politicians now think of the state in terms of television markets, rather than counties or senate districts as they used to." . . . By 1982, sixty-second television spots cost $15,000 in Los Angeles and $8000 in San Francisco, giving lots of advantages to candidates with lots of money.

[4] Ibid., p. 90.
[5] Terry Christensen and Larry N. Gerston, *The California Connection: Politics in the Golden State* (Boston: Little, Brown, 1984), p. 93.

California politicians pioneered special appeals to special interests. They have used, even invented, much of the technology of modern campaigns. Los Angeles Mayor Tom Bradley, the state's first serious black candidate for governor, solicited women's votes by sending out half-a-million letters, automatically but "personally" typed by machine, to all California women who used "Ms." before their names when they registered to vote. Reminding them that he "was committed to women's issues," he implied that his opponent was not.[6] Again and again in our story, we will meet San Jose and California, the quintessentially West Coast city in the quintessentially West Coast state. In sharp contrast stands a city in a state on the other side of America.

Bethlehem: Hub of a Declining Steel Industry

Pennsylvania is the cradle of the Union. In Philadelphia our American Constitution was signed in 1787. Even then, Bethlehem, the oldest of our four communities, existed.

In 1980, the population of Bethlehem, Pennsylvania, was 272,000, up by just 7 percent since the 1970 census. If San Jose stands for growth, then Bethlehem signals the decline many see when they look at the industrialized eastern seaboard. It is the headquarters of Bethlehem Steel, our second largest steel manufacturer. American steel in general and Bethlehem Steel in particular have fallen on hard times. Some cite the steel industry as a prime example of American's "sunset industry." Unemployment at Bethlehem is high, as layoffs have spread throughout the steel industry. In December 1983, Bethlehem's biggest American competitor, United States Steel, announced layoffs of 15,000 workers, 15 percent of its total work force. It justified its layoffs by pointing to its 1982 losses of $852 million. Bethlehem had already cut its work force by one-third in three years, saving a billion dollars in labor costs. These days, Beth-

[6] Ibid., p. 45.

Bethlehem, Pennsylvania. *In December 1982, workers lined up in an unemployment office in Bethlehem. Many, perhaps most, were laid-off steelworkers in this once-proud steel capital. But Bethlehem Steel and its main American competitor, United States Steel, have lost their dominance of the world market. Some say that steel is a basic industry, which government should assist. Others favor diverting government support to "sunrise" industries that could compete effectively with foreign industry. Traditionally Democratic, Bethlehem showed strong support for Ronald Reagan in 1984.*

lehem's biggest competitor is not U.S. Steel, but foreign manufacturers. One South Korean plant at Pohang produces 9.1 million tons a year. Its workers get $2.50 an hour, compared with Japanese wages of $18 an hour and wages of about $24 an hour at American plants like Bethlehem's. [7]

Bethlehem has long been a Democratic party stronghold. It has all the ingredients of pro-Democratic politics: heavily blue-collar, heavily Roman Catholic, heavily unionized, and heavily ethnic. Ever since Franklin D. Roosevelt forged a New Deal coalition during the dire days of the Great Depression, these groups have looked to the Democratic party to represent the masses against the classes. Yet Ronald Reagan fared surprisingly well here in 1980 and 1984. Some political scientists believed that the Democratic coalition that Roosevelt forged fifty years ago was breaking up. When places like Bethlehem tilt away from the Democratic party, then important shifts are taking place in American politics.

San Antonio: A High-Tech Capital Amid Poverty

San Antonio, Texas, is the nation's tenth largest city, far bigger than its image of a sleepy town surrounding the Alamo. [8] It is also the nation's largest city with a Hispanic mayor, Henry Cisneros, who supplements his meager mayoral pay by teaching political science. The computer company consortium, MCT (Microelectronics and Computer Technology Corporation), has located in Austin. Its president, Bobby Ray Inman, former deputy director of the Central Intelligence Agency, believes that the corridor between San Antonio and Austin (the state capital and home of the University of Texas) eighty miles north of San Antonio, will be the next decade's Silicon Valley.

But if San Antonio is going to catch a rising star, it has far to go: In 1980, it was the poorest of the nation's large cities. The Census Bureau counts 44 percent of San Antonio's population as Hispanic. Local officials believe that the Hispanic share is 54 percent, with blacks constituting 8 percent and "Anglos" (Texas lingo for whites) representing 38 percent. Some of these Hispanics (no one knows exactly how many) are illegal immigrants. The commissioner of the Immigration and Naturalization Service estimated that perhaps 12 million noncitizens were in our country illegally. [9] Many have come from Mexico. Among San Antonio's Hispanic voters, the vast majority are Democrats; but their turnout is low. Republicans have been eager to convert them to their ranks. President Reagan spoke to a Mexican-American gathering in San Antonio on Cinco de Mayo—a major Mexican national holiday—on May 5, 1983, appealing to their patriotism, their strong family ties, and their work ethic.

San Antonio Mayor Henry Cisneros. *San Antonio is the largest American city with an Hispanic chief executive. It is also the nation's poorest "big city." As mayor, Cisneros has tried to link San Antonio with the growing technological corridor from Bexar County to Austin, the Texas capital and site of the University of Texas. At the 1984 Democratic Convention, Cisneros strongly supported the Democratic ticket and platform.*

[7] Art Pine, "Third World's Gains in the Basic Industries Stir a Sharp Backlash," *Wall Street Journal*, April 13, 1984, p. 1f.

[8] On San Antonio, see the excellent collection of articles in David R. Johnson, John A. Booth, and Richard J. Harris (eds.), *The Politics of San Antonio: Community, Progress, and Power* (Lincoln: University of Nebraska Press, 1983). An earlier study of San Antonio is Robert L. Lineberry, *Equality and Urban Policy: The Distribution of Municipal Public Services* (Beverly Hills, Calif.: Sage, 1974).

[9] Cited in James Fallows, "The New Immigration," *Atlantic* (November, 1983): 46

The whole economic base of San Antonio is dependent on defense spending. Huge Air Force and Army bases are located there. So much money is pumped into the local economy through the defense budget that one local observed that "if the Cold War ever ends, San Antonio is in trouble."

San Antonio politics is part of Texas politics. Politics in Texas ranges from the mildly liberal to the wildly conservative. A moneyed, oil-rich elite has considerably influenced Texas politics. About an hour west of San Antonio is the Texas hill country, from which President Lyndon Baines Johnson hailed. Our old image of Texas as a rural state is belied by the overwhelmingly urban character of the Texas population. Three of the nation's ten biggest cities (Houston, Dallas, and San Antonio) are in Texas. From this big state and these big cities, we turn now to a very small city.

Smyrna: The Japanese Build a Factory

Smyrna, Tennessee, a town of about 9000 people located in central Tennessee in Rutherford County, is as typical a small, southern, agricultural town as you could find. Just one fact makes it different—very different—from hundreds (and thousands) of small farming centers elsewhere: Mighty Nissan Corporation, Japan's second largest automobile manufacturer, opened an American factory there in the summer of 1983.[10] It cost $85 million and, when fully operational, will employ 2,650 workers. Very likely, these will be non-unionized workers. Tennessee is a "right-to-work" state (on right-to-work laws, refer to Chapter 17, page 561) and unions have never found much favor with southern workers. (Union leaders even said that was why the Japanese picked Smyrna.) Despite the national attention given to Smyrna and its new plant, it was not the first Japanese-owned plant in our country, not even

[10] Michael Lenehan, "A Japanese Auto Maker Finds a Home," *Atlantic* (December, 1982): 12–19.

Smyrna, Tennessee. *On June 16, 1983, the first Nissan trucks rolled out of the Smyrna plant, where robots spit weld truck cabs on the assembly line. The first Nissan cars came less than two years later. Tennessee's efforts to attract Japanese industry have met with real success, proving that American communities are very much a part of a global economy.*

the first in Tennessee. ☐2 Eleven other Japanese firms preceded Nissan in Tennessee alone. Smyrna and Tennessee are very much a part of the global economy which we described in Chapter 1.

One result of Nissan's presence is a spin-off of new jobs. Hoover Universal, for example, makes seats for the new Nissan trucks, and it already has three factories in Tennessee and plans to build a fourth down the road from Smyrna in Murphreesboro, the county seat. A model of high-tech industrial efficiency, Nissan's and Hoover's assembly lines will communicate by computer so that inventories need never lag.

Tennessee would not have had so much to offer Nissan and other new investors had it not been for the role the federal government has played in Tennessee's history. During the 1930s, Tennessee and neighboring states benefitted from the federal government's creation of the massive Tennessee Valley Authority, a string of dams and locks on the Tennessee (and other) rivers. The TVA provided electricity for communities and energy for the whole region. For years, Tennessee politicians have been effective in bringing home federal dollars. The state of Tennessee received $1.7 billion in federal aid in 1983. Senator Howard Baker, the former minority leader of the United States Senate, won friends and influenced people through his ability to support projects back home. The Clinch River atomic breeder reactor was only one of Senator Baker's pet projects, funded to the tune of nearly $2 billion over a decade.

In these four communities we have taken a microscopic view of American politics. Let us now take a macroscopic view of our political system. Theories will help us do that, for there is much detail to be sorted out.

On March 24, 1985, Komatsu, the world's second largest manufacturer of construction equipment (after Caterpillar Tractor Company), announced in Tokyo that it would buy a plant in Chattanooga, Tennessee. By 1988, about 250 workers would be turning out heavy construction equipment, industrial robots, and other machinery there. Komatsu joined scores of other major Japanese plants in Tennessee. This map shows some of the major Japanese-owned plants in that state, together with the approximate number of employees in each.

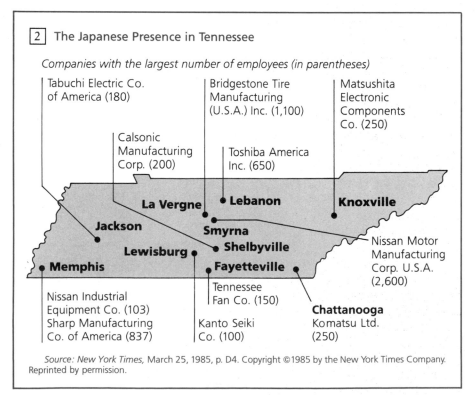

☐2 **The Japanese Presence in Tennessee**

Companies with the largest number of employees (in parentheses)

Tabuchi Electric Co. of America (180)

Calsonic Manufacturing Corp. (200)

Bridgestone Tire Manufacturing (U.S.A.) Inc. (1,100)

Toshiba America Inc. (650)

Matsushita Electronic Components Co. (250)

La Vergne • Lebanon   Knoxville

Jackson

Smyrna

Lewisburg • • Shelbyville

• Memphis   • Fayetteville

Nissan Motor Manufacturing Corp. U.S.A. (2,600)

Nissan Industrial Equipment Co. (103)
Sharp Manufacturing Co. of America (837)

Tennessee Fan Co. (150)

Kanto Seiki Co. (100)

Chattanooga
Komatsu Ltd. (250)

Source: New York Times, March 25, 1985, p. D4. Copyright ©1985 by the New York Times Company. Reprinted by permission.

USING THEORIES

Why We Need Theories

All bodies of knowledge use theories to simplify a mass of detail. In physics, there are Newtonian theories, atomic theories, and theories of relativity. The history of science can be written in terms of the theories which competed with one another over the centuries.

Theories of American politics are also plentiful. There are elite theories, rational choice theories, cultural theories, psychological theories, and many others. Each focuses on a key element as that theory views it and each reaches a somewhat different conclusion. Theories of American government and politics are essentially theories about who has power and influence. All, in one way or another, ask the key question: Who really governs in our nation?

Theories are of two types: theories about *what is* and theories about *what ought to be*. It is easy to confuse the two. Theories in such natural sciences as molecular biology or analytical chemistry are exclusively *empirical*. An **empirical theory** rests on observations relative to nature that can be verified with evidence. Its goal is to describe real-world phenomenon with accuracy and brevity. Some theories in political science are mainly empirical. They contain statements relative to the world of government and politics that can be verified. But other theories in political science are concerned with how things ought to be, and these make *normative* statements. A **normative theory** evaluates rather than merely explains. It labels things good or bad and deals with questions of "should" and "ought."

Consider the following statements about American politics, which can easily be categorized as empirical or normative theories;

1. The executive branch has become bigger and more powerful than it was originally. (empirical)
2. The American president has become too powerful for the nation's own good. (normative)

In *Government in America,* we will consider four theories of American politics. You are forewarned that they sometimes intermingle normative and empirical elements. You can, for example, believe that democratic theory is normatively desirable, that it is best to have a democratic government. You can simultaneously believe that American politics is not really a very close approximation of a true democratic government. You should not decide right now which of these theories is correct and which false. Indeed, it may trouble you to find competing theories of American politics here. You may prefer those branches of knowledge in which everything can be reduced to an equation or a formula. The study of American politics is not like that. Political science, like economics, sees many contending perspectives and fiercely debated theories. (President Harry Truman once grumbled that "if all the economists in the world were laid end to end . . . they wouldn't reach a conclusion.")

The strategy used in *Government in America* is to avoid the impression that there is a single "truth, whole truth, and nothing but the truth" about

American government. We deliberately present four contrasting theories of American politics and government. Quite likely, you will end up thinking that none of these perfectly describes American government. Yet they are not completely incompatible, although they do present very different views of American political life. Here, and throughout the book, we will focus on these four theories:

Democratic Theory. In a democratic government, the country is governed by the influence of citizens on policymakers. Because most Americans have a normative preference for democratic theory, it is easy (but perhaps not fully accurate) to conclude that the American system is an empirically democratic one.

Elite and Class Theory. All societies, including ours, are divided into social classes. When "the classes" have vast power and "the masses" have little, an upper-class elite rules. Then, of course, little democracy can exist.

Pluralist Theory. This theory contends that many centers of influence vie for power and control. Groups compete with one another for control over public policy. Bargaining, compromise, and trading are important ingredients in a pluralist system.

Hyperpluralist Theory. Hyperpluralism is pluralism gone sour. Just as it is said too many cooks spoil the broth, too many competing groups spoil government's ability to govern. Fragmentation threatens the effectiveness of government and produces rigidification.

THEORY 1: DEMOCRACY IN THEORY AND IN PRACTICE

Democracy is a much overused word. So utterly positive are its connotations today that the word takes its place among words like *freedom, justice,* and *peace* as a value that almost everyone favors but no one examines very carefully.[11]

Democracy was not always so popular. The writers of the American Constitution had no fondness for democracy as they understood it. Elbridge Gerry of Massachusetts told his fellow delegates to the Constitutional Convention, "The evils we experience flow from the excess of democracy." Alexander Hamilton spoke of the "imprudence of democracy." Perhaps emboldened (in what a contemporary politician might call an off-the-record remark), he told a fellow guest at a dinner party, "Your people, sir, are a great beast."

[11] One of the few Americans to argue seriously against values like freedom and democracy is behavioral psychologist B. F. Skinner, who thinks these values are simply impossible—even dangerous—in a society like ours. Needless to say, his arguments are not popular. You can examine his perspective for yourself in *Beyond Freedom and Dignity* (New York: Knopf, 1971).

Much later, Americans came to cherish democracy, even if they did not always know exactly what it meant. In the twentieth century, democracy is almost universally considered praiseworthy. But ideas that are so widely shared sometimes become almost emptied of meaning. The philosopher Carl Cohen remarked, "As a consequence of careless rhetoric, intellectual confusion, and even some deliberate deception, the term *democracy* has been largely drained of meaning. Applied to almost everything in the sphere of politics, it has come to mean almost nothing." [12] *Democracy* may be the sort of word about which Humpty Dumpty observed in *Through the Looking Glass*, "When I make a word do that much work, I pay it extra."

Today, most Americans would probably say that democracy is "government by the people." Lincoln's ringing rhetoric on "government of the people, by the people, and for the people" still echoes majestically. The best that may be said of this conception of democracy is that its informativeness does not match its brevity. Really, said E. E. Schattschneider, "we ought to get rid of confusing language such as 'government by the people.' To say that 200 million Americans 'govern' does not shed much light on the role of people in the American political system." [13] Two hundred million Americans could not do much governing if they wanted to. With a little rhetoric of his own, Schattschneider remarked:

> No one has ever seen the American people because the human eye is not able to take in the view of four million square miles over which they are scattered. What would they look like if (ignoring all logistical difficulties) they could be brought together in one place? Standing shoulder to shoulder in military formation, they would occupy an area of about sixty-six square miles.
>
> The logistical problem of bringing 200 million bodies together is trivial, however, compared with the task of bringing about a meeting of 200 million minds. Merely to shake hands with that many people would take a century. How much discussion would it take to form a common opinion? A single round of five-minute speeches would require five thousand years. If only one percent of those present spoke, the assembly would be forced to listen to two million speeches. People could be born, grow old and die while they waited for the assembly to make one decision.
>
> In other words, an all-American town meeting would be the largest, longest, and most boring and frustrating meeting imaginable. What could such a meeting produce? Total paralysis. What could it do? Nothing. [14]

Despite Schattschneider's reservations about government by the people, most Americans would still say that our government is democratic. What do they mean? Here is a basic definition, used throughout this book: **Democracy** is a means of selecting policymakers and of organizing government to ensure that policy represents and responds to the public's preferences.

---

[12] Carl Cohen, *Democracy* (Athens, Ga.: University of Georgia Press, 1971), p. xiii.

[13] E. E. Schattschneider, *Two Hundred Million Americans in Search of a Government* (New York: Holt, Rinehart and Winston, 1969), p. 63.

[14] Ibid., pp. 60–61.

Traditional Democratic Theory

What we call **traditional democratic theory** rests upon several principles.[15] These principles specify how a democratic government makes its decisions. One contemporary democratic theorist, Robert A. Dahl, suggests that "an ideal democratic process would satisfy five criteria."[16] Here are his cornerstones of traditional democratic theory:

1. *Equality in voting.* Giving whites two votes and blacks only one is undemocratic, because it violates the principle of equality in voting. When citizens have different preferences about policies or leaders, they need an equal chance to express their views.
2. *Effective participation.* Citizens must act on their opinions by participating effectively in political institutions. Political participation need not be universal, but it must be representative. If only high-income people vote, the result is the same as if the wealthy had literally been given extra votes.
3. *Enlightened understanding.* Democracy must be a marketplace of ideas. A free press and free speech are essential to civic understanding. When one group monopolizes or distorts information, citizens cannot develop enlightened understanding.
4. *Final control over the agenda.* Citizens should have the collective right to control government's agenda. If too much money, or too much manipulation, distorts the government agenda, then citizens have handed over control to those who have the money or do the manipulating.
5. *Inclusion.* The government must include, and extend rights to, all those subject to its laws. Citizenship must be open to all within a nation. Denial of the right to participate denies the right of a nation to call itself democratic.

Only by following these principles can a system qualify for the label "democratic." Only then can it observe **majority rule** and **minority rights.** In a democracy, choosing among alternatives (whether policies or officeholders) requires that the majority's desire be respected. Nothing is more fundamental to democratic theory than majority rule. Belief in it is deeply etched in the American mind. Alexis de Tocqueville, the great French traveller through America in the 1830s, wrote that "the very essence of democratic government consists in the absolute sovereignty of the majority. The power of the majority in America [is] not only preponderant, but irresistible."[17] Tocqueville, interestingly, was only describing, not approving. In fact, his observations about majority rule in America conclude with this harsh judgment: "This state of things is

[15] This conception of traditional democratic theory is derived from Robert A. Dahl, *Preface to Democratic Theory* (Chicago: University of Chicago Press, 1956), Chaps. 2, 3; Joseph A. Schumpeter, *Capitalism, Socialism, and Democracy* (New York: Harper & Row, 1942), Chap. 21; Anthony Downs, *An Economic Theory of Democracy* (New York: Harper & Row, 1957), pp. 22–24; and Cohen, *Democracy.*

[16] Robert A. Dahl, *Dilemmas of Pluralist Democracy* (New Haven, Conn.: Yale University Press, 1983), p. 6.

[17] Alexis de Tocqueville, *Democracy in America* (New York: Mentor Books, 1956), pp. 112–13.

harmful in itself, and dangerous for the future." Today, most Americans would disagree with Tocqueville. We believe that in a democracy majorities should rule, while guaranteeing minorities rights in order that they might sometime become majorities through persuasion and reasoned argument.

Majority rule and minority rights in a small town or civic group is one thing. Uprooting them from the small locale and superimposing them upon a vast and varied nation is quite another. Direct control by the citizens is replaced by indirect control at best. Obviously, in any government too large to make its decisions in open meetings, a few will have to carry on the affairs of the many. The relationship between the few leaders and the many followers is called **representation.** The closer the correspondence between representatives and their electoral majority, the closer the democratic approximation. But there are many reasons why representatives cannot, or will not, mirror majority preference on each issue. Representatives may think they have more information than their constituents (those they represent), and in some instances may be right. A campaign donation or an impressive presentation at a hearing has been known to modify a representative's view.

Some of the toughest problems with democracy in practice are problems of representation. If it does not work, democracy does not work. In San Jose, for example, there are locally elected representatives who serve on the city council; state assemblymen and senators in state government in Sacramento; a representative to the United States House of Representatives; and two United States senators from California. All are supposed to "represent" the majority of voters in the San Jose area—no easy task.

To enjoy effective representation, we need **electoral accountability,** the ability of the electorate to vote out of office anyone who has not accurately or honestly represented the majority's policy goals. Sometimes, though, representatives do not court public opinion; they may be motivated by other goals. Kenneth Prewitt, for example, studied city councils in the San Francisco Bay area and found that many council members, who were serving in low-pay or no-pay tasks, considered themselves volunteers. They saw themselves as performing tough jobs at considerable sacrifice and had no strong interests in political careers. They felt free, therefore, to ignore majority preference if it was not in agreement with their own policy goals. [18] You can see that guaranteeing effective representation in a democracy is no easy task.

A Gap or a Chasm? Democracy in Theory and in Practice

Almost all Americans believe in normative democratic theory. The question, though, is how well it lives up to these high ideals empirically. There is a gap—some would say a wide chasm—between democracy in theory and democracy in practice. Let us see why.

[18] Kenneth Prewitt, "Political Ambitions, Volunteerism and Electoral Accountability," *American Political Science Review* 64 (March 1907): 5–17.

Are the People Falling Down on the Job? Under the best of circumstances, it is difficult to maintain democratic government in a nation of 234 million people. But when citizens take little advantage of what powers they do have, democracy is threatened by those who are supposed to benefit from it.

Maintaining genuine equality of information and participation in a large society is a difficult—some might say impossible—task. There is plenty of evidence that Americans do not know much about their government's institutions or even who their United States senators and representatives are. And if they do not know the names of their elected officials, it is not likely that they will be able to pass intelligent judgment on the officials' actions. Patricia Hurley and Kim Q. Hill found that only 17 percent of the population could make an accurate guess about how their United States representatives voted on *any* issue before Congress.[19] Such widespread ignorance of our policymakers and their policies inspires little confidence in people's abilities to choose intelligently.

Nor is our record of participation in elections anything to brag about. There is an old saying, "You can't fight city hall." But less than a third of the adult population makes it to the polls for a local election. Just over half turn out for even that most publicized American political event, a presidential election. A high point in electoral turnout was reached in the late 1800s, and the roller coaster of participation in presidential elections has declined since.

If citizens are ignorant about politics, policy choices, and policymakers—and recent surveys (see pages 190–192) indicate that many are—and if their rate of political participation plummets—in short, if citizens are falling down on the job—then democratic theory cannot be translated into democratic reality.

Is Politics Too Dependent on Money? Another reason democracy seems to suffer in this modern age is the incessant intrusion of money into political life. American politics has become an expensive business. Campaigns involving costly television advertising, radio spots, newspaper advertisements, and airborne caravans are costly. Interest groups sometimes seem to outbid one another in their efforts to influence legislation and legislators. When money talks, politicians listen; to the degree that they listen more to contributors than to voters, democracy is weakened.

Numerous interest groups and individuals contribute generously to politicians. Corporations, unions, antiabortionists, Moral Majoritarians, farmers, and foreigners all put in far more than their two cents' worth. And there is ample evidence that monetary contributions have real impacts on the decisions of policymakers. Benjamin Ginsberg studied the effects of donations to the campaigns of members of Congress on their subsequent voting behavior on major bills. He concluded that "the greater the amounts of contribution received from an interest by congressional representatives, the more representatives' roll call support for

[19] Patricia Hurley and Kim Q. Hill, "The Prospects for Issue Voting in Contemporary Congressional Elections," *American Politics Quarterly* 8 (October 1980): 446.

that interest tends to change." [20] In extreme and (one hopes) infrequent cases, money passes from giver to taker under the table.

Democracy has problems enough when it has to contend with voter ignorance and apathy. When it confronts the might of money, the gap between theory and reality is widened even further.

Is Our High Technology a Threat to Democracy? At its base, democracy rests on the assumption that people have the good sense to reach judgments about their collective lives, and that government has the good sense to adhere to those judgments. President Andrew Jackson believed that any common man could fill any public office and perform any public trust. But today, someone must decide which drugs are safe for humans, which weapons system will buy the most effectiveness for the dollar, and which energy policy will most economically get us to the twenty-first century. These are highly technical questions. Ordinary people may have opinions on these matters, but they are no match for the opinions of experts. As Kharasch remarked:

> The complexity of modern life leaves us uneasily dependent upon the opinions of experts. Experts tell us what to eat to stay slim and, when laboratory animals get convulsions, other experts tell us to stop eating it.
> . . . Experts are the high priests. [21]

Few would be willing to let common folks decide highly complex issues of nuclear regulation, chemical waste cleanups, and banking regulations.

Democracy and technology have an uneasy co-existence. Telecommunications has brought political issues and political leaders into the living rooms of voters. Some communities have even experimented with telephone voting, in which voters can cast yes or no ballots by punching certain numbers on their telephones. But technology is expensive. Campaigns for office become more expensive. Only those who can afford it— or whose supporters can afford it—can make a real try for office.

With all these problems, democracy is hard to realize in practice. Some scholars go further and say that democracy is not only hard to attain, but an impossible dream. Every society, they claim, is divided into "the few and the many," as Alexander Hamilton put it. A few will rule, and many will follow.

THEORY 2: ELITE AND CLASS THEORY

Elite and class theory contends that our society is divided along class lines and that an upper class **elite** will rule, regardless of the formal niceties of governmental organization.

E Pluribus, A Few

There is nothing unusual, alien, or suspect about a class and elite analysis of American politics. It unites such otherwise diverse figures as James Madison and Karl Marx. Both argued that an awareness of the

---

[20] Benjamin Ginsberg, *The Consequences of Consent: Elections, Citizen Control, and Popular Acquiescence* (Reading, Mass.: Addison-Wesley, 1981), p. 232.
[21] Kharasch, *Institutional Imperative*, p. 66.

division of wealth among the classes unlocked our understanding of government and politics. President Woodrow Wilson took a stark view of elitism in American politics: "The masters of the Government of the United States are the combined capitalists and manufacturers of the United States."[22]

Elite theorists maintain that a handful of men (and a small but increasing number of women) hold the reins of power in American society. They are its movers and shakers. Sometimes they are elected officeholders in the public sector, but just as often, they hold key posts in the private sector. Obviously, to the degree that powerholders are not electable or defeatable in elections, they are not accountable to an electoral majority. Whether at the community level or at the national level, elite theory is inherently antagonistic to democratic theory. ⬚3

[22] Quoted in Benjamin I. Page and Mark P. Petracca, *The American Presidency* (New York: McGraw-Hill, 1983), p. 140.

⬚3 Power and Elites in Two Communities

Elites operate not only at the national level, but also in the American community. In two of our four cities, studies of local power structures provide insights into the pattern of class and elite influence.

After World War II, the San Antonio economy showed a major growth spurt. On December 7, 1954, Tom Powell, president of the local Chamber of Commerce, entertained sixty prominent San Antonio citizens in his home. Most were wealthy business or professional men and they voted to create the Good Government League. Its Board of Directors came to be the social, political, and economic elite of San Antonio and its hold on San Antonio was strong. For example, the GGL nominated candidates for mayor and city council, and of the eighty-one local councilman races for the next twenty-five years, GGL-backed candidates won seventy-seven of them. Almost all were Anglos; only six were Mexican Americans. But in the middle 1970s, Mexican-American leaders organized a group called COPS—Citizens Organized for Public Services. The political awakening of the city's Mexican-American community, combined with the U.S. Justice Department's enforcement of the Voting Rights Act of 1965, began a new era in San Antonio politics. Defeated and out of power, the GGL disbanded in 1976. City council members, even mayors, now came from the Mexican-American community. Mayor Henry Cisneros was first elected in 1981. When reelected, he received more than 90 percent of the vote. Power in San Antonio had been wrested from the old upper-class economic elite.

In San Jose, another local civic elite came to power at the end of the Second World War. The Progress Committee, dominated by the local business elite, won a major

election victory in 1944. (The Progress Committee's first campaign slogan was "San Jose is a Big Business." One of their candidates carried the slogan a step further in his own campaign ads: "San Jose is a Big Business—Let Business Run It." That was at least a frank statement about who had the power—or wanted it.) The local paper, the *San Jose Mercury*, was a major supporter of the probusiness, progrowth policies of the Progress Committee. Urban sprawl chewed up much of the valley's most fertile agricultural land. High-tech computer firms, research outfits, and defense contractors poured into the Valley.

Of all the members of the San Jose power structure, few had more influence, locally and nationally, than David Packard, partner in Hewlett-Packard. He was one of the wealthiest men in America, worth an estimated $700 million. HP had 42,000 employees and annual sales approaching $2 billion. Packard himself qualified as a quintessential member of the American economic and political elite. President Nixon appointed him Deputy Secretary of Defense in 1969. Although he was confirmed by the Senate, critics in Congress thought it inappropriate for a man whose firm did $94 million worth of business with defense to be running it.

Source: For more information on power in San Antonio and San Jose, on which our coverage relies, see John A. Booth and David R. Johnson, "Power and Progress in San Antonio Politics, 1836–1970," in David R. Johnson, John A. Booth, and Richard J. Harris, eds., *The Politics of San Antonio: Community, Progress and Power* (Lincoln, Neb.: University of Nebraska Press, 1983), chap. 1; Kenneth A. Betsalel, "San Jose: Crime and the Politics of Growth," in Anne M. Heinz, Herbert Jacob, and Robert L. Lineberry, eds., *Crime in City Politics* (New York: Longman's, 1983), Chap. 5; and Philip J. Trounstine and Terry Christensen, *Movers and Shakers: The Study of Community Power* (New York: St. Martin's Press, 1982), esp. Chap. 5.

The Concentration of Power. Elites control policies in America because they control key institutions. All American coins are impressed with the Latin words *E Pluribus Unum,* "out of many, one." But what is happening to our institutions could be given a slightly different description: out of many, a few. To the elite theorist, power in every sector of American life has become concentrated in a few hands.

In the first American century, many small businesses existed in the American economy; in the second American century, a few corporate giants dominated. In the first American century, farms were numerous and small; in the second American century, a few corporate organizations ruled American agribusiness. Once Americans lived in small towns; now they live in and near massive metropolitan areas. In almost every sector of American life, the large has come to displace the small. Especially in the second American century, power is concentrated in a few giant institutions and in the men and women who run them.

If you examine ☐4☐, you will see the largest institutions in America. Greatest of all, of course, is the federal government. The next seven biggest institutions in America are private corporations. Of the top fifty, forty are corporations; only ten are governments.

Everywhere, bigness is the order of the day. As recently as 1920, the average farm had 150 acres while today, it has more than 400. The 6.5 million farms in 1920 have dwindled to 2.3 million today. The technology of modern agriculture does not come cheaply. Small farmers were forced out of business by the high costs of farming. Fertile farmland in Santa Clara County and elsewhere was eaten up by the expansion of corporations and communities.

Nowhere is the concentration of power more obvious than in the news media. Three television networks account for about 90 percent of all televised news reaching the American public. Newspapers have also become concentrated as fewer and fewer cities have competing newspapers. Here, as in farming, the high costs of technology have helped promote concentration.

In every corner of American life, the story is the same: A few large institutions have displaced many small ones. To elite theorists, those who sit at the top of these vast institutional networks are those who have the power in American politics. [23]

Elite theorists stress the tight linkages and easy flow between government and corporations. Corporations provide our government with many things, including key policymaking personnel. Ronald Reagan turned frequently to a corporate elite to staff his administration. [24] The Bechtel Group, a San Francisco construction conglomerate and major defense contractor, supplied not one, but two, Reagan cabinet members. Bechtel—so large that it refuses to accept anything but "megaprojects" budgeted at a minimum of $25 million—is the leading constructor of nuclear power plants. Its former corporate counsel and vice-president is President Reagan's secretary of defense, Caspar Weinberger. When Alexander Haig was ousted as secretary of state, President Reagan called

---

[23] The best statement of this thesis remains the classic work by C. Wright Mills, *The Power Elite* (New York: Oxford University Press, 1956).

[24] On the Reagan administration from an elite theory perspective, see Thomas R. Dye, *Who's Running America? The Reagan Years* (Englewood Cliffs, N.J.: Prentice-Hall, 1983.)

4   The Concentration of Power in the United States

THE LARGEST INSTITUTIONS, 1983: INDUSTRIAL CORPORATIONS AND GOVERNMENTS[a]

1. *U.S. government*
2. Exxon Corp.
3. General Motors Corp.
4. Mobil Corp.
5. Ford Motor Company
6. IBM Corp.
7. Texaco Inc.
8. E. I. duPont de Nemours & Company
9. *California*
10. Standard Oil Company (Indiana)
11. Standard Oil Company of California
12. General Electric Company
13. Gulf Oil Corp.
14. *New York*
15. Atlantic Richfield Company
16. *New York City*
17. Shell Oil Company
18. Occidental Petroleum Corp.
19. U.S. Steel Corp.
20. Phillips Petroleum
21. Sun Company, Inc.
22. *Texas*
23. United Technologies
24. Tenneco, Inc.
25. ITT Corp.
26. Chrysler Corp.
27. *Pennsylvania*
28. Procter & Gamble Company
29. R. J. Reynolds Industries
30. *Illinois*
31. Getty Oil
32. Standard Oil Company (Ohio)
33. *Michigan*
34. AT&T Technologies
35. Boeing Company
36. Dow Chemical Company
37. Allied
38. Eastman Kodak Company
38. *Ohio*[b]
40. Unocal
41. Goodyear Tire & Rubber Company
42. Dart & Kraft
43. Westinghouse Electric Corp.
44. Philip Morris
45. *New Jersey*
46. Beatrice Foods Company
47. Union Carbide Corp.
48. Xerox Corp.
49. Amerada Hess
50. Union Pacific

FOUNDATIONS WITH MORE THAN $500 MILLION IN ASSETS[c]

Ford Foundation
Johnson (The Robert Wood) Foundation
Lilly Endowment, Inc.
Rockefeller Foundation
Kresge Foundation
Mellon (The Andrew W.) Foundation
Pew Memorial Trust
Kellogg (W. K.) Foundation

TELEVISION NETWORKS ACCOUNTING FOR 90 PERCENT OF NATIONAL NEWS REACHING THE AMERICAN PUBLIC[d]

ABC
CBS
NBC

MAJOR WIRE SERVICES

Associated Press
United Press International

PRIVATE UNIVERSITIES WITH MORE THAN $100 MILLION IN ENDOWMENTS[e]

1. Harvard
2. Yale
3. University of Chicago
4. Stanford
5. Columbia
6. MIT
7. Cornell
8. Northwestern
9. Princeton
10. Johns Hopkins

UNIONS WITH MORE THAN 500,000 MEMBERS[f]

1. International Brotherhood of Teamsters
2. United Automobile Workers of America
3. United Food and Commercial Workers International Union
4. American Federation of State, County, and Municipal Employees
5. International Brotherhood of Electrical Workers
6. United Steelworkers of America
7. United Brotherhood of Carpenters and Joiners of America
8. International Association of Machinists
9. Service Employees International Union
10. Communication Workers of America.

[a]Ranked by revenues. U.S. Department of Commerce, *Statistical Abstract of the United States, 1985* (Washington, D.C.: U.S. Government Printing Office, 1984); "The 500 Largest Industrial Corporations," *Fortune*, April 30, 1984, p. 276.
[b]Eastman Kodak and Ohio tie for 38.
[c]Thomas R. Dye, *Who's Running America: The Carter Years* (Englewood Cliffs, N.J.: Prentice-Hall, 1979), p. 120.

[d]Ibid., p. 98.
[e]Ibid., p. 134.
[f]U.S. Department of Commerce, *Statistical Abstract, 1985* (Washington, D.C.: U.S. Government Printing Office, 1984), p. 423.

Bechtel's president George Schultz (former secretary of labor under President Nixon), and made him secretary of state. Bechtel has hired numerous former policymakers as corporate officers. Richard Helms, former CIA chief and ambassador to Iran, is a Bechtel consultant. These close links persuade elitists that cozy relations exist between leaders of the capitalist economy and leaders of government.

As in the case of Richard Helms, easy movement often flows between positions in the corporate sector and positions in the government. Elites can thus be *interlocking*. A former member of Congress becomes an oil company lobbyist; corporate heads occupy key cabinet posts.

No one has collected more data on the American elite than Thomas R. Dye, who identified 7,314 elite roles in corporations, law, government, the media, foundations, the military, and cultural sectors. While most members of the American upper-class elite did not hold two key positions simultaneously, some 15 percent of them did, say, as corporation president and university trustee.[25] Almost 40 percent of the top elite held a government position at one time or another in their careers.[26] To elite theorists, these powerful Americans do not merely *influence* policymakers—they *are* policymakers. Moving freely among government posts, corporations, and the cultural and intellectual arenas, a small group (the corporate elite in Dye's sample controlled 55 percent of all our industrial assets in 1980) wields power far beyond their numbers.

Marx and Modern Politics. Karl Marx, the economist and philosopher, spent his life arguing that capitalist societies are divided into classes. One he called the *proletariat,* or the working class. The other class, the *bourgeoisie,* included those who owned the means of production, the capitalists. The European capitalist system Marx saw and described was an exploitative one. Power is unequal in capitalist societies because ownership of wealth is unequal. The government, he thought, was a key tool of the capitalist class. He predicted, and longed for, a time of social revolution in which the proletariat would rise up and overthrow the bourgeoisie. He believed a classless and stateless society would follow.

Marx's views of modern politics are important. Almost half the world's population lives in Marxist-influenced governments. Some elite theorists would find congenial Marx's view that the government is a tool of the upper classes. In one important book, James O'Conner describes the "fiscal crisis" of capitalist systems in Marxist terms.[27] More and more, he argues, capitalists expect government to spend money for services to the capitalist system. For example, government supports roads, police protection, and even makes loan guarantees to corporations. (Recently, Lockheed and Chrysler were two beneficiaries of large federal loans.) Yet the profits from these improvements are reaped by capitalists, not by the government, and so the costs of government soar out of control.

In the Marxist view, the government serves as an agent of social control. Unemployment compensation and welfare payments are not

[25] Ibid., p. 171.
[26] Ibid., p. 177.
[27] James O'Conner, *The Fiscal Crisis of the State* (New York: St. Martin's Press, 1973.)

distributed to the people because government has a big heart. Instead, they purchase obedience from the masses. Piven and Cloward, for example, argue that welfare payments rise in response to the troubles the poor cause, not to their numbers or level of poverty.[28] Riots, strikes, and protests prompt government aid to the poor.

To Marxist theorists, therefore, American politics is not democratic. Elections play a purely symbolic role by merely reassuring the working class that their views count. Real power lies elsewhere, in the holders of the means of production.

A Critique of Elite Theory: Heads I Win, Tails You Lose

In politics, critics of elite theory say, you win some and you lose some. Big business and corporate power win some issues; but they lose some, too. To its critics, elite theory is simpleminded and bull-headed. Elite theorists, of course, are fond of pointing to the issues that big corporations win. Business pressured Congress to defeat a proposed consumer protection agency; big oil companies resisted President Carter's efforts to break up "big oil." But corporate power is not invincible. Major corporations lose major policy issues, too. AT&T (the mighty Ma Bell) was split up by order of a federal court.

When mighty corporate powers lose an issue, elite theorists sometimes fall back on the view that the issue was not really important to them anyway. But this is a "heads I win, tails you lose" argument. If an upper-class elite wins an issue, it proves they have power; if they lose, it proves they did not care enough about the issue to fight for it. It is easy to show that a few Americans have disproportionate power in American government and politics. It is harder to prove that, issue after issue, they consistently set and win the policy agenda.

THEORY 3: PLURALISM

Neither Elitism nor Democracy

Pluralists see the political world in yet another way. Unlike democratic theorists, they doubt that electoral majorities can or do really rule. But unlike elite theorists, they see many groups vying for power and influence, rather than a concentration of power in the hands of the capitalist class alone. Thus, **pluralist theory** emphasizes that politics is mainly a competition among groups, each one pressing for its own preferred policies. One influential pluralist, Robert A. Dahl, had this to say about majority rule: "On matters of specific policy, the majority rarely rules."[29] Rather, he said, "A central, guiding thread of American constitutional development has been the evolution of a political system in which all

---

[28] Frances Fox Piven and Richard A. Cloward, *Regulating the Poor* (New York: Pantheon, 1971); *The New Class War: Reagan's Attack on the Welfare State and Its Consequences* (New York: Pantheon, 1982).

[29] Dahl, *Preface*, p. 124.

active and legitimate groups in the population can make themselves heard at some crucial stage in the process of decision." [30]

Group politics is certainly as American as apple pie. Alexis de Tocqueville called us a "nation of joiners." He should see us today. It is impossible to keep up with the number of groups in the United States. No one conducts a complete census of groups, but one type of special interest group, the Political Action Committee (PAC), is counted by the government. PACs that contribute money to political candidates must register their contributions with the Federal Election Commission. You can look at the burgeoning of PACs since 1974, when the FEC was created, in ⑤ . Plainly, PACs, like June in the musical *Carousel*, are "bustin' out all over."

Pluralists' views of American government are generally positive. There are, they say, multiple access points in our government. Because power is dispersed among the various branches of government, groups that lose here can take their case there. Civil rights groups, for example, were generally unsuccessful in getting civil rights legislation through Congress throughout the 1950s. Congress was controlled by senior southern senators and representatives, whose political careers could have gone up

[30] Ibid., p. 137.

---

5 | The Growth of PACs

It is impossible to know how many interest groups there are in our country, as no one keeps a precise tally. The growth in the number of Political Action Committees registered with the Federal Election Commission (FEC) is one good indicator of the interest group explosion. Here is the FEC's annual count since 1974:

Year	Number of PACS
1974	608
1975[a]	722
1976	1146
1977	1360
1978	1653
1979	2000
1980	2551
1981	2901
1982	3371
1983[b]	3460
1984[c]	3803

[a]through November
[b]estimate
[c]through July

Source: FEC data, cited in Jeffrey M. Berry, *The Interest Group Society* (Boston: Little, Brown, 1984), p. 24. Data for 1983 and 1984 from "1984 Races Become Battlefield for Competing Interest Groups," *Congressional Quarterly Weekly Report* (September 1, 1984): 2147–52.

Special Interest Groups. *All sorts of special interests are part of the American political landscape. Pro- and anti-abortion groups, pro- and anti-gun control advocates, and others put pressure on government to sway policies to their liking. A somewhat atypical group are these supporters of breeder reactors, atom-fusing machines that are supposed to produce more fuel than they consume. It is an unusual issue to attract protest marches, but this one shows that almost anything government contemplates will attract the attention of one or more groups.*

in smoke if they had hinted at—much less voted for—civil rights legislation. However, the courts were open to blacks, and blacks took advantage of it. Thurgood Marshall, now on the Supreme Court, was the general counsel for the National Association for the Advancement of Colored People, better known as the NAACP. He took scores of civil rights cases to court and won judicial approval for striking down much discriminatory legislation.

Groups are without doubt on the ascendency in American political life. Groups and their lobbyists—the groups' representatives in Washington—are becoming masters of the technology of third century politics. Computers, mass mailing lists, sophisticated media advertising, and high-sell techniques are their stock-in-trade.

Pluralism and Its Critics

Pluralism's critics believe that this view paints too rosy a picture of American political life. By arguing that almost every group can get a piece of the pie, pluralists may miss the larger question of how the pie is distributed. The poor may get their food stamps but the rich still get their tax deductions. Governmental programs may help minorities, but the income gap between blacks and whites remains wide.

John Manley has criticized pluralists for failing to recognize the importance of class and inequality in American life. Though admitting that leading pluralist theorists now pay more attention to inequality than they used to, Manley stoutly maintains that a class analysis of "American political economy seems more consistent with the fact of gross inequality in wealth, income, and power under capitalism."[31] Pluralists find it easier to explain bargaining, compromising, and logrolling than the long-run inequalities in a capitalist system.

THEORY 4: HYPERPLURALISM

Strong Groups, Weak Government

Pluralism may be a blessing, but **hyperpluralism** is not. Hyperpluralism is an extreme, exaggerated, or perverted form of pluralism. In this view, groups are so strong that government is weakened. Government may be big, but it is flabby and ineffective. Groups constantly outgun government. Pluralism may be a good thing, but hyperpluralism is too much of a good thing.

Lately, we have seen the rise of **single-issue politics** in our political system. A single-issue group is one that is singlemindedly concerned with one, and only one, issue and is reluctant to compromise. Single-issue groups are deplored by politicians and journalists alike. They may argue for anti-abortion legislation, oppose nuclear plants, shoot down gun control, or press for school prayer. ⑥ Whatever their favorite issue, these groups often see the world in black and white. They meticulously compile voting records of senators and representatives on "their" issues.

---

[31] John Manley, "Neo-Pluralism: A Class Analysis of Pluralism I and Pluralism II," *American Political Science Review* 77 (June 1983): 382.

Abortion Protests. *Group protests can turn ugly. In 1984, many protests against clinics performing abortions ended in violence or threatened violence against the clinics. Right-to-life groups claimed responsibility for the bombing of several abortion clinics, including this one in Florida. Matters of politics are often deeply felt, sometimes so much so that protest crosses the fine line into violence.*

The National Rifle Association (NRA), founded in 1871, is currently the most influential single-issue group on the American political scene. Gun control is the issue around which the NRA's extensive political activity is organized. In its efforts to block any proposed gun control legislation and prevent the election of public officials who sponsor such legislation, the NRA is a prime example of a *veto group*—a group that can exercise enough political power to prevent policy change.

To be successful, a veto group requires resources. For the NRA, those resources include approximately 2.8 million members, 54 state groups and 12,000 local gun clubs, a paid staff of 350, and a computerized information system that is used to monitor legislation and legislators and rally members through the mails at a moment's notice. Of its annual budget of $30 million, the association spends approximately $4 million on direct lobbying by five full-time lobbyists and contributes approximately $500,000 to political campaigns.

In the electoral arena, the NRA has had considerable success both in electing officials sympathetic to its cause and in defeating candidates supportive of gun control. Its political clout figured prominently in the failure of the re-election campaigns of Democratic Senators George McGovern of South Dakota and Birch Bayh of Indiana. Both had once advocated gun control, but they eventually succumbed to NRA pressures, not only abandoning their earlier positions, but when the election approached, actually supporting an NRA-backed bill to loosen controls.

In the legislative arena, the NRA's veto power has proven successful in defeating a number of gun control measures.

— A 1975 proposal to ban concealable weapons, sponsored by Illinois Representative Marty Russo, was approved by the House Judiciary Committee one Thursday. A barrage of telegrams over the weekend resulted in a reconsideration of the bill the following Monday and its subsequent defeat in the committee.
— In 1978, a series of regulations were proposed by the Bureau of Alcohol, Tobacco, and Firearms (ATF) to make it easier to trace guns used in crimes. After two months and 350,000 letters of protest (many of which asserted that the ATF was actually planning to confiscate all firearms), Congress pressured the bureau to drop the proposal.
— Beginning in 1981, a standoff between supporters of the Kennedy-Rodino Handgun Crime Control bill, a measure to impose rather stringent gun control, and the McClure-Volkmer Federal Firearms Reform bill, a decontrol measure considered the first step toward repealing the Gun Control Act of 1968, kept both proposals in committee for over a year. The failure of the Kennedy-Rodino bill to be approved by the committee is attributable both to NRA pressure and to the diversion of the procontrol lobby's efforts toward preventing the passage of the NRA-backed McClure-Volkmer bill.
— Early in 1982, the Reagan administration dismantled the Bureau of Alcohol, Tobacco, and Firearms, scattering federal policy responsibility for gun control among several agencies, including the Secret Service.

As these examples illustrate, the NRA has exercised considerable power in both the electoral and the legislative arenas where gun control has emerged as a hot political issue. It is among the most influential single-issue groups, primarily because it uses its resources effectively to veto policy measures in its area of concern. A hyperpluralist interpretation of the contemporary proliferation of such single-issue or interest groups as the NRA is that it will eventually cripple the policymaking capacity of the government.

Sources: "Magnum-Force Lobby," *Time*, April 20, 1981, pp. 22 and 27, and the Committee for Handgun Control, Inc.

These legislators "are judged on their stand on one highly charged issue by groups and voters with the resources and motivation to reward (or punish) their elected officials on the basis of their response to this one concern."[32] Presidents also experience pressures from these single-minded, single-issue groups. Former President Jimmy Carter spoke of the problems of this political fragmentation in his farewell address:

> Today, as people have become more doubtful of the ability of government to deal with our problems, we are increasingly drawn to single-issue groups and special-interest organizations to ensure that whatever else happens our own personal views and our own private interests are protected.
>
> This is a disturbing factor in American political life. It tends to distort our purposes because the national interest is not always the sum of all our single or special interests. We are all Americans together, and we must not forget that the common good is our common interest and our individual responsibility.

Our fragmented federal system also contributes to hyperpluralism. There are over 82,000 local, state, and federal governments. Too many governments can make it hard to coordinate policy implementation. Any policy requiring the cooperation of several levels of government can be hampered by the intransigence or reluctance of any one of them.

According to hyperpluralists, then, groups have become sovereign and government is merely their servant. Groups that lose policymaking battles in Congress these days do not give up the battle; they carry it to the courts. The number of cases brought to state and federal courts has soared recently, and many of these cases challenge the applicability or constitutionality of some new law or regulation. Environmentalists use legal procedures to delay the construction of nuclear power plants; businesses take federal regulatory agencies to court to win judicial nullification of safety legislation; religious groups drag local school districts into court to secure injunctions against sex education or the teaching of evolution. The courts have become one more battleground in which policies can be effectively opposed as each group tries to bend policy to suit its own purposes.

Interest groups can work so that policies may never be instituted, or if instituted, never implemented. Theodore Lowi called this situation **interest group liberalism.**[33] In interest group liberalism, groups are powerful but the government is fragmented and its authority weak. The government recognizes almost every group as the legitimate spokesman for its interest. Each group clamors to get or to prevent policies favorable or unfavorable to its interest. The multiplicity of special interest groups, said John Gardner, founder of Common Cause, has led to a "paralysis in national policymaking."[34] Politicians try to placate every group, and the result is confusing, contradictory, muddled policy—if government manages to make policy at all.

[32] William Crotty, *American Parties in Decline*, 2nd ed. (Boston: Little, Brown, 1984), p. 142.

[33] Theodore Lowi, *The End of Liberalism*, 2nd ed. (New York: Norton, 1979), Chap. 3.

[34] Quoted in John Herbers, "Deep Government Disarray Alarms Many U.S. Leaders," *New York Times*, November 12, 1978, p. 1.

Regardless of who is to blame for our current degree of hyperpluralism (and there are many culprits), the fact remains that hyperpluralism limits the ability of government to act, and no government that is unable to act will be very effective. Samuel Huntington put it like this: "The function of government is to govern. A weak government, a government which lacks authority, fails to perform its function and is immoral in the same sense in which a corrupt judge, a cowardly soldier, or an ignorant teacher is immoral."[35]

Hyperpluralists see government as weak, relatively powerless, and ineffective, and believe that what our government needs is a strong dose of power and authority. This need conflicts with much that Americans claim to believe about power. Americans prefer their power fragmented, dispersed, and decentralized. If schoolchildren learn only one thing about the American Constitution, it is that the Constitution promoted the separation of powers. It did so because Madison and the other Constitution writers feared concentration of power in any set of hands. Americans have seen divided government as good government. Power, they have believed, is something to be feared because it might be used for evil. So power should be decentralized.

The complexity of the American political system is fully consistent with this deeply ingrained American suspicion of power and authority. There are those who believe, however, that the effectiveness of the American political system has been reduced by such hyperpluralist complexity. The fragmented power that characterizes hyperpluralism may lead to a stalemate—nondecisions replace decisions, and policies destined not to work replace ones that might.

Hyperpluralism, Rigidification, and Other Evils

Kharasch remarks that "Nothing ever seems to work right. The chief products of our age are bafflement, frustration, and rage. The great agencies of government appear to be purposeless, ineffective, and yet curiously incapable of movement."[36] Americans rightly expect their government to be democratic; they also expect it to work. But more and more, government seems to function like the Rube Goldberg contraption we saw in 1.

The economist Mancur Olson offered a controversial theory, which linked the rise of interest groups to economic stagnation.[37] In free societies, Olson says, groups proliferate through the years. But groups are mainly interested in distributive advantages, that is, what they can get from government. The teachers union, environmentalists, and retired

[35] Samuel Huntington, *Political Order in Changing Societies* (New Haven, Conn.: Yale University Press, 1968), p. 28.

[36] Kharasch, *Institutional Imperative*, p. 5.

[37] Mancur Olson, *The Rise and Decline of Nations: Economic Growth, Stagflation, and Social Rigidities* (New Haven, Conn.: Yale University Press, 1983). For a critique of Olson's work, see David R. Cameron, "Creating Theory in Comparative Political Economy: On Mancur Olson's Explanation of Growth," a paper presented at the annual meeting of the American Political Science Association, Chicago, Illinois, September, 1983.

persons are only marginally concerned with the growth of the economy. They are mainly interested in the distribution of government benefits and care little for production and economic growth. It follows that the longer the interest group system has been around and the more entrenched it is, the less attention is paid to increasing the size of the national economic pie and the more attention is paid to how to carve it up. Olson argues that old, democratic nations like England have entrenched interest group systems, which slow down their economic growth. In the United States, a similar situation may be occurring.

Interest groups may work hard to *prevent* government from doing anything. Thurow reports that "in one major environmental group, delays are such a major part of their strategy that they even have a name for it—analysis paralysis." [38] Groups get Congress to write a morass of detail into legislation. Time-consuming procedural hurdles must be cleared. Failure to dot the "i's" and cross the "t's" delays projects and escalates their costs, and the project may be abandoned. Environmental groups are masters of the bureaucratic entanglement. A cobweb of rules and regulations ensnarl any major dam, roadway, or power plant. Groups can thus use the *procedures* of government to slow down—even halt—the *processes* of government.

Nowhere is the ability of groups to prevent coordinated action better evident than in Pressman and Wildavsky's tangled story of policy implementation in Oakland. 7

[38] Lester Thurow, *The Zero-Sum Society* (New York: Penguin Books, 1981), p. 13.

© Trevor 1985, reprinted with permission of the Albuquerque Journal.

The Case of Jobs for Oakland: How Hyperpluralism Reduces the Chances of Getting Policies Implemented

Oakland, California, has long had a troubled local economy, plagued by joblessness. On April 29, 1966, the Economic Development Administration announced a plan to create jobs in Oakland, whose unemployment rate was twice the national average. EDA's director, Eugene Foley, announced nearly $23.3 million in grants to be made available in Oakland. The main projects were to be an airport hangar and a marine terminal. The hangar would be leased by World Airways, a large charter service. The marine terminal would be built for the Port of Oakland. EDA projected that 3,000 jobs would be produced by the projects. Yet three years later, only thirty or so—not 3,000—jobs could be traced to the massive EDA investment. What happened?

A big part of the problem was the multitude of groups involved, each with its own priorities and interests. The further the project got, the more it seemed to run afoul of important agencies and groups. Here are a few examples:

— Minority group leaders in Oakland supported the jobs program, but wanted to make sure that minority groups, whose unemployment rates were higher than the city average, got first claim on any jobs created.
— The United States Navy, which operated an air base next to the proposed construction, discovered that cranes to be used in building would interfere with flight safety, and decided to oppose the project.
— Environmentalists, who certainly had no objection to creating more jobs in Oakland, discovered that a part of San Francisco Bay would be filled in by the construction and opposed it on those grounds.
— The Department of Labor was delighted to support job creation, but told EDA that apprenticeship and training programs belonged under its jurisdiction.

Pressman and Wildavsky counted the number of "decision points" needed before the contracts could be signed. Because an agreement to act was needed at each one before the next step could be taken, any single slowdown could bring the project to a standstill. And that was exactly what happened. Every group favored the idea in the abstract, but each had some objection that led to a veto of the idea's application. The outcome was no surprise: The program of jobs for Oakland failed.

The moral: Good intentions are nice, but they are no substitute for the capacity to coordinate joint action. Too much decentralization can produce stalemate.

Source: Jeffrey Pressman and Aaron Wildavsky, *Implementation: How Great Expectations in Washington are Dashed in Oakland, or, Why It's Amazing That Federal Programs Work at All, This Being a Saga of the Economic Development Administration as Told by Two Sympathetic Observers Who Seek to Build Morals on a Foundation of Ruined Hopes* (Berkeley: University of California Press, 1973).

THE THEORIES SUMMARIZED

In this chapter, we described four theories to aid our understanding of government in America. *Democratic theory* is both a normative standard and, to some people at least, a fairly accurate description of government in America. We called the second theory *class and elite theory* because it emphasizes that a small upper-class elite holds vast power in our government. *Pluralist theory* concerns competition among groups. But *hyperpluralist theory* contends that group politics has gotten out of hand. It is pluralism gone sour, where the ability of groups to veto or delay government policy threatens the very effectiveness of government.

You may want to make some tentative judgments about these four theories of government in America. You should reserve final judgment, though, until we have had time to review American government in action. We begin that in the next chapter, when we examine our constitutional foundations.

Key Terms

empirical theory
normative theory
democracy
traditional democratic
 theory
majority rule

minority rights
representation
electoral accountability
elite and class theory
elite
pluralist theory

hyperpluralism
single-issue politics
interest group
 liberalism

For Further Reading

Christensen, Terry, and Larry N. Gersten. *The California Connection: Politics in the Golden State* (1984). A breezy but informative text on California politics.

Dahl, Robert A. *Dilemmas of Pluralist Democracy* (1983). Dahl's analysis of the problems of pluralism in theory and practice won the 1983 American Political Science Association's Woodrow Wilson Prize.

Downs, Anthony. *An Economic Theory of Democracy* (1957). A classic study of democracy through the meticulous models of an economist.

Dye, Thomas R. *Who's Running America? The Reagan Years* (1983). Extensive evidence on elite and corporate influence in the Reagan administration.

Johnson, David R., John A. Booth, and Richard J. Harris, eds. *The Politics of San Antonio* (1983). A collection of very good articles on San Antonio government and politics.

Lowi, Theodore. *The End of Liberalism,* 2nd ed. (1979). "Interest group liberalism" makes government highly responsive to every interest group—so much so that its ability to govern is threatened.

Mills, C. Wright. *The Power Elite* (1956). Mills, the "godfather" of elite theorists, is still worth reading.

O'Conner, James. *The Fiscal Crisis of the State* (1973). A Marxist perspective on our political economy.

Olson, Mancur. *The Rise and Decline of Nations* (1983). This pretentious but important book on the rigidification of government shared with Dahl's *Dilemmas of Pluralist Democracy* the Woodrow Wilson Prize.

Piven, Frances Fox, and Richard A. Cloward. *The New Class War: Reagan's Attack on the Welfare State and Its Consequences* (1982). Argues that the Reagan administration commitment to corporate capitalism caused it to dismantle many federal social programs.

Pressman, Jeffrey, and Aaron Wildavsky. *Implementation* (1973). A classic, sometimes comic, case study of hyperpluralism in Oakland.

Troustine, Philip J., and Terry Christensen. *Movers and Shakers: The Study of Community Power* (1982). A journalist and a political scientist write this study of power and politics in San Jose.

CONSTITUTIONAL FOUNDATIONS

The Constitution, created in 1787 at Philadelphia, was written in a low-tech time. Now fully two centuries old, it continues to shape our government in these high-tech times. How this powerful document shapes our politics and our policies is the subject of the next three chapters.

In Chapter 3, we look at the making of our 200-year-old Constitution. We will trace its colonial background and the role of issues about equality and the economy on the Philadelphia agenda. Our Founding Fathers expressed very definite ideas about the nature of man, of government, and of political conflict; the government they created still reflects those views.

One important element in that government is the federal system, which we explore in Chapter 4. The array of governments in the United States is impressive indeed. Today, they compete with one another for economic advantage.

Our civil liberties are also an important part of our constitutional system. Civil liberties are the roadblocks we put in the way of government's efforts to interfere with our freedoms. The First Amendment and other parts of the Bill of Rights outline these civil liberties. In Chapter 5, we will see how old and new challenges to our freedoms affect the foundations of our constitutional system.

The First American Century: The Constitution

3

O N July 3, 1776, John Adams, attending the Philadelphia meeting of the Continental Congress, wrote his wife, Abigail:

> The Second Day of July 1776, will be the most memorable Epocha, in the History of America—I am apt to believe that it will be celebrated, by succeeding Generations, as the great anniversary Festival. . . . It ought to be solemnized with Pomp and Parade, with Shews [shows], Games, Sports, Guns, Bells, Bonfires and Illuminations from one End of this Country to the other from this Time forward ever more. [1]

Adams, later our second president, was mostly right: Pomp, parades, shows, games, and so forth, do characterize our Independence Day. His error was seemingly minor. It was July 2, not July 4, of which he waxed so eloquent. In fact, not his error but ours leads us to celebrate Independence Day on July 4. It was, as Adams said—he was there, after all—on the Second of July when the United States actually declared its independence.

This was a tumultuous period: battles with the British were brewing; war seemed inevitable, and it came. The decade 1776–1787—between the Declaration of Independence and the adoption of the Constitution—was our formative era. Begun in revolution, it ended in a Republic.

If longevity is a virtue, the Constitution penned in Philadelphia two centuries ago has been a smashing success. The words of the Constitution are largely intact; only a handful of amendments to it have been passed. Its institutions survive; the government it created lives on.

Today, the American Constitution is treated with the reverence usually reserved for religious documents. Like the Bible, the Constitution inspires criticism by learned people ("constitutional law scholars" are like "biblical scholars"), and acts incompatible with it are negatively labeled ("unconstitutional" is equivalent to "unholy"). This reverence for the Constitution is perpetuated by the myths that have grown up around the Founding Fathers. Sometimes they have been described as almost divinely inspired.

The Founding Fathers themselves contributed much to their own deification. Rarely have so few said so much about the wisdom of their own handiwork. In print and in public, they defended the document in the most glowing terms. And so they spoke of one another as well. Franklin called his colleagues "an assembly of notables." Madison said that they constituted the "best contribution of talent" the new nation could muster. "Never," he said, "was an assembly of men charged with a great and arduous trust, who were more pure in their motives, or more exclusively or anxiously devoted to the object committed to them than were the members of the Federal Convention of 1787."

Yet the Constitution makers were locked in a ferocious political battle that showed their strengths not only as political philosophers and governmental architects, but also as political strategists. Before we yield to the temptation to see these men as somehow above the political fray, we

[1] L. H. Butterfield, Marc Friedlaender, and Mary-Jo Kline (eds.), *The Book of Abigail and John: Selected Letters of the Adams Family* (Cambridge, Mass.: Harvard University Press, 1975), p. 142.

might note the events of the waning minutes of the Constitutional Convention.[2]

On the 109th day of the meetings, in stifling heat (the windows of the Pennsylvania statehouse having been kept closed to ensure secrecy), the final document was read aloud. Then Dr. Franklin rose with a speech he had written, but the enfeebled Franklin had to ask James Wilson to deliver it. In it, Franklin noted that "there are several parts of this Constitution of which I do not at present approve, but I am not sure that I shall never approve them." He then offered a few political witticisms, defended the handiwork, and concluded by saying, "On the whole, Sir, I cannot help expressing a wish that every member of the Convention who may still have an objection to it, would with me on this occasion, doubt a little of his own infallibility—and make manifest our unanimity, put his name to this instrument." Nonetheless, Edmund Randolph of Virginia rose to announce apologetically that he did not intend to sign. Gouverneur Morris of Pennsylvania announced his reservations about the compromises, but called the document the "best that was to be attained" and said he would "take it with all its faults." Alexander Hamilton of New York again made a plea for unity, but Elbridge Gerry of Massachusetts was adamant in opposition. Taking Franklin's remarks personally, he "could not but view them as levelled against himself and the other gentlemen who meant not to sign." He bluntly predicted that a "civil war may result from the present crisis of the United States."

On Franklin's motion, a vote was taken. Ten states voted yes, none voted no, but South Carolina's delegates were divided. As the records so quaintly put it, "The Members then proceeded to sign the instrument." Randolph, Gerry, and Mason, however, refused to sign. Franklin then made another short speech, saying that the sun pictured on the back of the president's chair was a rising, not a setting, sun. Then (quoting the records again) "The Constitution being signed . . . the convention dissolved itself by Adjournment." The members themselves adjourned to a tavern. (The experience of the last few hours, when conflict intermingled with consensus, reminded them they deserved a drink.) They realized that the job of implementing this new document would be no small feat.

It was an end and a beginning: the end of a marathon meeting that began on May 14, and the beginning of what sociologist Seymour Martin Lipset called "the first new nation."[3] To understand that beginning, we will first look at America before the Constitution.

THE ORIGINS OF THE NEW NATION

Today, in India, El Salvador, Malaysia, and elsewhere, nations are new and problems are fearsome. A strained world economy buffets the new nations. Great inequalities of wealth and power are apparent, and cor-

---

[2] This and other debates and activities at the convention are recorded somewhat imperfectly, because no one kept a transcript of the proceedings, and certainly no one would have taped them. The best source is Max Ferrand (ed.), *The Records of the Federal Convention of 1787*, 3 vols. (New Haven, Conn.: Yale University, Press, 1911).

[3] S. M. Lipset, *The First New Nation* (New York: Basic Books, 1963).

ruption too often rampant. Wars of revolution have recently been fought against colonial powers. Most nations of the world in the twentieth century are going through the process of nation building that the United States completed much earlier. Circumstances of equality, economic conditions, and the natural environment were different then, yet each shaped the context of the colonial period and the New Nation.

Equality, Economy, and Environment in the Early American Experience

Sometimes we think that the American experience started with the Declaration of Independence and a new Constitution for the Republic. Not so. Almost as many years passed from 1607 (the founding of the Virginia colony) to the writing of the Constitution as has passed from the Constitution until now. The circumstances of American life during colonial days shaped the American experience as much as the events of the 109-day convention.

Most of the colonists were English; but French, Dutch, Sephardic (Spanish and Portugese) Jews, and others piled on boats heading west across the Atlantic. Still others were involuntary immigrants: Slave traders hunted, trapped, and shipped hundreds of thousands of black Africans on boats to the English colonies. So much of our history is written by Easterners and English descendents, we sometimes forget that the Eastern/English heritage has no monopoly on the American experience. San Jose, California, was founded in 1777 by Spaniards, just a

Immigration and Nation-building. *Building a nation is more than writing a constitution. It is a symbolic process as well. Nationhood must implant itself in the hearts and minds of a people. Generations of immigrant Americans have undergone a nation-building experience that native-born Americans never had. In the 1890s, millions of immigrant children first learned what it meant to be Americans. Popular lore tells us that they entered the great "melting pot," but in fact the different immigrant groups maintained a high degree of diversity. Even today, newly naturalized citizens build themselves a new nation by adding their varied and unique experiences. On June 22, 1981, in Los Angeles, 10,000 new citizens took their oath of citizenship and watched the unfurling of the largest American flag in existence.*

year after the eastern colonists broke with their mother country. Of the European immigrants, the French traveller Michel de Crèvecoeur said,

> The rich stay in Europe, it is only the middling and the poor that migrate. In this great American asylum, the poor of Europe have by some means met together . . . Here individuals of all nations are melted into a new race of men, whose labors and posterity will one day cause great changes in the world. [4]

How right he was. In 1760, Crèvecoeur was already noticing the "melting pot" which would both enrich and complicate American nation building.

Equality in the Colonies. Today, we value equality in American life. In colonial times we experienced a taste of it that from that time forth left an indelible imprint on the American mind. Equality was not merely a dream, a noble goal, but within reach of the many. European travellers to the American shores were unaminous in "describing colonial America as a utopian middle-class democracy." One French visitor, Brissot de Warville, stopped in Boston in 1788 and "saw none of those livid, ragged wretches that one sees in Europe." He confirmed what Lord Gordon had seen there in 1764: "The levelling principle here [he wrote back to England] everywhere operates strongly and takes the lead, and everybody has property, and everybody knows it." [5] The careful study of American income inequality by Williamson and Lindert shows that the colonial period was one of "relative egalitarianism and stable wealth distribution." [6]

But even then, Americans were ambivalent about equality. The well-to-do sought ways to display their wealth, to distinguish themselves from their social inferiors. Dress codes divided people according to their station in life. In 1675, thirty young men in New England were arrested for wearing silk clothes, which were above their station. Social class lines were more rigid. In the late 1700s, Harvard College ranked its students not by academic performance but by family social status.

Today, stocks, bonds, tax deductions, and other investments are the key to wealth. Then, in that agricultural economy, land was the key to economic and political power; and the upper class was the landed class. "Land," said the great historian Louis B. Wright, "was the key to social status. . . . Most of the economic and political power was in the hands of the great landholders. . . . In Virginia and Maryland, they built great houses along the rivers, the James, the Rappahannock, the Potomac, the Patuxent and other deepwater outlets to the sea." [7] Land brought power. George Washington left an estate with an incredible 33,000 acres of land, valued at $530,000. He was easily one of the wealthiest men in the colonies—a Rockefeller of his day. (To give you an idea of how wealthy Washington was, note that today in the 1980s, after two centuries of

---

[4] Quoted in V. L. Parrington, *The Colonial Mind, 1620–1800* (New York: Harvest Books, 1927), pp. 144, 146.

[5] Quoted in Jeffrey Williamson and Peter Lindert, *American Inequality: A Macroeconomic History* (New York: Academic Press, 1980), p. 9.

[6] Ibid., p. 33.

[7] Louis B. Wright, *The Cultural Life of the American Colonies, 1607–1763* (New York: Harper & Row, 1957), pp. 3, 5.

Inequality in the Colonies. *George Washington is deservedly remembered as a revolutionary general, a leader of the Constitutional Convention, and the first president. But he was also the premier colonial aristocrat. Nothing highlights inequality in early America better than life at Mount Vernon. After the Revolution Washington added the splendid porch with graceful two-story pillars. In this tranquil picture, Lafayette visits Washington and his family. Martha, grandchildren, and servants complete the pastoral scene. One of the richest men in America, Washington agreed to serve as commander in chief without pay. But, as with executives in our own day, his expense account sometimes stretched a point. He billed the Continental Congress for $449,261.51. (To get today's value, multiply by a number between, say, ten and twenty.) Most of the bills were no doubt perfectly legitimate, but he was not above claiming reimbursement for wine, wig powder, portraits, and Martha's visit to the battlefront.*

inflation, only 2 percent of the American population have assets that exceed $100,000.)

Of course, the cruelest and sharpest inequalities were those between slave and free man. Americans engaged in a brisk slave trade. Rich planters (like William Byrd of Virginia) traded extensively in African and Indian slaves. Only 6 percent of slaves imported to the New World came to the soon-to-be United States. [8] But by 1800, almost a million slaves were in the United States—most, but not all, in the south.

It was a time, too, when sexual equality was scarcely imagined. John Adams, whose respect for Abigail and her keen mind was unbounded, once wrote her from France, "I must not write a Word to you about Politicks, because you are a womaen." Catching his error, he hastened to add, "What an offence have I committed?—a Woman!" [9] In the colonies, and later in the new Republic, women could not vote. The New Jersey Constitution of 1776 gave voting rights to any free person with a net worth of more than fifty pounds, thus including (by accident) propertied

[8] Robert W. Fogel and Stanley L. Engerman, *Time on the Cross: The Economics of American Negro Slavery* (Boston: Little, Brown, 1974), p. 14. On slavery, see also Kenneth M. Stamp, *The Peculiar Institution: Slavery in the Ante-Bellum South* (New York: Random House, 1956), and August Meier and Elliott Rudwick, *From Plantation to Ghetto*, rev. ed. (New York: Hill & Wang, 1970).

[9] *Book of Abigail and John*, p. 237.

women. When women began taking advantage of this, the State of New Jersey rescinded it in 1807.

For white male Americans, though, it was a period of equality. Americans believed in it and practiced it. Their incomes (despite the land speculator Washington and the slave trader Byrd) were probably more equal than ours are today. Americans respected equality but at the same time maintained some ambivalence about it. Paradoxically, the most admired men in the early republic were the great Benjamin Franklin, an "unpretentious commoner, drawn from the stock of the common people," [10] and haughty, rich, aristocratic George Washington. Few people worried too much about inequality then, because the economy was an agrarian one and land was there for the taking. Economic expansion seemed inevitable.

Yeoman Farmers and Urban Merchants: The Colonial Economy. As in most developing countries, the colonial economy was overwhelmingly agrarian. In 1790, the first official census counted only 5 percent of the population as urban. A *city* did not mean a metropolis with hundreds of thousands or millions of people. Philadelphia, the thriving metropolis of the Constitutional Convention, had 40,000 people, about as many as would fill a small major league baseball stadium today. America then was largely a nation of yeoman farmers.

Still, there was money to be made from commercial, and even industrial, pursuits. Yankee traders did a brisk business in rum, indigo, cloth, naval stores, and, of course, slaves. The first sign of industrialization was the emergence of iron forges (as in Valley Forge, Pennsylvania). By the time of the American Revolution, the colonies were producing more iron than England. A few men in New York and other cities began to see vaguely that what we call an *industrial revolution* might be as important as a political revolution. Wall Street was little more than a trail among forests and farms, but a few New Yorkers were beginning to make investments, accumulate capital, and consolidate production that would make Wall Street the center of an industrial economy. After the Constitution was written and the new government formed, differences between farmers and capitalists would help shape the origins of America's political parties.

People of Plenty: The Nonissues of Energy and Environment. Questions we now consider crucial about energy and the environment were mostly irrelevant to these colonists. Most of the country was one vast forest that would have to be cleared to make room for growth. Fewer than 4 million people were counted in the first census in 1790, and they had nearly 900,000 square miles of land at their disposal. "No man knew," says Clinton Rossiter,

> except in a casual way, that rich stores of coal, iron, copper, and other
> materials waited below the surface for the pick and shovel of industry;
> every man knew that the surface itself was a profligate treasure-house of the

[10] Parrington, *Colonial Mind*, p. 166. This "unpretentious commoner," though, had assets totaling about $150,000, an amount which would easily qualify him today as a multimillionaire. On Franklin's wealth, see Robert E. Brown, *Charles Beard and the Constitution* (Princeton, N.J.: Princeton University Press, 1956), p. 7.

one thing for which all men in that age longed: deep, well-watered, fertile soil, which commanded toil beyond our imagining yet often paid off in rewards beyond theirs. [11]

Exploitation of so vast a bounty was natural, despoliation but a problem for the distant future.

Imagining this vast expanse of open, free land with resources far more plentiful than available technologies could use to the full, and a population so small that exploitation and despoliation seemed trivial, we can understand that the environment and energy were not issues in colonial, nation building America. Not until 1798 would the English economist Thomas R. Malthus publish his pessimistic *Essay on the Principle of Population as it Affects the Future Improvement of Society,* in which he argued that population, when unchecked, increases faster than food supplies can be increased. The idea that a population would grow beyond nature's ability to support it would have seemed preposterous to most colonial Americans, who beheld nature's bounties as far as the eye could see.

Among Americans, only Thomas Jefferson—as brilliant a scientist and philosopher as he was a politician—anticipated Malthus. In his *Notes on the State of Virginia* (1781), he calculated his state's population growth through 1862. By his projections (about three times too high, incidentally), Virginia's population would be 4.5 million by 1862, more than the whole nation's at that time. "Yet I am persuaded," he wrote, "it is a greater

[11] Clinton Rossiter, *1787: The Grand Convention* (New York: Macmillan, 1966), p. 24.

The Colonial Environment. *In 1761, Bethlehem, Pennsylvania, looked like this. In that era of abundance, today's issues of energy and environment seemed irrelevant. Land was available for the taking and the tilling. Only a few people on this side of the Atlantic—Jefferson was one—even contemplated the possibility of limits to nature's bounty.*

number than the country spoken of, considering how much inarable land it contains, can clothe and feed, without a material change in the quality of their diet." [12] Jefferson anticipated Malthus, even as Malthus anticipated today's advocates of limited economic growth. [13] But what Jefferson saw, few others did. To most colonial Americans, the idea that there might be limits to growth was unthinkable.

The English Heritage: Ideas about Government

Whatever their differences in wealth, power, or interests, most colonists were English, not only in culture and citizenship, but also in their philosophical heritage. The political ideas behind the **Declaration of Independence** and the American **Constitution** were not the inventions of the Founding Fathers alone. Franklin, Jefferson, Madison, Morris, Hamilton, and other leaders of the new nation were learned and widely read men, steeped in the words and wisdom of the English, French, and Scottish political philosophers. They corresponded about the ideas they were reading, they quoted the philosophers in their debates over revolution and the Constitution, they applied these ideas in constructing a new government.

One of the most influential of these philosophers was John Locke, whose *Treatise of Civil Government* (1689) profoundly influenced American political leaders. His work was "the dominant political faith of the American colonies in the second quarter of the eighteenth century. A thousand pulpits thundered with its benevolent principles; a hundred editors filled their pages with its famous slogans." [14] There are in fact some remarkable parallels between Locke's language and Jefferson's language in the Declaration of Independence. ☐1

The rock on which Locke built his powerful philosophy was **natural rights.** Even before governments arise, Locke held, people exist in a state of nature, where they are governed only by the laws of nature. Natural law brings natural rights. Because natural law is superior to human law, it can even justify a challenge to the rule of a tyrannical king. Government, Locke said, must be built on the **consent of the governed.** It should be **limited government:** Certain things are out of bounds for government. This idea of limited government contrasted sharply with the old notion that kings had divinely granted absolute rights over their subjects.

There may be many limits on government, said Locke, but two stand out. First, there must be standing laws so people can know in advance—before they are arrested—if their acts are acceptable. Second—and Locke was very forceful on this point—"The supreme power cannot take from any man any part of his property without his consent." To Locke, "the preservation of property [was] the end of government." This idea of the sanctity of property is one of the few ideas with no direct parallel in Jefferson's draft of the Declaration of Independence. Even though Jeffer-

John Locke, 1632–1704. *English physician, philosopher, diplomat, and civil servant. Locke wrote the* Treatise of Civil Government *(1689), an important source of ideas reflected in both the Declaration of Independence and the Constitution.*

[12] Merrill D. Peterson (ed.), *The Portable Thomas Jefferson* (New York: Viking, 1975), p. 125.

[13] For a modern-day Malthusian analysis, see Donella Meadows et al., *The Limits to Growth* (New York: Universe Books, 1972).

[14] Rossiter, *1787*, p. 60.

son borrowed from and even paraphrased Lockean ideas, he altered Locke's phrase, "life, liberty, and property" to "life, liberty, and the pursuit of happiness." We shall soon see, though, how the Lockean idea of the sanctity of property figured prominently at the Constitutional Convention. One influential member of that body echoed directly Locke's line about the preservation of property being the object of government.

In the extreme case, said Locke, people have even a right to revolt against governments that no longer have their consent. Locke anticipated critics' charges that this right would lead to constant civil disturbances. He stressed that people should not revolt until injustices become deeply felt. The Declaration stressed the same point, emphasizing that "Governments long established should not be changed for light and transient causes." But when matters go beyond "patient sufferance," severance of old ties is not only inevitable but necessary.

---

1   **Locke and the Declaration of Independence: Some Parallels**

LOCKE	DECLARATION OF INDEPENDENCE
NATURAL RIGHTS "The state of nature has a law to govern it, which obliges everyone." "life, liberty, and property"	"Laws of Nature and Nature's God" "certain inalienable rights [of] life, liberty, and the pursuit of happiness"
EQUALITY "men being by nature all free, equal and independent"	"all men are created equal"
CONSENT OF THE GOVERNED "for when any number of men have, by the consent of every individual, made a community, with a power to act as one body, which is only by the will and determination of the majority"	"Governments are instituted among men, deriving their just powers from the consent of the governed."
LIMITED GOVERNMENT "Absolute arbitrary power, or governing without settled laws, can neither of them consist with the ends of society and government." "As usurpation is the exercize of power which another has a right to, so tyranny is the exercize of power beyond right, which nobody can have a right to."	"The history of the present King of Great Britain is a history of repeated injuries and usurpations."
RIGHT TO REVOLT "The people shall be the judge. ... Oppression raises ferments and makes men struggle to cast off an uneasy and tyrannical yoke."	"Prudence, indeed, will dictate that Governments long established should not be changed for light and transient causes; and accordingly all experience hath shown, that mankind are most disposed to suffer, while evils are sufferable, than to right themselves by abolishing the forms to which they are accustomed. But when a long train of abuses and usurpations, pursuing invariably the same Object evinces a design to reduce them under absolute Despotism, it is their right, it it their duty, to throw off such Government."

"FREE AND INDEPENDENT STATES": OUT OF MANY, ONE

Declaring Independence and Winning It

As colonial discontent with the English festered, the Continental Congress was in almost continuous session during 1775 and 1776. Tea taxes and other repressive—and costly—measures flowed from London. Talk of independence was common. Virginia, as it often did in those days, played a leading role at the Philadelphia meeting of the Congress. It sent seven delegates to join what would certainly be a serious discussion of repudiating the rule of King George III. They were joined subsequently by an eighth delegate, substituted at the last minute for Peyton Randolph, who was needed back in Williamsburg to preside over the House of Burgesses.

The substitute, Thomas Jefferson, was a well-educated Virginia lawmaker who had just written a resolution in the Virginia legislature objecting to new British policies. He traveled to Philadelphia attended by his slaves Richard and Jesse, and being in no great hurry to get there, stopped along the way to purchase some books and a new stallion, for which he paid fifty pounds.[15] In addition to his material possessions, Jefferson brought his talent as an author and the wide reading of a careful student of political philosophy. Jefferson was not a rabble-rousing pamphleteer like Thomas Paine, whose fiery tract *Common Sense* had appeared in January 1776 and fueled the already hot flames of revolution. He was steeped in the philosophical writings of French, English, and Scottish moral philosophers, and his rhetoric matched his reading.

In May and June of 1776, the Continental Congress began debating resolutions about independence. On June 7, Richard Henry Lee of Virginia moved "That these United States are and of rights ought to be free and independent states." A committee composed of Thomas Jefferson, John Adams of Massachusetts, Benjamin Franklin, Roger Sherman of Connecticut, and Robert Livingston of New York was busily drafting a document to justify the inevitable declaration. On July 2, Lee's motion to declare independence from England was formally approved. The famous *Declaration of Independence*, which might more properly be called "A Justification of Independence," was adopted two days later on the fourth.

The Declaration quickly became one of the most widely quoted and revered documents of American nationhood. Filled with fine principles and bold language, it can be read both as a political tract and as a philosophical treatise. Politically, it laid all sorts of evils at the doorstep of George III, who personally had little to do with Parliament's colonial policies. Poor George was even blamed for inciting the "merciless Indian savages" to war on the colonists.

Philosophically, the Jeffersonian pen put ideas on paper that were by then common on both sides of the Atlantic among those people who wished to challenge the power of kings. Some of these ideas were associ-

---

[15] Garry Wills, *Inventing America: Jefferson's Declaration of Independence* (New York; Doubleday, 1978), pp. 13, 77.

ated with John Locke, though Locke had no monopoly on them. As noted in [1] there are some remarkable parallels between Jefferson's declaration draft and Locke's *Second Treatise*, although there is no evidence that Jefferson ever read Locke's writings on politics. (To be sure, there is no evidence that he did *not* read them.) [16] Jefferson had once ordered a copy of Locke's treatise, but it was destroyed by a fire in his library immediately after he received it. Whatever its philosophical antecedents, the political effect of the Declaration was clear: It announced and defended a war of independence that had in fact already begun.

Declaring independence was easier than winning a war. John Adams wrote his wife Abigail, "You will think me transported with enthusiasm, but I am not. I am well aware of the toil, blood, and treasure that it will cost us to maintain this Declaration, and support and defend these states." Adams was right. The colonials seemed little match for the finest army in the world, whose size was nearly quadrupled by hired guns from the German state of Hesse and elsewhere. In 1775 the British had 8,500 men stationed in the colonies and had hired nearly 30,000 mercenaries. The colonists at the beginning had only 5,000 men in uniform, though their number waxed and waned as the war went on. How they eventually won is a story we shall leave to history books. How they formed a new government, though, is very much a part of our story of American nation-building.

Toward 1787: The Articles, the States, and the Power Shift

The Congress that adopted the Declaration of Independence was only a voluntary association of the states. In 1776, it appointed a committee to draw up a plan for a permanent union of the states. That plan, our first constitution, was the **Articles of Confederation.** [17]

The Articles of Confederation. The Articles established a government dominated by the states. The United States, it said, was a "league of friendship and perpetual union" among thirteen states that were themselves sovereign. The Articles established a national legislature with one house and a representative from each state. But there was no president and no national court, and the powers of the national legislature, the Continental Congress, were strictly limited. Most authority rested in the state legislatures.

Because unanimous consent of the states was needed to put them into operation, the Articles adopted by Congress in 1777 did not go into effect until 1781, when laggard Maryland finally ratified them. In the meantime, the Continental Congress barely survived, lurching from crisis to crisis (as when some of Washington's troops threatened to create a monarchy with him as king unless Congress paid their overdue wages).

All sorts of problems, logistical as well as political, plagued the Continental Congress. State delegations attended haphazardly. Thomas Jeffer-

---

[16] Wills, *Inventing America*, pp. 172–74.

[17] On the Articles, see Merrill Jensen, *The Articles of Confederation* (Madison: University of Wisconsin Press, 1940).

son, a Virginia delegate to an Annapolis meeting of the Congress, complained to his friend and fellow Virginian James Madison on February 20, 1784:

> We cannot make up a congress at all. There are eight states in town, six of which are represented by two members only. Of these, two members of different states are confined by gout, so that we cannot make a house [i.e., a quorum]. We have not sat above three days, I believe, in as many weeks. Admonition after admonition has been sent to the states to no effect. We have sent one today. If it fails, it seems as well we should all retire. [18]

The Continental Congress had few powers outside of maintaining an army and navy, and precious little money to do even that. Because it had no power to tax, it had to requisition money from the states. If states refused to send it (which they often did), Congress did without, resorted to selling off western lands to speculators, issued securities that sold for less than their face value, or used its own presses to print virtually valueless money. Congress had to disband the army, despite continued threats from British and Spanish armies and navies. It did manage to develop sound policies for the management of the western frontiers, however, creating the Northwest Ordinance of 1787, which encouraged the development of the Great Lakes region as soon as the British and the Indians were cleared out.

Power Shifts in the States: New Issues of Equality. What was happening in the states was more important than what was happening in the Continental Congress. The most important change in the states was that the old colonial economic elite no longer dominated the statehouses. Expanded political participation during the Revolutionary War brought a new middle class to power.

It was a middle class of yeoman farmers instead of manorial landholders, of artisans instead of lawyers. Before the Revolution almost all members of New York's Assembly were either urban merchants or wealthy landowners. In the 1769 Assembly, 57 percent of the legislators were nonfarmers, even though nearly 95 percent of New Yorkers were farmers. But *after* the Revolution a major power shift occurred. Farmers and craftworkers became a decisive majority, and the old elite saw its power shrink. The same change happened in other states as power shifted from a handful of wealthy men to a more broad-based group. [2] After a careful examination of the economic backgrounds of pre- and post-revolutionary legislators, Jackson Turner Main concluded, "The voters had ceased to confine themselves to an elite, but were selecting instead men like themselves. The tendency to do so had started during the colonial period, especially in the North, and had now increased so dramatically as almost to revolutionize the legislatures." [19] Members of the old colonial elite found this new turn of affairs troublesome, to say the least.

[18] Letter from Jefferson to Madison, reprinted in George Bancroft, *The History of the Formation of the Constitution of the United States of America* (New York: Appleton, 1900), pp. 342–43.
[19] Jackson Turner Main, "Government by the People: The American Revolution and the Democratization of the Legislatures," *The William and Mary Quarterly*, 3rd ser. 23 (July 1966): 405. Main's article is also the source of the data on New York.

2 Power Shift: Economic Status of State Legislators before and after the Revolutionary War

Status of Legislators	Three Northern States (N.Y., N.J., N.H.)		Three Southern States (Md., Va., S.C.)	
	Prewar	Postwar	Prewar	Postwar
Wealthy	36%	12%	52%	28%
Well-to-do	47%	26%	36%	42%
Moderate	17%	62%	12%	30%
Merchants and lawyers	43%	18%	23%	17%
Farmers	23%	55%	12%	26%

Source: Jackson Turner Main, "Government by the People: The American Revolution and the Democratization of the Legislatures," *The William and Mary Quarterly*, 3rd. ser. 23 (July 1966), Table 1. Reprinted by permission.

Economic Turmoil. James Madison was soon to observe that "the most common and durable source of faction has been the various and unequal division of property."[20] The postrevolutionary legislatures epitomized Madison's arguments that economic inequality plays an important role in shaping public policy. At the top of the political agenda were economic issues. A postwar depression had left many small farmers unable to pay their debts and threatened them with mortgage foreclosures. Now under control of people more sympathetic to debtors, the state legislatures listened to the demands of small farmers. A few states, notably Rhode Island, demonstrated their support by passing policies to help debtors, favoring them over creditors. Some printed tons of virtually worthless paper money and passed "force acts" requiring reluctant creditors to accept the paper money. Debtors could thus pay big debts with cheap currency.

This policy did not please the commercial elite and the men of wealth who had once controlled nearly all the state legislatures. Then in 1786— just as calls were being issued for a new convention in Philadelphia—a small band of farmers in western Massachusetts led by Revolutionary War Captain Daniel Shays started **Shays's Rebellion,** a series of attacks on courthouses to prevent foreclosure proceedings. Farmers in other states —though never in large numbers—were also unruly. Jefferson called Shays's attack a "little rebellion," but it was much on the minds of economic leaders in the states.

The Aborted Annapolis Meeting. In September 1786, a handful of continental leaders assembled at Annapolis, Maryland, to discuss the problems with the Articles of Confederation and what could be done about them. It was an abortive attempt at reform. Only five states—New York, New Jersey, Delaware, Pennsylvania, and Virginia—were represented at the meeting, and the twelve delegates were few enough in

[20] *The Federalist*, No. 10.

number to meet around a dinner table. Called to consider commercial conflicts that had arisen among the states under the Articles of Confederation, the Annapolis delegates decided that a larger meeting and a broader proposal were needed to organize the states. This small and rather unofficial band of reformers (who held most of their meetings in a local tavern) issued a call for a full-scale meeting of the states in Philadelphia the next May—in retrospect, a rather bold move to be made by so small a group. But it worked, and in May 1787, what we now call the Constitutional Convention got down to business in Philadelphia.

MAKING A CONSTITUTION: CONVENTIONEERING IN PHILADELPHIA

After the Annapolis meeting, the Continental Congress called a convention "to take into consideration the situation in the United States," to meet in Philadelphia "on the second Monday in May next, *for the sole and express purpose of revising the Articles of Confederation.*" (The Philadelphia delegates did not pay much attention to this order.) To the statehouse in Philadelphia came representatives from twelve states. Only Rhode Island, a stronghold of paper money interests, refused to send delegates, agreeing perhaps with Virginia's Patrick Henry, who "smelled a rat" in the developments in Philadelphia.

Gentlemen in Philadelphia

Who were these fifty-five men? They may not have been demigods, as Jefferson, perhaps sarcastically, called them, but they were certainly a select group of economic and political notables. They were mostly wealthy planters, successful (or once-successful) lawyers and merchants, and men of independent wealth. Many were college graduates, mostly from Princeton (nine alumni), Yale, William and Mary, Harvard, Columbia (then called King's College), and the University of Pennsylvania. Most were coastal residents, rather than residents of the growing West, and a significant number were urbanites in a rural America.

Philosophy into Action

Both philosophy and politics were prevelant in the constitutional dialogue. The founding fathers at Philadelphia were an uncommon combination of philosophers and shrewd political architects. In a brilliant article on the Philadelphia convention, Jillison and Eubanks have shown how the debates moved from high principles to practical politics.[21] The first two weeks were mainly devoted to general debates about the nature of republican government. After that, very practical, and very divisive, issues sometimes threatened to dissolve the meeting.

[21] Calvin C. Jillison and Cecil L. Eubanks, "The Political Structure of Constitution-Making: The Federal Convention of 1787," *American Journal of Political Science* 28 (August 1984): 435–58.

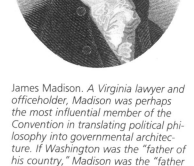

James Madison. *A Virginia lawyer and officeholder, Madison was perhaps the most influential member of the Convention in translating political philosophy into governmental architecture. If Washington was the "father of his country," Madison was the "father of its Constitution."*

Obviously, fifty-five men did not share the same political philosophy. Democratic Benjamin Franklin held very different views from aristocratic Alexander Hamilton, who hardly hid his disgust for democracy. Yet at the core of their ideas, even those of Franklin and Hamilton, a common center of gravity existed. The group agreed on questions of human nature, the causes of political conflict, and the nature of a republican government.

Views of Human Nature. Common to the times, delegates held a cynical view of human nature. People, they thought, were self-interested. Franklin and Hamilton, poles apart philosophically, reflected this sentiment. Said Franklin: "There are two passions which have a powerful influence on the affairs of men: the love of power and the love of money." Said Hamilton, in his characteristically blunt manner: "Men love power." The men at Philadelphia believed that government could play a key role in checking and containing the natural self-interest of people.

Views of Political Conflict. Of all the words written by and about the Founding Fathers, none have been more widely quoted than these by James Madison: "The most common and durable source of factions has been the various and unequal distribution of property." *The distribution of wealth* (property was the main form of wealth in those days) *is the source of political conflict.* "Those who hold and those who are without property," Madison went on, "have ever formed distinct interests in society."

These are strong and plain words. Arising from the unequal distribution of wealth are **factions,** as Madison called them (we might call them parties or interest groups). One faction is the majority, composed of the many who have little or no property. The other is the minority faction, composed of the few who hold much wealth. If unchecked, one of these factions will eventually tyrannize the other. The majority will try to seize the government to reduce the wealth of the minority; the minority will try to seize the government to secure its own gains. Governments run by factions, the founders believed, are prone to instability, tyranny, and even violence. The effects of factions have to be checked.

Views of the Objects of Government. To Gouverneur Morris, the preservation of property was the "principal object of government." Morris was outspoken and plainly overlooked some other objects of government, including security from invasion, domestic tranquility, and promotion of the general welfare. Morris's remark typifies much of the Philadelphia philosophy. John Locke, the intellectual patron saint of many of the Philadelphia gentlemen, had said a century before, "The preservation of property [is] the end of government," and few of these men would have disagreed. Propertyholders themselves, they could not imagine a government that did not make its principal objective an economic one: the preservation of individual rights to acquire and hold wealth. A few (like Morris) were intent on shutting out the propertyless altogether. "Give the votes to people who have no property," he claimed, "and they will sell them to the rich who will be able to buy them."

Gouverneur Morris. *This one-legged delegate from Pennsylvania, a man of considerable means and an extreme antidemocrat, held that protecting property was the "principal object of government." He was responsible for the style and wording of the Constitution.*

Views of Government. Human nature is avaricious and self-interested. The principal cause of political conflict is economic inequality. Either a majority or a minority faction will be tyrannical if it has too much power. Property must be protected against the tyrannical tendencies of faction. What sort of government, then, will work? The men at Philadelphia answered in different ways, but the message was always the same. "Ambition must be made to counteract ambition," said Madison. Power should be set against power, so that no one faction would overwhelm the others. The secret of good government is "balanced" government. A limited government would have to contain checks on its own power. So long as no faction can seize the whole of government at once, tyranny can be avoided. But a complex network of checks, balances, and separation of power would be required for a balanced government.

THE AGENDA IN PHILADELPHIA

The gentlemen in Philadelphia could not merely concoct a government from ideas. They wanted to design a government that would stand the test of time, but they also had to meet head-on some of the thorniest issues confronting the now independent colonies—issues of the economy, slavery, and other forms of inequality, and the new nation's relationship to the rest of the world.

The Equality Issues

The Declaration of Independence contained ringing rhetoric stating that all men are created equal; the Constitution is silent on the issue of equality. But some of the most important issues in the policy agenda at Philadelphia concerned equality. Three occupied more attention than almost any other issues: whether or not states were to be equally represented; what to do about slavery; and what to do about political equality.

Equality and Representation of the States. One crucial policy issue was how the new Congress would be constituted. Two views were presented. One side favored equal representation of the states, that is, a national legislature in which each state would have an equal number of representatives. The other side favored equal representation of people, in which each state would send representatives in proportion to its population.

One scheme put before the delegates by William Paterson of New Jersey is often called the **New Jersey Plan.** It called for each state to be equally represented in the new Congress. The opposing strategy was suggested by Edmund Randolph of Virginia and is often called the **Virginia Plan.** It would give each state a share of Congress that matched that state's share of the United States population.

The compromise was worthy of Solomon. Devised by a couple of delegates from Connecticut, it has been immortalized as the **Connecticut Compromise.** The solution: Create two houses in Congress. One body (the Senate) would have two members from each state, and the second body

Alexander Hamilton. *A New York delegate, born out of wedlock in the West Indies, Hamilton favored a strong central executive; in fact, he favored an elected king. He was less influential at the Convention than he became later as architect of the nation's economic policy.*

Benjamin Franklin. *A Pennsylvania delegate, Franklin was a philosopher, wit, scientist, inventor, diplomat, and folk-hero of the common man. One of the most democratic-minded delegates, he favored near-universal suffrage. He was the oldest (and, some would add, the wisest) of the delegates.*

(the House of Representatives) would have representation based on population. The United States Congress is still organized in exactly that way. Each state has two senators, but its representation in the House is determined by its population.

Sometimes historians and political scientists describe the conflict as between big and small states, each presumably looking for a plan that would maximize its representation. But the votes in Philadelphia do not support this interpretation. Eight states voted on the New Jersey plan (Georgia's delegation was split and did not vote), which supposedly favored the small states. In fact, three big states (New York, Maryland, and Connecticut) lined up with two small states (Delaware and, of course, New Jersey) to support equal representation of the states. The two Carolinas, small states at the time, voted against equal representation.[22] It was not a very sharp cleavage of small versus large. Rather, the vote depended on different views about the equality of representation, one side favoring equal representation of the states and the other favoring equal representation of people.

Slavery. The second equality issue was slavery. Slavery was legal everywhere except in Massachusetts, but it was concentrated in the South. Some delegates, like Gouverneur Morris, denounced slavery in no uncertain terms. Morris's position could not carry the day in the face of powerful southern opposition led by Charles C. Pinckney of South Carolina. The delegates did agree that Congress could limit future *importing* of slaves (they outlawed it after 1808), but nowhere did they forbid slavery itself. The Constitution, in fact, tilted toward recognizing slavery: It stated that slaves fleeing to free states had to be returned to their owners.

One further sticky question about slavery reared its head. How should slaves be counted in determining representation in Congress? Southerners were happy to see slaves counted toward determining their representation in the House of Representatives (though reluctant to count them to apportion taxation). Here the result was the famous **three-fifths compromise:** Representation and taxation was to be based upon the "number of free persons," plus three-fifths of the number of "all other persons," and everyone knew who those "other persons" were.

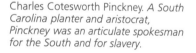
Charles Cotesworth Pinckney. *A South Carolina planter and aristocrat, Pinckney was an articulate spokesman for the South and for slavery.*

Political Equality. The delegates dodged one other issue on equality. A handful of delegates, led by Franklin, suggested that universal manhood suffrage should be required in national elections. But this democratic thinking did not appeal to men still smarting from Shays's rebellion. Many delegates wanted to put high property qualifications on the right to vote. Ultimately, as the debate wound down, they decided to leave the issue to the states. People qualified to vote in state elections could vote in national elections, too. ③

The Economic Issues at Philadelphia

The men at Philadelphia were deeply concerned about the state of the American economy. Economic issues were high on the Constitution writ-

---

[22] Paul Eidelberg, *The Philosophy of the American Constitution* (New York: Free Press, 1968), p. 82.

3	How Three Issues of Equality Were Resolved: A Summary	

PROBLEM	SOLUTION
SLAVERY	
How will slaves be counted for representation in the House of Representatives?	Count them as 3/5 of a person.
What should be done about slavery?	Basically, nothing. Congress was permitted to stop the importing of slaves after 1808, but the Constitution was mostly silent on the issue of slavery.
EQUALITY OF THE STATES	
Should states be represented equally (the New Jersey Plan) or in proportion to their population (the Virginia Plan)?	Both, according to the Connecticut Compromise. States would have equal representation in the Senate, but representation in the House would be proportionate to population.
POLITICAL EQUALITY	
Should the right to vote be based on universal manhood suffrage or should it be very restricted?	Finesse the issue. Let the states decide qualifications for voting.

ers' policy agenda. Historians still disagree as to whether the postcolonial economy was in shambles, as the Federalists claimed, or not. Kenyon notes that advocates of the Constitution stressed the economy's "weaknesses, especially in the commercial sector, and Antifederalists countered with charges of exaggeration."[23] The writers of the Philadelphia document, already committed to a strong national government, charged that the economy was indeed in disarray. Specifically, they claimed:

— States put up tariffs against products from other states.
— Paper money was virtually worthless in some states, but many state governments, which were controlled by debtor classes (those owing money), forced it on creditors anyway.
— The Continental Congress was having trouble raising money as the economy went through what we today call a business cycle.

Understanding something about these men and their economic interests gives us a clue as to their views on political economy. They were, by all accounts, the nation's *postcolonial economic elite.* Clinton Rossiter's authoritative study of the Constitutional Convention provides a profile of the members. What they saw as the sorry state of the economy was the "first complaint of the troubled men of 1787."[24] Some of these men were budding capitalists. Many of them were creditors whose loans were being wiped out by cheap paper money. Many were traders and merchants who could not even carry on trade with a neighboring state. Virtually all of them thought a strong national government was needed to bring economic stability out of economic chaos.

Historian Charles A. Beard took his cue from Madison himself to argue that the founders were highly self-interested in the outcome of their

[23] Cecelia M. Kenyon (ed.), *The Antifederalists* (Indianapolis, Ind.: Bobbs-Merrill, 1966), p. xxxv.
[24] Rossiter, *1787*, p. 42.

deliberations. In *An Economic Interpretation of the Constitution of the United States* (1913), he argued that the members of the Philadelphia convention, with a few exceptions, stood to gain personally from the adoption of the Constitution. [25] Most of the conventioneers, he said, had bonds and investments whose value would go up if the Constitution was adopted. This is not merely an argument that the Philadelphia gentlemen were propertied, upper-class men. Beard argued that these men would become richer if the Constitution was approved. After all, he suggested, it was Madison himself who spoke of the powerful economic motive in political affairs. The framers, too, had their economic motivations.

These charges from Beard are serious accusations to level at men we have now come to revere as our Founding Fathers. The notion of the Founding Fathers feathering their own nests suggests that the Constitution was a political document in the crudest sense of the word. Are Beard's charges true? Most historians today might say that Beard's arguments seem much exaggerated. In one painstaking review, historian Robert Brown tracked down information about the economic holdings of each member of the Philadelphia convention. [26] Only a minority, he concluded, could have been said to benefit from the new government, and a few of these ended up opposing the document in any case. But no one would dispute—and Brown emphasizes this—that most of the men at Philadelphia were far wealthier than the average American of their time, and few dispute that economic turmoil in the states was much on their minds.

Not surprisingly, therefore, the Constitution details very specifically the economic powers of the new national government. It forbids the states to print the hated paper money or interfere with lawfully contracted debts, and it gives significant economic powers to the new national government. Congress was to be the chief economic policymaker. Article I created the Congress, and Section 8 of Article I enumerated seventeen powers of the legislative branch. The first eight specified Congress's authority in economic policy. The civilian policy responsibilities of the president are brief and vague, summarized in nine words ("take care that the laws shall be faithfully executed"). But the economic powers of Congress are carefully spelled out. 4

In addition, the Constitution had one seemingly curious economic provision. It made all public debts of the Continental Congress binding on the new government. This provision appears a bit unusual at first glance for most people would use any excuse to *avoid* debts that they might argue are not really their responsibility. Today, most people view the size of the national debt with horror. Yet here were reasonable men enthusiastically saddling the new nation with (by standards of the day) a whopping national debt. Why?

Knowing what we know about the efforts by these men of Philadelphia to create a strong national government, the reasons should be obvious: A debt would have to be paid off, thus ensuring from the outset that revenues would flow into the federal treasury. There was a more impor-

[25] Charles A. Beard, *An Economic Interpretation of the Constitution of the United States* (New York: Macmillan, 1913).
[26] Brown, *Beard and the Constitution.*

tant reason: Alexander Hamilton, the first secretary of the treasury, stressed the link between a national debt and the emergence of capitalism. "It is a well-known fact," he said, "that in countries in which the national debt is properly funded, and an object of established confidence, it answers most of the purposes of money. Transfers of stock or public debt are the equivalent to payment in [money]."[27] When shares of the public debt can be bought and sold, they constitute a form of capital for investment. Even today, people trade in government debt (in the form of bonds) just as they do in the stocks of corporations. Thus did the Constitution help spur a capitalist economy.

The Global Connection

The new nation was small and surrounded by great nations. The United States did not become a powerful nation merely because it had defeated the English, any more than Vietnam became a major power after the Vietnam War. British, French, and Spanish colonies were to the north, west, and south of the United States. Troops from these nations surrounded our ill-defined borders. At a time when waterways were the major means of transporting goods, American commerce was weakly protected from foreign navies and pirates. Too bankrupt to pay for an army, never having more than a ragtag navy, the military posture of the new nation was underwhelming. Trade and commerce—indeed, the nation itself—were in jeopardy.

Foreign policy and the global connection were important issues on the agenda at Philadelphia. Although the first eight congressional powers dealt with economic policy, seven others dealt with Congress's power to create and maintain armies and navies and to declare war. The policy issues of the global connection shifted the constitutional spotlight from Congress to the president. It was an open secret that George Washington would be the first occupant of that office and the presidency was designed

[27] Alexander Hamilton, "A National Debt is a National Blessing," in Alpheus T. Mason (ed.), *Free Government in the Making* (New York: Oxford University Press, 1949), p. 313.

with him in mind. Thus the first policy responsibilities assigned to the president were to be commander-in-chief and to make treaties (with the consent of the Senate). To this day, the president has almost always held the upper hand in managing the nation's global affairs.

Separation of Powers, Checks and Balances: The Madisonian Model

We have described the policy agenda of the Philadelphia convention. We saw that policy issues about equality, the economy, and the global connection dominated the attention of these fifty-five men. We looked also at their views of human nature (self-interested), of the source of human conflict (inequalities of wealth), of the purpose of government (to preserve property), and of the structure of government (balanced). How these all were to be combined in an actual working structure can be understood if we examine the **Madisonian model.** [28] Madison was the principal architect of the government's final structure, and his blueprint still shapes our policymaking process.

Madison and his colleagues feared both majority and minority factions. Either could take control of the government and use it to their own ends. Factions of the minority, however, were easy to deal with; they could simply be outvoted by the majority. But factions of the majority were harder to handle. If a majority united around some policy (say, the redistribution of wealth) were to capture both houses of Congress, the presidency, and the Supreme Court, it could ride roughshod over the minority. To prevent that possibility, Madison's plan was to

1. Place as much of the government as possible beyond the *direct* control of a majority.
2. Separate the powers of different institutions.
3. Require a system of checks and balances.

To thwart a popular majority, first it was essential to *keep most of the government beyond the power of a majority.* Thus, if a unified majority were to seize control of one institution, others could stop it. Of the four elements of government in the Constitution's grand plan (the House of Representatives, the Senate, the presidency, and the Supreme Court), only one, the House of Representatives, could be reached directly by a voting majority. Senators were to be elected by the state legislatures and the president by special electors—not by the people themselves. Even if the majority seized control of the House of Representatives, they still could pass no policies without the concurrence of the Senate and the president. [5]

The Madisonian scheme also required a **separation of powers.** Each of the three branches of government—executive, legislative, and judicial— would be relatively independent of one another so none could control the

[28] Two brilliant expositions of the Madisonian model are found in books by past presidents of the American Political Science Association. One is by James M. Burns, *The Deadlock of Democracy: Four-Party Politics in America* (Englewood Cliffs, N.J.: Prentice-Hall, 1963), Chap. 1; the other is Robert A. Dahl, *A Preface to Democratic Theory* (Chicago: University of Chicago Press, 1956), Chap. 1.

others. The president, Congress, and the courts all hold different pieces of the power pie. Power is not separated absolutely, however, but shared among the three institutions.

Finally, Madison created a system of **checks and balances.** While separation of powers divided power, the checks and balances system was designed to limit government's power. This system reflected Madison's goal of setting power against power. If one institution is seized by a faction, it still cannot damage the whole system, he reasoned. The system of checks and balances is as elaborate and delicate as a spider's web. Presidents check Congress by holding veto power; Congress holds the purse strings of government and must approve presidential appointments.

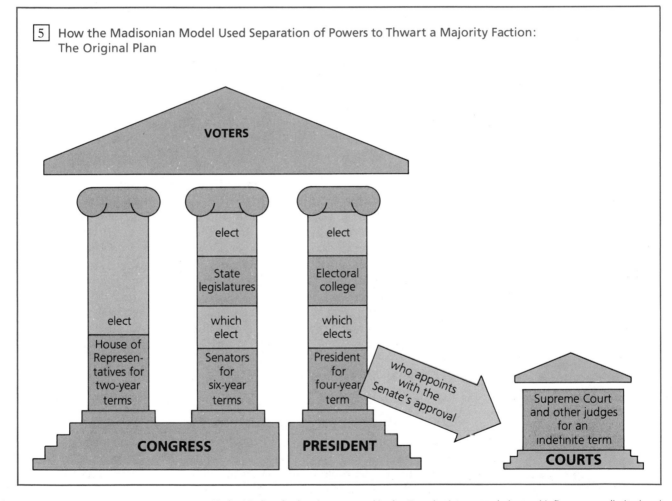

5 How the Madisonian Model Used Separation of Powers to Thwart a Majority Faction: The Original Plan

Under Madison's plan, incorporated in the Constitution, voters' electoral influence was limited and mostly indirect. Only the House of Representatives was directly elected. Senators and presidents were indirectly elected, and judges were appointed. Over the years, Madison's original model has been substantially democratized.

The Seventeenth Amendment (1913) made senators directly elected by popular majorities. Today, the electoral college has become largely a rubber stamp, voting the way the popular majority in each state votes.

The judiciary was the branch to which the Constitution devoted the shortest space, but the courts, too, figured in the neat system of checks and balances. Presidents could appoint judges, but only with the advice and consent of the Senate. Later the Supreme Court itself, in *Marbury* v. *Madison* (1803), asserted its power to check the other branches through judicial review: the right to hold policies of the other two branches unconstitutional. This right was a powerful trump card added to the checks and balances system and considerably strengthened the Court's initially rather weak hand. (For a summary of separation of powers and the checks and balances system, see ⑥ .)

The Constitutional Policy Settlement: An Overview

The Constitution signed at Philadelphia created a new government—but it did more than that; it also made policy. The policy agenda at Philadelphia was a long one. It contained thorny issues about equality—particularly slavery, representation of the states, and the right to vote. Some of those issues were deftly compromised (as in the conflict between the Virginia and New Jersey plans). Some were finessed (as in the issue of whether to have property qualifications for voting). Although conflict and compromise dominated the equality issues, there was a strong consensus on the economic ones. The men at Philadelphia wanted a strong national government to promote economic stability. They enumerated quite specifically the economic policy responsibilities of Congress. They knew, too, that the fledgling nation was a third-rate power on the global stage, and they intended to create an adequate American military force.

The government designed to achieve these policy goals was based on Madison's elaborate image of balanced government. The three branches were to check and balance one another. In that way, the governmental machinery could never be seized by any faction, whether a majority or a minority. When these men adjourned to the City Tavern for dinner and drinks on September 17, 1787, little could they have guessed that the Constitution they had drawn up would last for two centuries.

IMPLEMENTING THE CONSTITUTION

Federalists and Antifederalists

Our near-Biblical awe of the Founding Fathers sometimes blinds us to the bitter politics of the day. In that low-tech era before public opinion polls, we have no way of guaging the public's feelings about the new document. We do have it on good authority—arch-Federalist John Marshall's—that "It is scarcely to be doubted that *in some of the adopting states, a majority of the people were in opposition.*" [29]

---

[29] Quoted in Beard, *Economic Interpretation*, p. 299. My italics.

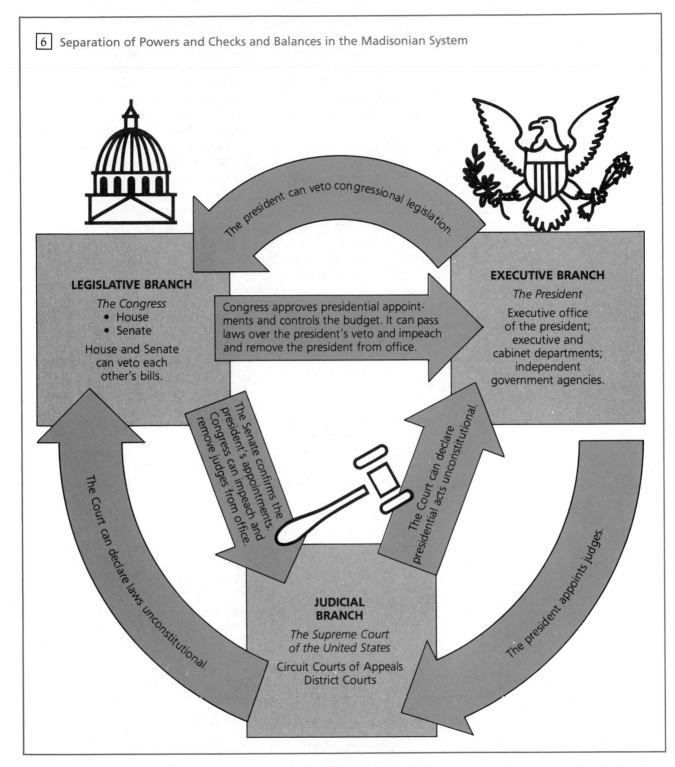

LEGISLATIVE BRANCH

The Congress
• House
• Senate

House and Senate can veto each other's bills.

The president can veto congressional legislation.

Congress approves presidential appointments and controls the budget. It can pass laws over the president's veto and impeach and remove the president from office.

EXECUTIVE BRANCH

The President

Executive office of the president; executive and cabinet departments; independent government agencies.

The Senate confirms the president's appointments. Congress can impeach and remove judges from office.

The Court can declare presidential acts unconstitutional.

The Court can declare laws unconstitutional.

The president appoints judges.

JUDICIAL BRANCH

The Supreme Court of the United States

Circuit Courts of Appeals
District Courts

The diagram shows how Madison and his fellow constitution writers used the doctrine of separation of powers to allow the three institutions of government to check and balance one another. Judicial review, the power of courts to hold executive and congressional policies unconstitutional, was not explicit in the Constitution but was asserted by the Supreme Court under John Marshall in Marbury v. Madison.

The Constitution itself required that nine states approve the document before it could be implemented. Throughout the states, a fierce battle erupted between the **Federalists** who supported the Constitution and the **Antifederalists** who opposed it. Newspapers were filled with letters and articles praising or condemning the document, many written under pseudonyms. In praise of the document, three men (James Madison, Alexander Hamilton, and John Jay) wrote a series of articles under the name of "Publius." These **Federalist Papers** have become documents second only to the Constitution itself in characterizing the minds of the framers. [30]

Beginning on October 27, 1787, barely a month after the convention ended, the Federalist Papers began to appear in New York newspapers. Eighty-five of them would eventually appear. They not only defended the Constitution detail by detail, but also represented an important statement of political philosophy; Madison's No. 10 is perhaps the most famous of all. Because they were written under a pseudonym, it was difficult at first to sort out the contributions of Madison, Jay, and Hamilton. Curiously, Alexander Hamilton laid claim to no less than sixty-three of the eighty-five, even though historians have demonstrated that he wrote only fifty-one. James Madison wrote twenty-five; John Jay, who became ill during the period, wrote only five; and three of them were jointly written.

Giving the Antifederalists Their Due. Far from being unpatriotic or unAmerican, the Antifederalists sincerely believed that the new government was an enemy of freedom, the very freedom they had just fought a war to ensure. Adopting names like Aggrippa, Philadelphiensis, and Monteczuma, the Antifederalists launched bitter, biting, even brilliant attacks on the Philadelphia document. They frankly questioned the motives of the Constitution writers.

One objection sung out above the rest: that the new Constitution was a class-based document. It was intended to ensure that a particular economic elite controlled the public policies of the national government. Let us hear these critics in their own quaint words. [31]

> From George Mason, a Virginian, one of the delegates at Philadelphia who refused to sign the document: "This government will commence in a moderate aristocracy; it is at present impossible to foresee whether it will, in its operation, produce a monarchy, or a corrupt, oppressive aristocracy."
>
> From an opponent whose pseudonym was Cornelius: "Thus, I conceive, a foundation is laid for throwing the whole power of the federal government into the hands of those who are in the mercantile interest; and for the landed, which is the great interest of this country to lie unrepresented, forlorn and without hope."

[30] A new and controversial interpretation of the Federalist papers can be found in Garry Wills, *Explaining America: The Federalist* (New York: Doubleday, 1981).

[31] The three quotations are from Kenyon, *The Antifederalists*, pp. 195, liv, and 1, respectively.

Amos Singletary of Massachusetts: "These lawyers, men of learning, and moneyed men . . . expect to get into Congress themselves . . . [so they can] get all the power and all the money into their own hands."

Remember that these charges of conspiracy and elitism were being hurled at the likes of Washington, Madison, Franklin, and Hamilton.

The Antifederalists had other fears. Not only would the new government be run by a few, but it would erode fundamental and hard-fought liberties. One James Lincoln was quoted in the records of the South Carolina ratifying convention as saying that "He would be glad to know why, in this Constitution, there is a total silence with regard to the liberty of the press. Was it forgotten? Impossible! Then it must have been purposely omitted; and with what design, good or bad, he left the world to judge." These arguments would prove persuasive: The First Congress adopted amendments to the Constitution—the **Bill of Rights**—to protect individual liberties.

Third, opponents said that the Constitution would weaken the power of the states (which, to be sure, it would—and did). Patrick Henry railed against it. "We are come hither," he told his fellow delegates to the Virginia ratifying convention, "to preserve the poor commonwealth of Virginia."[32]

Think about what would have happened if the Antifederalists had won the battle over the Constitution. At least at that time, we would not have had a unified Republic. States would have gone their own ways. Militarily, the American "nation" would have been weak. Today, we might be Virginians or New Yorkers, rather than citizens of the United States. Of course, antifederalist views did not prevail.

Ratification

Federalists may not have had the support of the majority, but they made up for it in aggressive politicking. They knew the legislatures of some states were cool to the Constitution, so they specified that it would have to be ratified in conventions in each of the states.

From Delaware's approval on December 7, 1787, only six months passed before New Hampshire made up the required nine. Virginia and New York then voted to join the new union. Two states were holdouts: North Carolina and Rhode Island made the promise of a Bill of Rights their price for joining the rest, and they finally came around a year later.

So sure were the delegates at Philadelphia that General Washington was likely to become the first president in the new Union, they gave him the convention's papers for safe-keeping. They were not wrong; the general was the unanimous choice of the Electoral College as our first president. He took office on April 30, 1789, in New York City, our first capital. Stern New Englander John Adams became "His Superfluous Excellency," as Franklin called the Vice President. Washington asked Thomas Jefferson to serve as the first Secretary of State. He called on

[32] On the Antifederalists, see also Jackson Turner Main, *The Antifederalists* (Chapel Hill: University of North Carolina Press, 1961).

Alexander Hamilton to become Secretary of the Treasury, and Hamilton launched his pet project of assuming all the colonial governments' debts, totaling $54 million, in order to put the nation on the road to a capitalist economy.

CONSTITUTIONAL CHANGE

"The Constitution," said Jefferson, "belongs to the living and not to the dead." The United States Constitution is frequently—and rightly— referred to as a living document. It is constantly being tested and altered.

Generally, constitutional changes are made either by formal amendments or by informal processes. Formal amendments change the letter of the Constitution. But there is an unwritten body of tradition, practice, and procedure—what political scientists sometimes call the **unwritten constitution**—that may be as important as the Constitution itself. Not all nations, even those (like Great Britain) that we call democratic, have written constitutions. Political parties and national conventions are not part of our written Constitution, but they are important parts of the unwritten constitution. Informal processes, including constitutional interpretation and political practice, alter this unwritten constitution and may thus change the spirit of the Constitution.

The Formal Amending Process

Article V of the Constitution outlines procedures for amending the letter of the document. There are two stages to the amendment process— proposal and ratification—and each stage has two possible avenues. 7 An amendment may be proposed either by a two-thirds vote in each house of Congress, or by a national convention called by Congress at the request of two-thirds of the state legislatures. An amendment may be ratified either by the legislatures of three-fourths of the states or by special conventions called in three-fourths of the states.

All but one of the successful amendments to the Constitution have been proposed by Congress and ratified by the state legislatures. The exception was a double exception—an amendment to repeal an amendment. Conventions called by the states repealed the short-lived Prohibition Amendment, the Eighteenth, with the Twenty-first. The reason conventions were used is simple: Proponents of repeal doubted that they could win in the Bible-belt legislatures, so they convinced Congress to require that conventions be called.

Today another proposed amendment is making the rounds of the state legislatures. It would call for a national convention to amend the Constitution to require a balanced national budget every year. By 1985, thirty of the required thirty-four states had formally requested such an amending convention. Opponents feared that it would open up a constitutional Pandora's box if hordes of special interest groups tried to grind their own favorite axes at such a convention.

Unquestionably, the amendments taken as a whole have made the

Constitution more egalitarian and democratic. The emphasis on economic issues in the original document is now balanced by amendments that stress equality and increase the ability of a popular majority to affect government. The amendments are headed by the Bill of Rights, the first eight amendments to the Constitution. [33] Included in the Bill of Rights are guarantees of equal treatment at the bar of justice and the great First Amendment rights of freedom of religion, press, speech, and assembly, which will be discussed in Chapter 5. Later amendments have forbidden certain inequalities (particularly political) based on race, sex, and age. Of all the amendments, few are so important as the brief Thirteenth Amendment abolishing slavery. Other amendments have democratized the political system, making it easier for voters to influence

[33] Some writers feel that the first *ten* amendments constitute the Bill of Rights, if for no other reason than that they were all adopted in a package. The first eight, however, deal with *individual rights*, whereas the ninth emphasizes that citizens have other, unspecified rights and the tenth reemphasizes the federal system. Surely it would be nitpicking to argue long over whether eight or ten amendments constitute the Bill of Rights.

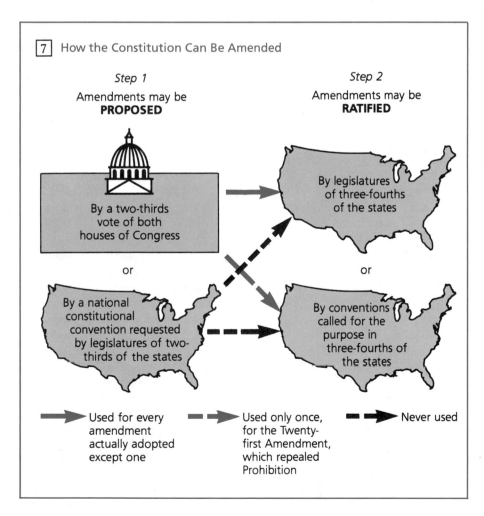

7   How the Constitution Can Be Amended

Step 1
Amendments may be
PROPOSED

Step 2
Amendments may be
RATIFIED

By a two-thirds vote of both houses of Congress

By legislatures of three-fourths of the states

or

or

By a national constitutional convention requested by legislatures of two-thirds of the states

By conventions called for the purpose in three-fourths of the states

Used for every amendment actually adopted except one

Used only once, for the Twenty-first Amendment, which repealed Prohibition

Never used

The Constitution set up two alternative routes for proposing amendments and two for ratifying them. Only one of the four possible combinations has really been used, but there are persistent calls for a constitutional convention to propose some new amendment or another. (Amendments to permit school prayers, to make abortion unconstitutional, and to require a balanced national budget are recent examples.)

the government. The Twelfth Amendment implicitly recognized the party system, and the Seventeenth permitted voters to elect United States senators directly.

Two recently proposed amendments were also intended by their promoters to expand equality. The Twenty-seventh Amendment was the controversial Equal Rights Amendment. It would incorporate into the Constitution language guaranteeing equal rights for women. But it generated almost unbelievable opposition in many state legislatures and was not ratified. In 1978, Congress sent to the states an amendment guaranteeing congressional representation to the District of Columbia's mostly black population. Supporters claimed that the District is the only political entity not officially represented in Congress and that its denial of voting power discriminates mostly against black Americans, who make up more than 70 percent of the district's population. Opponents claimed that Washington is not a state and should not be treated like one.

Only one amendment is specifically about the economy—the Sixteenth, or Income Tax, Amendment, whose practical side we note every April 15. None deals with the energy/environment policy arena and none with the global side of American policy. If the Constitution itself was primarily an economic document, its amendments have dealt mostly with the policy arena of equality.

The Informal Process of Constitutional Change

We can change the Constitution formally, as we do when we add an amendment to it. We can also change it informally by changing the meaning, but not the letter, of the document. There are two major ways in which the Constitution has changed informally over two centuries of the American republic: *judicial interpretation* and *political practice*.

Judicial Interpretation. Disputes arise about the meaning of the Constitution. If it is the "supreme law of the land," someone has to decide what it means when these disputes arise. Early in the first American century, that question was addressed in a very famous court case, ***Marbury v. Madison,*** in 1803. Here is what happened in this watershed case.

John Adams, our second president, was a starchy, staunch Federalist. His opponent in the 1800 election was Thomas Jefferson, and Jefferson won. Adams and his fellow Federalists devised a scheme to keep the Federalists in control of much of the government, despite the new administration. They made scores of "midnight appointments"—so called because they were made in the waning days, hours, even minutes, of the Adams administration. Adams was at his desk until nine o'clock of his last full night in office (March 3, 1801) signing commissions. Giving federal jobs to Federalists would insure years of continued Federalist power. One of those midnight appointments was to go to a chap named William Marbury, who would be a justice of the peace in the District of Columbia.

Unfortunately for the scheme, not all of the appointments were formally transmitted by the time Adams exited and Jefferson entered office.

Jefferson's new secretary of state, James Madison, refused to hand over Marbury's commission. Marbury sued Madison, taking his case straight to the Supreme Court. Heading the Court then was arch-Federalist John Marshall. (Marshall was something of a "midnight appointment" himself. Although he was Adams's fourth choice for the post of chief justice, he took his seat barely three weeks before Adams's term ended.) The furor over the Marbury case consumed national politics for a time. Jeffersonians threatened to impeach Marshall and his Federalist brethren if they ruled in favor of Marbury.

Always ingenious, Marshall hit upon a solution. He refused to order Marbury's commission delivered because, said the Court the law under which Marbury brought his case to the Supreme Court was constitutionally flawed and therefore invalid. He thus asserted for the Court the right to decide what the Constitution means, thereby sacrificing the battle over poor Marbury and his commission to score victory in a larger war. This power, called **judicial review,** gives courts the right to decide whether acts of legislative and executive branches of the national government and the states are in accord with the Constitution. Marshall's critics (and there was no shortage of them) claimed that the Court somehow "usurped" power which was not constitutionally theirs. This was untrue, since judicial review was commonplace in the states before and after the Constitution. The authors of *The Federalist Papers* wrote of judicial review as if it were clearly implicit in the Constitution.

The power of judicial review is infrequently invoked. But the whole process of judicial interpretation is central to the meaning of the Constitution in practice. In Chapter 5, when we look at civil liberties, and again in Chapter 14, when we look at the courts, we will see time and again the role of the courts in expanding or reshaping the letter of the Constitution.

John Marshall. *As chief justice, Marshall, along with his Federalist colleagues on the Supreme Court, strengthened first the power of the courts and then the power of the national government itself. Amid calls for his impeachment, Marshall deftly asserted the Supreme Court's power to declare the acts of other branches of government unconstitutional. Thus, Marshall left a lasting impact on American government.*

Changing Political Practice. The ways we practice politics also change the Constitution, stretching it, shaping it, and giving it new meaning. Probably no changes are more important than those related to parties and elections.

The political party did not exist when the Constitution was written. In fact, its authors would have disliked parties, which epitomize factions. But the party system was strong by 1800, and it plays a key role in policymaking today. Our government would be radically different if there were no political parties, even though the Constitution is silent about them. Practice has also reduced the role of the electoral college to a trivial one. The writers of the Constitution intended there to be *no* popular vote for the president himself; instead, the people would vote to select wise electors who would choose a "distinguished character of continental reputation," as the Federalist Papers put it, to be president. The electoral college would be the vehicle for this selection. Each state would have "electors," who would vote for the president.

Yet through the years electors have come to be bound to vote for the candidate winning their state's popular vote. Nothing in the Constitution prohibits an elector from voting for any candidate (even one with no "continental reputation"). For all practical purposes, though, electors are rubber stamps of the popular vote. Every so often, electors have decided to cast a vote for their own favorites; some state laws now require electors to vote with their state's popular majorities. The idea that the electoral college would exercise independent wisdom in choosing a president is now a constitutional anachronism, changed not by formal amendment but by political practice.

UNDERSTANDING THE CONSTITUTION

Evaluating anything depends on what standards you use and what you compare it to. If we evaluate the Constitution in terms of its stability and longevity, it is a very impressive document indeed, having survived a bloody civil war, industrial and urban revolutions, and other challenges. James Madison would hardly recognize the government he created, but he would find almost all the formal procedures and institutions still intact. (The actual Constitution may still be seen in the National Archives.) When we realize that the history of the modern world is littered with the dust from scraps of paper called constitutions, the survival of ours is all the more impressive. What standards, then, beyond its staying power, shall we use for evaluating the Constitution? Let us return for a while to the four models of American policymaking that we learned in Chapter 2, and see what sense we can make of the Constitution today.

The Constitution and Democracy

Millions of words have been written about the American Constitution. In none of them, so far as we know, has it been called a democratic document—hardly surprising considering the political philosophies of the men who wrote it. Among the "better classes," democratic government was roundly despised. If democracy was a way of permitting the majority's preference to become policy, the Constitution writers had no sympathy for democracy. Rather, they set up numerous roadblocks to a democratic majority's getting its way (see pages 88–90). It was to be a government of the "rich, well-born, and able," as Hamilton said, where John Jay's wish that "the people who own the country ought to govern it" would be a reality. That is not quite what we mean by democracy today.

Yet neither did the Constitution create a monarchy or a formal aristocracy. It created a form of representative government, modeled after Lockean tradition of limited government on which democracy depends. The Constitution also permitted extensive democratization through amendments. There are still familiar roadblocks to majority rule in America, but many of the highest hurdles have been lowered by constitutional amendments. The electoral college is virtually a rubber stamp of the popular vote, equality in suffrage is by and large universal, senators are now elected directly by the people. This undemocratic—even antidemocratic—document permitted substantial movement toward democracy.

The Constitution and
Class and Elite Theory

In Chapter 2, we also described a model of American politics called *class and elite theory*. According to this theory, an upper-class economic elite dominates government and politics. Clearly, Beard's work on the Constitution (see pages 85–86) is consistent with this thesis. The early American elite was firmly committed to establishing a capitalist economic system, and their principal agent was Alexander Hamilton. Delegate to the Constitutional Convention, author of many of the *Federalist Papers*, Hamilton, then thirty-two years old, was appointed by President Washington as the first secretary of the treasury. His ultimate goal was to "bind the moneyed interests firmly to the [Federalist] cause, to induce them to look to the central government rather than to the states for the security of their capital." [34] In this, he largely succeeded.

The structure of the Madisonian system made it easy for economic elites to protect themselves from popular majorities. In the original constitutional system the presidency, the Supreme Court, and the Senate were all indirectly selected.

The Founding Fathers themselves would have taken the charges of elitism in stride. Many would have been shocked at the idea that people should have political equality even if they were not economically equal. Yet it is important to remember that Madison and his constitutional colleagues believed that government should be protected from the greed of the rich as well as the greed of the poor.

The Constitution and Pluralism

As we noted in Chapter 2, *pluralism* refers to the multiplicity of interests and institutions in American politics that allows different groups some place in the political system where their ideas can be heard. The separation of powers and the checks and balances established in the Constitution are fully compatible with pluralist theory. Because many institutions share power, a group can usually find at least one sympathetic ear. The president is not all-powerful; even if he opposes policies you favor, Congress, the courts, or some other institution may support you. In the early days of the civil rights movement, for example, blacks found Congress and the president unsympathetic, but the Supreme Court sympathetic. They would have had a more difficult time getting their interests on the political agenda if the Court did not have important constitutional power. Groups advocating more equality for women had better luck getting Congress on their side to *propose* an equal rights amendment than they had convincing the state legislatures to *ratify* it. In pluralism, as the old saying goes, "you win some, you lose some." To a degree, the separation of powers and the system of checks and balances promoted the politics of bargaining, compromise, and playing one institution against another.

[34] Mason, *Free Government*, p. 307.

The Constitution and Hyperpluralism

A system of checks and balances implies that one institution is checking another. *Thwarting*, *blocking*, and *impeding* are synonyms for *checking*. But if I block you, you block him, and he blocks me, none of us is going to accomplish anything. The hyperpluralist argument suggests that so much checking was built into the Constitutional system that effective government is almost impossible. The historian and political scientist James M. Burns has argued:

> We have been too much entranced by the Madisonian model of government. . . . The system of checks and balances and interlocked gears of government . . . requires the consensus of many groups and leaders before the nation can act; . . . we underestimate the extent to which our system was designed for deadlock and inaction. [35]

If the president, the Congress, and the courts all pull in different directions on energy policy, the result may be either no energy policy at all or a makeshift and inadequate one. The outcome of hyperpluralism may be nondecisions when hard decisions are needed. If government cannot respond effectively because its policymaking processes are too fragmented, its performance will be inadequate. Perhaps the Madisonian model has reduced the ability of government to reach effective policy decisions.

FROM THE FIRST TO THE THIRD AMERICAN CENTURY

Of our four previously mentioned communities, only two—Bethlehem and San Jose—even existed on the eve of the first American century. During the revolution, Bethlehem served as a haven for part of the Continental Congress, which was scattered by the war. (Smyrna and San Antonio both came much later.) Prior to the Revolution, industries in Bethlehem were socialized and held in common by the community. The Hamiltonian system, though, made it easier for Bethlehem and other communities to develop an industrial, capitalist economy, in which changing technology played a key role. By the time of the Revolution, America was producing more iron than Britain.

The early creation of a strong national government was the doing of the Federalists. As Madison had shaped the Constitution and Hamilton the economic policies of government, so did John Marshall shape the judicial system. His Court's decision in *McCulloch* v. *Maryland* solidified the national government's involvement in the economy. (For more on *McCulloch*, see pages 107–108)

Thus, the current debate over government's role in the economy is an old one. Ronald Reagan is not the first to believe that government's role should be to strengthen the hand of capitalism. Hamilton, Marshall, and most of the Federalists supported similar policies.

---

[35] Burns, *Deadlock of Democracy*, p. 6.

Nor are issues on equality entirely new. Bethlehem, in fact, was founded by missionaries intending to work with Indians and blacks. A civil war settled the issue of slavery militarily, but not until the second American century would minority groups attain political, if not economic, equality.

The year 1987 marks the 200th anniversary of the American Constitution. A long, hot summer in Philadelphia brought forth a blueprint for government. The government that fifty-five delegates created has incorporated new groups (minorities and women, for example), expanded greatly its technology of war, and accommodated a party system. When we Americans celebrate its anniversary, few calls will be heard to rewrite the document itself. Two centuries ago our forefathers created American government; we are continually recreating it by formal and informal changes in our Constitution.

THE FIRST AMERICAN CENTURY SUMMARIZED

The year 1787 was crucial in American nation building. The fifty-five men who met in Philadelphia created a policymaking system that responded to a complex policy agenda. There were critical conflicts over equality, which led to key compromises in the New Jersey and Virginia plans, the three-fifths compromise on slavery, and the decision to toss the issue of political equality into the hands of the states. There was much more consensus, however, about the economy. These merchants, lawyers, and large landowners knew that the American economy was in a shambles, and they fully intended to make the national government an economic stabilizer. The specificity of the powers assigned to Congress left no doubt that it was to forge national economic policy. The Founding Fathers knew, too, that the global posture of the fledgling nation was pitifully weak. A strong national government would be better able to ensure its own security.

We should recall that 1787 was not the only year of nation building. The period before that reflected a crucial colonial and revolutionary heritage, the ideas and practices of which shaped the meetings in Philadelphia. Budding industrialism in a basically agrarian nation put economic issues on the Philadelphia agenda. What Madison was to call an "unequal division of property" made equality an issue, particularly after Shays's Rebellion. The greatest inequality of all, that between slave and free, was so contentious an issue that it was simply finessed at Philadelphia. Nor did ratification of the Constitution end the nation-building process. Constitutional change—both formal and informal—continues to shape and alter the letter and the spirit of the Madisonian system.

That system included the separation of powers, and checks and balances. Today Americans still debate whether the result is a government controlled by elites or a government too fragmented to be controlled by anyone. In Chapter 4 we will look at yet another way that the Constitution writers divided the government's power: between the national and the state governments.

Key Terms

Declaration of
   Independence
Constitution
natural rights
consent of the governed
limited government
Articles of
   Confederation
Shays's Rebellion

factions
New Jersey Plan
Virginia Plan
Connecticut
   Compromise
three-fifths
   compromise
Madisonian Model
separation of powers

checks and balances
Federalists
Antifederalists
Federalist papers
Bill of Rights
unwritten constitution
Marbury v. *Madison*
judicial review

For Further Reading

Beard, Charles A. *An Economic Interpretation of the Constitution of the United States* (1913). Argues that the men at Philadelphia had a personal financial interest in the Constitution.

Brown, Robert E. *Charles Beard and the Constitution* (1956). A thorough rebuttal of Charles Beard's thesis.

Eidelberg, Paul. *The Philosophy of the Constitution* (1968). An examination of the philosophical underpinnings of the Constitution.

Hamilton, Madison, and Jay. *Federalist Papers,* various eds. Key tracts in the campaign for adopting the Constitution.

Hofstadter, Richard. *The American Political Tradition and the Men Who Made It* (1948). Discusses the ideas not only of the Founding Fathers but also of other important figures in the American political development.

Jensen, Merrill. *The Articles of Confederation* (1941). Definitive treatment of the Articles.

Lipset, Seymour M. *The First New Nation* (1967). As a political sociologist, rather than a historian, Lipset sees the American experience as one of nation building.

Main, Jackson T. *The Antifederalists* (1961). Equal time for the opponents of the Constitution.

McDonald, Forrest. *We the People: The Economic Origins of the Constitution* (1958). Disputes Beard's thesis.

Rossiter, Clinton. *1787: The Grand Convention* (1966). Very well written study of the Constitutional Convention and its members.

Wills, Garry. *Inventing America: Jefferson's Declaration of Independence* (1978), and *Explaining America: The Federalist* (1981). Two volumes of a projected four-volume series reinterpreting the ideas of the Founding Fathers.

The American Governments: Federalism

It's natural to think of the United States as having *an* American government. As stated in Chapter 2, we have literally thousands of governments: one national, fifty state, and over 82,000 local. Nearly half a million elected officials, plus millions of bureaucrats and administrators, run them.

Constitutionally, the national government and the states constitute our federal system. In this chapter, I will show you that the states and cities are often "where the action is" in American politics and policymaking. I also argue that

- The central principle of American federalism has been the supremacy of the national government. It took a famous court case, a civil war, and a century of subsequent conflict to establish this principle. Today, though, it is indisputable.
- Contemporary federalism is often called *cooperative federalism*. States, cities, and the national government typically share costs and administrative responsibilities for many programs.
- State and local governments are best seen as competitors, just as firms and businesses are. Especially in our highly technological economy, states and cities want to carve the best deal for themselves, often at the expense of their neighbors. There are two principal games of federalism, the "economic growth game" and "the grantsmanship game."
- These games are quite serious. Because of shifts in population and production, some states—often those in the Sunbelt—are emerging as the leaders in the competition for jobs and economic growth. This has important consequences for the distribution of power in American politics.

AUTHOR JOHN NAISBITT claims that "real political power—that is, the ability to get things done—has shifted away from Congress and the presidency to the states, cities, towns, and neighborhoods."[1] Not every observer of federalism would agree, but the states and cities, once called governmental dinosaurs (and worse), are often where the action is in American government. Colorado's Governor Richard Lamm remarked that "the day of the state has come and gone—and come back again."

To many Americans the federal system is confusing. Everything government does seems to have more than one chef cooking the broth. Officially, the states and the national government are the two parts of our federal system. Your neighborhood school is run by a locally elected school board, but it also receives state and federal funds. With federal funds come federal rules and regulations. The local airport, the sewer system, the pollution control system, and the police department also receive a mix of local, state, and national funds. They also operate under a complex web of rules and regulations imposed by each level of government. Sometimes, federalism is almost impossible to understand. It is hard even to know exactly where the nearly $100 billion of federal aid to states and cities goes.[2] In 1972, when the U.S. Treasury Department first sent revenue-sharing checks to fifty states and 38,000 local governments, 5000 were returned by the Postal Service marked "addressee unknown." Even the Postal Service has trouble keeping up with all our American governments; pity the poor citizen.

Federalism may not always be the most exciting part of government in America, yet it is surely one of the most important. Consider these facts about federalism:

— An old issue of federalism—states rights versus national power—caused the only civil war we fought in American history. Particularly with respect to equality, federalism has been a battleground between states and the national government.
— Thousands of critical policy decisions are made annually by state and local governments. A "tax revolt" started in California; nuclear freeze referenda, though nonbinding on the federal government, first appeared on state and local ballots; social issues such as abortion and the teaching of evolution are hotly debated in state legislatures.
— States and their cities play key roles in economic development. As the federal government has backed away from its support for states and local governments, all fifty states and most cities now bolster economic development efforts by putting their money where their advertisements are.

Today's federal system is similar in form, but not in function, to the original design of the Constitutional Convention. How the federal system worked then and how it works today is our first topic.

---

[1] John Naisbitt, *Megatrends: Ten New Directions Transforming Our Lives* (New York: Warner Books, 1982), p. 108.
[2] Thomas Anton, *Moving Money.* (New York: Oxford University Press, 1982).

FEDERALISM THEN AND NOW

Federalism and Intergovernmental Relations

Federalism is a way of organizing a nation so that two levels of government have formal authority over the same area and people. The state of Tennessee has formal authority over its residents, but the national government has authority over the same land and people. Stand on any spot in Tennessee and you are subject to the constitutional authority of both a state and a national government. (Our language is a little confusing because we often call the *national* government the *federal* government.) In any federal system of government, each level of government must (1) have some domain in which its policies are dominant and (2) have some genuine political or constitutional guarantee of its authority. [3]

Federalism is not the most common way of organizing government. More governments today are unitary than federal. In a **unitary government,** all formal authority rests with a central government. Unitary governments may have geographical subdivisions, but these are merely administrative outposts of the central government, much as a giant corporation might have a headquarters in New York and administrative subunits in many places. Great Britain, France, and Japan have unitary governments. A unitary government can change the subunits' boundaries at will, make their officials mere flunkies of central authority, or abolish them altogether. But in a federal system, the subunits have power and authority of their own.

Today, we often refer to the workings of the federal system as **intergovernmental relations,** [4] by which we mean the entire set of interactions among the various units of government and their officials. The fine distinctions between the term *federalism* and the more encompassing term *intergovernmental relations* need not concern us here, but both describe how governments interact. There is a constitutional basis for much of that interaction.

The Constitutional Basis of Federalism

The word *federalism* is totally absent from the Constitution, and not much was said about it at Philadelphia. Loyalty to state governments was so strong that the Constitution would have been resoundingly defeated if it had tried to abolish them. It was clear to the delegates that the new nation would be a federal one. But it was going to be, if the gentlemen at Philadelphia had their way, a government in which the national government would be stronger, and the states weaker, than under the Articles of Confederation. And, as we know, they had their way.

---

[3] William Riker, *Federalism: Origin, Operation, Significance* (Boston: Little, Brown, 1964).

[4] Useful introductions to intergovernmental relations today are Deil S. Wright, *Understanding Intergovernmental Relations* (North Scituate, Mass.: Duxbury, 2nd ed., 1982); and David B. Walker, *Toward a Functioning Federalism* (Cambridge, Mass.: Winthrop, 1981).

The Constitution writers tried to define carefully which governments had—and did not have—which powers. [1] To be sure, the states were still to be vital cogs in the machinery of government. The Constitution guaranteed them equal representation in the Senate, and even made that provision an unamendable part of the Constitution. It made the states responsible for that most precious republican right, elections themselves. It required the national government to protect states against violence and invasion. And the Constitution virtually guaranteed the continuation of each state. Congress is forbidden to create new states by chopping up old ones, unless a state's legislature approves—an unlikely turn of events.

But the Constitution is silent on perhaps the most significant question of all: Where does power in the system really lie, and what happens when state and federal policies collide? According to some people, the **Tenth Amendment** gives part of the answer. It states, "The powers not delegated to the United States by the Constitution, nor prohibited by it to the states,

---

1   The Constitution's Distribution of Powers

Some Powers Specifically Granted by the Constitution

To the National Government	To Both the National and State Governments	To the State Governments
To coin money	To tax	To establish local governments
To conduct foreign relations	To borrow money	To regulate commerce within a state
To regulate commerce with foreign nations and among states	To establish courts	To conduct elections
To provide an army and a navy	To make and enforce laws	To ratify amendments to the federal Constitution
To declare war	To charter banks and corporations	To take measures for public health, safety, and morals
To establish courts inferior to the Supreme Court	To spend money for the general welfare	To exert powers the Constitution does not delegate to the national government or prohibit the states from using
To establish post offices	To take private property for public purposes, with just compensation	
To make laws necessary and proper to carry out the foregoing powers		

Some Powers Specifically Denied by the Constitution

To the National Government	To Both the National and State Governments	To the State Governments
To tax articles exported from one state to another	To grant titles of nobility	To tax imports or exports
To violate the Bill of Rights	To permit slavery (Thirteenth Amendment)	To coin money
To change state boundaries	To deny citizens the right to vote because of race, color, or previous servitude (Fifteenth Amendment)	To enter into treaties
	To deny citizens the right to vote because of sex (Nineteenth Amendment)	To impair obligations of contracts
		To abridge the privileges or immunities of citizens or deny due process and equal protection of the laws (Fourteenth Amendment)

are reserved to the states respectively, or to the people." To people advocating states' rights, the amendment simply means that the national government has only those powers and that authority *specifically* assigned it by the Constitution. Over any activity not mentioned there, the states or the people are supreme. But the Supreme Court in 1941 (in *United States* v. *Darby*) called the Tenth Amendment a constitutional truism, a mere assertion that the states have independent powers of their own. What really settled the question of how national and state powers are related was a famous court case, a civil war, and a civil rights movement.

Establishing National Supremacy

McCulloch v. *Maryland.* As early as 1819, the important issue of state versus national power came before the United States Supreme Court. The case was *McCulloch* v. *Maryland.* Here are the facts of the case and the principles decided by it.

The new American government had moved quickly to make economic policy. In 1791, it created a national bank. It was not a private bank like today's "First National Bank of Such and Such," but a government agency empowered to print money, make loans, and engage in many other banking tasks. A darling of such Federalists as Alexander Hamilton, the bank was hated by many Democrats (such as Jefferson), by farmers, and by state legislatures.

Railing against the "Monster Bank," the state of Maryland in 1818 passed a law taxing the national bank's Baltimore branch $15,000 a year. The Baltimore branch refused to pay, whereupon the state of Maryland sued the cashier, one James McCulloch, for payment. When the state courts upheld Maryland's law and its tax, the bank appealed to the United States Supreme Court. John Marshall, whom we first met in our discussion of judicial review (page 97) was still Chief Justice when two of the country's ablest lawyers argued the case before the Court.

Daniel Webster argued for the national bank and Luther Martin, a signer of the Declaration of Independence, for Maryland. Martin argued that the Constitution was very clear about the powers Congress had (you can read them in Article I of the Constitution). Among them was *not* the power to create a national bank. Thus, Martin argued, Congress had exceeded its powers and Maryland had a right to tax the bank. In behalf of the bank, Webster argued for a broader interpretation of the powers of the national government. The Constitution was not meant to stifle congressional powers, he said, but rather permitted Congress to use all means "necessary and proper" to fulfill its responsibilities.

Marshall, never one to pussyfoot about a big decision, had his decision in favor of the bank written before the arguments ended—some say before they even began. He and his colleagues set forth two great constitutional principles in their decision. The first is *the supremacy of the national government* over the states. Said Marshall in his decision, "If any one proposition could command the universal assent of mankind, we might expect it to be this—that the government of the United States, though limited in its power, is supreme within its sphere of action." (Notice the rhetorical flourish and exaggeration; of course national supremacy did not command the "universal assent of mankind." Marshall's rhetoric calls to mind the old story about the preacher who wrote in the margin of his sermon, "Weak point—pound the pulpit.") As long as the national government behaves in accordance with the Constitution, said the Court, its policies take precedence over state policies.

The Court also held that Congress *was* behaving consistently with the Constitution when it created the national bank. It is true, Marshall admitted, that Congress has certain **enumerated powers** listed in Article I, Section 8 of the Constitution. Congress can coin money, regulate its value, impose taxes, and so forth. Creating a bank is not enumerated. But the Constitution adds that Congress has the power to "make all laws necessary and proper for carrying into execution the foregoing powers." This, said Marshall, gives Congress certain **implied powers.** It can make economic policy in a number of ways consistent with the Constitution. The other key principle of *McCulloch,* therefore, is that the *national government has certain implied powers that go beyond its enumerated powers.*

Today, the notion of implied powers has become like a rubber band that can be stretched without breaking. Especially in the domain of economic policy, we have hundreds of congressional policies involving powers not specifically mentioned in the Constitution. Federal policies regulate our food and drugs, build our interstate highways, protect consumers, try to clean up our dirty air, and do many other things that have been justified as implied powers of Congress.

Equality: The Eternal Issue of Federalism. What *McCulloch* pronounced constitutionally, a Civil War (1861–65) confronted on the battlefield. Then, as now, many of the issues of states' rights versus national power were mere covers for the issue of equality. At least with respect to racial equality, the federal government, not the states, has been the source of policy changes and pressures. For much of American political history, *the battle for equality has essentially been fought on the terrain of federal power versus states' rights.* Take, for example, the issue of slavery. On hindsight, the Civil War seems to be a battle over slavery. Yet in a larger sense, it was a battle over national power and states' rights. In our zeal to make the Civil War a noble cause to free the slaves, we forget that Abolitionists were almost as roundly despised in the North as in the South. Few Americans today know that the Great Emancipator, Abraham Lincoln, announced in his inaugural address that he would even support a constitutional amendment to make the right to own slaves "express and irrevocable." [5] Defeat of the South in the Civil War was, of course, a victory for antislavery forces. It also settled an important issue concerning federalism: that our government is what the Supreme Court later called "the indestructible union of indestructible states."

A century later, national power and state power again collided over the issue of racial equality. In 1954, the Supreme Court held that the forced

[5] Richard Hofstadter, *The American Political Tradition and the Men Who Made It* (New York: Vintage Books, 1948), p. 126.

segregation of public schools was unconstitutional (see pages 495–496 for a discussion of this case). Massive resistance to the decision followed. In fact, some southern governors and legislatures openly defied the courts. When a federal judge ordered the admission of two black students to the University of Alabama at Tuscaloosa in 1963, an ugly confrontation between Governor George Wallace and federal authorities erupted. Wallace made a dramatic stand against integration. He stood in the doorway of the administration building to halt the enrollment of the two students. (In fact, the confrontation had been elaborately staged by representatives of Deputy Attorney General Nicholas Katzenbach and Wallace; chalk marks were carefully etched on the sidewalk to show each one where to stand during the showdown.) Since then, the national government has adopted law after law and policy after policy to end segregation.

Particularly during the 1960s, social programs, advocated to reduce inequalities, flowed from Washington to aid minority and other poor groups in the states and cities. Head Start programs helped disadvantaged preschoolers; job training programs aided the jobless; "model cities" programs were targeted to poor and minority neighborhoods. Browning, Marshall, and Tabb examined the impacts of these federal programs in ten California cities, including San Jose. The "federal presence," they concluded, "has had an important positive influence on the struggle by blacks and Hispanics for political equality."[6] People they

[6] Rufus P. Browning, Dale Rogers Marshall, and David H. Tabb, *Protest is Not Enough: The Struggle of Blacks and Hispanics for Equality in Urban Politics* (Berkeley and Los Angeles: University of California Press, 1984), p. 235.

George Wallace, Symbol of Segregation. *When a federal judge ordered the admission of two black students to the University of Alabama at Tuscaloosa in 1963, a confrontation between state and federal power erupted. Alabama Governor George Wallace made a dramatic stand in the administration building doorway to resist integration. Deputy Attorney General Nicholas Katzenbach led a contingent of federal marshals enforcing the court order. In 1979 Wallace said of his stand in the door. "I was wrong. Those days are over and they ought to be over."*

interviewed were nearly unanimous in believing that these federal programs were the key to a more powerful role for minority groups. In San Jose, one respondent remarked that "originally through its Model Cities programs San Jose organized advocacy groups. They continue to be politically active. With increased visibility and city assistance they have become a strong political force." [7]

Since the Reagan administration took office in 1981, the federal government has steadily whittled down its commitment to urban programs. Palmer and Sawhill traced the program-by-program reduction in urban and social programs in the Reagan years. [8] Whether newly powerful black and Hispanic groups will continue to play a major role in political action after recent cuts in federal aids to cities, no one can say.

From Dual to Cooperative Federalism

What has happened to American federalism over two centuries? There has been a gradual change from a system of dual federalism to one of cooperative federalism. [9] In **dual federalism,** states and the national government each remain supreme within their own spheres. The states are responsible for some policies, the federal government for others. The federal government had exclusive control over foreign and military pol-

[7] Ibid., p. 211.

[8] John Palmer and Isabell Sawhill (eds.) *The Reagan Experiment* (Washington: The Urban Institute, 1982).

[9] The transformation from dual to cooperative federalism is described in Walker, *Functioning Federalism*, Chap. 3.

Funding Federalism. *Today, fiscal federalism frequently involves joint funding of projects by the national government and the states or localities. The private sector often cooperates in funding these joint projects, as in this New York City housing rehabilitation project. Money for it came from the federal government's Department of Housing and Urban Development, from the City of New York, and from Citibank. Cutbacks in federal aid to cities have meant fewer of these joint ventures, but there is still close to $100 billion in federal aid to states and communities.*

icy, the postal system, and monetary policy, for example. States were considered to be exclusively responsible for schools, law enforcement, and road building. In dual federalism, the powers and policy assignments of the layers of government are distinct.

In **cooperative federalism,** however, powers and policy assignments are shared between states and the federal government. Costs may be shared, with the federal government and the states each paying a part. Administration may be shared, with state and local officials working within federal guidelines. Sometimes, even blame is shared when programs work poorly.

Of course, the American system was never neatly separated into purely state and purely federal responsibilities. We usually think of education as being mainly a state and local responsibility. But even under the Articles of Confederation, Congress set aside land in the Northwest Territory to be used for schools. During the Civil War, the national government adopted a policy to create land-grant colleges. Important American universities like the University of Illinois, Ohio State, North Carolina State, Iowa State, and Florida State owe their origins to this national government policy.

In the 1950s and 1960s, the national government began supporting public elementary and secondary education. In 1958, Congress passed the National Defense Education Act (largely in response to early Soviet dominance in the space race). The Act provided federal grants and loans for college students and financial support for education in science and foreign language. In 1965, Congress passed the Elementary and Secondary Education Act, which provided federal aid to numerous schools. Although these policies expanded the national government's role in education, they were not a sharp break with the past.

Today, the federal government's presence is felt in even the littlest little red schoolhouse. Almost all school districts receive some federal assistance. To do so, they must comply with numerous federal rules and regulations. They must, for example, maintain desegregated and non-discriminatory programs.

Highways are another example of cooperative federalism. In an earlier era, states and cities were mostly responsible for building roads, although the Constitution does authorize Congress to support "post roads." In 1956, Congress passed an act creating an Interstate Highway System. Hundreds of red, white, and blue signs were planted at the beginnings of interstate construction projects. The signs announced that the interstate highway program was a joint federal-state project and specified the costs and sharing of funds. In this as in other areas, the federal system has promoted a partnership between the national and state governments.

Cooperative federalism today rests on several standard operating procedures. For hundreds of programs, it involves:

— *Shared costs.* Washington foots part of the bill, but states or cities that want to get their share must pay part of a program's costs. Cities and states can get federal money for airport construction, sewage treatment plants, youth programs, and dozens of other programs, but only if they pay some of the costs.

— *Federal guidelines.* Most federal grants to states and cities come with strings attached. Congress spends billions to support state highway construction, for example, but to get their share states must adopt and enforce a 55-mile-per-hour speed limit.
— *Shared administration.* State and local officials implement federal policies, but they have administrative powers of their own. The U.S. Department of Labor, for example, gives billions of dollars to states for job retraining, but states have considerable latitude in spending it.

Fiscal Federalism: The Growing Role of the Federal Government

"Who should pay?" is a common query in the federal system. All sorts of worthy programs may be adopted by our governments, but someone has to pick up the tab. Democrats are often inclined to urge the federal government to pay for programs; Republicans often lean toward funding them through the states. Liberals typically argue that the federal government is a more efficient taxer and can take care of national needs. Conservatives counter with defenses of local responsibility for local problems. These and other issues are related to **fiscal federalism,** the patterns of spending, taxing, and grants in the federal system.

Two important trends in fiscal federalism are seen in 2 :

— The federal government's share of our governmental expenditures has grown rapidly since 1929. Then, the federal government spent only 2.5 percent of our gross national product; today it spends more than a fifth of our GNP.
— The proportion of our GNP spent by state and local governments has grown less rapidly than the federal government's share. Still, 7.4 percent of our GNP was spent by the states and localities in 1929, while almost 10 percent is spent today.

The Works Progress Administration. *Much of the growth of the federal government began during the 1930s in response to the Great Depression. President Franklin D. Roosevelt pressed Congress to create public service jobs, paid for by the federal government. The most significant of these programs was the Works Progress Administration (WPA). Bridges, schools, parks, and other public institutions—most of them still in use—were built as "WPA projects."*

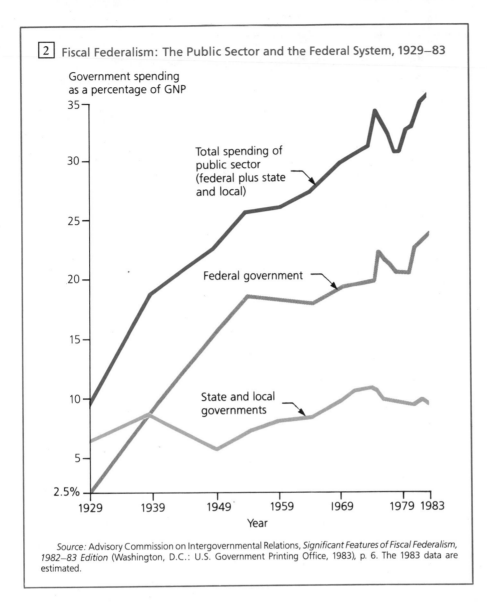

2 Fiscal Federalism: The Public Sector and the Federal System, 1929–83

Government spending as a percentage of GNP

Total spending of public sector (federal plus state and local)

Federal government

State and local governments

Year

Source: Advisory Commission on Intergovernmental Relations, *Significant Features of Fiscal Federalism, 1982–83 Edition* (Washington, D.C.: U.S. Government Printing Office, 1983), p. 6. The 1983 data are estimated.

Though the federal government is the heavyweight champion in the spending game, states and localities are strong middleweight contenders. A majority of Washington's spending is devoted to just two policies: national defense and social security. State and local governments are responsible for an array of spending: for schools, roads, colleges and universities, health care, and other policies. In addition, there are lots of local governments spending, too.

The States and Cities: How Many Governments Do We Need, Anyway?

The United States Bureau of the Census counts people, but it also counts governments. Its latest count, in 1982, continued to show plenty of American governments. 3

Certainly, better than 82,000 governments ought to be enough for any country. But are they too many? Americans value their state and local

113

3	How Many American Governments Are There?	
Federal government		1
State governments		50
Local governments		82,290
Counties	3,041	
Municipalities	19,076	
Townships	16,734	
School districts	14,851	
Special districts	28,588	
Total		82,341

Source: U.S. Bureau of the Census, *1982 Census of Governments,* Vol. 1, No. 1.

governments as grassroots government, supposedly able to stay close to the people. The multiplicity of governments helps sustain American pluralism. Beliefs and policy preferences unique to New Yorkers or Kansans can be reflected in the policies of New York or Kansas. Different states and regions also have different economic interests: oil in Texas, tobacco farming in Virginia, and copper mining in Montana, for example. The federal system ensures that each has a regional power base. James Madison, among others, valued this pluralism of interests within a large republic.

But where there is pluralism, hyperpluralism may not be far away. Too many governments, each with the power to delay, veto, or undercut policies, can make policy implementation difficult. A citizen in a typical metropolitan area may pay taxes to a dozen governments, some of which he or she knows nothing about. We saw in Chapter 2 (page 62) what happened when too many governmental players got into the act of implementing an employment policy for Oakland: stalemate. When policy goals can be thwarted by the fragmentation of governmental power, hyperpluralism dominates. America's federal system thus offers possibilities for pluralistic diversity and for hyperpluralistic stagnation.

The States: Friends and Critics. The states were here before the Union and are here to stay. Each state has its own written constitution, its own governor, public officials, legislature, and courts. But state governments have long been a source of consternation to both their friends and their critics. Former North Carolina governor Terry Sanford, certainly no bitter critic of the states, once called state governments "antiquated . . . ineffective . . . not responsive . . . and indecisive."[10] With friends making statements like this, you can imagine what the harshest critics of state government have to say. 4

Critics find that too much state power is held by particular economic elites (gambling interests in Nevada, copper companies in Montana, and oil producers in Texas and Oklahoma, for example). Others see the states and their officials as none too scrupulous in their management of the public purse. Many states could compete for the title of most corrupt.

114

[10] Terry Sanford, *Storm over the States* (New York: McGraw-Hill, 1967), p. 1.

Maryland would be a nominee: Spiro T. Agnew, former governor of Maryland and Richard Nixon's vice-president, was still receiving payoffs for old Maryland bargains while he was vice-president. Oklahoma would be another contender: In 1981, the federal government indicted scores of Oklahoma county commissioners for taking bribes and for assorted other scandals associated with local road building and repair.

But in defense of the states, Ira Sharkansky has claimed, "The states are maligned. They do not deserve to be the whipping posts of critics." [11] To the contrary, he said, states have taken the lead in many key policies, including transportation, higher education, urban aid, and mental health. They have been major policy innovators. States have often served as laboratories in which new policies are tested. Almost every public policy innovation began in one or more states before it caught on in the nation at large. The minimum wage, the income tax, driver training programs, urban renewal, child labor laws, open housing laws, and

[11] Ira Sharkansky, *The Maligned States* (New York: McGraw-Hill, 1977), p. 2.

---

4 Trials, Tribulations, and Texas

Few state governments have had a harder—or more colorful—time trying to enter the twentieth century than Texas. Texas still fancies itself as a rural, conservative state. Its legislature has often operated like a throwback to the nineteenth century. One of only seven states to have a biennial session (that is, meeting every two years instead of every year), Texas does not constitutionally permit its legislature to meet more than 140 days every two years. But "most Texans," says Agriculture Commissioner Jim Hightower, "think it'd be better if it only met for two days every 140 years." Legislators are paid only $600 for each month the legislature is in session. As recently as the 1960s, legislators did not even have offices. Public services and public welfare have been limited. Texas schooling has not been the envy of the nation.

In 1979, twelve moderate and liberal Democratic state senators went into hiding when a bill they opposed was up for consideration. Thus, the Senate lacked a quorum (the number of members required to be present) and could pass no legislation at all. The press called the delinquents the Killer Bees. The Texas Department of Public Safety was dispatched to find them, to no avail. The bill died and the Killer Bees returned to the floor of the Senate. It was only one of many trials and tribulations in Texas. Once, to show that members are not always paying attention to legislature business, a member introduced a resolution commending the population control efforts of the Boston Strangler. It passed.

More than many states, though, Texas and its state government has come to grips with its future. Oil and gas are a shrinking part of the Texas economy. Oil production has declined by more than a third since 1972. No new oil fields have been found for a quarter of a century. The state faced a $1.1 billion budget shortfall for the biennium beginning in 1985.

In response, Texas has committed itself to a research and technologically based economy. (Some call it "High Tex.") The Governor appointed Dallas electronics magnate H. Ross Perot to head a state task force on education. The Perot commission recommended a massive investment in elementary, secondary, and higher education. Said Perot: "We in this state have been lucky enough to sit on top of a whole bunch of oil and gas, but when we're in rocking chairs and that's all played out, we better make damn sure that our kids have something upstairs to keep the state going." In 1985, Governor Mark White pushed the legislature to quadruple its investment in pure research to $80 million. A San Antonio developer donated money and land to fund one of Mayor Cisneros' projects, an Institute of Biotechnology at the branch of the University of Texas Medical School there.

All in all, Texas was struggling to move quickly from the nineteenth to the twenty-first century.

Source: On the Texas legislature, Clifton McCleskey, et al., *The Government and Politics of Texas,* 7th ed. (Boston: Little, Brown, 1982), chapter 5, and Paul Taylor, "The Eyes of Texas Are Averted," *Washington Post National Weekly Edition,* February 4, 1985, p. 15; and on the problem of Texas oil, see Paul Taylor, "Going Dry," *Washington Post National Weekly Edition,* March 4, 1985, pp. 6–8.

The States, the Cities, and the Lures of Industry. *Federalism today includes a strong element of inter-state rivalry for economic development. Business magazines carry page after page of advertising supplements touting the advantages of locating here or there. Some 15,000 state and local agencies attempt to attract firms to their back-yards. South Carolina claims to have a corner on the goose that laid the golden egg—as well as low taxes, weak unions, and other features attractive to prospective relocators.*

scores of other policies were first proposed, passed, and implemented in one or more states. [12] States can also respond to their unique problems. Bilingual education is a problem in Texas, but not in North Dakota. Some states, such as Oregon, may decide not to pursue population growth. Other states may welcome it.

Local Governments: Hyperpluralism Prevails. You are now sitting within the jurisdiction of one national government, one state government, and perhaps ten to twenty local governments. The state of Illinois holds the current record for the largest number of individual governments—6,464 at the latest count. Chicago has 1,194 governments.

Local governments come in four major types. **Municipalities** are the city governments of Pittsburgh, Peoria, Pensacola, Phoenix, Portland, or your own hometown. Each municipality or township is located in one of about 3,000 counties. **Counties** are the least numerous local governments, but they provide important services for rural areas. Usually separate from both city and county governments are nearly 15,000 **school districts** responsible for elementary and secondary education. Most numerous but also most obscure are **special districts.** These nearly invisible governments handle such policy responsibilities as airport operation, mosquito abatement, and health care. Townships are numerous, but unimportant in their policymaking responsibilities.

Lone Jack, Missouri, is one of our 82,290 local governments. So small that it has no municipal employees, no city hall, and not even a telephone

[12] Jack L. Walker, "The Diffusion of Innovations among the American States," *American Political Science Review* 63 (September 1969): 880–99; Virginia Gray, "Innovations in the States: A Diffusion Study," *American Political Science Review* 67 (December 1973): 1174–85.

number, Lone Jack is one of the nation's 11,000 *toy governments*. Ross Stephens and Gerald Olson coined that term to describe the numerous local governments too small to exist except on paper.[13] Thousands of these governments, however, receive bits and dribbles of federal and state aid.

Having so many governments sometimes makes it hard even to know what governments are governing us. Exercising democratic control over them may be even harder. Americans speak eloquently about "government close to the people," but we participate in local elections at only about half the already low rate we participate in presidential elections.

One word characterizes the structure of American local government: hyperpluralism. In almost every American metropolitan area, fragmentation of the governing power prevails. Even within any city government, power is fractured. In many cities, for example, school committees set their own budgets; the city government must then set the tax rate to pay the bill. Within any metropolitan area, there will most likely be several municipalities, townships, special districts, and school districts. Critics of metropolitan fragmentation claim that having so many governments reduces the effectiveness of local government. One community may gain employment and tax advantages by attracting a new factory; citizens in neighboring communities will get no tax advantages but plenty of traffic congestion and air pollution. Overlapping jurisdictions may lead to contradictory policies, with one community trying to clean up its air while another tries to attract smog-producing industries.

Only a few metropolitan areas have attempted to solve their governmental fragmentation. One of them is Davidson County and Nashville, Tennessee, which consolidated their city and county governments. Even so, areas not far from Smyrna, in the next county, continue to grow outside the metropolitan jurisdiction.

Without all these subnational governments, we would have a very different political system. Their proliferation and fragmentation, though, encourages each of them to maximize their economic and fiscal advantage—typically at one another's expense.

THE GAMES OF FEDERALISM

We are all accustomed to the idea of firms competing in a marketplace. So, in a way, do states and cities. Businesses compete for profits and the goods and services (markets, skilled labor, raw materials, and the like) which bring them profits. Cities and states compete, too, not for "profits" in any narrow sense but rather, for countless particulars which benefit them at some other city's or state's expense. Peterson's study of cities found "the primary interest of cities to be the maintenance and enhancement of their economic productivity. To their land area cities must

---

[13] John Herbers, "Towns without Real Needs Getting U.S. Funds," *New York Times*, November 11, 1979, p. 1.

attract productive labor and capital."[14] Cities and states are devoted to promoting economic growth and benefits to their citizens.

Two factors above all stimulate competitive games among cities and states:

— States and cities compete for economic growth and development. New industries (like Smyrna's Nissan plant, which we described in Chapter 2) bring jobs, profits, and growth.
— States and their local governments compete for federal grants. Despite recent cuts in federal aid to states and cities, nearly $100 billion is available for distribution. The governor or mayor who does not bring home a piece of that pie is scorned by opponents as ineffective.

Competition for Economic Growth

Westmoreland County is at the opposite end of the state of Pennsylvania from Bethlehem, just east of Pittsburgh. It has suffered economic downturns similar to those in Bethlehem. In 1976, Governor Milton Shapp announced that Pennsylvania had "pulled the big Rabbit out of the hat." The massive Volkswagen Corporation announced that it would be pleased to accept $100 million in state and local government aid to take over an abandoned Chrysler auto plant and start turning out VW Rabbits. But it cost the state and local community a bundle: The state would finance a $10 million rail spur and give VW a $40 million, 1.75 percent long-term loan, while local government would settle for tax abatements (which meant that VW would pay less taxes annually than it charged for a single Rabbit).[15] Other states had desperately wanted "in" on the deal. Tennessee, which later got the Nissan plant in Smyrna, had

[14] Paul E. Peterson, *City Limits* (Chicago: University of Chicago Press, 1981), p. 14. For a similar argument about states and political entrepreneurs, see Susan Rose-Ackerman, "Does Federalism Matter? Political Choice in a Federal Republic," *Journal of Political Economy* 89 (1981): 152–65.

[15] The Rabbit story is told on pp. 1–8 of Robert Goodman, *The Last Entrepreneurs* (Boston: South End Press, 1979).

Hustling Industry in the States. *This is the Volkswagen plant in Westmoreland, Pennsylvania, which the state, county, and city paid so much to get. Subsidies, tax abatements, and other benefits helped to attract this VW Rabbit plant. Every state government tries to attract industry and commerce to its communities, hoping that new jobs will result. Advertisements, economic development offices, tax cuts, and industrial revenue bonds are just a few tried-and-true methods of pirating industry from other jurisdictions. In 1985, the whole nation waited on General Motors's decision about the location of its multi-billion dollar Saturn facility. Spring Hill, Tennessee, a stone's throw from Smyrna, was the lucky community chosen.*

formed a corsortium with Arkansas and Mississippi to bid for the Volkswagen plant. The three agreed that the winning state would encourage suppliers to locate in the two losing consortium members. All things considered, it was a genuine deal: States outbid one another, governors pleaded and wheedled one of the world's mightiest corporations, and concessions followed upon concessions.

These days, it is not enough to be a mayor or governor and attend to the services, schooling, and safety of your constituents. You must now hustle for them, too. San Antonio's mayor Henry Cisneros has taken up the mantle of local economic development, trying to identify his city as the labor-intensive element of the San Antonio-Austin "high tech corridor." Today, Robert Goodman reports, "there are more than 15,000 promotional agencies whose major function is to entice jobs from each other's state and local areas." [16]

Our state and local governments compete against foreign economic competitors, including Mexico, Hong Kong, Korea, and Taiwan; they also compete to attract foreign business. Cities and states may not agree on everything they find desirable or undesirable, but they probably agree that a new Toyota plant, a federal program to generate new electricity, a new federal office building promising hundreds of new jobs and some construction contracts, and an agreement to sell some local products directly to the Chinese mainlanders are good things. "Public bads" are equally apparent: Cities and states try to avoid being the recipients of the nuclear waste disposal plants or industries that attract large numbers of unskilled workers (who might end up on welfare).

Resource competition among jurisdictions essentially creates battles between cities and states to attract industry. There are two principal strategies in the resource competition game: One is to secure within your own borders the maximum number of activities that produce revenue, add jobs, and attract industry (preferably clean, nonpolluting, high-tech). States and cities spend hundreds of millions of dollars a year advertising their advantages in the pages of magazines and newspapers such as *Business Week, Fortune,* and the *Wall Street Journal.* They actively recruit industry by giving them policy advantages: cheap or free land, tax breaks, and job training for workers. States and cities often use **industrial revenue bonds** (often called IRBs) to promote new industry, putting the government's credit on the line to aid industries building a new plant or modernizing an old one. (The state of Washington found itself a bit overextended, though, when its creditors for the state's main nuclear industry thought the state should pay off bonds for the bankrupt utility.)

A second strategy is to shift costs and burdens to other units of government. Surely, each state wants to insure an adequate supply of inexpensive nonpolluting energy, but does not want to be the repository for the terrible by-products of nuclear power. The Department of Energy in trying to determine where to put the nuclear waste from a facility called Calvert Cliffs in Maryland, proposed to bury it in abandoned salt mines in Kansas. Kansas's droll Senator Dole remarked that "we're eager

---

[16] Ibid., introduction, n.p.

for new industry in Kansas, but we have grave doubts about whether this is the sort of industry we want." [17]

Increasingly, state governments have resorted to **severance taxes** to exploit their locational advantages. The most common are levied on minerals (oil, coal, and gas) exported to other states. ⑤ States use these severance taxes, and other means as well, to enhance their revenue base. But the federal government is also a major source of state and local revenue, and governments eagerly pursue the grantsmanship game.

The Grantsmanship Game: Competing for Federal Dollars

Distributing the Federal Aid Pie. Each year, the federal government publishes a massive volume called the *Catalogue of Federal Domestic Assistance*, in which is listed the host of federal programs available to states, cities, and other local governments. The listing includes federal support for energy assistance for the aged poor, housing allowances for the poor, drug abuse services, urban rat control, support for community arts programs, aid to state disaster preparedness, and so on.

There are three major types of federal aid programs for the states and

[17] The Calvert Cliffs story is discussed in David Davis, *Energy Politics*, 2nd ed. (New York: St. Martin's, 1978), pp. 195–96.

---

⑤ Federalism and Energy Policy: Does Wyoming Have a Right to Tax the Rest of the Country for Its Coal?

If Wyoming were a nation, it would be the world's fourth-largest coal producer. Richly veined with the less-polluting low-sulphur coal, Wyoming ships about ten mile-long trainloads a day from Rock Springs to the coal-consuming regions of the country.

To capitalize on this wealth of natural resources, Wyoming imposed a severance tax on its coal. A severance tax is an exit cost imposed on some such raw material as oil, coal, or natural gas. For every ton of Wyoming coal shipped to Illinois, an Illinois utility—and ultimately, the consumers of that utility's electricity—had to pay the state of Wyoming $1.12 in severance taxes. In 1980 one utility company, Chicago-based Commonwealth Edison Company, paid Wyoming $13.5 million in severance taxes. In fact, the funds reaped from the severance tax were just enough to meet the needs of the entire Wyoming state budget. Thus, Wyoming can do without a state income tax and a state sales tax and still have more than $1 billion in the state treasury.

Wyoming is not the only state with a severance tax. Many oil- and coal-rich states have it. None has outdone Alaska, which imposes a 12.25 percent severance tax on

oil produced from its North Slope. In two decades, the biggest state could be collecting an annual take of $10 billion in severance taxes. Texas, Colorado, Oklahoma, Montana, West Virginia, Kentucky, and Louisiana—all blessed by nature with energy resources—charge energy-poor states a severance tax.

When Montana imposed a 30 percent severance tax on coal exported from its borders, Commonwealth Edison took Montana to court to test the constitutionality of this practice. The utility argued that Article 1, Section 9 of the Constitution specifically stated that "no tax or duty shall be laid on articles exported from any State." Thus, it contended, Montana's severance tax was an unconstitutional and unreasonable burden on interstate commerce. The United States Supreme Court, however, did not agree. On July 2, 1981, in the case of *Commonwealth Edison* v. *Montana*, it held that Montana was within its rights to impose its severance tax.

Source: For more information on the Wyoming case, see James Coates, "It's Economic War among These United States," *Chicago Tribune*, July 27, 1981, p. 4.

Federal Aid as Carrot and Stick. *Billions of federal dollars available to states and cities stimulate their spending programs, especially when they come as matching funds for local dollars. The 41,000 miles of interstate highways were built with combined federal and state funds. But federal grants-in-aids are also a stick. Federal revenue sharing aid has been withheld from some cities until police departments have been racially and sexually integrated. Even when sharing funds, the federal piper can call some local tunes.*

localities. The largest, accounting for 80 percent of all federal aid to state and local governments, is **categorical grants.** These can be used only for specific purposes or "categories" of state and local spending. They also come with plenty of strings attached. One common string attached to categorical and other federal grants is a nondiscrimination provision: Aid may not be used for purposes that discriminate against minority groups, women, and other affected classes. Another common string is that Washington moneys may not support construction projects which pay below the local union wage. Virtually every categorical grant is inhibited by rules and requirements about its use. ⬚6

Thus, categorical grants function as both carrots and sticks. As a carrot, for example, Congress may entice local governments into spending money on water pollution control by *matching* local water pollution expenditures—that is, by putting up an amount of money equal to what the local government raises. To encourage urban revitalization, the federal government poured out billions in aid for that purpose, but localities had to ante up part of the money themselves. Federal aid can also be a stick. Concerned about the problem of teenage drunk drivers, President Reagan and Congress used the threat of taking away federal highway money for states that did not increase the drinking age to twenty-one.

Applications for categorical grants regularly arrive in Washington in boxes, not envelopes. Complaints about the cumbersome paper work and

If You Get Federal Aid, You Can't Teach Secular Humanism—
Whatever It Is

Ever since the federal government started aiding states and communities, it has attached conditions to that aid. Concerned about the high cost to urban school districts (such as Buffalo and St. Louis) in meeting court-mandated school desegregation, Congress in 1984 passed the Education for Economic Security Act. It authorized the Department of Education to spend up to $75 million to support "magnet schools" in districts undergoing desegregation efforts. Senator Orrin G. Hatch (R.—Utah) got Congress to add a "rider" to the legislation, requiring that no funds from the act could be used to support a course that the district "determines is secular humanism." Whatever secular humanism is, Religious Right groups have been against it. Senator Hatch was responding to their desires to keep secular humanism out of our schools and away from our young minds.

But what was it? Some linked it to Darwinism and evolution. One Fort Worth group handed out pamphlets ("Is Humanism Molesting Your Child?") and called it "a belief in equal distribution of America's wealth ... control of the environment ... the removal of American patriotism and the free enterprise system. ..." No one could quite point to where these evils were taught in the American schools, but Senator Hatch scored points with the Religious Right by including it in the legislation. Senators Moynihan (D.—N.Y.) and Eagleton (D.—Mo.), the bill's main sponsors, accepted the amendment because passage looked difficult without it. But the bill failed to define secular humanism and specifically forbade the Department of Education to define it. People for the American Way, a liberal interest group opposing the Religious Right, thought it opened a nest of problems. Now local groups could rail against some particular teaching practice, calling it secular humanism.

Whatever it is, schools getting money from the Education for Economic Security Act should not be using any of that money to teach secular humanism.

Source: The secular humanism story comes from Felicity Barringer, "A Ban on Teaching 'Secular Humanism,'" *Washington Post Weekly Review,* January 28, 1985, p. 32.

©Horsey For the Seattle Post-Intelligencer.

tedious strings of categorical grants led to the adoption of **block grants.** Block grants are more or less automatically given to states or communities to support broad programs in areas such as community development and social services. About 11 percent of all federal aid to state and community governments is in the form of block grants.

Another response to state and local governmental unhappiness with tedious categorical grants was **revenue sharing.** First proposed by economists in the Johnson administration, revenue sharing became a favorite of the Nixon administration. In it, virtually no strings were attached to federal aid payments. [18] An elaborate formula determined who got what. Revenue sharing, though a real help to hard-pressed states and localities, never amounted to more than 2 percent of all state and local revenues. It fell a partial victim to the Reagan administration's budgetary axes, though. Now states have been excluded from the revenue-sharing funds and only "substate" governments may get them. The Senate voted to eliminate revenue sharing altogether in 1985.

Despite these and other reductions, state and local aid from Washington still amounts to a tidy $98 billion a year. You can see the trend in its growth in 7 .

[18] On revenue sharing, see Paul R. Dommel, *The Politics of Revenue Sharing* (Bloomington: Indiana University Press, 1976); and David Caputo and Richard L. Cole, *Urban Politics and Decentralization* (Lexington, Mass.: D.C. Heath, 1974).

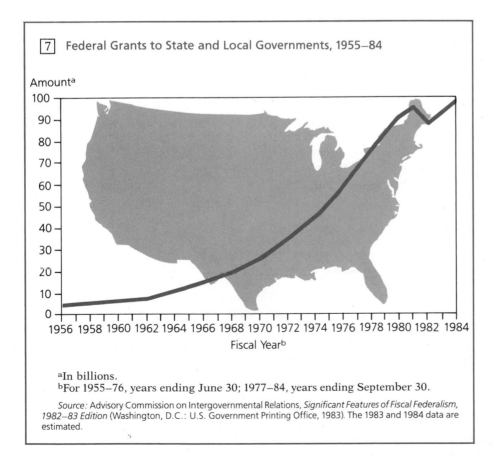

7 Federal Grants to State and Local Governments, 1955–84

Amount[a]

Fiscal Year[b]

[a]In billions.
[b]For 1955–76, years ending June 30; 1977–84, years ending September 30.

Source: Advisory Commission on Intergovernmental Relations, *Significant Features of Fiscal Federalism, 1982–83 Edition* (Washington, D.C.: U.S. Government Printing Office, 1983). The 1983 and 1984 data are estimated.

Grantsmanship Games. Hustling federal dollars is big business for states and communities (and also, of course, for businesses, universities, and other organizations). State and local agencies can obtain categorical grants only when they meet certain qualifications and when they specifically apply for the money. Full-time intergovernmental relations staffs in city hall or at the state capitol find out what programs they qualify for and make applications; more and more cities and states have their own lobbyists in Washington, D.C.

With so much money available from the federal government in the form of grants, most states and many cities have set up full-time staffs in Washington. Their task is to keep track of what can be gotten, and to help their states or cities be "firstest with the mostest." States and cities have even organized themselves into groups that act like other interest groups, including, for example, the National League of Cities, the United States Conference of Mayors, and the Council of State Governments. [19]

In playing the grantsmanship game, hard work is important, but luck counts as well. The *Wall Street Journal* once recounted how chancy the grantsmanship game can be.

> Well-to-do Palm Desert, California, got $2 million of federal funds designed to help unemployment. But Pittsburgh, Toledo, Seattle, and Phoenix—all cities with major unemployment problems—got nothing. Los Angeles, though, was a big winner. It worked hard to collect its $26.7 million, submitting eight cardboard boxes with applications weighing 400 pounds. Of its 253 applications, 34 were approved. All San Deigo got for its 44 applications was $1.6 million, even though its unemployment rate matched L.A.'s. The moral: Grantsmanship is a game played for high stakes, and hard work sometimes (but not always) pays off. [20]

Hard work and luck may pay off. The new airport renovation, the new water pollution program, the new university center for the handicapped may come to pass. But it often seems that having friends in high places helps, too. Senators and representatives regularly go to the voters with assurances that they are hustling for Hooperville and pushing for Pine Valley. Seniority in Congress and positions on key committees help the folks back home, they say. In Washington parlance, this is called "bringing home the bacon." [8]

FEDERALISM NORTH AND SOUTH

Regional Shift and the New War Between the States

Americans are a mobile people: The U-Haul may rank near the bald eagle as America's national symbol. At the beginning of this century Americans flocked to Detroit, where the automobile industry was turning out its first vehicles. Since 1979, however, half a million jobs have disappeared from the auto industry, many of them from Detroit. Some

[19] For coverage of these groups, see Donald Haider, *When Governments Come to Washington* (New York: Free Press, 1974).
[20] "How to Play the Game," *Wall Street Journal*, February 7, 1977. Reprinted by permission of *The Wall Street Journal*, © Dow Jones & Company, Inc., 1977. All Rights Reserved.

They used to say of former Congressman L. Mendel Rivers, chairman of the House Armed Services Committee, that if he brought any more naval bases or construction projects to his Charleston, South Carolina, constituency, it would sink into the Atlantic. Every politician is judged on his or her ability to provide specific benefits to the constituency. A new post office, a river improvement project, a brand new federal office building, a new building for the local university—these accomplishments and more are tests of a politician's clout in Washington. One after another, politicians have taken credit at election time for their ability to get things done for the folks at home. They have linked their seniority and power in Congress to their ability to deliver.

But clout in Washington is a poor guide to getting benefits for your state or district. Bruce Ray, for example, developed a number of measures of influence in Congress (including committee membership, leadership roles, and seniority) and tried to see whether the more powerful brought home more bacon than those with less congressional clout. In general, they did not. John Owens and Larry Wade, who found some evidence of clout in getting benefit to one's constituency, nonetheless remark that "the targeting of federal funds to particular districts on the basis of their representatives' congressional positions has become increasingly less manageable."

When the senator or representative comes to you and reports that his or her years of seniority, important committee positions, and general clout in Congress will get your district more from the federal aid wagon, be skeptical. Congressional decisions are universalistic, that is, they promise something for almost all constituencies and voters.

Source: For further evidence on the role of clout in providing benefits, see Bruce A. Ray, "Congressional Promotion of District Interests" and J. Theodore Aganonson, "Politics in the Distribution of Federal Grants: The Case of the Economic Development Administration," in Barry Rundquist (ed.), *Political Benefits* (Lexington, Mass.: D. C. Heath, 1980); and John R. Owens and Larry L. Wade, "Federal Spending in Congressional Districts," *Western Political Quarterly*, 37 (September, 1984): 404–423. (The quotation from Owens and Wade is on p. 409.)

Detroiters, like residents of other economically strapped areas, have moved to other locales in search of the American dream, or at least of a steady paycheck. By coincidence, the 1980 Census reported the loss of 321,841 people from Detroit in the past decade and a gain of 321,457 in Houston. At least 1,000 newcomers arrive in Texas's largest city every week. Some come with current issues of the *Houston Chronicle* or *Post*, whose help wanted ads—full of job openings in oil and other energy fields, in construction, and in every imaginable service industry—are popular reading even in Detroit.

The change in economic climate and the rising cost of energy, among other things, have led to this shift of population from the North and East to the South and West. If you take a map of the United States and draw a line across the country from Washington, D.C., to San Francisco it would be at about the thirty-eighth parallel. North of that line is the **Frostbelt,** and south of it is the **Sunbelt.** Increasingly, the area south of that line is the region of growth, and north of that line is the region of decline. Horace Greeley was quoted in the last century as saying, "Go west, young man." Today, jobs and population growth are going west—and south. The 1980 census found that 81.4 percent of the nation's population growth between 1970 and 1980 occurred in the Sunbelt.

125

Times Have Been Troubled in the Frostbelt. *Many families have decided to pull up stakes and move to the Sunbelt. There, they think, economic opportunities abound. Here—in Detroit, not Houston—workers buy Houston newspapers to get the "help wanted" section. Texas papers sell well outside the state and often serve as beacons beckoning the unemployed from elsewhere. Not all who move, though, find their opportunities increased.*

The implications of this shift for politics and public policy are just beginning to be noticed. Once dominant in politics and in industry, the northeast is rapidly becoming what the South was before—the problem child of the American federal system. David Cooley, president of the Dallas Chamber of Commerce, is fond of saying, "A second civil war is on, and we're going to win this one." The rise of the Sunbelt and the decline of the Frostbelt may well become the most important population shift since Americans left the farm for the cities during the first half of the twentieth century. Some of the reasons are economic; others relate to energy and the environment.

Economically, the Sunbelt states offer several attractions. Land and labor are cheaper there, offering attractions to industries thinking about relocating. Unions are weaker in the South than in the North, and wages are lower. Southern comfort may not be all that it is said to be, but southern living costs and taxes are both lower.

States in the South have not been shy in pointing out these advantages to business and industry. South Carolina ran ads in business periodicals depicting a state capitol building with a greedy tax collector's hand coming out of it. The ad said, "If this is what you think all state governments are like, have we got a surprise for you. The tax collectors of South Carolina . . . would love the pleasure of your company. But [they] demand very little in return." The ad was right. South Carolina has the third lowest tax burden per capita among states. People follow jobs to South Carolina, then more jobs follow the people.

Energy and the environment are also crucial in this regional shift. The South and West have a virtual monopoly on America's energy resources. The leading oil-producing states are Texas, Alaska, Louisiana, California, and Wyoming. Natural gas comes from the southwest and is moved all over the nation in an underground network of pipelines. Shale oil, which some have touted as a new energy source, is buried under the Rockies. In contrast, New England in particular and the northeast in general are energy poor.

The Federal Role in the Regional Shift

There is more than sunny climate and economic advantages to the transfer of people and production to the Sunbelt. The federal government has not been an idle bystander. Federal policies in general and congressional policies in particular, have long tilted toward some states rather than others. Some evidence suggests that federal policies give added advantages to southern and western states. An examination of per capita federal aid by region during the nineteenth century showed the South almost always ahead.[21] A much-discussed article in the prestigious *National Journal* in 1976 contributed to the debate about the tilt of federal benefits.[22] When the ratio of taxes to expenditures is totaled state by state, it concluded, southern states got back more than they sent to Washington; northern states got less. For some current evidence on which states get what, see 9 .

While the clout of grizzled southern senators and representatives may have something to do with this Sunbelt bias in federal aid, there is another reason for the Sunbelt's outdistancing of the Frostbelt. Even more than political power, aid formulas really determine what dollars go to which state. Federal aid often is written to aid poorer regions, and the South has always been the nation's poorest region.

Congress frequently writes a complex formula to tell the bureaucracy how to allocate aid to states and cities. But formulae are almost never purely arithmetic and neutral. When aid formulae included income levels as one trigger for extra support, southern states and local governments benefitted. But when northern Senators and members of Congress figured out the impact of aid formulae, they persuaded Congress to adopt new ones. Those, not surprisingly, tilted toward older northeastern states and their communities.[23] There are more than 146 specific formulae used for the sundry federal aid programs. Change the formulae and you change the beneficiaries.

Political Consequences of the Sunbelt Surge

One consequence of the Sunbelt surge is the shift in the center of political gravity in America.[24] This shift is reflected in the states from which our presidents hail. Among our post-World War II presidents, only John F. Kennedy (from Massachusetts) and Gerald Ford (from Michigan) were from the North. The others were from Missouri, Kansas, Texas, California (two), and Georgia. The political transformation is also reflected in the changing base of the electoral college, which is adjusted

[22] "Federal Spending: The North's Loss is the South's Gain," *National Journal* (June 26, 1976): 878–91.

[21] Morris P. Fiorina, David W. Rohde, and Peter Wiesel, "Historical Change in House Turnover," in Norman J. Ornstein (ed.), *Congress in Change* (New York: Praeger, 1975), pp. 36–37.

[23] One excellent discussion of the efforts of northeastern senators and representatives to recalculate formulae to their own interests is in Robert Jay Dilger, *The Sunbelt/Snowbelt Controversy: The War Over Federal Funds* (New York: New York University Press, 1982).

[24] A popularized account of the political changes associated with the rise of the Sunbelt is Kirkpatrick Sale, *Power Shift* (New York: Random House, 1975).

once a decade according to Census figures. California has replaced New York as the state where the presidential candidate can collect the most votes. In politics, there is an old saying: "Go where the ducks are." Increasingly, the ducks are in an arc from California through Texas to Florida. The power of the South and southwest in presidential politics is on the upswing.

---

9 How Your State Fares in the Federal Aid Game

The Tax Foundation, an independent institution specializing in tax patterns, provides an annual analysis of tax-benefit ratios by state. It compares the amount of federal income tax and other taxes contributed to the federal treasury with the amount of federal aid coming back to each state. The map shows how much each paid to get $1 back in federal aid. Some states put in more than they got back. Texas, despite its Sunbelt status, fared the worst, putting in $1.71 for each $1 in federal aid. Other states got back more than they put in. Among the fifty States, Vermont fared best, getting back $1 after contributing only $0.52 to the federal treasury. On balance, though, Sunbelt states fared better than Frostbelt states.

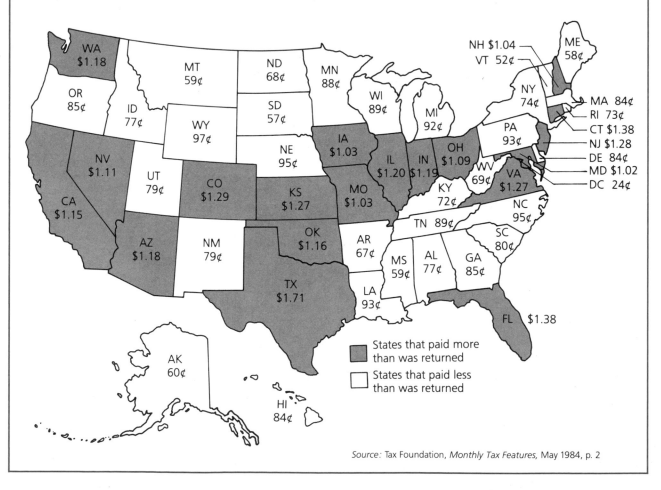

Source: Tax Foundation, Monthly Tax Features, May 1984, p. 2

The regional shift is likely to benefit Republicans and hurt Democrats —at least big-city, liberal, labor-oriented Democrats. Generally, the Sunbelt states are more conservative than the Frostbelt states. Slow-growth states like New York and Massachusetts have been bastions of Democratic liberalism. Fast-growing states like Arizona, Texas, and Florida have young, vigorous, and often successful Republican parties. The regional shift has made the "Solid South" less solid for the Democratic party. Republicans have moved to Dixie, and old Dixiecrats have abandoned their Democratic ties.

There are policy issues as well as political implications in this regional shift. The energy-poor and economically troubled northeast has tried to get its problems on the nation's policy agenda. Officials in northeastern states claim that the severest urban problems are in the northeast. Its unemployment rates are worse, and its taxes and cost of living are higher than in other regions. Southerners always claimed that "the South will rise again." They were right. But perhaps they will soon be saying in the energy-poor, economically troubled northeast, "The North will rise again."

FEDERALISM SUMMARIZED

Ours is a federal system of government, in which powers are distributed among the national and the state governments. It is a nation of states, but it is also an "indestructible union." The national government's supremacy over the states has been tested frequently but is today indisputable. In *McCulloch* v. *Maryland*, John Marshall and the Supreme Court affirmed this supremacy; a civil war reiterated the principle. Marshall also asserted that the national government has implied powers as well as those powers enumerated in the Constitution. This principle justifies much of the national government's growth over the decades. Today, the relationship between the national and the state governments can be described as cooperative federalism, in which both governments share the costs, tasks, and responsibility for many policies.

The existence of over 82,000 governments in America invites both pluralism and hyperpluralism. According to their critics, state governments are less efficient, less democratic, and more corrupt than the national government, and fragmentation is the hallmark of local governments.

With about $100 billion available in federal aid to states and cities, the grantsmanship game is a major effort of state and local officials. Getting categorical grants, block grants, and revenue-sharing money helps ease the fiscal stress in cities and states. Another way to ease the strained city or state budget is resource competition, a game in which economic advantage is pursued and costs are shifted to other players in the federalist system.

The regional shift of population and economic advantage to the South and the West (the Sunbelt) raises new questions about federalism in America. Federal aid continues to favor southern states, prompting renewed debate about the distribution of federal dollars. In addition to money, population and political power are also moving to the South and the West.

Key Terms

federalism	cooperative federalism	categorical grants
unitary government	fiscal federalism	block grants
intergovernmental	municipalities	revenue sharing
relations	counties	Frostbelt
Tenth Amendment	school districts	Sunbelt
McCulloch v. *Maryland*	special districts	
enumerated powers	industrial revenue	
implied powers	bonds	
dual federalism	severance taxes	

For Further Reading

Anton, Thomas. *Moving Money* (1982). A technical book, but a useful one in trying to figure out where all that money in the federal system flows.

Browning, Rufus P., Dale Rogers Marshall, and David H. Tabb. *Protest Is Not Enough* (1984). A study of ten California cities, particularly of the role played by federal programs in enhancing minority political power.

Dilger, Robert Jay. *The Sunbelt/Snowbelt Controversy: The War over Federal Funds* (1982). Traces the issue of federal aid to frostbelt and sunbelt regions.

Goodman, Robert. *The Last Entrepreneurs: America's Regional Wars for Jobs and Dollars* (1979). An account of the battle among state and local governments for jobs and economic growth.

Hale, George E., and Marian Lief Palley. *The Politics of Federal Grants* (1981). A useful account of who gets what, how, and when, from federal aid.

Riker, William. *Federalism* (1964). A highly critical account of American federalism.

Walker, David. *Toward a Functioning Federalism* (1981). A concise history of American federalism, with some blueprints for improvement.

Wright, Deil S. *Understanding Intergovernmental Relations*, 2nd ed. (1982). A review of state-local-federal relations.

Civil Liberties and Public Policy

MEMO

In a democracy, people retain certain rights against the government, called *civil liberties.* Questions about basic rights and liberties at first seem easy; but each turns on subtle interpretations of behaviors and the law. Government, through its police, legislatures, and courts, makes public policy decisions about civil liberties.

After describing the Bill of Rights, our Constitutional source of civil liberties, I will concentrate on three key elements:

- Our First Amendment rights, particularly the freedoms of religion, press, speech, and assembly.
- Rights at the bar of justice, and the ways those are balanced against society's need to protect itself against crime and criminals.
- The challenges to our civil liberties brought about by new technology: to manipulate life and death, to intrude upon privacy, and to use government security apparatus in the interest of "national security."

If the interpretation of civil liberties were easy, we could read the Bill of Rights and stop there. But simple words dissolve into complex cases. Throughout this chapter, you will note boxes called "You be the Judge." They sketch out the details of an actual issue brought before the courts. You should evaluate each one carefully, then render your most reasonable decision. Of course, I do not expect you to know as much about the law as a judge. However, I presume that your ethics and your sense of fairness are as dependable as a judge's. Try your hand at these test cases. The actual court decisions are collected toward the end of the chapter.

O N JULY 5, 1984, the last day of the Supreme Court's 1984 term, the nine justices—the Chief Justice and eight Associate Justices— had entered the elegant courtroom of the Supreme Court Building. It was only the second term in which a female associate justice, Sandra Day O'Connor, had ever participated in the deliberations. As the justices announced decisions, the agenda and the chambers were crowded. Again, the meaning of civil liberties was being defined and tested. Minnesotan Kathy Ebert had been fighting a five-year battle against the national Jaycees, a men-only group. She claimed that her state's law forbidding sex discrimination in service organizations did not infringe on their constitutional freedom of association. (She won a unanimous vote of the Supreme Court.) In another Minnesota case, six college students were claiming that a federal law denying education aid to men who do not register for the draft violated their rights against self-incrimination. Another Minnesotan, Chief Justice Warren Burger, wrote the opinion denying their contention.

But the greatest attention of the day was devoted to a set of cases involving the **exclusionary rule,** a long-standing judicial policy which forbids the admission of illegally seized evidence at a trial. If evidence is not properly gathered, it cannot be used by prosecutors. Opponents of the exclusionary rule had long argued that its good intentions nonetheless let criminals go free. In one of the exclusionary rule cases (*Massachusetts* v. *Sheppard*), a Boston police officer had suspected a man of murder and wanted to search his residence. Unable to locate a search warrant form for a homicide, he had reworked a standard form used for drug cases and gotten a judge to approve the search. But an appeals court in Massachusetts had thrown out the conviction because the form of the warrant was defective. Appealed to the United States Supreme Court, the case tested again the meaning of the civil liberties we enjoy under the Bill of Rights. (We will see later how that controversial case was decided.)

Civil liberties are our legal and constitutional protections against government. Claims about civil liberties often end up in court. *Somebody* v. *Somebody Else* is the way in which civil liberties issues make the news. A court case is filed alleging that government denied the right to counsel under the Bill of Rights; someone alleges that freedom of religion is denied by a city hall's putting up a nativity scene at Christmas; someone claims that her car was searched unjustifiably when the cops found a cache of heroin. Courts, police, and legislatures define the meaning of our civil liberties. But those liberties are formally set down in the Bill of Rights. This chapter is about them.

THE BILL OF RIGHTS—THEN AND NOW

The Bill of Rights was passed in the heady days following the American Revolution. British restraints on colonial opinion still stung. Newspaper editors had been jailed, citizens were arrested and tossed into jail, and confessions wrung out of them. Truly, our nation was "conceived in liberty." All the state constitutions contained a bill of rights (some of which survive to this day mostly intact). And although the new U.S. Constitution lacked one, the first Congress to meet wrote a set of rights to append to the federal Constitution.

Today, Americans are great believers in the Bill of Rights and its noble commitments to individual freedom—to a point. Here in the **Bill of Rights,** the first ten amendments to the Constitution, many of America's basic liberties—freedom of religion, of speech, of the press—are protected against arbitrary searches by the police, against being held incommunicado with no chance to talk to a lawyer, and so forth. We Americans do believe in these rights, yet there is often a distinction between how people see them in *theory* and in *practice*. Years ago, political scientists discovered that people were great devotees of political rights in theory, but sharply divided when it came time to apply those rights in practice.[1]

1 For example: We may believe in freedom of speech, but not all of us believe that it is a good idea to let Ku Klux Klansmen speak, parade, and demonstrate; we believe in freedom of speech, but not all agree that athiests or homosexuals should have the right to teach in our schools.

Ambivalence about specific applications of civil liberties is not surprising, for the issues involved are difficult. We are choosing, usually,

[1] James W. Prothro and Charles Grigg, "Fundamental Principles of Democracy: Bases of Agreement and Disagreement," *Journal of Politics* 22 (1960):276–94.

---

1 **American Commitment to Abstract Civil Liberties**

When the National Opinion Research Center asked 1,500 Americans whether they agreed with six important principles of civil rights and political tolerance, the results were warmly supportive, as you can see. But abstract support does not always translate into specific support for the political rights of unpopular groups.

	Agree	Uncertain	Disagree
1. People in the minority should be free to try to win majority support for their opinions.	89	9	2
2. Public officials should be chosen by majority vote.	95	3	2
3. No matter what a person's political beliefs are, he is entitled to the same legal rights and protections as anyone else.	93	4	3
4. I believe in free speech for all no matter what their views might be.	85	7	9
5. When the country is in great danger we may have to force people to testify against themselves even if it violates their rights.	35	16	48
6. Any person who hides behind the laws when he is questioned about his activities doesn't deserve much consideration.	52	16	32

Source: John L. Sullivan et al., "The Sources of Political Tolerance: A Multivariate Analysis," *American Political Science Review* 75 (March 1981): 98.

between two values. Social order is a good thing, but so is individual freedom—and the two often seem in conflict. Rule by the majority seems desirable, but so, too, does protection of the rights of the minority. Debate about applications of civil liberties often hinges on two questions: Is the scope of these freedoms unlimited? If not, where should we draw their limits? Take these examples:

- The Bill of Rights guarantees freedom of speech, but does it include the right to make a vicious speech against Jews or blacks?
- The Bill of Rights guarantees a free press, but does it include the right to publish a stolen document the government has stamped *Top Secret?*
- The Bill of Rights guarantees freedom of religion, but does it mean that religious cults can use any methods to wean teenagers away from their families without governmental interference?

Because we are going to discuss the Bill of Rights, and because the words describing our civil liberties in the Constitution have not been changed at all for nearly two centuries, this is a good time to read the first eight amendments carefully. ☐2 When you are reading these amendments, note that the **First Amendment**—where the key principles of free speech and press, religious tolerance, and freedom of assembly are all listed—begins with the words "Congress shall make no law." It does *not* say that neither Congress nor the states shall make a law abridging freedom of speech, press, religion, and so forth. A literal reading of the Bill of Rights suggests that it restrains the national government but not the states. The Bill of Rights was passed, after all, in a time of distrust of the new national government. It was the new, potentially monstrous, central government that made people nervous, not their state legislatures. Most states, in fact, already had a bill of rights in their constitutions.

What would happen, then, if your state government passed a sweeping law limiting free speech, censoring the press, and closing houses of worship? If the words of the First Amendment were both the beginning and the end of the story of the Bill of Rights, nothing would prevent your state from doing so. Hence, one of the most important questions about the Bill of Rights is the question of its applicability to the states.

The Bill of Rights and the States

In 1833, a man named Barron brought his legal troubles with the city of Baltimore to the Supreme Court. Complaining that Baltimore's wharf construction had ruined his drydock business, Barron argued that the Fifth Amendment forbade the city from depriving him of his property without due process of law. Though sympathetic, John Marshall's court refused to consider Barron's claim. The Bill of Rights, it said in **Barron v. Baltimore** (1833), restrained only the national government, not the states and cities.

Almost a century later, however, the Supreme Court first ruled that state governments must respect some First Amendment rights. The Court's new decision was based not on the wording of the First Amend-

(These amendments and the Ninth and the Tenth Amendments were passed by Congress on September 25, 1789, and ratified on December 15, 1791.)

AMENDMENT I — RELIGION, SPEECH, ASSEMBLY, PETITION
Congress shall make no law respecting an establishment of religion, or prohibiting the free exercise thereof; or abridging the freedom of speech, or of the press; or the right of the people peaceably to assemble, and to petition the Government for a redress of grievances.

AMENDMENT II — RIGHT TO BEAR ARMS
A well regulated militia, being necessary to the security of a free State, the right of the people to keep and bear arms, shall not be infringed.

AMENDMENT III — QUARTERING OF SOLDIERS
No Soldier shall, in time of peace be quartered in any house, without the consent of the owner, nor in time of war, but in a manner to be prescribed by law.

AMENDMENT IV — SEARCHES AND SEIZURES
The right of the people to be secure in their persons, houses, papers, and effects, against unreasonable searches and seizures, shall not be violated, and no warrants shall issue, but upon probable cause, supported by oath or affirmation, and particularly describing the place to be searched, and the persons or things to be seized.

AMENDMENT V — GRAND JURIES, DOUBLE JEOPARDY, SELF-INCRIMINATION, DUE PROCESS, EMINENT DOMAIN
No person shall be held to answer for a capital, or otherwise infamous crime, unless on a presentment or indictment of a Grand Jury, except in cases arising in the land or naval forces, or in the militia, when in actual service in time of war or public danger; nor shall any person be subject for the same offence to be twice put in jeopardy of life or limb; nor shall be compelled in any criminal case to be a witness against himself, nor be deprived of life, liberty, or property, without due process of law; nor shall private property be taken for public use, without just compensation.

AMENDMENT VI — CRIMINAL COURT PROCEDURES
In all criminal prosecutions, the accused shall enjoy the right to a speedy and public trial, by an impartial jury of the State and district wherein the crime shall have been committed, which district shall have been previously ascertained by law, and to be informed of the nature and cause of the accusation; to be confronted with the witnesses against him; to have compulsory process for obtaining witnesses in his favor, and to have the assistance of counsel for his defence.

AMENDMENT VII — TRIAL BY JURY IN COMMON-LAW CASES
In Suits at common law, where the value in controversy shall exceed twenty dollars, the right of trial by jury shall be preserved, and no fact tried by a jury, shall be otherwise reexamined in any Court of the United States, than according to the rules of the common law.

AMENDMENT VIII — BAILS, FINES AND PUNISHMENT
Excessive bail shall not be required, nor excessive fines imposed, nor cruel and unusual punishments inflicted.

ment, but on the wording of the Fourteenth, one of several amendments added to the Constitution after the Civil War. Basically, these amendments ended slavery and established legal protection for former slaves. Ratified in 1868, the **Fourteenth Amendment** declared:

> No State shall make or enforce any law which shall abridge the privileges or immunities of citizens of the United States nor shall any state deprive any person of life, liberty, or property, without due process of law; nor deny to any person within its jurisdiction the equal protection of the laws.

In 1925, the Supreme Court announced in *Gitlow* v. *New York* that freedoms of press and speech were "fundamental personal rights and liberties protected by the **due process clause** of the Fourteenth Amendment from impairment by the states." The Court had, in effect, interpreted the Fourteenth Amendment to say that states could not abridge a First Amendment freedom that the national government could not abridge. (Other people thought that if the writers of the Fourteenth Amendment had intended to extend First Amendment rights, they would have said so directly.)

At first, only a few rights guaranteed by the First Amendment were protected from state action by the Fourteenth Amendment. But especially during the 1960s, the Supreme Court broadened its interpretation to limit state action in most areas in which federal action is banned. "One by one," said constitutional scholar Samuel Krislov, "the provisions of the Bill of Rights have been held to apply to the states, not in their own right, but as implicit in the Fourteenth Amendment."[2] Many of these decisions, we will see, have been controversial. But today, for all practical purposes, the Bill of Rights guarantees rights against infringement by both state and national governments. Only the Second, Third, and Seventh Amendments have not been applied specifically to the states through the Fourteenth Amendment.

THE FIRST AMENDMENT FREEDOMS

The First Amendment to the Constitution contains many of our most crucial guarantees of rights and freedoms. If any rights are necessary to protect democracy and minorities, surely these are the ones. A democratic government depends on a free marketplace of ideas. Ideas that are muffled, speech that is forbidden, and meetings that cannot be held are the enemies of the democratic process.

But should we consider these rights *absolutes?* The Supreme Court Justice Hugo Black was fond of pointing out that the First Amendment said Congress shall make *no* law. To him, the Constitution meant just what it had said: "No law" means no law whatsoever. To others, the First Amendment has to be seen less absolutely, particularly when rights are in conflict. As we explore the meaning and interpretation of the First Amendment, we will see that absolute principles are sometimes hard to maintain in practice.

[2] Samuel Krislov, *The Supreme Court and Political Freedom* (New York: Free Press, 1968), p. 81.

Freedom of Religion

The Establishment Clause. The First Amendment says not one but two things about religion and government. First, in the **establishment clause,** it says: "Congress shall make no law respecting an establishment of religion." Some nations have an established church—one that is officially supported by the government and recognized as a national institution. (The Church of England in Great Britain is an example.) Clearly the First Congress did not want an established church here. There had been official churches in some colonies. But there has never been a significant effort in the United States to establish a national church. What else the establishment clause intended is less clear.

Some people argue that it meant only that the government could not favor one religion over another. In contrast, Thomas Jefferson argued that the First Amendment was designed to create a "wall of separation" between church and state. According to this interpretation, the First Amendment forbids not only favoritism toward one religion but also any support for religion in general. The government must avoid any entanglement with religion. These interpretations of the establishment clause continue to stir much argument.

Debate is especially intense over providing aid to church-related schools and saying prayers in public schools. In the 1960s, several state and federal programs included aid to church-related schools. Proponents of such aid could argue that it does not favor any particular religion. In *Lemon* v. *Kurtzman* (1971), however, the Court held unconstitutional several state programs helping parochial schools, fearing that direct state aid might be used to subsidize religious instruction. But the Court has allowed some aid to students in church schools. Tax funds can be used to provide secular textbooks or to reimburse parents for bus fares. In 1977, the Supreme Court permitted Ohio to subsidize certain testing services for parochial schools, provided that the testing took place off the school premises (*Wolman* v. *Walter*). There is a fine line between aid that is constitutionally permissible and aid that is not.

Prayer in the schools has been even more controversial than aid to parochial schools. In 1962, the Supreme Court incurred the anger of many people by holding that a prayer written by the New York State Regents to be recited by New York's schoolchildren violated the First Amendment (**Engel v. Vitale**). The next year, another sticky issue about religion in the schools confronted the Court: public Bible reading in the schools. ③ Some religious groups pushed for a constitutional amendment to allow prayers and Bible reading in the schools. Proposed amendments nearly passed Congress several times during the 1970s and 1980s. Finally, even with President Reagan's backing, supporters of the "prayer in the schools" amendment could not muster a majority in Congress. The House and Senate, though, passed a mild compromise in the summer of 1984: Schools getting federal funds would have to open their doors to groups, including religious ones, at the request of bona fide student organizations.

The Practice of Religion. The First Amendment also guarantees the free exercise of religion. This guarantee seems simple enough at first

| 3 | Does Bible Reading in Public Schools Conflict with the First Amendment?

In *School District of Abington Township, Pennsylvania v. Schempp* (1963), the Supreme Court confronted this question: Does a law requiring that public schools begin each day with a short reading from the Bible, but permitting parents to have their children excused, conflict with the First Amendment? The Commonwealth of Pennsylvania had a law that read: "At least ten verses from the Holy Bible shall be read, without comment, at the opening of each public school on each school day. Any child shall be excused from such Bible reading ... upon the written request of his parent or guardian."

A Unitarian family named Schempp objected to the policy. They filed suit against this Bible reading by intercom, charging that school Bible reading violated their religious beliefs. The Commonwealth of Pennsylvania, on the other hand, argued that the exercise was not required and that the Constitution had not meant to forbid religious exercises. According to the Commonwealth, the Constitution simply forbade favoring *one* religion over another. Nowhere, it claimed, does the Constitution forbid religious and moral teachings in the public schools, provided they do not single out one religion for preference.

You be the judge. Did the Pennsylvania statute violate the First Amendment's establishment clause? For the Supreme Court's answer, see 12, on page 166.

glance. Plainly, it means that whether you hold no religious belief, practice voodoo, or like to hear a Sunday sermon, you should have the right to practice your religion. But the matter is a little more complicated. Religious practices can disrupt society. Religious beliefs can forbid actions that society thinks are good or even necessary. What if, for example, someone's religion justifies polygamy, using illegal drugs, or disturbing the peace? What if someone's religious beliefs conflict with compulsory military obligations or compulsory health regulations (for example, vaccinations) or compulsory school attendance? Boxer Muhammad Ali, for example, refused induction into the armed services during the Vietnam conflict because, he said, participation would violate his Muslim faith. Amish parents often tangle with the law because they refuse to send their children to public schools. And the courts have often ordered Jehovah's Witnesses to accept medical treatment, especially blood transfusions.

Clearly, the Supreme Court has never permitted religious liberty to be an excuse for any and all behavior. Holding consistently to the view that people have an inviolable freedom to *believe* what they want, the courts are more cautious about the right to *practice* any belief. (The Court once asked rhetorically, "Suppose one believed that human sacrifices were a necessary part of religious worship. . . . ") Thus Congress permitted, and courts upheld, people to become conscientious objectors to military service on religious grounds, but the Supreme Court did not support a Mormon who justified his polygamy on religious grounds. Courts did, though, permit Amish parents to keep their children home from school. Reasoning that the Amish community was well established and that children would not become problems for the state, the Court in *Wisconsin v. Yoder* (1972) upheld religious freedom above the right of the state to make schooling compulsory.

The New Church-State Conflict. For nearly two centuries, Thomas Jefferson's view that there was (or should be) a "wall of separation" increasingly became the model for church-state relationships. There were, of course, skirmishes about where the wall meandered, but most

Americans stoutly agreed with Jefferson. In the last decade, though, some Americans have believed that governmental actions on behalf of religious issues were not only acceptable, but morally imperative. The 1984 presidential campaign was filled with debates about religion and politics. Catholic vice-presidential candidate Geraldine Ferraro was criticized by Catholic bishops and others for her views on abortion.

Conservative, fundamentalist groups have also sought to join religion and politics. Evangelist Pat Roberts once told a reporter, "we have enough votes to run the country." Reverend Jerry Falwell of Lynchburg, Virginia, captained the Moral Majority (bumper stickers against his movement claimed that "The Moral Majority Is Neither"). Moral Majoritarians and other conservative, protestant, fundamentalists waged holy and political wars on abortion, in behalf of public school prayers, and against the teaching of evolution in the schools. Reporter Tina Rosenberg argued that the power of the Moral Majority and other conservative, religious interests has been greatly exaggerated by the press. Hungry for news, the press consistently overstated the power of the new religious right. Groups opposing the Moral Majority used the exaggerated publicity to increase their coffers. The American Civil Liberties Union took in

Anti-Abortion Group. *Few issues in recent years have created the political fury of the Supreme Court's decision permitting abortions during the first months of pregnancy. In the years after the Court's decision, anti-abortion groups demonstrated at countless statehouses and courthouses, hoping to win a reversal of the decision. Abortions, though, increased in the aftermath of "Roe" v.* Wade. *Anti-abortion groups attempted to link the rights of the unborn with the civil rights of all U.S. citizens.*

$100,000 in contributions in a month, with a direct mail campaign headed, "If Jerry Falwell has his way, you'd better start praying. . . ."[3]

Evidence indicates that members of the so-called New Religious Right are, in fact, not very different in their political beliefs from other Americans. In fact, on many issues, their opinions are a mirror of general public opinion: Six in ten of them support gun registration, about the same percent as nonreligious right citizens. Almost 60 percent support the Equal Rights Amendment, slightly less than among the nonChristian right. On some issues (for example, abortion) there are sharp differences; but as George Gallup, Jr., remarked, "surprisingly little difference is found on those issues that dominate national elections."[4] Nonetheless, there are many favorite issues of the new Christian right, some of which have faced the legislatures and the courts.

One short-lived effort of some religious groups was to press state legislatures to forbid the teaching of evolution in the public schools. Arkansas passed such a law. But in 1968, in the case of *Epperson* v.

[3] Tina Rosenberg, "How the Media Made the Moral Majority," *The Washington Monthly* (October 1982):19–23. The quotation from Pat Roberts is also from Rosenberg.

[4] George Gallup, Jr., "Devining the Devout: The Polls and Religious Belief," *Public Opinion* (April/May, 1981):18–21.

From *HERBLOCK THROUGH THE LOOKING GLASS* (Simon and Schuster, 1984).

Arkansas, the Supreme Court held that such a law violated the separation of church and state by imposing a set of religious beliefs on the schools and students. Arkansas countered with a law requiring the teaching of "creation science," that is, the Bible's story of creation, alongside evolution. But a federal District Court in *McLean* v. *Arkansas* (1982), also held that law unconstitutional.

Whether the current Supreme Court will relocate the "wall of separation" between church and state is not yet clear. Some commentators think that the Court under Chief Justice Burger is more accommodating toward religion than earlier courts. In one celebrated case (*Lynch* v. *Donnelly*, 1984), it upheld the right of the city of Pawtucket, Rhode Island, to set up on public property a Christian nativity scene at Christmas. In its 1985 calendar, the Supreme Court faced other thorny issues about religion, including a test of an Alabama law setting aside a moment of silence each day "for meditation or silent prayer."

Freedom of the Press

The Founding Fathers, who were instrumental in drafting the Bill of Rights, lived in a low-tech time. To them, a weekly newspaper would have been a fairly sophisticated means of communication. When they spoke of a free press, they meant that anyone with the financial wherewithall to buy a paper ought to be able to get it printed without governmental intervention.

Times and technology have changed. Television beams news and other programs off satellites; some newspapers are even printed through satellite technology. The press is more than the daily newspaper; it also includes publishers of pornographic literature, available in the corner convenience store as well as the X-rated adult book store. Publishers, moviemakers, magazine dealers, and others claim their "First Amendment rights." The likes of Adams, Washington, Jefferson, and Madison would surely be stunned.

No Prior Restraint. In this complicated arena of policy, one thing has seemed clear. Time and time again, the Supreme Court has ruled that no prior restraint will be permitted against newspapers. **Prior restraint** is the government's preventing material from being published—a common way of limiting the press in other nations. Sometimes, of course, the article is not approved and cannot be published at all. But in the United States, the First Amendment has ensured that even if the government frowns on some newspaper, the paper's right to publish is almost inviolable. Typical is the case of ***Near* v. *Minnesota*** (1931).[5] A rather acid-tongued newspaper editor in Minnesota called local officials a string of ugly names, including "grafters" and "Jewish gangsters." The state of Minnesota closed him down. The Supreme Court ordered the paper reopened, holding that newspapers were protected by the First Amendment from "previous restraint." For another "prior restraint" case, see 4.

The Pawtucket Crèche and the First Amendment. *The First Amendment guarantees freedom of religion and ensures that there will be no establishment of religion by government. When the city of Pawtucket, Rhode Island, put up this nativity scene at Christmas, some objected and took their case to the federal courts. Eventually, the Supreme Court ruled that Pawtucket's crèche did not violate the First Amendment.*

---

[5] On *Near*, see Fred W. Friendly, *Minnesota Rag* (New York: Random House, 1981).

During the Johnson administration, the Department of Defense had prepared an elaborate secret history of American involvement in the Vietnam War. Hundreds of documents, many of them secret cables, memos, and war plans, were included. Many documented United States ineptitude and South Vietnamese duplicity. One former Pentagon official, Daniel Ellsberg, had become disillusioned with the whole Vietnam War, but had managed to retain access to one copy of these Pentagon Papers. Hoping that revelations of the Vietnam quagmire would help end American involvement, he decided to leak the Pentagon Papers to the *New York Times*.

The Nixon administration pulled out all the stops in its effort to embarrass Ellsberg and stop publication of the Pentagon Papers. Nixon's chief domestic affairs advisor, John Ehrlichman, approved a burglary of Ellsberg's psychiatrist's office, hoping to find damaging information on Ellsberg. (The burglary was bungled, and it eventually led to Ehrlichman's conviction and imprisonment.) In the courts, Nixon administration lawyers sought an injunction against the *Times* that would have ordered it to cease publication of the secret documents. Government lawyers argued that national security was being breeched, and that the documents were stolen from the government by Ellsberg. The *Times* argued that its freedom to publish would be violated if an injunction were granted.

In 1971, the case of *New York Times* v. *United States* was decided by the Supreme Court. You be the judge. The issue is: Did the *Times* have a right to publish secret, stolen Department of Defense documents? For the Supreme Court's answer, see 12 , on page 166.

Free Press versus Fair Trial. The Bill of Rights is an inexhaustible source of potential conflicts over rights. Clearly, the Constitution meant to guarantee the right to a fair trial as well as a free press. But a trial may not be fair if press coverage inflames public opinion so much that an impartial jury cannot be found. In one famous criminal trial an Ohio physician, Sam Sheppard, was accused of the murder of his wife. The extent of press coverage rivaled that of a military campaign, and little of it sympathized with Dr. Sheppard. Found guilty and sent to the state penitentiary, Sheppard appealed his conviction to the Supreme Court. He argued that press coverage had interfered with his ability to get a fair trial. The Supreme Court agreed, claiming that the press had created a virtual "Roman circus," and reversed Sheppard's conviction.

Reporters and editors seek full rights to cover all trials. They argue that the public has a right to know. They know, too, that juicy and lurid stories help sell newspapers. When a local judge in Nebraska issued a *gag order* forbidding the press to report any details of a particularly gory murder (and forbidding them even to report on the gag order itself), the Nebraska Press Association was outraged. They took the case to the United States Supreme Court, and in *Nebraska Press Association* v. *Stuart* (1976), the Court agreed with the editors and revoked the judge's order forbidding coverage. In 1979, the Supreme Court permitted a "pre-trial" hearing to be closed to the press, reasoning that excessive publicity might prejudice a defendant's right to a fair trial. A trial itself, though, was a different matter. In 1978, a Virginia judge closed the trial of a defendant named Stevenson (being tried for the fourth time on a murder charge) to the press and public. Again, the Supreme Court insisted that the press' right to collect and publish information should not be infringed on. "The trial of a criminal case," it said in *Richmond Newspapers* v. *Virginia* (1980), "must be open to the public."

Reporters like to have trials open to them, but they do not always like to open their files to the courts. Once in a while, a reporter is in possession of some information that the prosecution or the defense insists is essential evidence, but reporters often want to protect their confidential sources. More than one reporter has gone to jail because he or she refused to supply evidence gathered while preparing a story. Reporters argue that the freedom of the press guarantees them certain rights that other potential witnesses cannot claim. If they have to divulge their sources of information, there will be few informants. After all, reporters argue, much of what is said to them is said because people are confident that they will not be named as the source. Defendants and prosecutors do not hold the same view. Prosecutors argue that evidence is evidence. Defendants may argue that with their lives at stake, it is the height of journalistic arrogance for reporters to hide their sources.

You can see how entangled these arguments can become. (In 5 , a case involving these questions is discussed.) Several recent court decisions have limited a reporter's right to withhold information. In response, some states have passed *shield laws* to protect reporters' notes and information from being revealed in court. In most states, though, reporters have no more right to avoid presenting evidence than do other citizens.

Some of the conflicts between government and the press came to a head in the celebrated case of a police raid on the student newspaper at Stanford University. In 1971, nine police officers were injured in a confrontation with student protesters at Stanford University Hospital. In an effort to collect evidence on who was responsible, local police secured a search warrant and marched off to the *Stanford Daily*, which was reported to have pictures of the scene. The *Daily* contested the action and argued that the use of search warrants to rummage through newspaper files in search of evidence restricts First Amendment press freedoms. In **Zurcher v. Stanford Daily** (1978), the Supreme Court held that a proper search warrant could be applied to a newspaper as well as to anyone else without necessarily violating First Amendment rights.

All these issues of freedom of the press—the right of reporters to

---

5 The Case of Dr. *X* and the *New York Times*

Even by Hollywood standards, it was a bizarre case. But it was happening in suburban New Jersey instead of in a Hollywood script. Between 1965 and 1966, thirteen patients died mysteriously in a New Jersey hospital. Nearly a decade later, a *New York Times* reporter revealed that vials of poisonous curare were found in the locker of a certain "Dr. *X*," whom he did not name in the stories. Spurred by the *Times* stories, police renewed their investigation and arrested Dr. Mario Jascalevich for the murders. In 1978, the doctor came to trial and pleaded innocent. His attorneys demanded to see the notes of Myron Farber, the *Times* reporter. They might, the doctor's lawyers said, help the defense. Farber and the *Times* claimed protection under the First Amendment's "freedom of the press" clause. New Jersey also had a shield law protecting the security of reporters' sources. The

judge asked to examine all of Farber's notes to see if they qualified for protection under the shield law. Farber and the *Times* refused. Stressing that "a man is charged with murder and you say that Myron Farber should be the judge," the court jailed Farber and fined the *Times* $100,000 plus $5,000 a day until it produced the notes. The *Times* appealed to the Supreme Court to order Farber's release.

You be the judge. The issue is: When the First Amendment protects the freedom of the press, and the Sixth Amendment ensures a fair trial, can a reporter refuse to divulge information that the defense claims it needs and that an ordinary citizen would have to produce? For the Supreme Court's answer, see 12 , on page 166.

withhold evidence, the balancing of the government's right to keep secrets and the public's right to know, open trials—illustrate long-standing conflicts over the First Amendment. Two other thorny problems arise frequently in considering who can publish and express what.

Libel. **Libel** is the publication of knowingly false or malicious statements that damage someone's reputation. Press freedom is limited because individuals must be protected against outrageous defamations of their character. For the most part, the threat of libel action is inconsequential for the press. The constitutional battleground is over press criticism of public officials, who are sometimes agitated enough to sue the media. In a landmark case, the *New York Times* had published an advertisement (not an article) attacking the Birmingham, Alabama, police chief during the bloodiest days of the civil rights movement. The chief sued and an Alabama jury found some misstatements of fact in the advertisement and awarded a $500,000 judgment against the *Times*. Despite the *Times's* limited readership in Alabama (394), the judgment was more than ten times the previous highest libel award in the State. The Supreme Court, in **New York Times v. Sullivan** (1964), set aside the verdict. Vindicating the *Times*, the Court virtually exempted public officials from libel protection. Only when actual malice is shown—not mere errors—can public officials successfully sue for libel. A free press, the Court suggested, requires a spirited criticism of public officials even though some of that criticism may make public officials quite uncomfortable. (Implicitly, the court seemed to adopt Harry S Truman's fabled adage: "If you can't stand the heat, get out of the kitchen.")

The *Sullivan* precedent was busily tested during the winter of 1984–85,

General Westmoreland on the Battlefield and in Battle with CBS. *General William Westmoreland was the commander of American forces during the Vietnam war. This proud, four-star general commanded the only American army ever to be given an assignment it could not successfully complete. Later, when CBS News ran a documentary called* The Uncounted Enemy, *Westmoreland sued CBS. The network purported to show that Westmoreland and others had understated the number of enemy forces, so that American efforts would appear to be more successful than they were. Westmoreland heatedly denied the charges and sued CBS. But he threw in the towel before the case could go to a jury and accepted a CBS statement calling him "patriotic," but not withdrawing its charges.* Westmoreland v. Columbia Broadcasting System *(1985) was a vindication of the right of the press to criticize public officials. Not every news organization, though, has CBS's ability to bankroll a major libel case. Members of the press feared a "chilling effect" of Westmoreland-like suits.*

as two major public figures were claiming that the media had libeled them. In two separate New York courtrooms, Israeli General Ariel Sharon and American General William Westmoreland were suing *Time* magazine and CBS news, respectively. Sharon claimed that *Time* had libeled him by printing a story alleging that he had urged Christian forces in Lebanon to perpetrate a bloody revenge upon Palestinian refugee camps. To find against *Time*, the judge informed the jury, three things must be established: that the story was false; that Sharon's reputation was damaged; and that there was malicious intent to libel Sharon. The jury concluded that the first two elements of Sharon's case were proved, but not the third. General Westmoreland maintained he had been libeled by a CBS news special that alleged he had deliberately underestimated enemy strength in Vietnam in order to boost domestic support for becoming more involved in the war. He withdrew his case before it reached a jury. Most observers believed that he could not have won, and would have to bear the legal fees if he lost. Once again, the courts made it difficult for public officials to sue for libel. But—and media leaders made this clear—the threat of multimillion dollar libel awards might well have a chilling effect on free press.

Obscenity. In their gossipy portrayal of the inner sanctum of the United States Supreme Court titled *The Brethren*, Bob Woodward and Scott Armstrong recounted the tale of Justice Thurgood Marshall's lunch at Trader Vic's with some law clerks. Glancing at his watch about 1:50 (the story went), Marshall said to the clerks, "My God, I almost forgot. It's movie day, we have to get back." [6] The Supreme Court's "movie day" was a day when various motion pictures brought before the Court on some obscenity charge were shown in a basement storeroom. Several of the justices, arguing that obscenity should never be banned, consistently refused to attend these showings. Back in 1957, though, a Court majority had held that "obscenity is not within the area of constitutionally protected speech or press" (**Roth v. United States**). Defining what was obscene, however, was no easy matter. Former Justice Potter Stewart once remarked that although he could not define it, "I know it when I see it." Clerks at movie day from time to time echoed Stewart's oft-quoted remark, punctuating a particularly racy scene with calls of "That's it, that's it, I know it when I see it." In these breaks from the normally staid routines of the Court, Marshall often led the banter, once remarking to Justice Blackmun after a film, "Well, Harry, I didn't learn anything. How about you?"

Efforts to define obscenity have occupied various courts, including the Supreme Court, for years. Public perceptions, as well as judicial standards, vary from time to time and place to place. What many call obscene is perfectly legitimate entertainment to others. At various times, the works of Mark Twain and Aristophanes and the Tarzan stories of Edgar Rice Burroughs were banned as obscene. Courts are a battleground for these varying conceptions.

Sometimes what is acceptable in one place is brought into court elsewhere. The great variety of obscenity cases prompted the Supreme

[6] Bob Woodward and Scott Armstrong, *The Brethren* (New York: Avon, 1979), p. 233.

Civil Liberties, Privacy, and Pornography: The Case of the Policewoman in *Playboy*. When Barbara Schantz, a Springfield, Ohio, police officer, posed for Playboy magazine, the city fired her. She claimed that her right to privacy gave her the right to keep her personal decisions out of her professional life. The courts did not agree, however, and Ms. Schantz lost her job.

Court to try to bring order out of chaos. In 1973, the Court tried to define obscenity and made it easier to ban material (***Miller v. California***). Chief Justice Burger said that material would be legally obscene, if (1) the work, taken as a whole, appealed to a "prurient interest in sex," (2) it showed "patently offensive" sexual conduct, *and* (3) it lacked serious literary, artistic, political, or scientific merit. Unfortunately, one person's prurience is often another's pleasure. Whether material appeals to a "prurient interest," said the Court, should be determined by the *community's standards*. In *Miller*, the Court thus tried to define obscenity by avoiding defining it, leaving matters up to local and state authorities.

Obviously community standards differed, so *Miller* produced wildly inconsistent results. In decisions since *Miller*, the Court has limited the power of communities to censor materials and behaviors. In *Jenkins* v. *Georgia* (1974), it struck down a Georgia ban on the highly acclaimed movie *Carnal Knowledge*. A small town in New Jersey tried to ban a nude dancing parlor by using its zoning power to prevent any live entertainment in the area. But the Court said in *Schad* v. *Mount Ephraim* (1981) that this was far too broad. It would prohibit all sorts of live entertainment (perhaps even a community theater production). "Nor," the Court added, "may an entertainment program be prohibited solely because it displays a nude human figure." (States can use, and have used, their liquor licensing power to restrain some sorts of exhibitionist entertainment.) Some cities (including Minneapolis and Indianapolis) have tried to ban allegedly pornographic shows on the grounds that they impede women's civil rights. But the entire area of nudity and obscenity remains an unsettled area of constitutional law. Justice Blackmun once stated (or understated) the matter: There is "some ambiguity in this emerging area of law." You can see in ⑥ what happened when Jacksonville, Florida, tried to ban movies with nudity in them.

---

⑥ **When Can Obscenity Be Banned? The Case of the Drive-in Theatre**

Almost everyone might concede that *sometimes* obscenity can be banned by public authorities. One time might be when your right to show pornographic movies clashes with my right to privacy. Presumably, no one wants hardcore pornography shown in public places where schoolchildren might be passersby. Showing dirty movies in an enclosed theatre or the privacy of your own living room is one thing. Showing them in public is something else. Or is it?

The city of Jacksonville, Florida, wanted to limit the showing of certain kinds of movies at drive-in theatres. Its city council reasoned that drive-ins were public places and that drivers passing by would be involuntarily exposed to movies they might prefer not to see. (Some members of the council argued that drivers distracted by steamy scenes might even cause accidents.) So the council passed a local ordinance forbidding movies showing nudity (defined in the ordinance as "bare buttocks … female bare breasts, or human bare pubic areas") at drive-in theatres. Arrested for violating the ordinance, a Mr. Erznoznik challenged the constitutionality of the ordinance. He claimed that the law was overly broad and banned nudity, not obscenity. The lawyers for the city insisted that the law could be squared with the First Amendment. The government, they claimed, had a responsibility to forbid a "public nuisance," especially one that might cause a traffic hazard.

You be the judge. The issue is whether Jacksonville's ban on nudity in movies at drive-ins went too far or whether it was a constitutional limit on free speech. For the Court's answer, see ⑫, on page 166.

Pornography? *Here in San Francisco, but also in most major cities, issues swirl around the limits of pornography.* Deep Throat *actress Linda Lovelace became a crusader against pornography, claiming that she was a virtual slave to the moviemakers. Women's groups in Indianapolis, Minneapolis, and elsewhere tried to pass local ordinances to ban dirty movies because they degraded women. The Supreme Court debated whether pornography is constitutionally protected free speech. Defining it, though, is not easy.*

Freedom of Speech

Freedom of speech is essential for democratic dialogue. Totalitarian governments go to enormous trouble to limit expression. The First Amendment tells us plainly that our national government cannot place limits on freedom of speech. One can argue that the Constitution means just what it says, no more and no less, when it says, "Congress shall make no law . . . abridging the freedom of speech." The late Justice Hugo Black said, "I understand that it is rather old-fashioned and shows a slight naiveté to say that 'no law' means 'no law,'" but "there are absolutes in our Bill of Rights." [7]

Very few judges have taken this absolutist view of freedom of speech. Instead, courts have tended to divide speech into two kinds, protected speech and unprotected speech. This distinction presumes that there are some instances when some speech simply goes too far. The classic example of unprotected speech was offered by Justice Oliver Wendell Holmes, Jr., in 1919. "The most stringent protection of free speech would not," he argued, "protect a man in falsely shouting 'fire' in a theatre and causing a panic." The courts have constantly been called upon to decide what falls on either side of the line separating protected from unprotected speech.

Deciding on permissible and impermissible speech is not all the courts have had to do. They have also had to specify the very meaning of *speech* itself. If you are an ardent Reaganite arrested for making a rousing Reagan speech at a Reagan rally, you will have little trouble persuading any court that your First Amendment rights have been outrageously violated. Suppose, though, that you express your convictions in clear but wordless ways. During the turbulent Vietnam war years, a student named Tinker was suspended from a Des Moines school for wearing a black armband to protest American involvement in the war. The Supreme Court held in *Tinker* v. *Des Moines School District* (1969) that the suspension violated Tinker's First Amendment rights. Thus *speech* is

[7] Quoted in Krislov, *The Supreme Court and Political Freedom*, p. 96.

147

more than merely the spoken word. The guarantee of freedom of speech is in fact a guarantee of freedom of *expression*. Courts have often distinguished between *pure speech* (a neighborly chat, a candidate's campaign speech) and *symbolic speech* (Tinker's armband in Des Moines). All sorts of expressions are protected by the First Amendment. As the Supreme Court remarked in the Mount Ephraim nude dancing case, "Entertainment, as well as political and ideological speech is protected; motion pictures, programs broadcast by radio and television such as musical and dramatic works, fall within the First Amendment guarantee." Since the First Amendment casts such a long shadow, when, if ever, can the government limit one's freedom to express oneself?

Not surprisingly, governments have sometimes been zealous opponents of speech and behavior that opposes them and their policies. In one notable case during World War I, Charles T. Schenck, the secretary of the American Socialist Party, distributed thousands of leaflets designed to encourage young men to resist the draft. When arrested, Schenck claimed protection of the First Amendment. The Supreme Court, though, upheld his conviction in **Schenck v. United States** (1919). In doing so, Justice Holmes offered a "clear and present danger" test for speech. There may be times, he suggested, when speech provokes a **clear and present danger** to people. Then, and only then, can government restrain free speech. It is hard to say, though, when speech crosses that line between being merely controversial and being a "clear and present danger" to the body politic.

During the 1950s, the courts again confronted the question of free speech and its limits. American anticommunism was running strong. Senator Joseph McCarthy and others in Congress were persecuting people they thought subversive. The national government was intent on jailing leaders of the American Communist party. Its vehicle was the Smith Act of 1940, which forbids the advocacy of the violent overthrow of the United States government. In **Dennis v. United States** (1951), the Supreme Court permitted the government to jail several American Communist party leaders under the Smith Act. Pleas for free speech did little to stem the relentless prosecution of communists in the 1950s. By the 1960s, however, the Court had so narrowed the interpretation of the Smith Act that it is no longer used to prosecute dissenters.

The 1960s brought an era of protest that again strained and expanded the constitutional meaning of free speech. Although there was a great deal of unrest in the country over economic, racial, and social issues, the most bitter topic was the Vietnam War. To many people, war was an issue that should be decided by the government. They saw military duty as a necessity. To others, it seemed that a conflict should be justified before citizens were asked to die in it or pay for it. Organized protests on college and university campuses became common. People burned draft cards, occupied university buildings, marched, and demonstrated against the Southeast Asian conflict.

Times today are less turbulent; yet people still want to engage in public demonstrations and expressions. Courts have been quite supportive of your rights to protest, pass out leaflets, or gather political petitions —so long as you do it in public places. When you step on private property, however, constitutional protections of free speech diminish. In the case of the strange-sounding shopping center (*Pruneyard Shopping Center* v. *Robins*, 1980), the Supreme Court upheld the right of a shopping center to restrict political activities on its private property. But it also said that state governments could require access to semi-public places like shopping centers for leafleting, petition drives, and the like. Activities such as these are at the borderline between the right of free speech and the freedom of assembly.

Freedom of Assembly

The First Amendment also guarantees the right of assembly. Our other political liberties—speech, press, religion—would be pretty meaningless if we could never meet with like-minded people. Two separate rights are imbedded in this constitutional guarantee: One is the literal right to assemble, that is, to gather together in one place to make a political statement. The right to assemble anywhere, anytime, is not absolute; with some reasonable limits, it includes the right to parade, to picket, and to protest. These activities can cause inconvenience to others and can even turn violent. Thus governments may place some limitations on the right to picket, protest, and parade; but they cannot decide merely to prohibit the assemblage of groups they do not like. [7]

Inherent in the right to assemble is the right to associate. Parties and interest groups would not be legal if we did not have the right to associate with our fellow believers. In one famous case, the state of Alabama tried to weaken the National Association for the Advancement of Colored People (NAACP) by requiring it to publish its membership list. The Supreme Court found this an unconstitutional infringement on freedom of association (*NAACP* v. *Alabama*, 1958).

These are some of the First Amendment issues in civil liberties. There are other issues marked in the Bill of Rights, most of which have to do with protections against accusations of crime.

---

[7]   **The Nazis Apply to March in Skokie**

Hitler's Nazis, it is widely estimated, slaughtered six million Jews in death camps like Bergen-Belsen, Auschwitz, and Dachau. Many of the survivors migrated to the United States, and many settled in Skokie, Illinois. Skokie is a suburb of 80,000 people just north of Chicago. In its heavily Jewish population are thousands of survivors of German concentration camps.

The American Nazi party was a ragtag group of perhaps twenty-five to thirty members. Their headquarters was a storefront building on the West Side of Chicago, near an area of expanding black population. Denied a permit to march in a black neighborhood of Chicago, the American Nazis announced their intention to march in Skokie in 1977. Skokie's city government required that they post a $300,000 bond to get a parade permit. The Nazis claimed that the high bond was set in order to prevent their march and infringed their freedoms of speech and assembly. The American Civil Liberties Union defended the Nazis' claim and their right to march, despite its loathing of the Nazis. (The ACLU lost half its Illinois membership because it took this position.)

You be the judge. The issue is: Do Nazis have the right to parade, preach anti-Jewish propaganda, and perhaps provoke violence in a community peopled with survivors of the Holocaust? What rights or obligations does a community have to maintain order? For the Court's response, see [12] , on page 166.

Freedom of Assembly. *The First Amendment guarantees freedom of assembly. But guaranteeing freedom of assembly only to a community's teachers, doctors, or Democrats raises few questions. The questions about extending such rights to unpopular groups—a Ku Klux Klan rally, for example—are much tougher.*

THE CONSTITUTION, THE COURTS, AND CRIME

Most of the words contained in the Bill of Rights are actually about the rights of persons accused of crime. Only forty-four words guarantee the great democratic freedoms of speech, press, religion, and assembly. Most of the rest deals with rights at the bar of justice. These rights were originally intended to protect the accused in *political* arrests and trials. This is not to say that crime was not a major problem in the first American century. Some criminal historians have argued that crime in colonial America would rival present crime rates. [8] Today the protections in the Fourth, Fifth, Sixth, and Eighth Amendments are mostly applied in criminal justice cases. The Bill of Rights reminds us that we must protect the rights of the accused. On the other hand, society demands protection against the serious problem of crime.

The Crime Problem

Since the Federal Bureau of Investigation started collecting data on the crime rate in the 1930s, three little words have accurately described its trend: up, up, and up. The **crime rate** is recorded annually by the FBI and counts the numbers of serious personal (homicide and rape) and property (burglary and auto theft) crimes. In 1946, there were five serious crimes per 1000 Americans per year. By 1983, there were 52 serious crimes annually for every thousand Americans. Just short of one in three Amer-

[8] Roger Lane, "Urbanization and Criminal Violence in the Nineteenth Century: Massachusetts as a Test Case," in H. D. Graham and T. R. Gurr (eds.), *Violence in America* (Washington: Government Printing Office, 1969), Chap. 12.

ican households falls victim to a serious crime *annually* [9] and the problem is worse than official figures suggest. Only a fifth to a third of crimes are actually reported to the police and thus make their way into official statistics.

No one knows for sure why crime soared during the post-World War II period. There are many theories. Some criminologists argue that the increase is associated with demographic changes, particularly the increasing share of young, crime-prone people in the population. [10] Marxists argue that crime is a result of the extreme inequalities of wealth in a capitalist society. [11] You can see some explanations and descriptions of the rise of crime in ⁸.

[9] United States Department of Justice, *Justice Assistance News*, May, 1981, p. 1.

[10] An excellent review of the role of a youthful population, and other factors in crime can be found in Charles Silverman, *Criminal Violence, Criminal Justice* (New York: Random House, 1978).

[11] One Marxist interpretation of crime is found in Richard Quinney, *State, Class and Crime* 2nd ed. (New York: Longman, 1980).

---

⁸ Why Crime? Looking at the Growth of Crime Since World War II

Of all the startling statistics about crime, perhaps the most startling of all is this one: A male baby who is born in a big city today, and lives there the rest of his life, is more likely to die by homicide than a soldier was likely to die on the battlefield in World War II. This chart shows you how both violent and property crimes increased dramatically in cities over 50,000 since then. The 1960s—a period of social and political turmoil—were a time when the violent crime rate in particular soared. Crime rates followed a similar upward swing all over the western world, although America's crime rate is far higher than any other western nation's.

When Jacob and Lineberry examined crime in ten cities (Atlanta, Boston, Houston, Indianapolis, Minneapolis, Newark, Oakland, Philadelphia, Phoenix, and San Jose) over a thirty-one year period, they attempted to find some explanations for the rise of crime. Building on the work of several sociologists, they found that crime rates are connected to changing demography and life styles. Criminologists linked three factors with changing crime rates: First, there has been a steep rise in the "pool" of likely offenders, that is, young males in their teens and twenties. This age group commits most of our crime, and its share of the population increased significantly between the end of World War II and the 1970s. With a smaller share of the population in this age group today, crime rates are now declining slightly. Second, a change in our affluence and in the kinds of property Americans owned has occurred. Products born of technology—stereos, TVs, radios—are prime targets of crime. Our affluence and our technology combined to put more of them in our homes, stores—and, ultimately, in the clutches of criminals. These products are more attractive to thieves and easier to convert to cash. Third, there are important changes in our lifestyles. More women work outside the home than ever before. For this and other reasons, "guardianship" has declined; more homes are vacant much of the time. More people are out of the house putting themselves at risk of violent crimes. Statistically, these changes constitute powerful explanations for the rise of crime in America.

(box continues on next page)

None of these changes—demographic, economic, or life-style—is easily controlled by public policy. Still, that did not keep national, state, and local governments from promising more than they could deliver in solving the crime problem. The media also played up crime: in ten cities, between 15 and 20 percent of all front-page news stories concerned crime. The coverage was sometimes sensational and often bore little relationship to the actual seriousness of the crime problem. In San Jose, crime rates were the lowest of ten cities studied, but news about crime was greatest there. In the 1978 mayoral election in San Jose, crime was a major issue. The San Jose Peace Officers Association and other crime-conscious local groups supported hard-liner Al Garza for mayor. They accused incumbent Janet Gray Hayes of being soft on crime; but Hayes won, nonetheless. In other cities, too, crime has occupied a major place on the policy agenda.

Source: For more information on the rise of crime and San Jose as well, see Herbert Jacob, *The Frustration of Policy: Responses to Crime in American Cities* (Boston: Little, Brown, 1984); and Anne Heinz, Herbert Jacob, and Robert L. Lineberry (eds.), *Crime in City Politics* (New York: Longman, 1983). The statistics comparing crime and World War II are from Arnold Barnett, quoted in James Q. Wilson, *Thinking about Crime* (New York: Basic Books, 1975), p. 19.

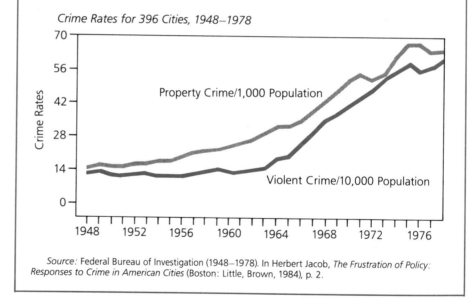

Crime Rates for 396 Cities, 1948–1978

Source: Federal Bureau of Investigation (1948–1978). In Herbert Jacob, *The Frustration of Policy: Responses to Crime in American Cities* (Boston: Little, Brown, 1984), p. 2.

American governments spend a significant sum of money to fight crime. In 1982, we spent $25 billion on police, courts, and corrections. We employ about 600,000 state and local police officers and a like number of private security guards. Yet there is very little evidence that more and more police officers guarantee less and less crime. Kansas City, Missouri, and the Police Foundation once conducted an important experiment. They divided up a part of the city into three kinds of areas—saturating one group with police officers, holding another group constant, and cutting back drastically in a third group. After the end of the year, there was no difference in the crime rates or citizens' feelings of security in the three groups of neighborhoods.[12] Nor does much evidence exist that "more aggressive" police officer behavior cuts crime.[13] People and politicians alike tend to expect too much of the police. Only a small portion of police time is spent on *Hill Street Blues*-style "crime fighting" activities. In the ten cities studied by Jacob and Lineberry (see 8), the average police officer made less than ten arrests per year for serious crimes. In San Jose, for example, the average officer made fewer than five arrests for serious crimes per year.[14]

The Stages of the Criminal Justice System and the Constitutional Umbrella

To understand the criminal justice system, let us first clear our minds of television crime stories. Most television episodes bear little connection to the realities of the police station or the courthouse. Instead, let us trace the stages of the criminal justice process. Think of the Bill of Rights as an umbrella, covering every stage of the criminal justice system. At every step—not just most of them—police, prosecutors, and judges must behave exactly in accord with the guarantees of the Bill of Rights. A misstep will invalidate a conviction if it is appealed; even one real hole in the constitutional umbrella is unacceptable.

Generally speaking, a *crime* is (sometimes) followed by an *arrest*, which is (sometimes) followed by a *prosecution*, which is (sometimes) followed by a *trial*, which (usually) results in a *verdict* of innocence or guilt. You may want to reread that last sentence; a lot of information is packed into it. The criminal justice system is like a series of smaller and smaller funnels, each one filtering into the next. Many more crimes occur than are reported, many more crimes occur than arrests are made (only about one in five crimes results in an arrest), many more arrests are made than prosecutors prosecute, and many more prosecutions occur than trials. In the next few pages, we will move through the stages of the criminal justice system, pausing at each point to see how the constitutional umbrella protects the rights of the accused.

Interpreting the Constitutional Umbrella. The Bill of Rights sets out a number of rights which would protect Joe or Mary Citizen if and when the dreaded day in court came. 9 The language of the Bill of Rights comes, of course, from the late 1700s. It is often quaint and, unfortunately, often vague. One may rightly ask, just how speedy is a *speedy trial?* How *cruel and unusual* is a punishment to be constitutionally cruel and unusual? Many cases are decided easily; a death penalty for a check forgery would easily qualify as cruel and unusual punishment. The

---

[12] George Kelling, et al., *The Kansas City Preventive Patrol Experiment* (Washington, D.C.: The Police Foundation, 1974).

[13] Herbert Jacob and Michael Rich, "The Effect of Police on Crime: A Second Look," *Law and Society Review* 15 (1981):109–122.

[14] Herbert Jacob and Robert Lineberry, *Governmental Responses to Crime in American Cities* (Evanston, Illinois: Center for Urban Affairs and Policy Research, Northwestern University, 1982), p. 65.

courts have had to rule on countless cases in which Joe or Mary Citizen claimed that their rights were violated. For example:

—Clearly, if the police burst into your home unannounced and confiscate everything in sight on the chance that you might harbor illegal substances, that is considered an "unreasonable search and seizure." But suppose that police order a suspect's stomach pumped after an arrest for the purpose of obtaining evidence? (The Supreme Court ruled that this was an unreasonable search and seizure.)

—The death penalty for stealing a $35 hubcap would be cruel and unusual punishment. Much more controversial, though, is the death penalty for rape, which many states permitted. In 1977, the Supreme Court held that the death penalty for rape was an unconstitutionally cruel and unusual punishment.

Somewhere, someplace, a crime is committed: perhaps a car theft, or a purse snatching from an elderly woman—just an average crime. But the

---

9   The Bill of Rights and the Stages of the Criminal Justice System

Although our criminal justice system is complex, it can be broken down into stages. The constitutional umbrella of the Bill of Rights protects the rights of the accused at every stage. Here are some key constitutional guarantees at various stages of the criminal justice system.

STAGE	PROTECTIONS
BEFORE A TRIAL	
Evidence gathered	"unreasonable search and seizure" forbidden (Fourth Amendment)
Suspicion cast	guarantee that "writ of habeas corpus" will not be suspended, forbidding imprisonment without evidence (Article I)
Arrest made	self-incrimination forbidden (Fifth Amendment); right to have assistance of counsel (Sixth Amendment)
Interrogation	excessive bail forbidden (Eighth Amendment)
AT A TRIAL	"speedy and public trial" by an impartial jury required (Sixth Amendment) "double jeopardy" (being tried twice for the same crime) forbidden (Fifth Amendment) trial by jury required (Article III) right to confront witnesses (Sixth Amendment)
PUNISHMENT	"cruel and unusual punishment" forbidden (Eighth Amendment)

average crime in America is *not* followed by an arrest. The *clearance rate,* that is, the proportion of crimes resulting in an arrest, is about 20 percent and has remained fairly stable at that rate for years. In San Jose, for example, only about one in eight serious crimes was followed by an arrest throughout the 1960s and 1970s.[15]

Collecting the Evidence. Police cannot arrest Joe or Mary Citizen on a whim; they need evidence to arrest and courts need it to convict. Police need what the courts call *probable cause* to believe that someone has committed a crime before making an arrest. Often they will need to get physical evidence (the car thief's fingerprints, the purse that was snatched) to use in court. Yet the Fourth Amendment is quite specific in forbidding **unreasonable searches and seizures.** To prevent unreasonable searches and seizures by the police, the Constitution usually requires that police obtain a **search warrant** from a court. It must specify the area to be searched and what the police seek.

A woman named Dollree Mapp, who lived in Cleveland, was under suspicion for illegal gambling activities. The police broke into her home looking for a suspect, and while searching the house from top to bottom, found a cache of obscene materials. She was subsequently tried and convicted of possessing obscene materials, and appealed her case to the Supreme Court, claiming that the Fourth Amendment should be applied to the states and local governments. In an important decision (**Mapp v. Ohio,** 1961), the Supreme Court ruled that the evidence was illegally seized and reversed her conviction. Since then, the exclusionary rule has applied to the states as well as the federal government.

Since 1914, the federal courts have used an *exclusionary rule* to prevent the introduction of illegally seized evidence. No matter how incriminating—even a shirt stained with the victim's blood—evidence cannot be introduced into a trial if it was not constitutionally obtained. The logic of the exclusionary rule is this: If police officers are forced to gather evidence properly, their competence will be rewarded in a conviction; if they are slipshod or ignore the rights of a suspect, they will not win a conviction. Yet critics of the exclusionary rule—and some of them sit on the Supreme Court—argue that its strict application may permit guilty people to be freed because of police carelessness or innocent errors.

In 1984, opponents of the exclusionary rule finally won an important victory in the Supreme Court. Two cases decided on the last day of the Supreme Court's term permitted a "good faith exception" for some evidence seized by police, even though officers may not have fully complied with the letter of the law. In *Massachusetts* v. *Sheppard* (the case reviewed at the beginning of this chapter) a 7 to 2 majority of the court held that a Boston officer acted in good faith, even though his warrant was technically defective. *United States* v. *Leon,* a federal equivalent of the *Massachusetts* v. *Sheppard* case we described at the beginning of this chapter, also invoked the "good faith exception" principle in federal cases.

[15] Herbert Jacob, *The Frustration of Policy* (Boston: Little, Brown, 1984), p. 110.

Making the Arrest. Suppose that evidence has been gathered and suspicion directed toward a particular person, and the police are ready to make an arrest. In our system, the burden of proof rests on the police and the prosecutors. You do not need to help them convict you, say, by blurting out a confession in the station house. The **Fifth Amendment** forbids forced **self-incrimination.** It says that no person "shall be compelled to be a witness against himself." Whether in a congressional hearing, a courtroom, or the police station, you need not provide evidence which can then be used against you. (Under law, though, the government may guarantee you *immunity*—or exemption—from prosecution in return for your testimony regarding your own and others' misdeeds.) Protection against self-incrimination begins at arrest.

You have probably seen television shows in which an arrest is made and the arresting officers recite, often from memory, a set of rights to the arrestee. These rights are authentic and originated from a very famous decision—perhaps the most important recent decision in criminal law — involving an Arizona man named Ernesto Miranda.[16]

Miranda was picked up as a prime suspect in the ugly rape-kidnapping of an eighteen-year-old girl. Selected by the girl from a police lineup, Miranda was questioned for two hours. During this time, he was told of neither his constitutional right against self-incrimination nor his right to counsel. In fact, it seems highly unlikely that Miranda had ever heard of the Fifth Amendment. He said enough to eventually lead to a conviction. The Supreme Court reversed his conviction on appeal (***Miranda v. Arizona,*** 1966). The Court also set guidelines for police questioning of suspected persons. Specifically, the Court said:

—Suspects must be told that they have a constitutional right to remain silent.
—They must be warned that what they say can be used against them in a court of law.
—They must be told that they have a right to have a lawyer present during questioning and that a public defender is available.

Police departments throughout the country were disgruntled by *Miranda.* Officers felt that interrogation was crucial to any investigation. Warning suspects of their rights and letting them call a lawyer were almost certain to silence them. When Neal Milner researched the effects of this decision, his data suggested that police departments often tended initially to ignore *Miranda,* partly because they did not understand it.[17] Most departments today, however, seem to take *Miranda* seriously. They usually read a "Miranda card" advising suspects of their rights. When Ernesto Miranda himself was murdered, the suspect was read his rights from a Miranda card.

A more conservative Supreme Court majority under Chief Justice Burger did not emasculate the *Miranda* rulings, as some civil liberties advocates feared they might. The Burger court remained strongly committed to a defendant's right to counsel.

[16] On the Miranda case, see Liva Baker, *Miranda: The Crime, The Law, The Politics* (New York: Atheneum, 1983).
[17] Neal Milner, *The Court and Local Law Enforcement* (Beverly Hills, Calif.: Sage, 1971).

The Right to Counsel. One of the most important of the *Miranda* rights is the right to secure counsel. Even lawyers taken to court hire another lawyer to represent them. (There is an old saying in the legal profession that a lawyer who defends himself has a fool for a client.) The **Sixth Amendment** assures this right to counsel in federal courts, but people who were tried in state courts did not have the right to counsel until relatively recently. Winning that right for poor defendants was a long fight. Until the 1930s, individuals were tried and sometimes convicted for capital offenses (those where the death penalty could be imposed) without a lawyer. In 1932, the Supreme Court ordered the states to provide an attorney for indigent (poor) defendants accused of a capital crime (*Powell* v. *Alabama*).

Not until 1963 did the Supreme Court extend that right to everyone accused of a felony. A man named Clarence Earl Gideon was in the Florida state prison, convicted of robbing a pool hall.[18] This nickel-and-dime burglary (the loss was mostly change from a vending machine) had netted Gideon a five-year jail term. Because he was too poor to hire a lawyer, he had never been represented by an attorney. Using the prison's law books, he wrote a "pauper's petition" and sent it to the Supreme Court. The Court reviewed the petition and held in Gideon's favor (***Gideon v. Wainwright,*** 1963). Gideon was released, retried (this time with a public defender handling his case) and acquitted. More than a thousand of Gideon's fellow Florida prisoners, plus thousands more in other states who had been convicted without benefit of counsel, were also released. Subsequently, the Court went a step further than *Gideon.* It held that whenever imprisonment is to be imposed, a lawyer must be provided

---

[18] The story of Gideon is eloquently told by Anthony Lewis, *Gideon's Trumpet* (New York: Random House, 1964).

Clarence Earl Gideon. *Gideon's "pauper petition" to the United States Supreme Court claimed that his constitutional right to a lawyer had been denied. The Court agreed, emphasizing that "lawyers in criminal courts are necessities, not luxuries." Thus did a very ordinary convict have a major impact on our criminal justice system.*

for the accused (*Argersinger* v. *Hamlin*, 1972). However poor you are, today you have the right to a lawyer. Thanks to the efforts of Clarence Gideon and others, the Supreme Court has universalized this Sixth Amendment right. Every court is required to appoint a lawyer to represent you if you do not have the money to hire one.

Your Rights in Court. The television image of the court and the trial is almost as dramatic as the television image of the men and women in blue. Yet there, too, myth and reality do not blend well. Highly publicized trials are high drama, but they are rare. The death of a wealthy diet doctor, the attempted murder of a Rhode Island socialite, the dramatic "recantation" of a rape story in Chicago, and the multiple rapes in a New Bedford, Massachusetts, barroom made headlines for weeks. (Cable News Network even carried live the trial of the barroom rapists.) In reality, most cases, even ones in which the evidence is rock-hard, do not get to trial.

If you ever go to a typical American criminal courtroom, you will rarely see a trial, complete with judge and jury. In American courts, 90 percent of all cases begin and end with a guilty plea.[19] Most cases are settled through a process called **plea bargaining.** A plea bargain results from an actual bargain struck between the defendant's lawyer and the prosecutor that the defendent will plead guilty to a lesser crime in exchange for the state's not prosecuting for the more serious one.

Critics of the plea bargaining system believe that it permits many criminals to avoid facing the music—or as much music as they could face if they were tried for a more serious offence. But the process works to the advantage of both sides: it saves time and money that would otherwise be spent on a trial; it permits the defendant who believes he might be convicted of a serious charge to settle for a lesser one. Critics of plea-bargaining argue that it works to the defendant's advantage and the public's disadvantage. If the truly guilty murderer enters a guilty plea on the lesser charge of manslaughter, justice is not served.

Whether plea bargaining lets the guilty defendant off easy is much debated by observers of our court system. Some research has dismissed the notion that the plea-bargaining system benefits defendants. David Brereton and Jonathan Casper studied sentencing patterns in three California counties. They discovered that a larger proportion of defendants who went to trial ended up going to prison than defendants who pleaded guilty and had no trial. This was true even when factors like previous record and the nature of the offense were taken into account. In answer to Brereton and Casper's question, "Does it pay to plead guilty?", their answer is a qualified yes.[20] But whether the plea-bargaining system serves the ends of justice, it is likely to remain with us for a long time. To bring every accused defendant to trial would require a vast increase in the resources we devote to our judicial system.

[19] Herbert Jacob, *Urban Justice* (Englewood Cliffs, N.J.: Prentice Hall, 1973), p. 98.
[20] David Brereton and Johnathan D. Casper, "Does It Pay to Plead Guilty? Differential Sentencing and the Function of the Criminal Courts," *Law and Society Review*, 16 (1981–82):45–70.

For those 300,000 cases that actually end up at trial, there is a multitude of rights available to the defendant. The Sixth Amendment insures the right to a speedy trial by an impartial jury. These days, defendants (at least those who can afford it) do not leave jury selection to chance. A sophisticated technology of jury selection has developed. Jury consultants, often psychologists or other social scientists, putting some of their statistical training to use, develop profiles of jurors likely to be sympathetic or hostile to the defendant. Lawyers for both sides spend hours questioning prospective jurors in a major case. One Chicago prosecutor reports that he would challenge "anyone who had one psychology or one sociology course in college," presumably fearing that these courses cause people to be more sympathetic to defendants. (No hard evidence suggests they do.) Only well-heeled defendants can afford this sophisticated technology of jury selection, however.

The Constitution does not specifically say how big a jury has to be. Theoretically it could be anywhere from one or two people to hundreds or thousands. Tradition in England and America has set jury size at twelve, though in petty (minor) cases, six jurors are sometimes used; traditionally, a jury had to be unanimous to convict. Yet the Burger Court has eroded these traditions, permitting states to use less than twelve jurors or even to convict with less than a unanimous vote.

Cruel and Unusual Punishment. If Mary Citizen is convicted of a crime, she can expect some punishment, which may range from mild to severe. The mildest is some form of probation, the most severe, of course, the death penalty.

The biblical injunction of an "eye for an eye" is tame compared with the reality of punishment through the ages. The English hung pickpockets while their fellow craftsmen rifled the pockets of the crowd.

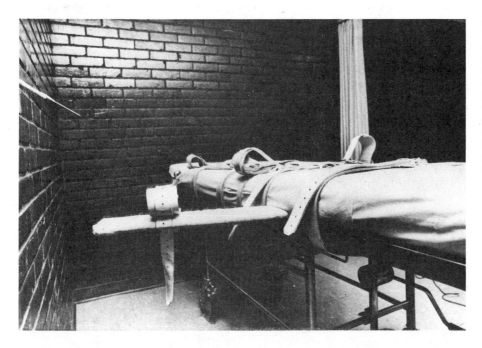

Capital Punishment: Making it "More Humane"? *Criminals sentenced to death by injection receive the lethal dosage intravenously while strapped to a stretcher like this one. This is the stretcher on which Charles Brooks was executed in the Texas State Penitentiary in Huntsville in 1982. Death by lethal injection was, its boosters claimed, "more humane." Chemical execution is a growing mode of death in the changing technology of the death penalty.*

Americans burned suspected witches, jailed the insane, and hung or shot people for what we would now call minor offenses. The **Eighth Amendment,** however, forbids **"cruel and unusual punishment."** As Justice William O. Douglas once remarked, "The Eighth Amendment expresses the revulsion of civilized man against barbarous acts" (*Robinson* v. *California*, 1962).

Today, the most controversial punishment is the death penalty. In 1968 (*Witherspoon* v. *Illinois*), the Court overturned a death sentence because people opposed to the death penalty had been excluded from the jury at the sentencing stage. This exclusion stacked the cards in favor of the extreme penalty. In ***Furman* v. *Georgia*** (1972), the justices first faced directly the question of whether the death penalty was inherently cruel and unusual. *Furman* had a constitutional message, but the message was garbled. Four judges said the death penalty was plainly not cruel and unusual. But the Court overturned Georgia's death penalty law. About all the majority of the Court agreed on was that in practice, imposition of the death penalty was often "freakish" and "random." Justice Marshall and others pointed out that death penalties were imposed disproportionately on blacks. Although blacks were only 12 percent of the United States population, a majority of those executed were black.

Furman stopped short of outlawing the death penalty. It did warn the states that the application of the death penalty needed clarification and uniformity. The legislatures of thirty-five states responded by passing new death penalty laws. North Carolina, for example, made the death penalty *mandatory* if the murder was "willful, deliberate, or premeditated" or if it was committed in connection with "any arson, rape, robbery, kidnapping [or] burglary." In *Woodson* v. *North Carolina* (1976), the Supreme Court ruled against mandatory death penalties. Failure to take account of the specifics of the crime, the background of the defendants, and their previous record all rendered North Carolina's law requiring the death penalty arbitrary and therefore unconstitutional.

Another new law was challenged in a Georgia case (***Gregg* v. *Georgia,*** 1976). Troy Gregg had murdered two hitchhikers and was awaiting execution in Georgia's state prison. But Gregg's attorney argued that the death penalty was cruel and unusual punishment. The Court this time did not agree. "In part," it said, "capital punishment is an expression of society's outrage at particularly offensive conduct. . . . It is an extreme sanction, suitable to the most extreme of crimes." In at least *some* circumstances, therefore, the death penalty is constitutionally acceptable. ⟨10⟩ Today many states are reinstituting death penalties. More than 1550 persons (a third of them in Florida and Texas alone) await the death penalty.

THE NEW TECHNOLOGY AND THE NEW CIVIL LIBERTIES ISSUES

The Founding Fathers who drafted the Bill of Rights had never experienced, heard of, or probably even imagined television, wiretapping, death-delaying machinery, medically induced abortions, national security clearances, satellite communications, or—heaven forbid—pornographic movies. In their simpler time, they were concerned with protecting people against the government's incarcerating them on a whim. Encased in the Bill of Rights is a set of protections against governmental caprice. How our government deals with the new technologies of the third American century is a major challenge for the courts and for proponents of civil liberties.

In Chapter 1, you learned that there are three technological transformations confronting us today: (1) the biomedical transformation, where life itself can be artificially manipulated; (2) the telecommunications and computer revolution, where our lives are more and more affected by the quantity and speed of information collected; and (3) the nuclear revolution, where our nation's war-making power has changed dramatically. Each of those transformations has affected the constitutional umbrella of our civil liberties, too. All constitute new threats to the privacy of the individual and the power of the government over him or her.

10 How They Die: The Death Penalty in the States

After a ten-year moratorium on the death penalty while the Supreme Court slowly worked out constitutional guidelines, executions increased rapidly in the 1980s. Ever since Socrates was condemned to die by drinking hemlock, there has existed a technology of death. In 1977, Gary Gilmore had faced a firing squad in Utah, a state which permits this old-fashioned practice for its executions. Today, more than 1550 men (and a few women) await execution in the states. (Florida alone accounts for about 200 death-row inmates, with Texas, Georgia, and California each having more than 100 awaiting their ends.) A plurality of death-penalty states use the electric chair. The first one, in New York's Sing Sing Prison, was built in 1890 and electrocuted 695 men and women. (It has a built-in fan above the chair to remove the smell of burning flesh after four currents of 2000 volts are passed through the body.)

In December 1982 a new technology of execution was first used. In the Texas state prison at Huntsville, Charlie Brooks, Jr., was strapped to a gurney—a hospital bed on wheels—and into his left arm (tattooed "I was born to die") was inserted a catheter needle. (Brooks, like a disproportionate number of persons executed in the history of the United States, was black.) At 12:10 a.m., Brooks was injected with two grams of sodium thiopental and at 12:16, he was pronounced dead. Five states now require lethal injection as a means of execution. Death penalty proponents hailed it as a "more humane" way for the state to take a life legally. The American Medical Association debated the physician's role in executions. It concluded that direct involvement of a physician would

violate his or her oath to preserve human life. In the Brooks case, a physician had helped locate the veins, but a technician had inserted the needle. Wisely, the vice chairman of the A.M.A.'s judicial council allowed that "the doctor may be forced to load the pistol, but he must never be the one to pull the trigger."

Here is a breakdown of the means of execution required or permitted in the various states:

Method of Execution[a]	State
Electrocution	Alabama, Arizona, Arkansas, Colorado, Florida, Georgia, Illinois, Indiana, Kentucky, Louisiana, Massachusetts, Nebraska, New York, Pennsylvania, South Carolina, South Dakota, Tennessee, Vermont, Virginia
Lethal Gas	California, Maryland, Mississippi, Missouri, Nevada, North Carolina, Oregon, Rhode Island, Wyoming
Hanging	Delaware, Montana, New Hampshire, Utah,[b] Washington
Lethal Intravenous Injection	Idaho, New Mexico, Oklahoma, Texas

[a]None: Alaska, Connecticut, Hawaii, Iowa, Kansas, Maine, Michigan, Minnesota, New Jersey, North Dakota, Ohio, West Virginia, Wisconsin
[b]or firing squad by choice

Source: Book of the States, (Lexington, Ky.: The Council of State Governments, 1980) p. 446. For information on the Brooks execution, see *Time,* December 20, 1982, pp. 28–29.

Life, Love, Privacy, and the Human Body

In the summer of 1972, Supreme Court Justice Harry Blackmun returned to the famous Mayo Clinic in Rochester, Minnesota, where he had once worked as its general counsel. Officers of the clinic gave Blackmun a tiny desk in a corner of the office of the assistant librarian, where he worked quietly for two weeks during the Court's summer recess. His research topic was the medical aspect of abortion. Laboring over his draft of the Court's opinion (Blackmun was chronically tardy in his opinion writing) he weighed the medical, moral, and legal issues. He mulled over the rights of the mother and the life of the fetus. Back in Washington, he finished the draft opinion and sent it to his brethren on the Court.

The decision was a difficult one. Blackmun had divided a pregnancy into three equal parts (or "trimesters"). The decision forbade state control over abortions during the first trimester; permitted states to limit abortions to protect the mother's health in the second trimester; and permitted states to protect the fetus during the third trimester. On January 22, 1973, the abortion case, ***"Roe" v. Wade*** (Roe was a pseudonym used by the plaintiff) was announced by the Court. A firestorm was unleashed. The Court's staff installed extra mailboxes to handle the heavy mail. Some contained death threats. Blackmun, who authored the opinion, received the brunt of the attacks. The Sisters of St. Mary's Hospital at the Mayo Clinic wrote outraged letters weekly. [21]

The abortion decision resulted in part because new technologies cause new controversies. Abortion is hardly new in history, but the ability to save many premature babies is. For all of us, new technologies present opportunities; to the Courts and the Constitution, they also present problems. In 1980, the Supreme Court was even called upon to decide whether new life forms, created through biotechnology, could be patented. The Court, in *Diamond* v. *Chakraharty*, decided they could be.

When you read the Bill of Rights, you never encounter the word "privacy." Clearly, though, the writers of the Bill of Rights had it in the back of their minds when they crafted those amendments. A freedom of religion implies the right to exercise private beliefs; protections against unreasonable searches and seizures leave a person secure in his or her private domicile; private property cannot be seized by government without "due process of law." The abortion decision in *"Roe"* v. *Wade* was justified by the Court largely on the grounds of the **right of privacy.** As early as 1928, Justice Brandeis hailed privacy as "the right to be let alone —the most comprehensive of rights and the most valued by civilized men." The right to privacy includes what Paul Bender calls "the right to keep the details of [one's] life confidential; the free and untrammeled use and enjoyment of one's intellect, body, and private property . . . the right, in sum, to a private personal life free from the intrusion of government or the dictates of society." [22]

---

[21] Woodward and Armstrong, *The Brethren*, pp. 271–284.
[22] Paul Bender, "Privacy," in Norman Dorsen (ed.), *Our Endangered Rights* (New York: Pantheon, 1984), p. 238.

Does the right to privacy include the right to die? More today than ever, issues of the "right to die" come to the legislatures and the courts. In response to the well-publicized plight of Baby Doe (which we discussed in Chapter 1) President Reagan issued a directive on April 30, 1982, forbidding federally aided hospitals from denying medical care or food to deformed infants. The American Academy of Pediatrics sued to prevent the adoption of these new rules. A federal district court in the District of Columbia forbade the Department of Health and Human Services from implementing the new rules (*American Academy of Pediatrics* v. *Heckler*, 1983). The department proposed new rules in January, 1984, and these were again the subject of a suit by the American Medical Association and the American Hospital Association.

Adults also confront the medical profession with right-to-die issues. Today, it is possible to prolong life far beyond nature's deadline; four out of five people die in a nursing home or hospital, where expensive, life-prolonging equipment is ready to be used. In 1981, Clarence Herbert, a security guard, lapsed into a coma in Los Angeles, and doctors pronounced his brain dead. With the family's consent doctors removed a respirator; but Herbert kept breathing and doctors, again with the family's consent, removed intravenous feeding. Eleven days later, Herbert finally succumbed, and Los Angeles prosecutors filed homicide charges against the doctors. (The charges were later dismissed.) In these situations, the edges of medical technology meet the edges of the law. As medical technology improves even more, the law and the constitution will continue to clash over medical and family judgments.

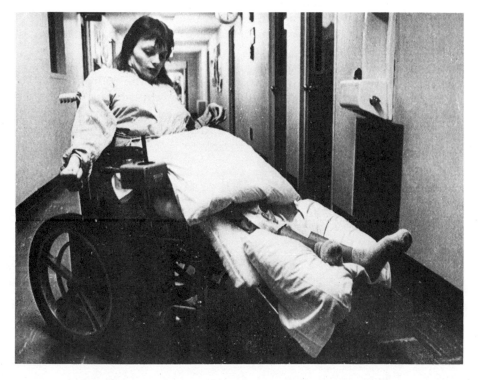

A Right to Die? *Elizabeth Bouvia, a cerebral palsy victim since birth, checked into a Riverside, California, hospital in 1983 with the intention of starving herself to death. Hospital officials refused to accommodate her desire to die. A new technology of medical care makes it possible to keep people alive beyond what nature might allow. Courts and other institutions of government are increasingly called upon to decide matters of life and death.*

The Eyes and Ears of Government: Civil Liberties and the Telecommunications Transformation

The computer has made possible the data bank. Government has created massive data banks on its citizens.[23] George Orwell's *1984* did not mention computers, but it is impossible to imagine the horrors he described without the computer and telecommunications transformations. Like the government, private firms keep countless records on you. Banks list your every financial transaction; phone companies can store your every call; credit card companies can track your every payment. The Office of Management and Budget estimates that the federal government maintains about fifteen files on every American citizen. Seemingly innocuous or routine information can be used to support government dragnets. The Social Security system, for example, loaned its tapes to the Selective Service System so that the latter agency could apprehend young men who had not registered for the draft.

In this era of modern technology, government's eyes and ears can be busy indeed. Hidden microphones can fit into the olive in a martini. A wiretap on your phone is easy to install. In 1967, the Supreme Court brought the use of indirect searches of people under the orbit of the Fourth Amendment. It held in *Katz* v. *United States* that the Fourth Amendment protects "people—and not simply 'areas'" against unreasonable searches, for example, through wiretapping or other electronic surveillance. Wiretapping reached a peak during the Nixon presidency. Obsessed that leaks were being seeped to the press on sensitive national security issues, Nixon and his national security advisor, Henry Kissinger, ordered scores of wiretaps on White House officials. In 1978, Congress passed a law sharply limiting the president's use of wiretaps. It created a special court to hear government petitions to "bug" suspected agents of foreign governments.

As technology makes possible more and more intrusions into our private lives, there will be more complex cases for the courts to decide. Today, our concerns for privacy and individual rights go well beyond the concerns of the Founding Fathers, partly caused by the overlapping of technology with the boundaries of our traditional concepts of justice and privacy.

National Security and the Bill of Rights

Even the strongest champion of free speech and the free press would agree that *sometimes* government can limit individual behavior on national security grounds. No one would find it peculiar or unconstitutional if a newspaper was hauled into court for publishing troop movement plans in a battle zone. In fact, the fine line between legitimate "national security issues" and freedoms in the Bill of Rights has been sharply debated. The awesome technology of nuclear war makes the clash between the Bill of Rights and national defense a vivid one.

---

[23] On the computer, privacy, and government, see David Burnham, *The Rise of the Computer State* (New York: Random House, 1983).

Normally the "no prior restraint" rule means that government cannot censor in advance what is published. But Howard Morland, a freelance writer, prepared an article for the small left-wing magazine, *The Progressive,* on how a hydrogen bomb works. Using nothing but published, nonsecret sources, Morland pieced together his story. *The Progressive*'s editors decided to send it to several nuclear scientists to review its accuracy. One gave his copy to MIT physicist George W. Rathjens, who sent the manuscript to Washington for a security review. Planning to publish the article in its March 1979 issue, the editors waited nervously for a call from Washington. It finally came. Department of Energy officials told the editors that the article included some classified material, and they suggested deletions. Arguing that everything in the article could already be obtained from public sources, the editors announced their intention to proceed with publication in May.

On March 8, government lawyers rushed to Wisconsin, where *The Progressive* is published, and secured a temporary restraining order from a federal judge, barring publication for ten days. A full-scale hearing followed. The government argued that publication would endanger national security, make the H-bomb available to more nations, and threaten world peace. Lawyers for the magazine insisted on their First Amendment rights and claimed that no secret material was used in gathering evidence for the article.

You be the judge. The issue: Does national security justify (or even demand) prior restraint against an article explaining how an H-bomb works? For the court's answer, see 12, on page 166.

Governments like to keep anything remotely related to national defense a secret. The Pentagon papers case (which we discussed on page 142 provided one fabled example. Other issues surface, too: Can an editor, for example, publish an article containing detailed instructions on how to make a hydrogen bomb? (For one case in point, see 11.) American government, under many presidential administrations, has been an active censor of information that it claimed might affect national security. Government has demanded the censorship of a book by former CIA agent Victor Marchetti and sued former CIA agent Frank Snepp for writing a book about Vietnam, even though no classified information was reviewed. (The Supreme Court upheld the government's suit in *United States* v. *Snepp*, 1980.) The Reagan administration went further than any other in its attempt to muzzle officials and former officials. On March 11, 1983, it adopted a new rule requiring that all speeches, commentaries, books or articles by policymaking officials and former officials be reviewed by the government—even if classified information is not discussed. Had such a rule been in effect before, everything written by former officials such as Alexander Haig, Henry Kissinger, Robert McNamara or perhaps even presidents themselves would have had to be screened by the government.

Civil libertarians believe that "national security" is often a cloak and a ruse for limiting debate and free speech. When national security is invoked, rights can be sorely tried.

CIVIL LIBERTIES SUMMARIZED

If our nation was truly "conceived in liberty," then the Bill of Rights is fundamental to our freedoms. Civil liberties are the protections that individuals enjoy against the government. Because the language of the Bill of Rights is quaint and simple, disputes develop about the meaning

165

3 The Court ruled that the establishment clause had definitely been violated. Although it noted, "The place of religion in our society is an exalted one," the Court majority held, "In the relationship between man and religion, the State is firmly committed to a position of neutrality."

4 In a 6 to 3 decision, a majority of justices (some of them reluctantly) agreed that the "no prior restraint" rule prohibited the government from seeking an injunction. But a majority also made it clear that criminal charges could be sustained against Ellsberg and the *Times* for theft of secret documents. No such charges were ever filed, though.

5 On October 6, 1978, the Supreme Court refused to order Farber released from jail and the *Times's* fine suspended. Farber stayed in jail throughout most of the trial and the *Times's* fine accumulated, finally totalling $285,000. In *New York Times* v. *New Jersey* (1978), the Supreme Court upheld Farber's contempt citation and the *Times's* fine, but the governor of New Jersey pardoned Farber.

6 In *Erznoznik* v. *Jacksonville* (1975), the Supreme Court held that Jacksonville's ordinance was unconstitutional. The city council went much too far, the Court said, and ended up banning movies which might not be obscene at all. The ordinance would end up banning a film "containing a picture of a baby's buttocks, the nude body of a war victim, or scenes from a culture where nudity is indigenous. ... Clearly," Justice Lewis Powell emphasized in this opinion, "all nudity cannot be deemed obscene even to minors."

7 A federal district court ruled that Skokie's ordinance did restrict freedom of association and the right of peaceable assembly. No community could use its power to grant parade permits in order to stifle the free expression of ideas. In October 1978, the Supreme Court, in *Collin* v. *Smith*, let this lower court ruling stand. As it happened, though, the Nazis did not march in Skokie. Chicago loosened its parade requirements, and the Nazis settled for a couple of poorly attended demonstrations there.

11 On September 19, 1979, while the case was pending, the Justice Department, without reversing its position, dropped its suit against *The Progressive*. Several newspapers had printed a letter to Senator Charles Percy containing much of the same information as the article. The case was thus rendered "moot," meaning that a substantive controversy no longer existed. The issue of prior restraint was not resolved.

of the constitutional umbrella. Legislatures, courts, and bureaucrats are constantly defining in practice what the Bill of Rights guarantees in theory.

The four great freedoms of the First Amendment are the freedom of religion, of speech, of the press, and of assembly. Sometimes, these rights clash with one another. One reporter's freedom to collect news may collide with a defendant's right to a fair trial. The Bill of Rights also contains protections of life, liberty, and property. These are especially important to those who have been accused of a crime. The crime rate soared between the 1930s (when we first started systematically collecting data on crimes) and the late 1970s. The Supreme Court extended many constitutional rights to persons in state courts, where most criminal trials take place. The right to counsel and protection from unreasonable searches and seizures are two key examples.

The Bill of Rights was written in a time of primitive technology. Today's technologies raise new issues for the police, citizens, and courts. Never explicitly mentioned in the Constitution is the right to privacy. Yet the Court has insisted that certain rights protect privacy from unwarranted intrusion by government. The right to an abortion is one extension of this right to privacy. Right-to-lifers claim that even the unborn has the right to be born; and there are conflicting issues related to the right to die. The telecommunications transformation and the sensitive problems of national security also create headaches for courts and citizens.

Key Terms

exclusionary rule
civil liberties
Bill of Rights
First Amendment
Fourteenth
    Amendment
due process clause
establishment clause

prior restraint
libel
clear and present
    danger
crime rate
unreasonable searches
    and seizures
search warrant

Fifth Amendment
self-incrimination
Sixth Amendment
plea bargaining
Eighth Amendment
cruel and unusual
    punishment
right of privacy

Key Cases

Barron v. *Baltimore*
    (1833)
Gitlow v. *New York*
    (1925)
Engel v. *Vitale (1962)*
Near v. *Minnesota*
    (1931)
Zurcher v. *Stanford*
    Daily (1978)
New York Times v.
    Sullivan (1964)

Roth v. *United States*
    (1957)
Miller v. *California*
    (1973)
Schenck v. *United*
    States (1919)
Dennis v. *United States*
    (1951)
Mapp v. *Ohio (1961)*
Miranda v. *Arizona*
    (1966)

Gideon v. *Wainwright*
    (1963)
Furman v. *Georgia*
    (1972)
Gregg v. *Georgia*
    (1976)
"Roe" v. *Wade (1973)*

For Further Reading

Baker, Liva. *Miranda: The Crime, The Law, The Politics* (1983). An excellent, book-length treatment of one of the major criminal justice cases of our time.

Burnham, David. *The Rise of the Computer State* (1983). A *New York Times* reporter examines the issues of computers and privacy.

Dorsen, Norman, ed. *Our Endangered Rights: The ACLU Report on Civil Liberties Today* (1984). A review from the perspective of the American Civil Liberties Union of the state of our liberties in various areas today.

Friendly, Fred W. *Minnesota Rag* (1981). The story of *Near v. Minnesota.*

Jacob, Herbert. *The Frustration of Policy* (1984). A study of crime and governmental responses in ten American cities, including San Jose.

Krislov, Samuel. *The Supreme Court and Political Freedom* (1968). A useful review of the history of the Supreme Court's interpretations of the First Amendment freedoms.

Lewis, Anthony. *Gideon's Trumpet* (1964). The story of how Clarence Gideon won the right to counsel in his case and for thousands of other defendants.

Silverman, Charles. *Criminal Violence, Criminal Justice* (1978). A perceptive author treats the problem of crime and criminal justice.

PEOPLE AND POLITICS

A democratic system demands that people participate in it. They do this not only by voting in elections, but through other linkage institutions as well. Party and group activities are other major ways in which Americans participate in setting the policy agenda.

In Chapter 6, we look at what politicians are fond of calling "the American people." There are so many of us that the mind cannot easily take in our size or diversity. We are from different ethnic and social groups, and our public opinions and political behaviors reflect our social, class, and ethnic backgrounds.

Chapter 7 deals with political parties. Some would sound their death knell, proclaiming that "the party's over" in American politics. I do not entirely agree. Many aspects of our parties have weakened in recent years—the old-fangled machines, voter support, and loyalty, for example. But parties are formidable political organizations and are here to stay.

Chapters 8 and 9 deal with elections in America. Chapter 8 describes the process of nomination and that great American institution, the political campaign. Chapter 9 analyzes the voting process itself.

In Chapter 10, we meet an old friend—the interest group, a political linkage institution discussed several times throughout *Government in America*. Many critics of "the lobbies" and the "special interest groups" believe that politicians pander to them too much. Yet they are important institutions for expressing citizen preferences.

The American People: Public Opinion and Political Action

I begin this chapter with a discussion of a made-for-TV movie called *The Day After*. Chances are you saw it; more than one in two adult Americans did. I was an extra in it, helping raid Rusty's grocery store in Lawrence, Kansas, hoarding food for the coming nuclear disaster. It was a fascinating experience, one which gave me some insight into our ability to work technological wonders, turning a movie made in Kansas into an event seen by 100 million Americans and countless more nonAmericans. What we think and believe is more and more shaped by technotronic wizardry.

Chapter 6 is about the American people—all 234 million of us. Abraham Lincoln said that ours is a government "of the people, by the people, and for the people." If our nation is truly to be a government *by* the people, instead of merely *of* the people, then people have to work their opinions and preferences into the political mainstream.

In this chapter, we will look first at

- *Who we are* politically. Demography shapes our democracy and so does technology. *Public opinion* is shaped by many forces, including our political socialization and our technologies.
- *How we learn* about politics is called political socialization. Through it we develop citizenship and attitudes toward politics, government, and public policy.
- *What we believe* about politics and policy is called public opinion. Of course, different people have different opinions; but opinion without action is unlikely to be heeded. You are easy to ignore if you do not speak up.
- *How we participate* in politics determines (in part) the degree to which our opinions count. Political participation includes many different activities designed to influence government. Voting is only one of those activities.

O N NOVEMBER 20 AND 21, 1983, one of the most watched television programs in the history of the world (more than 100 million people in the United States alone, almost one out of every two Americans) was shown by ABC. Entitled *The Day After*, it was about the day after World War III, a short, nuclear war which irradiated the earth and its inhabitants. Human flesh seared, nuclear fallout rained on the earth, civilization all but disappeared. Opinion about the movie ranged widely. Few thought it an artistic success, but many debated its political impact. The Reverend Jerry Falwell, Moral Majority's leader, demanded equal time on television to counteract this "two-hour political editorial." Some antinuclear groups feared that the movie might inspire hopelessness about nuclear war and hence political inactivity. Groups advocating a nuclear freeze—a moratorium on any new nuclear weapons by the United States and the Soviet Union—used the movie to increase support for their cause.

What, though, was the effect of the TV movie on public opinion? Perhaps public opinion on important issues is fragile and easily manipulated. Then again, perhaps public opinion is resistent to change, even from a powerful and graphic movie with political overtones.

Stanley Feldman and Lee Sigelman of the University of Kentucky conducted a local survey of the impact of *The Day After* on public opinion and attitudes toward nuclear war. Through telephone polling, they interviewed a sample of Lexington, Kentucky, residents about nuclear war before and after watching the movie on television. Despite its powerful drama, no significant changes occurred. Public opinions are developed over a long period and are not hastily changed. The impact of even this blockbuster movie was modest. They did note some small changes, however. The most educated viewers were more likely to conclude that Reagan's defense policies were unwise and that defense spending should be cut. Less educated voters concluded the opposite.[1] Let us consider another example: a social experiment, specifically designed to change people's values and opinions. It is summarized in 1 .

[1] The Feldman-Sigelman study is reported in "The Political Impact of Prime-Time Television: *The Day After*," forthcoming, *Journal of Politics*.

The Day After. *Millions of people throughout the world, including about 100 million Americans, watched* The Day After, *a controversial movie about the beginnings of World War III. This scene from the film depicts the city of Lawrence, Kansas after a nuclear blast. The important question about this and other episodes of politically charged television is: Can and do they change public opinion?*

Television is the most powerful technology of communication and persuasion ever invented. Political scientists, though, are still uncertain about its effect on our values, our thinking, and our public opinion. Only now are social scientists able to point clearly to some impacts on our opinions of this technotronic wonder.

Milton Rokeach and Sandra Ball-Rokeach, distinguished students of social psychology at Washington State University, conducted an ingenious experiment. Its goal was to test experimentally the impact of television on changing our basic values. Note that this test, called The Great American Values Test, was real, not a contrived laboratory experiment. A television show of that name was aired in the Tri-Cities area of eastern Washington on all three local network affiliates. To boost viewership, it was professionally produced and hosted by television personalities Ed Asner and Sandy Hill.

The show was about what Americans believe, specifically about how Americans ranked eighteen basic values (examples: family security, equality, freedom, wisdom, happiness, mature love, a world at peace). The Rokeachs knew from a number of national surveys how Americans ranked these values. Their goal: to use a television show to influence people to change their value priorities.

Here is how it worked: Early in the show, viewers were asked to rank the values. Then the hosts began, subtly yet perceptibly, to try to persuade people to rethink their priorities. For example, Hill tells the viewers that children begin with a natural appreciation of beauty, ranking "a world of beauty" high on their list of values. Teenagers rank it lower. Adults rank it lower still: seventeenth in a list of eighteen values. Perhaps, she says, "that explains why so many Americans are willing to live with pollution and ugliness." Subtle, yes, but a real effort to manipulate opinion on basic values.

After the show, the Washington State researchers used a variety of follow-up studies with their audience, including phone interviews, mailed questionnaires, and even invitations to viewers and nonviewers to contribute to causes representing these values (an environmental group, for example). What happened? Viewers gave clear evidence of changing their minds on basic values. When viewers and nonviewers were sent solicitations for causes representing targeted values, viewers were four to six times more likely to contribute than nonviewers.

There are ethical dilemmas in this sort of research, as the authors would be quick to admit. Even so, it shows that public opinion can be changed; and it can be changed by television.

Source: For a full report of the study, see Sandra J. Ball-Rokeach, Milton Rokeach, and Joel W. Grube, *The Great American Values Test* (New York: The Free Press, 1984).

In a democracy, we hope that public opinion can impact on politics, government, and public policy. Elite theorists, not surprisingly, believe that the impact of public opinion is skimpy. Our task here is to understand public opinion and political action. To understand what we believe, we first must understand who we are.

WHO ARE WE?

We live in what Zbigniew Brzezinski calls the "technotronic age." It is a time when "society is shaped culturally, socially, and economically by the impact of technology and electronics—particularly in the area of computers and communications."[2] It is a new and different period in the history of the American people. The third American century is not only a technotronic period, in which 97 percent of the population owns televisions, but also a time when our culture is changing. Lifestyles that our parents could not have imagined or accepted have become commonplace. Values they held fast are challenged.

One way of looking at those changes in American life that affect politics is to look at our changing **demography.** Demography is the science of population changes, and one valuable tool for understanding demo-

[2] Zbigniew Brzezinski, *Between Two Ages* (New York: Viking Press, 1970), p. 9.

173

graphic changes is the U.S. **census.** The Constitution mandates that the government conduct an "actual enumeration" of the population every decade. So every ten years (those ending in a zero) the United States Bureau of the Census goes to work, collecting a vast quantity of information about Americans, storing it in huge data banks on computers, and publishing tapes and books full of data on our incomes, education, jobs, and so forth. (Incidentally, during the 1890 census, the grandfather of the computer was born. A crude machine tallied punched cards with census data on them. The machine was named after its inventor, Herman Hollerith. He later took his Hollerith Machine and founded a company to market it and other business machines. Its name was International Business Machines, IBM for short.)

Some Minitrends

In Chapter 1, we looked at some "megatrends" that are shaping our political system. Here, we use census information to describe some "minitrends" which also have reshaped our government and the policy issues it faces.

The Regional Shift. Between 1970 and 1980, growth in the Sunbelt continued to surge, while growth in the Frostbelt sputtered (see pages 124–129). Florida added 43.4 percent to its population over the decade, Arizona 53 percent, Nevada 63.5 percent, and Texas 27.1 percent. Growth here was matched by decline there. New York, Rhode Island, and the District of Columbia actually lost people. Ohio, Massachusetts, and Pennsylvania had virtually "zero population growth." Cities, too, grew or shrank. As a rule, older northern cities did the shrinking and Sunbelt cities did the growing. San Antonio and San Diego displaced Washington and Cleveland among the top ten cities.

Demographic changes are often associated with political changes. States gain or lose congressional seats as their populations change. After the 1980 census, New York lost five members of Congress; Ohio, Pennsylvania, and Illinois lost two; Florida and Texas each added three more representatives in Washington. Almost all of these regional shifts seemed to bode well for the Republican party. Take a look at 2. It compares the recent political behavior of some high-growth and some low-growth states. First you can see how well Reagan and the Republicans fared in high- and low-growth states in 1984. In Colorado, for example, the Reagan-Mondale margin was a tidy 27 percentage points for Reagan. In Massachusetts, on the other hand, Reagan won by a hair, getting only 2 percent more than Mondale. You can also see how frequently each of these states voted Republican in the last six presidential elections.

One trend is evident: Republicans have a commanding lead in the fastest-growing states. Democrats, of course, need not give up the battle at hearing such news. One good guess is that Republicans have simply moved away, leaving Democrats behind in the Frostbelt but without affecting the total number of Republicans and Democrats. Even if the relative shares of the two parties remain unaffected by population dynamics, demographic change may leave its mark on partisan power. Because states, not individual people, play a role in the makeup of the

Political change is often connected to demographic change. Take a look at the map on page 176. You will quickly note that some states were rapidly growing in the 1970s; others were slow-growth states; a few even lost population. There are some important differences among these slow-growing and fast-growing states. Indeed, when we compare the political patterns of high- and low-growth states, some significant implications emerge.

The High-growth States. In nine states, population grew by more than 25 percent during the 1970s. Take a look at these states, their growth rates, and how big a margin Ronald Reagan got in 1984. You can also see how many of the six presidential elections between 1960 and 1984 were won by the Republicans in that state.

State	Growth Rate 1970–80 (percent)	Reagan Margin 1984 (percent)	Number of Republican Presidential Victories 1960–84
Nevada	64	35	5
Arizona	52	35	7
Florida	41	30	5
Wyoming	41	43	6
Utah	37	50	6
Alaska	32	37	6
Idaho	32	47	6
Colorado	30	27	6
Texas	26	28	3

The Low-growth States. In five states and the District of Columbia, populations remained static or even declined. Here are the slow-growth states. Compare the fortunes of Reagan and the Republicans in those states with the same information about high-growth states.

State	Growth Rate 1970–80 (percent)	Reagan Margin 1984 (percent)	Number of Republican Presidential Victories 1960–84
Ohio	—[a]	18	3
Pennsylvania	—[a]	8	3
Massachusetts	—[a]	2	2
Rhode Island	—[a]	4	2
New York	−4	8	3
Washington, D.C.	−16	−73[b]	0

[a]Less than 1 percent.
[b]A minus sign indicates a Mondale victory in that state.

(box continues on next page)

Senate and the electoral college, who controls which state is a matter of real interest to the parties.

Age: Getting Older. Until recently, it looked as if America was going to be overrun with children. A baby boom followed World War II and increased the demand for youth-oriented public policies, particularly

Demography and Politics: How Republicans Fare in High- and Low-Growth States (continued)

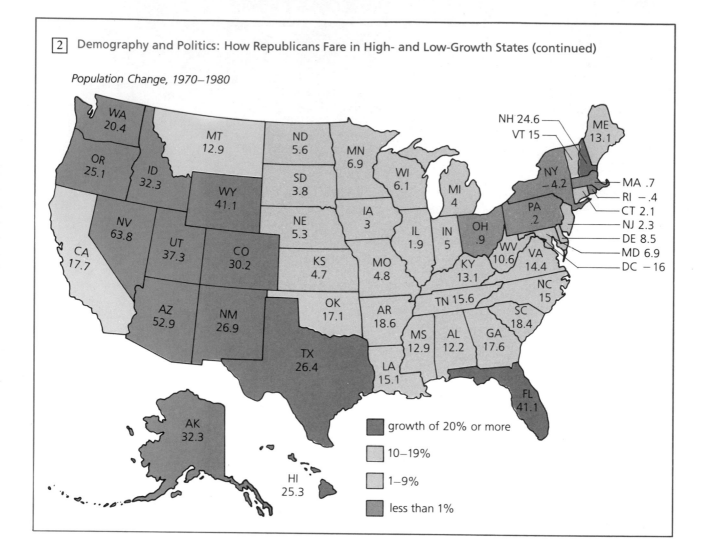

Population Change, 1970–1980

WA 20.4 · OR 25.1 · ID 32.3 · MT 12.9 · ND 5.6 · MN 6.9 · WI 6.1 · MI 4 · NY −4.2 · NH 24.6 · VT 15 · ME 13.1 · MA .7 · RI −.4 · CT 2.1 · NJ 2.3 · DE 8.5 · MD 6.9 · DC −16 · PA .2 · OH .9 · WV 10.6 · VA 14.4 · SD 3.8 · WY 41.1 · NE 5.3 · IA 3 · IL 1.9 · IN 5 · KY 13.1 · NV 63.8 · UT 37.3 · CO 30.2 · KS 4.7 · MO 4.8 · TN 15.6 · NC 15 · SC 18.4 · CA 17.7 · AZ 52.9 · NM 26.9 · OK 17.1 · AR 18.6 · MS 12.9 · AL 12.2 · GA 17.6 · TX 26.4 · LA 15.1 · FL 41.1 · AK 32.3 · HI 25.3

growth of 20% or more

10–19%

1–9%

less than 1%

schools. But the 1970s saw a "baby bust," and schools began to close down as fast as they had opened up in the 1950s. As a nation, we are now aging rapidly. Today's median age is thirty-one (meaning that half the population is older than thirty-one and half younger).

The rise of an aged population has meant the rise of new interests. Once tossed aside as no longer productive, the aged have now stressed "gray power."[3] In Florida, sunny retirement haven for millions, the state's senior citizens vote against nearly every referendum for school taxes, much to the chagrin of younger parents. They have managed to secure from the legislature tax breaks and service benefits for older Floridians. Senior citizens have discovered an old political dictum: There is strength in numbers. A large, growing, and potent group, the aged have one advantage of which almost no other group can boast: Every one of us will sooner or later be aged. The growing demands to take care of the aging population will become more acute in the decades ahead.

By 2020, our median age should be in the mid-thirties. By that date, every hundred working Americans may be matched by fifty-two Amer-

176

[3] See Henry J. Pratt, *The Gray Lobby* (Chicago: University of Chicago Press, 1977).

icans over sixty-five, most of whom will be retired and ready to collect social security. Today, nearly 30 million Americans are over sixty-five. The "over 85" group is our second fastest growing age group. The Social Security system, begun under the New Deal, is exceeded only by national defense as our most costly public policy. The current group of older Americans and those of us to follow can lay claim to nearly $5 trillion guaranteed them (and us) by the social security system. They also hold title to nearly $1 trillion in public and private pension plans. There is a political message in these numbers: People who have been promised benefits, especially ones for which they have made contributions, expect to collect them. Thus, even Ronald Reagan's budget-cutting policies treated social security benefits as virtually sacrosanct.

The American Mosaic

Pluralists are fond of pointing to the American mosaic of groups, one key indication that pluralism is alive and well. America has often been called a "nation of immigrants." Indeed, all of us except native Americans are the descendants of immigrants, and this includes the reluctant immigrants, namely, African blacks who were unwillingly imported to the United States. The English, Germans, Irish, Italians, Poles, and other groups who came during the 1700s and 1800s created a "melting pot." In the first decade of this century, more than 800,000 immigrants arrived annually to American shores and spread out to its cities and towns.

We are inclined to think of this wave of immigration as a matter of historical interest alone. You may not realize that the number of immigrants who legally come to America today, in the 1980s, is about 800,000 annually, approximately the same number who were coming in 1900. Each year, we add the equivalent of another San Antonio, the nation's tenth largest city, to our population through immigration. We live now in the era of the "second American melting pot." The first American immigrants came to seek political asylum or economic opportunity. And so it is

The Graying of America. *Older Americans are the fastest-growing segment of our population. These West Palm Beach, Florida, residents are being registered by the Republican party in 1984. In Florida and other states where older Americans have developed significant political power, school bonds and other issues which raise taxes without benefiting the elderly have had a hard time passing. As Social Security becomes the largest single item in the federal budget, the interest of older Americans in politics is certain to remain high and their numbers will add to their political influence.*

true of this generation of immigrants, who come from all parts of the world: Mexico, El Salvador, Cuba, Thailand, Vietnam, Nigeria, and elsewhere.

There is a difference between the first and the second melting pots. In the era of the first American melting pot, the immigrants were almost exclusively European. First came the northern Europeans: the English, Irish, Germans, and Scandinavians; then came the eastern and the southern Europeans: the Italians, the Czechs, the Poles, and the Russians. Today, the major sources of immigrants are Asia and Latin America, with strong representations from the Middle East, too.

The largest racial or ethnic group today in this country is the American black population—one in eight Americans. The presence of large numbers of black Americans has always been what Gunnar Myrdal called "the American dilemma." [4]

The prongs of this American dilemma are well known. A legacy of racism and discrimination has left our black population economically and politically disadvantaged. The familiar problems of black Americans tend to obscure the problems of other newly migrant groups, such as the second largest minority group in America—the Hispanic population, composed largely of Puerto Ricans, Cubans, Chicanos (of Mexican descent), and now Haitians. By the year 2000, the Hispanic population should outnumber the black.

All ethnic groups have myths associated with them. For Chicanos, it is the myth of the farm worker. Partly because California activist Caesar Chavez made headlines as an organizer of farm workers, it is easy to see Chicanos as mostly wandering, rural workers. In fact, 95 percent of Chicanos are urbanites. Several American cities, Denver and San Antonio being the largest, have elected mayors of Mexican lineage.

Chicanos would have more clout in politics if they voted more heavily. Only about a third of eligible Hispanic voters are registered to vote. Moreover, Chicanos and other Hispanics vote less because they are younger and less educated, key traits of underparticipation. In fact, when Wolfinger and Rosenstone adjusted for these traits, they discovered that Chicanos were about 3 percent more likely to vote than other Americans. [5]

The steady stream of illegal immigrants across the Rio Grande prompted Congress to consider an immigration reform bill. The Simpson-Mazolli bill, named after its sponsors, would have tightened up immigration requirements for new immigrants, but also permit amnesty for immigrants who had already been in our country. Its most controversial clause (and the one which led to its defeat) would have fined employers for hiring illegal immigrants. Mexican-American leaders successfully argued that this would lead to general discrimination against all Mexican-American workers.

Minority groups historically have been regionally concentrated. Blacks live disproportionately in the South and in big cities, Asians cluster on the west coast and in big cities, Chicanos are concentrated in

The New Immigration. *Before the Constitution was signed, America was called a melting pot. The greatest wave of immigration took place between the end of the Civil War and World War I. Today, though, we experience a "second American melting pot," where immigrants, like these recently arrived from Cuba, pose new challenges to state and local services. These people are waiting in a Miami detention center while their applications for entrance are reviewed.*

[4] Gunnar Myrdal, *The American Dilemma* (New York: Harper and Row, 1948).
[5] Raymond Wolfinger and Steven J. Rosenstone, *Who Votes?* (New Haven: Yale University Press, 1980), p. 92.

Rags and Riches: Native Americans. *Vast stores of coal and other resources lie embedded in some American Indian reservations. Coal is strip-mined on this Navajo reservation on Black Mesa in northern Arizona. For most Native Americans, the story is rags, not riches. They remain the poorest, least educated, and least healthy of any American group.*

the southwest and in big cities such as Chicago. Because many of these groups are literate mainly in their own language, the Supreme Court has insisted that ballots be multilingual in areas where nonEnglish-speaking persons are concentrated.

Among minority groups, by far the worst off are American Indians, whom we now usually call native Americans. Before Europeans arrived in America, twelve to fifteen million American Indians lived here. War and disease reduced their numbers to a mere 210,000 by 1910, and today, about a million descendents of the original Americans are left. Statistically, they are the least healthy, least educated, and poorest group in the American mosaic, as only a handful of Indian groups have found new power and wealth. Public interest lawyers in Maine helped Indians lay claim to vast portions of the state, and the Supreme Court upheld these claims. Our search for new energy sources has helped a few Indian tribes: The Navajo and Hopi reservations in the American southwest contain oil, gas, uranium, and about half of all the coal accessible to strip mining in the country.[6] Sadly, most native Americans remain economically and politically disadvantaged in our technological society.

Our second melting pot, like our first, will shape American politics. Culturally, we will become a more diverse country; as new groups vie for their piece of the political pie, conflicts will ensue. We may even debate the merits of a bilingual nation, as Canadians do. How we ultimately react to the new melting pot will be a function of our beliefs and attitudes.

HOW AND WHAT WE LEARN ABOUT POLITICS: POLITICAL SOCIALIZATION

"Man," said Aristotle, is a "political animal." But people are not born as political animals. Nor do we suddenly develop a whole set of political values and attitudes when we step into a voting booth at the age of

[6] Michael A. Dorris, "The Grass Still Grows, the Rivers Still Flow: Contemporary Native Americans," *Daedalus* 110 (Spring 1981):64.

179

eighteen. Instead, our views of politics and policy are best seen as a result of a process that begins very early. That process, political socialization, molds people into political beings and shapes our political beliefs and behaviors as adults. The sum of the socialization processes of a nation's citizens even shapes its political system and its policies. Americans are made, not born.

Political socialization may be defined as "the process through which an individual acquires his particular political orientations—his knowledge, feelings, and evaluations regarding his political world."[7] Put simply, studying political socialization means understanding *how* and *what* we learn about politics and policy.

How We Learn: The Process of Political Socialization

Some of our political learning is formal. We may take civics or government classes in high school or political science classes in college. In such formal settings, we learn some of the nuts and bolts of government—how many senators each state has, what presidents do, and so on. But formal socialization is to informal socialization what a puddle is to an ocean. Most of what we learn about politics, we learn without anyone's intending to teach it. In fact, there is little evidence that formal learning about politics is very long-lasting. Millions of American teenagers are required to take a high school civics course. But for the vast majority of white teenagers studied, taking civics makes virtually no difference in their political attitudes and beliefs.[8]

Informal learning is really much more important than formal, in-class learning about politics. Most informal socialization is almost accidental. Few parents sit their offspring down and say, "Johnny, let us tell you why we're Democrats." Words like *pick up*, *absorb*, and *acquire* perhaps best describe the informal side of socialization.

The **agents of socialization** are numerous.[9] The strong influence of family gives way to the multiple influences of school, television, and (the nagging worry of every parent) peer group (other children of about the same age).

The Family. Parents worry endlessly about the moral, religious, and sexual values of their offspring; politics is low on the list of parental worries. If their charges reach eighteen without bearing or fathering an unwanted offspring, if they make it through high school, if they avoid trouble with the law, and if they "appreciate the advantages your father and I never had," most parents consider their job well done, and could not

---

[7] Richard Dawson, Kenneth Prewitt, and Karen S. Dawson, *Political Socialization*, 2nd ed. (Boston: Little, Brown, 1977), p. 33.

[8] For black students, civics education is somewhat more significant. See Kenneth P. Langton and M. Kent Jennings, "Political Socialization and the High School Civics Curriculum in the United States," *American Political Science Review* 62 (September 1968):852–67.

[9] One of the most useful and succinct (though by now rather dated) reviews of the socialization process is Robert Lane and David O. Sears, *Public Opinion* (Englewood Cliffs, N.J.: Prentice-Hall, 1964), Chap. 3, "Forming and Weakening the Parental Opinion Tradition." See also Dawson, Prewitt, and Dawson, *Political Socialization*, Chaps. 7–10.

care less that their children are Democrats, Republicans, or Whigs. If "the family universally serves as one of the most important sources of socialization," [10] its role must be more informal than formal, more accidental than deliberate.

The family's role is central because of its monopoly on two crucial values in the early years: time and emotional commitment. The powerful influence of the family is not easily broken.

However, the family's influence can break down, usually due to adolescent rebellion against parents and their beliefs. Witnessing the outpouring of youth rebellion in the 1960s as students hit the barricades, many people thought a *generation gap* was opening up. "Radical" youth supposedly condemned their "reactionary" parents. Though such a gap did exist in a few families, the evidence for it in most is nonexistent. M. Kent Jennings and Richard Niemi were able to compare parents and their high school children in 1965. They reinterviewed those same parents and children eight years later, in 1973. They looked hard to find a gap between generations in party identification (a standing preference for one party) and political attitudes, but none appeared. Children and parents were not far apart originally. When they changed, their views moved in the same direction over the eight years. "The flow of the two generations over time," Jennings and Niemi concluded, "has, if anything, worked to bring them closer together." [11] This is another way of saying that the forces that change the opinions of one generation also work to change the opinions of the next.

Government and Its Schools. Political socialization is as important to a government as it is to an individual. Few political systems leave the rearing of society's next generation to chance. Learning positive things about the political system helps ensure that youth will grow up to be

[10] Dawson, Prewitt, and Dawson, *Political Socialization,* p. 114.

[11] M. Kent Jennings and Richard Niemi, "Continuity and Change in Political Orientations: A Longitudinal Study of Two Generations," *American Political Science Review* 69 (December 1975):1316–35.

Political Socialization. *Young Americans often have strong views about the parties, the presidency, and political issues. Those views often mirror the views of their parents, but parental influence is gradually weakened as young people encounter other influences at school and through peer groups and the mass media.*

supportive citizens rather than revolutionaries. David Easton and Jack Dennis have argued that "those children who begin to develop positive feelings toward the political authorities will grow into adults who will be less easily disenchanted with the system than those children who early acquire negative, hostile sentiments."[12] This is not always the case, of course. Well-fed, presumably well-socialized youths of the 1960s were in the vanguard of the opposition to the American regime and its policies. Governments care very much about political socialization—they cannot afford not to.

Authoritarian governments have often resorted to paramilitary youth organizations to instill acceptable beliefs and behaviors. The Hitler Youth in Germany and the Young Communist League in the Soviet Union are examples. Americans do not leave socialization to the private sector, either. Educational policy consumes over $170 billion annually. In this country, most schools are public schools, financed by the government, their textbooks are chosen by the local and state boards, and teachers are certified by the state government.

The schools have come a long way since Sir William Berkeley, a colonial governor of Virginia, said, "Thank God there are no free schools or printing; for learning has brought disobedience and heresy into the world, and printing has divulged them. God keep us from both." Schooling is the most obvious intrusion of the government into our socialization. The differences between the well educated and the less educated are enormous. Better-educated men and women:

— Vote and participate more often in politics.
— Show more knowledge about politics and policy.
— Are more tolerant of different (even radical) opinions.
— Are more supportive both of equal opportunity and of serious policy attention to energy and environmental issues.

School counts. It pays off not only in better jobs, but also in citizens more closely approximating the democratic model. A formal civics course may not make much difference,[13] but the whole context of education makes a big difference in attitudes and behavior.

Technology, TV, and Political Socialization. Grade school youngsters spend an average of twenty-seven hours a week watching television, more than they spend in school.[14] Contrary to popular impression, heavy TV watching by children does not seem to reduce, but rather increases, knowledge about politics and government. More and more television displaces parents as the chief source of information as children get older. Doris Graber, an authority on the impact of the media, calls the mass media, "the new parents."[15]

Television Socialization. *We learn about politics and political values more by absorption than through purposeful teaching. Children learn a great deal as they watch many hours of television each week. Their attitudes toward gender, the parties, authority, and perhaps even toward guns are shaped in the socialization process.*

[12] David Easton and Jack Dennis, *Children in the Political System* (New York: McGraw-Hill, 1969), pp. 106–107.

[13] Langton and Jennings, "Political Socialization and High School Civics."

[14] Doris Graber, *Mass Media and American Politics* (Washington: Congressional Quarterly Press, 1980), p. 120.

[15] Ibid., p. 121.

What We Learn: The Content of Political Socialization

Sociologist Talcott Parsons once remarked that the birth of new generations is like recurring barbarian invasions. He did not mean that children are naturally cruel and aggressive, but that they are untrained and uncivilized in our values and culture. The task of political socialization is, therefore, to turn "barbarians" into "citizens." What we learn makes us citizens. It also creates values and attitudes likely to be with us for a lifetime. Among the most important are attitudes toward authority, toward political leaders and elites, toward the parties, and toward public policies.

Socialization toward Authority. Parents, police officers, teachers, and presidents are all authority figures. How we relate to these authorities helps to mold our views toward political authority in general. Hostile, suspicious, and critical attitudes beget hostile, suspicious, critical citizens. Unquestioning respect for authority breeds passive citizens.

It is clear that American children accept authority but are not overawed by it. Fred Greenstein asked American, British, and French children what would happen if a police officer happened to stop a speeding car only to discover that the American president, British queen, or French president was driving.[16] The children were supposed to finish the scenario. Of the English children, 42 percent said the Queen would get away with it. A majority of French children (56 percent) thought that their president would get away with speeding. One French child simply observed, "The president, believing that everything is allowed because he governs France, will say that he is in a hurry." The American children were a little tougher on their errant president, less likely to think him above the law. Though 39 percent of white and 44 percent of black children thought he would get away with it, more American than French or English children thought their leader would be penalized as any other citizen. American children seem more likely to see the law applying equally to all, even people in high places.

Socialization toward Political Leaders and Elites. The first symbol of political life for American children is the president.[17] Many white middle-class children have impressions of the president that are almost too good to be believed. Greenstein reported that white middle-class children in New Haven in 1958 were almost unanimous in singing the praises of the president.[18] Elementary schoolchildren in Greenstein's study reported that the president "gives us freedom," "takes care of the U.S.," "makes peace," and even "builds parks and swings."

[16] Fred I. Greenstein, "The Benevolent Leader Revisited: Children's Images of Political Leaders in Three Democracies," *American Political Science Review* 59 (December 1975): 1371–98.
[17] Easton and Dennis, *Children in the Political System*, p. 391.
[18] Fred I. Greenstein, "The Benevolent Leader: Children's Images of Political Authority," *American Political Science Review* 54 (December 1960):934–43. See also his *Children and Politics* (New Haven: Yale University Press, 1965).

These are supporting sentiments indeed. Notice, though, that these attitudes are based on children studied in a particular place and time—New Haven in 1958, under the administration of grandfatherly, well-regarded Dwight D. Eisenhower. Some of this very same generation of children were, a decade later, carrying posters attacking President Lyndon B. Johnson and his Vietnam War policies ("Hey, hey, LBJ, how many kids did you kill today?"). How did the almost naive admiration of political leaders, especially the president, dissolve into placard-carrying denunciations during the Vietnam War years?

Lots of aspects about America seemed to come unhinged during the turbulent 1960s and the troubled 1970s. Civil rights demonstrations, urban racial disorders, and the Vietnam War all stripped bare some naive American optimism. Children were not immune to these changes. Television brought the Vietnam War into their line of vision.

The ugly events of Watergate (summarized on page 408) drove yet another nail into the coffin of political Pollyannas. Watergate news and the agonizing resignation of a president intruded into prime-time cop and comedy shows. Children were remarkably well informed about Watergate and its meaning for Richard Nixon. And Watergate helped to change children's naively benevolent images of presidents to much more human and fallible images.[19] Like most adult Americans, children today are more cynical about politics and politicians than they were in the 1950s.

Moreover, we should not confuse the beliefs of a white middle-class group of children sitting in a schoolroom in New Haven with the views of all children, or the views of Vietnam War protesters with those of all American youth. Jaros, Hirsch, and Fleron studied very poor children in Knox County, Kentucky, one of the nation's poorest counties.[20] Their images of the president were not very glowing. A plurality thought the president worked less hard than other men. They saw him as no better than other people. These views are shared widely by black youngsters, whose images, while not always negative, do not exhibit the "Goody Two-Shoes" image suggested by studies of white, middle-class children.[21] What seems to have happened in recent years is that white, middle-class impressions have come closer to those long exhibited by poorer and nonwhite children. No longer is the president thought to be above the law, better than anyone else, or incapable of doing wrong.

Socialization toward Parties. Even the least politically informed Americans know about the Democratic and Republican parties. So do children, even as early as the first or second grade.[22] Youngsters barely able to add double-digit numbers are perfectly prepared to announce,

[19] F. Christopher Arterton, "Watergate and Children's Attitudes toward the President Revisited," *Political Science Quarterly* 90 (Fall 1975):477–96.

[20] Dean Jaros, Herbert Hirsch, and Fredric Fleron, Jr., "The Malevolent Leader: Political Socialization in an American Subculture," *American Political Science Review* 62 (June 1968):566–75.

[21] Edward S. Greenberg, "Orientations of Black and White Children to Political Authority Figures," *Social Science Quarterly* 31 (December 1970):561–71.

[22] David Easton and Robert D. Hess, "The Child's Political World," *Midwest Journal of Political Science* 6 (August 1962):245.

"All I know is that we're not Republicans." [23] It requires little imagination to figure out that children's party identification coincides with that of their parents. Mom or Dad probably do not sit Mary or Johnny down and lecture on the evils of the Democratic and the virtues of the Republican party, or vice versa—political learning is less formal than that.

Children learn the most from informal socialization. Specifics not consciously taught may still be learned, and one of those is party identification. But things learned and felt strongly at the age of eight may be forgotten by eighteen. Rather remarkably, children are more strongly partisan in grade school than they seem to be when they enter the electorate a decade later. Perfectly convinced of their Democratic or Republican leanings as children in 1962, a majority of eighteen-year-olds who entered the electorate in 1972 declared themselves not Democrats or Republicans, but "Independents." [24] Perhaps ideas change over the adolescent years. We may intend to be police officers at some point, but most of us abandon the idea eventually.

Children of the 1960s and 1970s, of course, lived through an era when party ties weakened (see our discussion, "Is the Party Over?" in Chapter 7). Americans—especially young adults of parenting age—have become more independent recently. If parents pass along their party identification (when they have one), it stands to reason that they will also pass along their independence. The current cohort of schoolchildren may be even more independent in a decade, when they first pull a voting lever.

The Never-Ending Process of Socialization

Socialization does not abruptly stop when we reach political adulthood. There is nothing magical about the eighteenth year; it is merely an arbitrary, constitutional line separating voters from nonvoters. Instead of seeing political socialization as ending when we cast our first ballot, we should think of it as a never-ending process. Shakespeare's eloquent passage beginning "All the world's a stage" captures this message well. From infancy through retirement, we are changing politically. The lessons we learn at home and at school stick with us, but they are not unchangeable. Adult public opinion is the natural byproduct of childhood socialization. And public opinion is fluid, not fixed.

WHAT WE BELIEVE: PUBLIC OPINION AND POLICY

The public holds opinions about lots of things. Premarital sex, the reality of flying saucers, the virtues of jogging, and the lengths of women's skirts are all subjects about which people can hold opinions—sometimes very strong ones. Here we are interested in a particular kind of **public**

[23] Greenstein, *Children and Politics*, p. 71.
[24] Norman H. Nie, Sidney Verba, and John R. Petrocik, *The Changing American Voter* (Cambridge, Mass.: Harvard University Press, 1976), pp. 64–65.

opinion: the distribution of the population's beliefs about politics and policy issues. Saying that opinions are distributed among the population implies that there is rarely a single public opinion. If everyone were of one mind about some question, it would not be much of an issue. Policy issues arise when some people favor and other people oppose government job guarantees, a policy to close down polluting factories, the ERA, or other issues.

The Technology of Opinion Measurement

Understanding the content and dynamics of public opinion is, of course, important to political scientists, and even more important to politicians. Today, very sophisticated technology is available for measuring public opinion.

The first American century seemed to get along fine without public opinion polls. Indeed, it is hard to imagine Abraham Lincoln commissioning a poll to find out where the public stood on slavery and secession, or whether the Gettysburg Address increased his popularity. No George Gallup, Lou Harris, or Pat Caddell told Woodrow Wilson that his League of Nations was unpopular with the voters. No poll told Herbert Hoover that his policies during the Great Depression would result in a political calamity.

A young man named George Gallup perfected the public opinion poll, just as Herman Hollerith had perfected the Hollerith Machine. Gallup did some sampling for his mother-in-law, who was running for secretary of state in Iowa in 1932. From that little acorn, the mighty oak of public opinion polling has grown.

Let us see how public opinion polling works. Naturally it would be absurd (and expensive) to ask every citizen his or her opinion on an issue or a candidate. Instead, polls rely on a *sample* of the population. About 1500 to 2000 people can faithfully represent the "universe" of potential voters from which the sample is drawn. If the sample is accurately drawn, about 88 percent of the people polled will be white, about 50 percent will be women, and so forth, matching the population as a whole. All surveys have a *sampling error*. Because the population is randomly sampled, the poll is actually an estimate of what the population thinks. These estimates always contain a margin of error, the sampling error. For example, with 1500 *respondents*, the sampling error is normally about 3 percent.

An unrepresentative sample can produce a huge sampling error. In one of the most famous surveying errors—it cost a popular magazine its life—the *Literary Digest* predicted in 1936 that Republican Alf Landon would crush Democratic candidate Franklin Roosevelt. The number of people surveyed was staggering: 2,376,000! Unfortunately the poll had surveyed people from lists of telephone and car owners—an unrepresentative group in the midst of a depression. The moral: Accurate representation, not size, is the most important feature of a public opinion survey.

The newest technology will make surveying even less expensive and more commonplace. Typically, our image of a public opinion survey includes a well dressed middle-aged woman (sometimes men are pollsters, too) traipsing from door to door with a clipboard full of questions.

"*That's the worst set of opinions I've heard in my entire life.*"

Drawing by Weber; © 1975 The New Yorker Magazine, Inc.

In reality, most polling is now done with *random digit dialing*, or RDD. Calls are placed randomly to phones within a particular area code or neighborhood. Polling by RDD amounts to about a fifth of the cost of person-to-person interviewing, so that even candidates for minor offices can answer the question "to poll or not to poll" in the affirmative.

For good or ill, polling is here to stay. Polls help political candidates to distinguish which way people lean. Supporters of polling insist that it is a tool for democracy. With it, they say, public policymakers can be appraised of the majority preference on an issue. On the other hand, critics of polling think it makes politicians reactors, not leaders.

Dimensions of Public Opinion

The rhetoric of politicians is riddled with references to "public opinion demands that we . . . ," "public opinion is behind us on this issue . . . ," and the like. Yet, clearly there is no *one* public with *one* unanimous opinion. The late V. O. Key, Jr., once remarked that "To speak with precision about public opinion is a task not unlike coming to grips with the Holy Ghost." [25]

Public opinion is subtle and complex. To understand its meaning, we can distinguish three distributions of it: **Consensus** means agreement, that is, an opinion distribution in which a large majority sees eye to eye.

[25] V. O. Key, Jr., *Public Opinion and American Democracy* (New York: Knopf, 1963), p. 8.

Conflict characterizes issues on which opinion is sharply divided. **Change** refers to the degree that opinion is shifting or stable over time.

For a concrete example, let us look at several issues in the policy arena of equality. Overwhelming majorities of Americans exhibit consensus on great principles such as "all men are created equal." Herbert McClosky found that more than nine in ten Americans agree that "no matter what a person's political beliefs are, he [or she] is entitled to the same legal rights and protections as anyone else." [26]

Consensus on broad principles is easy; in practice, consensus often melts into conflict on specific applications. These days, there is a clear consensus that blacks and whites, for example, should have equal educational opportunity. In practice, people are sharply divided about one policy designed to achieve equal educational opportunity: mandatory busing for racial balance in the schools. Similarly, most Americans favor equal opportunity for minority groups and women in the workplace, but conflict displaces consensus when "affirmative action" is proposed as a remedy for past discrimination. ③

Technology and Public Opinion

The Bias of Information in the Technotronic Age. We live in a technotronic age, where electronic media surround us. "Television," says William Crotty, "is the new political god. It has supplanted the political party as the main conduit between candidate and voter." [27] Kevin Phillips has observed that ancient Sparta was a military state, nineteenth-century England was the world's first industrial state, and the "contemporary United States is the world's first media state." Phillips emphasizes that 30 to 40 percent of the U.S. gross national product is accounted for by the production and distribution of knowledge. [28] Among the chief purveyors of this knowledge are our television, newspaper, and magazine industries.

Elite and class theorists frequently point to substantial inequalities in American society: in income, wealth, and educational opportunities. An equally important gap between the classes and the masses is an ***information gap.*** Doris Graber stresses that "differences in media use patterns are particularly pronounced between income levels." [29] The poor and minority groups rely more heavily on television for information. The rich scan and absorb information from a variety of sources. About 57 percent of upper socioeconomic groups get information from multiple sources, as opposed to only a quarter of the poor. Thus, "the well-to-do have potentially much more information and a greater variety of information available to them. This helps them to maintain and increase their influence in American society." [30] Blacks and Hispanics are particularly likely to be

[26] Herbert McClosky, "Consensus and Ideology in American Politics," *American Political Science Review* 58 (June 1964): Table II.

[27] William Crotty, *American Parties in Decline* (Boston: Little, Brown, 2nd ed., 1984), p. 75.

[28] Kevin Phillips, "Power and the Knowledge Industry," in Dan Nimmo and William L. Rivers (eds.), *Watching American Politics* (New York: Longman, 1981), p. 194.

[29] Graber, *Mass Media and American Politics*, p. 128.

[30] Ibid., p. 129.

3 | Public Opinion on "Reverse Discrimination" to Compensate for Past Inequalities

Question: Some people say that to make up for past discrimination, women and members of minority groups should be given preferential treatment in getting jobs and places in college. Others say that ability should be the main consideration. Which point comes closest to how you feel on this matter?

	Give Preference	Ability Main Consideration	No Opinion
National	10%	83%	7%
By Sex			
Male	9	85	6
Female	11	82	7
By Race			
White	7	87	6
Nonwhite	29	57	14

Source: Gallup Report No. 185, February 1981.

"information poor" in a society where information is becoming as valuable as hard currency.

Influencing Public Opinion: Easy to Assume, Hard to Prove. Common sense suggests that long exposure to anything is likely to influence opinion. The average American spends twenty-eight hours and twenty-two minutes weekly glued to "the tube." (Contrary to popular opinion, teenagers are the least frequent TV viewers.) Thus Americans spend more time watching television than in any other single activity besides sleeping and working! On the average night, 100 million Americans—more than half the adult population—will be watching television.

Because of its pervasiveness, it is easy to *overestimate* the effects of the technotronic media on opinion change. For one thing, the vast majority of what people watch on television and read about in the papers is essentially nonpolitical. "Sitcoms," the NFL, *Hill Street Blues*, and *Star Search* are not exactly high political drama. Even watching television news produces only about as much information as a single newspaper page.

In the early days of research on media impact, it was assumed that there would be direct, visible impacts of the media on public opinion, but efforts to prove such direct effects usually failed. Most media effects are subtle; the most obvious is on "agenda setting." People pay attention to what the media pays attention to; what the media says is important, we assume is important. Because the media sets our priorities, we tend to adopt its world view of political issues. [31]

[31] The classic book on the media as agenda-setter is by Donald L. Shaw and Maxwell E. McCombs, *The Emergence of American Political Issues: The Agenda Setting Function of the Press* (St. Paul, Minn.: West Publishing Co., 1977). See also Lutz Erbring, Edie Goldenberg, and Arthur Miller, "Front-Page News and Real-World Cues: Another Look at Agenda Setting by the Media," *American Journal of Political Science* 24 (February 1980):16–49.

Joseph Wagner drew some conclusions about the effect of television, on the basis of a careful study of the media and public opinion. People who received most of their political information from TV during a campaign tended to see few differences between the candidates. Regular newspaper readers, though, are better able to see where the candidates stand on the issues. His conclusions are important:

> The direct behavioral impact of television's apparent muting of the political differences is a decline in voting turnout. . . . [T]elevision may have contributed to a general degradation of political culture in America. . . . It is then plausible that despite higher levels of education, the general decline in voting turnout since 1960 may in part be a function of the increased use of television. [32]

Sometimes the media are accused of being "purveyors of cynicism" about politics. It is, of course, easier for the stalwart reporter to dig up a scandal in Congressman Jones's past than to explain to readers how a $200 billion federal deficit affects their well-being. The former is fun and titillating; the latter is plain hard work. The media may have an impact on our cynicism about government and its officials. Miller, Goldenberg, and Erbring showed that people who regularly read newspapers with stinging criticisms of government responded by becoming more cynical about government. [33]

We live, some think, in a era of information glut. Yet for some, particularly those at the bottom of the socioeconomic order, an information gap exists. With our immense media system, one would think that Americans would be extremely well informed about politics and government. But are they?

How Informed Is American Public Opinion?

Two Views. Abraham Lincoln spoke stirring words about the inherent wisdom of the American public: "you can fool all of the people some of the time, some of the people all of the time, but you can't fool all of the people all of the time." Elitists, who have little faith in the wisdom of ordinary citizens, fear that Lincoln was wrong. Perhaps you can fool all of the people all of the time.

Two founding fathers, Thomas Jefferson and Alexander Hamilton, had very different views about the wisdom of plain people. Jefferson trusted people's good sense and believed that education would enable them to take their citizenship even more seriously. Toward that end, he founded the University of Virginia.

Hamilton held a contrasting view. His immortal words, "Your people, sir, are a great beast," do not exactly stir confidence in people's capacity for self-government. TV producer Norman Lear's ignorant and bigoted

---

[32] Joseph Wagner, "Media Do Make a Difference: The Differential Impact of Mass Media in the 1976 Presidential Race," *American Journal of Political Science*, 27 (August 1983):427.

[33] Arthur Miller, Edie Goldenberg, and Lutz Erbring, "Type Set Politics: The Impact of Newspapers on Public Confidence," *American Political Science Review*, 73 (March 1979):67–84.

Archie Bunker is a modern-day incarnation of Hamilton's view of the common folk and their political "wisdom."

Information and Ideology. Just before the 1976 bicentennial year, the Gallup Poll surveyed Americans on the subject of what they were celebrating. Fully three in ten Americans did not know why 1776 was an eventful year. Earlier, Gallup had asked people to identify a set of famous people. Though 92 percent knew who Columbus was, less than half could identify Marx, Aristotle, or Freud. [34]

No amount of Jeffersonian faith in the common people will erase the fact that Americans are not very well informed politically. Barely half will know the name of their member of Congress, much less how the elected official voted on key issues. Asking most people to explain the issues surrounding affirmative action, deregulation, or the MX missile would gain you mostly silence.

A coherent set of beliefs about politics and public policy is a **political ideology.** [35] (This stands in sharp contrast to views that are merely "gut reactions.") A *liberal*, for example, favors policies that "hang together": belief in a strong central government, support for policies to promote equality, and so on. A *conservative* also has closely related views: support of a smaller, less activist government, greater reliance on the private sector, and so on.

The authors of the classic study *The American Voter* first looked carefully at the ideological sophistication of the American electorate in the 1950s. [36] They divided the public into four groups according to their ideological sophistication. Their portrait of the American public was not a flattering one. Only 11.5 percent of the people were "ideologues or near-ideologues." These folks could connect politics with broad policy positions. They might know, for example, that the Republicans were the conservative and Democrats the liberal party. A plurality of Americans were called "group benefits voters." This 42 percent of the population thought of politics mainly by the groups they liked or did not like (for example, "Republicans support the farmers, and I'm a farmer"). About a quarter of the population were "nature of the times" voters. Their handle on politics was limited to whether the times seemed good or bad to them; they might vaguely link the party in power with their own good fortune or misfortune. About 18 percent of the voters were devoid of any ideological or issue content in their reactions to politics. They were the "no issue content" group. Overall, at least during the 1950s, Americans seemed to see politics through a muddy glass, if at all.

There has been much debate about whether this portrayal accurately characterizes our public today. Nie, Verba, and Petrocik took a look at the changing American voter from 1955 to 1972. [37] They argued that voters were more sophisticated in the 1970s than in the 1950s. Others have

One Image of the Average American: Archie Bunker. *Thomas Jefferson had a positive image of the innate wisdom of common citizens. Alexander Hamilton, elitist to the core, believed that the people were "a great beast." Television's Archie Bunker—bigoted, opinionated, and thoroughly ill-informed—would provide ample ammunition for Hamilton's view of the capacity of ordinary people to govern themselves. Clearly, Americans are not well-informed about many policy issues. Supporters of democratic government, though, believe that the average American's good sense is sufficient to permit him or her to make reasoned judgments about policymakers and specific policy courses.*

[34] Hazel G. Erskine, "The Polls: Textbook Knowledge," *Public Opinion Quarterly* 27 (1963):133–41.

[35] For a more extended definition, see Robert E. Lane, *Political Ideology* (New York: Free Press, 1962), pp. 13–16.

[36] Angus Campbell et al., *The American Voter* (New York: John Wiley, 1960), Chap. 10.

[37] Ibid., Chap. 7.

concluded that people seemed more informed and ideological merely because the wording of questions had changed. [38]

Political scientists are not of one mind about the ideological sophistication of the American public. Thus, it is hard for us to go far out on any limb. We may not be any more sophisticated in our political thinking today than a generation ago. Elite and class theorists would emphasize that information is a political resource (like money and power) and that it is more available to the upper classes than lower classes. Clearly, the level of knowledge possessed by the average American—knowledge often blurred by television—would not hearten Thomas Jefferson.

Ideology versus Self-Interest. Perhaps the beliefs of individuals regarding broad political issues do not matter much. Perhaps people respond to politics mostly on the basis of their own self-interest. Surely, it is one thing to support helping the poor if you are one of them, another if you are well off. It is one thing to support government aid to the unemployed because you are a liberal and believe in an active government; it is something else again if you support unemployment aid just after you lose your job.

Often, we think that self-interest motivates our public opinions. Being a crime victim may harden our views about "getting tough on criminals." Living in a school district with racial busing may lead us to oppose mandatory busing. Being unemployed means that we are more likely than not to think the president is doing a poor job of managing the economy. And so on. Most economic models of politics assume that voters are rational, that is, that they vote their self-interest.

Psychologist David Sears and his colleagues have challenged this widely held view that self-interest is the wellspring of political attitudes and behavior. [39] They compared the effects of self-interest with symbolic factors—party identification and political ideology in particular—on voting choice. One would assume that being unemployed, for instance, would cause a powerful political reaction, which would overcome factors of party loyalty or political ideology; but Sears and his colleagues found that people were *more likely* to vote on the basis of their beliefs and their ideologies than on the basis of their self-interest. The same story repeated itself in regard to other self-interest situations: being a crime victim and living in a district with mandatory racial busing, for example. According to this study, ideology matters in shaping political behaviors and can even overcome the powerful bond of self-interest. [40]

[38] See, for example, Christopher H. Achen, "Mass Attitudes and the Survey Response," *American Political Science Review,* 69 (December 1975):1218–31; John L. Sullivan, James E. Pierson, and George E. Marcus, "Ideological Constraint in the Mass Public: A Methodological Critique and Some New Findings," *American Journal of Political Science* 22 (May 1978):233–49.

[39] See, for example, David O. Sears, et al., "Self-Interest vs. Symbolic Politics in Policy Attitudes and Voting," *American Political Science Review* 74 (September 1980):670–84; David O. Sears and Richard R. Lau, "Inducing Apparently Self-Interested Political Preferences," *American Journal of Political Science* 27 (May 1983):223–252.

[40] For a very sophisticated extension of the Sears argument, see M. Stephen Weatherford, "Economic Voting and the 'Symbolic Politics' Argument: A Reinterpretation and Synthesis," *American Political Science Review* 77 (March 1983):158–174.

POLITICAL PARTICIPATION: ACTING ON OUR OPINIONS

What Political Participation Means

Consider some examples of political participation:

— A lobbyist for an influential group sits down for a two-martini lunch with a prominent senator to discuss a bill coming up for a vote.
— Voters in a tiny New England town stay up until after midnight on election eve so that they can be the first to cast their ballots in the presidential election.
— Protesters gather outside an abortion clinic to protest the "killing" which they believe goes on inside.
— Kathy Ebert, an officer of the Minnesota Jaycees, files a suit in federal court, claiming that the state's antidiscrimination law forbids the national organization from dropping her chapter's charter because it admitted women.
— Opponents of apartheid in South Africa demonstrate in front of the South African embassy in Washington, resulting in arrests of prominent members of Congress and other Americans.

All of these activities and many more are examples of political participation, the activities used by citizens to influence the selection of political leaders or the policies they pursue.[41] Too often, we think that the only way to participate in politics is voting, but there are many forms of participation, some peaceful and some not. Most are ordinary and undramatic: Your neighbor canvasses the block for "Joe Smith for Senator"; or you make a small contribution to the party or candidate of your choice. Other means of political participation are dramatic and unconventional. Saul Alinsky was a professional organizer who specialized in out-of-the-ordinary protests—to say the least. He once had a Chicago group concerned about rats in their homes carry loads of dead rodents to the mayor's home. Participation can also be violent; draft riots during the Civil War and urban riots in black communities in the 1960s are examples.

Participation: Conventional and Unconventional

Although the line is hard to draw, we can distinguish between two broad types of participation: conventional and unconventional. Under conventional participation occurs those widely accepted modes of influencing government: voting, trying to persuade others, doorbell ringing, running for office, and so on. Under unconventional participation occurs some activities that are dramatic or, to some at least, suspect. They include protesting, civil disobedience, even violence.

For a few, politics is their lifeblood; they run for office, work regularly in politics, and live for the next election. For others it is mere drudgery,

---

[41] This definition is a close paraphrase of one in Sidney Verba and Norman Nie, *Participation in America: Political Democracy and Social Equality* (New York: Harper and Row, 1972), p. 2.

and for still others, a civic obligation. The number of Americans for whom political activity is almost as important as food, drink, and sex is miniscule, numbering, at most, in the tens of thousands. They are the elites, the gladiators of political conflict: the activists, the party leaders, the "presidential timber, the group leaders, the judges and members of Congress. We will have plenty to say about them later. For now, let us concentrate on the masses."

Verba and Nie asked a sample of Americans about their participation in twelve kinds of political activities. Included were voting in presidential and local elections, contacting a government official, working in a campaign, and joining political groups, among others. The majority of Americans participated in only one of those twelve activities. That, not surprisingly, was voting in presidential elections. (Yet only 54 percent of the voting age population voted in the 1984 elections.) Less than a fifth had ever contacted a public official, given money to a candidate or party, or helped form a political group or organization. [42] Six of the twelve activities attracted less than 20 percent of the citizens.

Participation in politics, like other tasks, reflects specialization and division of labor. Just as people in an organization have different specialties, so do citizens in a country. Voting is a common denominator among most political activists, but other kinds of participation attract different clusters of people. In Verba and Nie's classification of American participants in politics, 22 percent are inactive; 11 percent are complete activists. In between are people who are specialized as contacters, communalists, or campaigners. (For a discussion of these types, see 4 .)

Protest as Participation

One form of participation missing from Verba and Nie's list of activities, though, is participation in unconventional activities. From the Boston Tea Party to our own day, Americans have engaged in countless political protests. **Protest** is a form of political participation designed to achieve policy change through dramatic and unconventional tactics. [43] The media's willingness to cover the unusual makes protest worthwhile. Giving a demonstration and having nobody come to cover it is a strategic mistake.

Throughout American history, individuals and groups have sometimes used **civil disobedience.** This means they have made a conscious decision to break a law they thought immoral and suffer the consequences. In the 1840s, Henry David Thoreau refused to pay his taxes in support of the Mexican War and went to jail (he stayed only overnight, because his friend Ralph Waldo Emerson paid the taxes). Influenced by India's Mahatma Gandhi, the Reverend Martin Luther King, Jr., won a Nobel Peace Prize for his civil disobedience of segregationist laws in the 1950s and 1960s. His "Letter from a Birmingham Jail" is a modern-day defense of civil disobedience.

[42] Ibid., p. 31.
[43] See the more extended definition in Michael Lipsky, *Protest in City Politics* (Chicago: Rand McNally, 1970), p. 2.

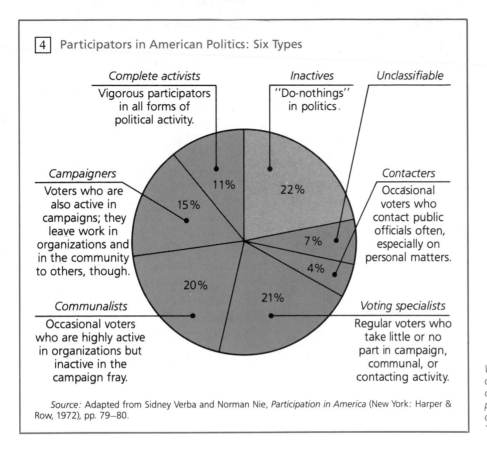

4 Participators in American Politics: Six Types

Complete activists
Vigorous participators in all forms of political activity.

Inactives
"Do-nothings" in politics.

Unclassifiable

Campaigners
Voters who are also active in campaigns; they leave work in organizations and in the community to others, though.

Contacters
Occasional voters who contact public officials often, especially on personal matters.

Communalists
Occasional voters who are highly active in organizations but inactive in the campaign fray.

Voting specialists
Regular voters who take little or no part in campaign, communal, or contacting activity.

11% 22% 15% 7% 4% 20% 21%

Source: Adapted from Sidney Verba and Norman Nie, *Participation in America* (New York: Harper & Row, 1972), pp. 79–80.

When Verba and Nie studied a sample of Americans, they found it useful to classify them into six basic types of political participants. (Their category of "parochial participants" is called "contacters" here.)

Sometimes political participation can be violent. The history of violence in American politics is a long one—not surprisingly, perhaps, for a nation born in revolution. One recent peak occurred in the turbulent 1960s when black areas of American cities erupted in violence.[44] College campuses were sometimes turned into virtual armed camps as protestors against the Vietnam war battled police and national guard units. At Kent State, Cornell, Columbia, and elsewhere, peaceful demonstrations turned ugly. Americans would do well never to forget that violence, however deplorable, is also a means of pressuring government to change its policies.

Class, Inequality, and Participation

In Chapter 2 we explored four theories of American politics: democratic theory, elite and class theory, pluralism, and hyperpluralism. Views about participation are entwined in all of them.

Those who believe that ours is a uniquely democratic country should be chagrined to discover that *participation is very unequal in American political life*. Virtually every study of political participation ever conducted comes to a similar conclusion: "Citizens of higher social and

[44] On the violence of the 1960s, see James Button, *Black Violence* (Princeton, N.J.: Princeton University Press, 1978).

economic status participate more in politics. This generalization . . . holds true whether one uses level of education, income, or occupation as the measure of social status."[45] Not surprisingly, elite theorists make much of the fact that the poor and undereducated play a scanty role in politics.

People who believe in democracy should not only be concerned about inequalities in participation, but also about our low levels of it. Voting turnout in the United States is lower than in almost any other industrialized nation. Those who participate are easy to listen to; nonparticipants are easy to ignore. In a democracy, citizenship carries the promise of self-government. At least one political scientist thinks that we could do a lot more to govern ourselves than we actually do. ⑤

Whatever Barber's hopes for a renewal of self-government, participation is still very unequal from one group to another. Many of the differences in conventional participation are explained by groups' different educational levels. On the average, blacks and Chicanos have low incomes and less education. Therefore, we might assume that they are always low participators in American politics; this is not the case. *If we compare blacks and Chicanos with whites of equal incomes and educations*, a higher percentage of blacks and Chicanos participate more, not less, in politics.[46] Compare, in other words, a black and white male, or a Chicano and Anglo female, with equal incomes and educational levels, and minority groups outparticipate the majority group.

[45] Verba and Nie, *Participation in America*, p. 125.
[46] On blacks, see Verba and Nie, *Participation in America*, Chap. 10; on Chicanos, see Wolfinger and Rosenstone, *Who Votes*, p. 92.

---

⑤ **Voting is Not Enough: One Political Scientist's Proposal for Strengthening American Democracy through Technology**

Many political scientists and other observers of American democracy are gravely concerned about its future. One is Benjamin R. Barber of Rutgers University. Voting, he says, is not enough to make democracy work. Americans have allowed large institutions to rob them of their real power as citizens. At best, Americans vote (and not all of them do even that). "As a consequence," he says, "we have become accustomed to attributing our problems to the defects of leaders. . . . Asking much of our leaders, we can afford to ask nothing of ourselves." But in a strong democracy, people are supposed to govern themselves, not merely pull a lever on a voting machine.

Barber has put forward a bold, ten-point program to strengthen true democracy. It would be built upon a set of local assemblies, each with 1000 to 5000 citizen-members. Through technology these assemblies should have ready access to information. More than a third of American homes are now wired for cable television and half will be by the end of the decade. Cable television could be used for electronic town meetings. (In 1982, two American communities, Los Angeles and Honolulu, experimented with electronic town meetings, with good results.) A "civic videotex service" should provide information on the civic agenda, everything from job retraining information to referendum issues.

Barber would encourage selective experiments with electronic balloting. There could be local or national referenda on issues like abortion or defense spending, which could be binding or nonbinding.

Barber's is a bold proposal indeed. It could take advantage of America's technotronic age to strengthen its oldest ideal: that citizens can actually govern themselves.

Source: For a brief sketch of the Barber proposal, see his article "Voting is Not Enough," *The Atlantic Monthly* (June 1984): 45–52. For an extended view, see his forthcoming book, *Strong Democracy* (Berkeley: University of California Press).

Political Participation Takes Many Forms. *Voting is the most obvious way in which ordinary people participate in politics, but it is not the only way. Political scientists sometimes divide participation into two types: conventional and unconventional. The former includes voting, collecting money for campaigns, and running for office. The latter includes protests, demonstrations (which can be peaceful, like the one against South African apartheid, left), and other unusual or dramatic forms of participation. Those exercising civil disobedience (like the nuclear waste protest, middle) accept the legitimacy of the law, even by disobeying the law and facing arrest.*

PEOPLE IN POLITICS SUMMARIZED

It is not easy to summarize 233.9 million Americans. No "typical" American stands out to exemplify all of us. In this chapter, we explored these 233.9 million Americans in politics by looking at who we are, how we learn about politics, what we believe, and how we act on these beliefs. Specifically, we covered

— *Political demography. Who we are* is determined partly by political demography. Some of the major traits of we Americans are our age (we're getting older), our race (about 12 percent of us are black), and our residence (more of us live in the suburbs and the Sunbelt). All these traits affect our opinions and, of course, our policy preferences.

— *Political socialization. How* and *what we learn* about politics is political socialization. Children become political animals through a

197

complex process, and what they learn affects their political lives. Most socialization occurs informally, especially in the family. Governments also try to influence children. In America, the schools are the government's main socialization tool. Since the 1950s, America's children have become less impressed by the president and less tied to any political party.

— *Public opinion. What we think* about politics and public policy is public opinion. Opinions are characterized by consensus, conflict, and change. American public opinion is not always as informed or as ideologically sophisticated as some people would like, but there is evidence that Americans are more informed and ideological today than they were a few years ago.

— *Political participation. How we act on our opinions* is political participation, which can take many forms. The most common way of participating is voting in presidential elections. But only about 54 percent of Americans over eighteen voted in 1984, and more than a fifth *never* participate in American politics in any way. There are very real inequalities in the level of political participation. Many are associated with race, sex, and social class. Those who are white, male, and well off are most likely to make their political opinions known.

Key Terms

demography	public opinion	information gap
census	consensus	political ideology
political socialization	conflict	protest
agents of socialization	change	civil disobedience

For Further Reading

Ball-Rokeach, Sandra J., Milton Rokeach, and Joel W. Grube. *The Great American Values Test* (1984). This experimental study suggests that the media can change public opinion, even basic values.

Bennett, Lance. *Public Opinion in American Politics* (1980). A good text on public opinion.

Campbell, Angus, et al. *The American Voter* (1960). The classic study of American voting behavior based upon data from the Survey Research Center at the University of Michigan.

Dawson, Richard, Kenneth Prewitt, and Karen Dawson. *Political Socialization*, 2nd ed. (1977). A good overview of the content and process of political socialization.

Graber, Doris. *Mass Media and American Politics*, 2nd ed. (1984). An excellent review of research on public opinion and the media, as well as on other aspects of the "media state."

Lane, Robert. *Political Ideology* (1962). A classic study of how common people think about politics.

Nie, Norman H., Sidney Verba, and John R. Petrocik. *The Changing American Voter* (1976). A controversial updating and rethinking of *The American Voter*.

Verba, Sidney, and Norman Nie. *Participation in America* (1972). A definitive study of American political participation.

The Political Parties

MEMO

The political party is America's most misunderstood political institution. It exists on ballots, in the phone book, and in our heads. As an organization, however, it is weaker than the parties in most other democracies.

One way of thinking about the parties is to think of them as firms (like Ford or General Motors) competing for voters (buyers). A party is in the market for voters; its products are its policies. Early in this chapter, we present a "marketplace model" of the two-party system. Here are some of the major issues we examine in this chapter.

■ The American party battle has been largely a two-party battle. Long periods of party dominance are followed by a critical election and a shift from one to another majority party.
■ The parties today are different from one another in their ideologies and organizational success. The Democratic party has emphasized representativeness, we call it the "party of representation." The Republican party has been less concerned with representativeness and more concerned with efficiency and effectiveness. We call it the "party of regeneration."
■ The party as an organization looks neat on an organizational chart, but the American party system remains organizationally imprecise at best.
■ There is much discussion today about the future of the two parties. The parties now have many rivals for the attention and affections of voters and politicians. Chief among these are the interest groups, the media, and—surprisingly—the candidates themselves.

Like most political scientists, I believe strongly that political parties are—or should be—a cornerstone of democracy. We have enjoyed a two-party system for the first and the second American centuries and it is likely that we will have one for the third as well. The question, though, is: What kind of party system will it be?

AFTER THE 1984 ELECTION, the votes were in and the chips were down for the Democrats. Speculation began anew about the future of the American political parties—the Democratic party in particular. For more than fifty years, the Democratic party has been our majority party, with more citizens claiming to be Democrats than Republicans. After the 1984 election, some writers thought the parties were realigning, and some even prophesied that the Democratic Party had been so trounced that the Republicans would be the new majority party. The *New York Times* reported that, for the first time in decades, the number of people who called themselves Republicans was almost identical to the number who called themselves Democrats. [1] *Time* asked, "Are the Democrats really done for?" [2] Democratic vice-presidential candidate Geraldine Ferraro spoke to a postelection audience at the University of Wisconsin: "Some have said," she commented, "that 1984 marked a great political realignment. But I don't see that." She implored Democrats to cling to their principles, because "the last thing this country needs is two Republican parties." [3] Amid all this speculation about the future of the parties, a *Washington Post* editorial asked, "Has there ever been an election in which the results were not spied by someone as the glimmerings of a political realignment?" [4] Perhaps, it allowed, there were some. But talk of the fate of the Democratic party was much in the air in postmortems of the 1984 Democratic defeat.

[1] Phil Gailey, "Permanance of G.O.P.'s New Strength is Debated," *New York Times*, December 24, 1984, p. 4.
[2] *Time*, November 19, 1984, p. 64.
[3] *Time*, December 24, 1984, p. 17.
[4] *Washington Post National Weekly Edition*, December 3, 1984, p. 26.

Election '84 Post Mortem. *The defeat of the Democrats in 1984 left many party leaders and political commentators worrying about the Democratic party and the future of the two-party system. Twenty years before, Republican leaders and political commentators were worried about the future of the Republican party and the two-party system. Speaking at the University of Wisconsin, vice-presidential candidate Geraldine Ferraro urged the Democratic Party to stick to its principles, because, she said, "the last thing this country needs is two Republican parties."*

Such talk, as the *Post* implied, is old hat in American politics. Twenty years before, the Republicans were down and, some thought, out. President Lyndon Johnson had trounced Republican candidate Barry Goldwater, winning the largest popular-vote victory in history. Pontificating after the 1964 election, Pulitzer Prize-winning political author (and Democrat) Theodore White sounded as though he was writing the Republican party's obituary:

> For the elections of 1964 had left the Republican party in a desperate condition. . . . The Republicans suffer, first, from a general condition—a continuing failure to capture the imagination of the American people. . . . Republicans suffer, next, from a specific political ailment—the lack of any agreed purpose for their Party. [5]

In 1984, the shoe was on the other foot; people were saying the same things about the Democrats.

Ups and downs of the two major parties are a staple of American political life. **Party competition** is the battle of the parties for control of public office. Americans have had a two-party system since the early 1800s, and despite the see-sawing, it will still be with us as the third American century dawns.

Americans have never really been fond of political parties. Overwhelming majorities agree that "the parties do more to confuse the issues than to provide a clear choice on them." [6] Some of the nastiest language in our political vocabulary—*party hack, party boss, party machine*—is linked to the parties. Yet, no one realistically has a chance of holding major office without the support of a party. Political scientists claim that parties are cornerstones of democracy, and in this chapter, we will see why. In addition, we will learn why political scientists believe that parties do not work as well as they should.

[5] Theodore White, *The Making of the President, 1964* (New York: Atheneum, 1965), p. 385.
[6] Jack Dennis, "Support for the Party System by the Mass Public," *American Political Science Review* 60 (September 1966):605.

THE MEANING OF PARTY

Some Definitions

William N. Chambers once remarked that "If the beginning of wisdom is to call things by their right name, some attention is due to what we mean by a political party." [7] A party is many things. In this country, it is all of the following:

— A symbol (donkey, elephant, rooster, or whatever) and a name on a ballot or voting machine.
— A psychological attachment in our mind, as when we say, "I am a Republican" (or Democrat, or Whig, or whatever).
— A national convention of women and men, young and old, black and white, meeting every four years to nominate "the next president of the United States. . . . "
— A legislative grouping or caucus, in which members of Congress actually sit together on their party's side of the aisle and share a cloakroom.
— A national office, with a national chairperson, staff, and office space.
— A loosely defined coalition of interests and ideologies, usually falling into line behind the party's presidential candidate, but coming partly unglued afterward.
— A legal entity empowered by state law to play a role in selecting candidates for office.

Parties are all of these things and more. Almost all definitions of political parties, American style, have one thing in common: Parties try to win elections. This is their core function and the key to their definition. Without this element, parties might be mere social groups, or pressure groups, or political organizations; their electoral efforts are what make them parties. Thus, Anthony Downs, an economist, defined a **political party** as a "team of men [and women] seeking to control the governing apparatus by gaining office in a duly constituted election." [8]

The word *team* is the slippery part of this definition. A party team may not be so well disciplined and single-minded as teams fielded by a fine football coach. Party teams are often running every which way (sometimes, it seems, toward the opposition's goal line), are poorly coached, and suffer serious problems of both recruitment and off-season confusion. In football, it is sometimes hard to tell the players without a scorecard. In American politics, it is sometimes hard to tell the players even *with* a scorecard. Unlike European parties, American ones have no official membership system. Even the parties' leaders often disagree about policy, and between elections the parties seem to all but disappear. So who are the members of these teams? Frank Sorauf has suggested that we think of American parties as "three-headed political giants." Each

---

[7] William N. Chambers, "Party Development and the American Mainstream," in William N. Chambers and Walter D. Burnham (eds.), *The American Party Systems* (New York: Oxford University Press, 1967), p. 5.

[8] Anthony Downs, *An Economic Theory of Democracy* (New York: Harper and Row, 1957), p. 25.

consists of a party-in-the-electorate, a party as organization, and a party-in-government. [9]

The largest component of the American party is the *party-in-the-electorate*. There are no dues or membership cards to distinguish members from nonmembers. We may register as Democrats, Republicans, or whatever, but registration is not legally binding and is easily changed. To be a member of a party, you need only claim to be a member. If you call yourself a Republican, you are one—even if you never talk to a party official, never work in a campaign, and often vote for Democrats!

The *party as organization* has a national office, a full-time staff, rules and bylaws, and budgets. Each party not only has a national office, but also state and local organizations. The party organization includes precinct leaders, county chairpersons, state chairpersons, state delegates to the national committee, and officials in the party's Washington office. These are the people who perpetuate the party between elections and make its rules; they keep the books and raise the funds to pay off campaign debts; they seek out new candidates for public office and organize conventions. From the party's national chairperson to the lowliest precinct captain, the party organization pursues electoral victory.

The *party-in-government* consists of those winning candidates who label themselves members of the party. It helps organize the government's agenda. Although presidents, members of Congress, governors, and lesser officeholders almost always run for election as Democrats or Republicans, they do not always agree on policy. Presidents and governors may have to wheedle and cajole their own party members to vote for their policies. Some of the party's politicians may put personal ambition—or principle—above loyalty to the party's leaders. Yet these officeholders are the main spokespersons for the party; between elections, their words and actions personify the party to millions of Americans. And if the party is to translate its promises into policy, the job must be done by the party-in-government.

Because parties are everywhere in American politics—present in the electorate's mind, as an organization, and in government offices—one of their major functions is to link the people of the United States to their government and its policies.

Tasks of the Parties

The Main Task: Parties as Linkage Institutions. The road from public opinion to public policy is long and winding. Masses of people cannot raise their voices to government and indicate their policy preferences in unison. In a large democracy, **linkage institutions** are necessary to put people's policy preferences on the government's agenda. [10] Well-functioning linkage institutions mean that popular preferences are heeded, not merely noted. In the United States, there are three main linkage institutions: parties, elections, and interest groups. Kay Lawson writes that

---

[9] Frank J. Sorauf, *Party Politics in America*, 5th ed. (Boston: Little, Brown, 1984), p. 8.

[10] The term linkage is introduced in V. O. Key's classic book, *Public Opinion and American Democracy* (New York: Knopf, 1963), Chap. 16.

"parties are seen, both by the members and by others, as agencies for forging links between citizens and policymakers."[11] [1]

Parties, of course, have many appeals to voters, for example, the attractiveness of their candidates and the staunch loyalties of their adherents. In a democracy, their ability to link voter preferences with actual government policies is especially important. Alan D. Monroe presents some evidence to show that the parties do a fairly good job of reflecting public opinion. He examined several hundred pledges made by the major parties in their platforms from 1960 through 1980. In each case, he looked at survey results to see whether or not the parties' positions

[11] Kay Lawson (ed.), *Political Parties and Linkage: A Comparative Perspective* (New Haven, Conn.: Yale University Press, 1980), p. 3.

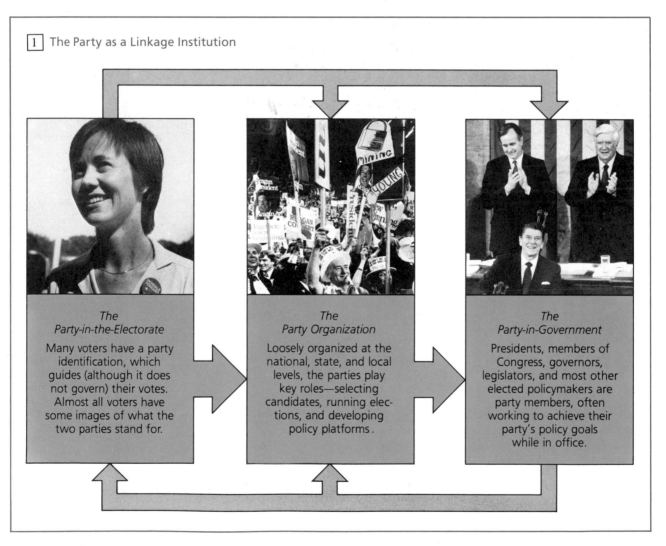

[1] The Party as a Linkage Institution

The Party-in-the-Electorate

Many voters have a party identification, which guides (although it does not govern) their votes. Almost all voters have some images of what the two parties stand for.

The Party Organization

Loosely organized at the national, state, and local levels, the parties play key roles—selecting candidates, running elections, and developing policy platforms.

The Party-in-Government

Presidents, members of Congress, governors, legislators, and most other elected policymakers are party members, often working to achieve their party's policy goals while in office.

Parties serve as one of the three main linkage institutions, helping to connect people's policy preferences with decisions of the policymaking institutions. They can do so because the party exists in the electorate, as an organization, and in the government itself.

reflected a popular majority opinion. The Republican party was consistent with majority opinion 64 percent of the time, the Democratic party 74 percent of the time. As we would expect from the more conservative party, Republicans were more often aligned with popular majorities when the status quo was favored. The Democrats were more in step with public opinion when change was favored.[12]

In Chapter 2, we drew a line between *normative* thinking and *empirical* thinking. Normative statements, we said, express preferences; they are statements about "should." Empirical statements are factual statements; they are statements about "do" or "is." When we say that the parties *should* perform some task, we do not mean that they do it handily. The party, like most political institutions, exists in theory and in practice. In theory, a party is a major linkage institution between people and politicians, and has several key tasks to perform.

What Parties Do: A Checklist. Parties do many things, some of them well, some not so well. Here is a checklist of the tasks parties perform, or should perform, if they are to serve as effective linkage institutions:

1. *Parties pick policymakers.* Political independents have a tough time winning office. No one above the local level (and often not even there) gets elected to a public office without winning a party's endorsement. A party's endorsement is called a *nomination*. (We examine nominations more closely in the next chapter.)
2. *Parties run campaigns.* Through their national, state, and local organizations, parties coordinate our political campaigns. They do not have a monopoly on campaigns, of course, because there are scores of players in the campaign game.
3. *Parties are cue-givers to voters.* Most voters have a **party image** of each party, that is, they know (or think they know) what the Republicans and Democrats stand for. Liberal, conservative, pro- or anti-union, pro- or antiblack—these are some of the elements of each party's image. Even in our antiparty era, many voters still rely on the party to give them cues for voting. 2
4. *Parties push policies.* Within the electorate and in the government, each political party peddles specific policy alternatives. The Democratic party has been a fervent backer of the Equal Rights Amendment; the Republicans have not. Republicans, on the other hand, are more likely than Democrats to favor higher spending on the military.
5. *Parties coordinate policymaking.* In our fragmented government, parties are essential for coordination among the branches of government. Each president, cabinet official, and member of Congress is also a member of one or the other party. Presidents try to have their way with Congress by working through its party leaders. Leaders of the two congressional parties normally line up on opposite sides of key roll-call votes.

[12] Alan D. Monroe, "Party Platforms and Public Opinion," *American Journal of Political Science* 27 (February 1983):27–42.

When the parties perform these functions well, they conform to the **responsible party model.** Many political scientists favor this notion of how parties should work: they should offer clear choices to the voters, who can use them as cues to their own choices of candidates. Once in office, the parties would carry out their promises made in the campaign.

The parties operate—at least in theory—as in a marketplace. They have something to sell (their candidates and policies) and the voters, in a democracy, can shop around.

Parties, Voters, and Policy: The Downs Model

Of all the normative conceptions of democracy, none is more universal than this: *Democratic government translates citizen preferences about policy into actual policy.* The political party can be a key instrument of this translation. Anthony Downs has provided a working model of the relationship of citizens, parties, and policy.[13] In a democracy, says Downs, both voters and parties have goals they want to achieve. Voters want to maximize the chances that policies they favor—particularly ones that will bring them individual benefits—will be adopted by government. Parties and candidates want to win office. In order to win office, the wise party selects policies which voters favor. Parties and candidates may do all sorts of things to win office—kiss babies, call opponents ugly names, run expensive political spots, even lie and cheat—but in a democracy the party will use its policy positions to attract votes. If Party A more

206

[13] Downs, *Economic Theory.*

accurately figures out the policy views of voters than Party B, then Party A will look forward to a joyful inaugural day.

Here is how Downs's model works. Assume first that both parties and voters are *rational*. Being rational means that we have a goal and we pick the logical, preferably the best, way to achieve it. (If your main goal is lower taxes, do not vote for the party that promises more spending for everyone, but the one that promises tightfistedness.) Not only voters, but parties are (to Downs at least) rational. If party leaders know that voters favor more environmental protection, they will propose environmental protection policies. And so on.

Take a look at 3 . It is based upon a Downsian assumption that voters are spread out on a continuum from extremely liberal to extremely conservative. A few voters are at the extreme liberal end, a few at the extreme conservative end, and the majority are in the middle of the road. Rational parties will locate themselves where the most voters are; foolish parties will not heed this advice, but will establish their positions elsewhere. If Downs is right, rational parties will win, and foolish parties will be condemned to a footnote in the history books.

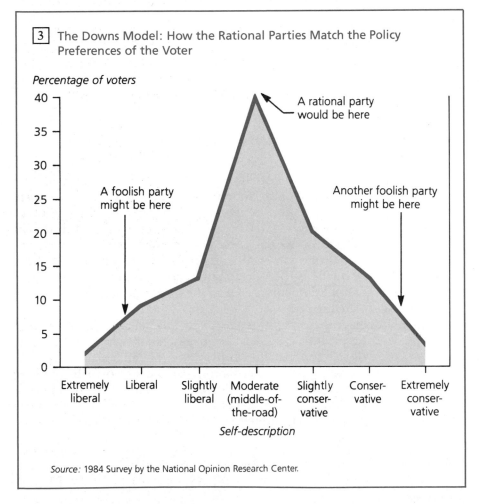

3 The Downs Model: How the Rational Parties Match the Policy Preferences of the Voter

Percentage of voters

A rational party would be here

A foolish party might be here

Another foolish party might be here

Self-description

Source: 1984 Survey by the National Opinion Research Center.

In 1984, the National Opinion Research Center asked a sample of the American electorate to classify themselves on a scale from extremely liberal to extremely conservative. The graph shows how the people located themselves and how rational (and foolish) parties would portray their stands.

The real world is more complex than a Downsian miniaturized world of democracy.[14] As Downs stresses, information will never be full and complete. Parties may misperceive where voters stand; voters may misperceive where parties stand. Parties are also educators. They may knowingly take positions unpopular with voters but favored by party leaders. They may stand on principle, hoping to persuade voters during the campaign. A major problem with Downs' model could be fatal: Voters may not neatly line up on a single dimension. If voters are concerned about too many different issues, the party cannot design a package to appeal to the average voter. This is why the rise of *single-issue politics* (see Chapter 2, pages 57–59) plagues the parties.

To summarize, understanding the party clearly in theory helps us to understand it better in practice. Downs's model stresses that the parties *can* be key instruments of democracy. The question is, *are they?*

THE RISE AND FALL OF THE PARTIES

In our discussion of parties, we need to remember the following: *Ours is a two-party system and always has been.* Most democratic nations—France, Italy, the Scandanavian countries, Israel, and others—have a multiparty system. Of course, even in the United States, an occasional third party will slip into the system. But only once—the Republicans in 1860—has a minor party become a major one, and they almost instantly became a major party.

The Two Major Parties: How Party Dominance Shifts

The two major parties do not simply seesaw after each election, one winning now, the other winning four years later. *Throughout our party history, one party has been the dominant majority party for long periods of time.* A majority of voters cling to the party in power, which tends to win a majority of the elections. We call these periods **party eras.** The majority party, of course, does not win everything in sight; sometimes it suffers from intraparty squabbles (as the Republicans did in 1912) and loses. Sometimes it nominates a real loser, and the opposition cashes in on the majority party's misfortune.

What punctuates these party eras is a **critical election.**[15] A critical election is an electoral earthquake: The ground shakes beneath the parties; fissures in the party's coalition appear and it begins to unravel; new issues appear, which divide the electorate. A new coalition is formed for each party, a coalition which endures for years. A critical election period may require more than one election before change is apparent; but in the end, the majority party will often be displaced by the minority party.

[14] A classic critique of the Downs model is Donald R. Stokes, "Spatial Models of Party Competition," *American Political Science Review* 57 (June 1963):368–77.

[15] The term is originally from V. O. Key, Jr. The standard source on critical elections is Walter D. Burnham, *Critical Elections and the Mainsprings of American Politics* (New York: Norton, 1975).

This process is called **party realignment.** One good predictor of a critical election period is a crisis in the nation's life. Two of the major realignments were associated with the Civil War of the 1860s and the Great Depression of the 1930s. Now we will explore the American party eras.

1800–1860: The First Democratic Era

Even though he was one of the authors of the celebrated *Federalist Papers,* which warned against "factions" or parties, Alexander Hamilton did as much as anyone to inaugurate our party system.[16] He was secretary of the treasury during the Washington administration. To garner congressional support for his pet policies (particularly a national bank) he needed votes. From this politicking and coalition building came the rudiments of the Federalist party, our first political party. The Federalists, though, were our shortest-lived major party. Only one American president, John Adams, is listed as a Federalist. The Federalists lost the election of 1800 to the Jeffersonians and then withered away.

The Federalists' rivals were Jefferson's party, then called the Democratic Republican party, but today called the Democratic party. It is the oldest surviving political party in the world. (The nickname of the Republican party is the GOP, for Grand Old Party, but the Republicans are newcomers compared to the Democrats.) Every political party depends upon a **coalition,** a group of individuals or a group of groups supporting it. The Democratic-Republican party derived its coalition from the agrarian interests, rather than the growing capitalists, who supported the Federalists. Southerners were a major element in the Jeffersonian coalition. As the Federalists disappeared, intraparty rivalries erupted within the old Jeffersonian coalition, soon to be called the Democratic party.

More than anyone else, it was General Andrew Jackson who founded the modern American political party. In the election of 1828, he forged a new Democratic coalition, which included westerners as well as southerners, new immigrants as well as settled Americans. The architect of this new coalition was Martin Van Buren, who succeeded Jackson as president ("a first class second rate man," one of his contemporaries called Van Buren). Opponents of Jackson formed the Whig Party, which included notables like Henry Clay and Daniel Webster, but it won the presidency only when it nominated aging but popular generals.

Andrew Jackson and the Democratic Party. *Jackson was more influential than anyone in creating the modern political party. He united the remnants of the old Jeffersonians with the westerners and many urban workers in an industrializing economy. Jackson's vice-president and successor, Martin Van Buren, was the mastermind of the new party organization, which was heavily dependent on the patronage system. The Democratic party of Jefferson and Jackson was the nation's dominant party until it was divided by the Civil War.*

1860–1932: The Republican Era

In the 1850s, one issue came to dominate American politics: slavery. The emerging Republican party was a single-issue party. Slavery, said Senator Sumner, one of the party's founders, "is the only subject within the field of national politics which excites any real interest."[17] This was a time of troubles. Congress battled over the extension of slavery to the new

---

[16] On the origins of the American party system, see William N. Chambers, *Political Parties in a New Nation* (New York: Oxford University Press, 1963).

[17] Quoted in James L. Sundquist, *Dynamics of the Party System,* rev. ed. (Washington, D.C.: The Brookings Institution, 1983), p. 88. Sundquist's book is an excellent account of realignments in American party history.

states and territories. The Supreme Court in the *Dred Scott* case had held that blacks could not be citizens and that former slaves could not be protected by the Constitution. Both sides had begun to mobilize.

The Republicans rose in the late 1850s as *the* antislavery party. Folding in the remnants of several minor parties, the Republicans in 1860 forged a coalition strong enough to elect former Illinois Congressman Abraham Lincoln. The Civil War was one of those political earthquakes that realigned the parties. After the Civil War, the Republican party was in ascendency for more than sixty years.

During this generally Republican era, the election of 1896 was a watershed, perhaps the most bitter battle in American electoral history. (For more on the election of 1896, see pages 267–269.) The Democrats nominated William Jennings Bryan, populist proponent of "free silver." The Republican party made clear its positions in favor of the gold standard, industrialization, the banks, high tariffs, and the industrial working classes against the "radical" western farmers and silverites. Republicans continued to preach about their role in freeing the slaves, and garnered the votes of almost every black who could vote. "Bryan and his program," remarks Sundquist, "were greeted by the country's conservatives with something akin to terror." [18] The *New York Tribune* howled that Bryan's Democrats were "in league with the Devil." A staggering turnout put William McKinley in the White House and brought into the Republican fold the new working classes as well as the new moneyed interests. Political scientists call the 1896 election a realigning one, because it shifted the two parties' coalitions and entrenched the Republicans for another generation.

For three decades more, until the Great Depression of the 1930s, the Republicans would continue as the nation's majority party. Only two Democrats (Grover Cleveland and Woodrow Wilson) were presidents during the entire period. The Republicans could have won just about every presidential election between 1860 and 1932 had they not done themselves in with an intraparty rivalry. In 1912 former president Teddy Roosevelt challenged his one-time protege and incumbent, President William Howard Taft. That splitting of the Republican vote permitted political scientist, former Princeton University president, and New Jersey Governor Woodrow Wilson to win the presidency.

Even after World War I, the Republicans settled back to claim another set of presidential victories. They nominated Ohio newspaper publisher and Senator Warren Harding in 1920. Harding was perhaps the most gullible and ineffectual man ever to serve in the White House. (Harding's speeches, said William McAdoo, were "like an army of pompous phrases marching across the landscape in search of an idea." Even Harding called his own speech-making "bloviating.") Harding presided over a government of charletans, who stole the country blind, either with or (worse) without Harding's knowledge. Republicans Calvin Coolidge and Herbert Hoover followed—as did the Great Depression. It began only months after Hoover had taken office in 1929. The Depression brought about another fissure in the crust of the American party system.

[18] Ibid., p. 155.

The Minority Party in a Major Party Era. *Historically, the two major parties have not seesawed from election to election. Instead, one has dominated for long periods of time, often until a social or economic earthquake disrupts our "normal" party loyalties. Nonetheless, the majority party does not win every election. In a dominantly Republican era, the Republicans in 1912 managed to split their own ranks (in a bitter nomination battle between Teddy Roosevelt and William Howard Taft) and permitted Democratic nominee Woodrow Wilson to become president. Wilson was a political scientist, a president of the American Political Science Association, and former president of Princeton University. Wilson presided over the American entry into World War I and also over the Senate's scuttling of his high-minded plans for a League of Nations after the war.*

1932–?: The Rise and Unravelling of the New Deal Coalition

Actually, the shifting and shuffling associated with a party realignment began before the 1932 election. New voters flocked to the electorate. Immigrant groups in Chicago and other cities had been attracted to the Democratic presidential candidacy of New York Governor Al Smith, a Catholic, in 1928. But "a single cataclysmic event—the Great Depression— . . . polarized the country."[19] President Hoover's handling of this critical situation hardly helped the Republicans. He solemnly pronounced that "economic depression cannot be cured by legislative action." Historian David M. Kennedy remarked that Hoover "proved [to be] no man on horseback to rescue his suffering people from the storm that enshrouded them in 1929. Salvation—of sorts—came instead from a man in a wheelchair, Franklin D. Roosevelt."[20] New York Governor Franklin Roosevelt, who handily defeated Hoover in 1932, promised a "New Deal." In his first hundred days as president, Congress passed scores of antidepression measures. Realignment began in earnest after the Roosevelt administration took office and attempted to get the country moving.[21] Roosevelt and the Democrats forged the **New Deal coalition,** which made the Democratic party a majority party for years thereafter.

[19] Ibid., p. 198.
[20] David M. Kennedy, "The Changing Image of the New Deal," *Atlantic Monthly* (January 1985):90.
[21] Jerome Clubb, William H. Flanagan, and Nancy H. Zingale, *Partisan Realignment: Voters, Parties, and Government in American History* (Beverly Hills, Calif.: Sage, 1980). Argues that realignments occur after, not before or during, a critical election.

Frankin D. Roosevelt, Coalition Builder. *Roosevelt towered over twentieth-century American politics as no other figure has done. He engineered the "New Deal" coalition that made the Democratic party our majority party for decades. This coalition, composed of union members, intellectuals, liberals, ethnics, and blacks, remained the base of Democratic party support long after Roosevelt's death in 1945.*

The basic elements of the New Deal coalition were these:

— *The urban working classes.* Such cities as Chicago and Philadelphia were staunchly Republican before the New Deal realignment; thereafter, they were Democratic bastions.
— *Ethnic groups.* After 1896, the Republicans were the party of the ethnic groups; after 1932, the Democrats were.
— *Catholics and Jews.* During and after the Roosevelt period, Catholics and Jews were strongly Democratic.
— *The poor.* Though the poor vote less than the rest of us, their votes went overwhelmingly to the party of Roosevelt, Kennedy, and Johnson.
— *Southerners.* Ever since the pre-Civil War days, white southerners were Democratic loyalists.
— *Blacks.* The Republicans freed the slaves, but the Democrats, especially after the 1960s, attracted most black Americans to their party.
— *Intellectuals.* Small in number, Democratic intellectuals nonetheless helped keep the Democratic party liberal.

The New Deal coalition dominated American politics from the 1930s to the 1960s. Harry S Truman, who succeeded Roosevelt in 1945, promised a "Fair Deal." After eight years of Republican Dwight D. Eisenhower, the Democrats regained the presidency in 1960 with the election of John Fitzgerald Kennedy. His "New Frontier" was in the New Deal tradition, with platforms and policies designed to help labor, the working classes, and minorities. Lyndon Johnson, picked as Kennedy's Vice-President largely because he could help garner the southern vote, succeeded to the presidency upon Kennedy's assassination in 1963. Johnson's "Great Society" programs included a major expansion of government programs to help the poor, the dispossessed, the cities, and the minorities.

Yet the recent history of the American parties can be written in terms of the crumbling of the New Deal coalition. By the 1970s, groups once solidly in the Democratic coalition began to waver. By 1984, union families, Catholics, southerners, and the urban working classes tilted to Ronald Reagan or split their votes about evenly between the two parties. Today, the Democrats fight fiercely to hold on to the coalition that Franklin Roosevelt brought together, or to find a new one. The Republicans hope to turn a string of presidential victories into status as the nation's majority party.

The Parties Today

The Democrats: Party of Representation. As the New Deal coalition became increasingly frayed, the Democratic party became more and more concerned with equality, pluralism, and representation. This concern began in the 1960s.

In 1968, the Vietnam War raged in Southeast Asia. Some of it seemed to rage here, too. The Democratic party was holding its annual convention in Chicago, Illinois. Demonstrators opposed to the war in Vietnam had come from many states to stage protests in Grant Park—just across

Michigan Avenue from the Conrad Hilton, where many of the delegates and dignitaries were housed. During one particularly boistrous rally attacking Democratic President Lyndon Johnson and probable nominee Hubert Humphrey, the Chicago police department sallied forth into the demonstrators. Thousands were arrested and hundreds were injured by the police. (An official inquiry later called it a "police riot.") Tear gas fumes seeped into the hotel rooms of party dignitaries, including Vice-President (and soon to be nominee) Humphrey.

Events outside the convention center captured more news than the convention itself. Still, much was happening at the 1968 Democratic convention that would reshape American's majority party. The party was hearing challenges to numerous delegations. Charges were made that delegates were unfairly selected, that state delegations underrepresented women, minorities, younger Democrats, and other groups. Charges of racial or sexual inequality always make Democrats especially sensitive. Barely able to struggle through the tumultuous convention, the Democrats nonetheless agreed to address those complaints. The delegates agreed to appoint a "special committee" to look into and recommend rules to make representation fairer.[22] That commission was chaired by South Dakota Senator George McGovern, who resigned to seek (successfully) the 1972 Democratic presidential nomination; Minnesota Representative Don Fraser succeeded McGovern as chairman.

---

[22] Accounts of the Democrats' reforms can be found in Austin Ranney, *Curbing the Mischiefs of Faction* (Berkeley: University of California Press, 1975); William Crotty, *Party Reform* (New York: Longman, 1983); and the articles by Longley and Casey in Pomper, *Party Renewal in America* (New York: Praeger, 1981).

Democratic Convention, 1968. *On August 29, 1968 Chicago police attempted to move demonstrators outside the Conrad Hilton Hotel, the convention's official hotel. The demonstrators were protesting the support of the Democratic party leaders for the Vietnam War.*

In addition to the highly-publicized riots, the 1968 Democratic Convention left an impact on its party like few others in the twentieth century. The party embarked on a new course to bring previously underrepresented groups, such as minorities, women, and youth, into the party. The McGovern-Fraser Commission finally codified these new policies. Senator George McGovern— later succeeded by Representative Donald Fraser—chaired this important commission of the Democratic party, charged with reforming the party's rules and representation. Its recommendations played a key role in making the Democratic party the party of representativeness, even while the Republican party was trying to resurrect itself from its minority party status. McGovern went on to run unsuccessfully for president as the Democratic nominee in 1972.

Thus, the **McGovern-Fraser Commission** brought massive changes to the Democratic party. The commission proposed sweeping reforms designed to make the Democratic party more representative of the people. It adopted guidelines in several areas. First, state parties were to take "affirmative steps" to provide blacks, women, and young people a share of delegate slots that mirrored the state's population. Second, it took other steps to pry open the party to participation by the rank-and-file, and to reduce the control of the conventions and the primaries by "party pros." By the 1972 convention, when these rules were fully in effect, the Democratic party came closer to mirroring our demography than any other American institution. Today, even though the McGovern-Fraser rules have been relaxed somewhat, the Democratic party still prides itself on being more representative of the electorate than the "other party."

Let us take a look at the Democratic party's convention delegates in 1984. You can see some comparisons between Democratic delegates and the party's rank-and-file in 4. Even with all the Democrats' reforms, some groups are still overrepresented: Better-educated and well-to-do Democrats are more likely to become delegates; union members are almost twice as likely to end up as delegates than their share of the party rank-and-file would predict; younger citizens under age thirty constitute a quarter of the Democrats, but less than 10 percent of the delegates.

You should also note the differences between the policy positions of the delegates and the rank-and-file Democrats. Typically, *delegates to the Democratic national convention are more liberal on issues than the party's rank-and-file members.* On social issues such as women's rights, on foreign policy issues, and on social policy issues, those selected as delegates to a national convention are more liberal than ordinary Democrats. (The reverse, incidentally, is true for the Republicans; more conservative people than the rank-and-file are selected as delegates to the Republican national convention. [23])

Today, the Democratic Party's main problem is not representation, but translating its representation into electability at the presidential level. Since 1952, there have been nine presidential elections. Democrats have won only three of them (1960, 1964, and 1976), two by razor-thin margins. The Democrats, despite the 1984 election, still have a lot going for them in American national politics. In recent decades, they have held a congressional majority more often than the Republicans have held the White House. Their control of the governorships and state offices is more solid now than two decades ago. For the Democratic party, the problem has been the elusiveness of the Oval Office.

The Republicans: Party of Regeneration. In 1968, as the Democratic party was enduring its convention agonies, the Republicans were nominating former Vice-President Richard M. Nixon for president. Only four

---

[23] See the evidence on the more extreme ideological views of the delegates for both parties in David Price, *Bringing Back the Parties* (Washington, D.C.: Congressional Quarterly, 1984), pp. 196–97.

| 4 | The Democratic Delegates and the Rank-and-File, 1984 |

The Democratic party has been strongly concerned about fair and full representation of various groups within the party. At one time, during the early 1970s, the party almost demanded "quotas" for younger voters, women, and minorities at its national convention. Today, these demands have weakened, but the Democratic party still sends to its convention a broader cross-section of delegates than does the Republican party. Here are some comparisons, both of demographics and of policy positions, between the 1984 Democratic delegates and rank-and-file people who identify themselves as Democrats.

	1984 Democratic Delegates (Percentage)	1984 Democratic Identifiers (Percentage)
EDUCATION		
High school or less	12	79
Some college	17	9
College graduates	23	8
Graduate school	49	4
HOUSEHOLD INCOME		
Under $12,000	3	37
$12,000–$20,000	8	18
$20,000–$30,000	16	23
$30,000–$50,000	31	17
$50,000 and more	42	5
RACE		
White	75	71
Black	17	20
Hispanic	6	6
Other	3	3
VIEWS ON POLICIES		
The Equal Rights Amendment should be ratified.	91	63
The U.S. can meet its national security obligations with a much smaller military budget than we have today.	85	56
The government should raise taxes now as one means of dealing with the federal budget deficit.	53	19
There should be a constitutional amendment outlawing abortion.	9	46

Source: Washington Post National Weekly Edition, July 23, 1984, pp. 8–10. © The Washington Post.

215

years before, the Republicans had suffered an electoral defeat never before or since equaled in American political history—the widest popular vote loss ever in a presidential contest (Johnson vs. Goldwater). A decade later, in 1974, the Republicans again faced a political catastrophe. Richard Nixon, resoundingly reelected in 1972, resigned the presidency after the scandals of Watergate (see pages 407–408 for more on Watergate). As often happens when a party is beset by multiple crises, friends of the party and of the two-party system feared for the Republican party's life.

They need not have worried. The Republican party went through very few of the intraparty reforms that so absorbed the Democrats. Crotty remarks that "there was little support for reform within the Republican party. . . . Despite their problems, Republicans are well satisfied with their party, whom it represents, and the way in which it operates."[24] Democrats, much more than Republicans, think they are the party of pluralism, committed to policies intended to bring minorities, women, the poor, and others into the American mainstream. It is not surprising that the Democrats decided to get their own house in order, too. There were few minorities and feminists in the Republican party to demand affirmative action and a fair share of delegates.

The Republicans had other work to do. They wanted to regenerate their party, regardless of its representational equity. To the Republicans, winning elections was more important than being balanced by race, sex, age, and ethnicity. After the embarrassment of Watergate, the Republican party turned to former Tennessee Senator Bill Brock in 1976.[25] Brock was a former naval officer, heir to a family candy business, and a master political craftsman. (President Reagan made him secretary of labor in 1985.) He wanted the Republican National Committee to be a service to state parties, not their watchdog. While the Democrats were making their party more representative, Brock was making the Republicans more effective.

The Republicans' Local Election Campaign Division not only put cash in the coffers of local Republican candidates, but held seminars on winning elections. The national party office bought a computer to track contributions and contributors. (It is symptomatic of the primitive state of national party organizations that they may have been the last major institutions in America to purchase computers.) Charles Manatt, elected chairman of the Democratic National Committee in 1981, described his goal as "trying to do the kind of job that Bill Brock did."[26]

In 1983, for example, the Republicans raised $93.4 million, mostly from direct mail and major donors—six times as much as the Democrats raised the same year. (One Democratic party executive remarked that "Just doing it on the back of a napkin, in 1981 and 1982, I think they made more in interest on their certificates of deposits than we raised.") The

[24] William Crotty, *American Parties in Decline*, 2nd ed. (Boston: Little, Brown, 1984), p. 193.

[25] Brock's effort to regenerate the Republicans is told in John F. Bibby, "Party Renewal in the National Republican Party," in Pomper (ed.), *Party Renewal in America*, pp. 102–115.

[26] The Manatt quotation is from Price, *Bringing Back the Parties*, p. 44.

Republicans, 1984. Ronald Reagan, evoked some real enthusiasm among younger voters at the 1984 Republican Convention. Young voters and a large percentage of women voters favored the Republican ticket. Despite the efforts of feminist groups to link Reagan and the Republicans with the defeat of the Equal Rights Amendment, the GOP fared well with women in 1984, though less well than with males, leading to discussions of a "gender gap" in American politics.

Republican party is a major source of cash for House and Senate candidates.[27]

These reforms reenergized the Republican party. Paying less attention than the Democrats to internal representation, they paid more attention to building an organization and a financial base. All these efforts were tremendous assets when Ronald Reagan first ran for the presidency in 1980.

Third Parties: Their Impact on American Politics

Election after election, the story of our party struggle is one of two mighty mountains and many small molehills. **Third parties,** those electoral contenders other than the two major parties, are not uncommon in American politics.[28] The landscape of American history is strewn with small and now-forgotten minor parties: the Free Soil Party (called the "Barnburners," a forerunner of the Republican Party); the American Party (called the "Know Nothings") in 1856; the Jobless Party of 1932; the Poor Man's Party of 1952; and others. [5]

Basically, third parties come in two varieties. First are the *single-issue* or *ideological* parties. These tend to support one single issue (prohibition of alcoholic beverages is one example) or a particular, often extreme,

[27] The quotation on the "back of a napkin" and the statistics on Republican and Democratic giving are from Thomas B. Edsall, "The GOP Money Machine," *Washington Post National Weekly Edition*, July 2, 1984, pp. 6–7.

[28] One standard book on third parties is Daniel Mazmanian, *Third Parties in Presidential Elections* (Washington, D.C.: The Brookings Institution, 1974).

ideological position, such as socialism or libertarianism. Second are *splinter* parties, which are offshoots of a major party. Teddy Roosevelt's Progressives in 1912, Strom Thurmond's States Righters in 1948, and George Wallace's American Independents in 1968 all claimed they did not get a fair hearing in their own party and left to form new parties.

Rosenstone, Behr, and Lazarus argue that third parties are more important than historians have realized. [29] They have controlled in one third of the last thirty-six presidential elections enough votes to have tipped the electoral college vote the other way. They have brought new groups into the electorate and have served as "safety valves" for popular discontent. Rosenstone and his colleagues argue that third parties are

[29] Steven J. Rosenstone, Roy L. Behr, and Edward H. Lazarus, *Third Parties in America* (Princeton, N.J.: Princeton University Press, 1984).

---

5 │ The "Major" Minor Parties

Election	Party	Its Claim to Fame
1832	AntiMasonic Party	As the name implies, this party was opposed to the Masons; it held the first national convention in 1831.
1860	Constitutional Union; Secessionist Democrats	Two of the four parties (together with the Democrats and the Republicans) who ran in the 1860 election.
1892	Populist	Agrarian opponents of banks and railroads; favored free silver.
1912	Progressive	The "Bull Moose Party," Teddy Roosevelt's splinter from the Republican Party; it got 88 electoral votes and cost the Republicans the election.
1924	Progressive	Another Republican splinter party.
1948	Progressive	Yet another Progressive Party, this one led by Democratic liberal Henry A. Wallace.
1948	States' Rights	A walkout by southerners at the Democratic convention led to this Dixiecrat party, whose candidate was Strom Thurmond (S.C.).
1968	American Independent	The party of segregationist Governor George Wallace of Alabama.
1980	Independent Party	Variously named, this represented losing Republican candidate John Anderson's effort to siphon off votes from the major parties.

often the unsung heros of American politics, bringing new issues to the public agenda. The Free Soilers of the 1850s were the first true antislavery party; the Progressives and the Populists put many social reforms on the political agenda. Many of these were incorporated into the major parties' platforms and later into governmental policy.

Despite the "also-rans" of third parties, we still have in this country a two-party system. Would it make a difference if we had a multiparty system like France, Italy, or Israel? Almost certainly.

Two Parties: So What?

The most obvious consequence of two-party governance is a moderation of political conflict. Because the best position is in the center, where the most voters are, the parties hate to go out on an ideological limb. If they follow the Downsian strategy outlined earlier, they will cling to a centrist position. The parties have often been criticized for this moderation. Their sternest critics think of them as a choice between "Tweedledum and Tweedledee." Third party candidate George Wallace in 1968 used to say that "there's not a dime's worth of differences between the parties." The two-party system throttles extreme or unconventional views.

The result is often policy ambiguity. Why should parties risk taking a strong stand on a controversial policy if it will only antagonize some voters? Ambiguity is a safe strategy. [30] Indeed, politicians often bend over backward to avoid taking a position on even the smallest issue. President Richard Nixon, after seeing the light musical comedy *No, No, Nanette*, told reporters, "My wife and I like musical comedy. I don't mean by that that they should always be old musicals. But I think that this musical that they call escapist—I don't look at it that way. I think that after a long day, most of us need a lift in the evening. I don't mean by that that sometimes I don't want to see a very serious play or something of that sort. . . . " If trivial issues elicit ambiguity, then controversial issues promote even more. As a result, it is sometimes difficult to distinguish the Democratic party from the Republican. Advocates of a responsible party model find this ambiguity most undesirable.

Clearly, if we had a multiparty system, each party would have more distinct policy positions than the two major parties do. Quite possibly, black groups might form their own party, pressing vigorously for more civil rights legislation. Environmentalists might constitute our newest party, vowing to clean up the rivers, oppose nuclear power, and rescue the wildernesses. We might have religious parties, union-based parties, farmers' parties, and all sorts of others. We might have—as several European countries do—ten or so parties represented in Congress. Guaranteed some power, each group (now a party) could stand strongly behind its special policy demands.

---

[30] For discussion of political ambiguity as a strategy, see Kenneth A. Shepsle, "The Strategy of Ambiguity: Uncertainty and Electoral Competition," *American Political Science Review* 66 (June 1972):555–68; and Benjamin I. Page, *Choices and Echoes in Presidential Elections* (Chicago: University of Chicago Press, 1978), Chap. 6.

THE PARTY IN THE ELECTORATE

In most European nations, being a party member means that you actually join a political party. You get a membership card to carry around in your wallet or purse, you pay dues, and you vote to pick your local and national party leaders. In America, being a party member takes far less work than becoming a member of the Rotary Club. There is no formal "membership" in the parties at all. If you believe that you are a Democrat or a Republican, then you *are* a Democrat or a Republican. Thus, one aspect of the "three-headed political giant," the party-in-the-electorate, consists largely of symbolic or psychological images and ideas. For most people, the party is a psychological label. They do not work for the party or its candidates but have images of the different parties' stances on issues and of their attitudes toward groups. These are very general pictures about which party is probusiness or prolabor, which is the party of peace, and which is the better manager of government. These pictures help shape people's party identification and consequently their voting behavior.

Party Identification

Even in our antiparty nation, most citizens are willing to claim "I am a Republican" or "I am a Democrat." This is their **party identification,** the self-proclaimed preference for one or the other party. Since 1937, Gallup has asked a sample of citizens the question: "Generally speaking, do you think of yourself as a Republican, a Democrat, or an Independent?" The repeated asking of this question permits us to trace party identification for three decades of modern American politics. 6

The clearest trend in 6 is *the decline of both parties and resultant upsurge of independence.* In 1937, the Democratic party could count on the allegiance of exactly half the American electorate (50 percent), and Republicans on well above a quarter (34 percent). But by 1985, the Democratic party could count on the allegiance of only 37 percent of the electorate. While Republicans had gained over these five decades, independents were growing at the expense of both parties.

During the 1960s and 1970s, the number of independents was on the upswing. Crotty observed that "the day is not far off when independent will clearly be the identification preferred by most Americans."[31] This is not true yet (the number of party identifiers has remained fairly stable through the 1980s), but "independence" is the choice of more Americans now than in any time since polling began.

Virtually every major social group—Catholics, Jews, poor whites, southerners, and so on—moved toward a position of increased independence between the 1950s and the 1970s. The exception was black voters. A decade of Democratic civil rights policy in the 1960s moved black Americans even more solidly into the Democratic party. Typically, a fifth of Democratic votes come from the 12 percent of the population that is black.[32] In 1984, black voters weighed in even more heavily: One in four voters for the Mondale-Ferraro ticket was a black voter.

[31] Crotty, *American Parties in Decline,* pp. 28–30.
[32] Norman Nie, Sidney Verba, and John Petrocik, *The Changing American Voter* (Cambridge, Mass.: Harvard University Press, 1976), p. 242.

For most white Americans, though, **party desertion**—the abandonment of either party for a nonparty attachment—is well advanced. This occurred at all age levels in the electorate, though it was more pronounced for those with the weakest party ties, that is, younger voters. [33]

Party identification is not only declining, but is not as closely tied to voting as in the past. In the 1950s, political scientists reported that party identification was the single best predictor of voting choice. [34] In the 1950s, 80 to 90 percent of the electorate could be expected to vote for their own party's candidate for president. Today, party identification—despite evidence of weakening over a generation—is still linked to the voter's choice. The last three presidential elections have shown a rebounding link between party identification and voting. [35] (See 2 on page 206.)

[33] The term "party desertion" and evidence on it comes from Helmut Norpoth and Jerrold G. Rusk, "Partisan Dealignment in the American Electorate: Itemizing the Deductions since 1964," *American Political Science Review* 76 (September 1982):522–37.

[34] See, for example, Angus Campbell, et al., *The American Voter* (New York: John Wiley and Sons, 1960).

[35] Crotty, *American Parties in Decline*, pp. 31–34.

---

6   Party Identification in the United States, 1937–85

	Percentage of People[a]		
Year	*Republicans*	*Democrats*	*Independents*
1937	34	50	16
1940	38	42	20
1944	39	41	20
1946	40	39	21
1949	32	48	20
1950	33	45	22
1952	34	41	25
1954	34	46	20
1960	30	47	23
1964	25	53	22
1968	27	46	27
1972	28	43	29
1975	22	45	33
1976	23	47	30
1977	21	48	31
1978	23	48	29
1979	22	45	33
1980	24	46	30
1981	28	42	30
1982	26	45	29
1983	25	44	31
1984	31	40	29
1985	35	37	28

[a]Those saying they have no party preference or who name other parties, 3–4 percent in the latest surveys, are excluded.

Source: Surveys by the Gallup Organization as reported in the *Gallup Reports*.

FROM THE GRASS ROOTS TO WASHINGTON: THE PARTY ORGANIZATIONS

An organization chart of any organization is usually shaped like a pyramid, with the bosses at the top and the lowliest staff workers at the bottom. You could draw such an organization chart of the American political party. You could put the national committee and national convention of the party at the apex of your pyramid, the state party organizations in the middle, and the thousands of local party organizations at the bottom. But when you got through, you would have a very incomplete picture of an American political party. ⑦ The president of General Motors is at the top of GM in fact as well as on paper. The chairperson of the Democratic or Republican national committee is on top on paper, but not in fact.

Here is the way an American political party looks on paper. But remember that real power in the party does not coincide with this neat hierarchical structure.

⑦ An Organization Chart of the American Political Party

National institutions

National convention

National chairperson   National committee

State institutions

State conventions and committees

Local institutions

County committees

Precinct and ward organizations

Party members

As organizations, our political parties are decentralized and fragmented. Frank Sorauf has written:

> Every four years [state and local] party organizations come together as a national party to select a presidential candidate and write a platform, but they have historically been careful to leave only an enfeebled national organization behind as they break camp. What appears to be pyramiding of state party committees into a single, integrating national party authority, therefore, is nothing of the kind. [36]

It is no accident that one leading study of the national party organization was called *Politics Without Power*. [37] We can imagine a system in which the national office of a party resolved conflicts among its state and local branches and stated the party's position on an issue, and then passed orders down through the hierarchy. We can even imagine a system in which the party leaders had the power to enforce their decision by offering rewards—campaign funds, advice, appointments—to national, state, and local officeholders who followed the policy and by punishing those who did not. (Many European parties work just that way.) The parties then would be accountable for the actions of their politicians. But in America the national parties have little such power. Power in the parties, as in the government itself, is fragmented among local, state, and national organizations.

Local Parties: The Dying Urban Machines

Today, urban party organization is pretty sleepy politics, except in a few places. County and city organizations may be the grass roots of the party, but the grass is often brown, especially if the party is a perpetual minority, doomed to certain defeat in every election. Even finding people to serve as unpaid party chairpersons becomes a chore. One Republican candidate for Congress in Texas, running in a district where a Democrat had held the office since the 1940s, had trouble tracking down the Republican county chairpersons in his district. When he found some, he encountered "what I call the Hereford look. You contact a person and ask them to do something and they agree, and you go back and ask if they've done it, and they just stand there and look at you." [38] In such places, parties are disorganized and demoralized after years of being the "out party." It takes real perseverance to track down the Republican committeeperson in Chicago, where Democrats walk away with everything. Trying to find Republican headquarters in the eleventh ward, the residence of every Democratic mayor of Chicago for four decades, one industrious researcher reported, "The outside doors to the headquarters are boarded up. . . . There are two alternative entrances, however, if one is

[36] Sorauf, *Party Politics in America*, pp. 114–115.
[37] Cornelius Cotter and Bernard C. Hennessey, *Politics without Power* (New York: Atherton, 1964).
[38] Robert L. Lineberry, John E. Sinclair, Lawrence C. Dodd, and Alan M. Sager, "The Case of the Wrangling Professors," in Alan L. Clem (ed.), *The Making of Congressmen* (North Scituate, Mass.: Duxbury, 1976), p. 188.

persistent enough to discover them; one behind the pin-setting machine in the bowling alley, and another through a tavern."[39]

Obviously, things are not always that bad, even for the minority party. In plenty of cases, both parties have well-oiled precinct, city, and county organizations. They get out the vote, conduct grass roots campaigns, and help state and local candidates. Sometimes independent (often liberal) reform organizations of amateur politicians are more active than the regular party organization. But as a rule, local politics is not a hotbed of party organization.

It was not always this way. Once, the urban political party was *the* political party organization in America. Roughly from the last years of the nineteenth century through the New Deal of the 1930s, scores of cities were dominated by party machines. A machine is a particular kind of party organization, different from the fragmented and disorganized political party typical in America. Edward C. Banfield and James Q. Wilson defined a **machine** as a "party organization that depends crucially on inducements that are both specific and material."[40] A *specific inducement* is one that can be given to someone and withheld from someone else: If you get the job, he cannot have it; if you get the paving contract, he loses it. A *material inducement* is something monetary or convertible into money. A job, cash, contracts, and so on, are examples of material inducements.

Patronage is one of the key inducements machines use. A patronage job is one that is given for political reasons rather than for merit or competence alone. Jobs are not the only form of patronage. A contract given to a friendly businessman may result from (or result in) a handsome campaign contribution.

Urban machines in Albany, Chicago, Philadelphia, Kansas City, and elsewhere depended heavily on ethnic group support. The Irish were leaders in New York's Tammany Hall, and they dominated Chicago's political machine. Some of the most fabled machine leaders were Irish politicians, including Tammany's George Washington Plunkett, Boston's James Michael Curley, and Chicago's Richard J. Daley. Daley's Chicago machine was the last surviving one, steamrolling its opposition amid charges of racism and corruption.

Still, the Chicago machine clings precariously to life.[41] Mayor Daley's protege and successor, Michael Bilandic, lost the mayoral election of 1979 to another of Mayor Daley's protegés, former consumer commissioner Jane M. Byrne. She, in turn, lost the 1983 Democratic primary election to Harold Washington, who went on to become the first black mayor in Chicago's history. Washington and the remnants of the Chicago machine are still engaged in a ferocious battle for control of patronage, policy, and political advantage. If the machine is not dead yet, it is at the least only one of several claimants to power in the city.

Chicago Mayor Harold Washington. *Chicago is the nation's third largest city (after New York City and Los Angeles) and its mayor is traditionally a powerful figure in Democratic politics. Former Congressman Harold Washington is Chicago's first black mayor. For four decades, Chicago was dominated by a predominantly white political machine. After the death of Mayor Richard J. Daley, the machine began to crumble, but its remnants are still strong enough to battle Mayor Washington on every appointment, every budget, and every policy.*

[39] Milton Rakove, *Don't Make No Waves, Don't Back No Losers* (Bloomington: Indiana University Press, 1975), p. 167.

[40] Edward C. Banfield and James Q. Wilson, *City Politics* (Cambridge, Mass.: Harvard University Press and the MIT Press, 1963), p. 115.

[41] See the articles in Samuel Gove and Louis Masotti (eds.), *Chicago Politics after Daley* (Urbana: University of Illinois Press, 1981).

The Fifty State Party Systems

The states are important elements in the national party system.[42] They are the proving grounds of national politics and of politically ambitious politicians. Our political system has little room at the top, but plenty of men and women who want to be there. Of the major candidates and contenders for presidential office in the last generation, only General Dwight D. Eisenhower did not serve first in some statewide elected post. These days, presidential timber is mostly chopped from the forests of senators, governors, and members of the House of Representatives.

Equally important, the states are the major pieces in the presidential election game. Our electoral college (see pages 288–290) makes the states, not the individual voters, the main campaign target. Each state delivers its electoral votes on a winner-take-all system. If the Democratic candidate for president wins 51 percent of the popular vote in a state with twenty-one electoral votes, he gets all twenty-one, not 51 percent of them. Obviously, winning big states with lots of electoral votes is the key to winning the presidency. Better to get the bishops and rooks of the electoral game—states like Texas, Florida, and California—than to make a clean sweep of the pawns—states with only a few electoral votes.

State Party Organizations: Weak But Getting Stronger. Our national parties are a loose aggregation of state parties, which are themselves a fluid association of individuals, groups, and local organizations. There are fifty state party systems, no two exactly alike. In a few states (Pennsylvania is one), the parties are well organized, have real staffs, and a reasonable budget. In other states, however, parties are weak. Christensen and Gersten say of the California party system that "to describe their [the parties'] function as minimal overstates the case . . . . The fact is that California has a political party system on paper, and that's about it."[43] Kay Lawson agrees. California, she says, "has political parties so weak as to be almost nonexistent; it is the birthplace of campaigning by 'hired guns'; and it has been run by special interests for so long that Californians have forgotten what is special about that."[44]

To give you an idea of the disorganized status of state parties, consider these facts about the state parties unearthed by John Bibby and his associates:[45] As recently as the 1960s, most state party organizations did not even maintain a permanent headquarters office. When the state party elected a new chairperson, the party organization simply shifted its office to his or her hometown. Today, almost all state parties have a physical headquarters, typically in the capital city or the largest city. Of course, a headquarters with no staff and budget is not much use. In the early 1960s,

---

[42] On the state parties, see Malcolm E. Jewell and David M. Olson, *American State Parties and Elections*, rev. ed. (Homewood, Ill.: Dorsey, 1982).

[43] Terry Christensen and Larry N. Gerston, *The California Connection* (Boston: Little, Brown, 1984), p. 37.

[44] Kay Lawson, "California: The Uncertainties of Reform," in Gerald M. Pomper (ed.), *Party Renewal in America* (New York: Praeger, 1980), Chap. 8.

[45] John Bibby, et al., "Parties in State Politics," in Virginia Gray, Herbert Jacob, and Kenneth Vines, *Politics in the American States*, 4th ed. (Boston: Little, Brown, 1983), pp. 76–79.

more than half the parties had a budget of less than $50,000 (in 1967 constant dollars), not much to employ fund-raisers and other key people. By the end of the 1970s, 37 percent of the state parties still limped along with less than $50,000 a year. By then, the average state party had a budget ranging from $50,000 to $150,000. (Compare these figures, by the way, to the contributions of interest groups in national campaigns. In 1980—just one year—just one Political Action Committee, the National Association of Automobile Dealers, gave $1,035,276 to congressional candidates.) [46]

Clearly, in headquarters and budgets, state parties are better organized than they used to be. Yet almost any second-rate national interest group in Washington will have a richer budget, a plusher headquarters, and a bigger staff than even the best-organized state party organization.

State Parties as Legal Organizations. The states, not the federal government, regulate the parties. Their statutes define a party and specify how it is to be organized. David Price notes that "in no western democracy are parties regulated as closely as in the United States." [47] California, Price points out, where "laws covering party organization and campaign practices cover several hundred pages, is a good example of the lengths to which such regulations can go." [48] California has traditionally been an antiparty state; its complex laws hamstring, rather than help, the parties. The party organization is effectively placed under the control of members of the State Assembly; party chairpersons are limited to nonconsecutive two-year terms and must rotate between southern and northern California. Other states have less complex regulations than California, but all set down party law in their statutes.

Sometimes, state legislation regarding the parties conflicts with national policy. Many years ago the Supreme Court held that a state could not turn its primary elections over to the party (as a "private organization") in order to prevent blacks from voting (*United States* v. *Classic*, 1940). More recently, the federal courts have upheld the national parties when national party policy has conflicted with state law. In cases involving Illinois and Wisconsin, the Supreme Court held that the national party convention's rules took precedence over state law governing how delegates to the convention were to be picked.

State Party Competition. Some states have two strong, competitive parties. Others have one dominant party and a lackluster opposition, which rarely wins anything. Historically, the southern states, from the end of the Civil War through 1964, were called the "Solid South." [49] This meant that they were solid for the Democratic party. Ever since 1952, the

[46] Cited in Jeffrey M. Berry, *The Interest Group Society* (Boston: Little, Brown, 1984), p. 172.
[47] Price, *Bringing Back the Parties*, p. 124.
[48] Ibid.
[49] On the old southern politics, see V. O. Key, Jr., *Southern Politics in State and Nation* (New York: Knopf, 1949).

Republicans have made steady forays into the old confederacy. In 1964, Republican presidential candidate Barry Goldwater even won the electoral votes of five southern states. The Republican party has become the more clearly conservative party, and most white southerners have become clearly conservative. Many northerners have moved to the south, some of them Republicans, and have brought their party affiliations with them. As you can see from 8, the south is no longer solid for the Democrats, who these days, are experiencing a significant dilemma there. Republican Congressman Trent Lott of Mississippi puts it this way: "They're in a bind with the national Democratic party. If they subscribe to the national . . . party principles, they are going to alienate an overwhelming majority of the white people of Mississippi. If they don't, they are going to offend the black folk in Mississippi." [50]

[50] Lott is quoted in Sundquist, *Dynamics of the Party System*, p. 375.

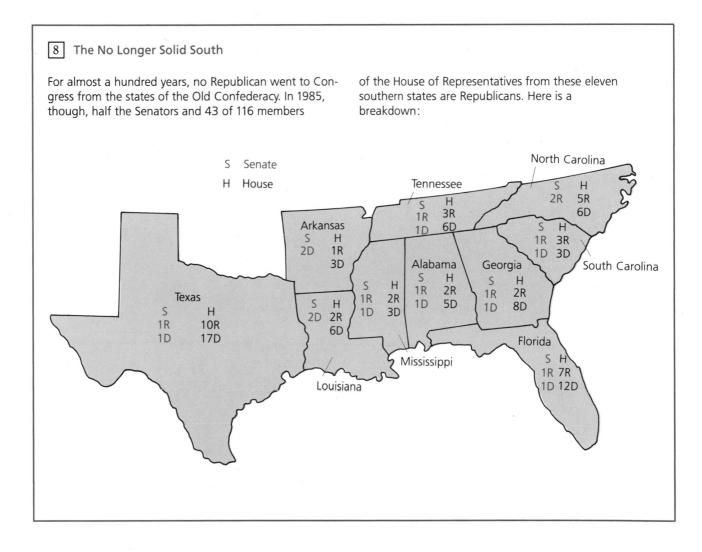

8 The No Longer Solid South

For almost a hundred years, no Republican went to Congress from the states of the Old Confederacy. In 1985, though, half the Senators and 43 of 116 members of the House of Representatives from these eleven southern states are Republicans. Here is a breakdown:

S Senate
H House

North Carolina
S   H
2R   5R
     6D

Tennessee
S   H
1R   3R
1D   6D

South Carolina
S   H
1R   3R
1D   3D

Arkansas
S   H
2D   1R
     3D

Alabama
S   H
1R   2R
1D   5D

Georgia
S   H
1R   2R
1D   8D

Texas
S   H
1R   10R
1D   17D

Mississippi
S   H
2D   2R
     6D

Florida
S   H
1R   7R
1D   12D

Louisiana

Bibby and his colleagues have classified the states into four types, depending upon their level of two-party competition. (See 9). Twenty-two of the states—less than half—are genuinely two-party; in these states, the parties seesaw for control. In the one-party states, year in and year out, one party tends to win all the main state offices.

No states are unabashedly in the Republican column. Only North Dakota is a "modified one-party Republican" state. The Democrats clearly have the edge in state politics, and it is growing wider. Since 1946, the number of states "locked up" for the Republicans has declined and the number of states tilting toward the Democrats has increased.[51] Here,

[51] Bibby, et al., "Parties in State Politics," p. 67.

9 Party Competition in the States

John Bibby et al. measured the competitiveness of the two parties in the various states from 1974 to 1980. Using state offices only (not counting national offices like the presidency), they rated the states on a scale from 1.000 (if the Democrats won everything in sight) to 0.000 (if the Republicans won everything in sight). A fully competitive state, therefore, rated .500. Maine and Kansas turned out to be the most competitive states, just above and just below the .500 mark. Here is a breakdown of the states on this measure of competitiveness.

States Classified According to Degree of Interparty Competition, 1974–1980

One-party Democratic	Modified one-party Democratic	Two-party	Modified one-party Republican
Alabama (.9438)	South Carolina (.8034)	Montana (.6259)	North Dakota (.3374)
Georgia (.8849)	West Virginia (.8032)	Michigan (.6125)	
Louisiana (.8762)	Texas (.7993)	Ohio (.5916)	
Mississippi (.8673)	Massachusetts (.7916)	Washington (.5806)	
Arkansas (.8630)	Kentucky (.7907)	Alaska (.5771)	
North Carolina (.8555)	Oklahoma (.7841)	Pennsylvania (.5574)	
Maryland (.8509)	Nevada (.7593)	Delaware (.5490)	
Rhode Island (.8506)	Hawaii (.7547)	New York (.5390)	
	Florida (.7524)	Illinois (.5384)	
	Connecticut (.7336)	Nebraska (.5166)	
	New Jersey (.7330)	Maine (.5164)	
	Virginia (.7162)	Kansas (.4671)	
	New Mexico (.7113)	Utah (.4653)	
	California (.7081)	Iowa (.4539)	
	Oregon (.6954)	Arizona (.4482)	
	Missouri (.6932)	Colorado (.4429)	
	Minnesota (.6680)	Indiana (.4145)	
	Tennessee (.6648)	New Hampshire (.3916)	
	Wisconsin (.6634)	Idaho (.3898)	
		Wyoming (.3879)	
		Vermont (.3612)	
		South Dakota (.3512)	

Source: John F. Bibby et al., "Parties in State Politics," in Virginia Gray, Herbert Jacob, and Kenneth N. Vines (eds.), *Politics in the American States: A Comparative Analysis,* 4th ed. Copyright © 1983 by John F. Bibby, Cornelius Cotter, James L. Gibson, and Robert Huckshorn. Reprinted by permission of Little, Brown and Company.

then, is a party paradox: Even though the Republican party has captured six of the last nine presidential elections, the Democratic party still has a firm, indeed an even firmer, foothold at the grass roots.

The National Party Organization

The supreme power within each of the parties is its **national convention.** It meets every four years, and its main task is to nominate the presidential and vice-presidential candidates of the party and then write the party's platform. (We will have more to say about conventions in Chapter 8.) In 1974, the Democrats also started a "mini-convention," held every two years. (Lately, though, it has become very "mini" indeed.) The conservative Republicans stuck to the tried-and-true four-year cycle.

Keeping the party operating between conventions is the job of two formal national institutions. The **national committee** is composed of representatives from the states and territories. (The Democrats also include assorted governors, members of congress, and other party officials.) Typically each state will have a *national committeeman* and a *national committeewoman* as delegates to the party's national committee. Day-to-day activities of the national party are the responsibility of the **national chairperson** of the party. He or she is usually hand picked by the presidential nominee of the party. (Walter Mondale, though, found it impossible to dislodge Charles Manatt from this post to make room for Georgian Bert Lance.) The national party chairperson hires the staff, raises the money, pays the bills, and attends to the daily duties of a party. (Earlier in this chapter, we looked at the Democratic and Republican parties today and learned how their national offices—particularly the vigorous Republican national office—operated.)

THE PARTY IN GOVERNMENT: PROMISES AND POLICY

Government is such a simple word to describe such a complex operation. The government includes the presidency, the Congress, the federal agencies, the governors and legislatures in the state capitals, and the courts. The winning party does not take over the entire government and throw its opponents out on the street (although Washington real estate agents practically salivate over a shift in partisan control of the national government), but party control matters to the various arms of the government. It matters because each party and the elected officials that represent it generally try to turn campaign promises into policies once they get into government. As a result, the party that has control will ultimately determine who gets what, where, when, and how.

Voters and coalitions of voters are attracted to the parties largely (though not entirely) by the policy promises and performance of the parties. What they promise to whom, and what they have done while in office, largely determine which coalitions will join them during the next elections.

Sometimes voters suspect that political promises are made to be broken, worth little more than the mimeograph paper on which they are printed. To be sure, there are notable instances of politicians straying—sometimes 180 degrees—from their policy promises. Lyndon Johnson repeatedly promised in the 1964 presidential campaign that he would not "send American boys to do an Asian boy's job" and involve the United States in a Vietnam war. But he did. Ronald Reagan was also charged with forgetting the promises he made. In the 1980 campaign he said he would oppose peacetime draft registration, but in office he continued it. His campaign rhetoric guaranteed a balanced budget, but his 1985 budget deficit grew to more than $200 billion. Reagan joined the ranks of every president before him in saying one thing and doing another.

Yet we are likely to forget how very often parties and presidents do exactly what they say they will do. For every broken promise, many more are kept. Ronald Reagan promised to step up defense spending and cut back on social welfare expenditures, and within his first year in office he did just that. He promised a major tax cut and provided one. He promised less government regulation and quickly set about deregulating natural gas prices, occupational safety, and environmental policies. The impression that politicians and parties never produce policy out of promises is largely erroneous.

In fact, the parties have done a pretty good job over the years of translating their platform promises into public policy. Gerald Pomper has shown that party platforms are excellent predictors of a party's actual policy performance in office. He tabulated specific pledges in the major parties' platforms from 1944 to 1978. Over that period, the parties made exactly 3,194 specific policy pronouncements. He then looked to see whether the winning party's policy promises were actually fulfilled.

Jesse Jackson's Candidacy. Chicago's Rev. Jesse Jackson, whose supporters cheered his speech at the 1984 Democratic national convention, was the first serious black candidate for president of either party. Jackson tried to assemble a "rainbow coalition" of minorities and the poor—people who had traditionally stood outside both parties. Few candidates exhibited as much charisma as Jackson. But black voters stuck with the national Democratic ticket despite Jackson's lukewarm support of it. In 1984, one in every four votes collected by Walter Mondale was from a black voter.

Nearly three-fourths of all promises resulted in policy actions. Others were tried but foundered for one reason or another. Only 10 percent were ignored altogether.[52]

If parties generally do what they say they will, then the party platforms adopted at the national conventions represent blueprints, however vague, for action. Consider what the two major parties promised the voters in 1984. 10

The Republican platform committed the new Republican president to cutting taxes, increasing defense spending, deregulating the economy, opposing school busing, deregulating natural gas prices, and reducing social spending. To those who read the Republican platform of 1980 carefully, Reagan's policies in office produced few surprises. If the voters decide they do not like the policies pursued by the winning party, they always have recourse at the next election.

IS THE PARTY OVER? REALIGNMENT, DEALIGNMENT, OR RENEWAL

Hard Times

People who support the party system worry regularly about its future.[53] They fear that we are in an era of **party dealignment,** when people and politicians are gradually disengaging from the parties. There is plenty of evidence that the parties have fallen on hard times. Party identification is shrinking. Young people entering the electorate for the first time tend to choose independence. In the 1950s about a quarter of the new voters at each election called themselves independents; by the 1970s, about half the new generation of voters chose independence.[54]

Other signs of hard times abound. **Ticket-splitting**—voting with one party for one office and another for other offices—is on the rise. In 1960, nearly two-thirds of the voters voted a "straight ticket." By 1972, only a third were.[55] Not only has ticket-splitting become the norm, but voters are voting for candidates for reasons other than their party affiliation. One major reason is simple incumbency. In recent years, more than 90 percent of the incumbents in Congress have run for office again; more than 90 percent of that 90 percent won.[56] Suppose that we had an "Incumbent Party" and a "Nonincumbent Party" in the United States. If we did, the Incumbent Party would overwhelm Democrats and Republicans alike.

The party in power is also experiencing hard times. One of the tasks of a responsible party is to coordinate policymaking. When members of each party stick together, they are able to carry out their platforms and

[52] Gerald M. Pomper, *Elections in America* (New York: Longman, 1980), p. 161.
[53] See, for example, David Broder, *The Party's Over* (New York: Harper and Row, 1971).
[54] This is a major argument in Nie, Verba, and Petrocik, *Changing American Voter.*
[55] Ibid., p. 53.
[56] Morris Fiorina, *Congress: Keystone of the Washington Establishment* (New Haven, Conn.: Yale University Press, 1977), p. 5. For more on the incumbency effect, see Chapter 12, pp. 368–373.

policy promises to the voters. But party cohesion in Congress is going down. [57]

All things considered, the parties seem to be having a tough go of it. Perhaps the party isn't over. But it seems to be winding down. And many of the guests are going home.

[57] Price, *Bringing Back the Parties*, pp. 51–59.

---

10 Party Platforms, 1984

In 1984, the *National Journal* contrasted the platforms of the major political parties. Here is a sampling of what they found in each of our four key issue areas:

REPUBLICANS

DEMOCRATS

THE ECONOMY

Oppose any attempts to increase taxes. Instead, favor reducing deficits by continuing the economic recovery, cutting government spending and providing incentives for more personal savings. Defend the three-year cut in income tax rates enacted in 1981 and oppose repeal of tax indexing. Say a "modified flat tax—with specific exemptions for such items as mortgage interest—is a most promising approach" for tax reform.

Support constitutional amendments requiring a balanced budget and line-item veto so that the president can reject individual items in appropriations bills.

Suggest the gold standard "may be a useful mechanism" for achieving stable prices. Call for reduced federal regulation.

Would reduce federal budget deficits by reassessing defense expenditures, creating a tax system that is "both adequate and fair," and controlling health costs. Oppose the "artificial and rigid restraint" of a constitutional amendment requiring a balanced budget.

Would cap the effect of Reagan tax cuts for the wealthy, limiting benefits of third-year reduction to individuals with incomes below $60,000 a year. Would partially defer tax indexation. Would impose a minimum corporate tax of 15 percent.

Would support tax reform aimed at "broadening the tax base, simplifying the tax code, lowering rates, and eliminating unnecessary, unfair and unproductive deductions." This "fair tax," unlike the GOP "flat tax," would retain some progressivity in the tax code.

EQUALITY

Civil Rights

Assert that Reagan adminstration has vigorously enforced civil rights laws. Reject use of quotas to remedy discrimination in employment, education and housing.

Call for affirmative action goals, timetables and "other verifiable measurements" to make up for past discrimination, but do not specifically endorse or oppose the use of quotas.

Accuse Reagan administration of eroding "constitutionally mandated and court-sanctioned remedies for longstanding patterns of discriminatory conduct." Promise an independent Civil Rights Commission with increased funding; strengthened civil rights enforcement and equal educational opportunity.

Women's Rights

Make no mention of proposed Equal Rights Amendment to the Constitution, but say that all Republicans "are free to work individually for women's progress" and demand that there be "no inhibition" of women's rights to "full opportunity and advancement within this society." Oppose concept of equal pay for jobs of "comparable worth."

Endorse adoption of the Equal Rights Amendment. Support equal pay for work of comparable worth.

Rivals of the Parties

The key problem of the parties today is this: The parties are "low-tech" institutions in a "high-tech" political era. The perceptive political columnist David Broder once noted that "a growing danger to the prospects for responsible party government is the technological revolution that

---

10 Party Platforms, 1984 (continued)

| REPUBLICANS | DEMOCRATS |

ENERGY/ENVIRONMENT

Energy

REPUBLICANS	DEMOCRATS

Would remove all remaining controls on natural gas prices in order to stimulate exploration and production. Would permit more coal mining and consumption, and development of oil and natural gas on federal properties. Would abolish windfall profits tax on oil and shut down federal Department of Energy.
 	
    Urge elimination of unnecessary regulations so nuclear power plants "can be brought on line quickly, efficiently and safely."
	Support increased coal production and promotion of coal exports. Endorse research and development of solar energy. Oppose offshore oil and gas exploration that would harm fisheries and coastal resources.
	
	    Oppose Reagan administration's "policy of aggressively promoting and further subsidizing nuclear power."

Environment

REPUBLICANS	DEMOCRATS
Would apply cost-benefit tests to environmental protection measures. Endorse strong efforts to clean up toxic waste, and would focus on acid rain research rather than controls.	Would increase budget of Environmental Protection Agency and would increase "superfund" financing to clean up toxic waste dumps. Would renew and strengthen Clean Air Act. On acid rain, would mandate a 50 percent reduction (from 1980 levels) in sulfur dioxide emissions within the next decade.

THE GLOBAL CONNECTION

Defense

REPUBLICANS	DEMOCRATS

Support Reagan administration's increase in defense spending and would make military spending an even larger share of the federal budget.
 	
    Endorse development and deployment of the MX missile. Support deployment of Pershing II and cruise missiles in Western Europe.
	Would reduce the rate of increase in defense spending. Support "military reform" that would produce more cost-effective military policies.
	
	    Would terminate production of the MX missile and B-1 bomber, and would prohibit production of nerve gas.

Arms Control

REPUBLICANS	DEMOCRATS
Would seek substantial mutual reductions in nuclear weapons. Would negotiate for verifiable arms control agreements while modernizing U.S. "deterrence capability." Oppose freeze on nuclear weapons, contending such a step would simply maintain Soviet superiority.	Would initiate immediately a "temporary, verifiable and mutual" freeze on testing of antisatellite weapons and underground nuclear weapons; on testing and deployment of all weapons in space, and of new strategic ballistic weapons now under development. Support negotiation of a "comprehensive, mutual and verifiable freeze on the testing, production and deployment of all nuclear weapons." Would pursue other arms negotiations with the Soviet Union, including updating and resubmitting SALT II treaty to the Senate.

Source: Diane Granat, "GOP, Democratic Platforms Collide … On Taxes, Defense and Social Issues," *Congressional Quarterly,* August 25, 1984. Reprinted by permission.

has affected campaigning in the past decade."[58] The party, through its door-to-door canvassers, is the only political institution that still makes house calls. Yet more and more of our political communication is not face-to-face, but conducted through the media.[59] The technology of campaigning—television, polls, computers, political consultants, media specialists, and the like—is available for hire to the candidates who can afford it. The underfinanced and understaffed parties (especially the Democrats) are ill-equipped to provide what candidates can buy themselves.

One reason, though, that the Republicans have lately been the "come-from-behind" party is their ability to capitalize on technology. At the national level, they have understood how to use technology in the campaign—and have had the money to pay for it.

No longer are parties the main source of our political information, attention, and affection. The party of today has rivals that appeal to voters and politicians alike. The biggest rival, of course, is the mushrooming media. Voters can now learn about candidates directly from television and the print media. They no longer have to listen to what and whom their party certifies. Television, says Crotty, "has supplanted the party as the main conduit between candidate and voter."[60] The interest group is another party rival. As we will see in Chapter 10, interest groups have grown on the body politic like crabgrass on a summer's lawn. They— not the parties—pioneered much of the technology of modern politics, including mass mailings and sophisticated fund-raising. Interest groups were housed in impressive steel and concrete buildings in Washington while state party organizations were still moving their headquarters to the hometown of the new chairperson.

Although it seems strange at first to say, even the candidates are rivals of their own parties—and they can be its deadliest ones. Presidential candidates typically set up their own organization outside the party structure. (In fact, doing so caused Richard Nixon to become embroiled in Watergate.) The incumbent president can even be the party's worst enemy. Presidents not only like to run *with* the party, they like to run *it*. Democrats and Republicans alike have been known to treat their party as a wayward stepchild. President Carter's advisors "seemed to regard the . . . parties more as potential antagonists to be neutralized than as potential allies to be nurtured."[61] Even the mighty Republican National Committee is sometimes frustrated with the Reagan White House. Said former GOP chairman Richard Richards in 1982: "Every clerk in the White House thinks he knows how to do my job."

No one, of course, knows what is in store for the parties. Some political

[58] Broder, *The Party's Over*, p. 236.

[59] Banfield and Wilson are among the first to note the impact of technology on erosion of the party, when they ascribe to television the weakening of the importance of the precinct committeeman's visits: "The precinct captain who vists in the evening interrupts a television program and must either stay and watch in silence or else excuse himself quickly and move on." See their *City Politics*, p. 122.

[60] Crotty, *American Parties in Decline*, p. 75.

[61] The observation about the Carter administration and the Democratic party and the quotation from Richards are both from Price, *Bringing Back the Parties*, p. 78.

scientists think we are entering a period of party realignment which, historically, may be overdue. The Reagan surges of 1980 and 1984 may push the Republicans into majority party status, and the resurgent Republican organization is poised to take advantage of shifting voter loyalities. Perhaps we face a period of party renewal. Both parties are now better funded, better organized, and better staffed than ever before. Their renewal, as Price rightly notes, "will critically depend upon the determination and ingenuity with which the parties help themselves."[62]

THE PARTIES SUMMARIZED

The political parties are one of our least beloved institutions. Yet political scientists see them as a major linkage between people and policymakers. The party is ubiquitous; we have described it as a force within the electorate, as an organization, and as a force in government. In a democracy, parties compete with one another in the political marketplace by using policies to attract voters to their cause. These policies are found in their platforms. Actually, American parties do a rather good job of enacting their platforms once elected.

Ours is a two-party system. This fact is of fundamental importance in understanding our politics. The parties do not seesaw with each election; rather, one party tends to dominate for long periods of time. These are party eras, punctuated by a period of party realignment following a critical election period. For the last fifty years or more, the Democratic party has been our majority party, but its hold on the old New Deal coalition has eroded. Some political scientists think we are on the threshold of a new party realignment.

If so, the Republicans are certainly prepared for it. While the Democrats spent time and energy making themselves more representative of the people, the Republicans spent their time and energy making themselves more effective—and better endowed.

Despite the efforts of parties to shape up, there is evidence that they are falling on hard times. Party identification is declining and party cohesion in Washington is weakening. There is much discussion, therefore, about the future of parties. Some political scientists see a party realignment ahead, others see a continuing dealignment in the offing, and still others believe that a party renewal is possible.

[62] Ibid., p. 301.

Key Terms

party competition	party realignment	machine
political party	coalition	patronage
linkage institutions	New Deal coalition	national convention
party image	McGovern-Fraser	national committee
responsible party	commission	national chairperson
model	third parties	party dealignment
party eras	party identification	ticket-splitting
critical election	party desertion	

For Further Reading

Crotty, William J. *American Parties in Decline,* 2nd ed. (1984). A thorough but concise review of research on the reason why the party seems to be in decline everywhere.

Downs, Anthony. *An Economic Theory of Democracy* (1957). A theoretical account of an economic theory of the parties and democracy.

Mazmanian, Daniel. *Third Parties in Presidential Elections* (1974). Documents and traces our minor parties.

Pomper, Gerald M., ed. *Party Renewal in America* (1980). A collection of articles on party reform and reorganization.

———. *Elections in America,* rev. ed. (1980). Presents evidence that parties and elections *do* affect policy.

Price, David E. *Bringing Back the Parties* (1984). A look at the possibilities of party "reengagement" instead of party decline.

Rakove, Milton. *Don't Make No Waves, Don't Back No Losers* (1975). A thoroughly informative and entertaining history of the Daley machine in Chicago.

Sorauf, Frank. *Party Politics in America,* 5th ed. (1984). The standard textbook on political parties.

Sundquist, James L. *Dynamics of the Party System,* rev. ed. (1983). An historical description of the realignments in post-Civil War American politics.

Running for Office: Nominations and Campaigns

MEMO

A nation can be democratic without many of the institutions we enjoy—without a president, a congress, states, and so forth—but not without competitive elections.

In America, nominations, campaigns, and elections are grueling races. Ideas and issues should prevail; sometimes stamina and sheer willpower are the winners. Some voters enjoy election campaigns as much as any drama, while others resent them as time away from their favorite TV show.

In this chapter, we study the drama of nominations and campaigns. I begin by describing the new technology of nominations and campaigns, and then move on to examine how they actually work.

The American presidential election can be described as a play in three acts, in which we close the final curtain at the inaugural parade in Washington, D.C. In this chapter and the next, we explore the scripts, the actors, and the staging of our three-act drama.

- Act I is the nomination game. The long road to the nomination begins well before the snowy New Hampshire primary; we face an almost perpetual campaign, as candidates declare earlier and earlier. Act I concludes at the national convention held, in the summer's heat, to nominate a candidate and write a platform.
- Act II is the campaign. Many candidates have been on the campaign trail working to get nominated, but the general election campaign between the Democratic and Republican nominees is the high drama of American politics, played with an abundance of media and money.
- Act III brings the voters to center stage. They play their part in Chapter 9. A tired extra, the electoral college, is introduced there.

THIS CHAPTER IS ABOUT an old American pastime: running for office. Nominations and campaigns are preludes to the election, a time of reckoning in American politics. Plenty of Americans run for office. There are nearly half a million elected public offices in the United States today, but most of them are minor local posts. Only a few are major offices like state legislator, governor, member of Congress, or senator.

Only one of them is the *big prize*—the presidency of the United States. In this chapter, we focus primarily on the nomination and campaign for the presidency.

ACT I: THE TECHNOTRONIC CAMPAIGN

The new machines of politics, which we described in Chapter 1, have changed the way we campaign for office. At the turn of the century, the candidate and his entourage piled onto a campaign train and tried to stop at as many places and speak to as many people as time, energy, and money would allow. An army of campaign workers would handle dozens of campaign chores: knocking on doors, writing letters, stuffing envelopes, and so forth. Today's candidate also needs an army of workers—but some of them can be machines. [1] Abramson, Aldrich, and Rohde remark that "technological advances provide . . . major advances in the electoral process of the 1970s and 1980s. Computerized mailing lists, polling techniques, marketing and advertising technology, and the capabilities of the print and broadcast media have transformed the art of campaigning."[1]

Today television, not the railroad, is the means to reach voters.[2] Thomas Patterson stresses that "today's presidential campaign is essen-

[1] Paul R. Abramson, John H. Aldrich, and David W. Rohde, *Change and Continuity in the 1980 Elections* (Washington: Congressional Quarterly Press, 1983), pp. 14–15.

[2] One useful review of elections in the TV era is Chapter 6 of Doris Graber, *Mass Media and American Politics* 2nd ed. (Washington, D.C.: Congressional Quarterly Press, 1984).

Technology and Campaigns. *Contemporary campaigns are technologically sophisticated. Computers keep track of contributors, job applicants, schedules, finances, and workers. The mass mailing list was pioneered by conservative Virginia fund-raiser Richard Viguerie. It can target highly specialized segments of the population and tailor specific requests to them. For a fee, conservative candidates can purchase Viguerie's mailing list. Generally, Republican and conservative groups have made greater use of contemporary technology in campaigns, though the Democratic party is attempting to close the gap.*

tially a mass media campaign. . . . It is no exaggeration to say that, for the majority of voters, the campaign has little reality apart from its media version."[3]

Throughout this chapter, we will see the technotronic campaign at work. From the lowliest candidate for sheriff to candidates for the presidential nomination, command of the technology of communication is important—and having access to electronic media demands money.

[3] Thomas E. Patterson, *The Mass Media Election* (New York: Praeger, 1980), p. 3.

---

1 Programmed for Victory

·Times have changed since President Dwight D. Eisenhower first used a bit of technology called a TelePrompter (an automated machine which can be used to magnify a speech so you do not have to look down at your notes) and found it totally confusing. He grumbled in front of national television, "How does this damn thing work anyway?"

We are well beyond the TelePrompter in making the candidate look attractive and efficient. After the invention of personal computers, candidates for national, state, and local offices turned increasingly to the new machines of politics. In 1984, Democratic presidential aspirants Gary Hart and John Glenn used a bank of IBM PCs to handle chores once relegated to volunteers; Walter Mondale's staff carried around Kaypros. Much campaign work is ideally suited to the computer: mailing lists of potential contributors, keeping track of past electoral trends, graphic analysis of voting patterns, tallying federal campaign finance reports, and many others.

Former President Carter's son Jeff designed a software program called *Statmap,* which graphically depicts demographic data on political units—counties, states, and so forth. (Ironically, President Reagan's campaign staff was one of its first users.) Said young Carter: "Computers are the biggest thing to hit politics since television." A multitude of software and hardware combinations have appeared in the marketplace seemingly overnight. For $16,000 you can purchase a full package of hardware and software called *Solon.*·It includes a powerful personal computer, two printers, a modem, data base management capacity, payroll management capacity, and plenty of politically specialized software. Other, less expensive programs are available for the less well-heeled candidate.

The mailing list is a technology which William Jennings Bryant would have envied. With it, he could have reached every potential voter who opposed the gold standard and had populist leanings. Richard Viguerie, the conservative

fund-raiser, pioneered the huge mass mailing list—which included hundreds of thousands of conservatively tilted voters, contributors, and workers. Although originally designed for big, mainframe computers, today you can purchase mailing lists for smaller campaigns and smaller computers. For example, American Mailing Lists Corporation in Falls Church, Virginia, advertizes The Viguerie Company's "Right of Center" mailing list on a rental basis.

Today, the computerized campaign is a necessity, not a luxury.

Source: For more information on the use of computers in campaigns, see Kimball Brace and Mark Jaede, "Computer Graphics: Campaign Targeting and Micro-Mapping," *Campaigns and Elections* (Spring 1984): 62–78; Jonathan Littman, "The New Political Machine," *PC World* (August 1984): 294–304. The Carter quotation is from the Littman article, p. 301.

THE NOMINATION: GETTING THERE IS HALF THE FUN

A **nomination** is the party's official endorsement of a candidacy for office. Anyone can play the nomination game, but few have any serious chance of victory. ☐2 The winner of the nomination game can go on to play the election game. Sometimes (particularly when a popular and powerful incumbent is running) the nomination game is easy. Typically, when the party is out of power, a flock of candidates comes forward eighteen to twenty-four months in advance of the convention and tests the waters. In the 1984 Democratic presidential race, seven serious contenders lined up for the race.

Generally, success in the nomination game requires *momentum, money,* and *media attention. Campaign strategy* is the way in which candidates attempt to manipulate each of these to achieve the nomination. Let us see how the nomination game works in practice.

A campaign, whether for a nomination or the election, can be unpredictable. Even with money, name recognition, and political savvy, victory

---

☐2 The Nomination Game

Board games are popular these days. Here is a rudimentary design for one we might call "the nomination game."

Players. Any number can play, but not everyone starts equally. Here are some who have a real shot at victory, and they should be handicapped accordingly:*

— *Incumbent Presidents.* Start at square 7; don't neglect to take square 7's bonus point for frequent meetings with party and world leaders. Other players should remember that no twentieth-century president who has tried to win the renomination game has ever failed.
— *Unemployed Notables.* Unemployed notables have three things going for them: They once occupied an important, visible office; they are not now formulating any policies that will antagonize voters; and they have lots of time on their hands. Ronald Reagan, Jimmy Carter, and Walter Mondale were all Unemployed Notables when they campaigned successfully for the nomination. Take a five handicap if you are an Unemployed Notable.
— *United States Senators.* Start at Square 3 (take bonus points).
— *Governors or Members of Congress.* Start at Square 2.

Goal. Your goal is to win a majority of the delegate votes at the party's summer convention. The final tally of points will be made in a cavernous convention hall in a major city in July or August; winner must make a speech and pick a running mate.

Rules. In the early version of this game, the rules were loose; today, they are rigid indeed. You must tally your finances exactly and agree to campaign spending limits; and if you do, the federal treasury will aid your campaign. In fact, it would be a good idea if you played with a good lawyer and a good accountant by your side.

Strategies. You are pretty much on your own here. You have a finite amount of time, energy, money, and staff. How you use them is up to you.

Ready to Play? Select a token, roll the die, and move according to instructions.

*Note: Although anyone over thirty-five years of age, who is a natural-born citizen and has resided in our country for fourteen years is eligible to play, be warned that no player has ever won who was not white, middle-aged or older, Protestant or Catholic, or male. Representative Geraldine Ferraro once told a black group that there was no longer a sign in front of the White House saying "Only white males need apply." Time will tell.

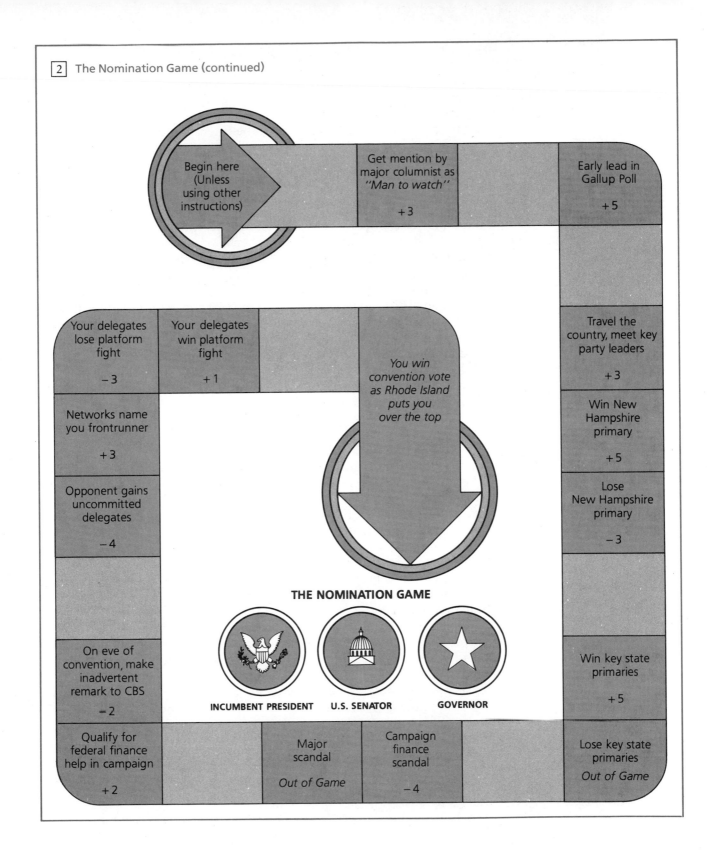

Begin here (Unless using other instructions)

Get mention by major columnist as "Man to watch"
+3

Early lead in Gallup Poll
+5

Your delegates lose platform fight
−3

Your delegates win platform fight
+1

You win convention vote as Rhode Island puts you over the top

Travel the country, meet key party leaders
+3

Networks name you frontrunner
+3

Win New Hampshire primary
+5

Opponent gains uncommitted delegates
−4

Lose New Hampshire primary
−3

THE NOMINATION GAME

INCUMBENT PRESIDENT   U.S. SENATOR   GOVERNOR

On eve of convention, make inadvertent remark to CBS
−2

Win key state primaries
+5

Qualify for federal finance help in campaign
+2

Major scandal
Out of Game

Campaign finance scandal
−4

Lose key state primaries
Out of Game

is not guaranteed. The press, of course, is eager to pounce on any blunder. What seemed a wise move at the moment may not look so good after a night's sleep and a peek at its interpretation by the press. In 1976, Jimmy Carter made a conscious decision to be interviewed by *Playboy* to overcome his stuffy, fundamentalist image. Unfortunately for him, it backfired. The press focused almost entirely on his admission that he "lusted in his heart" for other women. Sometimes, the magic just is not there. John Glenn may have soared into space, but he lacked "the right stuff" to galvanize voters in 1984. At other times, a single stroke of good judgement may make the margin of difference. In the 1960 presidential campaign, civil rights leader Martin Luther King, Jr., was jailed in Atlanta. John F. Kennedy called King's wife, Coretta, to offer support. His brother Bobby called the judge himself, and King was released. Martin Luther King, Sr., switched his allegiance to Kennedy (saying that he would vote for the Devil himself if he would wipe the tears from his daughter-in-law's face). "Ultimately," said Collier and Horowitz, that close election "may have turned on a gesture."[4]

Conscious choices and accidental factors help determine the outcomes of the nomination and election games. One thing, though, is certain: you do not get a ticket to play the election game until and unless you win the nomination game.

Many Are Called But Few Are Chosen

Believe it or not, every politician does not want to run for president. The rewards may be great, but the costs—emotional and financial—are staggering. Twelve percent of our presidents have been assassinated in office. David Rohde and John Aldrich have a theory of presidential ambition, which suggests that presidential candidates have to be risk-takers.[5] Many politicians reach political prominence nationally but decline to run for president, or make only half-hearted efforts. Two elections ago, someone accused Walter Mondale of not having the "fire in his belly" to run for president. If a politician decides to run for president, he or she must plan to spend at least two years at the task.

Candidates need an electoral base from which to begin. Rarely in history has a major party contender tried for the presidency without first holding a major elected office, although a few generals have made the grade. Two offices, U.S. senator and state governor, provided the electoral base for 80 percent of the major candidates since the end of World War II.[6] The same is true of the vice-presidency, and the candidates of 1984 were no exception. One incumbent president made the choice easy for the Republicans. Among the Democrats, one was a former vice-president and

[4] Peter Collier and David Horowitz, *The Kennedys: An American Drama* (New York: Summit Books, 1984), p. 248.

[5] The Rohde theory is in his "Risk-Bearing and Progressive Ambition: The Case of the United States House of Representatives," *American Journal of Political Science* 23 (February 1979):1–26; the Aldrich adumbrations are in his *Before the Convention* (Chicago: University of Chicago Press, 1980), Chap. 2.

[6] Aldrich, *Before the Convention*, p. 27.

Democratic Candidates, 1984. *Here is the whole group of the eight Democratic contenders who entered the race for the Democratic nomination in 1984. All but one had a strong electoral base to start. From left to right, they are Senator John Glenn of Ohio, Senator Alan Cranston of California, Senator Ernest Hollings of South Carolina, former Senator George McGovern of South Dakota, Senator Gary Hart of Colorado, former Vice-President Walter Mondale of Minnesota, Rev. Jesse Jackson of Illinois, and former Governor Reuben Askew of Florida. This photo was taken at a well-publicized debate among all eight. The primaries serve to narrow a large field down to a few contenders. Those left seem to the press and the public to have "momentum." Most of these contenders dropped out of the race, leaving Mondale, Hart, and Jackson to struggle to the end.*

a former senator (Mondale); four were senators (Hart, Glenn, Cranston, and Hollings); one was a former governor (Askew); and only one candidate had never held elective office (Jackson).

Two Roads to the Convention

In some ways, the nomination game is tougher than the general election game. It whittles a very large number of players down to two. The goal of the nomination game is to win the majority of delegate ballots at the **national party convention.**

There are fifty different roads to the national convention, one through each state. (Actually, given the representation from Democrats Abroad, the District of Columbia, Overseas Republicans, Puerto Rico, and elsewhere, there are more than fifty roads; but let's keep our story simple.) These roads converge into two main thoroughfares: the presidential primaries, and the caucuses. From February through June of the election year, states busily choose their delegates to the national convention. Candidates hustle to try to win state caucuses or primaries.

The Caucus Road. Once, all state parties selected their delegates to the national convention in a meeting of state party leaders called a **caucus.** Sometimes one or two party "bosses" ran the caucus show. By controlling the state caucus, they could control who went to the convention and how the state's delegates voted.

Today's caucuses are different. In the states which have them, party rules mandate openness and strict adherence to complex rules of representation. The caucuses can sometimes be very important. Iowa holds the earliest one, and an obscure former Georgia governor named Jimmy Carter took his first big presidential step by winning it in 1976. Caucuses usually are organized like a pyramid. Small, neighborhood, precinct-level caucuses—often meeting in a church, an American Legion hall or even someone's home—pyramid to county-level, then state-level meetings. Each level elects delegates to the next one. Supporters of Candidate X or Y jockey to get elected so that they may represent their candidate ultimately (they hope) at the national convention.

The Presidential Primary Road. Today, three quarters of the delegates to the Democratic and Republican conventions are selected in **presidential primaries,** where voters in a state go to the polls and vote for a candidate (or delegates pledged to him). The presidential primary was promoted around the turn of the century by reformers, who wanted to take nominations out of the hands of the party bosses. Their idea was this: Let the people actually vote for the candidate of their choice; then bind the delegates to vote for that candidate at the convention. In 1910, Oregon passed the first presidential primary law that required delegates to vote according to the primary results. In 1984, twenty-nine states had Democratic presidential primaries and twenty-four had Republican presidential primaries.

Few happenings have transformed American politics as much as the proliferation of presidential primaries. Presidential election watcher Theodore White calls the primaries the "classic example of the triumph of goodwill over common sense." Says White:

> An entirely new breed of professionals has grown up, voyaging like Gauleiters from state to state, specializing in get-out-the-vote techniques, cross sectionings, media, ethnic breakdowns, and other specialties. . . . Most of all, delegates, who were supposed to be free to vote their own common sense and conscience, have become for the most part anonymous faces, collected as background for the television cameras, sacks of potatoes packaged in primaries, divorced from party roots, and from the officials who rule states and nation. [7]

The primary season usually begins in a New Hampshire winter. If Virginia was the "mother of presidents" in the early days of the Republic, New Hampshire is today's midwife. Tiny New Hampshire always manages to schedule its presidential primary first, thus magnifying the importance of this atypical state in electing presidents (if there *is* a "typical" American state, New Hampshire is not it). Network and newspaper reporters play up the New Hampshire results. Democrats in New Hampshire cast 82,381 votes in 1976 and got 2,100 seconds of nightly network news coverage. New York's 3,746,414 Democrats voted in a

---

[7] Theodore White, *America in Search of Itself: The Making of the President 1956–1980* (New York: Harper & Row, 1982), p. 285.

primary but got only 560 seconds. Each New Hampshire voter received 170 times as much TV attention as each New York voter.[8]

Other state primaries follow New Hampshire's. The laws determining how the primaries are set up, who may enter them, and who may vote in them are made by state legislatures and state parties, leading to an array of rules confusing even to the candidates and the press. But month after month, the primaries serve as elimination contests. They are important not only because they select delegates, but also because they "represent an ostensibly objective indication of whether a candidate can win the election. The contestants stand to gain or lose far more than the growing number of votes that may be at stake."[9] Politicians, press, and public all love a winner. The losers in the early primaries usually get labeled losers and eventually drop out. Losers spend a lot of their time trying to explain their losses away: "I didn't really campaign there"; "It was my opponent's strong state anyway"; "I wasn't really organized there." But the relentless sorting continues.

In the 1980 delegate chase, one memorable term was coined. After George Bush scored a surprise victory over Ronald Reagan in the Iowa Republican caucuses, he proudly claimed to possess "the big mo" —momentum. (Actually, Bush had only a little "mo," and quickly fell victim to Reagan in New Hampshire's primary.) The term, however, neatly describes what candidates for the nomination are after. Primaries and caucuses are more than an endurance contest, though they are certainly that. They are proving grounds. Week after week, the challenge is to do better than expected, for doing better than your opponents is not enough. To get "mo" going, you have to beat people you were not expected to beat, collect margins above predictions, and never, above all else, lose to people you were expected to trounce. (So stunned was Ronald Reagan after his Iowa caucus defeat that he fired his campaign manager before the New Hampshire primary.) Donald Matthews put it thus:

> More often than not, winning a presidential primary means doing better than expected; losing means disappointing expectations. The media find a winner in this curious contest by arriving at a rough consensus on how candidates should do and then measuring the vote and delegate outcomes against this rubbery yardstick.[10]

Scoring big on this "rubbery yardstick" of success in any particular primary means that you take one giant stride toward the nomination.

Picking up momentum involves other endeavors too: more media attention, higher standings in the polls, more name recognition, and —last but hardly least—more money flowing into the campaign coffers. No one has studied the momentum phenomenon more closely than John Aldrich. Take a look at ⬛3 and you can see how Jimmy Carter in 1976 came from obscurity to capture the nomination because of his early successes in Iowa's caucuses and New Hampshire's primary.

The Importance of Being New Hampshire. *New Hampshire has managed to keep its presidential primary first on the hit parade of primaries. Candidates who do well in New Hampshire get an extra boost in "momentum." Those who are frozen out in New Hampshire may never get any momentum. Colorado's Gary Hart (shown here speaking right after the primary) fared fairly well in New Hampshire's 1984 primary, thus closing some of the gap between himself and leader Walter Mondale. Because there are spending limits in the primaries, Mondale had exhausted much of his campaign treasury, while Hart had yet to raise and spend much of his.*

[8] Michael J. Robinson, "TVs Newest Program: The Presidential Nominations Game," *Public Opinion* (May/June 1978):42–43.

[9] Nelson W. Polsby and Aaron Wildavsky, *Presidential Elections*, 4th ed. (New York: Scribner's, 1976), p. 108.

[10] Donald R. Matthews, " 'Winnowing': The News Media and the 1976 Presidential Nomination," in James David Barber (ed.), *Race for the Presidency* (Englewood Cliffs, N.J.: Prentice-Hall, 1978), p. 63.

"The Big Mo": How Carter Had It in 1976

The primary season is a long one. Events during this period do not occur in a vacuum, but are determined by the whole sweep of the campaign. Nothing helps more than to ride the escalator of momentum. Early victories—especially unexpected ones—produce (1) more name recognition, (2) more media attention, (3) more campaign coverage, and normally, (4) a wider lead over your opponents.

For the 1976 primaries, in which Jimmy Carter took an early lead in the first caucus (Iowa) and the first primary (New Hampshire), John Aldrich tallied Carter's standings as his momentum developed. Aldrich examined Carter's standing in the Gallup poll; he looked at the media attention by counting the number of *New York Times* stories about Carter; he got data from the Federal Election Commission on contributions to Carter's campaign; and he looked at Carter's "competitive standing (CS)," his lead over the next closest rival. An early success often brings later successes. Here is a graph showing how Carter fared as he gained that "Big Mo."

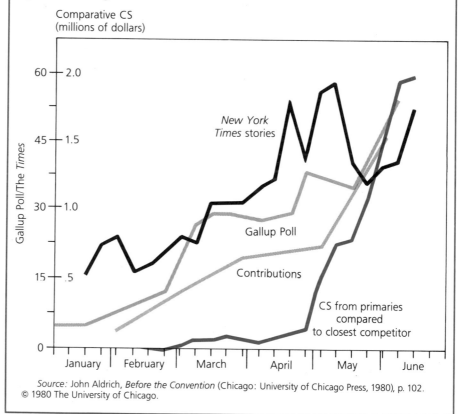

Source: John Aldrich, *Before the Convention* (Chicago: University of Chicago Press, 1980), p. 102. © 1980 The University of Chicago.

Describing what happened to the Republicans in 1984 is simple enough. An incumbent president (unless for some reason he has major liabilities) normally begins and ends with the momentum to be renominated. No incumbent president in the twentieth century has been denied his party's renomination. (Nevertheless, Harry Truman in 1952 and Lyndon Johnson in 1968 would have had tough battles on their hands, had they tried for an additional term.) In January 1984, President Reagan announced his desire to be renominated for the presidency; no Republican thought seriously of challenging him.

For the 1984 Democrats, though, it was a freewheeling show on the primary trail. Although Massachusetts Senator Edward M. Kennedy declined to toss his hat into the nomination game, a sizable number of Democratic aspirants wanted to play. There were two southerners (South Carolina Senator Ernest Hollings and former Florida governor Reuben Askew), a Californian (Senator Allan Cranston), two Fritzes (Hollings and former Vice-President Mondale were both nicknamed Fritz), a charismatic black minister (Jesse Jackson), a former astronaut (Ohio Senator John Glenn), and a Kennedyesque senator from Colorado (Gary Hart). An eight-man race dwindled to a two-man race, between Mondale and Hart. Jesse Jackson, however, persevered to the end, trying to hold on to enough delegate votes to influence the Democratic platform.

Assessing the Primaries. Clearly, the primaries are here to stay; though how well the primary serves our democratic process is widely debated. Turnout in the primaries, for example, is low, at least by comparison with general election turnouts. Slightly more than half the eligible population votes in the November election for president. Only about half of that half will vote in a presidential primary.[11] Moreover, participation in primaries is unrepresentative of the public at large. Primaries attract better educated and more affluent citizens, leaving the poor and less educated largely without a role in selecting their party's nominee.

The primary system was established to return the nomination process to the people. This it has done—at least to *some* of the people. The system has also turned a part of our nomination process over to the media, who pick winners and bestow or withhold that precious commodity, momentum—and with momentum comes money. In addition, the virtually random staging of primaries across the country contributes to the confusion of the nomination process. For these reasons, some commentators have advocated a single national primary or a series of regional primaries.

Conventioneering

Convention cities love the business. Many cities will bid for the next convention, guaranteeing rooms and rates, special deals on the convention center, and other support. In 1984, San Francisco was the lucky winner for the Democrats and Dallas for the Republicans.

Once the main job of the convention was to select the candidate of the party. He would then select his vice-presidential running mate. Today, though, the winner of the nomination is usually a foregone conclusion. Delegates selected in primaries, and usually those selected in caucuses, have known preferences. The losers may put up a brave front, as did Ted Kennedy in 1980 and Gary Hart in 1984, but simple addition told them they had no chance.

[11] Information on participation and equality in primary turnout is reviewed in David E. Price, *Bringing Back the Parties* (Washington, D.C.: Congressional Quarterly, 1984), pp. 193–94.

Today, the main job of the conventions is to get the campaign ball rolling. A massive send-off to the candidates for president and vice-president is orchestrated carefully. The party's leaders are there in force, plus many of its most important followers—people whose input will be important during the campaign. Thus the convention is an important rallying point for them.

Meeting in an oversized, overstuffed convention hall in some big city, a convention is a short-lived affair. For four days in late July or August, a couple of thousand delegates—outnumbered several times by reporters—transact their business and then scatter back home again. Presumably, party conventions believe that if God could create the world in six days and rest on the seventh, they can nominate a presidential and vice-presidential candidate and write their platform in four.

Delegates spend the first day hearing reports of the Credentials Committee. When there is some challenge to delegate eligibility, the committee decides who shall be seated which, in turn, can determine who gets nominated. Credentials fights are notoriously vigorous. At the end of the first day, smart convention organizers will have scheduled a rip-roaring "keynote speaker," who will recall party heroes, condemn the opposition party, and tout the nominee-apparent. In 1984, the Democrats chose New York Governor Mario Cuomo, whose keynote speech was a spellbinder. The Republicans chose the rather obscure (and, as it turned out, lackluster) treasurer of the United States, Katherine Ortega, presumably to show that Republicans appeal to women and minorities, too.

The second day includes debates on a party platform. Like struggles over disputed credentials, votes on the proposed platform often give clues to who's ahead in the nomination game.

Day three is devoted to the nominations and voting. One of the candidate's eminent supporters will give a speech extolling his virtues (and hiding his vices); a string of seconding speeches will follow. Demonstrations erupt as if spontaneous, even though thousands of dollars are spent orchestrating them. Balloting begins as states and territories announce their votes. ("Guam, where America's day begins, casts its vote for. . . .") By midnight, the convention's real work is over: The presidential candidate has been selected. The victor huddles with his aides in his hotel suite trying to nail down a running mate and polish an acceptance speech.

The vice-presidential nomination and the acceptance speeches occupy the fourth day, as delegates are transformed from actors in the drama to mere audience. No longer needed, they then go home, presumably looking back on their handiwork and deciding that it was good.

Conventions today are not as important in the nominating process as they once were. They still contain the same hoopla, the same demonstrations—even though those are now organized by pros—and the same long speeches; but because so many delegates are selected by the primaries, we know who they support before the convention begins. Today, only a handful of the delegates are really uncommitted when they get to the convention city, and they almost always come knowing who will be offering the acceptance speech. It took the Democrats 46 ballots in 1912, 44 in 1920, and a record 103 in 1924 to nominate their presidential standard-bearer. Not since 1952 has a convention taken more than one

The Democrats' Keynote Speech, 1984. *New York Governor Mario Cuomo was the keynote speaker at the 1984 Democratic national convention. The keynote speaker is supposed to provide a tough, rip-roaring speech, heralding the party's past achievements and leaders, and signalling support for the party and its nominees. Cuomo disappointed no one; in fact, his speech was widely acclaimed and was believed by many to boost his own chances for getting into a national office.*

The Orchestrated Convention. *Especially when an incumbent president is about to be renominated, a convention focuses on show as well as substance. Nancy Reagan played her part in the show in 1984. By tradition, contenders are not supposed to be in the convention center until they are finally nominated. Tradition apparently does not forbid their video image from the big screen.*

ballot. Of recent conventions, only the 1976 Ford-Reagan contest really kept anyone guessing until the votes were totaled.

The conventions may be less important in determining nominations today, but they are more important in developing the party's policy positions and in promoting political representation. Once, a convention was essentially an assembly of state and local party leaders, gathered together to bargain over a candidate. Almost all delegates were white, male, and over forty. Lately, party reformers, especially among the Democrats, have worked hard to make the conventions more representative.

Once the business of conventioneering is out of the way, the successful nominees can then enter the campaign game.

ACT II: THE CAMPAIGN GAME

Once nominated, candidates concentrate on campaigning. These days the word *campaign* is part of our political vocabulary, but it was not always so. The term was a military one: Generals mounted campaigns, using their scarce resources, men and materials, to achieve strategic objectives. Political campaigns are like that, too: Resources are scarce, expenditures are limited by federal law, and both have to be timed and targeted. Should you spend your money early, hoping to build up an early lead, or concentrate it in the last few days? The most precious resources of all—your candidate's time and energy—are also finite. Should your candidate spend more time in big industrial states or in the south?

More than generalship is involved in campaigns. Artistry is also a part, for campaigns deal in images. The campaign is the canvas on which artist-strategists try to paint portraits of leadership, effectiveness, caring, and other images we value in presidents. The art form of campaigns is impressionism, not photography. Backgrounds on a canvas may be hard to manipulate, for voter-viewers of this artistry bring strong preferences with them: their party identifications, their issue positions, and their ideologies. Yet the images they form of the candidates and their positions are carefully crafted by the artist-generals of campaigns. To project the right picture to the voters, three ingredients are needed: a campaign organization, money, and media attention.

Organizing the Campaign

In every campaign, there is too much to do and too little time to do it. You will want to prepare yourself psychologically for pounds and pounds of rubbery chicken and cold peas served at banquets, as well as for sleepless nights and sleepy days and hands sore from too many handshakes. But there are more important details to consider. (If you just won your party's nomination, you will, of course, have already handled some of these details. If you are just starting on the caucus and primary road of the nomination game, you have even more details to deal with.) You will want to

— *Line up a campaign manager.* If you do not have one left over from an earlier campaign, there are plenty of professionals around who have won other battles.
— *Get a fund raiser.* Money may not buy happiness, but as we will shortly see, it helps win elections.
— *Get a campaign counsel.* With all the federal regulation of campaign finance these days, you need a lawyer to keep you honest and in compliance with the laws. (Watergate burglar G. Gordon Liddy started out as the Nixon 1972 campaign counsel, so watch who you hire.)
— *Hire some media and campaign consultants.* You may have a clever idea for campaign bumper stickers, but you have better things to do with your time than plan ad campaigns, contract for buttons and bumper stickers, or buy TV time and newspaper space. Professionals can do these better than you can, anyway.
— *Round up a campaign staff.* Include as many professionals as you can afford, but get a "volunteer coordinator," too.
— *Plan the logistics.* You do not want to be campaigning in Alaska on the day before the election, when your opponent is in New York. And you do not want to arrive for the annual United Auto Workers dinner on the wrong day. Hire some advance people to handle the complicated details of your schedule.
— *Get a research staff and policy advisors.* You will barely have time to read the papers, much less master the complex issues reporters will ask about. Get people—distinguished academics, if possible—who will feed you information and ideas.

Campaign 1984. *It was off to a rocky start for the Democratic ticket of Walter Mondale and Geraldine Ferraro in 1984. Vice-Presidential candidate Geraldine Ferraro's family finances seemed to be the major issue for the first month of the campaign. On August 21, though, she spent more than an hour in a grinding press conference detailing her and her husband's tangled taxes and finances, a performance which many considered one of her finest hours. Campaigns, though, need momentum and the Democratic one lost weeks of momentum in the agonies of Ferraro finances.*

— *Hire a pollster.* There are dozens of professional polling firms who will (for a fee, of course) tell you how you are going over with the voters and what is on their minds.

— *Get a good press secretary.* If you are running for a major office, you are going to have reporters dogging you every hour of the day and every step of the way. They need news, and a good press secretary can think of some to give them.

You will notice that most of these tasks cost money. Campaigns are not cheap (though they are not as expensive as many people think they are), and the role of money in campaigns is a controversial one.

Money May Not Buy Happiness, But Does It Win Elections?

There is a simple, symbiotic relationship between candidates and campaign supporters: Our high-tech elections have made campaigning expensive and candidates need money to win; our highly regulated society has made government important to many groups and they need access to elected officials. Those who need money get it; those who have it to spend give it away.

Are Our Campaigns Too Expensive? Particularly after 1972, when Richard Nixon packed away so much extra money from his campaign that his staff was doling it out to Watergate burglars as "hush money," there has been grave concern about money in politics. One key aspect of this concern is the worry over the cost of elections. In 1984, our nation footed a bill of more than $1 billion for elections. (However this included all elections—national, state, and local—and presidential expenditures are incurred only once every four years.) Horror stories about expensive campaigns have become a staple of American journalism.

Here is a rundown of approximately what we spend on elections: According to Herbert Alexander, the 1980 elections cost our nation $1.203 billion. The sum splits about equally between what candidates for national office spend (about $275 million for the presidency and about $239 for congressional elections) and what the hundreds of thousands of state and local candidates spent. True, campaign costs have increased considerably faster than inflation. Alexander estimates that campaign costs increased by 759 percent between 1952 and 1980, compared to a general inflation increase of 210 percent. [12]

More than a billion dollars may seem like a staggering sum of money, but try to put it in a larger perspective: For example, half of our 1980 election costs would be spent by Procter and Gamble in one year to advertise soap and related items. Compared to most other goods and services on which Americans spend their money, campaigns are a good buy. 4

---

[12] These data are from Herbert Alexander, *Financing the 1980 Election* (Lexington, Mass.: Lexington Books, 1983).

4 | The Cost of American Elections: Frankly, A Bargain

Journalists have nearly succeeded in persuading us that the costs of American elections are a national scandal. Yet they are low in comparison to those in other nations. Concretely, American elections cost about as much per voter as a meal at your favorite fast-food franchise. (In Israel, the cost is more than $20 per voter.) The best way of assessing the costs of elections—our basic tool of democracy— is to compare them to other expenditures Americans willingly make annually. In 1984, the estimated cost of the presidential election was about $100 million. This was a sizable share of money, to be sure, but compare it with what Americans spent in one recent year on a few other consumer goods and services:

Item	Annual Cost
Apparel and accessories	$54.0 billion
Automotive repair	39.1 billion
Toiletries	18.4 billion
Laundry and cleaning	10.6 billion
Beauty and barber shops	8.9 billion
Color TVs	6.7 billion
Microwave ovens	2.6 billion
Videotape cassette machines	2.3 billion
Video game software	1.7 billion
Telephones	1.2 billion
Coffee makers	.4 billion
Tanning shops	.3 billion
Hair dryers	.3 billion
Cornpoppers	.2 billion
Air purifiers	.1 billion

As you can see, the cost of electing presidents is closer to the costs of our tanning, our coffee makers, our hair dryers, and our cornpoppers than it is to our TV purchases or our beauty and barber shop appointments. After all, we only elect a president every four years but we pay these tidy sums for consumer goods and services annually. Frankly, electing a president is a bargain. Even if you include all the costs of electing Congress and state and local officials, the costs of elections would not hold a candle to what we spend on clothes, car repairs, or toiletries.

Source: Costs of our consumer goods and services are based on sales or value in 1983, *Statistical Abstract 1985* (Washington: Department of Commerce, 1984), various tables. On tanning industry expenditures, see *Newsweek's* estimate, February 25, 1985, p. 82.

Does Money Buy Victory? The "bottom-line" question about money in political campaigns is "Does money buy victory?" To some degree, of course, the answer is yes; candidates must always spend something to win. In our era of high-tech campaigning, pollsters, public relations people, programmed campaign packages, press releases, and posters are necessary and do cost money.

But surely the charge that "money buys elections" implies more than just the fact that all campaigns cost something. The real fear is that of a direct correlation between dollars spent and votes received.

Polsby and Wildavsky have conducted a thorough review of the role of money in campaigns and candidly conclude that "even in the era when the parties were free to spend whatever they could raise and were not subjected to the limitations of the public finance law, money did not buy election victories." [13] In modern presidential elections, Republicans have nearly always outspent Democrats. Yet, since 1932, the Democratic candidate outpolled the Republican candidate in eight national elections; the Republicans won five. Only in 1968, when Nixon greatly outspent Humphrey, is it conceivable that more money for the loser could have swayed the final verdict. To be sure, as Polsby and Wildavsky remark, "it would be nice to have more money to spend than the other fellow." [14] But money does not always produce victory.

A similar story is true in Congress, though the evidence is complicated by the fact that so many of the candidates in congressional elections are incumbents. In fact, Gary Jacobson's careful analysis of money in congressional elections shows that "the more incumbents spend, the worse they do." [15] This paradoxical result does not mean that you should donate money to your opponent's campaign to improve your candidate's chances! Jacobson's finding simply means that incumbents who face a tough challenger hustle more money to defeat him or her. Facing an easy win, they can afford to campaign cheaply.

If Money Does Not Buy Elections, Why are People Willing to Give so Much of It? Individuals and groups give money for lots of reasons. Unions and businesses each hope to tilt candidates toward pro-union or pro-management policies. Some give money for ideological purposes. (General Motors heir Stewart Mott has given millions to left-of-center candidates.) Some individuals and groups (let us be realistic) hope to "buy" votes on specific issues. Gun dealers, environmentalists, teachers, postal clerks, farmers, chemical companies, and a host of American interest groups target candidates for obvious reasons: They expect a sympathetic ear (and vote) when issues come up in Congress. At a minimum, such groups are buying *access*, the certain knowledge that their positions will be noted when critical issues come up for a vote. Sometimes, the access can be pretty direct: Several Philadelphia congressmen helped engineer federal funds for a Philadelphia hospital, which had donated heavily to their campaigns. There is little hard evidence that donations directly determine decisions of senators and representatives; to some critics, though, the smell of influence is there. [16]

---

[13] Nelson Polsby and Aaron Wildavsky, *Presidential Elections*, 6th ed. (New York: Scribner's, 1984), p. 56.

[14] Ibid, pp. 58–59.

[15] Gary Jacobson, "The Effects of Campaign Spending in Congressional Elections," *American Political Science Review* 72 (June 1978):469.

[16] One writer who smells influence in the role of money in politics is *New Yorker* Washington correspondent Elizabeth Drew. See her *Politics and Money: The New Road to Corruption* (New York: Macmillan, 1983). For a stinging critique of Drew's cynical assessment, see Robert J. Samuelson, "The Campaign Reform Failure," *The New Republic* (September 5, 1983):28–36.

The Maze of Campaign Finance Reforms

Richard Nixon made many contributions to American politics. Among them, he almost single-handedly reformed campaign finance in America, although, no doubt, this was not his intention. In 1968, Nixon relied heavily on wealthy contributors. (Chicago insurance magnate W. Clement Stone contributed a tidy $2.8 million to the Nixon campaign.) When his 1972 campaign brought campaign finance to a new art form and his expenditures to a new level of suspiciousness, the movement for reform was on. What public interest groups had long called for—bringing campaign finance under the federal regulatory umbrella—Nixon accomplished handily.

Richard Nixon's questionable financing brought about the campaign reforms of the early 1970s. Several public interest lobbies (see pages 318–319), notably Common Cause and the National Committee for an Effective Congress, led the drive. In 1974, the Senate and House passed the **Federal Election Campaign Act.** The Supreme Court declared a few of its provisions unconstitutional. In *Buckley* v. *Valeo* in 1976, it struck down part of the campaign finance law that had limited the amount an individual could contribute to his or her own campaign. In essence, here is what the act, with subsequent amendments, did:

— *It created a* **Federal Election Commission (FEC).** A bipartisan body, supposedly not favoring one party or the other, the six-member FEC administers the campaign finance laws and enforces compliance with their requirements.
— *It provided public financing for presidential primaries and general elections.* Presidential candidates who raised some money on their own in at least twenty states could get a check from the United States Treasury to help pay for their primary campaigns. For the general election campaign, presidential (but not congressional) candidates get almost all expenses federally supported *if* they are willing to accept campaign spending limits.
— *It limited presidential campaign spending.* If the candidates accept federal support, they agree to limit their campaign expenditures to an amount prescribed by federal law.
— *It required disclosure.* Candidates must file periodic reports with the Federal Election Commission listing who contributed and how the money was spent.
— *It tried to limit contributions.* Originally, the Federal Election Campaign Act tried to draw the reins on PAC expenditures. Section 9012(f) prohibited PACs that were not authorized by the candidate (for example, any PAC other than those specifically formed by the candidate) from contributing more than $1000 to any presidential or Congressional campaign. It forbade them from spending more than $25,000 a year total. But on March 18, 1985, in the case of *FEC* v. *National Conservative Political Action Committee*, the Supreme Court ruled that these limits denied freedom of speech. It was, the Court said, "like allowing a speaker in a public hall to express his views while denying him the use of an amplifying system."

Put another way, if you will agree to certain limitations on your fund-raising and spending, the federal government will help you foot the bill for your presidential campaign. This is true of both the nomination phase, and the postnomination phase when the Democratic and Republican nominees meet head-on. Naturally, it is comforting to the candidate to know that there is money in the bank. Strategic gambles must be taken because total expenditure is limited. In 1984, each candidate was permitted to spend up to $20.2 million on the primaries. Walter Mondale wanted desperately to capture "the Big Mo" early, so by the end of 1983, he had already spent $7.8 million of his allotted primary funds—even before a single primary ballot had been printed. His emerging leading rival, Gary Hart, had expended only $1.4 million on primary advertising and organization by the end of 1983. Thus, Walter Mondale had spent thirty-eight cents of every dollar he could spend, and Hart only seven cents of every dollar he could spend, before the New Hampshire primary. Mondale's gamble almost backfired; as Hart kept closing the gap, Mondale had less and less money to spend to defeat him. [17] Presidential politics is always played for high stakes. When your well runs dry before your opponent gains his momentum, you face the loss of high stakes indeed.

In strategic decisions concerning resources, having a good computer program helps. Having a good accountant helps, too. These days, campaign finance regulations have become so complicated that even certified public accountants have trouble keeping up with them. The FEC is constantly required to rule on one tangled interpretation or another, for there are plenty of gray areas. In one, groups can support your candidacy supposedly without your either knowing about it or controlling their efforts (though most savvy political operatives would be drummed out of their profession if they played by these rules). Today, campaign finance regulations are a maze. Unless you plan to run for president, you need not master it; but if you do, you had better hire someone adept at finding his way through the labyrinth of restrictions.

Overall, there is no doubt that the campaign finance reforms of the 1970s have made American campaign financing more open and honest. Small donors are encouraged and the rich restricted. It is unlikely that any campaign coffer will contain enough idle cash to fund a burglary of its opponent's headquarters, as did Nixon's campaign in 1972. These are gains; but some think that the proliferation of PACs is a real loss.

The Proliferation of PACs. Before the 1974 reforms, corporations were technically forbidden to donate money to political campaigns. Unions could, although limits were set on how they could aid and abet candidates and parties. The 1974 reforms created a new way of contributing to campaigns. Corporations, unions—everybody—could get in on the act. To some critics, the new mode was a financial monster. The term coined for

---

[17] These figures are from Herbert E. Alexander, the "dean" of America's campaign finance watchers, in his article "Matching Funds and Momentum," *Campaigns and Elections* (Spring 1984):48.

From HERBLOCK THROUGH THE LOOKING GLASS (Simon and Schuster, 1984).

**"ACTUALLY, I THINK IT CAME
BEFORE THE VIDEO GAME"**

the funding vehicles created by the campaign reforms was **Political Action Committees—PACs** for short. Few happenings since the Watergate crisis have generated so much heat as the parade of PACs in our political system.

Here is how the PACs work. A corporation, union, or some other interest group decides to channel some of its money into political campaigns, supporting candidates who support their goals. The corporation, union, or group creates a PAC, registering it with the Federal Election Commission, and then puts money into it. The PAC can collect money from stockholders, members, and other interested parties, and can donate it to any campaign of its choosing. There is one very important ground rule: All expenditures must be meticulously accounted for to the FEC.

PACs have proliferated in recent years. The FEC counted 3,803 PACs in 1984. Independent PAC outlays in that year amounted to about $120 million.

Candidates need PACs because high-tech campaigning is expensive. Senate races can cost a million dollars for television alone; tightly contested races for the House of Representatives can easily cost a candidate a million dollars. PACs make those burdens more bearable. Thus, there emerges a symbiotic relationship between the PACs and the candidates. Candidates need money, which they insist can be used without compromising their integrity. PACs want access to office-holders, which they insist can be achieved without buying votes. (Justin Dart, of Dart Industries, a close friend of President Reagan, remarks of his PAC that "Talking to politicians is fine, but with a little money, they hear you better." [18]) An abundance of PACs are around to help out the candidates. There are big ones, such as the Realtors Political Action Committee and the American Medical Association Political Action Committee. There are little ones, too, representing smaller industries or business associations: EggPAC, FishPAC, FurPAC, LardPAC, and—for the beer distributors, of course—SixPAC. [19] You can see in ⑤ some of the biggest PACs in terms of contributions.

We said earlier that money does not—at least in any direct and obvious way – buy electoral victory. But does it buy something just as important: control over the votes of the winners? A direct link between a PAC's support for Candidate X and X's vote on some issue favoring the PAC is tantamount to buying votes, a practice we find revolting in a democracy.

In order to establish a direct connection between campaign aid and a successful candidate's vote, several conditions would have to be met: First, the PAC has to back the right horse. Pouring money into a losing campaign is not very useful in influencing public policy. PACs typically give about two-thirds of their money to incumbents, because they usually win. Second, the supported candidate would have to vote other than he might have without PAC dollars; in any event, most PACs support those who agree with them in the first place. The anti-abortion PACs will not waste their money supporting outspokenly pro-abortion candidates.

Sometimes, on some issues, it is clear that PAC money makes a difference. The Federal Trade Commission, for example, passed a regulation

[18] Quoted in Jeffrey Berry, *The Interest Group Society* (Boston: Little, Brown, 1984), p. 162.
[19] Cited in ibid., pp. 162–163.

---

⑤ **The Big Spenders**

According to the Federal Election Commission, which monitors PAC spending carefully, here are the ten largest PAC contributors to all federal candidates:

	Amount Contributed, January 1983–June 1984
Realtors Political Action Committee	$890,736
American Medical Association PAC	$792,962
Seafarers Political Activity Donation	$758,222
National Education Association PAC	$715,078
Build PAC (National Association of Home Builders)	$669,453
UAW Voluntary Community Action Program	$649,039
Machinists Non-Partisan Political League	$609,902
Active Ballot Club (United Food and Commercial Workers Union)	$596,356
BANKPAC (American Bankers Association)	$496,125
American Federation of State, County, and Municipal Employees PAC	$494,497

Source: Federal Election Commission, *Record*, December, 1984, p. 6.

requiring that car dealers list known mechanical defects on the window sticker of used cars. The National Association of Automobile Dealers quickly became the fourth largest donor in the 1980 congressional elections, contributing just over $1 million to candidates of both parties. Then, 216 Representatives co-sponsored a House resolution nullifying the FTC regulation. Of these, 186 had been aided by the used car PAC. [20]

The impact of PAC money on presidents is more doubtful. Presidential campaigns, of course, are partly subsidized by the public, through the Federal Election Commission, and so are less dependent upon PACs. Moreover, presidents have well-articulated positions on most important issues. A small contribution from any one PAC is not likely to turn a presidential candidate's head. And, let's face it, groups need the president, once in office, more than he needs them.

To summarize: Money matters in campaigns. Because it matters then, it also matters when legislative votes come due. Scare stories about the proliferation of PACs may be exaggerated, [21] but campaign finance is an old issue which is not likely to go away, even if there is a round of new reforms.

The Media and the Campaign

Money matters, and so does the media. Media coverage is determined by two factors: how a candidate uses his or her advertising budget, and the "free" attention he or she gets as a newsmaker. The first, obviously, is relatively easy to control; the second harder, but not impossible. "In the television age," says Doris Graber, "media people do the casting for presidential hopefuls, whose performance is then judged according to the assigned role." [22] Every decision in the campaign—where to eat breakfast, whom to include on the rostrum, what to say about Israel, everything—is calculated according to its intended media impact. During an election year, about 13 percent of all newspaper political news and 15 percent of TV political news are about the candidates and their campaigns. [23] Candidates must use that massive amount of news attention to their advantage.

Years ago, say in the election of 1896, the biggest item in a campaign budget might have been campaign train rental. Today, the major item is unquestionably television advertising. About half of the total budget for a major campaign will be targeted toward television advertising. (Networks and their affiliates, by the way, think of campaigns and political parties as poor credit risks. They usually insist on "cash up front" before agreeing to air commercials for candidates.) Television has done much to shape our new high-tech politics. ⑥

The Selling of the President. These days, no candidate can go without what political scientist Dan Nimmo calls "the political persuaders." [24]

Symbols and Substance. *Campaigners need both symbols and substance to put together a confident public image. In December, 1983, Rev. Jesse Jackson, then gearing up for his campaign for the Democratic nomination, helped negotiate with the Syrians for the release of a captured American pilot, Lt. Robert Goodman. Chicago ministers do not develop much experience in foreign policy, and this effort presumably helped to show that Jackson could handle a delicate matter with discretion and diplomacy.*

[20] This is discussed in ibid., p. 172.
[21] Frank J. Sorauf, "Who's in Charge? Accountability in Political Action Committees," *Political Science Quarterly* 99 (Winter 1984–85):591–614.
[22] Graber, *Mass Media and American Politics*, p. 181.
[23] Ibid., p. 189.
[24] Dan Nimmo, *The Political Persuaders: The Techniques of Modern Campaigning* (Englewood Cliffs, N.J.: Prentice-Hall, 1970).

Today a new profession of political consultants has emerged, and for the right price, they can turn a losing campaign into a winning one. They can do it all—polling or hiring the pollster, molding your image, advising you on your spouse's behavior, handling campaign logistics, managing payrolls, and so forth. Not only candidates, but incumbents, too, use professional consultants. When the days of the Carter presidency were dark, Carter hired Atlanta public relations man Gerald Rafshoon, who became a close advisor.

---

6 | TV and Politics: Some Great and Not-So-Great Moments

1952: The Checkers Speech. The 1952 presidential election was the first ever that utilized TV. Television was in its infancy. The star of TV campaigning in 1952 was California Senator Richard M. Nixon, then Dwight Eisenhower's running mate. Nixon was accused of hiding a secret slush fund from campaign donations. He took to television to denounce the charges. It came to be called "The Checkers Speech" because he claimed that the only personal item he ever took from a campaign contributor was his little dog Checkers. His wife, Pat, he said, proudly wore a "Republican cloth coat," not a fur coat. Ike kept him on the ticket after the speech.

1960: The First Great Debates. Again in 1960, Nixon was present, this time as Republican presidential candidate against youthful Senator John F. Kennedy from Massachusetts. The first nationally televised presidential debate took place in Chicago. Too rushed to shave before the debates, Nixon used a product called Lazy Shave to hide his five-o'clock shadow; he looked unshaven and drawn. Nixon answered questions like the college debater he once was, but JFK aimed his remarks directly to the TV audience. The debates did much to dispel the idea that Kennedy was too young and inexperienced for the presidency. Many believe the debate turned the tide in Kennedy's favor.

The '60s: Refining TV's Powerful Role. By the Johnson-Goldwater campaign of 1964, campaigns were following the lead of detergent and deodorant manufacturers. Clever sixty-second "spots" came into being. Most famous was the "daisy girl" commercial. Goldwater was in favor of nuclear testing, so the Democrats put on an advertisement in which a little girl is shown picking the petals off a daisy in the meadow. A voice counts down: 10-9-8-7 . . .—and the world explodes. Republicans were furious at the implication that Goldwater would start a nuclear war. Democrats withdrew the commercial after only one day. Few politicians took television to heart as

Richard Nixon did in the 1960s. He believed that his performance in the 1960 presidential debates had cost him the presidency, and he determined to package himself effectively. Journalist Joe McGuinniss wrote a best-seller called *The Selling of the President* about Nixon's effort to create the perfect public image for himself in 1968.

TV Today. By the middle of the 1970s, television was *the* dominant medium of presidential campaign politics. No longer could candidates decline to debate their opponents. Challenger Jimmy Carter demanded and got three debates with President Gerald Ford in 1976. Having set a precedent, it was hard for Carter to duck a debate with Ronald Reagan in 1980 (though try he did). So important are presidential debates that Walter Mondale temporarily closed Ronald Reagan's lead in 1984, following a lackluster performance by the President in the first debate. Again in 1984, TV was the medium with the message. Perhaps the most effective ad depicted a bear wandering around the forest—an obvious allusion to the Soviet Union—and indicated that the Reagan policies would quell the danger of that menacing bear.

These days, television can make or break the candidate. Though John Kennedy pioneered its political use, it nearly broke his youngest brother Teddy. Deciding to run against incumbent Jimmy Carter in 1980, Kennedy consented to a television interview with Roger Mudd, an old friend of the family. On the air, though, Mudd was a professional, pressing Kennedy on Chappaquidick, on his wife's alcoholism, on his ambitions. Mudd asked why Kennedy wanted to be president. Kennedy folded. He said: "Well, I'm—were I to—to make the announcement . . . is because I have a great belief in this country, that it is, has more natural resources than any country in the world. . . ." Television made one Kennedy president; it played a key role in keeping another Kennedy out of the job.

The Presidential Debates. *The institution of the presidential debate became an almost permanent part of the American political landscape in 1960. Then Vice-President Richard Nixon, the Republican candidate, consented to debate Massachusetts Senator John F. Kennedy. The debate took place in Chicago, when television was still a relative newcomer to American political life. Kennedy seemed well-informed and used television to speak directly to the viewers; Nixon looked jowly and sounded like the college debater he once was. The 1960 debates established Kennedy as a credible candidate for president. In 1976, presidential debates returned, as President Ford agreed to debate challenger Jimmy Carter. By 1980, President Carter found it hard to dodge Ronald Reagan's request for a debate. In many ways, the 1980 debate did for Reagan what the 1960 debate did for Kennedy: it established him as a credible candidate for president. By 1984, debates were a staple of the campaign. They had become less of a debate and more of a joint press conference, where each candidate made a general opening and closing statement but largely answered questions from a panel of reporters. In 1984, Reagan and Mondale debated twice, once on foreign policy and once on domestic policy. Mondale's zesty performance in the first debate sent him temporarily into the lead in presidential polls. Vice-presidential debates have now also taken their place alongside presidential debates as a staple feature of the campaign game. In October, 1984, Vice-President George Bush and Congresswoman Geraldine Ferraro debated in Philadelphia.*

All these public relations efforts to mold a candidate's image worry some observers of American politics. They fear a new era of politics in which the slick slogan and the image salesman will dominate, an era when Madison Avenue will be more influential than Wall Street or Main Street in American politics.

Most political scientists are increasingly persuaded that the advertising and public relations explosion is not importing all the vices of Madison Avenue to the presidential campaign. There are some virtues as well. Advertising can be a source of information about issues as well as about images. Two political scientists, Thomas Patterson and Robert McClure, examined the information contained in TV advertising and found it impressive. In fact, they concluded, you could learn more about how candidates stood on the issues from watching their ads than from watching TV news coverage. Most news coverage stressed where the candidates went, how big their crowds were, and other campaign details. But it rarely delved into how the candidates stood on the issues. Their ads, though, often did. [25]

Perhaps there is less conflict between *issues* and *images* than first appears. The candidates' positions are a crucial part of their images. Getting that across to voters is as important as persuading them that a candidate is honest, competent, and a real leader.

News Coverage. Candidates attempt to manipulate their images through advertising and image-building. But they have less control of the other face of the media, coverage of the news. To be sure, most campaigns have press aides who feed "canned" news releases to reporters too preoccupied to dig up their own news. Still, the media largely determine for themselves what is happening in a campaign. Campaign coverage seems to be a constant interplay between "hard" news about candidates and their issues and the "human interest angle," which most journalists think sells newspapers or interests television viewers.

Apparently, news organizations believe that policy issues are of less interest to voters than the campaign game itself. The result is that news coverage is disproportionately devoted to campaign strategies, guesses about who is ahead, poll results, and other aspects of the game, and not to information about substantive issues. Patterson tabulated the amount of media attention to the campaign itself and the amount of attention to such substantive issues as the economy in the 1976 presidential campaign. Examining several newspapers and news magazines as well as television network news, he found that attention to the game far exceeded attention to substance. [26] The attentive voter may try very hard to become informed. He or she may follow television news, read newspapers regularly, and subscribe to a multitude of news weeklies. But the attentive voter would find much more information about who was where in the polls than about what the candidates stood for. The new Harris poll showing that Smith is ahead of Jones is somehow more newsworthy than their positions on the issues.

[25] Thomas Patterson and Robert D. McClure, *The Unseeing Eye* (New York: Putnam's, 1976).
[26] Patterson, *Mass Media Election*, pp. 22–25.

The Reagan Image. *Campaigns traffic in two key commodities: issues and images. Part of the task of a campaign staff is to convey a particular image of the candidate. Ronald Reagan gave potential voters a set of signals that added up to an image: He was, they were supposed to believe, casual but determined, at ease on the job and on the ranch, and of course, a devoted family man.*

The Impact of Campaigns: Summing It Up

Politicians are great believers in campaigns. Almost all of them figure that a good campaign is the key to victory. Political scientists doubt that. Reviewing the evidence, Dan Nimmo concluded, "Political campaigns are less crucial in elections than most politicians believe."[27] For years, researchers studying campaigns have stressed that campaigns have three consequences for voters: **reinforcement, activation,** and **conversion.** They can reinforce the voter's preference for his or her candidate. They can activate the voter, getting him or her to contribute money or ring doorbells instead of just voting. And they can convert, changing the voter's mind.

Three decades of research on political campaigns lead to a single message: Campaigns mostly reinforce and activate; only rarely do they convert. The evidence on the impact of campaigns points clearly to the conclusion that the best-laid plans of campaign managers change few votes. This does not mean, of course, that campaigns never convert, or that converting a small number of voters is unimportant. In tight races, a good campaign can make that crucial marginal difference. And a bungled campaign can cost you the close one.

[27] Nimmo, *The Political Persuaders*, p. 5.

Because of the millions of dollars spent on campaigns, it may be surprising that they have no more impact than they do. But several factors tend to weaken their impact:

— People have a remarkable capacity for *selective perception:* paying most attention to things they already agree with and tuning out items that attempt to convert them.
— Most people pay little attention to campaigns.
— Such factors as party identification, though less important than they used to be, are still important reasons for voting behavior, regardless of what happens in the campaign.
— Some people—surveys usually report a third to a half of the electorate—have decided who they are going to vote for before the campaign starts.

And in a way, campaigns tend to cancel one another out. Points scored by one candidate may be counterbalanced by points scored by the other.

NOMINATIONS AND CAMPAIGNS SUMMARIZED

Our campaigns and nominations, and our elections generally, have changed throughout the two American centuries, and two of these changes are important. Nominations and campaigns have become more democratic, and they have become more technocratic.

Americans have spent two centuries trying to reform their electoral process in order to make it more democratic. Through the introduction of presidential primaries, they have tried hard to get "the bosses" out of the act. Today, about three-quarters of all the delegates to the national convention are selected by presidential primaries; but primaries have also raised other questions. Because the media is so prominent in election politics, winning early and winning often is important to claim momentum. Money also matters in political campaigns. We have tried to regulate political money, too, though the proliferation of PACs has caused new concerns.

Nominations and campaigns are an intricate part of the life of American politics. Selecting a president, as well as other officeholders, is crucial to the workings of our democratic system. How well the whole process works we examine after we have completed our review of nominations, campaigns, and elections.

Key Terms

nomination	Federal Election	Political Action
national party	Campaign Act	Committees (PACs)
convention	Federal Election	reinforcement
caucus	Commission	activation
presidential primaries	(FEC)	conversion

For Further Reading

Aldrich, John. *Before the Convention* (1980). The best scholarly assessment of the politics of nomination.

Alexander, Herbert E. *Financing the 1980 Election* (1983). Alexander is the most respected observer of American campaign finance, and this and other Alexander books are meticulous reviews of who gives what and how it is spent.

Drew, Elizabeth. *Politics and Money: The New Road to Corruption* (1983). A very critical view of the role of money in politics.

Kessel, John. *Presidential Campaign Politics* (1980). A good review of campaign strategies in building coalitions.

Patterson, Thomas. *The Mass Media Election* (1980). A coverage of the role of the media in the election of 1976.

Polsby, Nelson, and Aaron Wildavsky. *Presidential Elections*, 6th ed. (1984). A standard, and excellent overview of the presidential election game.

Elections:
The Voters Decide

MEMO

There comes a time in every campaign when the last poll is polled, the last speech is spoken, and the last television commentator has commented—the time to vote. The candidates exit center stage and the voters move on. Voters are to political scientists what genes are to biologists and atoms are to physicists: the raw material of their inquiry. More energies have been spent by political scientists examining elections than on any other subject.

In this chapter, we look at three American elections, those of 1796, 1896, and 1984. Elections have changed from early low-tech times to current high-tech times. They have become much more democratic than they were in the earlier American centuries. One reason for this evolution is that suffrage, the right to vote, has been expanded.

Eligibility to vote means little if people do not exercise their franchise. In recent years, we have become concerned in our country about the empty voting booth signalling a decline in voter participation. So we take a close look at voter turnout, to see who votes and who doesn't. If a citizen chooses to vote, many factors enter into his or her thinking in casting a ballot. Some of those factors relate to the candidate, others to the policy issues, still others to the party.

Even after the polls close and the votes are counted, the election is not over. There is a quaint American institution called the electoral college, and we will learn how it works.

Having glimpsed all of this, I will focus your attention on the models of American politics we introduced in Chapter 2. I will discuss how elections measure up to the various theories of American government we examine throughout *GIA.*

ONE OF THE MOST astute observers of American politics, the sage journalist Walter Lippman, once remarked that

We call an election an expression of the popular will. But is it? We go into a polling booth and mark a cross on a piece of paper for one of two, or perhaps three or four names. Have we expressed our thoughts on the public policy of the United States? Presumably we have a number of thoughts on this and that with many buts and ifs and ors. Surely the cross on a piece of paper does not express them. [1]

Americans—not just pollsters, pundits, and political scientists—search for meaning in elections. Are they mandates for change, as winners often claim? Are they disconnected tabulations of millions of crosses on ballots and pulls of levers? Elections are like tea leaves. Reading them is hard work, sometimes guesswork. This chapter will give you a perspective on American elections. We provide no hard-and-fast interpretations of elections in general nor of any one in particular. We do show how they function in the American system, how voters behave, and how you can make some sense of American elections. This chapter is mainly about presidential elections. Later, in Chapter 12, we will examine congressional elections.

Constitutionally, we pick our presidents once every four years. Given the length of the process, perhaps that is often enough. The road to the White House is tedious and tiring for voters as well as for candidates. Today we have virtually a permanent campaign, in which candidates for the next election line up almost before the Inaugural Parade is cleaned up. Short on news at the Republican's predictable 1984 convention, networks focused on the 1988 candidates, a *full four years and three months* before the election. Tennessee Senator Howard Baker frankly admitted that he "badly wanted" to be president. (Presumably he did, for he had left the Senate to find time to campaign for the job.) Senator Robert Dole, who would succeed Baker as majority leader, told the press that his hotel in Dallas had given him room 1988. His wife, Secretary of Transportation Elizabeth Dole, when asked about a 1988 vice-presidential bid, said that if George Bush wanted to keep the job, she'd consider him.

Fifty-one presidential elections have produced thirty-four men elected to the presidency. (Five others—John Tyler, Millard Fillmore, Andrew Johnson, Chester Arthur, and Gerald Ford—were vice-presidents who became presidents without ever having been directly elected.) Times change, and so do elections. Today, campaigns are slick and scientific. Imagine our high-tech elections transported to an earlier day: Think of John Adams and Thomas Jefferson, standing under the TV lights, perhaps powdering and adjusting their wigs, waiting for the "Presidential Debate of 1796" to begin. Or Abraham Lincoln securing the nomination and then lining up an ad agency and a professional pollster. Woodrow Wilson did not have an early-day network exit poll to report whether he had won; he had to find out on his own. A glance at three American elections should give us a good idea of how they have changed over nearly two centuries.

[1] Cited in Stanley G. Kelley, Jr., *Interpreting Elections* (Princeton, N.J.: Princeton University Press, 1983), pp. 3–4.

THE MAKING OF OUR PRESIDENTS: A TALE OF THREE ELECTIONS

1796: Adams Beats Jefferson

By our standards, 1796 was not much of an election at all: no primaries, no nominating convention, no campaign, no speeches, no entourage of reporters, no press releases, not even parties as we know them. Outgoing President George Washington apparently assumed that his vice-president, John Adams, should succeed him. He reviewed matters of state with Adams before announcing his decision to retire. Adams's archrival and subsequent opponent, Thomas Jefferson, had quit the Washington cabinet and was living quietly at Monticello.

The election was fairly simple. Neither Adams nor Jefferson needed to campaign, since there was no popular vote. The Electoral College chose the president. Communication was so slow that most people knew nothing about the contest until the election was over. But there was plenty of backroom bargaining. Alexander Hamilton, never fond of flinty, abrasive John Adams, thought he could persuade members of the electoral college to vote for Adams's vice-presidential running mate, Thomas Pinckney, and not for Adams. The plan failed, but it produced a curious result: Adams was elected president and Jefferson, his rival, got enough electoral votes to become vice-president. (The Twelfth Amendment to the Constitution arranged procedures so that this sort of thing would not happen again.)

1896: Republicans Solidify Their Coalition with Gold

Exactly a century later, the election of 1896 was fought largely over economics. Voters were still smarting from the depression of 1893. Candidates were nominated by national conventions. Republicans, meeting in St. Louis for their convention, had a clear front-runner, former Congressman William McKinley. McKinley had the look and style of a president. He also had the money. His campaign manager, Mark Hanna, bankrolled McKinley's campaign for the nomination, largely with dollars from prosperous manufacturers. The issues were gold and tariffs. Republicans were for both. Hanna, McKinley, and the Republican platform all supported the gold standard and high tariffs. The gold standard linked money to gold, which was scarce. Thus, debtors never got a break from inflation. Tariffs protected capitalists and their workers from foreign competition. After piling up a commanding majority on the first ballot at St. Louis, McKinley sat back to see what the upcoming Democratic convention would do.

The Democrats met in Chicago's sticky summer heat, in July 1896. They had an issue—unlimited coinage of silver—but no candidate. Their incumbent president, Grover Cleveland, was blamed for the Panic of 1893, and a resolution praising the Cleveland administration was hooted down. The high point of the Chicago convention was a speech by young William Jennings Bryan of Nebraska, known as the "Boy Orator of the Platte." (Bryan's critics maintained that the river Platte was a "mile wide and an inch deep at the mouth.") Bryan's "Cross of Gold" speech pro-

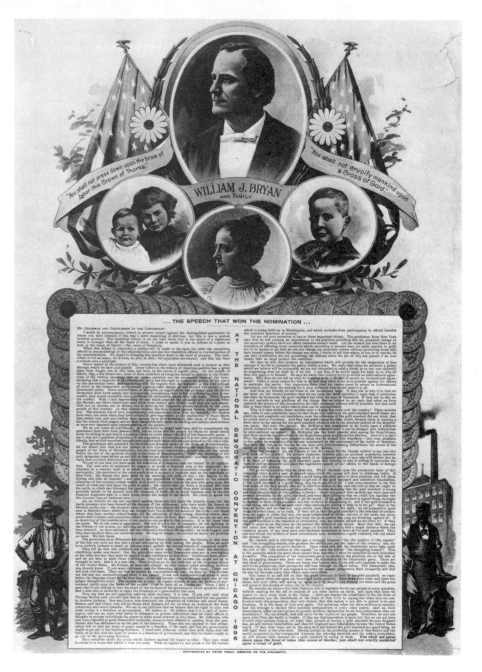

The Campaign of 1896: A Poster for William Jennings Bryan. *Even in this era of television, fast transportation, and political image-makers, no election has matched 1896 in intensity or turnout. McKinley's and Bryan's campaign attracted a higher percentage of the eligible population to the polls than any presidential election in the twentieth century.*

claimed the virtues of "free silver." "You shall not crucify mankind on a cross of gold," he concluded, and clinched the nomination on the fifth ballot.

The campaign contrasted flamboyant Bryan—who took a train through twenty-six states, logging 18,000 miles, and gave 600 speeches— and the serene McKinley. Debtors and silver miners were especially attracted to Bryan's pitch for cheap silver money. Hanna advised McKinley to sit home in Ohio and run a front-porch campaign. He did, and managed to label the Democrats as the party of depression ("In God We Trust, with Bryan We Bust").

Bryan won the oratory, but McKinley won the election. Eastern manufacturers contributed a small fortune—perhaps as much as $15 million —to the Republicans. (Not until 1964 did any party spend as much to win the presidency.) A few manufacturers told their workers not to report back to work if Bryan won. Blacks (those few who could vote), urban workers, industrialists, and easterners of all kinds voted Republican, and most of them stayed with the GOP until the 1930s. Southerners and rural debtors (plus the silver-producing states) lined up behind Bryan, but McKinley got 7.1 million votes to Bryan's 6.5 million. Nearly 80 percent of the eligible electorate voted.

1984: Reagan Wins Another One

Democratic nominee Walter Mondale, in an attempt to gain ground, chanced two bold strokes within a two-week period.[2] As it turned out, neither worked very well. First, just before the July Democratic convention in San Francisco, he announced his vice-presidential candidate. Mondale had interviewed a cross-section of political leaders at his home in North Oaks, Minnesota. There were women: Queens Congresswoman Geraldine Ferraro, Kentucky Governor Martha Collins, and San Francisco Mayor Diane Feinstein. One potential candidate was San Antonio Mayor Henry Cisneros of Mexican-American heritage; Los Angeles and Philadelphia mayors Tom Bradley and Winston Goode were black contenders. Only one white establishment senator, Lloyd Bentson of Texas, rounded out the interviewees. It was vintage Democratic pluralism. Mondale picked Geraldine Ferraro, the first major-party, female vice-presidential candidate. "This," said Mondale, "is an exciting choice."

It needed to be. Every available poll showed Mondale behind in all fifty states as the Democratic convention opened. Just after forging the Mondale-Ferraro ticket, the duo travelled to San Francisco and the national convention. Like virtually all modern conventions, this would contain no surprises. Despite dogged challenges from Colorado Senator Gary Hart (who had actually won twelve primaries to Mondale's eleven), and from Reverend Jesse Jackson, Mondale's delegates were solidly for him. The delegate count had been largely settled by the presidential primaries. Thus, appearing unified and in command of the issues was the key to an orchestrated convention. In his acceptance speech, therefore, Mondale tried a second bold stroke: He announced that the $200 billion federal deficit was the nation's most important problem and that he would raise taxes to reduce it. Rarely had a candidate come out so foursquare on the side of a tax increase.

Underdogs need all the euphoria they can muster; the Democrats came out of San Francisco serene, if not euphoric. Not for long. Soon Mondale and Ferraro ran into their first crisis, even before the August Republican convention began in Dallas. Reporters found flaws in Geraldine Ferraro's financial reporting of her congressional campaigns; her realtor husband, John Zacarro, was said to be involved in questionable real estate practices (and was later convicted of fraudulent real-estate dealings). After much vacillation, the couple finally released their

[2] On the 1984 elections, see the excellent journalistic account by Elizabeth Drew, *Campaign Journal: The Political Events of 1983–1984* (New York: Macmillan, 1985) and the articles in *P.S.* (Winter 1985).

The National Convention as Party Unity Builder. *Once the principal role of the national convention was to select the party's candidate for president. Today, that process is mostly routine at the convention itself. All the delegates have been selected in presidential primaries and caucuses and their individual preferences are hardly a secret. More and more, a convention has become a unity-building institution. Even though the party may have been divided during the primaries, party leaders—winners and losers—rally around the presidential candidate. In 1984, the unsuccessful candidates shared the rostrum with presidential nominee Mondale and vice-presidential nominee Ferraro. A solidified party stands a better chance of emerging victorious in November. For the Republicans, as for any party with a popular incumbent president, party unity was easier to achieve. These podium-sharings suggest that conventions are symbolic, as well as substantive, parts of our political process.*

tax returns to the press; they were minutely scrutinized. The media had a field day, and for a time it seemed that the Ferraro family finances were the only issue in the campaign. If campaigns depend on momentum, the Democrats lost much of it then. Every poll still showed Reagan soaring to victory.

The first televised presidential debate in Louisville, Kentucky, on Sunday, October 7, renewed a flicker of hope in the Democratic party. More than a hundred journalists had been rejected as potential questioners by the two sides. The debate's sponsor, the League of Women Voters, grumbled that "the process [of selecting panelists] has been abused." Nonetheless, it was Walter Mondale's finest hour. President Reagan appeared old, tired, and unsure of the facts. The short-lived age issue reared its head again with reporters pointedly musing whether a man who reportedly napped during cabinet meetings was too old to be president. President Reagan even slipped a bit in the polls after the first debate. For the second and last debate in Kansas City, however, Reagan returned to form, and the polls showed a clearcut victory for him.

And such a victory it was! Ronald Reagan in 1984 won the electoral votes of every state but Minnesota and the District of Columbia: 525 to Mondale's 13. Predictably, Jewish voters gave Mondale majorities of their votes; 65 percent, as opposed to 35 percent for Reagan. So did black voters, an overwhelming 91 percent for Mondale, 9 percent for Reagan. Poor and union voters favored Mondale, and women split almost evenly between Mondale and Reagan. The differences between men and women in their support for Reagan led to discussions of a gender gap in politics. [1] But overall, it was a sweep—regionally and demographically—for Ronald Reagan.

Elections Today

The election of 1984 was as different from the election of 1896 as the Bryan-McKinley race was from the election of 1796. For one thing, the right to vote has been greatly expanded since 1796 (when there was no popular voting at all), and since 1896 (when the right to vote was limited mainly to white males).

The Founding Fathers did not perceive elections the way we do today. They did not expect men like George Washington or John Adams, elitists to the core, to hit the road to muster support from the masses; the very idea of campaigning would have been loathsome to them. Instead, they created the electoral college (see page 288) to choose a president. But since then several waves of democratization have washed over the electoral shoreline.

---

1 | A Gender Gap?

The 1984 presidential election saw a new term popularized in American politics: "gender gap." It meant that female voters were somehow different from male voters, particularly in their support of Ronald Reagan for president. Throughout the election, and even in the final vote, women were less loyal to Reagan than were men.

In July, 1983, the National Women's Political Caucus held its annual meeting in San Antonio, Texas. Some 800 delegates heard female members of Congress and other state and national officials detail the meaning of the "gender gap." Queens Congresswoman Geraldine Ferraro, destined for a bigger and better role in politics, said that "We've got the issues, we've got the gender gap on our side, and at long last the men are going to pay attention to us." Women political leaders pointed with pride to the fact that they had come a long way. In 1971, there were fifteen women in Congress, 362 women in state legislatures, and seven mayors of cities with more than 30,000 people. By the time of the 1983 convention, only twelve years later, there were twenty-four women in Congress, 992 state legislators, and 76 mayors. In the four states we have examined throughout *Government in America,* there were significant changes, too. In Tennessee, the number of women legislators doubled between 1975 and 1985. It grew from 4 to 8 percent in Texas. In California, women numbered 2 percent of the 1975 legislature and 12.5 percent of the 1985 group. In Pennsylvania, their share had grown from 3.5 percent to 5 percent.

As women have become more powerful in politics, so has their influence increased within the electorate. Women voted less heavily for the Republicans and

Reagan in 1984 than men did. But there are two more components of the gender gap that are more important than a single electoral result:

— Women are more likely than men to be registered voters. They constitute about 53 percent of all registered voters.
— Women are more likely to be Democrats than are men. Among men, Democrats and Republicans are split almost equally, with Democrats holding a slight edge. Among women, though, Democrats hold a significant lead. Almost half of American women are Democratic party identifiers, compared with less than 40 percent of men.

There is no clear evidence that having a woman as the vice-presidential nominee helped or hurt the Democrats in 1984. Geraldine Ferraro probably cost the Democrats momentum, as valuable weeks had to be spent explaining to the press and public her family's complicated financial dealings. The loss of momentum may have meant the loss of votes as well. Nonetheless, differences between men and women in politics transcend any particular election. In registration rates, in party identification, and on some issue positions, women do differ from men.

Source: For the specific evidence quoted above, *Time,* July 25, 1983, pp. 12–13; Haynes Johnson and Thomas B. Edsall, "Will the Next President Owe His Election to Women?" *Washington Post National Weekly Edition,* August 20, 1984, p. 11. See also Vicky Randall, *Women and Politics* (New York: St. Martins, 1982) and Ethel Klein, *Gender Politics* (Cambridge, Mass.: Harvard University Press, 1984).

The American Electorate. *Over our two centuries of American politics, elections have become much more democratic. They really did not exist at all in 1796. A century later, they existed but the electorate consisted almost entirely of white males. The twentieth century saw the addition of blacks, women, and younger Americans to the electorate. Even residents of Washington, D.C., whom you see here at their polling place, can now vote for presidential electors.*

Nearly two centuries have resulted in widespread eligibility to vote. Women, minorities, and young adults have been brought into the electoral arena (to learn how, see page 274). Parties reach out to more and more groups—Asian Americans, Latinos, older people, younger ones—hoping to bring them into the fold.

Hard to fight for, the vote is easy to waste. Curiously, as the right to vote has been extended to more and more Americans, proportionally fewer and fewer of those eligible to vote have chosen to exercise that right. Gerald Pomper remarked that, paradoxically, "as the ballot has become more available, it has become less valued." [3] In the last hundred years, the election of 1896 was a high point for turnout in presidential elections; the election of 1980 a low point. In 1984, only 53 percent of eligible adult Americans voted.

This chapter is about those voters—and nonvoters—who do—and do not—go to the presidential polling place. The voter has long been at the center of the inquiry of political scientists. Scores of books and thousands of articles have probed the mysteries of the individual voter and the election. [4] Only one thing is certain: Voters are complex individuals, tougher to study than genes or atoms.

THE STRUCTURE OF AMERICAN ELECTIONS

How Elections Work

Elections are an American commonplace. Because they are so numerous—there are nearly half a million elected public officials in our country—and so complicated—moreso than in any other democratic nation—we should carefully examine their workings. In our system, the *states*, not the federal government, are mainly responsible for elections. There is a Federal Election Commission, but it does not run our national elections. It mainly keeps candidates financially accountable and doles out federal aid to presidential candidates. So long as states do not violate the Constitution or a few federal laws (mostly against discrimination at the polls), states run our elections, even for national offices like the president and Congress.

There are two different kinds of elections in the United States: those elections that *select candidates and officeholders,* and those elections in which voters engage in *direct legislation*. Most attention focuses on elections that select officeholders, although there are plenty of examples of direct legislation each election season. [2]

Most American elections either select candidates for office (called **primaries**) or select the officeholders from those nominated by the parties (called **general elections**). We met one kind of primary in Chapter 8, the *presidential primary*. In addition, most states use primaries to select candidates for United States Senate, the House of Representatives, governors, and other state offices. These we call **direct primaries,** to distinguish

---

[3] Gerald M. Pomper, with Susan Lederman, *Elections in America*, 2nd ed. (New York: Longman, 1980), p. 4.

[4] One of the best reviews is the collection in Richard Niemi and Herbert Weisberg (eds.), *Controversies in Voting Behavior*, rev. ed. (Washington: Congressional Quarterly Press, 1984).

them from primaries to choose delegates to a presidential nominating convention.

Elections for particular offices occur at fixed intervals. Presidents are elected for four years, senators for six, members of the House of Representatives for two, and so on. This may seem too obvious to mention, but it is not that way in most democracies. In parliamentary systems, elections

---

2 The "Other American Elections" and the Case of the Denture Services Act

In 1984, voters in Montana, like those everywhere else, went to the polls to choose between Reagan and Mondale. They also had another choice: A chance to vote on the Freedom of Choice in Denture Services Act. Yes, you read correctly. Montana voters passed a law that would permit professionally trained "denturists," and not only dentists, to fit false teeth. As you might expect, the Montana dental lobby strongly opposed the measure, which proponents claimed would save denture wearers as much as 50 percent of the cost.

In Montana and most other state and local governments, there are many "other elections" that do not select candidates but rather constitute policy decisions by voters. In twenty-three states, the State Constitution permits an **initiative** petition. This permits a certain percentage of the state's voters (typically about 10 percent of the number who voted in the most recent statewide election) to put a proposed law directly on the ballot. If a majority of the voters vote in favor of this law, it becomes state policy even if the legislature does not act. A **referendum** is another example of direct legislation. In a referendum, voters are given the chance to approve or disapprove a law passed by the legislature or some constitutional amendment. Forty-nine of the fifty states permit some use of the referendum (Delaware is the lone exception).

Perhaps the most famous legislation-by-the-people in modern times took place in California. Howard Jarvis, "a rugged bastard who's had his head kicked a thousand times by government" (those are his own words), organized a statewide initiative to cut property taxes. He collected 1.2 million signatures (twice that required by law) to force an election on what came to be called *Proposition 13*. It meant cuts in California property taxes of $7 billion. Acting with too little, too late, neither Governor Jerry Brown nor the legislature could counter Jarvis's groundswell of tax revolt. In June 1978, Prop 13 passed. California governments set about doing with less.

Year in and year out, direct legislation is on state and local ballots. In 1984, for example, voters in forty-three states voted on more than 200 statewide referendums. In California, Oregon, Michigan, and elsewhere, voters

Howard Jarvis: Crusader Against Taxes. *Few people in America had more to do with the recent tax revolt than Howard Jarvis. In 1977, he launched a statewide campaign against high property tax rates in California. The state constitution provision permitting referendums enabled Jarvis to bring his issue to the voters. Collecting signatures across the state, Jarvis and his supporters succeeded in getting a referendum question on limiting residential property taxes on the ballot. In June 1978, voters approved the proposition.*

decided against measures that would have started another round of fiscal cuts in state and local governments. Voters in California, Missouri, Oregon, and West Virginia approved state lotteries. Washington voters turned down a proposal that would have forbidden state abortion fundings, while Arizona voters upheld a similar one. Through initiatives and referendums, voters in the states can make public policy directly, bypassing the legislatures if they desire.

Source: On the 1984 referendums, see Austin Ranney, "Referendums and Initiatives in 1984," *Public Opinion* (December/January 1985): 15–17.

may be called irregularly. In Great Britain, for example, elections must be called at least every five years. They may be called earlier, however, if the majority party thinks it can boost its control of parliament or if a government looses the support of its parliamentary coalition (as it often does in Italy). Unlike citizens in most of these other countries, Americans who want to vote confront a complex process called registration.

Registration: Getting to the Polling List on Time

Years ago, machine politicians used to say, "Vote early and vote often." Partly to prevent the corruption associated with the names on headstones voting or paying cash to vote, states adopted voter **registration** systems, which began in the 1890s. Usually voters must register well in advance of election day, although virtually instant registration is permitted for presidential elections in some states.

American electoral turnout is well below that of other democratic nations, even nations such as India. Our complex registration system is one reason. [5] One way to see how registration systems encourage or discourage voting is to compare voter turnout in easy-to-register states with turnout in hard-to-register states. Raymond Wolfinger and Steven J. Rosenstone did just that. [6] Some states make it easy for you to register and vote. Those in the upper great plains and the Pacific northwest have easy-to-meet registration requirements. States in the south, however, with a legacy of using all available means to keep blacks from voting, typically have difficult registration systems. See for yourself in [3] how voter turnout differed in 1984 between facilitative and frustrating states. Wolfinger and Rosenstone estimate that if all the states adopted the registration requirements of the most facilitative states, our national turnout would probably increase by more than 9 percent. [7] Then it would be on a par with India's.

Once registered, at election time the voter has *two* key decisions to make: First, he or she has to decide *whether to vote*. Then, if the answer to that is yes, the voter must decide *how to vote*. Then begins Act III of the electoral drama, when the voters are on stage.

WHETHER TO VOTE: THE VOTER'S FIRST CHOICE

Eligibility: Toward More Equality

Eligibility is the very first hurdle to clear on the road to decisions about whether to vote. Expansion of the right to vote has been an important part of the gradual democratization of the American electoral process. From our tale of three elections, we learned that elections have become more democratic since 1796.

---

[5] One of the first strong, empirical arguments to this effect is in Stanley G. Kelley, Jr., Richard E. Ayres, and William G. Brown, "Registration and Voting: Putting First Things First," *American Political Science Review* 61(June 1967):359–79.

[6] Raymond Wolfinger and Steven J. Rosenstone, *Who Votes?* (New Haven, Conn.: Yale University Press, 1980), Chap. 4.

[7] Ibid., p. 73.

The history of this evolution can be told as a story of expanding equality. **Suffrage,** the legal right to vote, was limited to a handful of the population in the early Republic. No one thought about letting blacks (most of whom were slaves) and women vote. Consistent with John Jay's dictum, "The people who own the country ought to govern it," most states limited suffrage to adult white males who owned property. By the Civil War, though, all states had abandoned property qualifications. An era of universal (white) manhood suffrage had arrived. The post-Civil War history is a story of the gradual extension of the vote to blacks, women, and other previously disenfranchised groups.

The **Fifteenth Amendment** guaranteed suffrage to blacks. Adopted in 1870, it said, "The right of citizens to vote shall not be abridged by the United States or by any state on account of race, color, or previous condition of servitude." Yet the gap between these constitutional words and their implementation remained wide for a full century. Only the Supreme Court took the Fifteenth Amendment seriously. States seemed to outdo one another in imaginative policies to thwart Negro voting.

Some states used poll taxes to deter voting. These were small charges levied on the right to vote, often falling due during the time poor black voters had the least cash on hand. States sometimes used literacy tests as a criterion for voting. These also deterred less well educated voters—again, often black. One by one, these and other barriers fell to challenges before the United States Supreme Court.

The civil rights movement of the 1950s and the policy changes of the 1960s helped end both formal and informal barriers to black suffrage. Civil rights groups led voter registration drives. Congress passed the **Voting Rights Act of 1965.** Under that law, federal registrars went to many southern states and counties to register blacks, many of whom had never voted before. Just before Independence Day of 1982, Congress passed and President Reagan signed into law a twenty-five year extension of the Voting Rights Act. In Chapter 18, we will describe more specifically how public policy brought blacks into full citizenship. For now, though, we stress that blacks have the same rights to suffrage long enjoyed by whites.

The first instance of women's suffrage was an accident. When the New Jersey constitution failed explicitly to prevent women from voting, a few tried. The state legislature quickly amended their constitution to make it clear that voting was for men only. Not until 1869, when the territory of Wyoming permitted women to vote, was the first nonaccidental women's suffrage policy adopted.

The battle for women's suffrage was fought mostly in the last years of the nineteenth and first years of the twentieth century. Such suffragists as Susan B. Anthony and Elizabeth Cady Stanton preached that a new era of morality would emerge when women could vote. The suffragists used parades, protests, and even civil disobedience, offering a preview of conflict destined to erupt two generations later over civil rights and the Equal Rights Amendment. These courageous suffragists emerged vic-

Suffragettes. The first question potential voters confront is, "Am I eligible?" Being eligible to vote requires gaining suffrage—the right to vote—and getting registered. The twentieth century opened the doors of suffrage to hitherto ineligible groups. Women first got the right to vote in the western states. The Nineteenth Amendment (1920) forbade denying the right to vote on account of sex.

torious in 1920, when the **Nineteenth Amendment** was ratified, guaranteeing women the right to vote.

Blacks and woman are not the only groups to have recently won the right to vote. Especially in the 1960s, young people began to notice their disenfranchisement. Historically, the minimum voting age had been set at twenty-one, although a few states (Georgia, for example) had lower ages, apparently without catastrophic results. Youths in the 1960s in particular were active politically. They took to the barricades (sometimes literally) against the Vietnam War and played key roles in such campaigns as that of antiwar Senator Eugene McCarthy, who tried to win the Democratic presidential nomination in 1968. The passage of the **Twenty-sixth Amendment** in 1971 extended suffrage to everyone over the age of eighteen. The **Twenty-third Amendment,** passed in 1961, gave residents of the District of Columbia the right to select presidential electors just like a state.

An Election Paradox: More Suffrage, Less Participation

As we have said, in comparison with other democratic nations, Americans are not very vigorous participants in elections. West Germany, Italy, and Australia have rates of participation of 90 percent or more of those eligible to vote; France, Holland, and Denmark score at 80 percent or better; Japan, Britain, and Canada are in the 70s; even poverty-ridden India counts six in ten of its citizens as voters. [8] There is a significant participation gap in American politics between voter turnout and both what we might expect it to be and what it is in other nations.

One by one, the barriers to voting have fallen. First women, then minority groups, then young people have been added to the electorate by federal and state policy. There are several reasons why we should hypothesize that the participation rate in elections would have soared in the last half of the twentieth century:

— More and more money is spent to court voters.
— Americans are better educated today than fifty years ago, and education is one of the strongest predictors of voter turnout. [9]
— Television brings the campaign into our living rooms; formerly, campaign trains only brought it to the nearest train station.

In fact, though, electoral participation has not risen, but has actually declined. Our task is to find out why.

First, consider the long-run trends. Let us not go all the way back to 1896, when the counting of votes was more dubious and before the female half of the population could even vote. Let us instead begin with the election of 1924, the first in which all women could legally vote for president. Take a careful look at 4 . It depicts the percentage of the eligible population that actually voted for the president and for members of the House of Representatives.

[8] Ibid., p. 17.
[9] William Crotty, *American Parties in Decline*, 2nd ed. (Boston: Little, Brown, 1984) p. 5.

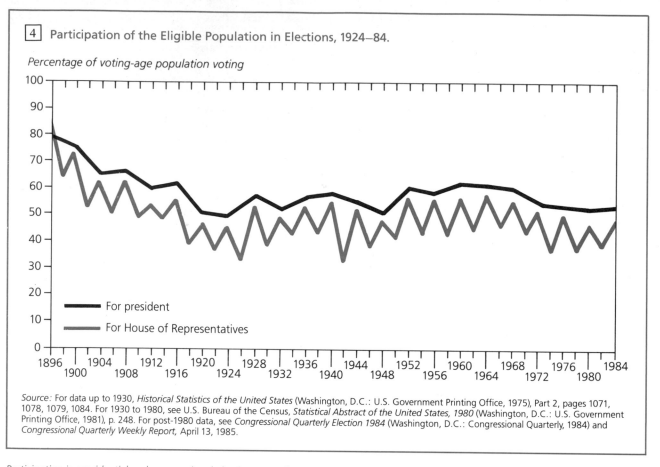

4   Participation of the Eligible Population in Elections, 1924–84.

Percentage of voting-age population voting

Legend:
— For president
— For House of Representatives

Source: For data up to 1930, *Historical Statistics of the United States* (Washington, D.C.: U.S. Government Printing Office, 1975), Part 2, pages 1071, 1078, 1079, 1084. For 1930 to 1980, see U.S. Bureau of the Census, *Statistical Abstract of the United States, 1980* (Washington, D.C.: U.S. Government Printing Office, 1981), p. 248. For post-1980 data, see *Congressional Quarterly Election 1984* (Washington, D.C.: Congressional Quarterly, 1984) and *Congressional Quarterly Weekly Report,* April 13, 1985.

Participation in presidential and congressional elections actually rose somewhat after women were granted suffrage in 1924, peaked in 1960 in the Kennedy-Nixon race, and has dropped by about 10 percentage points since then.

Clearly, since 1924, electoral participation has remained relatively steady. Over this fifty-year period from 50 to 60 percent of the adult, eligible population has voted for president. The rate drops during mid-term elections, when people turn out to vote for Congress in "off-year elections."

Explaining the Participation Gap. Since 1960, when 63 percent of those eligible voted, turnout has declined steadily. By 1984, the percentage had shrunk to 53 (just a hair greater than in 1980), a decline of more than 10 percentage points in two and a half decades. Politicians and political scientists have wasted no time decrying the "empty ballot box" and asking "where have all the voters gone?"[10] Politicial scientists have also tried to explain the phenomenon.

Part of the reason lies in the changing composition of the electorate. Throughout the twentieth century, we have opened up the ballot box to new groups. But each of those groups, when admitted, has participated at lower-than-average rates. First women, then minority groups, then

[10] Everett Ladd, *Where Have All the Voters Gone?* (New York: Norton, 1982).

278

young voters all were low participators. (If we start with a roomful of six-footers, then admit some persons of medium height, then some really short people, we will inevitably decrease the average height.) Although women's voting rates now equal men's, this did not happen overnight; nor have the voting rates of black and young people yet reached the average of white and middle-aged people. But, as we'll see, more is involved in this complex issue.

Who Votes and Who Stays Home? These days, about half of the population votes in a presidential election; about half stays home.[11] Here we look at the voters and the stay-at-homes.

The most useful study of nonvoting in American elections was done by Raymond Wolfinger and Steven J. Rosenstone.[12] In ⑤ you can see for yourself which groups supply most of the voters and most of the non-voters. Several conclusions become apparent from that evidence:

— *Voting is a class-biased activity.* Persons with higher-than-average incomes and educational levels vote more than people with lower incomes and educational levels. Among all factors affecting turnout, this one is the most important.
— *Voting is not very strongly related to gender.* In an earlier period, a woman's place may have been in the home, not in the voting booth. Today, women vote just about as frequently as men do.
— *Whites vote with greater frequency than members of minority groups.* Blacks, Puerto Ricans, and Chicanos are all underrepresented among the ranks of voters. But this may be explained by other factors. Blacks and other minority groups with high levels of income and education vote more than whites with high levels of income and education, but they are a smaller percentage of the total black population.
— *Southerners do less voting than northerners.*
— *Voting is a middle-aged activity.* Smaller shares of the young (those under thirty) and the very old (those over seventy-nine) are likely to vote.
— *Not surprisingly, people who work for the government are heavy participators in the electoral process.* Having something at stake (their jobs and the future of the programs they work on) and being in a position to know more about government seems to impel government workers to high participation levels.

These differences are often cumulative. Possessing several of these traits (say, being well-educated, white, and a government worker) adds to one's likelihood of voting. Conversely, being young, black, poor, and southern is likely to add up to a very low probability of voting.

[11] A note of caution: When we say that "half the population" votes or does not vote, we mean "the half of the population that the Census Bureau counts." Remember that the census counts all sorts of people who are not citizens, even illegal aliens if they can be found. Thus, comparing highly accurate voting figures with very imperfect census figures overestimates the proportion of nonvoters—by how much no one can say.
[12] Wolfinger and Rosenstone, *Who Votes?*,

Raymond Wolfinger and Steven Rosenstone have examined the voting rates of various groups in the population. Some of their results are shown in the following table. The figures in the last column indicate whether a group is over- or underrepresented in elections.

A ratio of 1.00 means that the group is neither over- nor underrepresented; that is, its share of the vote is equal to its share of the population. Women come closest to a representation ratio of 1.00. They constitute 53.2 percent of the population and 52.7 percent of voters, so their ratio is 0.99; that is, they are only very slightly underrepresented at the polls. A representation ratio of less than 1.00 indicates that a group is underrepresented in the voting. People who have less than a high-school education, for example, account for 36.4 percent of the adult citizen population but only 29.0 percent of those who vote. This group is greatly underrepresented, as reflected in its representation ration of 0.80.

A ratio of more than 1.00 means that a group is overrepresented. People making more than $15,000 a year account for 19.3 percent of the adult citizen population but 23.8 percent of the voters. Their ratio is 1.23. Because their percentage of the voting population is higher than their percentage of the adult citizen population, they are overrepresented.

Ideally, if a group constitutes a third of the population it should account for a third of the voters (a representation ratio of 1.00) in order to be adequately represented. If it accounts for less than a third of voters, it is underrepresented (representation ratio of less than 1.00). If it accounts for more than a third of voters, it is overrepresented (representation ratio of more than 1.00).

The implications of these statistics are important for election outcomes and, ultimately, for the policies that the winners will support. Because certain groups are underrepresented, it might be more difficult for their interests to be represented adequately and for policies helpful to them to get passed. On the other hand, if some groups are overrepresented, policies that benefit them may have a better chance of passing: Politicians know that these groups make their voices heard during the election.

A Policy Approach to the Voter's Decision

Let's be realistic. When 90 million people vote in a presidential election (as they did in 1984), your chance of affecting the outcome is slim. Once in a while, of course, an election is decided by one vote or a handful of votes. (In 1948, Lyndon B. Johnson won a race for the United States Senate by a total of 88—very suspicious—votes, earning him the nickname of "Landslide Lyndon.") But almost no elections are truly decided by what a single voter does.

Not only does your vote probably not make much difference, but voting is somewhat costly. You have to spend some of your valuable time becoming informed, making up your mind, and getting to the polls. If you are truly a rational person, careful to calculate your time and your expenditure of energy, you might decide perfectly rationally that nonvoting is more sensible than voting.

Economist Anthony Downs, in his model of democracy, tries to explain why a rational person would bother to vote. Rational people vote, he said, if they believe that the policies of one party will bring more benefits than the policies of the other party.[13] Thus, people who see *policy differences* between the parties are more likely to join the ranks of voters. If you expect the Democrats to pass more environmental legislation than the Republicans, and you are an environmentalist, then it is rational to vote and vote Democratic. If you think the Republicans will do more to control

[13] Anthony Downs, *An Economic Theory of Democracy* (New York: Harper & Row, 1957), Chap. 14.

Overrepresentation and Underrepresentation: A Look at Some Groups (continued)

Comparison of Voters with the Adult Population 1972

Group	Percentage of adult citizen population[a]	Percentage of voters[b]	Ratio of group's voter turnout to its share of the adult citizen population (column 2 ÷ column 1)
EDUCATION			
Less than high school	36.4	29.0	.80
High school	37.6	38.7	1.03
College	26.0	32.3	1.24
INCOME			
Less than $10,000	55.2	48.0	.87
$10,000–$15,000	25.6	28.1	1.10
More than $15,000	19.3	23.8	1.23
AGE			
31 and under	32.5	27.9	.86
32–36	8.2	8.3	1.01
37–69	49.7	54.8	1.10
70–78	6.5	6.6	1.02
79 and over	3.1	2.4	.77
WOMEN	53.2	52.7	.99
SOUTHERNERS	25.6	21.6	.84
GOVERNMENT EMPLOYEES	10.2	12.6	1.24
BLACKS	9.8	8.2	.84
PUERTO RICANS[c]	.6	.3	.50
CHICANOS[c]	1.9	1.3	.68

[a]Citizens age eighteen and over for whom turnout was reported.
[b]Voters in the general election.
[c]Estimated using 1974 data.
Source: Raymond Wolfinger and Steven J. Rosenstone, *Who Votes?* (New Haven, Conn.: Yale University Press, 1980), pp. 106–107, Table 6.1.
Copyright © 1980 by Yale University.

inflation, and you are sick and tired of seeing your income eaten away, then you will vote and vote Republican. But you may be indifferent to the parties. You may think that the two parties offer no real choice about the policies they advocate. Or you may believe that the Democrats' proenvironmental platform is balanced by the Republicans' control-inflation platform. If you are truly indifferent—that is, if you see no difference whatsoever between the two parties—you may rationally decide to abstain. Still, even if you are indifferent about the outcome, you may decide to vote anyway, simply to support democratic government. You might, Downs suggested, even cast a random vote for one party or the other just to show that you believe elections contribute to the workings of a democratic government. In that case, you are impelled to vote by a sense of *civic duty*.

Now, suppose that you do detect a difference between the parties. You are an environmentalist and can see that party *A* has a strong environmental platform and party *B* a weak one. Even so, there is at least one circumstance when it might be rational to decide not to vote. A reasonable person is more likely to vote if he or she believes that *his or her vote matters*. If party *A*'s chances of winning are so slim or so great that your vote is not likely to affect the outcome, you may decide to take election day off. As William Riker and Peter Ordeshook have pointed out, your calculations about whether to vote depend somewhat on your assessment of the probability that you can affect the election results.[14] In fact, people who see the election as a close one are more likely to vote than those who see it as a foregone conclusion.[15] If your party is a hopeless underdog, you may decide to stay at home on election day. (The fact that voters think, or know, that third parties have very little chance of winning may be a major reason for their lack of success in American politics.)

If we assume that voters are rational (and we hope that is better than assuming that they are irrational), their decision to vote will be a product of three reasons:

1. They can see a *policy difference* between the parties and believe that one party would provide them more policy benefits than the other one would.
2. They see some possibility that *their vote matters* and would affect the outcome of the election. (Some voters will say to themselves, "My God, what if I didn't vote, and my preferred candidate lost by one vote? I'd feel like killing myself.")[16]
3. Even if they do not see a policy difference or think they will affect the election, they may still have a sense of *civic duty* and believe that elections are important to democracy.

Why, then, is there so much inequality in voting, with the rich and the well educated doing it more than the poor and less educated? First, in nearly every election, on nearly every issue, the upper classes are more likely to see a party difference than the lower classes. If the decision to vote is determined by whether you see a real difference between the parties, then richer and better-educated voters are more likely to vote. Second, if voters vote because they see their vote as making a potential difference, then the upper classes again score. Upper-class people score higher on **political efficacy,** the belief that their participation really matters. Lower classes turn out less because they think that their votes do not really matter. (People subscribing to an elitist interpretation of American government, of course, think the poor are right.)

[14] William Riker and Peter Ordeshook, "A Theory of the Calculus of Voting," *American Political Science Review* 62(1968), 25–42.

[15] Angus Campbell, et al., *The American Voter: An Abridgement* (New York: Wiley, 1964), p. 54.

[16] John A. Ferejohn and Morris P. Fiorina, "The Paradox of Not Voting: A Decision Theoretical Analysis," *American Political Science Review* 68(1974): p. 535.

HOW WE VOTE: EXPLAINING THE DECISIONS

Ronald Reagan's pollster and political advisor, Richard Wirthlin, noted in 1980 that there was a "substantial ideological gap" between candidate Reagan and the average Republican, not to mention the average voter. Wirthlin was right: Most Americans, even most Republicans, considered themselves more liberal than Ronald Reagan. In 1984, the president's good friend and chairperson of the Republican National Committee, Senator Paul Laxalt, allowed that "people have deep differences with his [President Reagan's] policies." The evidence from opinion polls was clear. When surveyed, Americans favored cutting defense spending and maintaining spending on social programs, policies just the opposite of Reagan's. Even on issues dear to the heart of President Reagan's right flank, the voters were not with him. Less than a third *of Reagan voters* in 1984 favored the president's proposal of a constitutional amendment to end abortion.[17] Yet the president mustered enough votes in 1984 to overwhelm his Democratic opponent.

How, then, do we explain voter choices? Plainly, more is involved than calculating one's own position and the candidates' positions and voting accordingly. Voters make up their minds for many reasons, some of which we explore here.

Voters, of course, do not make their choices in isolation from the stream of campaign events; campaign managers do not make their decisions in isolation from voters' thinking. Through the technology of opinion polling, it is now easier to know what voters are thinking during a campaign. The candidates and their managers know that three factors stand out above all others in shaping the electoral decision:

1. Voters' *party identification*.
2. Their *candidate evaluation*.
3. The match between their own issue positions and those of the candidates and parties, which we call *policy voting*.

Party Identification: Down But Not Out

Most voters (although the proportion is shrinking) have a standing allegiance to one of the major parties. We call this *party identification*. (See our discussion of party identification on pages 220–221.) These identifications—other things being equal—can be a useful guide to voters' choices. "Presumably," Niemi and Weisberg say, "people choose to identify with a party with which they generally agree. . . . As a result they need not concern themselves with every issue that comes along, but can generally rely on their party identification to guide them."[18] Parties tend to rely upon these pools of partisanship for their basic coalition. Even before the election campaign begins, Republicans must virtually write

---

[17] The quotations from Wirthlin and Laxalt and the poll data cited in this paragraph are from Seymour M. Lipset, "The Elections, the Economy and Public Opinion, 1984," *P.S.* (Winter 1985):29–30.

[18] Niemi and Weissberg, *Controversies in Voting Behavior*, pp. 164–65.

off blacks, most Jews, Mexican Americans, and most intellectuals. Democrats have an uphill struggle with groups that are staunchly Republican in their leanings.

The hold of the party on the voter is eroding year by year.[19] In the 1950s, the authors of *The American Voter* could single out the party as the best single predictor of a voter's decision.[20] Since then, the party has declined as a predictor of voting choice in presidential elections. As we would expect, there is an upsurge in **ticket splitting**, that is, voting for one party's candidate, say, for president, and another's for senator.[21]

Let us not, however, count the party out altogether as an influence on voters. Hill and Luttbeg looked at elections from 1956 through 1980 and found that, "with the exception of the 1972 presidential election, party identification has prevailed over the other determinants of voter choice, but only narrowly in 1980."[22] It is younger voters, whose party affiliations are the weakest, who are least likely to use party as a guide to voting.

Candidate Evaluation: How We See the Candidates

All candidates try to present an image of trust, decisiveness, attractiveness, and command. In 1976, Jimmy Carter told us that "I will never lie to you." Even going down to bitter defeat in 1980, Carter still was seen as an honest president.[23] But more than honesty is required in candidate evaluations. People want an ephemeral quality they call "leadership." (*Time* columnist Hugh Sidey once remarked that Jimmy Carter was a "decision maker, not a leader.") Candidates carefully cultivate their images in campaigns. Walter Mondale in 1984 tried to show that he was better in command of the facts of government than Ronald Reagan. Reagan cultivated his image as sincere, trustworthy, and in overall command of the ship of state, if not the details of administration. Hill and Luttbeg found that candidate image has remained an important factor in decisions of voters from 1956–80.[24] Only in 1972, when the hapless George McGovern challenged Richard Nixon, did it exceed the impact of party.

Policy Voting: On the Rise?

Policy voting occurs when people base their choices in an election on their own issue preferences. If Ronald Reagan believes that aiding covert forces in Central America and building lots of MX missiles is good foreign

[19] For some important qualifications to this view, though, see David W. Brady and Patricia A. Hurley, "The Prospects for Contemporary Partisan Realignment," *P.S.* (Winter 1985):63–68.

[20] Campbell, et al., *The American Voter.*

[21] Crotty, *American Parties in Decline*, pp. 34–36.

[22] David B. Hill and Norman Luttbeg, *Trends in American Electoral Behavior*, 2nd ed. (Itaska, Ill.: Peacock, 1983), p. 49.

[23] Warren E. Miller, "Policy Directions and Presidential Leadership: Alternative Interpretations of the 1980 Presidential Election," paper presented at the annual meeting of the American Political Science Association, New York, September 3–6, 1981.

[24] Hill and Luttbeg, *Trends in American Electoral Behavior*, p. 50.

policy, and you agree and vote for him for those reasons, you have engaged in policy voting of a sort. If Mondale believes that the federal budget deficit should be cut by raising taxes, and you agree and vote for Mondale, then you, too, are engaging in policy voting. Only when several conditions are met can we speak of real policy voting. First, you must have a clear view of your own policy positions. If you haven't made up your mind on issues like Central America, MX missiles, and the deficit you cannot be much of a policy-oriented voter. Second, you must know where the candidates stand on policy issues. If you think that Reagan was opposed to the funding of antigovernment guerillas in Nicaragua, your policy voting will be off the mark. Third, you must in fact vote for the candidate whose policy positions coincide with yours.

Sometimes, policy voting is not easy. Candidates may try to befuddle you. They may cloud their positions in rhetoric, as they did on the Vietnam War issue in 1968. [25] Policy ambiguity can be a conscious political strategy. The media may not be of much help. They often focus more on the "horse-race" aspects of the campaign—who's ahead by how much —than on where candidates stand on the issues. To engage in policy voting, the voter has to work very, very hard.

In the early days of voting research, the evidence was clear: Voters rarely engaged in policy voting, preferring to rely on party identification or candidate evaluation to make up their minds. In the 1950s the authors of the *American Voter* stressed that only a small percentage of the American electorate relied on issues to decide. [26] Nie, Verba, and Petrocik challenged this claim. [27] They argued that voters became more sophisticated about issues. Voters, they said, became more willing to use policy positions to guage candidates. The 1950s may have been a time of issue apathy, but by the 1970s, Americans at all educational levels were more policy oriented in their voting. Not all political scientists accept these conclusions. [28] Most would agree with Hill and Luttbeg that "issue orientation" (or policy voting) is more significant in voting than twenty years ago. Nonetheless, attentiveness to the issues in a campaign still plays second fiddle to party and candidates in cueing voters to their decisions. [29]

Party voting, candidate evaluation, and policy voting all play a role in elections. Their impact is not exactly equal from one election to another, but main factors they are in affecting voter decisions.

Voters are unpredictable; they will engage in some party voting, some candidate voting, and some policy voting. From voter to voter, and election to election, the mix may differ. Because elections are so complex, a few—very few—political scientists have tried to simplify this complex process. [6]

[25] Benjamin Page and Richard Brody, "Policy Voting and the Electoral Process: The Vietnam War Issue," *American Political Science Review* 66(1972):979–95.

[26] Campbell, et al., *The American Voter*, Chap. 6.

[27] Norman Nie, Sidney Verba, and John Petrocik, *The Changing American Voter* (Cambridge, Mass.: Harvard University Press, 1976).

[28] See, for example, John L. Sullivan, et al., "Ideological Constraint in the Mass Public: A Methodological Critique and Some New Findings," *American Journal of Political Science* 22(May 1978):233–49; George Bishop, et al., "Change in the Structure of American Political Attitudes: The Nagging Question of Question Wording," *American Journal of Political Science* 22(May 1978):250–69.

[29] Hill and Luttbeg, *Trends in American Electoral Behavior*, p. 50.

THE ELECTORAL CURTAIN FALLS

The networks station TV crews at the headquarters of the candidate. In a hotel ballroom somewhere, probably near the headquarters of the candidate, the staff will be setting up. There is just enough booze to get everyone through the evening; balloons are hung in nets from the ceiling for the candidate's triumphal or saddening entrance; workers and supporters begin to gather as the last voters are swinging by the polling places on their way home from work. The evening is young yet, and the candidate is ensconced in his or her suite upstairs—quiet, tired, probably pensive and reflective. Even if they never shared a moment or an idea during the campaign, the candidate and the voters now share something in common: they will both find out who won by watching television. And yet it is all, in its own way, anticlimactic. These days, poll predictions are so accurate that only in the closest elections should a candidate be under any illusions about the outcome.[30] Tonight is high drama and excitement. Tomorrow, hotel crews will clear away the debris in an empty hall.

[30] On the accuracy of polls and other election forecasts, see Michael Lewis-Beck, "Elections Forecasts in 1984: How Accurate Were They?" *P.S.* (Winter 1985):53–62.

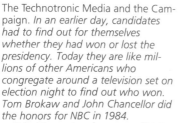

The Technotronic Media and the Campaign. *In an earlier day, candidates had to find out for themselves whether they had won or lost the presidency. Today they are like millions of other Americans who congregate around a television set on election night to find out who won. Tom Brokaw and John Chancellor did the honors for NBC in 1984.*

Television networks can predict the electoral outcome early in the evening through the use of exit polls. Congress has debated legislating against exit polls or their announcement before all the nation's polls have closed.

Tonight belongs to the candidate and the workers. They will be watching television, our quickest source of knowledge about what is happening in politics. The next president of the United States gets the firm news of his election from the Columbia Broadcasting System or from another television network. Learning from his own reports and from the networks that he was losing his presidency in 1980, Jimmy Carter decided to concede early. "I told you," he said to his assembled workers, "that I would never lie to you and I can't say it doesn't hurt."

But how does Dan Rather know, and know so confidently, that he can deliver the news to the next president of the United States? The answer in large part lies in our highly sophisticated technology of public opinion surveying. Pollsters for all major media—the *New York Times*, *Time*, and *Newsweek*, *USA Today*, and the networks—have developed very precise **exit polls** to predict with precision the winner of the presidential sweepstakes. 7

---

7   The Exit Polls

Political scientist Michael Lewis-Beck remarks that "one autumn out of four, election forecasting surpasses baseball as America's national pastime.... With the ballots carefully counted, forecasters await their awards." These days, predicting elections is not a matter of idle academic curiosity. Something more significant is at stake: TV network ratings.

During the 1960s, CBS tried a new technology in order to provide more color to its election analysis. It caught voters outside their polling places and asked them a string of questions. One asked simply how they voted in presidential and other key races. Other questions asked were personal, for example, their income, race, and so forth. The pollsters choose a sample of precincts across the nation: so many upper middle-class areas, so many mostly black areas, so many in the south, and so on. Taken together, the precincts constitute a representative sample of each state. Network employees (thousands have to be used on election day) fan out to the precincts to jot down voter responses on their clipboards. Quickly fed into central computers, the results of these exit polls add up to the winner.

One key question about exit polls, though, stems from the fact that polls close at different times across the country. Due to a three-hour time difference, voters in the east are through balloting by the time California voters are voting on their way home from work. Suppose Smith and Jones are running for president, and news of Smith's stunning victories in eastern states is broadcast to California voters on their way to the polls. On hearing this news, perhaps Jones's supporters on the West Coast will not waste their time voting and will throw in the towel. Just as bad, perhaps Smith's voters will save themselves the trouble of voting for what they now consider a foregone conclusion.

There is some disturbing evidence that exit polls affect the propensity to vote or not to vote. John E. Jackson, for example, looked at the 1980 election and the impact of these exit polls on voters who had heard the announcement of the Reagan "victory." Hearing the news did indeed erode turnout among those who had not yet voted. Republicans, more than Democrats, decided not to participate. Of course, 1980 was not a close election. In a razor-thin election, though, many people deciding not to vote because their side had "already won" could snatch defeat out of the jaws of victory.

Congress has made some forays into the exit poll problem. In the 1986 congressional elections, it secured from the networks a commitment not to report exit poll results until the polls closed. However, the ratings war is in presidential, not congressional races. Time will tell what happens in 1988.

Source: On the origins and importance of exit polls, see Percy H. Tannenbaum and Leslie J. Kostrich, *Turned-On TV/Turned-Off Voters* (Beverly Hills, Calif.: Sage, 1983). The Jackson data are reported in his article, "Election Night Reporting and Voter Turnout," *American Journal of Political Science* 27 (November 1983):615–35. The quotation from Lewis-Beck is in his article "Election Reporting in 1984," *P.S.* (Winter 1985):53.

WITH ONE PER CENT OF THE VOTE IN, OUR COMPUTER AT ELECTION CENTRAL PREDICTS WILBUR FUNT WILL WIN THE U.S. SENATE SEAT IN OHIO... IN 1985 HE WILL MARRY HIS DEVOTED SECRETARY.... THEY WILL HAVE TWO CHILDREN ... IN 1989 HE WILL BECOME SERIOUSLY ILL AND...

© Peters for the Dayton Daily News.

Knowing the results of the presidential sweepstakes, most Americans, as well as both candidates, can take a well-deserved respite from campaign politics. Officially, though, the electoral drama is not over.

THE LAST BATTLE:
THE ELECTORAL COLLEGE

The ballots are counted, the defeated candidate calls to congratulate the victor, and the president-elect mixes a needed rest with cabinet selection. These events in early November seem to wind down the presidential electoral process for another four years. Yet there is one more hurdle to clear. The **electoral college,** not the popular vote, determines the next president of the United States. This is a unique American institution, created by the Constitution, and numerous efforts to abolish it have failed. Many (but certainly not all) political scientists oppose it. The American Bar Association called it "archaic, undemocratic, complex, ambiguous, indirect and dangerous." [31] Worse, most voters do not understand it.

The Founding Fathers wanted the president to be selected by the nation's elite, not by the people directly, so they provided for presidential electors. Fortunately, political practice has made the electoral vote responsive to popular majorities. Today, the electors normally vote for the candidate who won their state. Some states even make it illegal to vote for someone other than the statewide winner. These changes have helped democratize the electoral college.

[31] American Bar Association, *Electing the President* (Chicago: ABA, 1967), p. 3.

Here is how this quaint system works today:

— Each state, according to the Constitution, has as many electoral votes as it has United States senators and representatives. [32] The state parties select slates of electors.
— In each state, there is a "winner-take-all" system. Electors vote as a bloc for the winner, whether the popular winner got 32 percent [33] or 95 percent.
— Electors meet in their states in December after the November election, and then mail their votes to the president of the United States Senate (who is the incumbent vice-president). The vote is counted when the new congressional session opens in January.

[32] The Twenty-third Amendment (1961) permits the District of Columbia to have at least three electors, too.

[33] The 32 percent with which Woodrow Wilson won Idaho in 1912 was the lowest percentage with which any candidate has ever won a state. The incumbent Republican, William Howard Taft, got 31 percent, and Theodore Roosevelt and several small-party candidates split the rest.

Curtain Call in the Electoral Drama: Voting. *No question about elections is more important or harder to answer than this one: Do elections serve primarily as symbolic reassurance for the masses, as elite theorists claim, or are they crucial in helping the masses influence public policy, as democratic theory insists?*

The men at Philadelphia even decided what to do if no candidate got an electoral college majority. The House of Representatives votes, each *state* delegation casting only a single vote. Had this happened in 1976, a ticklish situation would have developed. More states went for Ford than for Carter (27 to 23), but most members of the House were Democrats. The vote in the electoral college, however, gave a clear majority to Carter (297 votes to Ford's 241).

The electoral college is important to the presidential saga for two reasons. First, it introduces a bias into the campaign and electoral process. It gives extra electoral clout to big states. The winner-take-all rule means that winning big states like California, New York, Texas, and Ohio is more important than piling up big leads in small states.[34] Politicians would rather get California's forty-seven votes than Utah's five, New York's thirty-six than North Dakota's three. Steven Brams and Morton Davis demonstrated that both Democratic and Republican candidates since 1960 have spent more time in big than in small states.[35] Furthermore, big states are likely to have big cities (New York has New York City, Texas has Houston, California has Los Angeles, Illinois has Chicago, and so on). Thus the big-state bias produces an urban bias in the electoral college. And big cities are more likely than small ones to have ethnic, black, Catholic, and unionized voters.

The electoral college attracts special attention when it fails to reflect a popular majority. Only rarely has the result in the electoral college failed to coincide with the people's choice. But in almost every close election, a few changes here and there would produce an incompatible result.

ELECTIONS AND PUBLIC POLICY

Understanding Elections: Four Views

Democratic theorists, elitists, pluralists, and hyperpluralists all see elections differently. The line outside the voting booth in early November (or at other times) is the same line, but its meaning is different, depending on your perspective on American politics.

To the democratic theorist, if you take away elections, you take away democratic government. Not just any election will do. Almost every nation has some facade of elections. Even if there is only one candidate on the ballot, people troop to the polls, sometimes under the watchful eyes of government troops. But only freely contested elections need apply for the label *democratic*. If you lock up your opponents and then declare an overwhelming electoral victory, your election does not qualify.

Elections accomplish two tasks in democratic theory: First, and most obviously, they *select the policymakers*. The morning-after headlines that proclaim "It's Reagan over Mondale" or "Brown Crushes Black" remind us of this first task. Second, and more widely disputed in some ways,

---

[34] Lawrence D. Longley and Alan G. Brown, *The Politics of Electoral College Reform* (New Haven, Conn.: Yale University Press, 1972).

[35] Steven J. Brams and Morton D. Davis, "The ⅔'s Rule in Presidential Campaigning," *American Political Science Review* 68(March 1974):113–34.

elections are supposed to help *shape public policy*. In the mythical world of pure democratic theory and the Downs model (see pages 206–208), elections do just that.

Americans appear to have bought this democratic view of elections. They do not care much for parties and interest groups, but they are definitely fans of elections. [36] Politicians, too, espouse stirring words about elections. Former President Lyndon Johnson said, while signing the Voting Rights Act of 1965, "The right to vote is the most basic right without which all others are meaningless. . . . The vote is the most powerful instrument ever devised by man for breaking down injustice."

Elitists think remarks like these are little more than political rhetoric. To them, elections provide mainly symbolic reassurance to the masses. [37] Voters delude themselves about their importance. People are led to believe that elections are the place where crucial choices are made. The elites who actually run the country encourage people to overestimate the importance of elections because as long as people believe that elections give them a say in government, they will continue to support the government. Benjamin Ginsberg and Robert Weissberg have shown that right after an election, the percentage of people seeing the government as responsive to the people goes up. Even people who voted for the loser feel that elections give them a real voice in running government. [38] According to elitists, however, power in the system lies outside the electoral system. To them, as we have seen, the people with most power are often people whose names never appear on a ballot.

Pluralists are great believers in elections, but they too try not to overestimate their importance. Robert Dahl wrote, "A good deal of traditional democratic theory leads us to expect more from national elections than they can possibly provide." [39] Elections do a great job of picking policymakers, pluralists argue, but they do only a mediocre job of controlling policy. Rarely does an election send a clear policy message from the voters. Pluralists reject the *mandate theory of elections,* which sees elections as mandates from the voters to pursue the winner's policies. In fact, there are hundreds of policy issues, and thousands of reasons why millions of voters voted as they did. Elections pick policymakers; policymakers pick policy. To pluralists, policies are influenced more by groups than by elections.

Hyperpluralists, as we said, see the American system as pluralism carried too far. They see fragmentation and diffusion of responsibility, and want coordination and centralization. Looking at American elections, the hyperpluralist views the hundreds of thousands of elections and heaves a sigh of hopelessness. A real majority can never get control of

[36] Jack Dennis, "Support for the Institution of Elections by the Mass Public," *American Political Science Review* 64(September 1970):819–35.

[37] One argument along these lines is in Murray Edelman, *The Symbolic Use of Politics* (Urbana: University of Illinois Press, 1967).

[38] Benjamin Ginsberg and Robert Weissberg, "Elections and the Mobilization of Popular Support," *American Journal of Political Science* 22(February 1978):31–55.

[39] Robert A. Dahl, *Preface to Democratic Theory* (Chicago: University of Chicago Press, 1956), p. 131.

government. If today a majority of the people wanted a strong consumer protection bill, they would have to:

— Elect the right president, who is elected at four-year intervals.
— Elect the right House of Representatives, whose members are elected at two-year intervals.
— Elect the right Senate, only a third of whose members are up for election every two years.
— Be sure the courts do not prevent the implementation of the consumer protection bill, but federal judges are not elected.
— Be sure that the governors and state legislatures do not thwart their goals, but there are thousands of elections in the states.

Small wonder, hyperpluralists say, that the people rarely rule. Too much fragmentation in the electoral process limits popular majorities. But that, let us recall, is how the Founding Fathers wanted it.

All four theories zero in on one question: What is the relationship between elections and public policy? The question is crucial, but the evidence is scattered and often circumstantial. We argue here that the connection between elections and public policy is a two-way street. Elections—to some degree at least—affect public policy, and public policy also affects electoral outcomes.

Elections Affect Public Policy

We saw earlier in this chapter that voters these days pay more attention to policy differences between the parties and candidates than they used to. If elections are really to affect public policy, then two other things must happen: Parties and candidates must offer a genuine policy choice, and the winners must do in office what they promised during the campaign.

A generation of research by political scientists has not answered with finality the question of how much elections affect public policy. The broad contours of the answer, however, seem reasonably clear: *When the parties and candidates offer voters a genuine choice, electoral results make an important difference in government's policies.* Over the long span of American history, the parties have been most sharply divided during periods of party realignments (see pages 208–209). Ginsberg has linked those periods with major shifts in our public policies. [40] When individual candidates offer a plain choice to the voters (what Senator Barry Goldwater once called "a choice, not an echo") voters are more able to determine policy directions of government. No one familiar even in passing with Ronald Reagan's campaign stances could have doubted the policies he would pursue once elected.

The parties and candidates do not always do their best to unmuddy the issue waters. Controversial or complex issues are sometimes sidestepped. A controversial position can lose as many voters as it attracts. One result is that the policy stands of parties and candidates are often shaped by what Benjamin Page once called "the art of ambiguity," by which

[40] Benjamin Ginsberg, *Consequences of Consent,* (Reading, Mass.: Addison-Wesley, 1982) pp. 133–41.

"presidential candidates are skilled at appearing to say much while actually saying little." [41] So long as parties and candidates can take refuge in ambiguity (and the pitifully skimpy coverage of issues in the media does little to destroy that refuge), the possibility of democratic control of policy is lessened.

Public Policy Affects Election Outcomes

If elections affect policy, then policy can also affect elections. Politicians do not sit waiting for cues from voters, but choose their policies for many reasons. One reason is that they think their stance will attract votes. Every policy, no matter how trivial it may seem, attracts some voters and repels others. A strong government stand against smoking will delight cancer fighters and enrage tobacco farmers. Proconsumer legislation may win friends among consumer lobbyists, but not among business interests.

Nothing makes incumbent politicians more nervous than the state of the economy, for good reasons. Inflation and unemployment are the twin enemies of incumbents running for reelection. As we saw in our review of the 1896 election, people tend to blame the party or the person in power (like Grover Cleveland) for their economic misfortunes.

In presidential elections, people unhappy with the state of the economy tend to blame the incumbent. [42] Republican Herbert Hoover was in office when the stock market crash of 1929 sparked the Great Depression. Poor Hoover became so unpopular that the shanty towns occupied by unemployed people were called "Hoovervilles" and the apples they sold were called "Hoover apples." Hoover and his fellow Republicans were crushed by Democrat Franklin Roosevelt in the 1932 elections. Knowing perfectly well that their management of the economy will affect their reelection chances, presidents and their advisors use policy to try to minimize inflation and maximize employment. (*How* they try to do this is considered in Chapter 17.)

Congressional candidates also gain or suffer from the state of the economy. Economic downturns hurt incumbents and help challengers. [43] When times go bad, voters want a change. People can throw the president out only every four years. They can throw all the members of the House of Representatives and about a third of the Senate out every two years. Curiously, the president's party seems almost always to do badly in these off-year elections. Edward Tufte has shown that the economy is usually

---

[41] Benjamin Page, *Choices and Echoes in American Presidential Elections* (Chicago: University of Chicago Press, 1978), p. 153.

[42] Morris Fiorina, "Economic Retrospective Voting in American National Elections," *American Journal of Political Science* 22(1978):426–43. See also Gerald Kramer, "Short Term Fluctuations in U.S. Voting Behavior, 1896–1964," *American Political Science Review* 64(1971):131–43.

[43] In this somewhat unsettled body of research, this appears to be the dominant conclusion, suggested by Howard S. Bloom and Hugh D. Price, "Voter Response to Short-Run Economic Conditions," *American Political Science Review* 69(1975):1240–54. For some contrary views, see Francisco Arcelus and Allan H. Meltzer, "The Effect of Aggregate Economic Variables on Congressional Elections," *American Political Science Review* 69(1975):1222–39; and Fiorina, "Economic Retrospective Voting."

performing worse in these years and that the voters tend to vote against the president's party.[44]

The 1984 election was no exception to this general pattern of links between economic circumstances and voting choice. Reagan won, said William Schneider, "because twice as many voters believed their personal financial situation had gotten better rather than worse under Ronald Reagan."[45] He pointed out that those who believed that our economy was at the beginning of a long-term recovery voted overwhelmingly (92 percent) for Reagan to 8 percent for Mondale. Those who felt that the economy was not getting any better favored Mondale 87 to 13 percent.

Clearly, elections affect policy, but public policy—at least the perception of economic policy impacts—can affect elections. Politicians, once in office, work very hard to keep the mighty engine of the American economy running at full speed. If that economic machine breaks down or slows down, voters point their collective fingers at incumbent policymakers, and those fingers are more likely to pull the lever for the challengers on election day.

ELECTIONS SUMMARIZED

We have examined the final act in the electoral drama in this chapter. Once the parties have made their nominations and the campaign has concluded, voters take over center stage. Elections have changed dramatically since 1796, when Adams ran against Jefferson. By 1896, it was fashionable to campaign, and William Jennings Bryan campaigned with a vengeance. Then, suffrage was still limited mostly to white males. The democratization of elections has made suffrage available to virtually all adult Americans. Though hard to win, the franchise can too often be easy to ignore. The 1984 election between Ronald Reagan and Walter Mondale was another in a long string of low-turnout elections.

American elections are numerous and complex. We have elections to select candidates (called primaries) and officeholders (called general elections), plus elections on issues (called referendums).

Voters make two basic decisions at election time. The first is whether to vote. Our right to vote is called suffrage and it is determined by law; in the United States, you must also register to vote. Our registration systems are clearly associated with a reduction in voter turnout, which varies from group to group.

Second, voters must decide (presuming that they have already chosen to vote) which way to vote. While a generation of research on voting behavior has failed to unlock every secret of the voter, it has helped us to understand the dominant role played by three factors in voters' choices: party identification, candidate evaluation, and policy positions.

We examined elections through the theoretical eyes of our four perspectives on American politics. Of course, elections are the centerpiece of

[44] Edward R. Tufte, "Determinants of the Outcomes of Midterm Congressional Elections," *American Political Science Review* 69(1975):812–26.

[45] William Schneider, "An Uncertain Consensus," *The National Journal* (November 10, 1984):21–30, cited in Lipset, "Elections, Economy, and Public Opinion," p. 33.

democratic interpretations of American politics. Class and elite theorists think of elections as largely symbolic, legitimizing devices in which the non-elites are persuaded that they have a major role in governing. Elections are critical to pluralist theory, yet pluralists try not to overstate their importance. Particularly as our system becomes more hyper-pluralistic, elections may become less important than the ability of groups to wheedle their demands out of government. Regardless of your own view of these theories, there is some clear evidence that elections do affect public policy, and vice versa.

Key Terms

initiative	Fifteenth Amendment	Twenty-third
referendum	Voting Rights Act of	Amendment
primaries	1965	political efficacy
general elections	Nineteenth	ticket splitting
direct primaries	Amendment	policy voting
registration	Twenty-sixth	exit polls
suffrage	Amendment	electoral college

For Further Reading

Abramson, Paul R., John H. Aldrich, and David W. Rohde. *Continuity and Change in the 1980 Elections* (1983). Even though this is about just one election, it is an excellent overview of electoral research.

Asher, Herbert B. *Presidential Elections and American Politics*, 3rd ed. (1984). Reviews changes in American elections and the American electorate since 1952.

Campbell, Angus, et al., *The American Voter* (1960). The classic study of American voting from the perspective of the Survey Research Center at the University of Michigan.

Drew, Elizabeth. *Campaign Journal: The Political Events of 1983–1984* (1985). A perceptive journalist writes about the 1984 campaign.

Ginsberg, Benjamin. *Consequences of Consent: Elections, Citizen Control, and Popular Acquiescence* (1982). Explores elections as both instruments of popular control and as devices for controlling the populace.

Hill, David B., and Norman Luttbeg (1983). *Trends in American Electoral Behavior.* An analysis of five key trends of voting behavior.

Kelley, Stanley G., Jr. *Interpreting Elections* (1983). Presents a theory of "the simple act of voting."

Nie, Norman, Sidney Verba, and John Petrocik. *The Changing American Voter* (1976). Challenges some of the assumptions of *The American Voter.*

Page, Benjamin. *Choices and Echoes in American Presidential Elections* (1978). An analysis of how well the American electorate performs its democratic function when elections and issues are clouded in ambiguity.

Pomper, Gerald M., with Susan Lederman. *Elections in America*, 2nd ed. (1980). A historical examination of elections in America, paying particular attention to the role of democratic control in American politics.

Rosenstone, Steven J. *Forecasting Presidential Elections* (1983). A methodology for forecasting presidential elections on a state-by-state basis.

Tannenbaum, Percy H., and Leslie J. Kostrich. *Turned-On TV/Turned-Off Voters.* (1983). On the problem of the exit poll and its distorting effect on the election outcome.

Wayne, Stephen J. *The Road to the White House*, 2nd ed. (1984). A useful text on presidential election politics.

Interest Groups

MEMO

Like parties and elections, interest groups are a linkage institution. And like these other linkage institutions, they have been dramatically reshaped by our high-technology politics. In this chapter, we will see how.

Interest groups—sometimes called special interests, pressure groups, or lobbies—seek favorable public policies from government and want to side-track unfavorable ones. No part of the government is immune from interest groups.

Frankly, interest groups these days have had bad press. People usually think of them as representing some narrow, special, and selfish interest. Press and public alike suspect that they exert a corrupting influence on our political system. I, for one, believe these charges are partially true but greatly oversimplified. There is a significant bias in the interest group system; not all groups are created equal. But interest groups are a vital part of our political system.

Keep the following in mind as we discuss groups and government:

- The American political system teems with an amazing array of groups. Some of them will seem trivial to you, but they have interests and members work to achieve their policy goals.

- Groups, unlike parties, view the whole political system as fair game. Lobbying, electioneering, litigation, and appeals to the public are major group strategies.

- Small groups, curiously, have a distinct advantage over large ones.

- We can try to understand interest groups by looking at them from the perspectives of democratic theory, elite and class theory, pluralism, and hyperpluralism.

Here is a paradox in American politics: As the exercise of our fundamental democratic right, the right to vote, has declined in recent years, the number of groups and group members has mushroomed. Jack Walker reports that "the American public is more extensively organized for political action today than ever before, and there is no reason to believe that the process will soon be reversed." [1]

One secret of group success is that groups have used contemporary technology effectively. Today, they ably organize their memberships to lobby Congress on bills important to the groups. Andrew McFarland observes that

> [A]dvances in technology have made the coordination of constituents' activities and efforts of lobbyists much easier. Many lobbyists, for example, have available computerized lists of names and phone numbers of group members that can be easily arranged by congressional district or state. Address labels can be printed automatically or members can be called by WATS line from a group's headquarters. For example, friends of a member of Congress can be called and urged to telephone the member on behalf of the bill. [2]

Technology may not have created interest group politics, but it has surely eased the job of the interest group trying to influence government and its agencies.

The nation's capital is a citadel of group politics. On any given day, you could watch Washington group politics in action. You could breakfast in the Senate dining room and see committee staffers going over today's testimony with representatives of agricultural groups. You could wander over to the Supreme Court in the morning and watch an environmental lawyer arguing a pollution suit. Catch lunch at a nice Washington restaurant and note a lobbyist taking a member of Congress to lunch.

The afternoon could be spent in any department of the executive branch (such as agriculture, labor, or commerce), where you could watch bureaucrats working out rules and regulations with friendly or unfriendly representatives of the interests they serve or regulate. If you have a few minutes over coffee, you might look through the Washington, D.C., Yellow Pages and skim the scores of listings under "associations." If the weather is pleasant, stroll past the headquarters of the National Rifle Association, the AFL-CIO, or the National Association of Manufacturers (NAM). Drop by 1 Dupont Circle, where all the higher education groups have their offices. They lobby for student loans and scholarships and aid to educational institutions, among other things. After dinner (find a lobbyist with an expense account), you can surely find one of those famous Georgetown cocktail parties where ambassadors, lawyers, senators, cabinet secretaries, and maybe even a lobbyist or two mingle.

The United States may run out of all kinds of natural resources, but we are in no danger of running out of groups. Today, about 42 percent of the

---

[1] Jack L. Walker, "The Mobilization of Political Interests." Paper delivered at the annual meeting of the American Political Science Association, Chicago, Illinois, September 1–4, 1983, p. 35.

[2] Andrew McFarland, *Common Cause: Lobbying in the Public Interest* (Chatham, N.J.: Chatham House, 1984), p. 1.

American population report active membership in at least one group.[3] While very few such groups are primarily political, we will see shortly that the number of policy-oriented groups is impressive. Most of them are admittedly self-interested, although the rise of self-styled "public-interest groups" is an important new development. Our task in this chapter is to explore how these groups enter the policymaking process and what they get out of it.

WHAT ARE INTEREST GROUPS, AND WHY ARE PEOPLE SAYING SUCH AWFUL THINGS ABOUT THEM?

All of us have interests we want represented. Butcher (high meat prices), baker (good bread prices), beggar (a job), thief (a fair trial)—we all have interests. Organizing to protect these interests is a natural part of democracy. The right to organize groups is even protected by the Constitution, which guarantees people the right "peaceably to assemble, and to petition the Government for redress of grievances." This important First Amendment right has been carefully defended by the Supreme Court. The freedom to organize is as fundamental to democratic government as freedom of speech or of the press.

Defining Interest Groups

The term *interest group* seems simple enough. *Interest* refers to a policy goal that some people have in common; a *group* is a combination of people. An **interest group**, therefore, is an organization of people, with policy goals, entering the policy process at several points to try to achieve those goals.[4] Whatever their goals—lower prices or higher ones, more pollution or less—interest groups pursue them in many arenas. Every branch of government is fair game. Every level of government, local to federal, is a possible target. A policy battle lost in Congress may be won on the fields of policy implementation, in the bureaucracy, or in the courts.

This multiplicity of battlegrounds helps distinguish interest groups from political parties. The party's main arena is the electoral system; parties run candidates for public office. Interest groups may support candidates for office (sometimes lavishly), but they rarely run their own candidates. Everyone may know that Smith got the nod because he was the oil industry's boy and that Jones won because she was supported by women's groups, but Smith and Jones face the voters as Democrats or Republicans.

There is one other key difference between parties and groups. *Groups are often policy specialists, whereas parties are policy generalists.* An inter-

---

[3] Surveys by the National Opinion Research Center, *Cumulative Codebook, 1972–1984* (Chicago, IL: National Opinion Research Center).

[4] This definition is similar to one offered by Jeffrey Berry, *The Interest Group Society* (Boston: Little, Brown, 1984), p. 5: "An interest group is an organized body of individuals who share some goals and who try to influence public policy."

est group has a handful of key policies to push: A farm group cares little about the status of blacks, but worries about farm prices; an environmental group has its hands full if it brings polluters into court, without worrying about the minimum wage. Groups do not know the constraints of trying to appeal to everybody. Each group has a policy goal and can pursue it relentlessly.

Why Interest Groups Get Bad Press

Despite their importance to democratic government, interest groups—like parties—have had a bad press in America. The authors of the Federalist Papers thought interest groups were no better than political parties, which, you will recall, they did not care much for either. (In fact, we have not found many things the Founding Fathers *did* like, given their strong opposition to pure democratic government, to parties, and to groups.) Madison's term *faction*, which he deplored, was general enough to include both parties and groups. Today, our image of lobbies, special interests, and pressure groups is no more favorable. On a slow news day, editorial cartoonists can always depict lobbyists as skulking around in the congressional hallways, pockets stuffed with money, just waiting to take a representative out to a three-martini lunch.

These cartoons are not mere muckraking. Many of the Watergate-related events showed the seamy side of lobbying. Richard Nixon yielded to the campaign contributions of milk producers and authorized a windfall increase in milk subsidies. After Nixon's fall, charges of undue influence-peddling and money-taking by Congress added to the view that interest groups were up to no good.

These and other revelations about pressure politics color public perceptions of interest groups. People see the government as much too dominated by groups. The Survey Research Center reports steady increases in the number of people who believe "government is run for the benefit of a few special interests." One of presidential candidate Walter Mondale's many heavy burdens in 1984 was the charge that he was the "candidate of special interests."

We could argue that a few rotten apples do not spoil the whole interest group barrel. No doubt for every lobbyist who peddles favors, there are a hundred who try only to document the soundest case for their group's goals. For every Watergate and Koreagate (a 1977 scandal in which a South Korean businessman was accused of lavishing "gifts" on several congressmen), there are hundreds of basically honest transactions between Congress and interest group leaders. It would be easy to make those arguments, and they would probably be right. But if this chapter has a single theme, it is that dishonest lobbying is less of a problem for democracy than honest lobbying. Understanding why lobbying—and interest groups generally—present problems requires a close look at their growth in American politics.

The Group Explosion

The number of groups in the United States is increasing rapidly. Although no one has ever compiled a *Who's Who* of interest groups, your local telephone directory—or even better, the Washington, D.C., directory—will give you a taste of the range and variety of groups, but only a taste. The closest thing to a census of groups is the annual *Encyclopedia of Associations*.[5]

Although not an exhaustive inventory, the *Encyclopedia of Associations* shows the variety of groups in the United States. You can see a sampling of the *Encyclopedia's* 18,000 entries in ⎡1⎤. If you skim that listing, you will get several messages: Most groups have their headquarters in Washington, D.C.; New York is the next biggest headquarters city; there is an

[5] Denise Akey (ed.), *Encyclopedia of Associations*, 20th ed. (Detroit: Gale, 1984).

⎡1⎤ A Group Profile: A Very Incomplete Sampling of Groups

Name (Date of Founding)[a]	Headquarters	Membership	Staff	Publications
GROUPS INTERESTED IN ECONOMIC POLICY				
National Electrical Manufacturers Association (1926)	Washington, D.C.	550	100	News Bulletin
National Association of Manufacturers (1895)	Washington, D.C.	13,000	220	Enterprise
Underwear-Negligee Associates (1946)	New York	130	—[b]	—[b]
Pharmaceutical Manufacturers Association (1958)	Washington, D.C.	130	100	Newsletter
Air Line Pilots Association, Int'l. (1931)	Washington, D.C.	33,000	250	Air Line Pilot
AFL-CIO (1955)	Washington, D.C.	13,800,000	500	American Federationist; Free Trade Union News
Glycerine and Fatty Acid Producers Council (1983)	New York	18	—[b]	—[b]
National Consumers League (1899)	Washington, D.C.	2,500	7	Bulletin
National Peanut Council (1941)	Washington, D.C.	250	7	Peanut News
American Farm Bureau Federation (1919)	Park Ridge, Ill.	3,297,224	102	Farm Bureau News
American Mushroom Institute (1955)	Kennet Square, Pa.	300	5	Mushroom News
National Potato Council (1948)	Denver, Colo.	14,000	4	Spudletter
GROUPS INTERESTED IN EQUALITY POLICY				
National Organization for Women (1966)	Washington, D.C.	260,000	—[b]	National NOW Times
National Association for the Advancement of Colored People (1909)	Washington, D.C.	500,000	132	Crisis; Report
National Urban League (1910)	New York	50,000	2,000	The Urban League Review; State of Black America
National Women's Political Caucus (1971)	Washington, D.C.	75,000	15	Women's Political Times

(box continues on next page)

A Group Profile: A Very Incomplete Sampling of Groups (continued)

Name (Date of Founding)[a]	Headquarters	Membership	Staff	Publications
GROUPS INTERESTED IN ENERGY/ENVIRONMENT POLICY				
American Petroleum Institute (1919)	Washington, D.C.	7,500	500	—[b]
American Mining Congress (1897)	Washington, D.C.	600	72	Journal; Washington Concentrates
Sierra Club (1892)	San Francisco, Ca.	350,000	185	Sierra; National News
Water Pollution Control Federation (1928)	Washington, D.C.	30,000	49	Highlights
SOME OTHER INTEREST GROUPS				
Navy League (1902)	Washington, D.C.	48,000	27	Sea Power; Now Hear This
Veterans of Foreign Wars (1899)	Kansas City, Mo.	1,965,000	250	VFW Magazine; Washington Action
Common Cause (1970)	Washington, D.C.	250,000	152	Common Cause
American Medical Association (1847)	Chicago, Ill.	250,000	—[b]	Journal; American Medical News

[a]All data based on reports from individual groups.
[b]No data reported.
Source: Denise Akey (ed.), Encyclopedia of Associations, 1985. (Detroit: Gale Research Company, 1984).

enormous number (our listing is a tiny sample) of such highly specialized, obscure, seemingly trivial groups as the National Potato Council; and almost every group, however small, has a staff and publications, which keep group members up-to-date on the latest technologies, products, appeals, and, of course, impending policies.

Many groups' interests are primarily economic. The trade, commercial, and business section of the *Encyclopedia* lists 3,622 groups, beginning with Accounting Research International Associates and ending with the National Association of Wholesaler-Distributors. (Yes, there is a Glycerine and Fatty Acid Producers Association, and yes, there is even an American Cricket Growers Association.) Other groups are more interested in the issues of equality, and still others focus on energy and environmental policy.

The growth rate of groups has been phenomenal. Jack Walker studied 564 groups listed in the *Washington Information Directory* and tried to trace their origins and expansion.[6] The origins of important interest groups—80 percent in Walker's study—reflect occupational, industrial, or professional membership. Very few occupations or industries go without an organized group to represent them in our nation's capital. Walker also found that more than half of these 564 groups were born after World War II. Recently, the birth rate of groups has increased and groups have

[6] Jack L. Walker, "The Origins and Maintenance of Interest Groups in America," *American Political Science Review* 77 (June 1983):390–406.

increasingly gravitated to Washington, D.C. In 1960, only about 66 percent of our national interest groups were headquartered in metropolitan Washington. Today nearly 90 percent are housed there.

There are many reasons for this group explosion. Such cheaper means of communication as low long-distance rates and computerized mailing lists have enabled groups to contact and recruit more potential members. Many groups found patrons (foundations, wealthy donors, and even the government itself) to subsidize their start-up costs, and many (legal service agencies, environmental groups, and so on) receive government support.

The organizational explosion of the past forty years has contributed to the increased number of groups in our society, most of them with political interests. One characteristic still applies to most groups: They are relatively small compared to the whole population, and most represent a very narrow and specific interest. There is a reason for this, and it is found in the difficulty of organizing a large group.

The Surprising Ineffectiveness of Large Groups

A lone voice is not likely to be heard. Two voices can at least talk to one another. But successful group politics depends on organizing a number of voices. The first secret of success is organizing. Staff, money, volunteers, and power come to those who get organized.

Presumably, the more people who join an organization the better. A million-member group is surely better, and more potent, than a hundred-member group. However appealing initially, this view of groups—the bigger the better—is simply wrong. We will see in this section that, as a rule, *the larger the group, the less effective it is.*

E. E. Schattschneider wrote perceptively, "Pressure politics is essentially the politics of small groups. . . . Pressure tactics are not remarkably successful in mobilizing general interests."[7] There are perfectly good reasons why consumer groups are less effective than producer groups, environmentalists are less effective than polluters, patients are less effective than doctors, and energy conservationists are less effective than oil companies. As we will see, small groups have both organizational and policy advantages over large groups.

To shed light on this point, let us distinguish between a potential group and an actual group. Potentially, every group is as big as the number of people who share its interest. Theoretically, every consumer could be a member of a consumer group, every black could be a member of a civil rights organization, every airline pilot could be a member of the Air Line Pilots Association, every teacher could be a member of the National Education Association, and every pickle manufacturer could be a member of Pickle Packers International. A **potential group** is composed of all people who might be group members because they share some common

[7] E. E. Schattschneider, *The Semisovereign People* (New York: Holt, Rinehart and Winston, 1960), p. 35.

interest. [8] An **actual group** is composed of that part of the potential group who do join. Potential groups are almost always larger than actual groups. There are more people who could be converted to the cause than actually buy a membership or actively support the organization.

When we look closely at some examples, shown in 2, we see that groups vary enormously in the degree to which they enroll their potential membership. Organizations of consumers are minuscule when compared with the total number of consumers, which is all of us. Some organizations, however, do very well in organizing almost all of their potential members. The United States Savings and Loan League, the Tobacco Institute, and the Air Transport Association include most of their potential members as actual members. Compared to consumers, blacks, and women, these groups are tightly organized. Big potential groups are likely to have a larger gap between potential and actual membership than small potential groups.

Economist Mancur Olson explained this paradox. [9] Each group is providing some collective good to its members. A **collective good** is something of value (money, a tax write-off, prestige, clean air, and so on) that cannot be withheld from a group member. If one member of a group gets a collective good, everyone gets it. Unlike bread or sofas or cars, collective goods cannot be packaged and sold separately. When person A benefits from clean air, his neighbor B benefits as well.

To Olson, all groups are in the business of providing collective goods. When the AFL-CIO wins a higher minimum wage, all low-paid workers benefit. When the automobile lobby convinced Congress to delay implementation of auto emission controls, all the automobile makers saved money. *Collective goods are automatically available to everyone similarly situated, whether or not they paid for the costs of securing the collective good.* Even if the low-wage worker did not join the AFL-CIO, he or she still got a minimum wage boost. The automobile manufacturer who refused to aid the lobbying effort for emission-control delays still saved money. In other words, *members of the potential group share in benefits that members of the actual group paid to secure.*

If potential members share in the collective goods and policy gains that the actual group secures, an obvious and massive problem results: Why pay for something if you can get it for free? Why join the group, pay dues, and work hard when you can get any policy benefit the group wins at no cost? By all means, you should, behaving rationally, "Let George do it." Unions call this the **free-rider problem.** If other people are contributing dues, time, and energy to get better wages, hours, and working conditions, then by *not* joining you can have your cake (what you would usually pay in dues) and eat it too (share the gains won). Unions are not alone in facing the free-rider problem. Whatever consumer advocate Ralph Nader wins for consumers, all consumers share even if they never kicked in a dime to support Ralph Nader's group activities.

The bigger the group, the more serious the free-rider problem. That is

---

[8] David B. Truman, *The Governmental Process* (New York: Knopf, 1951), p. 511.
[9] Mancur Olson, *The Logic of Collective Action* (Cambridge, Mass.: Harvard University Press, 1965), especially pp. 9–36.

2 Potential versus Actual Groups

Some groups organize most of their potential membership. Others suffer an enormous shortfall between their actual membership and the group they claim to speak for. Obviously, estimating the true potential membership of a group is difficult, but if you will tolerate some very rough approximations, we can compare groups' actual to potential membership:

Some groups have a tiny fraction of their potential membership.

Consumers	National Consumers League, a Washington-based consumer action group	Potential: 234,000,000 (Every American) Actual: 2,500
Blacks	National Association for the Advancement of Colored People, the largest civil rights organization	Potential: 28,000,000 (Every black) Actual: 500,000
Women	National Organization for Women, a leading women's rights organization	Potential: 120,000,000 (Every woman)[a] Actual: 260,000
Taxpayers	National Taxpayers Union, a "taxpayers' rights" group advocating tax and government spending cuts	Potential: 172,000,000 (Every adult 18 and over) Actual: 120,000

Other groups have a very high proportion of their potential members.

Physicians	American Medical Association, a professional organization of medical doctors	Potential: 510,000 (All M.D.s) Actual: 250,000
Savings and Loan Associations	U.S. League of Savings Institutions, an organization of local savings and loan associations	Potential: 3,513 (All S&Ls) Actual: 3,513
Tobacco	Tobacco Institute, the organization of tobacco manufacturers	Potential: 14 (All cigarette manufacturers) Actual: 11
Airlines	Air Transport Association of America, the organization of U.S. airlines	Potential: 96 (All U.S. air carriers) Actual: 31

---

[a]NOW membership is open to both women and men, but the interests it espouses are women's interests, so, practically speaking, its potential membership is all women, and most all of its actual members are women.

Source: For data on organization memberships, Denise Akey (ed.), *Encyclopedia of Associations,* 1985 (Detroit Gale Research Company, 1984). For data on size of potential membership and actual membership of the U.S. League of Savings Institutions, the various compilations in U.S. Department of Commerce, *Statistical Abstract of the United States,* 1985.

the gist of what we can call **Olson's law of large groups:** "The larger the group, the further it will fall short of providing an optimal amount of a collective good." [10] Small groups thus have an organizational advantage

[10] Ibid., p. 35.

The Groups: Organizing for Influence. *Interest groups need organization to be effective. These lobbyists are planning strategy on a portico of the U.S. Capital. There is a paradox about group organization: larger groups are often less effective because they are harder to organize. Bigger is not necessarily better in the world of interest group politics.*

over large ones. In a small group, a given member's share of the collective good may be great enough that he or she will try to secure it. Favorable airline regulations are so important to the United States airlines that each clearly has a vested interest in lobbying for those regulations. But, in the largest groups, each member's share of the policy gained is so tiny that it is rational to let George (or Ralph Nader or the Sierra Club) do it. The larger the potential group, Olson argued, the less likely potential members are to contribute to the group.

This distinct advantage of small groups helps explain why public interest groups have a hard time making ends meet. Consumer groups and environmentalists claim to seek "public interest" goals. The gains they win are usually spread thinly over millions of people. But the costs imposed on business are concentrated. Suppose that consumer advocate Ralph Nader wins a major victory over some wrongful practice of the airline industry. Suppose his victory nets a saving to airline passengers of $10 million, and a corresponding $10 million loss to airlines. The consumers' $10 million benefit is spread over 234 million Americans, about four cents per person. (Actually, the benefit is a little higher if we divide only by the number of people who use airplanes.) But the $10 million airline loss is shared by thirty carriers at $333,333 apiece. You can quickly figure out which side is going to be better organized in that struggle.

Olson's law of large groups suggests several important truths about groups. Most obviously, it explains why small is beautiful in the interest group system. It suggests why such big interests as consumers often lose out to such small interests as producers. Finally, it suggests that the main problem the public interest group faces in trying to get certain policies enacted may not be dishonesty in government, but the inherent logic of group size. Small potential groups have an easier time organizing themselves for political action than large potential groups. Large groups, once organized, may be much more effective than small ones, but it is harder for them to get together in the first place.

HOW GROUPS TRY TO SHAPE POLICY

Small or large, no group has enough staff, money, or time to do everything at once. You cannot launch a massive membership drive today, file a major lawsuit tomorrow, and lobby every member of Congress the next day. Intelligent choice of strategies and tactics is important. Three traditional strategies of interest groups are lobbying, electioneering, and litigation. In addition, groups have lately developed sophisticated techniques to appeal to the public for general support.

Lobbying

The Lobbyists. The term *lobbying* comes from the legislative lobby itself, where petitioners used to collar their legislators. Lobbying is not confined solely to the legislative branch, however. There is also plenty of

administrative lobbying. (We will meet groups as actors in the administration process in Chapter 14.) Lester Milbrath offered a more precise
definition. He said that **lobbying** is a "communication, by someone other
than a citizen acting on his own behalf, directed to a governmental
decision-maker with the hope of influencing his decision." [11]

The lobbyist, in other words, is a political persuader. ☐3☐ He or she is
the representative of an organized group, normally works in Washington
(even if the group's headquarters is elsewhere), and handles the group's

[11] Lester W. Milbrath, *The Washington Lobbyists* (Chicago: Rand McNally, 1963), p. 8.

☐3☐ The Lobbyists

Washington lobbyists have a bad reputation. They are depicted by cartoonists as
men (and, increasingly, women) with too much ready cash to channel into too
many corrupting purposes. Yet they see themselves as people accomplishing an
important representative mission.

Lobbying is a high-pressure job. Turnover is heavy; the average Washington
lobbyist has been in his or her job less than five years. Most are extremely well
educated, and a lobbyist for a major group will be paid well in excess of $50,000
a year (which you surely need to live well in costly Washington). Although
women are increasingly seen in the public interest lobbying role, 94 percent of
the representatives of business and professional associations are men.

Basically, lobbyists are of two types. First are regular, paid employees of a
corporation, union, or association. They may hold a title such as vice-president
for government relations, but everyone knows that their office is in Washington
for a reason, even if the company headquarters are in Milwaukee. Second are
lobbyists available for hire on a temporary basis. One group may be too small to
afford a full-time lobbyist; another may have a unique, but temporary, need for
access to Congress or the executive branch. Several thousand Washingtonians
are available as "lobbyists for hire." One prime source is the Washington law
firm, where the number of Washington lawyers grew three-fold between 1970
and 1980. Senior partners can earn a quarter of a million dollars a year; starting
salaries can range up to $35,000. Public relations firms are another source of
lobbyists.

A handful of individuals, some of them former officeholders or government
officials, are what Jeffrey Berry calls the "superstars of lobbying." They may
charge $350 per hour for lobbying services. Among the most successful is Charls
E. Walker, who was Richard Nixon's deputy secretary of the treasury. His specialty
is tax law. Corporations like Eastern Airlines, Ford, Procter and Gamble, and other
corporate giants pay him handsomely to watch and work for minuscule changes
in tax laws that could gain (or cost) them millions of dollars. Walker rarely prowls
the halls of the Capitol, but works mostly by phone and over lunches. Contacts
are important to him, much more so than any electoral threat he poses. Few
voters would know or care what Charls Walker wanted them to do, but a great
many powerful people think of him as a conduit to power.

Source: For more information on the Washington lobbyists, from which this overview is taken, see
Jeffrey Berry, *The Interest Group Society* (Boston: Little, Brown, 1984), Chap. 6.

legislative business. Ornstein and Elder listed five ways lobbyists can help a member of Congress:

— Lobbyists are an important source of information. Harried members of Congress, amateurs and laymen at nearly everything they vote on, eagerly seek information to help them make up their minds.
— They can help a member with political strategy. Lobbyists are politically savvy people, and they are free consultants.
— They can help formulate campaign strategy and even get their members behind your reelection campaign.
— They are a source of ideas and innovations. Politicians are often eager to link their name with an issue that will bring them political credit. Lobbyists cannot introduce bills, but they can peddle their ideas to politicians eager to find the idea whose time has come.
— They provide friendship. It is a rare member of Congress who could not say, "Some of my best friends are lobbyists."[12]

Like anything else, lobbying can be undertaken crudely or gracefully. Lobbyists can be heavy-handed. They can threaten or cajole the legislator, implying that electoral defeat is a certain result of not "going along." They can even imply that money flows to those who cooperate. Most men and women in Congress are not much different from you and me and are likely to view heavy-handed lobbyists as a pain. No one knows for sure where the fine line is drawn between lobbying as shady business and as strictly professional representation of legitimate interests. We do not even know how many lobby groups there are, how much they spend, or who they spend it on.

One reason we know so little about lobbyists is that Congress has never made it easy to find out about them. The **Federal Regulation of Lobbying Act** of 1946 required lobbyists to register and state their policy goals. However, the Supreme Court intrepreted the law to mean that only groups whose "principal" purpose is lobbying were legally required to register. A good many do register and state quite directly their legislative goals; but many do not. Then, too, most groups use an extremely narrow definition of lobbying when the time comes to file expenditure reports to Congress. Thus, the biggest spender, according to official records, is always Common Cause. Common Cause makes a habit of accounting for every nickel it spends in legislative lobbying. Groups like the AFL-CIO, the National Association of Manufacturers, and the oil lobbies typically file reports so low as to strain belief. Common Cause pressed hard for a Lobby Disclosure Act in several recent Congresses. Proving that politics can make strange bedfellows of conflicting groups, Ralph Nader, the NAM, the Sierra Club, labor, and nearly every other interest group opposed the act, and it failed to pass. (For more on lobby regulation, see pages 396–397.)

Assessing the Impact of Lobbying. Political scientists are not entirely in agreement about the effectiveness of lobbying. Most evidence suggests that lobbyists' power over policy is much exaggerated by the political

---

[12] Norman Ornstein and Shirley Elder, *Interest Groups, Lobbying and Policymaking* (Washington, D.C.: Congressional Quarterly Press, 1978), pp. 59–60.

cartoonist. Bauer, Pool, and Dexter studied the work of groups in making foreign trade policy. [13] Convinced before they started that they would find potent, well-oiled lobbies hustling Congress, they found instead lobby groups that were ineffective, understaffed, and underfinanced. Usually, the lobbyists offered too little too late to be effective. Members of Congress often had to pressure the pressure groups to get behind the legislation. Bauer and his colleagues even took a look at the role of giant Du Pont, headquartered in tiny Delaware. Delaware's congressional delegation heard nothing from Du Pont and eventually voted against what it assumed was Du Pont's position on foreign trade. Milbrath bluntly concluded his own analysis of lobbying by arguing, "There is relatively little influence or power in lobbying per se." [14] Lobbyists are most effective, he claims, as information sources, and relatively ineffectual in winning over legislators who are opposed to their goals.

Yet there is plenty of contrary evidence suggesting that lobbying can carry the day. The National Rifle Association, which has for years kept major gun control policies off the congressional agenda, is one of Washington's finest examples of the successful lobby. Soon in this chapter, we will look at several policies in which interest groups, and their lobbying activities, played major roles. Again, in our examination of Congress in Chapter 12, we will address and assess the lobbyists.

Nailing down the specific effects of lobbying is difficult, partly because isolating the effects of lobbying from other policy influences (such as party leadership or the president) is difficult. It works best on persons already committed to the lobbyist's policy position. Thus, lobbyists, like political campaigns, try to *activate* and *reinforce* their supporters, and realistically expect to *convert* only a few opponents. Because lobbying works best with those already on your side, getting the right people into office in the first place is also a key strategy of interest groups.

Electioneering

Electioneering directly involves groups in the electoral process. These groups aid candidates financially, testify to urge the party to adopt favorable positions, and get their members out working for the candidate. Group involvement in campaigns is nothing new. In the first McKinley-Bryan campaign (1896), silver-mining interests poured millions into Bryan's campaign, which advocated unlimited silver coinage.

The PAC explosion is the modern-day effort to get dollars into campaigns. (We met PACs in Chapter 8, pp. 255–258.) The number of political action committees has mushroomed from 608 in 1974 to 3803 in 1984. To political candidates they donated about $12.4 million in 1974 and an estimated $120 million in 1984. 4

One candidate described his experiences trying to get on the PAC bandwagon. When Democrat Steve Sovern ran for Iowa's Second Congressional District in 1980, he (like hundreds of other candidates for national office) made his pilgrimage to Washington to meet with poten-

[13] Raymond A. Bauer, Ithiel de Sola Pool, and Lewis A. Dexter, *American Business and Public Policy* (New York: Atherton, 1963).

[14] Milbrath, *The Washington Lobbyists*, p. 354.

tial contributors. "I found myself in line with candidates from all over," he reported. Each PAC had eager candidates sit down and fill out a multiple-choice questionnaire on issues important to it. Candidates who answered right and who looked like winners got the money. Sovern reported later that "the process made me sick." After his defeat, he went back home and organized a PAC called LASTPAC (for Let the American System Triumph). It urged candidates to shun PAC-backing.[15] The grandfather of public interest lobbies, Common Cause, has also waged war on PAC support.[16] A nonpartisan group called Citizens Against PACs paid for full-page newspaper ads in the hometown papers of large PAC recipients. (Said one in Representative Dan Rostenkowski's neighborhood paper: "What is Representative Dan Rostenkowski going to do with half a million dollars in leftover campaign funds? Take it with him?") Only a few candidates have resisted the lure of PAC money. Only two senators (David Boren of Oklahoma and William Proxmire of Wisconsin) and eight representatives specifically decline all PAC money.

[15] The Sovern story is told in "Taking an Ax to PACs," *Time,* August 20, 1984, p. 27.
[16] On Common Cause, see McFarland, *Common Cause.*

Litigation

Litigation may be a more effective group strategy than lobbying in affecting policymaking. Taking your policy goals to court offers a way of neutralizing your lost legislative battles. Karen Orren has linked much of the success of environmental interest groups to their use of lawsuits. "Frustrated in Congress," she wrote, "[they] have made an end run to the courts, where they have skillfully exploited and magnified limited legislative gains."[17]

The law explosion (see Chapter 15, pages 502–505) has made the courts the prime object of interest group attention. Civil rights groups paved the litigation way in the 1950s with major victories in cases concerning school desegregation, equal housing, and labor market equality. More recently, consumer groups and environmentalists have used suits against business and polluters and also against federal agencies enforcing consumer and pollution regulations. Any federal agency involved in environmental regulation has hundreds of suits outstanding against it at any given time. As long as law schools churn out lawyers, groups will fight for their interests in court.

Going Public

Groups are also interested in the opinions of people outside Washington, D.C. Public opinion may ultimately trickle back to policymakers, so interest groups cultivate their public image carefully. Business firms, as well as other interest groups, market not only products but reputations as well. Labor likes to be known as a united organization of hardworking men and women, rather than as a racketeer-infested bed of corruption. Big business wants people to see it as what made America great, not as a bunch of greedy capitalists. Farmers cultivate the image of a sturdy family working to put bread and meat on your table, rather than that of huge agribusiness reaping high profits. All groups try to create a reservoir of good will in the public at large.

Lately, more and more interests and organizations have launched expensive "public interest" public relations efforts. Soft sell and rational analysis—even presenting both sides of the issue—are the hallmarks of this new era of public interest PR. Mobil Oil has spent millions on advertising to present the oil company's side of the energy crisis. Caterpillar, the manufacturer of massive earth-moving and strip-mining machinery, has inundated *National Geographic* and other magazines with balanced, two-sides-to-everything ads. No one knows just how effective these image-molding efforts are, but this is the era of advertising. Unions, teachers, businesses, and other groups seem to believe firmly what detergent makers learned long ago: Advertising pays.

Groups go public not only by professionally advertising to get their messages across, but also by energizing and activating their members. The colorful and dramatic gesture is intended to generate news coverage. The farmer's plight is highlighted by a public slaughtering of pigs, whose costs are greater than the prices they command; the push for the Equal

---

[17] Karen Orren, "Standing to Sue: Interest Group Conflict in Federal Courts," *American Political Science Review* 70 (September 1976): 724.

Groups Use PR. *In this age of modern electronic communications, groups need to utilize public relations as well as old-fashioned lobbying. A full page advertisement in the New York Times (preferably the widely-read Sunday edition) is a common vehicle for bringing a group's views to the attention of elite groups, those able to influence public opinion. An ad such as this one often includes as standard equipment a list of signatories and an appeal for funds. Here, a group of opinion leaders is urging the government to support opposition to the Sandinista regime in Nicaragua. No one can say whether these public relations ventures actually enhance the influence of a group. But most groups feel that public relations is too important to be ignored.*

Rights Amendment is dramatized by a hunger strike in Illinois; opposition to a new nuclear plant is demonstrated by a sit-in. These attention-getting tactics are intended to get the message across to the public and its representatives.

GROUP PORTRAITS: TYPES OF INTEREST GROUPS

Whether they are lobbying, electioneering, litigating, or appealing to the public, interest groups are ubiquitous in our political system. As with other aspects of American politics and policymaking, we can loosely categorize interests into clusters. Some deal mainly with economic issues, others with equality issues, and still others with issues of energy and the environment.

All groups do not confine their attention to just one of our three policy boxes. The American Petroleum Institute and the American Mining Conference, for example, are economic heavyweights as well as energy heavyweights. Our classification at least suggests that most groups mind their own policy business most of the time. (The Pharmaceutical Manufacturers are not likely to spend their valuable resources lobbying for or against environmental bills or school busing policies.) Not all groups are easily molded into our three policy arenas. Veterans, military groups, public interest groups like Common Cause, and various professional associations exist as well.

The Economic Interests

In the most general sense, everyone has an economic interest. But some economic interests are much better organized than others. The big three economic interests have historically been business, labor, and agriculture, although recently consumers have organized.

All economic interests are ultimately concerned with wages, prices, and profits. In our mixed economy, government does not determine wages, prices, and profits directly. Only infrequently has government imposed wage and price controls and usually during wartime, although the Nixon administration briefly used wage and price controls during peacetime to control inflation. More commonly, public policy in America has economic effects through *regulations, tax advantages, subsidies and contracts,* and *international trade policy.*

Business, labor, and farmers all fret over the impacts of government regulations. Even a minor change in government regulatory policy can cost industries large amounts or bring windfall profits. Tax policies also affect the livelihoods of farmers, firms, and workers. How the tax code is written determines whether people and producers pay a lot or a little of their incomes to the government. Because government often provides subsidies (to farmers, small businesses, railroads, minority businesses, and others), every economic group wants to get its share of direct aid and of government contracts. And in this day of the global economic connection, business, labor, and farmers alike worry about import quotas, tariffs (fees placed on imports), and the soundness of the dollar. In short, white-collar business executives, blue-collar workers, and khaki-collar farmers seek to influence government because regulations, taxes, subsidies, and international economic policy all affect their economic livelihoods. Let us take a quick tour of some of the major organized interests in the economic policy arena.

Labor. Numerically, labor is the biggest interest group. More than 14 million workers are members of unions affiliated with the AFL-CIO, itself a union of unions. Several million others are members of non-AFL-CIO unions, especially the International Brotherhood of Teamsters, which represents those knights of the open road, the truck drivers.

Like labor unions everywhere, American unions press for policies to ensure better working conditions and higher wages. Recognizing the seriousness of the free-rider problem, unions have fought hard for the *union shop.* The union shop requires that new employees join the union representing them. In contrast, business groups have supported "right-to-work" laws, outlawing union membership as a condition of keeping a job. (Notice the political symbolism involved in the phrase "right-to-

As Old as the Boston Tea Party. Protest in America is as old as the Boston Tea Party and as contemporary as the efforts of these protestors to have their say about President Reagan's proposed expenditure reductions in March 1985. Protesting is not to be confused with violent actions. It can be as peaceful and powerfully moral as Martin Luther King's quiet civil disobedience against segregation in the south in the 1960s. Protest depends upon the visibility of the protest, and the media are crucial to this effort.

work." Unions, in their own symbolic rhetoric, described the Taft-Hartley Act of 1947 as a "slave labor law" because it permitted states to adopt right-to-work laws.) Boosts in the minimum wage are also a top union priority.

Unions in the 1980s are more concerned with the global economy than ever before. Low wages elsewhere have diminished the American job market. Steel once made by workers in Bethlehem is now made more cheaply in Korea. Cars once manufactured in a near-monopoly by Detroit and its United Auto Workers are now made in Japan. The global connection has increased labor's interest in international economic policy.

Agriculture. American agriculture has changed dramatically. The family farm has given way to massive agribusiness. Family farms are to agriculture what small business is to commerce, a shrinking share of the producing units. To city dwellers, the tangled policies of acreage controls, price supports, and import quotas are confusing. Yet to farmers, the policies of the government may be more important than the whims of nature.

There are several broad-based agricultural groups (the American Farm Bureau Federation, the National Farmers' Organization), but equally important are the commodity associations. These join together peanut farmers, Angus ranchers, potato growers, dairymen, tobacco farmers, and other commodity producers. The United States Department of Agriculture and the congressional agriculture committees are organized along commodity lines, with separate divisions for different products. This organizational system leads to very cordial relations among agricultural commodity groups, congressional subcommittees, and bureaucratic agencies, promoting a classic example of what hyperpluralists call subgovernments.

Business. Last in our review of the three big economic interests, we come to business. If the elite theorists are right, and there is an American power elite, certainly it would be dominated by leaders of the mighty banks, insurance companies, and multinational corporations.

This view may or may not be exaggerated, but business is certainly well organized for effective action. Two umbrella organizations, the National Association of Manufacturers and the Chamber of Commerce, include most corporations and businesses. They can speak for business when general business interests are at stake. Corporate taxation, consumer policy, and labor legislation are policy issues on which almost all businesses agree. On many other issues, however, business interests compete. More international free trade would help some kinds of business. Others find that foreign competition threatens their profits. Sears and Montgomery Ward want an easing of import restrictions on cheaper, foreign-made clothes and TVs, but American clothing and TV manufacturers want to limit foreign competition. Trucking and construction companies want more highways, but railroads do not. Thus, business interests are both unified and fragmented.

The hundreds of trade and product associations are far less visible than the NAM and the Chamber of Commerce, but they are at least as important in seeking policy goals for their members. From Angus cattle and angora goats through pickles and potatoes to theatre owners and TV networks, trade associations run the alphabetical and political gamut: They fight regulations that would narrow their profits, seek preferential tax treatment, pursue import restrictions to protect themselves against foreign competition, seek government subsidies and contracts. The tax code and the schedule of tariffs are monuments to the activities of the trade associations. Although the least visible of Washington lobbies, their successes are scored in amendments won, regulations rewritten, and exceptions made.

Consumers. If ever a lobbying effort was spurred by a single person, it was the consumer movement.[18] Almost single-handedly, gaunt, ascetic activist Ralph Nader took on American business in the name of consumerism. He was propelled to national prominence by a book (*Unsafe at Any Speed*) that attacked General Motors' Corvair as mechanically deficient and downright dangerous. Mighty GM made the mistake of having him tailed and hiring a private detective to dig into his background. No one who knows the abstemious young lawyer would have imagined that the best private eye in the world could find anything adverse about Nader. Consequently, Nader sued GM for invasion of privacy and won. He used the proceeds to launch a consumer group in Washington, D.C. Soon he became the dean of consumer advocates.

Though consumer groups advocated a national Consumer Protection Agency with cabinet-level status, and lost, they have won many other legislative victories. In 1973, during the Nixon administration, Congress responded to consumer advocacy and created the Consumer Product Safety Commission. It launched regulations against products ranging from children's sleepwear (some of which contained a carcinogen) to hot

[18] On the origins of the consumer movement, see Mark Nadel, *The Politics of Consumer Protection* (Indianapolis, Ind.: Bobbs-Merrill, 1971).

Consumer Crusader Ralph Nader. *A small General Motors car, the Chevrolet Corvair, first propelled Ralph Nader to national prominence. His book,* Unsafe at Any Speed, *attacked Corvairs (and other automobiles) as mechanically deficient and dangerous. Speaking out against shoddy products and practices, Nader became the self-appointed dean of consumer advocates. He ran the Center for the Study of Responsive Law, which spun off a dozen or so policy research and advocacy groups. "Nader's raiders" looked into health care costs, tax reform, congressional practices, and other interests of consumers.*

Nader did not singlehandedly create the consumer movement in American politics, but few have done as much to focus national attention on the issues that affect consumers.

tubs to lawn mowers. (Household products kill 30,000 Americans annually.) Congress authorized the CPSC to regulate all consumer products, and even gave it the power to ban particularly dangerous ones. (Other lobbying groups for guns and tobacco persuaded Congress to exempt firearms and tobacco from CPSC's power.) However, the Reagan administration reduced the personnel of the agency by 32 percent, forcing cutbacks in its testing and regulatory activities. By the middle of the first Reagan administration, CPSC inspections of manufacturers had dropped 56 percent.[19]

Interest Groups and Equality

Two large segments of the American population, minority groups and women, have made equal rights their main policy goal.

The history of the civil rights movement is a long one, and this is not the time to repeat it. We are concerned here with its policy goals and organizational base. Equality at the polls, on the job, in schooling, housing, and college admissions, and in all other facets of American life has been the dominant goal of black groups. Oldest and still largest of these groups is the National Association for the Advancement of Colored People (the NAACP). It argued and won the monumental *Brown* v. *Board of Education* case in 1954. In that decision, the Supreme Court held segregated schools unconstitutional. The NAACP and other civil rights groups lobbied and litigated for policies forbidding discrimination in voting, jobs, and housing. Almost all of these policy goals were adopted by Congress. Battles between southern opponents and northern supporters preceded the enactment of the Civil Rights Act of 1964, the Voting Rights Act of 1965, open housing legislation in 1968, and other policies.

Having won these victories, civil rights groups today face even harder policy issues. Substantial housing segregation, job discrimination, and school segregation still exist. Affirmative action (see pages 29 and 577–578) is not a popular cause, but civil rights groups have a long history of pushing unpopular causes.

The rise of organizations of women both preceded and postdated the civil rights movement. Even when the NAACP was a fledgling organization, suffragists were in the streets and the legislative lobbies, demanding the right to vote. The Nineteenth Amendment, ratified in 1920, guaranteed women the vote; but other guarantees of equal protection were not in the Constitution. Equal pay, equal access to jobs, and equal treatment in family law were policy goals of the second generation of women's groups, such as the League of Women Voters and the American Association of University Women, joined later by new activist groups. The National Organization for Women (NOW) was created in 1966. It was followed by several other groups, including the National Women's Political Caucus and the Women's Equity Action League. Though they lobbied for a variety of policies, the centerpiece of their efforts was the Equal Rights Amendment. [5] With the demise of the ERA, many women's groups have turned their attention to the thorny issue of comparable worth (see page 577).

[19] On the recent perils of the CPSC, see Jean Cobb, "Recalling Consumer Safety," *Common Cause* (May–June 1983): 29–30.

Groups, Energy, and Environment

Among the newest interest groups are the environmentalists. Perhaps as many as 3,000 organizations are interested in the environment.[20] Some of these, like the Sierra Club and the Audubon Society, have been around since the nineteenth century, but many others trace their origins to Earth Day, April 22, 1970. On that day, ecology-minded people marched

[20] Walter A. Rosenbaum, *The Politics of Environmental Concern*, 2nd ed. (New York: Praeger, 1977), p. 76.

---

5 | A Case Study in the Politics of Equality: The Demise of the Equal Rights Amendment

First proposed in Congress in 1923 by the nephew of suffragist Susan B. Anthony, the Equal Rights Amendment had to wait almost fifty years before Congress passed it and sent it to the states for ratification. When the Senate and House approved it overwhelmingly in 1972 (the vote was 354 to 23 in the House, and 84 to 8 in the Senate), it seemed to be an issue whose time had finally come. Simply worded, the ERA read as follows:

> Section 1. Equality of rights under the law shall not be abridged on account of sex.
> Section 2. The Congress shall have the power to enforce by appropriate legislation, the provisions of this article.
> Section 3. This amendment shall take effect two years after the date of ratification.

At first, it was an easy race against the seven-year deadline Congress had established. State legislatures even seemed to outdo one another to ratify. Hawaii had arranged with Senator Inouye's office to signal the island legislature when the Senate passed the ERA, so that Hawaii could be the first state to ratify. Within the first month, fifteen state legislatures had ratified, all with overwhelming majorities. Even Texas and Kansas, fairly conservative states, voted decisively for the ERA. Women's interest groups seemed to be coasting to victory.

While the ERA was zipping through the legislatures, conservative publicist Phyllis Schlafly of Alton, Illinois, became a one-woman movement against the ERA. Mrs. Schlafly's whirlwind schedule took her to talk shows, speeches, rallies, and interviews, where she ticked off the evils of ERA. It would, she and her fellow opponents argued, lead to women in combat, destroy the integrity of the family, encourage homosexuality, and eliminate the legal protections women already had.

The quiet, consensual politics of ERA's early days became boisterous, bizarre politics. Pro-ERA groups tried to present the most rational possible arguments and always be "ladylike." But placards carried by "Lesbians for ERA" did not always help their cause. Both sides sent apple pies (and other items) to legislators. Legislative leaders in one state turned the floor over to an anti-ERA group that staged a skit depicting the presumed negative impacts of ERA—communal bathrooms, abortions on demand, military fatigues for mothers, and homosexual marriages. One legislator reasoned that if God had meant for women and men to be equal, he would have had six female and six male apostles. A female legislator voted against ratification because "I like having men open doors for me." A few legislatures that had ratified the ERA later rescinded their ratification, a constitutionally dubious but politically significant reaction. By 1978, a year short of the traditional seven-year deadline for ratification, the ERA was still three states short of the required thirty-eight.

ERA proponents turned their attention to two spots. One was Illinois, the last holdout against ERA ratification among northern states. But Illinois was also the home of Phyllis Schlafly, ERA's leading opponent. Illinois once again turned down ERA (and repeated that performance annually until 1982). The other focus of attention was Washington, D.C. There, proponents got the House and Senate to extend the time limit for ratification through June 1982.

Opposing groups not only continued their opposition in the legislatures, but also launched a litigation campaign. Late in 1981, opponents won an important judicial victory when a federal judge in Idaho ruled that states could rescind their *yes* votes during the extension period.

In June 1982 the deadline neared, and supporters turned their attention to several states that had not yet ratified the amendment. In Illinois, ERA boosters chained themselves to railings in the state capitol and went on hunger strikes, but to no avail. Last-minute pushes in North Carolina, Oklahoma, and Florida also came to nothing. And the amendment whose time seemed to have come in 1972 simply passed away.

Source: For a more extensive analysis of the early politics of ERA ratification, see Janet Boles, *The Politics of the Equal Rights Amendment* (New York: Longman, 1979).

on Washington and other places to symbolize their support for environmental protection. They have organized and have supported pollution-control policies, wilderness protection, and population control. What they have opposed may be even more significant. Supersonic transports, strip-mining, the Alaskan oil pipeline, offshore drilling, chemical waste dumps, nuclear power, loggers, DDT, and polluters of all kinds have been on the environmentalists' hit list.

Almost all of the environmental groups are busy not only lobbying, but also litigating. Using the courts as effectively as they use legislative lobbies has been a hallmark of the environmental action movement. Hundreds of young public interest lawyers grind out hundreds of suits against agencies and polluters annually. These suits may not halt environmentally troublesome programs, but the constant threat of suits increases the likelihood that agencies will consider the environmental impact of what they do.

For a while, the environmentalists seemed unstoppable, but their goals often seem in conflict with energy goals. Environmentalists insist that, in the long run, energy supplies can be ensured without environmental danger. Yet short-run conflicts between energy needs and environmental protection have blunted the environmentalists' impact. Energy producers argue that environmentalists oppose nearly every new energy project. Nuclear power plants, the Trans-Alaskan pipeline, offshore drilling, liquefied natural gas, strip-mining, and supertankers have all been attacked as unsafe. (One of the most famous antinuclear pitches of environmentalists is the ad asking, "What do you do if a nuclear power plant blows up? Kiss your children goodbye.") Despite environmentalist opposition, Congress subsidized the massive Trans-Alaskan pipeline, which a consortium of oil companies use to transport oil from Alaska's north slope. The strip-mining of coal continues despite the opposition of environmentalists. When two public interests—environmental protection and an ensured supply of energy—clash, group politics intensifies.

The Rise of the Public Interest Lobbies

So frequently is the term **public interest** invoked that one might think everyone knew what it was and worked hard to achieve it. The term suggests that there are some interests superior to the private interests of groups and individuals, interests we all have in common. Albeit, often what is everybody's business becomes nobody's business. Recently a new breed of interest group has arisen, claiming to represent the public interest. These groups seem to defy the grim logic of Olson's law of large groups by showing that people do, at least once in a while, organize for policy goals that do nothing for them directly. Jeffrey Berry's analysis of these **public interest lobbies** defines them as organizations that seek "a collective good, the achievement of which will not selectively and materially benefit the membership or activists of the organization." [21] There are many aspects of the public interest represented by these groups, as some examples from Berry's study shows: the Children's Foundation,

[21] Jeffrey M. Berry, *Lobbying for the People* (Princeton, N.J.: Princeton University Press, 1977), p. 7. See also Andrew McFarland, *Public Interest Lobbies: Decision-making on Energy* (Washington, D.C.: American Enterprise Institute, 1976).

Jerry Falwell. *Bumper stickers claiming that "The Moral Majority is Neither" reflect the growing opposition to the likewise expanding influence of a religious-based interest group headed by the Reverend Jerry Falwell. Falwell founded the group in 1978 and spread the word on his syndicated Sunday-morning television show and at his frequent public appearances. Within a year or so, the Moral Majority claimed a membership of more than half a million and a budget of $1 million.*

Issues supported by the group include constitutional amendments banning abortions and allowing prayer in the public schools. The Moral Majority is only one of numerous religious interest groups that are typically conservative in their political views. Estimates that as many as one in five adult Americans calls himself a fundamentalist make the potential membership—and influence—of these groups large indeed.

Common Cause, the American Horse Protection Association, the Wilderness Society, the Fund for Animals, the Washington Peace Center, and the American Civil Liberties Union.

Environmentalists are not the only ones claiming to be public interest groups. Groups speaking up for those who cannot speak for themselves push protection for children, animals, and the mentally ill; good government groups such as Common Cause and ideological groups such as the Americans for Democratic Action are political coalitions; peace groups, temperance groups, pro-life (antiabortion) groups, church groups, and tax reform groups all stake out their own claims on the public interest.

Recently a new group has organized to address such "moral issues" in American politics as homosexuality, abortion, sex education, and TV programming—the Moral Majority, a political group founded and heavily funded by the Reverend Jerry Falwell, minister of the Thomas Road Baptist Church in Lynchburg, Virginia. Falwell's Moral Majority was born in 1979 and claimed credit (too much credit, no doubt) for the election of Ronald Reagan and the defeat of liberal senators (George McGovern of South Dakota, Birch Bayh of Indiana, Frank Church of Idaho) in the 1980 elections. Opposed to the many policies that recognize alternative (Moral Majoritarians would call them "sinful") life styles, Falwell and other conservative religious leaders have brought religion once more into our political agenda.

Public Interest or Single Issue?
The Growth of Single Issue Groups

Almost all groups claim to represent some version of the public interest. A free term, costing nothing to use, public interest immediately associates your interest with everyone else's. Nonetheless, we have lately

319

seen the growth of **single issue groups.** These single issue groups differ significantly from such traditional interest groups as labor, business, and farmers in both the range and intensity of their interests. Single issue groups have three general features.

— First, *their interest is narrow* rather than broad. As their name implies, group members care little about the broad range of issues buffeting the American political system. Traditional interest groups (the Chamber of Commerce, the AFL-CIO) usually have numerous issues to address, although they are not as broadly focused as a political party.

— Second, *they tend to dislike compromise,* fearing that compromise weakens their posture, which is not merely politically correct but morally imperative. Fervor, whether ideological or religious, is a major weapon in the arsenal of the single issue group. Traditional interest groups, on the other hand, are often willing to trade off a gain on some issue for a loss on another one.

— Third, *these groups often draw membership from people new to politics.* The ranks of some single issue groups are filled with people who previously had no interest in political action.

Any interest can be pursued single-mindedly. Anti-Vietnam War activists in the 1960s and 1970s may have been the first modern single issue group. Proponents or opponents of nuclear power plants might qualify as single issue groups. Today, many single issue groups have a moral, religious, or evangelical basis.

The abortion issue has attracted its fair share of these groups. The February 1973 Supreme Court ruling in *"Roe"* v. *Wade* upholding the right of a woman to secure an abortion during the first trimester of pregnancy spurred a wave of group formation. [22] The National Right to Life Committee (NRLC) and the Life Amendment Political Action Committee (LAPAC) were founded by Judie and Paul Brown to oppose abortion and secure a constitutional amendment forbidding it. Organizing at the state level, these and other anti-abortion groups trained their fire on candidates for and incumbents in state and national offices, sometimes with success. Anti-abortion groups were strongly felt in the presidential election campaign of 1984. Democratic Vice Presidential candidate Geraldine Ferraro, a Catholic, defended women's right to choose, though claiming that she herself could not imagine circumstances in which she found abortion acceptable for herself. Anti-abortion groups picketed her speeches throughout the country, and New York's Archbishop O'Conner criticized her stand. In response to the activities of anti-abortionists, pro-abortion groups like the National Abortion Rights Action League (NARAL) began to organize and support or oppose candidates as well.

As with other interest groups, single issue groups are not likely to run their own candidates or generate a majority needed for victory. They can, however, sometimes make a marginal difference in the election of a senator, governor, or legislator. In a close election, a group with as little as 2 or 3 percent of the vote can ensure the defeat of a candidate it opposes.

---

[22] Roger Williams, "The Power of Fetal Politics," in Alan Shank (ed.), *American Politics, Policies, and Priorities,* 3rd ed. (Boston: Allyn and Bacon, 1981), pp. 175–81.

"Senator, according to this report, you've been marked for defeat by the A.D.A., the National Rifle Association, the A.F.L.-C.I.O., the N.A.M., the Sierra Club, Planned Parenthood, the World Student Christian Federation, the Clamshell Alliance . . ."

UNDERSTANDING INTEREST GROUPS

Our group profile, sketchy though it has been, certainly shows that there are plenty of groups seeking policy goals. These days, no interest lacks some organized group speaking for it, although groups vary widely in their ability to turn potential members into actual ones. The right to organize groups is constitutionally protected in the First Amendment's freedom of assembly clause. Americans today have taken full advantage of that right, producing an alphabet soup of group names and initials— NRA, NAM, AFL-CIO, ACLU, and thousands more—making Tocqueville's observation about a "nation of joiners" truer today than when he wrote it.

To assess our complex interest group system, we return once more to the four theories of American politics outlined in Chapter 2.

Groups and Traditional Democratic Theory

Passed over lightly in the writings about traditional democratic theory, groups can still fill key gaps in it. When the parties and the electoral system fail to represent interests effectively, groups can take their claims directly to the government, providing another linkage between people and policy. Groups bring representation to the unrepresented; without them, the voice of the unorganized would be faint indeed. Black Americans would still be merely struggling for equal opportunity if they had to depend solely on the electoral system—where blacks were often disenfranchised or easily outvoted—and the party system—where the parties were reluctant to antagonize the segregationists among their supporters. Using lobbying and litigation, and effectively taking their case to the larger public, civil rights groups secured policies difficult to win by the electoral process alone. Women, Mexican Americans, native Americans, and homosexuals have tried to follow in the steps of the black civil rights movement.

Nonetheless, group politics can produce expensive public policies. Pleasing groups with policies costs money, and pleasing even more groups demands even bigger bites of the budget. Almost all groups, of course, attempt to externalize the costs of their policy benefits—that is, to pass the costs along to others, either as bigger tax bills or as price increases. Environmentalists who win regulations promoting cleaner air, older citizens who receive social security benefits, and younger ones whose families want tax credits for college tuition—these and other groups inflate the cost of government or of products. Groups are, and will remain, an important political linkage, but nothing comes free—not even the politics of group representation.

Pluralism and Group Theory

Pluralist theory rests its case on the multiplicity of power centers in the American political system. The extensive organization of competing groups is seen as evidence that power is widely shared. In group politics, you win some and you lose some, but no group really loses all the time. In effect, a group is never shut out completely. A considerable body of writings by pluralist theorists offers a *group theory* of politics,[23] which contains several essential arguments:

1. *Groups provide a key linkage between people and government.* Almost all legitimate interests in the political system can get a hearing from government once they are organized.
2. *Groups compete.* Labor, business, farmers, consumers, environmentalists, blacks, and other interests constantly make claims on one another.
3. *No one group is likely to become too dominant.* When one group throws its weight around too much, its opponents are likely to intensify their organization and thus help bring a balance to the whole system.
4. *Groups usually play by the "rules of the game."* In the United States, group politics is a fair fight, with few groups lying, cheating, stealing, or engaging in violence to get their way.
5. *Groups weak in one resource can use another; group resources are substitutable.* Big business may have money on its side, but labor has numbers. No legitimate group is totally unable to affect public policy by one means or another.
6. *A rough approximation of the public interest emerges out of the group struggle.* However hard to define, the public interest is well served when groups compete fairly for their own policy goals.

[23] The classic is Truman, *The Governmental Process.*

Pluralists would never deny that some groups are stronger than others, or that all interests do not get an equal hearing. Still, they can point to plenty of cases in which a potential group got organized and then got action. Blacks, consumers, and women are groups who were virtually ignored by government, but once organized, began winning.

Elites and the Denial of Pluralism

Whereas pluralists are impressed by the vast number of organized interests, elitists are impressed by how insignificant most of them are. *Real* power, elitists say, is held by relatively few key groups and institutions. Elitists are fond of pointing to the concentration of power in a few hands. Where pluralists find dispersion of power, elitists find interlocking elites. Almost 40 percent of top institutional positions—corporate boards, foundation boards, university trusteeships, and so on—are occupied by people who hold more than one such position.[24] Elitists see the rise of mighty multinational corporations as further tightening the control of corporate elites. Vast oil companies are key examples. Robert Engler has tried to show that government has always bent over backward to maintain high profits for the oil industry.[25] Alongside the power of these multinational corporations, small interests such as consumers are political lightweights.

To elitists, the interest group system looks like this:

1. The fact that there are numerous groups proves nothing because groups are extremely unequal in their power.
2. The groups and institutions with awesome power are those in control of the largest corporations.
3. The power of a few is fortified by an extensive system of interlocking directorates.
4. Other groups may win many individual policy battles, but the real game of group politics is the one played by the corporate elites; and they almost always win.

Hyperpluralism and Interest Group Liberalism

Hyperpluralism sees pluralism as being carried too far—so that the relationship between government and interest groups is much too cozy. As we saw in Chapter 2, Theodore Lowi coined the term *interest group liberalism* to refer to excessive deference to groups.[26] Interest group liberalism is characterized by the philosophy that *all* interests are almost equally legitimate and the job of government is to advance them all. If environmentalists want clean air, government imposes clean air rules; if businesses complain that cleaning up pollution is expensive, government gives them a tax write-off for pollution control equipment. If the direct mail industry wants cheap rates, government gives it to them; if people complain about junk mail, the Post Office gives them a way to take their

[24] Thomas R. Dye, *Who's Running America? The Reagan Years* (Englewood Cliffs, N.J.: Prentice Hall, 1983).
[25] Robert Engler, *The Brotherhood of Oil* (Chicago: University of Chicago Press, 1977).
[26] Theodore Lowi, *The End of Liberalism*, 2nd ed. (New York: Norton, 1979), Chap. 3.

name off mailing lists. If cancer research gets government to launch an antismoking campaign, tobacco sales may drop; if they do, government subsidizes tobacco farmers to ease their loss. In an effort to please and appease every interest, agencies proliferate, conflicting regulations expand, programs are multiplied, and, of course, the budget skyrockets.

Interest group liberalism is promoted by the network of **subgovernments** in the American system. These subgovernments (which are also known as *iron triangles*, and will be discussed in greater detail on pages 472–473) are composed of:

1. Key interest group leaders interested in policy *X*.
2. The government agency in charge of administering policy *X*.
3. The members of congressional committees and congressional subcommittees handling policy *X*.

The interests of these elements are remarkably similar. The network of subgovernments in agricultural policy areas is an excellent example. Take tobacco. Interest groups include the Tobacco Institute, the Retail Tobacco Distributors of America, and the tobacco growers. Various agencies in the Department of Agriculture administer tobacco programs. And most of the members of the House Tobacco Subcommittee are from the tobacco-growing states. All of these elements have a common interest in maximizing tobacco sales and exports. They may not agree on everything —growers want higher prices and buyers do not—but their close relationships permit them to iron out their differences without major battles. Similar *iron triangles* of group-agency-committee ties exist in dozens of other policy areas.

Hyperpluralism at Work. *Hyperpluralism leads government to pursue contradictory policies. Satisfying this group and that one means that government can do one thing with its left hand and another with its right. Nothing better illustrates hyperpluralism than the war against cigarette smoking combined with government's continued efforts to subsidize tobacco farmers. North Carolina's Senator Jesse Helms is a conservative about almost all government spending—except that spending which supports his state's tobacco farmers. He even declined to give up his chairmanship of the Senate Agriculture Committee for the powerful Foreign Relations Committee so that he could tend to the needs of his state's farmers, heavily dependent upon tobacco. But at the same time, Surgeon General C. Everett Koop—like all recent surgeon generals—was railing against the health hazards of tobacco.*

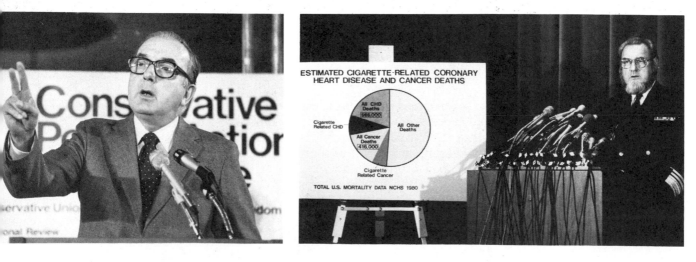

The problem with this hyperpluralist system, its critics say, is that groups become too powerful. Hard choices about national policy never get made. We are so eager to favor polluters *and* environmentalists that we cannot make effective environmental policy. We favor business *and* labor, highways *and* mass transit, poor *and* rich, railroads *and* truckers, tobacco interests *and* cancer fighters. Instead of making choices as to whether we want *X* or *Y*, we pretend we do not really have to choose at all, and try to favor them both—surely a prescription for policy paralysis. In short, the hyperpluralist position on groups is that:

1. The groups have become too powerful in the political process, as government tries to aid every conceivable interest.
2. This interest group liberalism is aggravated by numerous subgovernments—cozy relationships among a government agency, the interest group it deals with, and congressional subcommittees.
3. The result is contradictory and confusing policy.

The rise of so-called single issue groups also exacerbates hyperpluralism. From fragmented government, it is but a short step to stalemated government. Absolute opposition to a government action by some single-minded single interest group makes it difficult for policymakers to make policy. In our new era of partyless politics, the rise of the strong uncompromising group can only serve to complicate our political life.

THE ROOT OF ALL EVIL?

It used to be said that money was the root of all evil. These days, it seems to be the special interests. Let us review the main charges against our current interest group system and try to assess them.

1. Interest groups are "harmful to economic growth, full employment, coherent government, equal opportunity, and social mobility." [27] This sweeping charge comes from economist Mancur Olson, who believes that interest groups are—collectively—very conservative institutions. From government they gain guarantees, which leave their built-in advantages built-in. Unions insist upon job protection even in declining industries; corporations insist upon protection from foreign competition; teachers' groups want protection from the threat of enrollment declines; and so forth. Rather, societies need change in order to grow. The rigidification of the interest group system, says Olson, is its great defect. And the more the system has become entrenched, the greater its stranglehold on growth and change.
2. The interest group system is corrupting American elections. Democratic elections require free and open exchanges of ideas. Candidates and voters should be able to hear one another out. But PACs, the source of so much money in elections, distort the process, permitting those who have the most to spend to buy the most of a

---

[27] Mancur Olson, *The Rise and Decline of Nations* (New Haven, Conn., Yale University Press, 1982), p. 237.

candidate. Moderate Republican Representative Jim Leach of Iowa thinks that "it's a myth to think they [the PACs] don't want something in return."[28] PACs can link money to politics at the highest levels. The old party machines may have bought votes in the voting booth; the new PACs are accused of buying votes in the legislative chambers. Technology—television especially—makes our elections expensive; candidates need money to pay for campaigns and PACs are able to supply that money. In return, they ask only to be remembered on one or two crucial votes.

3. The interest group system is biased. Senate Majority Leader Robert Dole remarked once that he had not been recently approached by any Poor People's PAC. His implication: PACs and interest groups more often aid class and elite interests in American government. In the last generation, control over money was important; today, control over information and the technology of communication is equally important. Groups rich in both money and technology are groups whose influence is enhanced in the public policy battle.

There is no doubt that groups are under attack—at least everyone else's group. I may see my group as the embodiment of the public interest and your group as a special, selfish interest. Nevertheless, group participation is one way in which Americans can influence public policy. Poor people's movements as well as rich people's associations are ways of affecting the policy agenda. Not only the rich take advantage of interest groups. Environmentalists in Colorado, opponents of nuclear power in New Hampshire, and nuclear freeze advocates everywhere have formed into pressure groups.

Groups, like parties, have been around for a long time in American politics. More than parties, they have been able to take advantage of the high technology of the third American century. Parties, says Professor Berry, "are the natural counterweight to interest groups, offering citizens the basic means of pursuing the nation's collective will. . . . When there is little confidence that parties are capable of providing a meaningful link between the ballot box and the policies that affect one's life, suspicion grows that government is being directed by well-organized groups."[29]

INTEREST GROUPS SUMMARIZED

Our whirlwind tour of group politics should have convinced you that there is a vast array of interests in American society, all vying for policies they prefer and trying to prevent policies they oppose. We saw that large groups often fall victim to the free-rider problem, which we called Olson's law of large groups. Thus, groups representing large numbers of people, with some exceptions, generally find it harder to get organized than smaller ones.

Once organized, groups can choose among four basic strategies to maximize their effectiveness. Lobbying is one well-known group strategy. Although the evidence on its effectiveness is mixed (and may never be

[28] "Taking an Ax to the PACs," *Time*, August 20, 1984, p. 27.
[29] Berry, *The Interest Group Society*, p. 220.

beyond dispute), it is clear that lobbyists are most effective with those legislators already on their side. Thus, electioneering becomes important, because it helps put supportive people in office. More and more these days, groups operate in the judicial as well as the legislative process and use litigation to achieve their ends. Most also find it important to shape a good image, going public to stress their legitimate needs.

Our group profile peeked at some of the major kinds of interest groups, particularly those concerned with economic, equality, and energy/environment policy. The public interest lobbies claim to be different from other interest groups, representing, they say, an important part of the public interest. Recently we have seen the growth of single issue groups, which differ from traditional interest groups in that they are narrowly focused on one issue on which they will not compromise.

Interest groups play a role in each theory of American government, but they are the centerpiece of pluralist theory. Pluralists see groups as the most important way people can have their policy preferences represented in government. Yet, as even pluralists are quick to admit, groups vary enormously in their ability to get organized.

Though groups are an important linkage between people and policy, it is also useful to ask how much group politics is enough. However you answer that question, though, remember that neither James Madison's fear of faction nor modern-day politicians' worries about single-issue groups have deterred groups from organizing for policy purposes.

Key Terms

interest group	Olson's law of large	electioneering
potential group	groups	public interest
actual group	lobbying	public interest lobbies
collective good	Federal Regulation of	single issue groups
free-rider problem	Lobbying Act	subgovernments

For Further Reading

Berry, Jeffrey. *The Interest Group Society* (1984). One of the best contemporary textbooks on interest groups.

————. *Lobbying for the People* (1977). The major study of public interest lobbies.

Boles, Janet K. *The Politics of the Equal Rights Amendment* (1978). The trials and tribulations of the ERA in its quest for ratification by the state legislatures.

Cigler, Allan J., and Burdette A. Loomis, eds. *Interest Group Politics* (1984). An excellent collection of original articles on the modern interest group system.

Lowi, Theodore. *The End of Liberalism*, 2nd ed. (1974). A critique of "interest group liberalism."

McFarland, Andrew S. *Common Cause: Lobbying in the Public Interest* (1984). A study of the major public interest lobby.

Nadel, Mark V. *The Politics of Consumer Protection* (1971). Describes the goals, strategies, and origins of the consumer protection movement.

Olson, Mancur. *The Logic of Collective Action* (1968). Develops an economic theory of groups, showing how the cards are stacked against larger groups.

————. *The Rise and Decline of Nations* (1982). Olson blames many of the ills of the modern democracies on groups. This is a difficult and controversial book, but a provocative one.

THE POLICYMAKERS

Politics in Washington revolves around four formal institutions of government—the presidency, the Congress, the bureaucracy, and the courts—plus a host of informal ones. Chapter 11 gives you a brief tour of Washington politics. In Washington, the formal institutions of government are surrounded by interest groups, political consultants, the media, and other unofficial, but very active, players in policymaking.

Chapters 12 to 15 consider the four principal policymaking institutions individually. I cannot stress strongly enough that these institutions interact, and do not make decisions in isolation from one another. Still, it makes sense to describe each one in turn. You will quickly note that each of these chapters is organized similarly. In each, we first describe who the policymakers (presidents, members of Congress, bureaucrats, and judges) are, how they got there, and what they do. Second, we explain how the institution is organized to make policy. Third, we discuss the policymaking process within the institution.

The Founding Fathers considered Congress, the subject of Chapter 12, our main policymaking institution. But in our technological era, power has drifted away from our "Congress of amateurs" to the professionals of the executive branch, that is, the president and the bureaucracies. Thus, Congress is often a source of frustration to its members as well as to its critics. More and more, national agenda building is the responsibility of the president, whom we discuss in Chapter 13. The president is the titular head of the nation's bureaucracy, which is the subject of Chapter 14. The sprawling federal bureaucracy, though, is never easy to control.

Neither the bureaucracy nor the courts (the subject of Chapter 15) are elected policymakers. The Founding Fathers never intended that the courts should be a democratic institution. They could scarcely have imagined today's vast federal executive establishment and its powers to regulate the economy and so many other facets of our lives. Both the courts and the bureaucracies are critical, and often misunderstood, policymakers in the American system.

Of course, almost every policy adopted by government costs money. We set aside a whole chapter (16) to describe the budgetary process, which spends about a quarter of our gross national product. Especially at a time of staggering federal deficits, an understanding of the budgetary process is one key to understanding American government.

Politics and Policy in Washington

11

MEMO

Much of our government and politics takes place in a tiny ten-square-mile area called the District of Columbia. Its only city is Washington, D.C. Its only real industry is government. Government is to Washington what steel is to Bethlehem and computers are to San Jose. Washington is a gossipy, goldfish bowl sort of place. Public policy is made at cocktail parties as well as in Congress and the agencies. Our purpose here is to understand Washington and its politics and government.

Chapter 11 sketches a big picture of government in Washington, while the next four fill in the details. It is intended to bridge the gap between our coverage of the linkage institutions (Chapters 6–10) and the next four chapters, which cover Congress, the president, the bureaucracy, and the courts. The linkage institutions, if they are working well, present to the government a *policy agenda*. This is the set of issues that government actually addresses. After we take a guided tour of our nation's capital, here is what we will cover in this chapter:

- *Official* and *unofficial* Washington are bound inextricably together. Official Washington is housed in well-known edifices: the White House, the Capitol, the Supreme Court Building, the halls of the bureaucracies. Unofficial Washington, composed of the politicos and the press, is housed all over Washington.
- The *public agenda* and the *governmental agenda*. These are what the people want government to pay attention to, and what government actually pays attention to.
- The *shapers of the policy agenda*. Policy entrepreneurs take hold of an issue and make it theirs. Their goal is to put it high on the governmental agenda.
- The *Washington media* are important, both because they control information going out of Washington and also because they control information among the power-holders of Washington.

"**W**ASHINGTON," says former Secretary of State Henry Kissinger,

is like a Roman arena. Gladiators do battle, and the spectators determine who survives by giving the appropriate signal, just as in the Coliseum. Barely noticed by the rest of the country, leaks to media serve Washington as clues to power and influence. . . . The journalists act simultaneously as neutral conduit and tribunal, shielding their witnesses by the principle of "protection of sources. . . ." The people may have a "right to know"—but only what the press chooses to tell it. [1]

This is a hard-edged and hard-boiled view of Washington. Henry Kissinger, though, was in a position to know. Washington can be a city of intrigue and of ruthless competition for power and prestige. It is also a place where men and women grapple with the tough questions of domestic and foreign-policy making. None of them—not even the centerpiece of official Washington, the president—is omnicient. All are human; most are well-meaning.

There is, of course, official Washington. In it are the edifices and the institutions of government: the executive, legislative, and judicial branches. Schoolchildren learn that our government in Washington is a "separation of powers." Harvard political scientist Richard Neustadt thinks that description is misleading. Our government is, he says, "separated institutions sharing powers." [2] Rarely does one institution work independently of the others. The legislative process involves the bureaucratic agencies, the Congress, the president, and, often later on, the courts. Thus, government takes place in and between the edifices of Washington.

Yet politics takes place everywhere, permeating both official and unofficial Washington. Let us take a closer look at this small area, in which so much of our nation's politics takes place.

THE WASHINGTON COMMUNITY

A Washington Tour

All things considered, Washington, D.C., is one of America's most attractive places. Once a swamp on the banks of the Potomac, it is now home to 623,000 people and is the heart of a metropolitan area of over 3 million. Culturally, it rivals other world capitals and other cultural centers such as New York City.

Some cities (such as Detroit or Pittsburgh) grew because they were major centers of industrial production. Some (such as Miami Beach or Las Vegas) grew because they were tourist meccas. Some (such as Carl Sandburg's Chicago) grew because they were "hog butcher to the world." Washington grew for one reason alone: It housed the federal government. As government grew, so did Washington. Like Smyrna and Bethlehem, Washington is a one-industry city.

You can ride one of the nation's finest mass transit systems (the Metro) into and out of downtown Washington. Interstate 95 provides easy access

[1] Henry Kissinger, *Years of Upheaval* (Boston: Little, Brown, 1982), p. 421.
[2] Richard Neustadt, *Presidential Power* (New York: John Wiley, 1960), p. 34.

by car to the heart of America's government, though you might find driving *in* Washington a challenge. French engineer Pierre L'Enfant, who designed the American capital in 1791, avoided the grid system of streets and laid out the main arteries like the spokes of a wheel. 1 Many tourists prefer to catch taxis downtown. Taxi rates are regulated directly by Congress, which keeps fares in the government district quite low.

If you prefer to stroll, one good route will take you down Pennsylvania Avenue through the heart of governmental Washington. The formal address of the White House is 1600 Pennsylvania Avenue, although you should not have to look for the street number. If you start there, you can see the locations of all three branches of government, and a good sample of its bureaucratic offices, by heading southeast on Pennsylvania Avenue. You will have to go around the block that holds the massive Treasury Department building, guarded by a statue of our first secretary of the treasury, Alexander Hamilton. They do not print our money there (the Bureau of Engraving and Printing is on the river), but they do much to regulate its value. Your continued journey will take you past the Department of Commerce, a cabinet department, and the Interstate Commerce Commission, the first of the regulatory agencies that are sometimes called "the fourth branch of government." The Internal Revenue Service, which collects your taxes, is next, followed by the Department of Justice. Across the street from Justice is the headquarters of the Federal Bureau of Investigation, whose design was minutely supervised by one of the most powerful Washington bureaucrats in the twentieth century, the late FBI director J. Edgar Hoover. Off to your right you can see the Mall, the location of some of the world's finest museums.

Another few blocks will bring you to the United States Capitol. Once almost the entire government was housed in the Capitol building. Now only the Congress is located there and even the Congress has expanded into huge office buildings that surround the Capitol and are connected to it by a labyrinth of underground passes and tramways. If you went in to watch the House or Senate in action, chances are you would be disappointed. Even when Congress is in session, action in the House or Senate chambers is usually slow. One member may be making a speech to a small audience mostly interested in answering its mail. Most members are likely to be found in committee or subcommittee meetings, or in their offices taking calls and meeting lobbyists or constituents. If it is necessary for all members to assemble for a vote, the action changes rapidly. Buzzers and bells all over the Capitol and its office complexes summon the representatives and senators to their posts.

Just behind the Capitol is the Supreme Court building, above the portals of which are carved the words, "Equal Justice under Law." The Supreme Court, consisting of nine justices who do most of their own work, is the quietest branch of government. Yet as Justice Oliver Wendell Holmes once remarked, "We are quiet here, but it is the quiet of a storm center." In 1857, for instance, the Supreme Court had held, in the *Dred Scott* case, that slaves were barely human and not at all citizens. Almost a hundred years later, another Supreme Court held that school segregation by race was unconstitutional, unleashing decades of debate about desegregation and busing. Today, it remains very much a quiet eye in the midst of a storm.

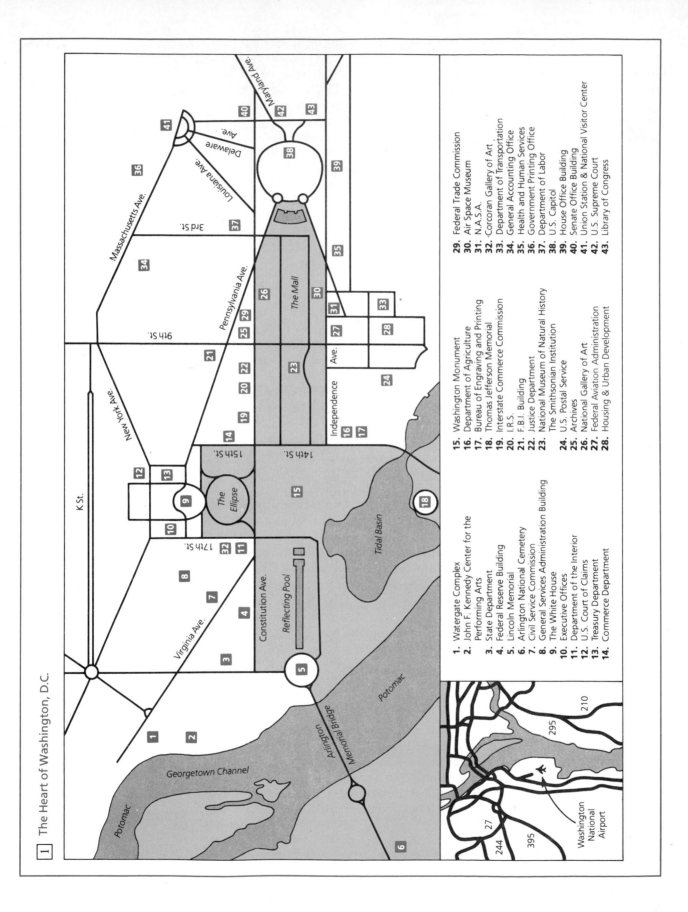

1 The Heart of Washington, D.C.

1. Watergate Complex
2. John F. Kennedy Center for the Performing Arts
3. State Department
4. Federal Reserve Building
5. Lincoln Memorial
6. Arlington National Cemetery
7. Civil Service Commission
8. General Services Administration Building
9. The White House
10. Executive Offices
11. Department of the Interior
12. U.S. Court of Claims
13. Treasury Department
14. Commerce Department
15. Washington Monument
16. Department of Agriculture
17. Bureau of Engraving and Printing
18. Thomas Jefferson Memorial
19. Interstate Commerce Commission
20. I.R.S.
21. F.B.I. Building
22. Justice Department
23. National Museum of Natural History
   The Smithsonian Institution
24. U.S. Postal Service
25. Archives
26. National Gallery of Art
27. Federal Aviation Administration
28. Housing & Urban Development
29. Federal Trade Commission
30. Air Space Museum
31. N.A.S.A.
32. Corcoran Gallery of Art
33. Department of Transportation
34. General Accounting Office
35. Health and Human Services
36. Government Printing Office
37. Department of Labor
38. U.S. Capitol
39. House Office Building
40. Senate Office Building
41. Union Station & National Visitor Center
42. U.S. Supreme Court
43. Library of Congress

That is the official side of Washington. But there is an unofficial Washington too—Washington is not only the home of the government, but the home of those who seek something from it, the Washington lobbies that seek to secure favorable policies or to prevent unfavorable ones. There are thousands of lobbies in Washington. Almost every major interest group has its headquarters there. The big ones are housed in gleaming buildings, and the little ones in rented walk-ups. They are in Washington to have easier access to Congress and the bureaucracies. The United Egg Producers at 499 South Capitol Street in southwest Washington has ready access to the House subcommittee on Livestock, Dairy, and Poultry and the Senate subcommittee on Agricultural Production, Marketing, and Stabilization of Prices. The egg producers also have easy access to the Department of Agriculture's Poultry and Dairy Quality Division, located in the Agriculture building at 14th and Independence. And lobbyists need to see one another. The Poultry and Egg Institute of America is across the Potomac in Arlington, Virginia. The National Turkey Federation is in Reston, Virginia. Small interest groups and big ones interact regularly and repeatedly with government and its agencies, and with each other. Thousands of interest groups are headquartered on the great avenues of the capital city.

Getting Ahead in Washington

To describe Washington as a city of government buildings and interest group headquarters is to give an incomplete picture. Washington does not live by government alone, but also by politics, an occupation that attracts a singular set of men and women. One theme uniting almost all politicians is ambition. In the 1930s, a young man came to Washington as a secretary to Texas Congressman Richard Kleburg. The young man (who lodged at a former women's hotel, the Dodge), soon discovered that his congressman was less interested in legislating than in socializing, and Lyndon Johnson quickly took charge of the office. Few specific political or policy beliefs intruded on Johnson's ambition. Said a young contemporary of his: "Lyndon Johnson believed in *nothing*, nothing but his own ambition. Everything he did—*everything*—was for his ambition." [3] That ambition impelled him to his own seat in Congress, to the Senate, and later to the vice-presidency. He became president after John Kennedy's assassination in 1963.

Ambition is still a driving force in Washington. Newly appointed as legal counsel to President Richard M. Nixon, young John Dean observed ambition and the pursuit not only of power, but also of the trappings of power: "Everyone jockeyed for a position close to the president's ear, and even an unseasoned observer could sense minute changes in status. Success and failure could be seen in the size, decor, and location of offices." [4]

Ambition is required to be a success in Washington, D.C. The city is full of ambitious people with new ideas, proposals, and solutions. The

[3] Robert A. Caro, *The Years of Lyndon Johnson: The Path To Power* (New York: Knopf, 1982) p. 274.

[4] John Dean, *Blind Ambition* (New York: Simon and Schuster, 1976), p. 20.

Official Washington. *Four institutions—the presidency, the Congress, the bureaucracies, and the courts—make up official Washington. Each has one or more buildings that symbolize and house its work. The president is often at work with key aides in the Oval Office, located in the west wing of the White House and separated by a long hallway from the living quarters of the president and his family. Members of Congress (here is Representative Claudine Schneider of Rhode Island) work in a crowded honeycomb of offices, committee rooms, and chambers in and around the United States Capitol. Although bureaucracies are intimately involved in Washington politics, most federal employees perform routine work, such as sorting mail for the Postal Service. (Actually, less than 10 percent of all federal civil servants work in Washington.) The last of the four major official institutions is the courts. The Supreme Court is the pinnacle of the American judicial system, but it hears only a tiny fraction of all legal cases. In Washington and elsewhere, the federal district courts hear the bulk of cases brought to the federal courts.*

engines of ambition are sometimes fueled at the expense other values, however. A handful of Nixon men, Dean included, followed their ambition and forgot their commitments in the ugly events of Watergate in 1972 through 1974. On your walking tour of Washington, you may have detoured past the most famous apartment building in Washington, the Watergate complex. There, men employed by Richard Nixon's reelection committee let their ambition and their good sense run amok when they burgled the headquarters of the Democratic National Committee in the Watergate Towers. Where there is too much unbridled ambition, the potential for corruption is enhanced.

More often, ambition is channeled into plain hard work. Although some members of Congress deliberately set an unhurried pace, the more typical member bounces from one committee meeting to another (members are not infrequently scheduled for four to seven subcommittee meetings, all at the same hour of the morning), takes a hurried call from a worried constituent, and pulls together information on tomorrow's legislative agenda.

In the relatively small physical space of Washington, ambitious men and women pursue political power and shape our public policies. The institutions these politicians inhabit shape our lives, through the public policy choices that are made and through the enforcement and implementation of these policies. Most of the rest of this book is devoted to the people and institutions of Washington, D.C. Before we study them in detail (beginning with Chapter 12), we will take a general look at the four major official policymaking institutions and at two unofficial but extremely influential institutions.

OFFICIAL WASHINGTON

Official Washington consists of the policymakers and the policymaking institutions of government. Each of the four major policymaking institutions—the Congress, the presidency, the courts, and the bureaucracies—is a separate institution, jealous of its powers, perquisites, and prerogatives. But none of them make policy in isolation, even though we study them individually. Institutions are on the policymaking stage together, in chorus. All four major institutions in Washington have two things in common: they have goals which they want to achieve, and they have constituencies they want to satisfy.

Congress: The Politics of Representation

Congress makes our laws, levies our taxes, and spends our federal budget. In earlier years, Congress was a simpler place. When young Lyndon Johnson arrived in Washington in the 1930s, each senator and member of the House of Representatives had only a secretary. Today, a staff of 39,000 serves the 435 representatives and 100 senators in Washington and in their home state or district. Those 535 members are divided along many lines: liberals and conservatives, Democrats and Republicans, farmbelt and city, Frostbelt and Sunbelt. Every one of them has at least one thing in common with the other 534: They are all politicians, willing to invest hours of time and thousands, even millions of dollars (usually someone else's) getting and keeping their seats.

Every individual has countless goals, priorities, and preferences, and members of Congress are no exception. Many are there to foster some political cause or belief. North Carolina's Senator Jesse Helms carried a variety of causes with him to Washington, including opposition to school busing and abortion. Most are there to advance their district's or state's economic interests. In the 1970s Senators Magnuson and Jackson of Washington "spent two years trying to sustain government [support] for Boeing's supersonic transport," knowing that it would benefit employment in Seattle. But "in the end they failed and thousands of constituents were thrown out of work."[5] Others succeed in returning benefits—dams, industrial and agricultural subsidies, business loans, government projects, and so on—to their constituencies.

One reason politicians provide these benefits is the pursuit of a key goal: reelection. Services to constituents can be performed out of sheer altruism and goodness of heart, but both the noble of heart and the less noble work hard at constituency service because it is fundamental to their reelection.[6] Almost everything members of the House and Senate do is intended to enhance reelectability. Kiewiet and McCubbins even found evidence that the federal budget (particularly those parts providing such constituency-oriented services as farm loans) increases more in election years than in nonelection years.[7] The way members of Congress vote on major bills is also shaped by their guesses about the constituency's reaction.

The Presidency: The Politics of Leadership

At the epicenter of Washington is the Oval Office, the president's office, thirty-four feet long by twenty-eight feet wide. We depend on the president for that amorphous quality called leadership. When asked what quality they valued most in a president, a plurality of people put leadership at the top.[8]

In our awe of the presidents we think great and our anger at the ones we think let us down, we may lose sight of the fact that presidents have goals, too. Paul Light identifies three main presidential goals.[9] First, reelection is a goal of most first-term presidents. Even those who are completing their constitutionally limited second term would like their party and their protégés to do well. Second, says Light, presidents seek a place in

---

[5] R. Douglas Arnold, *Congress and the Bureaucracy: A Theory of Influence* (New Haven, Conn.: Yale University Press, 1979), p. 32.

[6] Morris Fiorina, *Congress, Keystone of the Washington Establishment* (New Haven, Conn.: Yale University Press, 1977).

[7] D. Roderick Kiewiet and Mathew B. McCubbins, "In the Mood: The Effect of Election Year Considerations upon the Appropriations Process," paper delivered at the annual meeting of the Midwest Political Science Association, Cincinnati, Ohio, April 15–18, 1981.

[8] Stephen J. Wayne, "Great Expectations: What People Want from Presidents," in Thomas E. Cronin (ed.), *Rethinking the Presidency* (Boston: Little, Brown, 1982), p. 194.

[9] Paul Light, "Presidents as Domestic Policymakers," in Cronin (ed.), *Rethinking the Presidency*, p. 362.

history: "Each corridor in the White House contains subtle reminders of a president's potential place in history; each portrait hanging in the halls suggests the impact of historical judgment." [10] Late one night, just before he decided to resign the presidency in disgrace over the ugly events of Watergate, Richard M. Nixon called Secretary of State Henry Kissinger to the White House. The atmosphere was cheerless as Kissinger talked with the first man ever to be driven from the presidency. What Nixon wanted to talk about, though, was his "place in history." Kissinger assured him that future historians would treat him more kindly than the Washington community was then treating him. [11] Third, presidents want to enact their policy agenda, get their platform put into law, keep the economy humming, and introduce policy innovations. In a word, presidents want to make good policy, however they define it.

The Bureaucracies: The Politics of Administration

If the bureaucracies are not the unsung heroes of American government, then they are at least unsung. People who work for government are often called *bureaucrats*, by which term we at least mean them no disservice. Only 8 percent of the 3 million Americans who work for the federal government actually work in or near Washington, D.C., but all the headquarters are located there. They are in the ancient Treasury building, the old State Department at "Foggy Bottom," the Central Intelligence Agency in suburban McLean, the National Science Foundation around the corner from the White House, and others scattered all over the city and its environs.

Bureaucracies are a diverse group; even so, they have goals in common. One, of course, is for their own job security and pay. Few bureaucrats admire the Reagan administration. One reason is that Reagan's first director of the Office of Personnel Management (the government's personnel office), political scientist Donald Devine, implied that bureaucrats are lazy, overpaid, and none too competent. When President Reagan began his second term with a $200 billion budget deficit, he proposed, as one solution, to cut the pay of government workers by 5 percent. But most public employees see the work they are doing as important, deserving of public support. The lawyers working for the Environmental Protection Agency, the postal clerks, and the secretaries in the Bureau of Indian Affairs each see their own work as important. One presumes that the public gets better service from those who value their missions and are fairly compensated for them, than from those who do not care.

Douglas Arnold lists three bureaucratic goals: budget stability, budgetary growth, and a mission of public service. [12] Agencies prefer budget stability for a good reason: People desire to work in an environment of certainty rather than chaos. To enhance their budgets and for other

[10] Ibid., p. 363.
[11] Kissinger, *Years of Upheaval*, pp. 1207–09.
[12] Arnold, *Congress and the Bureaucracy*, p. 21.

reasons, agencies work closely with interest groups. Agency officials are naturally committed to the groups with which they work. No one watches the Department of Agriculture dairy division closer than the dairy lobby. Over every bureaucratic shoulder is an interest group. When the relationships between bureaucratic agencies, congressional committees, and interest groups become cozy, we call them "iron triangles" (see pages 472–473).

The Courts: The Politics of Justice

More than any other policymaking institution, the courts foster an image of splendid isolation. Members of Congress want all the press coverage they can get. In contrast, even when *The Brethren*, a gossip-filled and often unflattering book on the Supreme Court, was published, the Supreme Court's press office tactfully declined to comment.

Federal judges, including those on the Supreme Court, are appointed by presidents, with Senate approval, essentially for life. They have no electoral needs to fulfill and, being an inexpensive part of government, make few budget claims on other institutions. But the judges also have goals and constituencies. Like presidents, judges—especially the select few on the Supreme Court—are conscious of their place in history. Presidents seek to be associated with good policy; justices want to be remembered for good decisions, well articulated and firmly grounded in the constitution and the law. Though unelected, justices and judges also have constituencies. One important one is the legal profession itself. Lawyers weigh a judge on the basis of his or her opinions; a judge's place in history is determined by what lawyers think of these opinions.

Even this self-isolated branch of government interacts with other elements of the Washington community. The judicial norm is to avoid any compromising contacts with political Washington (although former Justice Fortas used to advise President Lyndon Johnson, and Chief Justice Burger was free with his advice to President Richard Nixon). Still, the shadow of the Court looms large. More than anything else, it was the Supreme Court's decision in *United States* v. *Nixon* (1974) that led to Nixon's resignation and his cheerless discussion with Henry Kissinger about his place in history. Having discovered that Richard Nixon taped conversations in the Oval Office, both Congress and the courts trying the Watergate cases wanted them as evidence. When Nixon refused to turn them over, the courts ordered the president to do so. When the Supreme Court upheld the order, the beginning of the end of the Nixon presidency had come.

UNOFFICIAL WASHINGTON: THE POLITICOS AND THE PRESS

The Politicos

It is hard enough to understand official Washington. Harder still is it to understand unofficial Washington and to realize that it is bound like a tangled skein to the official government. Author Theodore H. White speaks of

> not the schoolbook Washington of tradition, but the real Washington, the jungle of special interests, claimants, lobbies, and cause groups. It is difficult to describe this Washington, that shifting menagerie of cold-eyed money men and hot-eyed moralists who shuffle through the marble anterooms of the Capitol, who slink or stalk through the corridors of the Senate and House office buildings. [13]

This "menagerie of cold-eyed money men and hot-eyed moralists" makes up unofficial Washington. We call them "the politicos," and there are many breeds. We met one in Chapter 10 when we described the lobbyists, a cornerstone of unofficial Washington. There are other Washington politicos, too.

In 1967, when Richard Nixon made a guest appearance on the Mike Douglas show, he met a brash, twenty-eight-year-old producer named Roger Ailes, who lectured the former vice-president about the importance of television in politics. [14] Impressed with Ailes, Nixon hired him to produce television commercials when he ran for president in 1968. Today, Ailes Communication, Inc. is a leading, Republican-leaning "media consulting" firm. It handled the media, for example, for Phil Gramm's successful Senate bid in 1984. Ailes, like other Washington politicos, is a political consultant.

The **political consultant** is a relative newcomer to the Washington establishment. A political consultant, says Larry Sabato, is "a campaign professional who is engaged primarily in the provision of advice and services (such as polling, media creation and production, and direct mail fundraising) to candidates, their campaigns, and other political groups. . . ." [15] The political consultant is the high priest of modern political technology. Not all, but most, political consultants have their offices in Washington. Their job as "hired guns" is to help candidates win elections. Sabato quotes one: "When it comes to political consulting, the name of the game is winning on election day. We do everything we are legally and morally able to do to win." [16] The *National Journal* called consultant Robert Squier the "campaign coach of the year" in 1984. [17] He created television commercials for six Democratic candidates and five of them won. One was Tennessee's new Senator Albert Gore, Jr. Political consulting firms, of course, do not come cheap. A half a million dollars can easily be sunk into a Senate campaign's media budget.

Some political consultants are quite specialized. For example, V. Lance Tarrance, who polled for victorious Senator Phil Gramm in 1984, specializes in polling for Republicans. Pat Caddell's Cambridge Survey

The Politicos. *Unofficial Washington includes the politicos and the press. Political consultants and pollsters make Washington their headquarters because most politicians are there, or would like to be there. Patrick Caddell is a Democratic-leaning pollster, whose services to President Carter firmly established him as a political professional. Caddell's home base is Boston, but much of his business is in Washington and in the congressional constituencies. Politicos are hired by campaigns and by interest groups to conduct surveys, to manage campaigns, to lobby, and to alter public images.*

[13] Theodore H. White, *America in Search of Itself* (New York: Harper and Row, 1982), p. 203.

[14] The story of the first Nixon–Ailes meeting is in David Halberstam, *The Powers That Be* (New York: Dell Books, 1979), p. 824–25.

[15] Larry Sabato, "Political Consultants and Campaign Technology," in Allan J. Cigler and Burdett A. Loomis (eds.), *Interest Group Politics* (Washington, D.C.: Congressional Quarterly Press, 1983), p. 146.

[16] Ibid., p. 148.

[17] *National Journal*, November 10, 1984, p. 2173.

Research, Inc. is a leading pollster for Democratic candidates; his most prominent client was Georgia Governor and then President Jimmy Carter. Still other firms specialize in political public relations. ☐2

Pollsters, consultants, public relations specialists, and other professional politicos have their offices in Washington for good reason. That is where the politicians are (or want to be) and that is where the political media are.

The Washington Media

Washington is a city of news. More news is leaked in Washington than in any city in the world. And more reporters are there to scoop it up than anywhere else. Ronald Reagan once called Washington "one gigantic ear."

The Washington media sit astride two key streams of communication: news flowing out of Washington and news flowing within it. Controlling the flow of information within and out of Washington is in the hands of a relatively small number of institutions. Stephen Hess has identified an "inner ring" of Washington media, those institutions that truly define what is news and thus shape the nation's policy agenda.[18] The "inner ring" consists of the three major networks (NBC, CBS, and ABC), the two wire services (AP and UPI), and three major newspapers (the *New York Times*, the *Washington Post*, and the *Wall Street Journal*). These media heavyweights do not merely mirror events and doings; they shape them. They define for official Washington—presidents, members of Congress, agency officials—what is important and what is being discussed by whom. Two pieces of information are made available every morning to

[18] Stephen Hess, *The Washington Reporters* (Washington: The Brookings Institution, 1981), Chap. 1.

☐2 Signing on a PR Firm Can Even Help a Nation's Image

Of course, corporations have public relations units. Today, more and more groups, lobbies, and PACs spend money on "PR" firms to tidy up their public image. Even nations have gotten into the act, hiring public relations firms to improve their public image in the United States. Manheim and Albritton report that "the 1970s saw a veritable explosion of lobbying and public information campaigns on the part of foreign governments." Much is at stake. Aid and trade are important to every nation, and the United States is the world's largest aider and trader. Thus foreign nations, like corporations and groups, have started hiring PR firms to boost their image here.

But does it work? In an innovative study, Manheim and Albritton studied six nations (the Republic of Korea, the Philippines, Yugoslavia, Argentina, Indonesia, and Zimbabwe) that hired American public relations firms to improve their image in the United States. (They also selected one other country, Mexico, which had considered doing the same thing, but declined to do so.) Each of these countries had some image problems with Washington and the American public. The authors then systematically compared coverage of these seven nations in the *New York Times* both before and after signing on their PR consultants. The result: in the six nations hiring their PR firm, positive images presented in the *Times* increased; Mexico's image was unchanged.

If Manheim and Albritton's evidence can be generalized, it appears that even foreign countries—much less American corporations or politicians—can alter a public image through successful public relations activities.

Source: Jarol B. Manheim and Robert B. Albritton, "Changing National Images: International Public Relations and Media Agenda Setting," *American Political Science Review* 78 (September 1984): 641–58.

The Press. *NBC's Connie Chung graduated from correspondent to anchorwoman. The importance of the Washington press in defining the governmental and public agenda is well-known. It also plays another key role: it is the communication system for the nation's policymakers. The three television networks and a handful of major newspapers are a leading source of information about happenings in Washington for those in Washington who get things done.*

the president of the United States: One is a daily intelligence briefing on developments around the world; the second is a set of extracts from national media coverage.

Later in this chapter, we will explore how the media shape the Washington agenda. Both the politicos and the media interact closely with each other and, of course, with official Washington. Collectively, they shape the Washington policy agenda.

THE POLICY AGENDA

When someone says to you, what's your agenda?, he or she wants to know something about your priorities: what you will do first and what you will save till later. Governments have agendas, too. John Kingdon describes the **policy agenda** as "the list of subjects or problems to which government officials, and people outside of government closely associated with those officials, are paying some serious attention at any given time."[19] One way of looking at politics in Washington is to see it as a gigantic effort to alter the priorities of government. Interest groups, the press, public relations firms, bureaucracies—and, of course, the president and members of Congress—constantly try to get their priorities first on everyone else's priority agenda.

The public has an agenda, too. As Cobb and Elder put it, "in a democratic policy, the formal agenda of government presumably should reflect the problems, priorities and concerns of the community at large," that is, the people.[20] If the public's agenda and the government's agenda coincide, linkage institutions are working well.

[19] John Kingdon, *Agendas, Alternatives, and Public Policies* (Boston: Little, Brown, 1984), p. 3.
[20] Charles D. Cobb and Roger W. Elder, "Agenda-Building and the Politics of Aging," *Policy Studies Journal* 13(September 1984):118.

The Two Agendas

The **public agenda** consists of issues the public as a whole considers important. The **governmental agenda** consists of those issues policymakers actually consider. In a democratic government, there should be a close correspondence between what people think government should be handling and what government is handling. The linkage institutions (parties, groups, and elections) should work to put the public's concerns at the top of the government's priorities, as we have seen in the last three chapters. The more distant the two agendas, the more government is ignoring popular preferences. If government institutions are responding to issues that people do not care about, or ignoring the ones that really matter to them, linkage institutions have failed.

The Public Agenda. The public agenda represents public opinion about which issues are most important. Different groups, of course, have different priorities. Gay rights activists in California are not likely to want their elected representative to concentrate on farm problems. They may be willing for the representative to be concerned about such problems, but they will want gay rights to be his or her first concern. Kentucky tobacco farmers do not want their representative to get so wrapped up in peddling national health insurance that he or she forgets to push for tobacco-oriented policies.

Even though different individuals and groups have different agendas, it is possible to locate some overall concerns of the public. These concerns and priorities change over time. For many years, the Gallup Poll has asked its respondents this question: "What do you think is the most important problem facing this country today?" Answers to this question give us some clues to people's priorities. ③ During the 1950s, people thought foreign affairs—what we call *the global connection*—was the country's biggest problem. In the 1960s, the Vietnam War dominated our political lives and kept foreign policy in first place among the country's problems. Social issues—civil rights, crime, racial conflict, drug use and abuse, and other social problems—rivaled foreign affairs as a national worry in the 1960s and early 1970s. But for most of the 1970s, the state of the economy won the battle for first place on the public agenda. High taxes, high inflation, and high unemployment added up to high public concern over the (apparently sorry) state of the American economy. Public concern over the economy waned somewhat in the 1980s, because of growth in the GNP and great reductions in inflation.

The Governmental Agenda. Every group and every political actor wants his or her issue placed prominently on the policy agenda. In Congress, there are almost 10,000 bills and resolutions introduced by members each year. The claims on the Supreme Court's agenda have grown, too. In 1940, less than 1000 cases were appealed to the nation's highest court; by 1960, 2000 petitioners wanted the Supreme Court to hear their cases; in the 1980s, about 5000 petitions annually will come to the Court. Every edifice in Washington will face competition for its scarce time and energy.

Faced with this escalation of demands, policymakers have to say "first

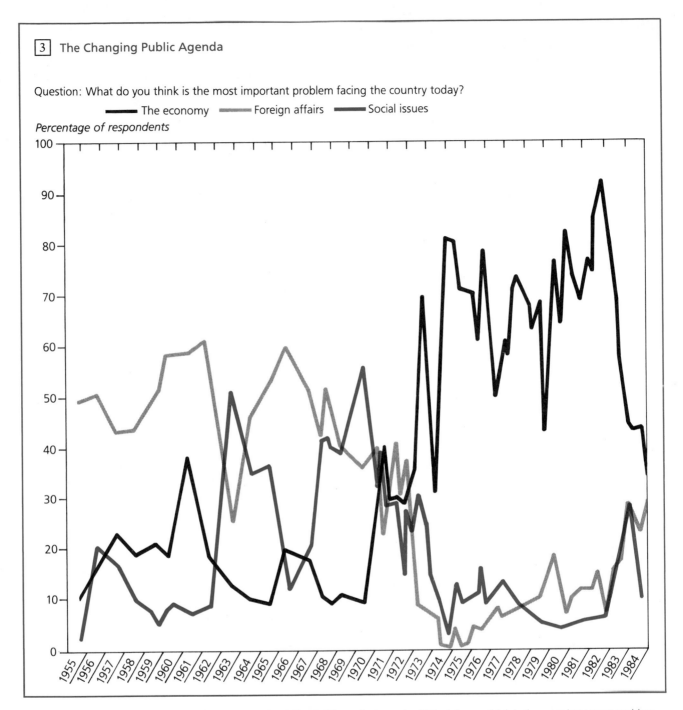

Question: What do you think is the most important problem facing the country today?

—— The economy ━━━ Foreign affairs ━━━ Social issues

Percentage of respondents

For years, the Gallup Poll has asked people: "What do you think is the most important problem facing this country today?" Here is a look at how Americans have answered this question in terms of three broad clusters of issues—foreign affairs, social issues, and the state of the economy—from 1955 to 1984.

things first." Every institution of government develops a set of **gatekeeping** mechanisms to regulate their flow of business. Congress uses a powerful committee system to winnow down the thousands of bills into a manageable number. The Supreme Court focuses only on issues its justices think represent important cases. Presidents rely on their key aides to screen issues and organize the president's agenda.

345

The institutions of government, of course, shape one another's agenda. The president, as chief legislator, sends a budget and a set of legislative priorities to Congress. Congress, in turn, will try to shape the administration's agenda. One way is to hold hearings on administration policies. There, a cabinet secretary may joust with congressional committee members about administration policies on Nicaragua or cleanups of chemical dumps.

How Issues Get on the Policy Agenda

John Kingdon, who more than anyone else has studied the process of agenda formation, offers a useful metaphor for thinking about the policy agenda. Borrowing from the biologists who posit a kind of primeval soup out of which the molecules of life were born, he suggests that we think of a "policy primeval soup." Thousands of ideas for policy are floating around in the primeval soup. As with the molecules of life itself, only a few will survive.[21] Many of these ideas come from what Jack Walker has called **policy communities**,[22] loose-knit groups with no formal structure. Each policy area—drugs, aging, water pollution control, and so on—has its own policy community. They are the gatekeepers of ideas; being policy specialists, they are supposed to know what will work and what will not. A policy community will include a number of policy specialists:

— *Bureaucratic officials*, typically expert in the subject matter of their agency.
— *Scholars, academics, and "think tank" members* who write and research in the particular area.
— *Lobbyists* who are interest groups' knowledgeables.
— *Congressional staff members* who work regularly in the policy area.

Members of policy communities know one another, read one another's writings, and see one another at meetings. Often, an academic specialist will go to work—perhaps part-time as a consultant—for some bureaucratic agency. A congressional staff member may take a job as an executive of a professional association, even as a lobbyist. All these members of policy networks are specialists; their specialty is knowledge.

But in this blooming, buzzing confusion of ideas, someone has to get an idea moved from the policy primeval soup to the concrete policy agenda. Someone has to be the broker for any new policy idea.

Policy Entrepreneurs. In economics, an *entrepreneur* is one with capital to invest in an idea for making money. In politics, a **policy entrepreneur** is one who invests his or her political "capital" in an issue.[23] Kingdon says that the policy entrepreneur "could be in or out of

---

[21] Kingdon, *Agendas, Alternatives, and Public Policies*, pp. 122–23.

[22] Jack L. Walker, "The Diffusion of Knowledge and Policy Change: Toward a Theory of Agenda Setting," paper presented at the Annual Meeting of the American Political Science Association, Chicago, Illinois, August 29–September 2, 1974.

[23] One important entrepreneurial study of politics is Norman Frohlich, Joe A. Oppenheimer, and Oran R. Young, *Political Leadership and Collective Goods* (Princeton, N.J.: Princeton University Press, 1972).

government, in elected or appointed positions, in interest groups or research organizations."[24] The entrepreneur has to believe in the policy idea, to commit to it, and to persuade others of its wisdom, even its necessity. Said one policy participant to Kingdon:

> If you try to sell an idea by saying, "Well, this might work, but on the other hand there are problems with it, but the data show this, but there are problems with the data, so we have to qualify it, but nevertheless I think we should perhaps try this out," you won't get anywhere. You have to go in there and say, "This is the greatest thing to come along in years."[25]

The policy entrepreneur who leads a winning campaign gains reputation and power. "Far-sighted politicians," says Robert Eyestone, "may anticipate the direction an issue will take and act in advance of public sentiment."[26] Representative Jack Kemp of New York and Senator William Roth of Delaware were "supply-side" policy entrepreneurs, urging for years that government ought to cut taxes to free money for investment and economic growth. The 1980 Republican platform endorsed their idea. And when the Reagan administration came into office, it peddled the same policy idea. Senator Bill Bradley and Congressman Richard Gephardt put a tax reform measure on the policy agenda in 1983. It proposed a drastic overhaul of the taxing system, eliminating many deductions and moving toward simpler taxpaying categories. It was seriously considered as Congress labored over tax reform in 1984 and was picked up by the Reagan administration in 1985.

Of course, policy entrepreneurs can miscalculate and get behind an issue that turns out to be a political disaster. Eyestone adds, "The response to the anticipated issue may not work correctly . . . leaving the politician holding the bag, and what is worse, credited with an unnecessary failure."[27] This is why politicians often use *trial balloons* or *leaks* to put forward a new idea. "Unidentified administration sources" are quoted in the media. The government is planning, the press says, a new tax reform or a cutback in tobacco subsidies. If the hue and cry is explosive, the government can deny it ever thought of such an outrage.

Nongovernmental actors are also policy entrepreneurs. Sometimes they aspire to public office, but often they do not. Sometimes they are leaders of an interest group, but not always. Here are some examples:

— *Ralph Nader,* consumer protection advocate. No other person in America is quite so identified with a single major issue as Nader. Operating at first out of his apartment in Washington, he has become a leader of several organizations (commonly called "Nader's raiders") who research and lobby for consumer protection legislation.
— *Arthur Laffer,* a University of Southern California business school professor, who (it is said) drew what came to be called the "Laffer Curve" on the back of a cocktail napkin. It purported to show that

Policy Entrepreneurs. *A policy entrepreneur can be inside or outside government. The entrepreneur invests his or her political capital in an issue, intending to move it to a higher place on the governmental agenda. Florida's Senator Paula Hawkins is a conservative Republican, typically opposed to federal intervention in social problems. But even she became an entrepreneur for legislation to punish and identify child abuse. She testified to her own experience as an abused child, helping to put child abuse on the congressional agenda.*

[24] Kingdon, *Agendas, Alternatives, and Public Policies,* p. 129.
[25] Ibid., p. 134.
[26] Robert Eyestone, *From Social Issues to Public Policy* (New York: Wiley, 1978), p. 37.
[27] Ibid., p. 37.

the more government taxed, the more disincentives to work it built in to the economy, and, thus, higher taxes never yielded higher returns for the government. Laffer became a guru of the Supply-Side Economics School, and much cited and quoted by Reagan administration economists.

— *Mary Lasker*, wealthy philanthropist and cancer crusader. After her husband died of cancer, Lasker set out to make cancer research a national priority. Working behind the scenes in committees and with policymakers, she deserves much of the credit for the billions of dollars the federal government has invested in the crusade against cancer.[28]

— *Phyllis Schlafly*, an Alton, Illinois, housewife who led what was at first almost a one-woman campaign against the ratification of the Equal Rights Amendment. Long a leader in conservative causes, Schlafly helped persuade many state legislatures that the ERA would have far-reaching—and pernicious—consequences. No friend of women's rights groups, she demonstrated that entrepreneurs can oppose as well as support policy change.

Yet policy entrepreneurs can also cry in the wilderness without being heard. They can invest their capital in a lost cause or an idea whose time never comes. In a government running partly on inertia, the opportunities for change may be few. What Kingdon calls the **policy window** is open only sporadically. A policy window, he says, "is an opportunity for advocates of proposals to push their pet solutions, or to push attention to

---

[28] A valuable study of how cancer got on the policy agenda, largely through the efforts of Mary Lasker, is in Robert Rettig, *Cancer Crusade* (Princeton, N.J.: Princeton University Press, 1977).

Phyllis Schlafly: Campaigner Against the ERA. *Often billed as "an Alton, Illinois housewife," Phyllis Schlafly is much more than that. She has earned a law degree and run a successful campaign against the passage of the Equal Rights Amendment.*

Schlafly's conservative credentials were established by her authorship of five books and the Phyllis Schlafly Report, *a periodic newsletter sent to thousands of conservatives across the country. In 1972, she created a group called "Stop ERA," which quickly opened chapters in twenty-six states and signed up thousands of members. "Stop ERA" became the organizational backbone of opposition to the Equal Rights Amendment.*

their special problems." [29] The time must be ripe. The national mood and public opinion must be ready for change; governmental officials, whether the president or in the agencies, must push for it; the Congress must be receptive. No one can say exactly when a policy window is ready to open or why it will close.

The stream of events, of course, can open a policy window. A **crisis** is a sudden, often unexpected event, almost sure to open a policy window. A major plane crash triggers demands for new airline regulation; a toxic waste disaster opens the window for the reform of chemical regulation. Sometimes, a major book can help pry open a long-stuck window. Michael Harrington's *The Other America* (1963), a moving account of poverty in America, was found on President John Kennedy's desk after his assassination. It did much to bring the issue of poverty to the presidential agenda and thus helped launch the "war on poverty" in 1964. Presidents may use commissions to create a climate for policy change. A bipartisan National Commission on Social Security was created by President Reagan in 1982. It was designed to help shape understanding of the crisis in social security, paving the way for legislative reform.

THE WASHINGTON MEDIA AND THE POLICY AGENDA

Policy entrepreneurs depend heavily upon the media to get their ideas out of the primeval soup and onto the policy agenda. Media scholar Doris Graber says of politicians and the media that

> There is a love-hate relationship between government officials and the media. To perform their functions adequately, each needs the other. . . . [But] government wants its portrait taken in its Sunday best, from the most flattering angle. The media, however, want to take candid shots, showing government in awkward poses and off its guard. [30]

However strained their relations, the policymakers and the press need one another. Policymakers and their press aides want the "best press" possible; reporters (the good ones anyway) try to get beyond and behind the sheen of official Washington's handouts. Or, as President Reagan's press secretary, Larry Speakes, once told reporters: "Don't tell me how to manage the news, and I won't tell you how to cover it." [31]

Especially in the last two decades—since the media brought the Vietnam War into our living rooms and also helped unseat President Richard Nixon—the power of the media has itself been an issue on the political agenda. In late 1984, no fewer than three suits against the media brought by public figures were being tried: Moral Majority leader Jerry Falwell was suing *Hustler* publisher Larry Flynt; General William Westmoreland was suing CBS's *Sixty Minutes;* and Israeli General Ariel Sharon was

[29] Kingdon, *Agendas, Alternatives, and Public Policies*, p. 173.
[30] Doris Graber, *Mass Media and American Politics*, 2nd ed. (Washington, D.C.: Congressional Quarterly Press, 1984), p. 221.
[31] John M. Barry, "Washington's Powerhouse Press Corps," *Dun's Business Month*, July, 1984, p. 28.

suing *Time* magazine. The outcomes were mostly victories for the media. Falwell won a symbolic, but non-monetary victory. General Westmoreland finally threw in the legal towel; all CBS had to do was promise to pay its own court costs and issue a statement describing him as "patriotic." General Sharon won a battle (the jury decided that *Time* made a factual error) but lost the war when the jury found that no malice was intended.

As their role has widened, the media have become more than a mirror and a recorder of American political life. They help shape, rather than merely report, the policy agenda. British television producer Anthony Smith took a hard look across the Atlantic and summed up nicely the concerns of many Americans:

> It is more than a fashionable observation, it is a prevailing conviction, that American television, in the last fifteen years, has become a major unelective source of power, the cause of changes in social behavior, in the operations of the Constitution, in the management of the economy, *in the ordering, so to speak, of the whole national (and therefore international) agenda.* [32]

Conservatives fear that the media make up a new elite, shaping a policy consensus of essentially liberal dimensions. Liberals have less objection to the news and opinion presented by the media, but find plenty of things to criticize, too, particularly the alleged overemphasis of violence on TV. We cannot determine here whether one or the other or neither side is right, but we can look more closely at what the media do and how they are structured.

A Linkage for the Linkage Institutions

Linkage institutions—the parties, the interest groups, and the elections—cannot do much linking of people to policymakers if they cannot communicate. Although some political communication happens face to face, much of it depends on reaching a broad audience. A political party convention not only writes a platform and selects candidates, but also functions to get the party's message to the people. That would be nearly impossible these days without radio, TV, and newspapers. Once nominated, candidates depend on the media to get their pitch across to the voters. They try hard to communicate both their issue positions and their image. Duplicating machines churn out tons of press releases from each candidate's headquarters. Media budgets typically consume about half of a campaign chest. Interest groups are no less dependent on the linkage function of the media. A well-organized protest demonstration will usually be preceded by calls to the press. Groups peddling policies in Congress like to see the glare of TV lights when their officials testify in committees.

So we can think about the media as a linkage institution for the linkage institutions. The parties, groups, and elections would not disappear if all the media went out of business tomorrow, but they would have a tougher time performing their linkage functions.

[32] Anthony Smith, " 'Just a Pleasant Way to Spend an Evening'—The Softening Embrace of American Television," *Daedalus* 197(Winter 1978):195. Italics added.

Structure of the Media

Journalists divide the world of the media into two types: *print* and *broadcast*. The print media include newspapers and magazines. The broadcast side includes radio and the glamour stock of the journalistic trade, television. There are in Washington today between 8,000 and 10,000 journalists, working for the newspapers, the magazines, and the broadcast media. [33]

About 1700 newspapers are published daily in the United States. But in 1914 there were as many *foreign language* papers published in the United States as there are daily papers published today. Strikes, low profit margins, and fierce competition have all taken their toll. Today, fewer than 4 percent of all cities have competing daily newspapers. Many papers are owned by chains, making the fiercely independent editor-owner-publisher largely an image of the past. In addition, newspapers depend heavily on the two wire services, the Associated Press and United Press International, for their national and international coverage. Only the very largest papers—the *Washington Post*, the *Chicago Tribune*, the *New York Times*, the *Los Angeles Times*, and a few others—have their own far-flung bureaus generating news from around the nation and the world.

Of course, the networks (CBS, NBC, and ABC) are the largest and latest entrants onto the media stage. And large they are. Each of them has annual sales of well over $1 billion; each is safely located on the *Fortune* 500 list of our largest corporations (NBC through its parent company, RCA). So powerful and so profitable are the networks that they are likely prospects for corporate "takeovers." In March 1985, Capital Cities Broadcasting, with 1984 revenues of $934 million, acquired ABC, with 1984 revenues of $3.7 billion. Rumors flew that CBS would be bought next. About 13 percent of all American households will watch the networks' evening news and information programs, just a bit fewer than will turn on mysteries, situation comedies, and other fluffier fare. Network "anchorpersons" compete with sports and motion picture stars among America's highest paid wage earners.

Both print and broadcast journalists produce a product, just as San Jose produces computers and Bethlehem produces steel. They produce news.

What Is News?

Defining "News." As every journalism student will quickly tell you, "news" is what is new and different. The oft-repeated speech on foreign policy or the well-worn statement on school busing is less newsy than the odd episode. Getting into a presidential helicopter is not news. But bumping your head as you board the helicopter—as Gerald Ford once did—for some reason is news. In its search for the new and the different, the news media can give us a very peculiar view of "objective conditions" and of policymakers.

There are millions of new and different events happening every day. Someone decides which of them are newsworthy. No one has taken a

---

[33] Barry, "Washington's Powerhouse Press Corps," p. 27.

more careful look at the definition and production of news than Edward J. Epstein. Given a unique opportunity to observe NBC's news department for a year, Epstein wrote *News from Nowhere*, a surprising inside account of the TV news business. [34]

Some of the important characteristics of the TV news business, Epstein found, come from the nature of the viewing audience. Contrary to popular opinion, regular viewers of the evening news are less educated than the average American. News shows are tailored to a very low level of audience sophistication.

Still, news is a business with a budget. Camera crews are expensive. Their numbers are limited, and they cannot be sent out to cover every story, many of which will not be on the news. It is thus important to cover events that are predictable—press conferences, for example. News is more likely to be covered if it happens near where camera crews are stationed, mainly New York, Washington, and Chicago. Unless it happens early in the day, important news from California cannot be covered on the evening news because of the time difference between the east and west coasts. Unless the story is of monumental importance, news divisions are reluctant to spend the high costs of transporting film electronically from the west coast.

Finding the News. Although Epstein called his book *News from Nowhere*, news does not, of course, come from nowhere. Our popular image of news-gathering is that the correspondent or reporter somehow ferrets out news. Some do. Yet a surprising amount of news comes from other sources. Much comes tailor-made in press releases, "trial balloons," and leaks by politicians. Interestingly, however, most news tips and stories originate from *other news media*. Epstein tracked down the sources of 440 major stories during his tenure at NBC. The correspondents—those attractive men and women who read news stories so sonorously—accounted for exactly 1 percent of new stories. The AP and UPI wire services accounted for 70 percent of television news. [35]

Not only the networks rely on other media to answer the question, What is news today? So do newspapers, local TV and radio stations, and magazines. Mark Fishman studied how the New York City media reported crime news. He found that one editor of a television news show started his day by reading the morning papers, listening to an all-news radio show, and then listening to his TV competitors. He told Fishman, "I'm not proud. I'll steal any source of news." [36] Similarly, print reporters read other newspapers, watch television news, and listen to the radio to find their news.

Despite this pyramiding—or pirating—of news from one medium to another, the enterprising and hardworking reporter has many opportunities to live up to the image of the crusading truth-seeker. Reporters Carl Bernstein and Bob Woodward of the *Washington Post* almost single-

---

[34] Edward J. Epstein, *News from Nowhere: Television and the News* (New York: Random House, 1973). Many of our observations on TV news come from Epstein.
[35] Ibid., p. 42.
[36] Mark Fishman, "Crime Waves as Ideology," *Social Problems* 26(June 1978):537.

handedly cracked the Watergate case. Columnists like Jack Anderson expose the uglier side of government corruption and inefficiency. Pulitzer prizes regularly go to reporters who get their stories from legwork instead of other media.

Once the news has been "found," it has to be neatly compressed into a thirty-second news segment or squeezed in among the advertisements in the newspaper.

Presenting the News. If you had to pick a single word to describe news coverage by the print and broadcast media, it would be "thin." Generally, TV news is little more than headline reading. Except for the highly regarded MacNeil-Lehrer News Hour on PBS and the late-night *Nightline* on ABC, "in-depth" analysis rarely covers more than a minute. Patterson's careful analysis of campaign coverage (page 261) found only skimpy attention to the "issues" of the presidential campaign. Clearly, if coverage of political events in the high season of an election campaign is thin, coverage of policy questions is even thinner. Policy issues of nuclear power, money supply, and pollution policy are complex, and complex issues are difficult to treat in a short news story or a thirty-second news clip.

However thin it may be, news coverage contributes significantly to shaping our images of ourselves, our government, and our politics. 4 It could hardly be otherwise: The average American child spends more time watching television than he or she does in school. The average American adult spends more leisure time watching television than on anything else. [37] Between 1960 and 1970, television watching increased by 50 percent, from about ten to fifteen hours a week. Not all of this is news, but TV is our main source of news.

[37] U.S. Department of Commerce, *Social Indicators III* (Washington, D.C.: U.S. Government Printing Office, 1980), p. 546.

A "Media Event." *As its name suggests, a "media event" is one contrived for the media. It is staged and orchestrated, often carefully timed, to be completed before the network evening news deadlines. There is nothing spontaneous or very real about this meeting between a Republican congressional candidate and the president and vice-president of the United States. A presidential visit to a disaster area or to a hungry family in a rural area can also be a media event.*

Television news, for most Americans, is *the* medium through which impressions of government are shaped. If an average American were asked, "What sort of government do we have in this country?," his or her answer would largely be determined by television's portrayal of government. Dahlberg put it like this:

> Network TV news has emerged over the last two decades as the dominant vehicle for interpreting national politics to the United States citizenry. It is through TV news that the [government] makes itself visible to most people on a regular basis. [38]

Few have studied the image television news paints of government more carefully than Richard Joslyn. He watched a lot of television news—four years of it on three networks—and coded the images TV presented of our government. [39] Generally, he found that TV painted a positive image of government. Government was depicted as a problem-solver, as decisive, and as strong. In our television-inspired image of government, though, citizens play only a passing, passive role. A scant 1 percent of all television news references to government over the four-year period involved government responding to citizen input. If a democratic govern-

[38] Peter Dahlberg, "TV News and the Suppression of Reflexivity," *Urban Life* 9(July 1980):201; cited in Richard A. Joslyn, "The The Portrayal of Government and Nation on Television Network News," paper delivered at the annual meeting of the Midwest Political Science Association, Cincinnati, Ohio, April 15–18, 1981, p. 5.

[39] Joslyn, "The Portrayal of Government."

---

4 The Media and Technology: The Case of Nuclear Power

In Chapter 6, we pointed out (page 173) that one experimental study showed a significant impact of the media in reshaping people's values. Doris Graber looked into another case of media impact, this time on shaping the public agenda and attitudes toward nuclear technology.

To be sure, it is easier to report political scandals and to print leaks and trial balloons than it is to cover complex scientific and technological issues. Yet increasingly, in our technologically sophisticated society, the media are called upon to cover highly technical issues: the economy, the biomedical revolution, nuclear energy, and so forth. Graber looked specifically at how the media covered the controversial and complex issue of nuclear power.

Well before the Three Mile Island accident in 1979, public support for nuclear power was declining. Some suspected that this was because scientists were doubtful of its advantages. Yet evidence indicated clearly that overwhelming majorities of scientists—even those close to but not directly in nuclear work—urged continued development of nuclear power. But analyses of mass media coverage showed that media coverage tilted negatively. By 1976—three years before Three Mile Island —negative stories outnumbered positive stories by a 2–1 ratio. One key reason was the attitude of reporters. In one survey, scored on a scale of +9 to −9, indicating strong support of to strong opposition to nuclear power, scientists scored +5. But science writers for major media sources scored only +.5, just straddling the neutral fence. Television reporters were at −1.9. Stories on nuclear power tended to quote heavily the Union for Concerned Scientists and Ralph Nader, neither of whom reflected a clear majority of scientific opinion.

No one could prove, of course, that the bias of media coverage pushed nuclear energy off the policy agenda. Graber speculates, though, that policymakers "are loathe to challenge scientific findings that the media have labelled as 'expert' opinion, and they are loathe to take actions that may engender widespread fears among the citizenry."

Source: Doris Graber, *Mass Media and American Politics* (Washington, D.C.: Congressional Quarterly Press, 1984), pp. 270–73. Graber relies heavily upon a study of scientific and journalistic opinion by Stanley Rothman and S. Robert Lichter, "The Nuclear Energy Debate: Scientists, the Media and the Public," *Public Opinion* 5 (August/September 1982): 47–48.

"WE HEAR YOUR SON MAY BE A CASUALTY IN THE BEIRUT BOMBING. GIVE US SOME COLOR ON THAT— LIKE ANGUISH, GRIEF, HOW YOU FEEL ABOUT IT..."

ment rests on a cornerstone of popular control of government, the televised image of government is not a very democratic one. It is, though, an image not conducive to complacency. More than half (52 percent) of all the portrayals of the nation coded by Joslyn showed the nation as "threatened"—by a foreign nation, by a disaster, by some immoral or illegal behavior, by economic problems, and so forth. If our images of the world are shaped by TV news, then it is a hostile world indeed.

Some conservative groups have felt strongly that the world of media news is hostile, even unpatriotic and unwholesome. In the corporate merger mania of 1985, the media were a common target, and at least one effort was made to take over CBS news. Dan Rather, the CBS anchorman, was unpopular with the far right ever since he needled President Nixon during Watergate as the White House reporter. North Carolina's conservative Republican Senator Jesse Helms announced a campaign to buy out CBS in early 1985. His supporters claimed they would buy enough CBS stock to "become Dan Rather's boss." But CBS would cost $4 billion. Even to well-heeled conservative financiers, it was not much of a bargain, and the effort to buy it out fizzled.

The Media and Policymakers: A Communications Network

Actually, Washington policymakers pay a lot more attention to news than ordinary people do. Nothing better illustrates how much the media pervade policymakers' attention than the minutes of cabinet meetings leaked during President Carter's term. As Robert Sherrill summarized them in *Nation*, "Carter and his crowd spent an amazing amount of time poring over newspapers or sitting and staring at television shows and then talking about them."[40] In the cabinet meeting of April 25, 1977, Carter expressed his regret that he missed Secretary of Energy

[40] Robert Sherrill, "Message of the Leaked Minutes," *The Nation*, September 30, 1978.

Schlesinger on *Face the Nation*. At the June 20 meeting, Secretary of State Vance recommended an article on the U.S.S.R. in the *Washington Post*. On October 17, Carter carped to his cabinet about an article by Evans and Novak which, he said, was inaccurate. Even at cabinet meetings, an inordinate amount of attention is devoted to who is saying what in the media.

Ordinary voters may skim or even skip the front page; they may prefer prime-time TV to news. But politicians follow the media voraciously. President Johnson kept a television with three screens—one for each network—in the White House. Policymakers pay plenty of attention to the media partly because they hope to read about or see themselves. They use the media to try to influence people and the policy agenda, and they watch to see how they are doing.

But Washington policymakers also use the media to get their policy messages across to one another. Joseph Califano, advisor to President Johnson and later Secretary of Health, Education, and Welfare under Jimmy Carter, explained the key role the media play in the president's communication network.

> For the president, one of the key functions of the print media in the nation's capital is to serve as a major, if not paramount means of communication with the Congress and the federal bureaucracy. . . . Only a handful [of the members of Congress] ever read most presidential messages to Congress. Except for a few hardworking members who study particular legislation in detail, representatives and senators rely on the *Washington Post* and the *New York Times* reporting of those messages, and perhaps read whatever verbatim excerpts those newspapers print. [41]

What members of Congress know about the president and his policies, they know mostly because they read about them. What the president knows about Congress, his bureaucracy, and the courts, he knows partly because his aides prepare a detailed summary of the news, available bright and early every morning.

Presidents, members of Congress, and other policymakers use the media just like everyone else: to find out what's going on in the world. To busy policymakers, they have built-in virtues. The media's news is virtually instantaneous, already distilled, with its meaning interpreted in black and white. Those are the virtues of the media as a means of communication, but also their defects.

POLITICS IN WASHINGTON SUMMARIZED

In this chapter, we introduced a small but extremely important group of people, those who work in official and unofficial Washington. The "big four" policymaking institutions—the presidency, the Congress, the bureaucracy, and the courts—have their own edifices in Washington. But they are not the only actors on the Washington stage. Unofficial Washington contains two kinds of actors. One is the politicos, those pollsters,

[41] Joseph A. Califano, Jr., *A Presidential Nation* (New York: Norton, 1975), p. 116.

consultants, and public relations specialists who try to shape the political and governmental agenda. The other, the media, are better known to the public.

Everyone in Washington is concerned about the policy agenda. This represents the priorities of government, the issues to which government is paying attention. In a democracy, one hopes that the public's agenda and the government's agenda coincide. Because there are so many demands upon the institutions of government, each institution uses gatekeeping mechanisms to control its agenda. Even so, the claims on government have grown in recent years.

The media are the "gigantic ear" of Washington; they play two key roles in shaping policy agenda. First, they communicate what Washington wants communicated to the rest of us. Second, they are a vital communication linkage among the policymakers. The media are hardly just neutral recorders of events. Their biases in reporting the news can and do help shape the policy agenda itself.

Key Terms

political consultant	governmental agenda	policy entrepreneur
policy agenda	gatekeeping	policy window
public agenda	policy communities	crisis

For Further Reading

Cobb, Roger D. and Charles Elder. *Participation in American Politics: The Dynamics of Agenda-Building* (1975). A classic study of agenda-building.

Epstein, Edward J. *News from Nowhere: Television and the News* (1973). After you read this, you will never have quite the same faith in the evening news.

Eyestone, Robert. *From Social Issues to Public Policy* (1978). A brief review of how social questions become public policy issues.

Gans, Herbert. *Deciding What's News* (1980). The news is what the news media say is news. This book helps explain who decides and how.

Graber, Doris A. *Mass Media and American Politics*, 2nd ed. (1984). Contains excellent coverage of the media and official Washington.

Halberstam, David. *The Powers That Be.* (1979). A study of four media powers: The *Washington Post*, the *Los Angeles Times, Time,* and *CBS*.

Hess, Stephen, *The Washington Reporters* (1981). An excellent study of the men and women who cover official Washington.

Kingdon, John. *Agendas, Alternatives, and Public Policies* (1984). Perhaps the best work on the formation of the policy agenda in Washington.

Sabato, Larry J. *The Rise of Political Consultants* (1981). The best study to date of the political consulting game and its Washington base.

Congress

MEMO

In Chapter 11, we looked at Washington politics. In this chapter, we focus on just a few square blocks of Washington, the beehive of activity called Capitol Hill. Its centerpiece is the Capitol Building, with the Senate at one end and the House of Representatives at the other. Here, the Founding Fathers intended, national policymaking should take place.

Today Congress is a source of frustration, and our job is to figure out why. Its process is a labyrinth. Its power is now so fragmented—especially in the Senate—that orderly policymaking is no certainty. Caucus builds upon caucus, group upon group, rule upon rule, subcommittee upon subcommittee. Today's Congress is a haven of pluralism; and, where pluralism resides, hyper-pluralism is lurking.

Outsiders are not alone in noting the frustrations of Congress. Members feel them, too. These men and women spent years to get themselves there. Their elections exact a high social, economic, and political price; once there, most plan to stay. One of the most important motives in congressional politics is the desire for reelection. Casework and the pork barrel are two ways which members of Congress try to get themselves reelected.

In this chapter, we discuss:

- Who our senators and representatives are and how they got there.
- What members do as policymakers and representatives of their constituents.
- The structure of power and leadership in Congress and the strong role of its committees.
- The many influences on legislative decision making, particularly the role of the president as "chief legislator."

Last, I try to step back and give you the big picture, a picture of the congressional labyrinth and why it is a source of consternation to its critics and even its members.

Tᴴᴇ ᴛᴀꜱᴋꜱ ᴏꜰ Cᴏɴɢʀᴇꜱꜱ become more difficult with each passing year. Conceived by the Founding Fathers as our national legislature, Congress, of course, still makes our laws. It passes our federal budget and declares our wars (if the president has not beaten Congress to it). But the rush of legislation through the congressional labyrinth has never been more complicated. During a single week in late March 1985, Congress wrestled with these issues:

— The House of Representatives voted, after eleven years of testing and $13 billion already spent, to spend $1.5 billion for twenty-one MX missiles. President Reagan had requested them, lobbied for them, and wheedled for them, and the House finally joined the Senate in approving them.
— Both the House and the Senate continued to struggle with a $200 billion dollar federal deficit and budget cuts to pare it down. The Senate Republican leadership's plan to cut spending substantially was strongly opposed by many interest groups.
— The Senate voted, 92–0, to approve a nonbinding resolution asking President Reagan to insist that Japan open up its markets to American exports. Reports were that the Japanese planned to raise their yearly automobile exports from 1.8 to 2.3 million cars a year, thus further eroding American jobs in the steel and automobile industries. Senator John Danforth, a Missouri Republican, claimed that President Reagan's administration was letting the United States be a "punching bag" for the Japanese.
— Amid the largest number of farm bankruptcies since the Great Depression of the 1930s, the Senate Agriculture Committee was beginning hearings on new farm legislation.

These were only the tips of congressional icebergs. On any day, a representative or senator could be required to make a sensible judgment about nuclear missiles, nuclear waste dumps, abortions, trade competition with Japan, the $200 billion federal deficit, the soaring costs of social security, and countless other issues.

Facing this disjointed agenda has become increasingly difficult. For one thing, most important congressional activity is done in individual offices and in committee rooms, not in the House and Senate chambers. The Senate ("the world's greatest deliberative body," it likes to call itself) has little time for deliberation. Former Senate Majority Leader Howard Baker said that moving the Senate is like "trying to push a wet noodle." Republican Senator Warren Rudman of New Hampshire said: "My personal fear is that we're becoming an anachronism. If we're going to become a House of Lords, at least we should get peerages."[1] Much the same story is true in the House. Unlike the Senate, though, the House of Representatives has allowed its floor debates to be televised. There is a minuscule but devoted national following of gavel-to-gavel coverage called C-SPAN (the show which one cable TV trade publication says "dares to be boring").

[1] Helen Dewar, "Is the 'World's Greatest Deliberative Body' Over the Hill?" *Washington Post Weekly Review*, December 10, 1984, p. 12.

C-Span. *The cable network called C-Span features gavel to gavel coverage of the House of Representatives in session. Here Speaker of the House Thomas P. ("Tip") O'Neill is opening a session. Conservative Republican members made use of C-Span in staging a mini-revolt. They made long speeches at the end of the day attacking the Democrats. The Speaker solved that problem by ordering cameras to pan around the chamber, which by then was empty.*

For many within and outside the Congress, there is frustration. Oklahoma Representative Michael Synar swears that while visiting a Cub Scout pack in Grove, Oklahoma, he asked if any of the boys could tell him the difference between Congress and the Cub Scouts. And one little cherub replied: "We have adult supervision."[2]

One sign of members' frustration is that voluntary turnover rates from the House almost doubled between the 1960s and the 1970s.[3] Observers of Congress once suspected that members of Congress "leave only in pine boxes or . . . kicking and screaming on the heels of electoral defeat."[4] These days, the frustrations of the job drive many members to other lines of work.

Why do such frustrations exist in a body that each member put blood, sweat, tears, and a great deal of money into joining? Some are frustrated with the tremendous, disjointed agenda of Congress. Said one perceptive midwestern senator:

> We are losing control of what we are doing here. . . . There isn't enough time in a day to keep abreast of everything we should know to legislate responsibly, dealing with so many bills, having to attend so many committee and subcommittee meetings, listening to lobbyists, having to worry about problems of constituents, and, of course, keeping a close watch on politics back home. You know, one *has* to get reelected.[5]

[2] Gregg Easterbrook, "What's Wrong with Congress?" *Atlantic* (December 1984):57.

[3] John R. Hibbing, "Voluntary Retirement from the U.S. House of Representatives: Who Quits?" *American Journal of Political Science*, 26 (August 1982):467–84.

[4] Stephen Frantzich, *Computers in Congress* (Beverly Hills, Calif.: Sage Publications, 1982), p. 467.

[5] Quoted in Tad Szulc, "Is Congress Obsolete?" *Saturday Review*, March 3, 1979, p. 20.

Other frustrations concern the lobbying explosion, which we met in Chapter 10. On key votes, as senators and representatives stream into the chambers from all over Capitol Hill, lobbyists stand near the doorways buttonholing waverers or slashing a thumbs-up or thumbs-down sign to their supporters. Thousands of dollars in campaign contributions ride on the outcome. Still others are frustrated with the fragmentation of power in the Congress itself. Members of Congress can be, and often are, fiercely independent. (Senate Majority Leader Robert Dole once dryly observed that "We have a lot of self-starters here. The last time I counted, there were 100." The Senate, said his predecessor, Howard Baker, was as unwieldy as "hogs on ice.") Many retirees report their unwillingness to stick it out when seniority in Congress no longer leads unambiguously to power.

Frustrating or not, there is no shortage of men and women clamoring for congressional office. Let us take a look at these national legislators.

THE REPRESENTATIVES AND SENATORS: WHO THEY ARE, HOW THEY GOT THERE, AND WHAT THEY DO

The Myth and the Reality

There are two myths about Congress. One is flattering; the other decidedly is not.

First is the flattering myth of the representative as a national policymaker, deliberating carefully, debating opponents about the issues, and casting a reasoned vote. After all, the Constitution itself makes our senators and representatives the national policymakers. Congressional freshmen have high hopes of making an impact on national issues.

The second myth is an ugly one. It sees most members of Congress as corrupt, incompetent, or—worse—both. Little did the famous "Abscam" (the FBI's name for Arab scam) help the image of the diligent member of Congress. In a sting operation, seven representatives and one senator were videotaped and later convicted for taking bribes from an undercover agent posing as an Arab businessman. ("I've got larceny in my blood," one burbled in front of the hidden camera; another literally stuffed money into his pockets.)

The realities of congressional life depart from both of these myths. For one thing, the freshman who expects to have time for reasoned deliberation about national policy—is the MX missile really a strong deterrent to Soviet aggression? is the administration's farm bill the solution to farmers' woes?—is bound to be disappointed.

Today's representative is a member of 5.15 committees and subcommittees; a senator is a member of 9.75.[6] Contrary to the laws of physics, members are scheduled regularly to be in two places at the same time. Representatives and senators, most of whom are ambitious, hard-work-

---

[6] Steven S. Smith and Christopher J. Deering, *Committees in Congress* (Washington, D.C.: Congressional Quarterly Press, 1984), p. 53.

ing men and women, deeply resent popular beliefs that they are overpaid, underworked, corrupt, and ineffective. Members have even done their own time-and-motion studies to demonstrate that they do work hard. [1]

Who They Are

There are 535 of them. An even hundred, two from each state, are members of the Senate. The other 435 are members of the House of Representatives. The Constitution states only that members of the House must be at least twenty-five years old and have been citizens for seven years, that senators must be at least thirty and have been citizens for nine years, and that all must be residents of the states from which they are elected.

By no stretch of the imagination could anyone call the members of Congress "typical" or "average" Americans. Elite theorists are quick to point out that members come mostly from occupations with high status and usually have substantial incomes. Although calling the Senate a

---

[1] A Representative's "Average Day"

Activity		Average Time
In the House chamber		2:53 hours
In committee/subcommittee work		1:24 hours
Hearings	26 minutes	
Business	9 minutes	
Markups	42 minutes	
Other	5 minutes	
In his/her office		3:19 hours
With constituents	17 minutes	
With organized groups	9 minutes	
With others	20 minutes	
With staff aides	53 minutes	
With other representatives	5 minutes	
Answering mail	46 minutes	
Preparing legislation, speeches	12 minutes	
Reading	11 minutes	
On telephone	26 minutes	
In other Washington locations		2:02 hours
With constituents at Capitol	9 minutes	
At events	33 minutes	
With leadership	3 minutes	
With other representatives	11 minutes	
With informal groups	8 minutes	
In party meetings	5 minutes	
Personal time	28 minutes	
Other	25 minutes	
Other		1:40 hours
Total average representative's day		11:18 hours

Source: U.S. House of Representatives, Commission on Administrative Review, *Administrative Reorganization and Legislative Management* (95th Congress, 1st session, 1977, H. Doc. 95–232): pp. 18–19.

"rich man's club" is an exaggeration, the proportion of millionaires and near-millionaires in Congress is higher than in an average crowd of 535 people. If we look at a collective portrait of the Congress, as in [2], we quickly discover what an atypical collection of Americans it is. Law is the dominant occupation, with other elite occupations—business and academia—also well represented. Only a handful (nineteen) of representatives are black (compared to about 12 percent of the total population), and almost all of them are elected from overwhelmingly black constituencies. No state is mostly black, and there are now no blacks in the Senate. There are eleven Hispanics in the House. In terms of their numbers, though, women are the most underrepresented group. Half the population is female, but only two senators and twenty-two representatives are female.

[2] A Portrait of the 99th Congress: Some Statistics

	House (435)	Senate (100)
PARTY		
Democrat	253	47
Republican	182	53
SEX		
Men	413	98
Women	22	2
RACE		
Black	19	0
Hispanic	11	0
White and other	405	100
AVERAGE AGE	49.7 years	54.2 years
RELIGION		
Protestant	241	58
Roman Catholic	125	19
Jewish	30	8
Other and unspecified	39	15
OCCUPATION[a]		
Law	190	61
Business and banking	144	30
Education	37	10
Public service/politics	65	11
Agriculture	24	7
Journalism	21	8

[a]Some members specify more than one occupation.
Source: Congressional Quarterly Weekly Report, November 10, 1984.

The Congressional Staff. *No member of Congress could function well without a strong staff. Staff members handle scheduling, constituent services, press relations, and information gathering. One part of the staff works in the constituency, tending to local business; another works in cramped quarters in the Senate or House office buildings. Here is Democratic Congressman Romano Mazzoli of Kentucky with his staff on Capitol Hill. (The congressman is holding the coffee cup.)*

One thing all members have in common is their willingness to spend considerable time, trouble, and money getting a crowded office on Capitol Hill. To the nineteenth-century humorist, Artemus Ward, their quest was inexplicable: "It's easy to see why a man goes to the poorhouse or the penitentiary. It's because he can't help it. But why he should voluntarily go live in Washington is beyond my comprehension." Yet today the job seems attractive enough. The salary is not bad and the little things that go with it make the job tolerable. You can get:

— A salary of $72,600, high by most Americans' standards, although well below that of 400 corporation presidents, who earn over $200,000 annually.
— Free office space in Washington and in your constituency, usually cramped with staffers who practically sit on top of each other.
— A staff allowance of almost $367,000 for each member of the House and anywhere from about $850,000 to about $1,500,000 for each senator, depending on the size of the state.
— Handsome travel allowances to see the home folks each year, plus opportunities to travel at low fares or even free to foreign nations on congressional inquiries (what critics call *junkets*).
— Virtually unlimited franking privileges—the free use of the mails to communicate with constituents—costing Congress almost $50 million a year, on top of the $4 to $5 million it spends on machines that duplicate a member's signature in real ink (it will even smear if a constituent should test its authenticity).
— Generous retirement benefits.
— Plenty of little goodies, like free flowers from the National Botanical Gardens, research services from the Library of Congress, exercise rooms and pools, and cut-rate meals and haircuts.

Despite the salaries, the perquisites, and the 39,000 staff members, the cost of Congress really is pretty cheap. Per citizen, we spend annually

365

about the equivalent of the cost of a hamburger, fries, and coke at your favorite fast-food franchise on running our nation's legislature.

How They Got There: Congressional Elections

A Tale of Four Cities. Congressional elections are wearing, expensive, and, as we will see, generally foregone conclusions. As much as $200,000 is required in a typical House of Representatives contest; ten times that amount is required in tough Senate races in big states like Texas or California. [7]

Off and on throughout *Government in America* we have looked at four American communities. Each, of course, is represented by two senators, as guaranteed by the Constitution. Each will have at least one representative in the House. Bigger cities, like San Antonio and San Jose, will normally have more than one district, each with its own representative. In the House, each representative will stand for election every two years. In the Senate, a six-year term enables senators to concentrate on legislative business—or on presidential ambitions. Roughly one in three Senate seats will be elected every two years. Thus in 1984, Bethlehem, Smyrna, San Antonio, and San Jose were all electing members of the House of Representatives; Texas and Tennessee were also electing United States senators.

In San Jose, Norman Mineta, like most incumbents, was a shoo-in for reelection to his House seat. A more interesting contest was taking place in Bethlehem, Pennsylvania's Fifteenth District. Allentown, Bethlehem, and Easton are its core. Steel is the dominant industry in a district in which 40 percent of all jobs are blue collar. It would be an ideal district to be represented by an old-fashioned, New Deal Democrat. Instead, its representative was the only Ph.D. scientist in Congress, metallurgy professor Don Ritter, a Reagan Republican. His opponent was almost equally unlikely—Jane Wells-Schooley, a former vice-president of the National Organization for Women. She argued that Ritter had done too little to help the district where "steel jobs are gone, garment jobs are gone, and not enough defense contract money comes into the district." Ritter, though, earned credit with steelworkers by urging (though unsuccessfully) President Reagan to impose quotas on steel imports from abroad. Rewarded presumably for his efforts, Ritter returned to Washington in 1985 with the Fifteenth District's blessing.

The Twenty-third District of Texas rambles from the city itself through part of the San Antonio suburbs all the way to Laredo on the Mexican border. One of our most heavily Mexican-American districts (53 percent of its population is Hispanic) its representative had never been of Mexican-American heritage. But in 1984, Bexar County Judge Albert Busta-

---

[7] Gary Jacobson, *The Politics of Congressional Elections* (Boston: Little, Brown, 1983), pp. 41–42. An excellent review of the costs of congressional campaigns and the uses to which money is put in them is Edie N. Goldenberg and Michael W. Traugott, *Campaigning for Congress* (Washington: Congressional Quarterly Press, 1984). In 1984, the citizen's group Common Cause estimated that the 802 House candidates on the November ballot spent $165 million on their campaigns. This actually represented a decrease of 5.4 percent since the 1982 congressional election. See George Lardner, Jr., "How Much for a House Seat?" *Washington National Weekly Edition*, April 28, 1985, p. 14.

mante defeated incumbent Congressman Abraham Kazen in the primary election to become Democratic nominee, tantamount to election in the Democratic Twenty-third District. Defeating an incumbent, as we will soon see, is a rare event in congressional elections. Kazen was one of only three incumbents to lose renomination by his party in 1984.

There was no incumbent in the Sixth District of Tennessee, which Albert Gore had vacated to run for the Senate. Candidate Bart Gordon took full advantage of technology in his campaign, using a computerized phone bank and extensive direct mail efforts. His tight primary race against three other prominent local Democrats bypassed one nasty issue to be raised later by his Republican opponent: the charge that Gordon was named in a paternity suit. Gordon mostly ignored it, stressing instead his credentials as a moderate Democrat in favor of a balanced budget. He received 63 percent of the district's vote.

At the state level, few 1984 Senate elections generated more heat than the Texas senatorial contest between Republican Phil Gramm and Democratic State Senator Lloyd Doggett.[8] Gramm was a one-time Democrat who changed parties and asked his east Texas constituency to reelect him to Congress as a Republican. They did, and he decided to run for the Texas Senate seat when Republican John Tower announced his retirement. It was a spirited campaign. Doggett had spent many of his resources in a close Democratic primary against Congressman Ken Hance and former San Antonio Congressman (and onetime dean of arts and sciences at Duke University) Bob Krueger. This left him slightly cash-poor in the general election. Gramm's ads shouted that Doggett had raised some

[8] One race that did generate even more heat in 1984 was the contest between Governor James Hunt and Senator Jesse Helms of North Carolina. For a review of that race, see William D. Snider, *Helms and Hunt: The North Carolina Senate Race, 1984* (Chapel Hill: University of North Carolina Press, 1985).

Texas Elections, 1984. Here are two winners from the 1984 Texas congressional elections. Left is Senator Phil Gramm, who ran a spirited race against State Senator Lloyd Doggett. Gramm, an economics professor before he went to Congress, once shifted parties from the Democratic to the Republican fold. At the right is Congressman Albert Bustamante, the first Hispanic ever to represent heavily Hispanic San Antonio in Congress.

money from a male, gay striptease show in San Antonio. (Doggett eventually returned it.) Gramm wore his conservative credentials as a badge of honor. Doggett was, he said, too liberal for Texas. Gramm won decisively.

Open seats (such as the one in Texas) almost always produce more competition than ones already occupied by an incumbent. In fact, the role of incumbency is an important key to understanding congressional elections.

Incumbents Run Away with Congressional Elections. Everyone in Congress is a politician. Every politician has his or her eye on the next election. The players in the congressional game are the incumbents and the challengers. Here we will see how very often incumbents run away with congressional elections.

Incumbents are those already holding office. Sometime during each term, the incumbent has to decide whether to run again or to retire voluntarily. Most will decide to have another go at it and will enter their party's primary, almost always emerge victorious (recall that Albert Bustamente was one of only three candidates who defeated an incumbent in the 1984 primaries), and typically win in the November general election, too. In fact the most important fact about congressional elections is this: *Incumbents usually win.*

Thus, the most important resource to ensure your opponent's defeat is *not* having more money than your opponent, although that helps. It is *not* being more photogenic, though that helps, too. The best thing to have going for you is simply to be the incumbent. ⟨3⟩

Gary Jacobson's study of congressional elections puts it like this: "the picture could not be clearer. . . . On the average, fewer than 2 percent of [House] incumbents are defeated in primary elections; fewer than 7 percent lose in general elections."[9] Not only do they win, but they tend to win with big electoral margins. Perhaps most astonishing of all, the evidence is that even when challengers' positions on the issues are closer to the voters' positions, incumbents still tend to win.[10] The picture for the Senate is a little different. Though senators still have a better-than-even chance of beating back a challenge, their odds are hardly as handsome as for House incumbents. One reason is that senators are forced to take positions on many more sensitive policy positions than representatives. Some of these may alienate groups in the state. Members of the Senate also draw more visible challengers, many of whom, one might suspect, know that the Senate is one steppingstone to national prominence and even the presidency.

Jacobson, though, feels it worth stressing that incumbents are not always shoo-ins. Toting up the actual results of elections to the House, he found that incumbents were no more likely to win than they did in the 1950s, and by margins similar to those three decades ago.[11] Incumbents

[9] Jacobson, *The Politics of Congressional Elections*, p. 26.

[10] John L. Sullivan and Eric Uslaner, "Congressional Behavior and Electoral Marginality," *American Journal of Political Science* 22 (August 1978):536–53.

[11] Gary C. Jacobson, "The Marginals Never Vanished: Incumbency and Competition in Elections to the U.S. House of Representatives, 1952–1982," paper presented at the annual meeting of the Midwest Political Science Association, Chicago, Illinois, April 17–20, 1985.

still pile up vast reelection warchests, send service signals to any who will hear, and work tirelessly to stay in touch with groups and the folks back home. They may continue to win frequently, but it is not through sheer good luck.

Why Incumbents Do So Well. There are several possible explanations for the success of incumbents. One is that voters know how their elected representatives vote on important policy issues and agree with their stands, sending them back to Washington to keep up the good work. This is not the case. In fact, voters are rather oblivious to how their senators and representatives actually vote.[12] Another possibility is that voter assessments of presidential candidates influence their voting for Congress. Stories of presidential "coattails" (so called because other candidates were said to ride into office by clinging to presidential coattails)

[12] Actually, only about 17 percent of the population can make an accurate guess about how their representative had voted on *any* issue in Congress. Patricia Hurley and Kim Q. Hill, "The Prospects for Issue Voting in Contemporary Congressional Elections," *American Politics Quarterly* 8 (October 1980):446.

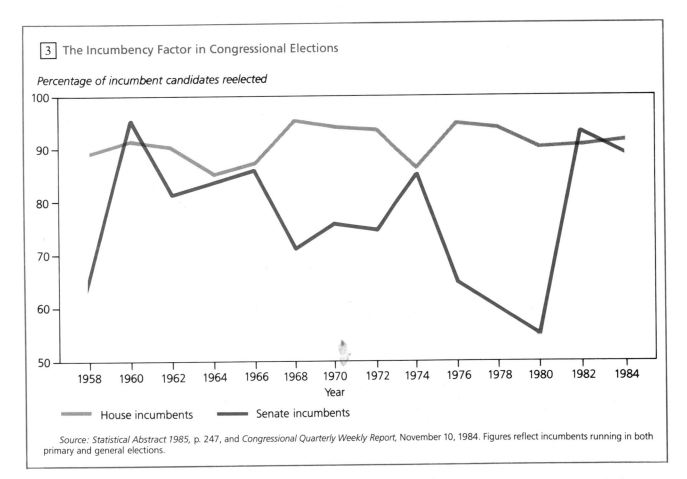

3 The Incumbency Factor in Congressional Elections

Percentage of incumbent candidates reelected

House incumbents   Senate incumbents

Source: Statistical Abstract 1985, p. 247, and *Congressional Quarterly Weekly Report,* November 10, 1984. Figures reflect incumbents running in both primary and general elections.

The effect of incumbency is more impressive in the House than the Senate, but even in the Senate, whopping majorities of incumbents who seek reelection win.

seem to be just stories. [13] Nor do members of Congress gain or lose very much from the ups and downs of the economy. [14] So if voters know little about how their representatives and senators vote, if presidential effects are unconnected with congressional races, and if economic conditions do not have much impact, what accounts for the success of congressional incumbents?

One important factor is *visibility*. Members of Congress work hard to get themselves known in their constituencies. They usually succeed. The Center for Political Studies at the University of Michigan surveyed a sample of voters in the 1978 elections. [15] People were asked whether they had had any direct or indirect contact with their representative or senator. The level of visibility of incumbent senators and representatives is nothing short of phenomenal. Consider for a moment how very difficult it is to permeate the consciousness of the average American voter. Only about a third to half of the population claims to read newspapers regularly, and there are even fewer regular news watchers. [16] Less than half will bother to vote in a congressional election. Yet *90 percent of the population reports some form of contact with their congressman or senator*. [17] Specifically,

— 50 percent of the population reports having seen their representative on TV.
— 71 percent got mail from him or her.
— 20 percent saw their representative at a meeting.
— 23 *percent met him or her personally.*

Now reflect for just a moment on the fact that 23 percent of the people in an average congressional district claim to have met their House member personally. In an actual congressional district with almost half a million people, a member of congress has met—or, perhaps more likely, persuaded people to believe that he or she has met—about 85,000 adult constituents. Not surprisingly, members concentrate on staying visible. Trips home are frequent. The average member will make about thirty-five trips back to the home district every year. [18] One member told Richard Fenno about the image he tried to cultivate there:

> [I have] a very high recognition factor. And of all the things said about me, none of them said, "He's a conservative or a liberal," or "He votes this way on such and such an issue." None of that at all. There were two things said. One, "He works hard." Two, "He works for us." Nothing more than that. So we made it our theme, "O'Connor gets things done"; and we emphasized the dams, the highways, the buildings, the casework. [19]

[13] That presidential elections and congressional elections are not closely related is an argument made in Lyn Ragsdale, "The Fiction of Congressional Elections as Presidential Events," *American Politics Quarterly* 8 (October 1980):375–98.

[14] John R. Owens and Edward C. Olson, "Economic Fluctuations and Congressional Elections," *American Journal of Political Science* 24 (August 1980):469–93.

[15] The first analyses of the CPS study are reported in three articles in the *American Political Science Review* 74 (September 1980), and the entire issue of *American Politics Quarterly* 8 (October 1980).

[16] Thomas Patterson, *The Mass Media Election* (New York: Praeger, 1980), pp. 59–60.

[17] Thomas E. Mann and Raymond E. Wolfinger, "Candidates and Parties in Congressional Elections," *American Political Science Review* 74 (September 1980):Table 11, p. 627.

[18] Richard F. Fenno, Jr., *Home Style* (Boston: Little, Brown, 1978), p. 32.

[19] Ibid., pp. 106–7.

Like most members, this representative quickly discovered that service spells success. [20] His campaign literature stressed 14,000 individuals "helped with problems involving the federal government," 25,000 "incidental requests" met, 20,000 letters on "national issues" answered, the 700 "community projects" assisted, and his 93 percent attendance record in Congress. Not how you vote, but how many folks know you and how they size up your service to them is what counts for reelection. Contrast the incumbent, who has this rich experience and visibility, with the typical challenger, unknown, unsung, and underfinanced. [21]

Morris Fiorina has stressed this close link between service and success. Members of Congress, he says, *can* go to the voters and stress their policymaking record. They *can* make promises about their stands on new policy issues on the agenda. But the problem with facing the voters on your record—past, present, and future—is that policy positions make enemies as well as friends. Your vote for reducing government spending may win some friends. But it will make an enemy of voters who happen to connect your vote with service cutbacks. Besides, you can almost never show that you were single-handedly responsible for a major policy. Being only one of 435 members of the House or of 100 senators, you can hardly promise to end inflation, cut taxes, or achieve equal rights for women by yourself.

One thing, though, always wins friends and almost never makes enemies: *servicing the constituency.* There are two ways you can service your constituency: through casework and the pork barrel. **Casework** is helping constituents as individuals, cutting through some bureaucratic red tape to get people what they think they have a right to get. The **pork barrel** is the mighty list of federal projects, grants, and contracts available to cities, businesses, colleges, and institutions in your district.

Do you have trouble getting your check from the Social Security Administration on time? Call your congressman, who can cut red tape. Do you have trouble getting federal bureaucrats to respond to Pottsville's request for federal construction moneys? Call your congressman. Representatives and senators can single-handedly take credit for each of these favors.

Casework and the pork barrel are the secrets of congressional reelection success. Fiorina put it like this:

Congressman Norman Mineta. *Incumbents almost always have a heavy edge in congressional campaigns. Typically, they are more visible and have access to vastly greater sums of money than their opponents. Norman Mineta has represented San Jose since 1974. He is a member of the Committee on Science and Technology and the Select Committee on Intelligence.*

> Even committee chairmen have a difficult time claiming credit for a piece of major legislation, let alone a rank-and-file congressman. Ah, but casework, and the pork barrel. In dealing with the bureaucracy, the congressman is not merely one vote in 435. Rather he is a nonpartisan power, someone whose phone calls snap an office to attention. He is not kept on hold. The constituent who receives aid believes that his congressman and his congressman alone got results. Similarly, congressmen find it easy to claim credit for federal projects awarded in their dis-

[20] The "service spells success" argument is made in Morris Fiorina, *Congress: Keystone of the Washington Establishment* (New Haven, Conn.: Yale University Press, 1977), and, with a slightly different emphasis, in Glenn R. Parker, "The Advantages of Incumbency in Congressional Elections," *American Politics Quarterly* 8 (October 1980):449–61.

[21] Because of the massive edge that incumbents have, challengers are typically underfinanced, as Gary Jacobson shows in *Money in Congressional Elections* (New Haven, Conn.: Yale University Press, 1980).

tricts. The congressman may have instigated the project in the first place, issued regular progress reports, and ultimately announced the award through his office. Maybe he can't claim credit for the 1965 Voting Rights Act, but he can take credit for Littletown's spanking new sewage treatment plant. [22]

As long as constituents need help hurdling a bureaucracy, as long as there is a project to build or grants to send to the home district, incumbents do well. They can more easily overwhelm their opponents because they are the link between little citizens and big government. Getting things for the folks back home gets you the chance to serve them again.

Notice that the benefits of serving constituents have a spin-off effect: There is a built-in incentive for members to tolerate, even to expand, an already big government. The more policies there are, the more bonuses to send home to the constituency. The more bureaucracies there are, the more red tape you can help cut. Big government helps you get back to Washington and even gives you good reason to support making it bigger.

Add party to incumbency and you have an "almost unbeatable combination" in House elections. [23] In the 1978 studies, only 5 percent of the voters who belonged to the incumbent's party voted for the challenger. [24]

Therefore, says, Jacobson, "Since most incumbents do work hard to remain in office and are therefore extremely difficult to defeat, it is not absurd to ask why . . . anyone challenges them at all." [25] One of the main reasons, he suggests, is simply that challengers are often naive about their chances of winning. Not blessed with top dollars for expensive polls, they rely on friends and local party leaders, who often tell them what they want to hear. Sometimes they do get some unexpected help. Incumbents almost have to beat themselves, and some do.

An incumbent who lands in a scandal or a corruption charge does himself or herself little good. Peters and Welch examined what happened to members of Congress and challengers caught up in corruption charges. Clearly, voters *do* take out their anger at the polls. Democrats mired in corruption charges over a ten-year period lost about 11 percent of their expected vote; Republicans lost about 6 percent. [26] In a close election, erosion like that can turn easy victory into certain defeat.

The incumbent may also be redistricted out of his or her familiar turf. After each federal census, Congress reapportions its membership. Big population gainers among the states will be given more seats; big losers will lose one or more of their seats. The state legislatures have to redraw their states' district lines. One incumbent may be tossed into another's district, and left to battle it out. A state party majority is more likely to toss two of the opposition party's representatives into the same district than two of its own.

[22] Fiorina, *Congress: Keystone of the Washington Establishment*, pp. 44–45.
[23] Mann and Wolfinger, "Candidates and Parties," p. 621.
[24] Ibid., p. 620.
[25] Jacobson, *The Politics of Congressional Elections*, p. 46.
[26] John G. Peters and Susan Welch, "The Effects of Corruption on Voting Behavior in Congressional Elections," *American Political Science Review* 74 (September 1980):697–708. A cynic, one supposes, might interpret the same findings differently, like this: "Corrupt politicians lose a mere 6 to 11 percent of their expected vote."

In a nutshell, here are some of the pluses that can help you get elected to Congress:

— Be an incumbent. Perhaps no factor is more important than this.
— Be a good provider of constituency services. Take casework and the pork barrel seriously.
— Be from your district's majority party. The effects of incumbency, good casework, and the right party label are almost unbeatable.
— Stay clean. One thing that can cost an incumbent the election (even one with a fine service record and the right party) is a scandal.
— Have enough money, or access to enough money, to scare any potential opponents away.

Money in Congressional Elections. It costs a great deal more money to elect a Congress than to elect a president. Each of the two presidential candidates in 1984 received about $40 million from the federal treasury, which covered nearly the entire cost of each presidential campaign. The quarter-billion mark for congressional elections was passed in 1982. In the 1984 Senate races alone an estimated $175 million was spent. [27] Political Action Committees (PACs) accounted for about $120 million in donations in the 1984 congressional elections (see Chapter 8). One in every four dollars spent in congressional races comes from PACs. A look at spending in congressional elections can be found in 4.

Critics of PACs specifically and congressional fund-raising generally offer plenty of complaints about the present system of campaign finance. Why, they ask, is money spent to pay the campaign costs of a candidate already heavily favored to win? Representative Dan Rostenkowski, the Chicago Democrat who is chairman of the House Ways and Means Committee, had acquired $613,000 in campaign funds in 1984. Yet Rostenkowski had won his last three elections by 80 percent of the vote. Tennessee Republican John Duncan collected more than $200,000 from PACs in his last election—and that with no primary or general election

[27] Federal Election Commission, *Record*, vol. II, no. 7, July, 1985, p. 8.

Ways and Means Chairman Rostenkowski. *The chairman of the House Ways and Means Committee, which writes tax legislation, attracts PAC money like a magnet. Representative Dan Rostenkowski (second from right), a Chicago Democrat, is the current Ways and Means chairman. His political accounts are always filled with PAC money, even though he rarely attracts serious opposition for reelection. PAC critics think that contributions to people like "Rosty" are truly unnecessary, and signal only that PACs intend to buy influence.*

In 1984, we spent a little over $200 million electing members of the House of Representatives and about $175 million electing the Senate. Since the Federal Election Commission first started keeping records in the 1976 elections, our expenditures on congressional elections have increased. In that year, neither House nor Senate elections reached the $50 million mark. Costs of elections have climbed steadily since then, although there was a small dip (about .2 percent) in House spending between 1982 and 1984. Despite the growth of PACs,

the major portion of money spent in congressional races still comes from the traditional source—independent contributions to the candidate. The median Senate candidate spent more than $1,000,000; the median House candidate spent more than $100,000 in 1984.

The total cost of a campaign depends on whether the candidate is a challenger or an incumbent or is battling for an open seat, that is, one not now occupied by an incumbent. Below is the breakdown for the 1984 House elections:

Spending by House candidates, 1984ᵃ

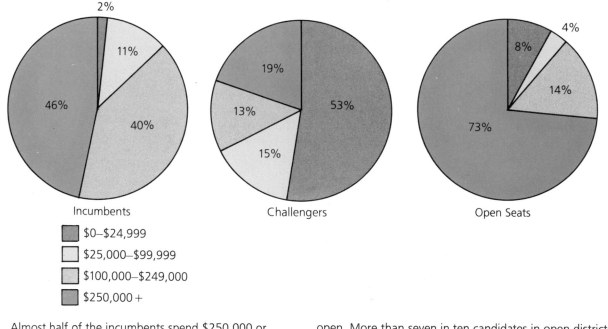

Incumbents — 2%, 11%, 46%, 40%

Challengers — 19%, 13%, 15%, 53%

Open Seats — 8%, 4%, 14%, 73%

- ▮ $0–$24,999
- ▯ $25,000–$99,999
- ▨ $100,000–$249,000
- ▮ $250,000 +

Almost half of the incumbents spend $250,000 or more to get themselves reelected; another four in ten spend between $100,000 and $250,000. Challengers, though, are typically underfinanced. This, of course, is one reason incumbents do so well. More than half of the challengers in 1984 were unable to raise more than $25,000 in their bids to unseat incumbents. The real spending contest, though, is in districts where the seat is

open. More than seven in ten candidates in open districts spend more than a quarter of a million dollars.

ᵃGraph covers all campaign spending (primary, runoff, and general) of major party candidates running in the general election.

Source: The source of information on total spending since 1976 is the Federal Election Commission *Record,* July 1985, p. 8. The source of the information on spending by House candidates in 1984 is the Federal Election Commission's report *The First 10 Years,* p. 7.

opponent at all. It gave the appearance of a "preemptive strike" or of "preventive maintenance," that is, money spent to prevent any opposition from developing.

Evidence like this convinces PAC critics that PACs are not trying to elect, but to influence. They are fond of suggesting links between donations and votes. Here is one of their favorite examples: In November 1983, the 250 House members who voted to retain dairy price supports had received $1.7 million—about $6,800 each—from a dairy PAC. [28] Connection, of course, is not causation. Most senators and representatives are firm in their conviction that he who pays the piper does not necessarily call the tune. Most critics, however, fear the worst. Congressional critic Gregg Easterbrook puts it thus: "Money rarely buys elections. . . . Money can, however, buy individual congressmen's votes on a bill, or distort congressmen's thinking on an issue—normally all an interest group needs to achieve its ends." [29] Political scientists, though, have been harder to persuade that the PAC piper calls the political tune. [5]

What They Do: The Congressional Roles

Policymaker. The Constitution assumes, indeed requires, that policymaking be the primary role of Congress and its members. Considering bills, voting intelligently for policy in the national interest, and doing your legislative homework means making policy. Of all the senator's or representative's roles, this one is toughest. One reason is the frenzy of work combined with the shortage of time. Little time is available for even the most conscientious member to examine policy alternatives. Instead, when ringing bells announce a roll-call vote, representatives or senators rush into the chamber from their offices or a hearing, often unsure of

[28] *U.S. News and World Report,* May 28, 1984, p. 50.
[29] Easterbrook, "What's Wrong with Congress?", p. 70.

---

[5]   The PACs as Pipers: Do They Really Call the Tune?

These days, PACs are the favorite "bad boys" of journalists and other political commentators. They are said to influence Congress in two major ways: first, they use campaign contributions to elect people who agree with them; second, they use those contributions to influence the behavior of incumbents by withdrawing (or threatening to withdraw) or promising contributions in future campaigns. Stories of the extent of PAC influence are a staple of Washington reporting.

But are PACs really this influential? John R. Wright has conducted perhaps the most careful analysis of the influence of PACs to date. He conducted an exhaustive study of five PACs and their efforts to influence congressional elections and congressional incumbents. The PACs were: the American Medical Political Action Committee, the physicians' PAC; the DEAC (Dealers Election Action Committee), a PAC for car dealers; the American Bankers' Association (BANKPAC); the Realtors Political Action Committee; and the Associated General Contractors Political Action Committee. Wright interviewed Washington officials of the PACs, and then studied the links between contributions and the actual voting behavior of members of Congress.

One very important limitation on PAC power is that the people who do the Washington lobbying are not usually the people who determine where the campaign contributions go. *Local* contributors and not *national* PAC leaders decide to aid Congresswoman Jones or her challenger. One national director of a PAC said, "If we have someone who raised $10,000 at the local level, but wants to support someone who we don't think is especially deserving, we usually go along with him. If we didn't, he might not raise that kind of money for us the next time around." This considerably weakens the bargaining power of the PAC's Washington lobbyist.

Wright saw that the link between contributions and voting is a weak one. On votes crucial to each PAC, he found that "in none of the cases were the effects of contributions enough to change the outcome" of the congressional vote. Wright concluded that his findings "cannot support a claim that PACs never have, or never will, determine voting outcomes, but they do indicate the probable rarity of such influence."

Source: John R. Wright, "PACs, Contributions and Roll Calls," *American Political Science Review* 79 (June, 1985):400–414.

what is being voted on. Often, "uncertain of his position, he will seek out one or two men who serve on the committee which considered and reported the bill, in whose judgment he has confidence." [30] Congressional policymaking is so varied and confusing that members frequently resort to these "cue givers," other, more knowledgeable members who can help them make up their minds. [31]

Members are short of time, and of expertise as well. Almost all amateurs, they are surrounded by people who know (or claim to know) more than they do—lobbyists, agency administrators, even their own staffs. Even if they were all, in David Halberstam's phrase, "the best and the brightest," making wise national policy would be difficult. If economists disagree about policies to fight unemployment, how are legislators to know which ones may work better than others? Faced with the frustrating responsibility for solving national problems, members of Congress as a whole do what anyone else would do: They delegate authority to those who, they hope, are able to find the answers. In particular, they delegate authority to committees made up of fellow members who have an interest in specific policy areas.

Budgetmaker. Congress has the power of the purse in American politics. The Constitution is quite specific about Congress' power over the budget, and each member of Congress plays a role in the budget process. Some play major roles by sitting on budget, taxation, or appropriations committees. Some play a role mainly when they vote on the various budget bills in the House or Senate. These responsibilities cannot be

[30] So says House majority leader Jim Wright, *You and Your Congressman* (New York: Putnam's, 1976), p. 190.

[31] Donald R. Matthews and James Stimson, *Yeas and Nays: Normal Decision-making in the House of Representatives* (New York: Wiley, 1975).

Congressman William Gray. *Pennsylvania's Congressman William Gray is a minister and also chairman of the powerful House Budget Committee, a post he took over from Oklahoma Congressman James Jones. The House and Senate Budget Committees are responsible for the important (and sometimes impossible) task of recommending total limits for spending and keeping Congress to their own timetables for budget-writing.*

shirked, especially in a time of immense deficits. Members must go back to their constituents and defend their budgetary votes. Sometimes, though, budget voting can be so confusing that it is possible to attack or defend voting on either side of the issue. By one count, there were thirty-six "test votes" on the funding for MX missiles during the Reagan administration. Snarled in the maze of the legislative process, a representative might have to vote "yes" on one and "no" the next time just to stay consistent.

Committee Member. Committee member is another role members play. Here most of the policymaking work goes on. The Ninety-ninth Congress has 22 standing committees and 149 subcommittees in the House, 16 committees and 105 subcommittees in the Senate, plus four joint committees and five joint subcommittees. Committee work nurtures specialization and expertise. If a member is on a committee long enough, he or she may become a policy expert, one whose advice is sought by colleagues. If you are on the right committee, you should also be able to play your role of constituency representative more effectively.

Representative. The member of Congress is also a representative, expected by his or her constituents to represent their interests in Washington. Sometimes, the job of representative itself requires a balancing act. If some representatives favor more defense spending but suspect their constituents do not, what are they to do? Some political philosophers argue that representatives should always vote their best judgment (*virtual representation*); others say they should vote their constituencies' beliefs (*actual representation*). The English politician and philosopher Edmund Burke came down on the side of voting by conscience. He favored the concept of a legislator as a *trustee*, using his or her best judgment to make policy for people. Others prefer the concept of the representative as *instructed delegate*, voting the preferences of constituents as if constituents themselves were present and voting. The difference is a bigger problem to political scientists than it seems to be to legislators. About half the legislators think they can balance the two roles without much problem. [32]

Constituent Servant. Members represent their constituents not only through their voting decisions but also as constituent servants. Casework and the pork barrel are the raw materials of constituent service. Generally, a constituency well served is a constituency well satisfied, especially at the next election. So important is constituency service that legislators do it almost in assembly-line fashion. (One rule of thumb in handling constituents' problems: If you can get a satisfactory resolution to the problem—"Yes, your social security check will now come on time," sign the representative's name to the letter; if the response is unfavorable—"I regret to inform you, . . . " have an aide sign it.)

[32] Roger H. Davidson, *Role of the Congressman* (Pegasus Press, 1969). Davidson asked a sample of congressmen whether they saw themselves as "trustees" or "delegates." About a quarter voiced support for each, but almost half Davidson called "politicos," members who thought they could do both at the same time.

Members of Congress as Constituent Servants. *Of all congressional roles, none is more critical than that of constituent servant. Former Congressman Ken Hechler emphasized this role when talking with his West Virginia constituents.*

Time spent servicing constituents means time not spent making policy. These small but time-consuming tasks take up hours of a congressional day, even though routine ones are delegated to the staff. Kenneth Olson suspects that "the chances are good that a careful analysis of the total time expended by members and their staffs [would find constituent] casework the leading activity."[33]

Politician. In itemizing congressional roles, we cannot ignore the most universal one: politician. Men and women may run for Congress to forge new policy initiatives. But they also run because they are politicians, they enjoy politics, and a position in Congress is near the top of their chosen profession. Even if they dislike politics, without it they will not be around long enough to shape policy.

To say that thinking about reelection occupies every waking moment of a congressman's time is an exaggeration. But "because reelection is so important, and because it may be so difficult to ensure, its pursuit can become all-consuming."[34] As policymakers, budgetmakers, representatives, committee members, and constituent servants, legislators are also playing the biggest role of all, the role they play for keeps, politician.

HOW CONGRESS IS ORGANIZED TO MAKE POLICY

Congress is a collection of generalists trying to make policy on specialized topics. Power in modern society has largely drifted to the specialized institutions: the professions, whose practitioners dispense

---

[33] Kenneth G. Olson, "The Service Function of the United States Congress," in Alfred deGrazia et al., *Congress: The First Branch* (Washington, D.C.: American Enterprise Institute, 1966), p. 344.

[34] Lawrence C. Dodd, "Congress and the Quest for Power," in Lawrence C. Dodd and Bruce I. Oppenheimer (eds.), *Congress Reconsidered* (New York: Praeger, 1977), p. 271.

increasingly complex legal and medical advice; the bureaucracies, whose mighty armies of technocrats are specialists incarnate; and the universities, whose specialties are enshrined as academic disciplines. Congress' constitutional organization gave it just a hint of specialization, when it was split into the House and the Senate. The demands of contemporary times require much more specialization. Congress tries to cope with these demands through its elaborate committee system.

American Bicameralism

A **bicameral legislature** is one divided into two houses. The United States Congress and every American state legislature except Nebraska's are bicameral. As we saw in Chapter 3, the Connecticut Compromise at the Constitutional Convention created a bicameral Congress. Each state is guaranteed two senators. Its number of representatives is determined by the population of the state. (California has forty-five representatives; Alaska, Delaware, North Dakota, South Dakota, Vermont, and Wyoming have just one each.) By creating a bicameral Congress, the Constitution set up yet another check and balance: No bill can be passed unless both House and Senate agree on it; each body can thus veto the policies of the other.

Americans sometimes blur the distinction between senators and representatives, but the members of Congress see sharp differences between the two bodies. These differences are shown in ⬚6. Members even hold stereotypes of "the other body." Senators are seen by their House counterparts as grandstanders, eyeing the White House instead of tending to legislative business. Through Senate eyes, the House is a bit unimaginative and even parochial.

The House. More than four times larger than the Senate, the House is also more institutionalized, that is, more centralized, more hierarchical,

---

⬚6   House versus Senate: Some Key Differences

	House of Representatives	Senate
Constitutional powers	Must initiate all revenue bills; must pass all articles of impeachment	Must give "advice and consent" to many presidential appointments; must approve treaties; tries impeached officials
Membership	435 members	100 members
Term of office	2 years	6 years
Centralization of power	More centralized; stronger leadership	Less centralized; weaker leadership
Political prestige	Less prestige	More prestige
Role in policy	More influential on budget; more specialized	More influential on foreign affairs; less specialized
Turnover	Small	Moderate
Role of seniority	More important in determining power	Less important in determining power

less anarchic. Party loyalty to leadership and party-line voting are more common than in the Senate.[35] Partly because there are more members, leaders in the House do more leading than leaders in the Senate. Freshman House members are still more likely to be seen and not heard, with less power than senior representatives have.

Both the House and the Senate set their own agendas. Both use committees, which we will examine shortly, to winnow down the thousands of bills introduced. One institution unique to the House, though, plays a key role in agenda-setting: the **House Rules Committee.** It reviews all bills (except revenue, budget, and appropriations bills) coming from a House committee before they go to the full House. Performing a traffic-cop function, it then gives each bill a "rule," which schedules the bill on the calendar, allots time for debate, and may even specify what kind of amendments may be offered.

If the Rules Committee were no more than a traffic cop for crowded calendars, no one would have minded. But for years it was dominated by southern representatives who strongly opposed policies promoting equality for blacks. Conservative members had an easy solution to the problem of civil rights legislation: Deny it a rule, thus burying it. But the power of the Rules Committee was decreased in the 1960s, and as conservative members have died, retired, or been defeated, the conservative majority has gradually been replaced by a liberal majority more responsive to the House leadership. The Speaker of the House now appoints directly the membership of the Rules Committee.

The Senate. The Founding Fathers thought the Senate would protect elite interests against the tendencies of the House to protect the masses. Thus, to the House they gave the power of initiating all revenue bills and of impeaching officials; to the Senate they gave responsibility for ratifying all treaties, for confirming important presidential nominations (including nominations to the Supreme Court), and for trying impeached officials. Until the Republicans gained control in 1980, the Senate was just as liberal as (some say more liberal than) the House. The real differences between the bodies lie in the Senate's organization and decentralized power.

Smaller than the House, the Senate is also less disciplined and centralized. Today's senators are more equal in power than representatives are. They are also more equal than senators have been in the past. Some years ago, Donald Matthews described the insignificance of freshman senators, even calling the first term an "apprenticeship." Freshmen confided to Matthews that senior members advised them thus: "You may think you are smarter than the older fellows, but after a time you find that this is not true"; "Keep on asking for advice, boy, that's the way to get ahead around here."[36] In 1981, though, the Senate had sixteen newcomers, none of them eager to take a back seat to oldtimers. Even very new senators get top committee assignments; some even became chairmen of key subcommittees.

[35] Nelson W. Polsby, et al., "Institutionalization of the House of Representatives," *American Political Science Review* 62 (1968):144–68.

[36] Donald R. Matthews, *U.S. Senators and Their World* (Chapel Hill: University of North Carolina Press, 1960), p. 93.

Committees and the party leadership are important in determining the Senate's legislative agenda, just as they are in the House. Party leaders do for Senate scheduling what the Rules Committee does in the House. One item unique to the Senate is the **filibuster.** In the House, debate can be ended by a simple majority vote. Priding itself on freedom of discussion, the Senate traditionally permitted unlimited debate on a bill. But if debate is unlimited, opponents of a bill may try to talk it to death. Strom Thurmond (R.—S.C.) once held forth for a full twenty-four hours. Yielding at times to a fresh voice, filibusterers can tie up the legislative agenda until proponents decide to give up their battle. Filibusters were a favorite device of southern senators to prevent civil rights legislation. In 1959, 1975, and again in 1979, the senate adopted rules to make it easier to close off debate. Today, sixty members present and voting can halt a filibuster.

Leadership in the House

Leading 100 or 435 men and women in Congress, each jealous of his or her own power, responsible to no higher power than the constituency, is not an easy task. "Few members of the House, fewer still in the Senate," Robert Peabody once wrote, "consider themselves followers." [37] We spoke in Chapter 7 of the party-in-government. Much of the leadership in Congress is really party leadership. There are a few formal posts, whose occupants are chosen by non-party procedures. But those who have the real power in the congressional hierarchy are those whose party put them there.

Chief among these in the House of Representatives is the **Speaker of the House.** This is an office mandated by the Constitution. ("The House of Representatives," it says, "shall choose their speaker and other officers.") In practice, the majority party does the choosing. Before each congress begins, the majority party puts forward its candidate for Speaker, who turns out—because he attracts the unanimous support of his party—to be a shoo-in. Typically, the Speaker is a very senior member of the party. (Thomas P. "Tip" O'Neill, elected Speaker in 1977, had been in Congress since 1953. His likely successor, Representative Jim Wright, is a long-time congressman from Texas.) Today, the Speaker is two heartbeats away from the presidency, being second in line (after the vice-president) to succeed a deceased president.

Years ago, the Speaker was king of the congressional mountain. Autocrats like "Uncle Joe Cannon" and "Czar Reed" ran the House like a fiefdom. A great revolt in 1910 whittled down the Speaker's powers and gave some of them to committees. But six decades later members of the House restored some of the Speaker's powers. Today, the Speaker of the House has some important formal powers:

— He presides over the House when it is in session.
— He plays a major role in making committee assignments, coveted by all members to ensure their electoral advantage. The Speaker appoints, for example, eight members of the Democratic Steering

[37] Robert L. Peabody, *Leadership in Congress* (Boston: Little, Brown, 1976), p. 4.

and Policy Committee, which functions as the "Committee on Committees" for House Democrats.

— He appoints or plays a key role in appointing the party's legislative leaders and the party leadership staff.

— He exercises substantial control over which bill gets assigned to which committee.

In addition, the Speaker has a great deal of informal clout inside and outside Congress. When the Speaker's party is different from the president's party, he is often a national spokesman for his party. The bank of microphones in front of the Speaker of the House is a commonplace feature of the evening news. A good Speaker also knows the members well, where their skeletons are buried, what ambitions they harbor, and what pressures they are under.

Leadership in the House, though, is not a one-man show. The Speaker's principal partisan ally is the **majority leader,** a job which has been the main stepping-stone to the Speaker's role. The majority leader is responsible for scheduling bills in the House. More important, he is responsible for rounding up votes in behalf of the party's position on legislation. Working with him are the party's **whips,** who carry the word to party troops, counting votes beforehand and leaning on waverers whose votes are crucial to a bill.

The minority party is also organized, ever poised to take over the Speakership and other key posts if it should win a majority in the House. The Republicans have been the minority party in the House since 1955, although they have had a president to look to for leadership for most of the last three decades. Lately, a group of younger, more conservative, Republicans has made life for the Republican **minority leader** difficult. One of their ringleaders was Representative Newt Gingrich of Georgia, a four-term Representative and proponent of a "Conservative Opportunity Society." [38] In 1984, he began using the House's television coverage to make stirring speeches (to empty chambers) condemning the Democrats. In 1985, when the Democratic majority in the House refused to seat a Republican from a close race in Indiana, the Young Turk Republicans went into open revolt. Using parliamentary obstreperousness to block legislation, they made life less easy for both the Democratic majority, as well as their own minority leader, Robert Michel of Illinois.

Leadership in the Senate

The Constitution makes the vice-president of the United States the president of the Senate. This is the vice-president's only constitutional job. But even the mighty Lyndon Johnson, who had been the Senate majority leader before becoming vice-president, found himself an outsider when he returned as the Senate's president. Vice-presidents usually ignore their senatorial chores, leaving power in the Senate up to party leaders. Senators typically return the favor, ignoring the vice-president except in the rare case when his vote can break a tie.

[38] On Gingrich, see Nicholas Lemann, " 'Conservative Opportunity Society,' " *Atlantic Monthly,* May, 1985, pp. 22–36.

Thus the Senate majority leader, aided by the majority whips, is his party's wheelhorse, corralling votes, scheduling the floor action, and influencing committee assignments. No majority leader left quite the imprint that Lyndon Johnson did. He got the job in 1955, during his first term. Johnson was a small-town Texas boy who thrived on power. He was almost mesmerizing in his mixture of tall tales, crude talk, boundless energy, and attention to legislative detail. In the lobbies and offices, the Capitol cloakrooms, and the Washington bars, the "Johnson treatment" was legendary. He combined wheedling, needling, charm, flattery, pressure, promises, near physical abuse, obscenities, bear hugs, and stories to cajole congressmen into compromise. When LBJ became vice-president, the Senate traded his Texas wildcatter style of leadership for that of a taciturn Montana history professor, Mike Mansfield. Under Mansfield's guiding but gentle leadership, senators grew more independent. When Mansfield retired, he was replaced by West Virginia's Robert Byrd, whose fiddle playing has enlivened many a Washington social function. In 1980, the Republicans garnered a majority of the Senate, whereupon Senator Howard Baker, who had been minority leader, became majority leader in the 97th Congress. Thus did Tennessee's Baker achieve a post that his father-in-law, Illinois Senator Everett Dirksen, minority leader from 1959 to 1969, never obtained.

With Senator Baker's retirement from the Senate, the Republicans elected a new party leader as the 1985 congressional session opened. Five candidates were in the running, and Senator Robert Dole of Kansas was selected by his colleagues. A man of rapier wit, Dole was a master legislative strategist. He would have to be, because the major issue he faced as the new majority leader was putting together a plan to deal with a $200 billion budget deficit.

The Doles and Leader. *In November, 1984, the Senate Republicans elected a new Majority Leader after the retirement of Tennessee's Senator Howard Baker. They chose Kansas Senator Robert Dole, whose wife Elizabeth is Secretary of Transportation. She bought the Senator a new dog for the occasion, which was named Leader. Asked at his morning news conference if he was thinking about the presidency, Dole replied that, "Right now, I'm thinking about lunch."*

The Committees and Subcommittees

Will Rogers, the famous Oklahoma humorist, once remarked that "outside of traffic, there is nothing that has held this country back as much as committees." [39] Members of the Senate and the House would apparently disagree. Most of the real work of Congress goes on in committees. In fact, South Carolina's Senator Ernest Hollings once remarked that so little is done on the Senate floor that a senator could run naked through the chamber and no one would notice. Most senators would be handling committee business. Committees dominate congressional policymaking in all its stages, although they usually attract little attention.

Only twice in recent years has the nation's attention been riveted on a congressional committee; both occasions involved the Watergate affair. Senator Sam Ervin (D.—N.C.) chaired the Senate Select Committee on Campaign Activities, which looked into the misdeeds and duplicity of the 1972 campaign. Later, the House Judiciary Committee, chaired by Peter Rodino (D.—N.J.), voted under the glare of television lights to recommend that the House impeach the president of the United States. Ten days later, Richard Nixon was flying back to private life in California.

[39] Quoted in Smith and Deering, *Committees in Congress*, p. 1.

Only once have committees driven a president from office. Regularly, though, they hold hearings to investigate problems and possible wrong-doings and to oversee the executive branch. Most of all, they control the congressional agenda and guide legislation from its introduction to its send-off for the president's signature. Committees can be grouped into four types, of which the first is by far the most important:

1. **Standing committees** are subject-matter committees, handling bills in different policy areas. ⑦ Each house of Congress has its own standing committees; members do not belong to a committee in the other house.

2. **Joint committees** exist in a few subject-matter areas; their membership is drawn from both the Senate and the House.

3. **Conference committees** are formed when the Senate and the House pass a particular bill in different forms. Appointed by the party leadership, a conference committee consists of members of each house chosen to iron out Senate and House differences and report back a single bill.

4. **Select committees** are appointed for a specific purpose. The Senate select committee that looked into Watergate is one well-known example.

The Committees at Work: Legislation and Oversight. With more than 8,000 bills submitted by members every year, some winnowing is essen-

---

⑦ Standing Committees in the Senate and in the House

Senate Committees	House Committees
Agriculture, Nutrition, and Forestry	Agriculture
Appropriations	Appropriations
Armed Services	Armed Services
Banking, Housing, and Urban Affairs	Banking, Finance, and Urban Affairs
Budget	Budget
Commerce, Science, and Transportation	District of Columbia
Energy and Natural Resources	Education and Labor
Environment and Public Works	Energy and Commerce
Finance	Foreign Affairs
Foreign Relations	Government Operations
Governmental Affairs	House Administration
Judiciary	Interior and Insular Affairs
Labor and Human Resources	Judiciary
Rules and Administration	Merchant Marine and Fisheries
Small Business	Post Office and Civil Service
Veterans' Affairs	Public Works and Transportation
	Rules
	Science and Technology
	Small Business
	Standards of Official Conduct
	Veterans' Affairs
	Ways and Means

The Senate Budget Committee at Work. *The Senate and House each has its own budget committee. The task of that committee is to focus congressional attention on the "forest and not just the trees" of budgeting. The budget committees have targets for submitting a "budget reconciliation resolution" to their respective chambers. These resolutions are supposed to bind Congress to an overall total expenditure. Yet as budget deficits have worsened and relationships between the Democratic House and the Republican Senate have been strained, the job of the Budget Committees has ranged from the tough to the impossible.*

tial. Every bill goes to a committee, which then has virtually the power of life and death over it. Only bills getting a favorable committee report are considered by the whole House or Senate.

New bills sent to a committee usually go directly to a subcommittee, which can hold hearings on the bill. Sizable committee and subcommittee staffs conduct research, line up witnesses for hearings, and write and rewrite bills. One output of the committees and their subcommittees is their report on proposed legislation, typically bound in beige or green covers and available from the Government Printing Office. Their most important output, though, is the "marked up" (rewritten) bill itself, submitted to the full House or Senate for debate and voting.

The work of committees does not stop when the bill leaves the committee room. Members of the committee will usually serve as "floor managers" of the bill, helping party leaders hustle votes for it. They will also be the "cue givers" to whom other members turn for advice. And, when Senate and House pass different versions of the same bill, some committee members will be on the conference committee.

The committees and subcommittees do not leave the scene even after legislation is passed. They stay busy in legislative **oversight,** the process of monitoring the bureaucracy and its administration of policy. Oversight is handled mainly through hearings. When an agency wants a bigger budget, the use of its present budget is reviewed. Even if no budgetary issues are involved, members of committees constantly monitor how a law is being implemented. Agency heads and even cabinet secretaries testify, bringing graphs, charts, and data on the progress they have made and the problems they face. Committee staffs and committee members grill agency heads about particular problems. A member may ask a Small Business Administration official why constituents who are applying for loans get a runaround. On another committee, officials charged with listing endangered species may defend the grey wolf against a member of Congress whose sheep-rancher constituents are not fond of wolves. Oversight, one of the checks Congress can exercise on the

385

executive branch, gives Congress the power to pressure agencies and, in the extreme, to cut their budgets in order to secure compliance with congressional wishes, even congressional whims.

Getting on a Committee. If you are an incoming freshman member of Congress, one of your first worries (after paying off your campaign debts and taking the family on that much-needed vacation) is getting on the right committee. Although it is not always easy to know what the right committee is, it is fairly easy to figure out some wrong committees. The Iowa newcomer does not want to get stuck on the Merchant Marine and Fisheries committee; the Brooklyn freshman would like to avoid Agriculture. Members seek committees that will help them achieve three goals: reelection, influence in Congress, and the opportunity to make policy in areas they think are important.[40]

Just after their election, new members write to the party's congressional leaders and members of their state delegation, indicating their committee preferences. Every committee includes members from both parties, but a majority of each committee's members as well as its chairman come from the majority party. Each party in each house has a slightly different way of picking its committee members.[41] Party leaders almost always play a key role. Generally, freshmen will do a little better in getting their first committee choice than nonfreshmen wanting to shift committees.[42] Freshmen have nothing and want something; nonfreshmen have something already and want a better assignment.

Getting Ahead on the Committee: Chairmen and the Seniority System. If committees are the most important influencers of the congressional agenda, **committee chairmen** are the most important influencers of the committee agenda. They play dominant—though no longer monopolistic—roles in scheduling hearings, hiring staff, appointing subcommittees, and managing committee bills when they are brought before the full house.

Until the 1970s, there was a simple rule for picking committee chairmen, the **seniority system.** It worked like this: If you had served on the committee longest, and your party controlled Congress, you got to be chairman—whatever your party loyalty, your mental state, or your competence.[43]

This system gave a decisive edge to members from "safe" districts. They were least likely to be challenged for reelection and most likely to achieve seniority. In the Democratic party, most safe districts were in the South. As a result, southern politicians had power beyond their numbers.

[40] Richard Fenno, *Congressmen in Committees* (Boston: Little, Brown, 1973), p. 1.

[41] The way this process works for the Democratic party in the House is described by David W. Rhode and Kenneth A. Shepsle, "Democratic Committee Assignments in the House of Representatives," *American Political Science Review* 67 (September 1973):889–905. See also Charles S. Bullock, III, "Freshman Committee Assignments in the House of Representatives," *American Political Science Review* 66 (September 1972):996–1007.

[42] Rhode and Shepsle, "Democratic Committee Assignments in the House of Representatives," p. 898.

[43] On the pre-reform seniority system, see Barbara Hinckley, *The Seniority System in Congress* (Bloomington: Indiana University Press, 1971).

They chaired many committees, sometimes dominating them as if they were plantations. For years it seemed to some that southerners may have lost the Civil War but won the Congress as a consolation prize. James O. Eastland of Mississippi chaired the Senate Judiciary Committee, which handled civil rights legislation, a policy arena not dear to Eastland's plantation-owning heart. L. Mendel Rivers of South Carolina chaired the House Armed Services Committee, engineering military bases, shipyards, and defense contracts for his district. Today, the South may be rising again, but its hold on congressional chairmanships is dwindling. The South is becoming a two-party region, and electoral losses, aging, and mortality have taken their toll of southern committee chairmen.

Once Woodrow Wilson, a political scientist before he became a politician, could say that the government of the United States was really the government by the chairman of the standing committees of Congress. So powerful were the chairs for most of the twentieth century that they could bully members or bottle up legislation any time—and with almost certain knowledge that they would be chairs for the rest of their electoral life. But in the 1970s, the Congress faced a revolt of its younger members. First the Republicans in the House and, later, both parties in both branches permitted members to vote on committee chairmen. In 1975, the House Democrats dumped three chairmen. Today, seniority remains the *general rule* for selecting chairmen, but there are exceptions. You can look at the overthrow of one key chair in 1985 in [8].

These and other reforms have somewhat reduced the clout of the chairs. Today, two authorities on congressional committees could actually write: "In the 1980s . . . chairs are far less able to mold the decision-making processes of their committees. Indeed, the most common complaint we heard about committee leadership from committee members and staff was that chairs are no longer responsible for their committees' actions." [44] Such an observation would have been unthinkable two decades ago.

[44] Smith and Deering, *Committees in Congress*, p. 177.

---

8 Armed Services Gets a New Chairman, 1985

On January 4, 1985, House Democrats convened to vote on their organization for the upcoming congressional session. Attention focused on a potential revolt against Representative Melvin Price, the eighty-year-old chairman of the House Armed Services Committee. The party caucus voted 121–118 to remove Price. Ironically, Price had succeeded to the chairmanship during the first revolt of the members in 1975, when he replaced the unpopular Edward Hebert of Louisiana. Old and frail, Price himself had allowed that, if reelected, this term would be his last. Members decided not to wait.

The surprise came with the selection of Price's successor. House Democratic leaders nominated the second-ranking member of the Armed Services Committee, Charles Bennett of Florida. From the floor, however, members nominated Les Aspin, the seventh most senior member on the panel. Aspin defeated Bennett on a 125–103 vote. Aspin and his supporters had waged a vigorous campaign for the post.

For the first time in recent congressional history, a congressional committee on defense was in the hands of a major critic of the Defense Department. Traditionally,

(box continues on next page)

members of the Armed Services Committee had been veterans, conservative regardless of their party, and eager to work as Pentagon handmaidens in Congress. Aspin was different. He had long been a critic of the profligacy of the Pentagon. An early opponent of the MX missile, he changed his mind and helped keep it alive. His support in 1985 votes was indispensible to the MX approval by the Congress. Still, it would be a new day at Armed Services. No longer could the Pentagon find sustenance in a virtual "blank check" mentality at the committee.

Source: "House Seniority System Jolted; Price Dumped, Aspin Elected," *Congressional Quarterly,* January 5, 1985, pp. 7–9.

Changing of the Guard. *In January, 1985, the House Democrats voted not to continue aging Representative Melvin Price of Illinois (left) as chairman of the Armed Services Committee, the powerful committee which oversees the Pentagon. Instead, the House Democrats selected Representative Les Aspin of Wisconsin as the new chairman. It was the first time since the Cold War began that the Armed Services Committee was led by a critic of the Defense Department, rather than a supporter. Aspin, though, was a congressional leader in efforts to create an MX missile system.*

The Mushrooming Caucuses: The Informal Organization of Congress

The formal organization of Congress consists of its party leadership and its committee structures, but equally important is the informal organization of the House and Senate. The informal networks of friendship and mutual interest can spring from numerous sources. Friendship, ideology, and geography are long-standing sources of informal organization.

Lately, these traditional informal groupings have been dominated by the growing number of caucuses. A **caucus** is a grouping of members of Congress sharing some interest or characteristic. In the 99th Congress there were more than seventy of these caucuses, most of them containing membership from both parties and some from both the House and the

Senate.[45] The goal of all caucuses is to shape the agenda of Congress. They do this by elevating their particular issues or interests to a prominent place in the day-to-day workings of Congress. They are rather like interest groups, but with a difference: Their members are members of Congress, not petitioners to Congress on the outside looking in. Mulhollan, Hammond, and Stevens emphasize that "much of the activity of informal groups is directed toward agenda-setting in Congress."[46] The caucuses, interest groups within Congress, are nicely situated to pack more punch than the interest group outside Congress.

Consider the sampling of caucuses in ⑨. Some caucuses are based on characteristics of the members, such as the Black Caucus, the Congresswomen's Caucus, and the Hispanic Caucus. Some of them are based on regional groupings, such as the Sunbelt Caucus and the Northeast-Midwest Congressional Coalition. Some are ideological groupings, such as the Moderate/Conservative Democrats. Still others are based on some economic interest important to a set of constituencies, such as the Steel, Travel and Tourism, Coal, and Mushroom caucuses. (Yes, there is a Mushroom Caucus, composed of members interested in protecting the interests of mushroom growers.)

The activities of these caucuses are directed toward their fellow members of Congress and toward administrative agencies. Within Congress, they press for committees to hold hearings, they push particular legislation, and they pull together votes on bills they favor. The Steel Caucus, for example, contains 160 members whose districts include major steel-

[45] Daniel P. Mulhollan, Susan W. Hammond, and Arthur G. Stevens, Jr., "Informal Groups and Agenda-Setting in Congress," paper delivered at the annual meeting of the Midwest Political Science Association, Cincinnati, Ohio, April 16–18, 1981. See also Burdett Loomis, "Congressional Caucuses and the Politics of Representation," in Dodd and Oppenheimer (eds.), *Congress Reconsidered*, 2nd. ed. (Washington: Congressional Quarterly Press, 1981), Chap. 11.

[46] Mulhollan, et al., "Informal Groups and Agenda-setting in Congress," p. 4.

---

⑨   The Congressional Caucuses: An Incomplete Sampling

Whether based on region, constituency characteristics, or member characteristics, caucuses have grown in recent years. Some have their own professional staffs. Most meet regularly to share ideas. All press their fellow members of the House and Senate to be more attentive to the problems of coal or steel or textiles or Hispanics or the arts or whatever. Here are some of the caucuses operating today:

— The Democratic Study Group, a set of liberal Democratic House members.
— The Concerned Senators for the Arts, a group interested in more federal money for the arts.
— The Travel and Tourism Caucus, interested in more travel and tourism, no doubt because they represent

constituencies in Nevada, Florida, and other tourist meccas.
— The Blue-collar Caucus, a group representing heavily unionized districts or members who themselves were blue-collar workers (not a large caucus, incidentally). The Vietnam-era Veterans Caucus, a group of congressmen who are Vietnam War veterans.
— The Jewelry Caucus, representing the plight of the jewelry industry.
— The Mushroom Caucus, representing the plight of the mushroom industry.
— The Auto Task Force, representing the plight of the auto industry.

One Caucus. *The proliferation of caucuses in Congress has added one more layer of pluralism in the legislative process. Caucuses are normally composed of legislators whose districts share common economic characteristics (for example, steel production or tourism) or who share some personal or political characteristic in common. Here is a meeting of the Hispanic Caucus.*

producing enterprises. (Nearly one in five Pennsylvanians is employed in the steel industry.) It pushed the House Ways and Means Committee to hold hearings on the plight of the steel industry. The Mushroom Caucus successfully pressured the executive branch to ban the importing of canned mushrooms, hoping to help domestic mushroom producers.

This explosion of informal groups in Congress has made the representation of interests in Congress a more direct process, cutting out the middleman, the lobbyist. The caucuses proceed on the assumption that no one is a more effective lobbyist than a senator or representative. And they may be right.

As with other lobbyists, the caucuses seek to influence the legislative process, the way bills become law. We will now study this process, which we might term "labyrinthine"; that is, getting a bill through Congress is very much like completing a difficult, intricate maze.

THE CONGRESSIONAL PROCESS

The Legislative Labyrinth

In the last chapter, we described the government's *agenda*. Congress' agenda, of course, is a crowded one. About 10,000 bills are introduced annually. A **bill** is a proposed law, drafted in precise, legal language. Anyone—even you or I—can draft a bill. The White House and interest groups are common sources of polished bills. However, only members of the House or the Senate can formally submit a bill for consideration. What happens to a bill as it works its way through the legislative labyrinth is depicted in ☐10☐. Most bills are quietly killed off early in the process. Some are introduced mostly as a favor to a group or a constituent. Some are private bills, granting citizenship to a constituent or paying a settlement to the lady whose car was demolished by the Postal Service truck. But some bills may alter the course of the nation.

Basically, Congress is a reactive and cumbersome decision-making body. Rules are piled upon rules and procedures upon procedures. Some congressional strategists are masters of the art of the "rider," an amendment, typically unrelated to the bill itself, intended to be carried along on the back of another bill. Legislators often use riders to pass a bill that on

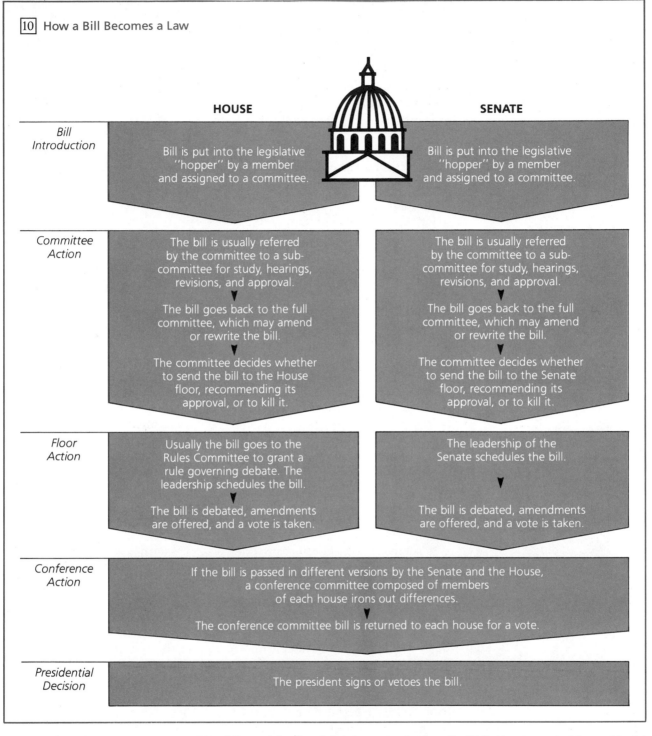

HOUSE

SENATE

Bill Introduction

Bill is put into the legislative "hopper" by a member and assigned to a committee.

Bill is put into the legislative "hopper" by a member and assigned to a committee.

Committee Action

The bill is usually referred by the committee to a sub-committee for study, hearings, revisions, and approval.

The bill goes back to the full committee, which may amend or rewrite the bill.

The committee decides whether to send the bill to the House floor, recommending its approval, or to kill it.

The bill is usually referred by the committee to a sub-committee for study, hearings, revisions, and approval.

The bill goes back to the full committee, which may amend or rewrite the bill.

The committee decides whether to send the bill to the Senate floor, recommending its approval, or to kill it.

Floor Action

Usually the bill goes to the Rules Committee to grant a rule governing debate. The leadership schedules the bill.

The bill is debated, amendments are offered, and a vote is taken.

The leadership of the Senate schedules the bill.

The bill is debated, amendments are offered, and a vote is taken.

Conference Action

If the bill is passed in different versions by the Senate and the House, a conference committee composed of members of each house irons out differences.

The conference committee bill is returned to each house for a vote.

Presidential Decision

The president signs or vetoes the bill.

Many bills travel, in effect, full circle, coming first from the White House as part of the presidential agenda, then returning to the president at the end of the process. In the interim, there are two parallel processes in the Senate and House, starting with committee action. If a committee gives a bill a favorable report, the whole chamber considers it. When it is passed in different versions by the two chambers, a conference committee drafts a single compromise bill.

its own doesn't have enough support to pass. A bill must pass one procedure after another to get through the system. So complex is the system that President John F. Kennedy once remarked that "it is very easy to defeat a bill in Congress. It is much more difficult to pass one."[47] Even presidents, as we will shortly see, find it hard to influence Congress.

There are, of course, countless influences on this legislative process. Presidents, parties, constituents, groups, the congressional and committee leadership structure—these and more offer members cues for their decision making. Let us look at a few of the major influences on Congress, starting with the President.

Presidents and Congress: Partners and Protagonists

In late March 1985, President Reagan rode by motorcade to Capitol Hill. He went for lunch just five hours before the Senate was to vote on $1.5 billion for the MX missile. He met with Republican senators and emphasized how essential the MX was to successful arms negotiations with the Soviet Union. (He won the vote in the Senate, 55–45.) He had started his intensive lobbying effort three weeks before, hosting 8 a.m. breakfasts for small groups of 25 to 35 senators and representatives at the White House. Each included the secretary of state, the secretary of defense, and the national security advisor. Dozens of other members of Congress were personally called by the president. (The White House switchboard tracked down New York Senator Alphonse D'Amato in Manhattan's Little Italy section, eating dinner at a favorite restaurant. Thinking it was a practical joke by his old friend Congressman Guy Molinari, D'Amato shouted into the phone: "Molinari, you creep, cut out this crap.") There were promises, too. No one made them public, of course, but one White House aide insisted that there was nothing "illegal or expensive" about the commitments President Reagan gave those who supported his position.[48]

It seems a wonder that presidents—even with all their power and influence—can push and wheedle anything through the cavernous congressional process. Light remarks that "The President must usually win at least ten times to hope for final passage: (1) in one House subcommittee, (2) in the full House committee, (3) in the House Rules Committee to move to the floor, (4) on the House floor, (5) in one Senate subcommittee, (6) in the full Senate subcommittee, (7) on the Senate floor, (8) in the House-Senate conference committee to work out the differences between the two bills, (9) back to the House floor for final passage, and (10) back to the Senate floor for final passage."[49] Presidents are partners with Congress in the legislative process. But all presidents are also Congress' antagonists struggling with Congress to control legislative outcomes.

Presidents have their own legislative agenda, based in part on their party's platform and their electoral coalition. Their task is to persuade

The Chief Legislator. We call the president the Chief Legislator, even though he rarely appears in the Capitol Building itself. His legislative aides make most of the contacts with Congress. From time to time, though, on a particularly critical issue, the president will get into the legislative act, calling key supporters and trying to persuade waverers.

[47] Paul Light, *Artful Work: The Politics of Social Security Reform* (New York: Random House, 1985), p. 13.

[48] The MX lobbying story is told in *Time*, April 1, 1985, pp. 20–21.

[49] Light, *Artful Work*, p. 13.

Congress that the president's agenda should be its own. Lyndon Johnson once claimed (with perhaps a touch of that famous Johnsonian overstatement), "If an issue is not included on the presidential agenda, it is almost impossible—short of crisis—to get the Congress to focus on it."[50] Political scientists sometimes call the president the "chief legislator," a term that might have appalled the Constitution writers, with their insistence on separation of powers. But facts are facts. Presidents do help create the congressional agenda. They are also their own best lobbyists.

A president has many resources with which to influence Congress. (We will look carefully at his political clout in Chapter 13.) He may try to influence members directly—calling up the wavering member and telling him or her that the country's future hinges on this one vote, for example—but not often. If the president picked just one key bill and spent ten minutes on the telephone with each of the 535 members of Congress, he would spend eighty-nine hours chatting with them. Instead, he wisely leaves most White House lobbying to his congressional liaison office. He himself works mainly through regular meetings with his party's leaders in the House and Senate.

It is hard to measure one person's power over another, and especially hard to measure presidential power over Congress. The *Congressional Quarterly* regularly calculates a "presidential success score." 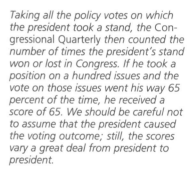 It is

[50] Doris Kearns, *Lyndon Johnson and the American Dream* (New York: New American Library, 1976), p. 146.

Taking all the policy votes on which the president took a stand, the Congressional Quarterly then counted the number of times the president's stand won or lost in Congress. If he took a position on a hundred issues and the vote on those issues went his way 65 percent of the time, he received a score of 65. We should be careful not to assume that the president caused the voting outcome; still, the scores vary a great deal from president to president.

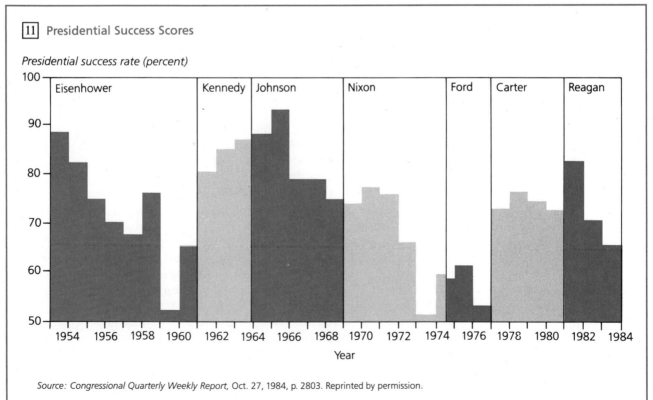

11 Presidential Success Scores

Presidential success rate (percent)

Source: *Congressional Quarterly Weekly Report*, Oct. 27, 1984, p. 2803. Reprinted by permission.

based on the proportion of congressional votes in which the president's position won. Nevertheless, supporting a winning position does not prove the president caused the victory.

At least one political scientist, Aage Clausen, thinks that presidential influence on Congress is overrated, particularly on domestic matters. Not surprisingly, he found that presidents are potent bargainers on foreign policy matters, as President Reagan was on the MX missile. But on domestic matters, the president is only one of many claimants for the attention of Congress. [51]

On domestic policy issues, certainly the president cannot be completely ignored. He has a fair-sized arsenal of weapons to deal with Congress. Popular presidents can lend campaign support to a congressional campaign (presumably unpopular presidents can promise to stay in Washington). They can use the bureaucratic apparatus to tilt federal aid dollars in favor of a senator's favorite project back home. They can lend a sympathetic ear when Congressman So-and-So wants his campaign chairperson appointed to a federal commission. And presidents can simply confer prestige. Even if those MX breakfasts in the White House changed no minds, the men and women there were pleased to be present. The president, however effective with Congress on a particular issue, is still the president of the United States.

Party and Constituency

Presidents come and go; the parties linger on. Presidents do not determine a member's electoral fortunes; constituents do. Where presidents are less influential, on domestic policies especially, party and constituency are more important.

Party Influence. On some issues, members of the party stick together like a marching band. They are most cohesive when Congress is electing its official leaders. A vote for Speaker of the House is a straight party-line vote, with every Democrat on one side and every Republican on the other. On other issues, the party coalition may come unglued. Votes on civil rights policies have shown deep divisions within each party.

Differences between the parties are sharpest on questions of social welfare and economic policy. [52] When voting on labor issues, traditionally Democrats cling together, leaning toward the side of the unions, whereas Republicans vote with business. On social welfare issues—poverty, unemployment aid, help to the cities—Democrats are more generous than Republicans. That the parties split this way should not be too surprising if you recall the party coalitions described in Chapter 7 (page 209). Once in office, party members favor their electoral coalitions.

Party leaders in Congress help "whip" their members into line. Their power to do so is limited, of course. They cannot drum a recalcitrant member out of the party (as party leaders in Britain can). But leaders

---

[51] Aage Clausen, *How Congressmen Decide: A Policy Focus* (New York: St. Martin's, 1973), p. 209.

[52] Clausen, *How Congressmen Decide.*

have plenty of influences, including some say about committee posts, the power to boost a member's pet projects, and the subtle but significant influence of information.

Recently, the parties in Congress, especially the Republicans, have been a growing source of money for congressional campaigns. Once the Democratic and Republican Congressional Campaign committees were informal organizations which did little, and collected little, for party campaigners in the constituencies. Lately, though, the congressional campaign committees of both parties have energized. They help recruit candidates, run seminars in campaign skills, and conduct polls. Equally important these days, the congressional campaign committees have money to hand out to promising candidates. As recently as 1975, the Democratic congressional campaign committee was doling out only about half-a-million dollars annually, and the Republicans more than a million. As with the Republican party in general, the Republican Congressional Campaign Committee by the 1980s was handing out more than $7.5 million each election to promising Republican incumbents and challengers. [53] Although these figures were dwarfed by individual contributions and by PAC moneys, they have also given the congressional parties a role they never had before: The parties can make an impact on the kinds of people who sit in Congress on either side of the aisle.

Constituency Influence. The best way constituents can influence congressional voting is simple: elect a representative or senator who agrees with their views. John Sullivan and Robert O'Connor discovered that congressional candidates tend to take policy positions different from each other. Moreover, the winners tend to vote on roll calls pretty much as they said they would. [54] If voters use their good sense to elect candidates who match their policy positions, then constituents *can* influence congressional policy.

If voters miss their chance and elect someone out of step with their thinking, it may be difficult to influence his or her votes. It is hard even for well-intentioned legislators to know what people want. Some pay careful attention to their mail, but mail is a notoriously unreliable indicator of people's thinking. Individuals with extreme opinions on an issue are more likely to write than those with moderate views. Some members send questionnaires to constituents. Some try public-opinion polling, but it is expensive if professionally done and unreliable if not.

Dislodging an incumbent, as we have seen, is no easy task. Even legislators whose votes are out of step with their constituents tend to return. Most voters have trouble recalling the names of their representatives and senators, let alone keeping up with their roll-call record. Most issues are obscure. On those, legislators can ignore constituency opinion safely.

[53] Congressional Quarterly, *Elections '84* (Washington: Congressional Quarterly Press, 1984), p. 137.
[54] John L. Sullivan and Robert E. O'Connor, "Electoral Choice and Popular Control of Public Policy: The Case of the 1966 House Elections," *American Political Science Review* 66 (December 1972):1256–68.

On some controversial issues, however, legislators ignore constituent opinion at great peril. For years, civil rights votes fit that bill for southern congressmen, who would not have dared to vote for a civil rights bill. Lately, representatives and senators have fretted about the new "single-issue groups." Such groups care little about a member's overall record. To them, a vote on one issue—gun control, abortion, the ERA, or whatever—is all that counts. Ready to pounce on one wrong vote and pour money into an opponent's campaign, these new forces in constituency politics make every legislator nervous.

Lobbyists and Interest Groups

Lobbyists have a dismal image, one made worse by the scandal called "Koreagate." A South Korean lobbyist named Tongsun Park unloaded cash on dozens of congressmen to secure support for favorable trade policies. Following the scandal, there was a *Time* cover story on "The Swarming Lobbyists." *Time* announced its estimate that lobbyists spent more than $1 billion annually to pass or defeat legislation. It quoted House Speaker O'Neill as saying (*Time* said he "grumbled" it), "Everybody in America has a lobby." [55]

Such stories give lobbyists a bad press, no doubt often deserved. But lobbyists have a job to do. Their job is to represent the interests of their organization. Lobbyists, some of them former members of Congress, can provide members with crucial information and often with assurances of financial aid in the next campaign.

There are an estimated 10,000 Washington representatives. [56] Forty groups alone are concerned with the single issue of protecting Alaska's environment; the bigger the issue, the more representatives are involved in it. Charls Walker is probably the king of Washington lobbyists. Bethlehem Steel is one of the corporations he represents and it is only one of many, including General Electric, Ford Motor Company, Procter and Gamble, ITT, Goodyear, CBS, Alcoa, Inland Steel, Republic Steel, American Airlines, and the Chase Manhattan Bank. The Nissan Motor Corporation, which runs the plant in Smyrna, has a Washington office on Pennsylvania Avenue and its own lobbyist, Corporate Public Affairs Manager Franklin J. Crawford. Washington law firms represent many interests also. Both station WLAC-TV in Nashville and station WLVT in Bethlehem are represented by Washington firm Dow, Lohnes, and Albertson. States and cities either hire Washington representatives or send their own. The city of San Antonio is represented by the firm of Creamer Dickson Basford, while the state of Texas has hired Sarah Weddington as director of the Office of State Federal Relations. Washington representatives can be a formidable group.

Before we decide that lobbyists hold all the high cards in their relations to members of Congress, we should note some trumps that repre-

[55] *Time*, August 7, 1978, p. 15.
[56] Arthur C. Close, ed., *Washington Representatives 1984* (Washington: Columbia Books, 1984), p. 5. The material on Washington representatives in the rest of this paragraph comes from Close.

sentatives hold. The easiest way to frustrate a lobbyist is to ignore him or her. Lobbyists make little headway with their opponents anyway. The lobbyist for General Motors arguing against automobile pollution controls would not have much influence with a card-carrying Sierra Club legislator. Members of Congress can make life uncomfortable for lobbyists, too. They can embarrass them, expose heavy-handed tactics, and spread the word among an organization's members that it is being poorly represented in Washington. Last but not least, Congress *can* regulate lobbyists, although it has never done so very well.

For more than thirty years, lobbyists have been regulated mainly by the 1946 Federal Regulation of Lobbying Act. Paid lobbyists whose principal purpose is to influence or defeat legislation must register and file reports with the secretary of the Senate and the clerk of the House. In theory, by forcing publicity regarding who the lobbyists are, who finances them, and what bills they are trying to pass or defeat, the law would not only prevent shady deals between lobbyists and Congress but also curb the influence of special interests. In fact, the law has been largely unenforceable; only four cases have been prosecuted under it. Few organizations are even required to register as lobbyists. The law covers only direct contacts with Congress and only those whose principal activity is lobbying. And special interest groups seem to be thriving. Indirect, grassroots lobbying—such as computerized mailings to encourage citizens to pressure their representatives on an issue—has grown. So, too, have efforts to tighten the regulation of lobbyists.

In 1978, the House did pass a bill that strengthened the requirements for disclosure of lobbying activities, but the bill died in a Senate committee. Again in 1979, efforts to reform regulation of lobbying failed. Cynics might be ready to view the failure as further evidence of greed or corruption or inertia in high places. But among those opposing the 1978 House bill were the American Civil Liberties Union, the Sierra Club, and the United Church of Christ. That bill would have required groups to report such grassroots activities as letter-writing campaigns and contributions by organizations. The result, critics claimed, would have been to discourage some groups from making their views known. The bill's time-consuming and costly record-keeping requirements would even have forced some small lobbying groups out of existence. The proposed regulations thus posed a familiar kind of problem: how to balance the need for disclosing the activities of lobbyists with the need to protect privacy and freedom of speech.

UNDERSTANDING CONGRESS

There is no shortage of congressional frustrations on the inside, nor criticism on the outside. Congress is a complex institution. Its members want to make sound national policy, but they also want to be there after the next election. We have now reviewed how Congress is organized and how it works. To understand Congress, we turn to the theories we have used throughout *Government in America*.

Democratic or Elitist?

The success of democratic government in a large nation depends on the quality of representation. In a tiny decision-making body, people can cast their own votes. But we could hardly hold a national referendum on every policy issue on the governmental agenda. Instead, we delegate decision-making power to representatives. If Congress is a successful democratic institution, it will have to be a successful representative institution.

Certainly, some aspects of Congress make it very *un*representative. Its members are an American elite. Its leadership is chosen by its own members, not by any vote of the American people. Voters have little direct influence over the men and women who chair key committees or lead congressional parties. Voters in just a single constituency control the fate of committee chairmen and party leaders. Voters in the other 434 House districts and the other 49 states have no real say about who chairs the energy committee, a committee considering defense buildups, or a committee making economic policy.

Nevertheless, the evidence in this chapter should demonstrate that Congress does not callously write people's opinions off as worthless. Who voters elect makes a difference in how votes turn out; which party is in power affects policies. Linkage institutions *do* link voters to policymakers. No doubt Congress could do a better job at representation than it does. Legislators find it hard to know what constituents want. Groups may keep important issues off the legislative agenda. Members may spend so much time servicing their constituencies that they have little time left to represent those constituencies in the policymaking process.

Pluralism or Hyperpluralism?

Pluralism describes a system of government in which there are multiple centers of power, loosely coordinated to make policy. Hyperpluralism describes a system of power with multiple centers, but where coordination is difficult or even impossible. Pluralism implies a decentralized system of decision making. Hyperpluralism implies a decision-making system so decentralized that the system's effectiveness is compromised. Recent reforms of Congress have certainly made it a more open, decentralized institution. They may also have made it so open and decentralized that congressional effectiveness is weakened.

The legislative process has become a labyrinth. Easterbrook reports the following story:[57]

> Because of the regularity with which redundant floor votes occur, Congress "never finishes anything, never arrives at a decision," according to Senator Ted Stevens of Alaska. "Always they are just preliminary decisions that will be addressed again anyway. It's totally confusing to the public, and even to ourselves." By my count there have been thirty-six "test votes" in the House and Senate on the MX missile since Reagan took office, most of them necessitated by some whorl in the legislative process. These test votes have been accompanied by tension, packed press galleries, ringing debate—all

[57] Easterbrook, "What's Wrong with Congress?", p. 61.

the drama of a decision, but no decision. On a Tuesday in December of 1982 the House worked late into the night debating whether to cut nearly $1 billion from MX funding. The vote was headline news nationwide and was played as HOUSE KILLS MX. Then, on Wednesday—*the following day*—the House voted to retain $2.5 billion for MX research and development.

In 1983, there were eight votes in the Senate on what language to use in condemning the Soviet destruction of a Korean Air Lines plane. Over a three-month period in 1983, the House took twenty-seven recorded votes on a nuclear freeze resolution, eleven in a single week. [58]

Faced with a staggering legislative calendar and workload, Congress has struggled for years to meet its information needs. Thomas Jefferson wisely remarked that "there is, in fact, no subject to which a member of Congress may not have occasion to refer." The problem is that the number of subjects has become incredibly large and the subjects highly technical. The House Select Committee on Committees itself said that [59]

> During the 19th century, America had many distinguished senators, presidents, congressmen . . . but most of these men dealt in their entire political life. . . . with only four or five major problems. . . . Now the problems swarm across the desks of political leaders.

Wrestling with a plethora of problems, coupled with a glut of demands, has not been easy for Congress. Congress has tried—and tried, and tried—to reform itself to deal more effectively with its agenda. Unfortunately, the reforms themselves have made the Congress a more pluralist, even hyperpluralist, institution.

Reforming Congress

At least since the revolts against the autocratic Speakers Reed and Cannon in the early twentieth century, reformers have tried to promote a more open, democratic Congress. To a large degree, they have succeeded. Looking at Congress in the 1950s, one could say that it was like a stepladder. The members advanced one rung at a time toward the heights of power with each reelection. At the top was real power in Congress. Committee chairmen were automatically selected by seniority. Their power on the committee was unquestioned. Bills disappeared forever into the chairman's "vest pocket" if he did not like them. He alone created subcommittees, picked their members, and routed bills to them. If committees controlled bills from the cradle to the grave, the chairman was both midwife and undertaker. At the bottom of the ladder, the norm of apprenticeship—"be seen and not heard"—prevailed. The standing Washington joke about seniority was this: "Son, the longer you're here, the more you'll come to appreciate the seniority system." The system was democratic—one person, one vote—when the roll call came. But it was not democratic when the bill itself was shaped, shelved, or sunk.

The waves of congressional reform, in the 1960s and especially the 1970s, changed all this. Lyndon Johnson had started the reform ball

[58] Ibid.
[59] This quotation and the Jefferson quotation are both from Stephen E. Frantzich, *Computers in Congress* (Beverly Hills, California: Sage Publications, 1982), pp. 9 and 10.

rolling during his majority leadership with the "Johnson rule," which limited senators to one key chairmanship. This reform allowed for more room for junior members at the top.

By the 1970s the reform movement, bent on democratizing Congress, picked up speed. It tried to create more democracy by spreading power around. First to go was the automatic and often autocratic dominance of the most senior member as committee chairman. Instead, the chairman was elected by the majority party, and some of the most objectionable ones were dropped. The power of chairman was also cut by the proliferation of subcommittees, which "has spread authority, visibility, and resources around in both chambers."[60]

Subcommittees became the new centers of power in Congress. Freshman senators and representatives came to chair major subcommittees. In the House, five separate subcommittees focus on consumer legislation, a dozen on welfare policy, and six on energy. Legislative hurdles are harder to pass because of the proliferation of subcommittees.

Not only the formal reforms of Congress, but also the proliferation of informal caucuses has tended to decentralize power in Congress. Burdett Loomis remarks that "the proliferation of caucuses illustrates the shoring up of particularistic forces in Congress. . . . And while members decry the increase in single-issue politics, they have only to consider their own behavior."[61]

All these recent changes in Congress—seniority reform, the subcommittee explosion, and the burgeoning caucuses—have fragmented the power of Congress. Richard Fenno, a veteran observer of Congress, once remarked that the "performance of Congress as an institution is very largely the performance of its committees," but that the committee system is the "epitome of fragmentation and decentralization."[62] The fragmentation of power in Congress promotes, hyperpluralists would say, fragmented policy. The agriculture committees busily tend to the interests of tobacco farmers, while committees on health and welfare spend millions for lung cancer research. One committee wrestles with domestic unemployment while another makes tax policy that encourages business to open new plants out of the country.

Interest groups grow on committees and subcommittees like barnacles on an ocean liner. After a while, these groups develop intimacy and influence with "their" committee. Committee decisions usually carry the day on the roll-call vote. Thus, the committee system links congressional policymaking to the multiplicity of interests, rather than to a majority's preference. When special interests usually win, hyperpluralists worry that the public's interest may lose. Pluralists see Congress as a place where many interests compete for a spot on the policy agenda. Hyperpluralists wonder if so many groups get attention that policy is as uncoordinated and fragmented and decentralized as the committee system itself.

[60] David E. Price, "Congressional Committees and the Policy Process," in Dodd and Oppenheimer (eds.), *Congress Reconsidered*, 2nd ed., p. 175.
[61] Loomis, "Congressional Caucuses," p. 218.
[62] Richard Fenno, "If, as Ralph Nader Says, Congress Is the 'Broken Branch,' How Come We Love Our Congressmen So Much?" in Norman Ornstein (ed.), *Congress in Change* (New York: Praeger, 1975), p. 282.

Political scientist Samuel Huntington offered a curious observation about Congress: "Congress is in a legislative dilemma because public opinion conceives of it as a legislature."[63] Indeed, not public opinion alone, but the Constitution itself conceives of Congress as our policymaking institution. The Madisonian system intended that Congress make policy, the president implement it, and the courts enforce it. Is there something wrong with the Madisonian model? Congress is a modern manifestation of Madison's checks and balances and separated powers. Itself fragmented and divided, Congress has let its power to make policy slip to interest groups, to the bureaucracies, and to the president. Congressional scholar Lawrence C. Dodd bluntly predicted that future congressional policymaking in this decentralized system will be "incremental at best, immobilized and incoherent as a norm."[64]

CONGRESS SUMMARIZED

According to the Constitution, Congress is the policymaking branch of government. But legislative policymaker is only one of the roles of a member of Congress. Congressmen are also politicians, and politicians always have their eye on the next election. Success in congressional elections is determined more by constituency service—casework and the pork barrel—than by policymaking. Senators and representatives have become so skilled at constituency service that incumbents have a big edge over challengers. Not only do incumbents tend to win, but they tend to win by big margins.

The structure of Congress is so complex that it seems remarkable that legislation gets passed at all. Its bicameral division means that bills have two sets of committee hurdles to clear. Recent reforms have decentralized power, so the job of leading Congress is harder than ever.

[63] Samuel P. Huntington, "Congressional Responses to the Twentieth Century," in David Truman (ed.), *The Congress and America's Future* (Englewood Cliffs, N.J.: Prentice-Hall, 1965), p. 29.
[64] Lawrence C. Dodd, "Congress, the Constitution, and the Crisis of Legitimation," in Dodd and Oppenheimer (eds.), *Congress Reconsidered*, 2nd ed., p. 412.

ONLY SOME CONGRESSMEN SAY ONE THING AND DO ANOTHER —

THE REST OF THEM SAY IT AND DO NOTHING —

6-7

BRICKMAN

Brickman, The Washington Star

Presidents try hard to influence Congress, and parties and elections can also shape legislators' choices. Their impact clearly differs from one policy area to another. Party impacts are clearest on issues for which the party's coalitions are clearest—social welfare and economic issues in particular. Constituencies influence policy mostly by the initial choice of a representative. Members of Congress do pay attention to voters, especially on visible issues, but most issues are not visible. On these, lobbyists are more influential.

Evaluating Congress, we found that it had some undemocratic and unrepresentative features. Its members are hardly average Americans. Even so, they pay some attention to popular preferences, when they can figure out what they are. People inside and outside the institution, however, think Congress is ineffective. Some even suggest that it redefine its role, becoming less a policymaker and more a link between little citizen and big government.

Key Terms

incumbents	Speaker of the House	select committees
casework	majority leader	oversight
pork barrel	whips	committee chairmen
bicameral legislature	minority leader	seniority system
House Rules	standing committees	caucus
Committee	joint committees	bill
filibuster	conference committees	

For Further Reading

Davidson, Roger H., and Walter J. Olesek. *Congress and Its Members* (1981). Readable review of the people in Congress and the way they work.

Dodd, Lawrence C., and Bruce I. Oppenheimer, eds. *Congress Reconsidered,* 3rd ed. (1985). Excellent essays on the problems of Congress in the 1980s.

Fenno, Richard. *Home Style* (1978). How members of Congress mend fences and stay in political touch with the folks back home.

Frantzich, Stephen E. *Computers in Congress* (1982). How Congress is trying to cope with its information needs.

Goldenberg, Edie N., and Michael W. Traugott. *Campaigning for Congress* (1984). A good book on congressional campaigns.

Jacobson, Gary. *Money in Congressional Elections* (1980). Money talks, and it also helps to elect the Congress.

——— . *The Politics of Congressional Elections* (1983). An excellent review of congressional elections.

Light, Paul. *Artful Work: The Politics of Social Security Reform* (1985). An excellent case study of social security reform, involving both the president and the Congress.

Malbin, Michael. *Unelected Representatives* (1980). A study of congressional staffs.

Ornstein, Norman, and Shirley Elder. *Interest Groups, Lobbying, and Policymaking* (1978). A good examination of lobbying, with several informative case studies.

Smith, Steven S., and Christopher Deering. *Committees in Congress* (1984). A thorough overview of the complex committee structure in the House and Senate.

The President

MEMO

There is a paradox about the American presidency: A powerful office, the presidency can never quite do enough to satisfy our craving for policy solutions.

Our presidency has become a "media presidency," in which presidents resort to technology to maximize their visibility and image with the American public. Often, the news media exaggerate the power of the presidency; particularly in domestic policy, more power is attributed to the president than he actually has. Thus, Americans develop unrealistic perceptions of presidential power. The result is heightened aspirations and dashed expectations.

A basic question about the presidency is this: Are the powers of the president too great, about right, or too small for the responsibilities he commands? I cannot answer this question for you, because it is appropriate that each citizen reach his or her own conclusions with respect to the problem of presidential power. I can, though, give you some perspectives on the presidency. Specifically, they include the following:

■ Who are the presidents, how did they get there, and what do they do?
■ How is the presidency organized to make policy?
■ How does the president shape our domestic and foreign policy agendas?
■ How shall we understand the presidency in terms of the four theories of American government we discussed in Chapter 2?

"**P**UT NOT YOUR TRUST IN PRINCES," the Bible says. Yet Americans have placed an enormous amount of trust in their presidents. Not content to settle for the numerous constitutional responsibilities of the president, we have added many of our own. Today, we make the president responsible for our economic well-being, our energy supplies, and—most awesome of all—nuclear war and peace.

Americans badly want to believe in a powerful president, one who can do good. They look back longingly on the great presidents of the first American century—Lincoln, Washington, Jefferson—and some in the second as well—especially Franklin D. Roosevelt and the short-lived John Kennedy. 1

Very recently, Robert Shogan, a distinguished Washington correspondent, titled his book on the presidency *None of the Above*. We often hope for more than the modern presidency can deliver. Shogan contends that we have seen a "substantial enlargement of presidential responsibility,

---

1 The Presidential Greatness Rating Game

Almost a hundred years ago, the perceptive British observer of American politics, James Bryce, titled one of his chapters "Why Great Men are Not Chosen President." Says Bryce:

> Europeans often ask, and Americans do not always explain, how it happens that this great office, the greatest in the world to which any one can rise by his own merits, is not more frequently filled by great and striking men. In America, which is beyond all other countries the country of a "career open to talents" ... it might be expected that the highest place would always be won by a man of brilliant gifts.

Bryce admits that some great men became presidents in the early Republic. But, he says, "who now knows or cares to know anything about the personality of James K. Polk or Franklin Pierce? The only thing remarkable about them is that being so commonplace they should have climbed so high."

These days, Americans like to rate everything from basketball teams and TV shows to American presidents. Historians play the ratings game, too, in evaluating American presidents. The most recent effort has been undertaken by Pennsylvania State University historians Murray and Blessing, who polled 1997 historians. Here is their ratings of presidents:

The Great Presidents: Lincoln, Franklin D. Roosevelt, Washington, and Jefferson
The Near Great Presidents: Teddy Roosevelt, Wilson, Jackson, Truman
Above Average: John Adams, Lyndon Johnson, Eisenhower, Polk, Kennedy, Madison, Monroe, John Q. Adams, Cleveland
Average: McKinley, Taft, Van Buren, Hoover, Hayes, Arthur, Ford, Carter, Benjamin Harrison
Below average: Taylor, Tyler, Fillmore, Coolidge, Pierce
Failures: Andrew Johnson, Buchanan, Nixon, Grant, Harding

Source: Robert K. Murray and Tim H. Blessing, "The Presidential Performance Study: A Progress Report," *Journal of American History* 70 (December, 1983): 535–55. William H. Harrison, Garfield, and Reagan are excluded because they were not in office long enough for the historians to form judgments. The Bryce quotation is from *The American Commonwealth* (New York: Macmillan, 1893), p. 78.

both explicit and implied, without a corresponding increase in presidential power."[1]

It is certainly true that we've come to expect a great deal from our president. We expect him to manage the world, preventing civil strife here, anti-American actions there, and nuclear war everywhere. We expect him to manage the American economy, and we reward and punish him with our approval or disapproval. The scores for these follow the indicators of our economic health (such as inflation and unemployment) closely. We expect him to solve our social ills, our racial tensions, and our health cost problems. We expect him to resolve our crises, including threats from hostile missiles and leaking nuclear power plants, and to keep a cool head while doing it.[2]

We have come to expect, quite simply, that the president be our chief policymaker. Take a look at the survey results reported in [2]. Surveyors asked a sample of Americans whether the president or the Congress should have the major responsibility for making policy, or whether it should be shared equally. The results would no doubt shock our Founding Fathers. While they intended that the president should be our chief *foreign*-policy maker, they had no intention of making the president generally responsible for policymaking. That was to be Congress' job. Yet barely a third of the population think that the general responsibility for policymaking properly rests with the Congress. Either the president has taken or the public has given him far more power and responsibility than the Founding Fathers intended.

Consider, as you read this chapter, the possibility that we expect too much of our presidents. David Gergen, who works for President Reagan as a communications assistant, drew attention to the fact that "we've had

[1] Robert Shogan, *None of the Above* (New York: Mentor Books, 1982), p. 13.
[2] On our expectations of presidents, see Stephen J. Wayne, "Great Expectations: What People Want from Presidents," in Thomas E. Cronin (ed.), *Rethinking the Presidency* (Boston: Little, Brown, 1982), Chap. 15.

Harry Truman's Slogan. *President Harry Truman made famous the line "The Buck Stops Here," after the old witticism about "passing the buck." Truman even had a sign made for his desk with the aphorism on it. Jimmy Carter, a great Truman admirer, had another sign made for his office. This photograph of Carter at his desk became a "White House handout photo."*

a series of presidents from Kennedy through Carter who have left office in death, tragedy, disgrace, or disappointment." [3] For years, a famous motto of the presidency was captured in the sign President Harry S Truman had on his desk: "The buck stops here." (Jimmy Carter put one on his desk, too.) If our expectations exceed the president's resources or resourcefulness, future presidents may find a new motto for the office: "High expectations followed by dashed hopes." (One reason is surely that presidential candidates, during their campaigns, make exorbitant promises about peace, inflation, unemployment, poverty, and almost everything else.) The question of whether or not we expect too much from our presidents is one you may wish to evaluate seriously, but withhold judgment until we have examined the presidents, their powers, and their roles.

THE PRESIDENTS

The presidency was tailor-made for its first occupant, George Washington. He initially defined the office, but its thirty-eight subsequent occupants each have changed the office, its powers, and its responsibilities. Our image of the president is a mixture of myth and reality shaped largely by the media, so we should begin our study of the president by setting the record straight and disentangling some presidential myths from presidential realities.

[3] "How Much Can Any Administration Do?" *Public Opinion* 4 (December–January 1982): 7.

Presidential Myth and Reality

The Myth of the Overworked President. Although most Americans have never been inside the White House, we have images of the president's job. We can imagine, for example, the heavy workload. The president is supposedly our chief policy maker, responsible for solving myriad problems. Nuclear missile systems, the budget deficit, tax reform, peace in the Middle East, Central American conflicts, the urban problem, joblessness, high interest rates—a mighty array of issues can become presidential problems. The nation's agenda seems to be his agenda. We are psychologically close to the President. Thinking of this vast range of problems, we can almost imagine a presidential day. Up before dawn dealing with a grueling schedule before breakfast—discussing energy issues with a congressional delegation, signing laws over eggs and bacon, making snap decisions about a budget deficit of $200 billion while buttering a roll— then on to a grinding schedule of daily activities. He is tired by dusk, but there are still dinners to host, speeches to give, or concerts to attend. Lyndon Johnson kept two full-time staffs busy, taking an afternoon nap to refresh himself for another full day's work in the evening.

This image of presidential life leads easily to the myth of the overworked president. George Reedy, a press secretary to President Johnson, remarked, "There is far less to the presidency, in terms of essential activity, than meets the eye. The psychological burdens are heavy, even crushing, but no President ever died from overwork and it is doubtful whether any ever will." [4] Ronald Reagan is certainly one president unlikely ever to collapse from overwork. His tenure has often been called "the 9 to 5 presidency." He sleeps until a respectable 7:30 A.M.—aides once declined to wake him to report that United States fighter jets had shot down Libyan planes during the night—and works at a relaxed pace.

As a matter of fact, most presidents find enough time for secondary activities. Nothing better illustrated how much time the president can fritter away than **Watergate.** [3] Richard Nixon promoted the public image of a decisive man, carrying a stack of yellow legal pads to the presidential retreat at Camp David, Maryland, to make momentous decisions and write orders. In fact, Alexander Butterfield, one of his aides, told the Senate Watergate Committee that Nixon took time to select menus and music for state dinners, arrange their seating charts, even select uniforms and buttons for the White House guards. Nixon spent hours chatting with aides about the personalities and events of Watergate. He rarely reached any conclusions, much less decisions about what to do. If the need for a momentous decision intruded on these Watergate ramblings, Nixon must have made it in a moment.

Even as the Nixon family tearfully packed their belongings and watched the death throes of the administration, the government went on. "For a unique interlude," Hugh Heclo remarked, "the President had virtually ceased to exist as a political force in Washington." [5] Yet the Department of Defense was announcing $1 billion in new contracts, the

[4] George Reedy, *The Twilight of the Presidency* (New York: Mentor, 1970), p. 31.
[5] Hugh M. Heclo, *A Government of Strangers: Executive Politics in Washington* (Washington, D.C.: The Brookings Institution, 1977), p. 8.

Department of Transportation was finalizing a $500-million program in mass transit aid, a presidential staffer was trying to sell the administration's position on various policies to Congress.

The Watergate story suggests that the government continues even if the president is temporarily out of business. The challenge to the presi-

---

3 | **Watergate: What Was It?**

If a novelist had invented Watergate, it would have made a fascinating but not very believable story. As reality, it caused the resignation of the president who was elected by the then largest popular majority in American history, Richard M. Nixon.

Tangled threads of dozens of events and decisions produced the Watergate affair. Many centered on Nixon's 1972 reelection campaign. His campaign manager, former Attorney General John Mitchell, hired a man named G. Gordon Liddy as counsel to the Committee to Re-elect the President (CREEP). Liddy did little lawyering at CREEP, but he did develop an expensive "counterintelligence" program.

On January 2, 1972, Liddy presented his multimillion-dollar plan to Mitchell. Mitchell later described it as including "mugging squads, kidnapping teams, prostitutes to compromise the opposition, and electronic surveillance." He ordered Liddy to scale down the program.

One offshoot of Liddy's plan was the planting of a wiretap at the headquarters of the Democratic National Committee (DNC) in Washington's Watergate complex. On June 17, 1972, five men were caught inside the DNC headquarters with burglary tools, bugging devices, and a stack of $100 bills. Their links to CREEP soon became known, and Liddy himself was arrested. Nixon's press secretary Ron Ziegler dismissed it as a "third-rate burglary," and Nixon assured the press that the White House had no involvement whatsoever in the bungled break-in.

To this day, no one has demonstrated that Nixon had prior knowledge of the break-in. But within hours after the arrests, paper shredders at the White House and CREEP were destroying documents that might link the burglars to the White House. CREEP and White House officials pressured Nixon's personal lawyer, Herbert Kalmbach, to collect funds quietly to "support the families" of the accused. A former New York policeman, Anthony Ulasewicz, working for the White House, later regaled the Watergate Committee with stories of leaving money in paper bags hither and yon to be picked up and delivered to the accused burglars. *Washington Post* reporters Woodward and Bernstein began an investigation, which eventually tracked the Watergate break-in and its coverup to the very door of the Oval Office.

As the trail got closer, Nixon's aides resigned one by one. Chief of Staff Bob Haldeman, Domestic Policy Advisor John Ehrlichman, and others were writing their resignations and ringing up their lawyers simultaneously. On May 17, 1973, hearings of the Senate Select Committee on Campaign Activities opened, chaired by Senator Sam Ervin (D.–N.C.). Nixon's former White House Counsel, John Dean, claimed that Nixon had known more than he was admitting and had played fast and loose with the truth about White House involvement. Haldeman and Ehrlichman defended the president. One White House functionary, Alexander Butterfield, broke the news that Nixon had a secret taping system, which recorded every conversation in the Oval Office. The battle for control of the tapes began. The Ervin committee demanded them. Courts trying the Watergate defendants subpoenaed them. Nixon asserted that executive privilege permitted him to refuse to disclose them. Finally, the Supreme Court, in *United States* v. *Nixon* (1974), ruled that Nixon had to hand over the tapes to courts trying the Watergate burglars.

As the Watergate coverup unraveled, more became known about what John Mitchell called "the White House horrors." Nixon's White House aides and CREEP officials sponsored a burglary of a psychiatrist treating Daniel Ellsberg, an opponent of the Vietnam War who leaked classified documents to the press; had the administration's opponents' income tax records audited; tapped phones illegally; collected campaign contributions (preferably cash) in return for specific favors; and engaged in some funny business over Nixon's own tax returns.

The House launched impeachment hearings in 1974. On July 31, 1974, the Judiciary Committee recommended Nixon's impeachment. Facing almost certain impeachment by the House and possible conviction by the Senate, Nixon resigned ten days later. Shortly after assuming the presidency, Gerald Ford pardoned Nixon, arguing that years of trials and appeals would aggravate bitterness over Watergate. But most of Nixon's aides were not so lucky—many were convicted and served prison sentences.

A President in Disgrace. *In Richard Nixon's emotional farewell speech to his assembled staff, he reviewed his childhood and his struggles in public life. Then Nixon, the only American president ever to resign his office, retired to California. The Watergate scandal, involving suppression of evidence and other crimes by Nixon's principal advisors and Nixon's own Oval Office assurance that "we could get" a million dollars in bribe payments, sealed the fate of the Nixon presidency.*

dency is not somehow to run the government. A central feature of the American presidency, in fact, is this: *The president has to work hard to keep the government from running without him.* With its rules and hierarchies and routines, the government will move along even in his absence. The real presidential challenge, more difficult than administering the routines, is to *shape a government's policy agenda,* to make his policy goals the goals of the whole government. It would be easier if the president were really the political powerhouse people sometimes think he is.

The Myth of the Powerhouse President. Powerful, strong, leader of the free world, a superman in American politics, commander in chief—these have been common images of the American president. The president epitomizes American government. The only place in the world where television networks assign a permanent camera crew is the White House. The presidency is power. Or so we usually think.

These images are all part of the president-as-powerhouse myth. In this myth, the president is the government's command center. Problems are brought to his desk; he decides the right course of action, issues an order, and an army of marching foot soldiers carries out his commands. Nothing could be further from the truth, as presidents themselves soon discover. Thomas Cronin interviewed various presidential aides about the work of the presidency, and one put his finger on the problem of getting things done: "Every time you turn around, people resist you."[6] As Harry Truman was getting ready to turn over the Oval Office to Dwight

[6] Thomas E. Cronin, *The State of the Presidency,* 2nd ed. (Boston: Little, Brown, 1980), p. 223.

Eisenhower, a former general, he mused: "He'll sit here and he'll say, 'Do this! Do that!' *And nothing will happen.* Poor Ike—it won't be a bit like the army. He'll find it very frustrating."[7]

Sometimes nothing happens even when the president tries hard to pull the levers of power. Shortly after his inauguration, Jimmy Carter and his special assistant for national security affairs, Zbigniew Brzezinski, were briefed on plans for evacuating the president and his key staff from Washington in the event of a nuclear attack.[8] A helicopter would whisk the president to Andrews Air Force Base in Maryland, where he would board a $250-million plane (called simply The Plane by the Air Force) filled with the most sophisticated technology of modern warfare. It would take off instantly and permit the president to command a nuclear war from the skies.

A few days later, Brzezinski put the system to a test. Wandering up to the fellow in charge of the operation at the White House, Brzezinski casually asked if he could really get the president out before the missiles arrived. Assured that he could, Brzezinski announced that Mr. Carter had asked him to test the system, with Brzezinski standing in for the president. "Pretend an alarm has sounded," said Brzezinski. "Get me to safety." Told that it was snowing outside, Brzezinski insisted. Once airborne in the helicopter—five minutes later—Brzezinski barked orders to call the joint chiefs of staff. A crewman put the call through the White House switchboard. Brzezinski pointed out that if this had been a real attack, the White House would already have been destroyed. When Brzezinski arrived at Andrews, The Plane—supposedly ready to go within three minutes—was still not ready. All things considered, the experiment was a flop.

All presidents, at least those from Franklin Roosevelt to Ronald Reagan, have complained that moving their own administration into action was tough. Although the presidency is the center of vast powers, sometimes the vast powers of the president do not work very well. A look at presidential reality helps to explain why.

The Presidential Reality. The main reason presidents have trouble getting things done is that other policymakers with whom they deal have their own agendas, their own interests, and their own sources of power. Congress is beholden not to the president but to the individual constituencies of its members. Even cabinet members push their departmental interests and their constituencies (the Department of Agriculture has farmers as its constituency, the Department of Labor unions, and so on). Even President Reagan, whose cabinet mirrors well his conservatism, had trouble persuading his cabinet to accept cuts in their departmental budgets. Secretary of Defense Caspar Weinberger organized promilitary groups, took to television, and personally lobbied the president to prevent cuts in defense spending in 1985. The president operates constitutionally in an environment filled with checks and balances; he operates

---

[7] Quoted in Richard E. Neustadt, *Presidential Power*, rev. ed. (New York: Wiley, 1976), p. 77.

[8] The story of The Plane and Brzezinski's test is told in Blythe Babyak, "The Plane: Cruising to Armageddon," *Washington Monthly* (December 1978): 32–36.

politically in a pluralistic setting. The president must mix persuasion with command. However, not everyone bends easily to the will of even the most persuasive president.

Presidents with the power of persuasion are not born, but made. The president's background and experiences make a great deal of difference in his success.

Who They Are

When Warren G. Harding, one of our least illustrious presidents, was in office, Clarence Darrow remarked, "When I was a boy, I was told that anybody could become president. Now I'm beginning to believe it." The Constitution simply states that the president must be a natural-born citizen at least thirty-five years old. In fact, all have been white, male, and, except for John Kennedy, Protestant. In other ways, however, our recent collection of presidents suggests considerable variety. Since World War II, we have had a Missouri haberdasher; a war hero; a Boston Irish politician; a small-town Texas boy who grew up to become the biggest wheeler-dealer in the Senate; a California lawyer described by his enemies as "Tricky Dick" and by his friends as a misunderstood master of national leadership; a former Rose Bowl player who had spent his entire political career in the House; a former governor who had been a Georgia peanut wholesaler; and an actor who was also a former governor of California. 4

All manner of men have occupied the Oval Office. Thomas Jefferson was a scientist and scholar who assembled dinosaur bones when presidential business was slack. Woodrow Wilson, the only political scientist ever to become president, combined a Presbyterian moral fervor and righteousness with a professor's intimidating style of leadership and speech-making. His successor, Warren G. Harding, became president because Republican leaders thought he looked like one. Poker was his pastime. Out of his element in the job, Harding is almost everyone's choice as the worst American president. His speech-making, said opponent William G. McAdoo, sounded "like an army of pompous phrases marching across the landscape in search of an idea." Harding's friends stole the government blind, prompting his brief assessment of the presidency: "God, what a job!"

In this potpourri of personalities, James David Barber has looked for some patterns in order to understand how presidents perform. He suggested that we examine presidents by looking at their *presidential character.* 9 Presidents, he claims, vary in their *activity* or *passivity* toward the job. Some, like Lyndon Johnson, throw themselves into the job and work furiously at being president; others, like Calvin Coolidge (who sometimes slept eleven hours a night), do not. Presidents also vary in their *positive* or *negative* evaluation of politics. Some, like Franklin Roosevelt or John Kennedy, claim to love politics and enjoy the job of being president; others, like Richard Nixon, feel that duty impels their perfor-

---

9 James David Barber, *The Presidential Character,* 2nd ed. (Englewood Cliffs, N.J.: Prentice-Hall, 1977). See especially pp. 11–14.

Harry S Truman (1945–53), Democrat from Missouri. A haberdasher by trade, Truman worked his way up through the political machine in Kansas City to become United States senator from Missouri. Tapped by Roosevelt to be his vice-presidential running mate in 1944, Truman had barely taken office when FDR died. Truman had to decide whether to drop atomic bombs on Japan (he ordered them dropped) and then presided over the trying times of postwar recovery. A man of strong opinions, Truman often shot from the lip. Never popular while in office (partly because FDR was a hard act to follow), his stature seemed to grow once he retired to Independence, Missouri.

Dwight D. Eisenhower (1953–61), Republican, born in Texas and reared in Kansas. "Ike" was the commander of Allied Forces in Europe during World War II, but had never voted until he became the Republican nominee in 1952. He presided over the relatively tranquil 1950s, offering to the public a grandfatherly image of sternness and compassion. His public image remained high, and he crushed the Democratic nominee, Adlai Stevenson, in the 1952 and 1956 presidential elections. He made Richard Nixon his vice-president but never his friend; he even declined to invite him inside his house at Gettysburg, Pennsylvania.

John F. Kennedy (1961–63), Democrat from Massachusetts. JFK is remembered most for his leadership style, his elegant wife, Jackie, and his tragic assassination in Dallas, Texas, on November 22, 1963. Kennedy was a senator before he ran for president in 1960. Handsome, virile, and graceful, he touted culture and made *charisma* a household word. Kennedy's legislative record was not enviable and is little remembered, and his popularity with the public was never too impressive. Once he was assassinated, though, public estimation of him escalated. According to a 1977 Harris Poll, Americans rank him as our best president of the last four decades, an incredible opinion to students of the presidency.

Lyndon B. Johnson (1963–69), Democrat from Texas. As Senate majority leader, Lyndon Johnson was one of the most skilled politicians ever to walk the Capitol corridors. In private, he was simultaneously charming, cunning, and coercive. After the culture and charisma of the Kennedy years, his public image seemed coarse and he was easily ridiculed. Johnson was frustrated that he, unlike Kennedy, somehow lacked the "right background" to mix with Harvard-educated elites. Nonetheless, he tackled the presidency with energy, launching a War on Poverty at home and escalating the Vietnam War abroad. The latter caused the unmaking of his presidency. In March 1968, he announced that he would neither seek nor accept renomination.

Richard M. Nixon (1969–74), Republican from California and later New York. Ike's vice-president, Nixon was a natural candidate for the Republicans in 1960. He was defeated by John F. Kennedy. Trying again in 1968, he edged out Democrat Hubert Humphrey and the American Independent party's George Wallace. Though the Vietnam War continued to rage during his term, he did establish American links with China. Running for reelection in 1972, he crushed George McGovern. During that campaign, though, the Watergate break-in started the beginning of the end of the Nixon presidency. After the House Judiciary Committee voted to recommend his impeachment for high crimes and misdemeanors, Nixon resigned on August 9, 1974.

Gerald R. Ford (1974–77), Republican from Michigan. Ford spent his political career in the House of Representatives before becoming president. He was "the accidental president," becoming vice-president when Spiro T. Agnew left office under a cloud of scandal. He became president when the same thing happened to Nixon. Though cartoonists depicted him as personally clumsy and none too intelligent (Lyndon Johnson said nasty things about his intelligence), he re-established respect for a Watergate-tainted presidency. But his pardon of Nixon caused him to slip in the polls and, he maintained, cost him reelection.

Jimmy Carter (1977–81), Democrat from Georgia. Carter had been a naval officer, a peanut warehouser, and a governor. He surprised the nation by winning the Democratic nomination in 1976 and then defeating the incumbent president, Gerald Ford. "If I had to choose one politician to sit at the Pearly Gates and pass judgment on my soul," wrote his ex-speech writer James Fallows in the *Atlantic,* "Jimmy Carter would be the one." But he also, claimed Fallows, lacked the sophistication, the ability to communicate his goals, and the passion necessary to be an effective leader. Once in office, Carter demonstrated that being a Washington outsider may help get you elected, but makes it hard to influence the Washington community. Carter was defeated in his bid for reelection by Ronald Reagan.

Ronald W. Reagan (1981–   ), Republican from California. Born in Illinois, Reagan moved to California and pursued a show-business career, becoming an actor of middling stature. His presidency of the Screen Actors' Guild brought him into politics. As governor of California, he was ideologically conservative but more liberal in his policies than opponents had feared. As president, he managed to convey genial affability, using power with poise. Resoundingly reelected in 1984, his efforts to pare domestic spending and boost defense spending, while coping with massive deficits, were his second-term goals.

mance and have a grim, self-sacrificial attitude toward the job. Not all presidential scholars agree with Barber's typology of active positives, active negatives, passive positives, and passive negatives. Garry Wills describes Barber's analysis as an example of "games academics play." [10] There are many opinions, but no single answer, to the question of what makes a successful president.

Regardless of their background or character, all presidents must come to the job through one of two basic routes. Although some presidents might dispute it, no one is born to be the future president as someone is born to be the future king or queen of England.

How They Get There: The Presidential Cycle

Elections: The Normal Road to the White House. Most presidents take a familiar electoral journey to 1600 Pennsylvania Avenue: they run for president in the electoral process, which we described in Chapters 8 and 9. Once in office, presidents are guaranteed a four-year term by the Constitution; but the **Twenty-second Amendment,** passed in 1951, limits them to two terms.

Only eight of our thirty-nine presidents (not counting Ronald Reagan) have actually served two full terms in the White House: Washington, Jefferson, Madison, Jackson, Grant, Wilson, Franklin Roosevelt, and Eisenhower. A few decide against a second term ("Silent Cal" Coolidge said simply "I do not choose to run"). Four presidents (Polk, Pierce, Buchanan, and Hayes) threw in the towel at the end of one full term. Six others (both of the Adamses, Van Buren, Taft, Hoover, and Carter) thought the voters owed them a second term, but the voters disagreed.

The Vice-Presidency: Another Road to the White House. For better than 10 percent of our history (28 of 200 years), the presidency has actually been occupied by an individual not elected to the office. (This includes part or all of the terms of Tyler, Andrew Johnson, Arthur, Teddy Roosevelt, Coolidge, Truman, Lyndon Johnson, and Ford). Not quite one fourth of our presidents got the job not through the normal road of elections, but because they were in the right place at the right time when the then president either died, was assassinated, or (in Nixon's case) resigned. In the twentieth century almost a third (five of sixteen) of our presidents were "accidental presidents." The most accidental of all was Gerald Ford, who did not run for either vice-presidency or presidency.

Neither politicians nor political scientists have paid much attention to the vice-presidency. Once the choice of a party's "second team" was an afterthought; now it is mostly an effort to placate some important symbolic constituency. The occupants have rarely enjoyed the job. John Nance Garner, one of Franklin D. Roosevelt's vice-presidents, said the job was "not worth a bucket of warm spit." Some have performed so poorly as to be an embarrassment to the president. (After Woodrow Wilson's debilitating stroke, almost everyone agreed that Vice-President Marshall —a man who shirked all responsibility, including cabinet meetings— would be a disaster as acting president.)

[10] Garry Wills, *The Kennedy Imprisonment* (Boston: Atlantic-Little, Brown, 1982), p. 186.

Once in office, a vice-president's main job is waiting. Constitutionally, he is assigned the minor task of presiding over the Senate and voting in case of a tie. Recent presidents, though, have taken their vice-presidents more seriously, involving them in policy discussions and important diplomacy.

The End of the Presidential Cycle: Impeachment and Succession.
Getting rid of an unwanted president before the end of his term is no easy task. The Constitution prescribes how to do it through **impeachment,** which is roughly the political equivalent of an indictment in criminal law. The House of Representatives may impeach the president, by majority vote, for "Treason, Bribery, or other high Crimes and Misdemeanors." Once impeached by the House, the case goes to the Senate, which tries the accused president, with the chief justice presiding. By a two-thirds vote, the Senate may convict the president and remove him from office. [11]

Only once has a president been impeached: Andrew Johnson, Lincoln's successor, who was impeached by the House in 1868 on charges stemming from his disagreement with Radical Republicans. He escaped conviction in the Senate by one vote. Richard Nixon came as close to impeachment as any president since. On July 31, 1974, the House Judiciary Committee voted to recommend his impeachment to the full House. Nixon escaped a certain vote for impeachment by resigning.

Constitutional amendments cover one other ticklish problem concerning the presidential term: presidential disability and succession. Several times a president has lain disabled, incapable of carrying out his job for weeks or even months at a time. After Woodrow Wilson suffered a stroke, his wife became virtual acting president. The **Twenty-fifth Amendment** (1967) tidied up the Constitution's vagueness about disability. It permits the vice-president to become acting president if both he and the president's cabinet determine that the president is disabled, and it outlines how a recuperated president can reclaim the Oval Office. Other laws specify the order of presidential succession, from the vice-president, to the Speaker of the House, to the president pro tem of the Senate, and down through the cabinet.

The Twenty-fifth Amendment also created a means for selecting a new vice-president when the office becomes vacant—a not infrequent occurrence. The president nominates a new vice-president, who assumes the office when Congress approves the nomination.

What They Do: Presidential Power and Roles

At the American Constitutional Convention in 1787, there was a spirited debate about the role of the proposed presidency. Old Republicans wanted a weak chief executive, but the prevailing group preferred a strong executive. [12] Article II of the Constitution says that "The executive

[11] On the impeachment process, see a book that remarkably was published exactly a year before Nixon's impeachment became an issue: Raoul Berger, *Impeachment: The Constitutional Problems* (Cambridge, Mass.: Harvard University Press, 1973).

[12] Donald L. Robinson, "The Inventors of the Presidency," *Presidential Studies Quarterly* 13 (Winter 1983): 8–26.

power shall be vested in a President of the United States of America" and then sets out his relatively limited constitutional responsibilities. From these little acorns has grown the mighty oak of presidential power.

Constitutional Powers. There have always been two presidencies—a domestic and a foreign. Neither is fully defined in the Constitution itself, but the detail sketched out for the global presidency is far more specific than for the domestic one. The president is given some specific worldly powers, among them the following:

— To be commander in chief of the armed forces.
— To make treaties with other nations, subject to the agreement of two-thirds of the Senate.
— To appoint our ambassadors and receive other nation's ambassadors, thereby conferring diplomatic recognition on other governments.

These are small acorns indeed. Technology is partly responsible for reshaping the global presidency. George Washington's ragtag militias (mostly disbanded by the time the first commander in chief took command) are of a different order than the nuclear arsenal that today's president commands.

Alongside the specificity of global powers, the powers of the domestic president sound almost clerical. A full thirty-seven words of the Constitution are taken up with the exact presidential oath of office; only ten words are devoted to his job of administering the federal government ("he shall take Care that the Laws be faithfully executed"). There are appointing powers and legislative powers as well. Presidents (with senatorial consent) appoint their own cabinet officers, other officials, and new federal judges. The president is also constitutionally mandated to report on the state of the nation and to review or even veto congressional legislation.

All in all, a close reading of the Constitution makes presidential power sound so routine, so mechanical, so ordinary, that we find it hard to believe that the president is the character to whose power the word "awesome" is most often applied. Today there is more to presidential power than the constitution alone suggests, and that power is derived from innumerable sources. Presidents can summon up a report on the activities of a foreign ruler or a domestic challenger, relying on the complex organs of the intelligence and law enforcement bureaucracies. A call to a head of state, a senator, a network executive, or a military commander never goes unanswered. Presidential power is far greater than the constitutional niceties imply.

Textbooks on American government (and this one is no exception) usually describe several crucial presidential roles: head of state, commander in chief, foreign-policy maker, agenda builder, chief executive, chief legislator, economic leader, crisis manager, and party leader. We add another to this standard collection: politician.

Head of State. In some countries, including most parliamentary democracies like England, the jobs of head of state and head of government are occupied by different people. For example, the queen is head of state in England, but she holds little power in government and politics. In

The President as Head of State. *The American president is not only our chief executive but our head of state as well. One of his tasks as head of state is to welcome foreign dignitaries. Here are President and Mrs. Dwight D. Eisenhower with Queen Elizabeth and her husband, Prince Philip, of the United Kingdom.*

America, these roles are fused. As head of state, the president is our ceremonial leader and symbol of government. Trivial but time-consuming activities—tossing out the first baseball of the season, lighting the White House Christmas tree, meeting some extraordinary Boy Scout—are part of the ceremonial function of the presidency. Meeting foreign heads of state, receiving a new ambassador's credentials, and making global goodwill tours symbolize the global side of this role. These ceremonial activities give the presidency an important symbolic aura and much press coverage.

Commander in Chief. Because the presidency was tailored for George Washington, it was natural that the Constitution made the president commander in chief of the armed forces. As president, Washington actually led troops to crush the Whiskey Rebellion in 1794. Today presidents do not take the task quite so literally, but their military decisions have changed the course of history. Once he became president, Harry Truman was told about a major new weapon, the atomic bomb. Truman contemplated the consequences of using this frightful weapon to defeat the Japanese and end World War II. "The final decision," he said, "on where and when to use the atomic bomb was up to me. Let there be no mistake about it."[13] He personally selected the target and the date. Three decades later, Lyndon Johnson personally selected targets and ordered bombing missions to North Vietnam. Richard Nixon personally made the decision to invade Cambodia in 1970. Ronald Reagan joined the ranks of presidents exerting their prerogatives as commander in chief when he sent American troops to invade the Caribbean island of Grenada and to serve as "peacekeepers" in fractious Lebanon.

When the Constitution was written, the United States did not have—nor did anyone expect it to have—a standing or permanent army. Today, the president is commander in chief of two million uniformed men and

[13] Harry S Truman, *Year of Decision* (New York: New American Library, 1955), p. 462.

women. Even more important, the president is the nuclear warmaker. Never more than a few steps from the president is "the football," that macabre briefcase with all the codes needed to unleash nuclear war. Movies like "The Day After" remind us of this apocalyptic power of the president. The Constitution, of course, dutifully requires that only the Congress has the power to declare war. But it is farfetched to believe that Congress can convene, debate, and vote on a declaration of war in the nuclear age. The House and Senate chambers would be gone—*literally* gone—before conclusion of a debate.

Foreign-policy Maker. Constitutionally, the president dominates American foreign policy. He alone extends diplomatic recognition to foreign governments, as Jimmy Carter did on December 14, 1978, when he announced the exchange of ambassadors with the People's Republic of China and the downgrading of the United States embassy in Taiwan. The president has sole power to negotiate treaties with other nations, although the Constitution requires the Senate to approve them by a two-thirds vote. Sometimes presidents win and sometimes they lose when presenting a treaty to the Senate. Woodrow Wilson lost his effort to persuade the Senate to approve the League of Nations treaty in 1920. After extensive lobbying, Jimmy Carter convinced the Senate to approve a treaty returning the Panama Canal to Panama (over such objections as that of Senator Hayakawa [R.—Calif.], who said, "We stole it fair and square"). Later in this chapter we will examine the president's global role in more detail.

Agenda Builder. The president is the nation's key agenda builder. What his administration wants sets the parameters of Washington debate. John

The President as Commander in Chief and Chief Foreign-policy Maker. *President Harry Truman proved his mettle as commander in chief when he fired General Douglas MacArthur as American commander in Korea in 1951 for disobeying orders. Truman's decision was not popular. Congress even invited MacArthur, who was a hero in World War II, to speak. But Truman stuck by his guns, at the cost of considerable popularity, proving once again that the president is himself commander in chief.*

Kingdon's careful study of the Washington agenda found that "no other single actor in the political system has quite the capability of the president to set agendas in given policy areas." As one lobbyist told Kingdon: "Obviously, when a president sends up a bill [to Congress], it takes first place in the queue. All other bills take second place."[14] In setting the global agenda, the president is often the only fish in the political sea; in setting the domestic agenda, the president is at least the biggest fish in the sea.

Because each of the president's appointees and departments will have its own agenda, the president needs a clearinghouse. (Presidents can hardly have twenty spokespersons each out peddling their own policy wares.) Thus, presidents use the Office of Management and Budget to clear ideas before an agency proposes them to Congress. Presidential speeches, press conferences, telephone calls, and meetings are all ways in which presidents try to keep an issue in top position on the Washington agenda. The OMB meticulously reviews major legislative proposals from the cabinet and other executive agencies, assesses their budget implications, and advises the president on them.

Chief Executive. All the Constitution says about the role of chief executive is that the president "shall take Care that the Laws be faithfully executed." In the early days, this clerical-sounding function was fairly easy. Today the sprawling federal bureaucracy spends nearly a trillion dollars a year and numbers nearly 3 million employees. Although they are nominally responsible to the president, he never meets more than a handful of them. Protected by civil service laws, most are safe from the threat of a presidential firing.

One of the president's resources for controlling this sprawling bureaucracy is his power to appoint top-level administrators. New presidents have about 300 of these high-level positions available for appointment—cabinet and subcabinet jobs, agency heads, and other non-civil service posts—plus 2000 lesser jobs.[15] Since the Budgeting and Accounting Act of 1921, presidents have had one other important executive tool, the power to recommend agency budgets to Congress.

Chief Legislator. Nowhere does the Constitution use the words *chief legislator.* It is strictly a term invented by textbook writers to emphasize the president's importance in the legislative process. The Constitution does require that the president give a State of the Union address to Congress and instructs him to bring other matters to its attention "from time to time." In fact, as we saw in Chapter 12, the president is a major shaper of the congressional agenda.

The Constitution also gives the president power to **veto** congressional legislation. Once a bill reaches his desk, he may (1) sign it, making it law; (2) veto it, sending it back to Congress with his reasons for rejecting it; or

---

[14] John Kingdon, *Agendas, Alternatives, and Public Policies* (Boston: Little, Brown, 1984), p. 25. On presidential agenda setting, see Paul Light, *The President's Agenda* (Baltimore: John Hopkins University Press, 1983).

[15] Heclo, *A Government of Strangers*, p. 94.

10:00 a.m.
10-5-78

To Members of Congress

The Producers Price Index for finished goods rose 0.9% in September (an annual rate of 11½%).

I urge you to help me Control inflation and to set an example of leadership for the nation by supporting my veto of the public works bill.

Jimmy Carter

The President as Chief Legislator. *The president proposes new policies to Congress, presents a budget to Congress, and can veto legislation after Congress passes it, as Jimmy Carter is shown doing here. The Constitution requires a president to state his reasons for vetoing a bill, and allows Congress to override the veto. The veto is a powerful weapon, but the president often must use the informal powers of his office to convince Congress not to override him. In 1978 Carter convinced Congress to sustain his veto of a public works bill only after he used notes, meetings, and phone calls to lobby Congress.*

(3) let it become law within ten working days by not doing anything. Congress can pass a vetoed law, however, if two-thirds of each house vote to override the president. But at one point in the law-making process the president has the last word. If Congress adjourns within ten days after submitting a bill to the president, he can simply let it die by neither signing nor vetoing it. This process is called a **pocket veto.**

The presidential veto is usually effective; Congress rarely overrides a vetoed bill. From 1961 to 1984, presidents vetoed 230 bills (including pocket vetoes); Congress overrode only twenty of them. Even the hint of a presidential veto is often enough to convince Congress that the president's preferences should count in shaping legislation. Only about 4 percent of all vetoed bills have been overridden by Congress since the nation's founding.

Economic Leader. Increasingly, the president has become our chief national economic leader. A president's political fortunes, measured monthly in the polls, often rise and fall with the nation's economic well-being. So it is not only in the nation's interest but also in the president's own political interest that he play a major economic role. We give our presidents many tools to manage the economy. The budget is one of them.

The Council of Economic Advisors is charged with giving the president economic advice, but in the role of economic leader, as in his other roles, the president should make policy choices consistent with his party's platform and his own policy preferences.

Crisis Manager. Hostages in Iran, Russian missiles in Cuba, Three Mile Island—these and other crises are challenges to the president; he has become the nation's crisis manager. **A crisis** is a sudden, unpredictable, and potentially dangerous event. Risks and tempers often run high and quick judgments are needed, despite sketchy information. Crises are rarely of the president's making but, badly handled, they can be his unmaking.

Three elements are key to the successful handling of a crisis by the White House: *staff, secrecy,* and *skillful strategy.* A president rarely works alone during a crisis. Typically, a team is quickly assembled. John Kennedy assembled a group from the National Security Council to meet regularly in response to the Cuban missile crisis in 1962. President Nixon's national security advisor and later secretary of state, Henry Kissinger, became a globe-trotting practitioner of "shuttle diplomacy" to deal with crises, especially in the Middle East. President Carter's advisor, Hamilton Jordan, became a key go-between in the Iranian hostage crisis.

Handling a crisis, domestic or foreign, usually involves secrecy. During the Cuban missile crisis, President Kennedy kept the public unaware until he was ready; he adhered strictly to his public schedule. Traveling to Paris to meet with Iranian intermediaries over the hostage crisis, Hamilton Jordan wore wigs and dark glasses to hide his identity from the press.

Strategy works best if the options are multiple and no doors are closed early in crisis management. During the Cuban missile crisis, President Kennedy and his advisors considered six options, ranging from doing nothing to launching an invasion of Cuba (as one advisor put it, "Go in there and take Cuba away from Castro"). [16] The president kept his options open for several days before settling on a naval blockade of Cuba. President Carter tried at least that many options in the management of the Iranian hostage crisis. Economic pressure, diplomatic entreaties, a sudden, heroic rescue attempt—all failed until quiet diplomacy by two French citizens with close ties to the Iranian government laid the groundwork for release of the hostages. [17]

Party Leader. The president is his party's leader, not by any authority of the Constitution, whose authors abhorred parties, but by strong tradition and practical necessity. Presidents campaign for their party's candidates, appoint party stalwarts to key jobs, and name, or at least approve, the party's national chairperson. Their portraits and achievements are highlighted at party conventions, where they can slip into a presidential box and hear speeches extolling their achievements. The president's policies become the party's policies. His successes are recalled in the

[16] Theodore Sorensen, *Kennedy* (New York: Bantam Books, 1965), p. 769.
[17] Hamilton Jordan, *Crisis* (New York: Berkley Books, 1982).

The President as Politician. *Presidents must be good politicians to get elected, but once in office they must also be politicians to be effective. The president must convince other politicians and bureaucrats to follow his lead. If they resist him, the ability to go out and "press the flesh," as Gerald Ford is doing here, and demonstrate public support for presidential policies may be a powerful weapon against opponents.*

party's election campaigns, and his failures haunt his party at the polls. This role of party leader blends easily with the one role the president must play if he is to handle the other roles effectively: the role of politician.

The Ultimate Role: The President as Politician. The many roles of the president cannot be easily separated in theory or in practice. The president cannot be foreign-policy maker from 8:00 to 9:00, chief executive from 9:00 to 10:00, commander in chief from 11:00 to 12:00, and chief legislator over lunch. His performance as commander in chief will enhance his stature as leader of his party. The frustrations of Vietnam during Lyndon Johnson's term contributed significantly to the unmaking of his presidency in 1968 and also hurt his party. [18]

The thread linking all these other roles is the role of politician. In Chapter 12 we learned that members of Congress are politicians as well as policy makers, always eyeing the next elections. The president is like that, too. As all politicans, he seeks to win not only elections but issues, to be powerful and to appear powerful.

HOW THE PRESIDENCY IS ORGANIZED

The Cabinet

Although the group of presidential advisors known as the **cabinet** is not mentioned in the Constitution, every president has had one. George Washington's cabinet was small, consisting of just three secretaries

[18] See Herbert Y. Schandler, *The Unmaking of a President: Lyndon Johnson and Vietnam* (Princeton, N.J.: Princeton University Press, 1977).

(state, treasury, and war) and the Attorney General. Presidents since Washington have increased the size of the cabinet by requesting that new executive departments be established. These requests must be approved by Congress, which creates the department. Today twelve secretaries and the Attorney General head executive departments and constitute the cabinet.

— *The Department of State*, founded in 1789, which is responsible for foreign-policy making, including treaty negotiations.
— *The Department of Treasury*, the government's banker, founded in 1789.
— *The Department of Defense* (DOD), created in 1949 by consolidating the former departments of the Army, the Navy, and the Air Force.
— *The Department of Justice* (whose head is the Attorney General), created in 1870 to serve as the government's attorney.
— *The Department of the Interior*, created in 1849, which manages the nation's natural resources, including wildlife and public lands.
— *The Department of Agriculture*, created in 1862, which administers farm and food stamp programs and aids farmers.
— *The Department of Commerce*, created in 1903 as the Department of Commerce and Labor, which aids businesses and conducts the United States census.
— *The Department of Labor*, separated from the Department of Commerce in 1913, which runs manpower programs and aids labor in various ways.
— *The Department of Health and Human Services*, which runs health, welfare, and social security programs; created as the Department of Health, Education, and Welfare in 1953, it lost its education function in 1979.
— *The Department of Housing and Urban Development*, created in 1966, which is responsible for urban and housing programs.
— *The Department of Transportation*, created in 1966, which is responsible for mass transportation and highway programs.
— *The Department of Energy*, created in 1977, which is responsible for energy policy and research, including atomic energy.
— *The Department of Education*, created in 1979, which is responsible for the federal government's education programs.

In addition, presidents may designate other officials (the ambassador to the United Nations is a common choice) as cabinet members.

The Executive Office

Next to the White House sits an ornate (some would say unsightly) building called the *EOB*, or Executive Office Building. It houses a collection of offices and organizations loosely grouped into the Executive Office of the President. Some of these offices (such as Council of Economic Advisors) are created by legislation, and some are organized essentially by the president. Starting small in 1939, when established by President Roosevelt, the Executive Office has grown with the rest of government. In the Executive Office are housed three major policymaking bodies: the

National Security Council, the Council of Economic Advisors, and the Office of Management and Budget.

The **National Security Council (NSC)** is the committee that links the president's key foreign and military policy advisors. The president, vice-president, and secretaries of state and defense are its members, but its informal membership is broader. The president's special assistant for national security affairs plays a major role in the NSC. This post, made famous by Henry Kissinger and later occupied under Jimmy Carter by Zbigniew Brzezinski, is occupied by Robert McIntyre in Reagan's administration.

The **Council of Economic Advisors (CEA)** has three members, each appointed by the president, who advise him on economic policy. They prepare the *Annual Report of the Council of Economic Advisors* and help the president make policy on inflation, unemployment, and other economic matters.

The **Office of Management and Budget (OMB)** grew out of the Bureau of the Budget (BOB), created in 1921. President Nixon revamped the BOB in 1970 in an attempt to make it a managerial as well as a budgetary agency. (We discuss OMB and its budgetary role in Chapter 16.)

Though smaller and less unwieldy from the president's point of view than the cabinet departments, the Executive Office is still filled with people performing jobs required by law. Although institutionalized, it is still less so than the cabinet departments. There is, however, one part of the presidential system that the president can truly call his own—the White House staff.

The White House Staff

The White House Staff consists of the key aides the president sees daily —his chief of staff, his congressional liaison people, his press secretary, his appointments secretary, and a few others. They are the people who owe almost total loyalty to the president and to whom he turns for advice on the most mundane and the most serious matters of governance. Good staff people are self-effacing, working only for the boss and hiding from the limelight. So important are their roles, though, that their names quickly become known. Woodrow Wilson's Colonel Edward M. House, Franklin Roosevelt's Harry Hopkins, Dwight Eisenhower's Sherman Adams, John Kennedy's Pierre Salinger and Theodore Sorensen, Lyndon Johnson's Bill Moyers and Larry O'Brien, and Jimmy Carter's Hamilton Jordan and Jody Powell did much to shape the contours of domestic and global policy. Few staff people became as famous as Richard Nixon's staff —H.R. "Bob" Haldeman, John Ehrlichman, John Dean, Charles Colson, and the rest—all of whom became embroiled in the Watergate scandal.

In his first term, President Reagan preferred to operate through a "troika" of presidential aides; advisors James Baker, Michael Deaver, and Edwin Meese. Baker was chief of staff, Deaver tended to Reagan's pristine public image, and Meese focused on details of domestic policy. As his second term began, Baker and treasury secretary Donald Regan literally swapped jobs. Regan, who was a former Wall Street powerhouse, "considers the executive branch to be like a corporation. Cabinet mem-

Colonel E. M. House (*near right*). *A western progressive who helped unite the Democratic party behind Woodrow Wilson at its 1912 convention, Colonel House—the title was an honorary one given him by his home state of Texas—became President Wilson's closest advisor. He had no official title, but his power was enormous; at times he almost seemed to be co-president. His was one of the most important voices in persuading the president that the United States had to enter World War I, and later he supervised the working committee that drafted Wilson's famous "Fourteen Points" and laid the groundwork for the armistice. An affable man and a skillful political operator, House provided a necessary contrast to the aloof, intellectual president.*

Sherman Adams. *Chief of staff for President Dwight Eisenhower, Adams (top right) was the former governor of New Hampshire. His tough chain-of-command style easily suited the managerial preferences of the former general. But Adams got himself entangled in a minor scandal, accepting a vicuna coat from a powerful friend, and was forced to resign his White House post.*

Arthur M. Schlesinger, Jr. *Many of President John Kennedy's aides were drawn from the ranks of the Harvard faculty. They were, author David Halberstam sarcastically remarked, "the best and the brightest." One important Kennedy advisor was Arthur Schlesinger, Jr., a distinguished historian. Schlesinger, along with former Harvard dean McGeorge Bundy and MIT economist Walt W. Rostow, were major advisors on Vietnam, urging Kennedy to send American military advisors to assist the South Vietnamese.*

bers are vice presidents, the president is the chairman of the board, and the chief of staff is the chief operating officer," said one aide.[19]

These sorts of changes are not merely cosmetic, because presidents rely heavily on their staffs. Different presidents, of course, have different relationships with their staffs. President Johnson could be abusive one minute, wheedling the next. President Nixon presented a macho image with his subordinates, but shied away from executing unpleasant personnel decisions, using Chief of Staff H.R. Haldeman as his alter ego. Said top Nixon aide John Ehrlichman, "Once Nixon's decision had been made,

424

[19] *Time*, January 21, 1985, p. 10.

H. R. Haldeman. *Haldeman (far left) was Nixon's chief of staff. A former advertising executive who had played a managerial role in Nixon's presidential campaign, Haldeman, with his colleague John Ehrlichman, formed what some called a "Berlin Wall" around Nixon. A stern disciplinarian, Haldeman ran the White House with an iron grip, insisting on a "zero-defect" system. Haldeman, Ehrlichman, and other Nixon aides served time in federal prison for their involvement in the Watergate scandal.*

Jody Powell and Hamilton Jordan. *Powell (left) and Jordan (right) were two of President Jimmy Carter's senior aides. Powell was press secretary to the president, but also participated in numerous key decisions. Jordan was Carter's chief of staff and alter ego. He personally handled much of the negotiation for the release of the hostages in Iran, traveling incognito to Panama and Paris to work out details of the American response to the Tehran crisis.*

Donald T. Regan. *In his first term, President Reagan preferred a three-member team of key advisors. In his second term, he moved toward a centralized model, with former Treasury Secretary and Wall Street power Donald Regan serving as White House chief of staff. Regan saw himself and the presidency in corporate terms: he would be the chief executive officer while Reagan was chairman of the board, a style that dovetailed nicely with the president's penchant for delegation.*

Haldeman became the enforcer. . . . Dozens of assignments, instructions, and inquiries came from Haldeman every day. For example, one day this memo came from 'H':

> Memorandum for: John Ehrlichman
> From: H.R. Haldeman
> Billy Graham raised with the President today the point that postal rates for religious publications are being increased 400% while postal rates for pornography are only being increased 25%.
> Needless to say, the President was horrified to learn of this state of affairs and wants to know what we are doing about it." [20]

[20] John Ehrlichman, *Witness to Power* (New York: Pocket Books, 1982), p. 61.

425

On the memo, Ehrlichman scribbled back, "shall we lower religious mail or raise the rates for porn?" Haldeman replied, "You'll have to raise that question w/ RN or BG—I am only qualified to report the horror, not act upon it." Nixon, like many other chief executives maintained a *chain-of-command* organization in the White House. Haldeman maintained tight discipline—he called it a "zero defect system"—among White House staff members. Other presidents (for example, John Kennedy) maintain a more *pluralistic* system of White House management. In that system, many aides are consulted, even balanced against one another, before the president decides. See pages 424–425 for a look at some key presidential aides.

No presidential management styles contrast more sharply than those of Presidents Carter and Reagan. Carter was a detail man, pouring endlessly over memorandums and facts. (He was, said presidential observer Hugh Sidey, "not a leader but a decision maker.") President Reagan is the consummate delegator. So adept at dispersing authority is Reagan that his advisors—the news media often call them "his handlers" —feel it periodically necessary to have the president insist that "I am the boss" in media interviews. How the Reagan White House "works" is seen best through the research of presidential scholar John Kessel.

The Reagan White House, Kessel found, is a fairly open place for discussion. In large staff meetings, said one aide, "he [Reagan] does not mind disagreements on philosophical points or details of strategy and that sort of thing." Sometimes, Reagan will simply say, "What do you fellows think?" He is least flexible when an issue triggers one of his deeply held conservative beliefs. [21]

At the beginning of his second term in office, President Reagan made a major overhaul in his staff. Once divided into a pluralistic organization, it came to be much more centralized in the hands of Donald Regan, one-time Wall Street powerhouse and President Reagan's former treasury secretary. Regan ran a tighter ship in the White House than Reagan had in his first term.

PRESIDENTIAL POWER

Texas journalist Ronnie Dugger was interviewing President Lyndon B. Johnson during the days of the Vietnam War. Dugger had reflected, he told Johnson, on the awesome power of the presidency, on his impression that "this immaculate White House is what it actually is, a house wired for universal death, instant after instant, president after president." Raising the specter of nuclear war with Johnson, Dugger asked uncomfortably, "But how do you feel about it?" (The *it* presumably was the power of the president to order nuclear war.) Johnson rambled, talking about Russian power, telling stories bearing only obliquely on the issue, and working himself into a feverish anger. Finally, Dugger reports, "He shouted at me with a terrible intensity, jamming his thumb down on an

[21] John H. Kessel, "The Structure of the Reagan White House," *American Journal of Political Science* 28 (May 1984): 231–58.

imaginary spot in the air beside him, "*I'm* the one who has to *mash* the *button.*" [22] In foreign policy especially, though less so in domestic policy, presidents are powerful indeed. Let us examine that presidential power, its sources and its uses.

The Technology of Presidential Power

Franklin D. Roosevelt was the first president to use modern mass communication to enhance presidential power. During the Great Depression of the 1930s, he went on radio in a series of "Fireside Chats" from the White House. Harry S. Truman, his successor, was the first to use television. It was Dwight D. Eisenhower who hired the first media coach for the president—actor Robert Montgomery.

The American president is powerful today in large part because the presidency was the first institution of American government to realize the vast power of the media of mass communication to enhance its own power. President Woodrow Wilson typed much of his own correspondence. This simple mode of communication has given way to the most elaborate communication system yet devised—that of presidential communication with the American people. Even today, only half the Congress (the House) is televised. Yet the presidency has understood the power of television for a generation.

Washington politics is fragmented. Interest groups, congressional committees, bureaucratic agencies—each competes for policy dominance. Presidents have learned to go beyond Washington intrigues in their effort to hold power. They resort to the technology of mass communication, the cutting edge of which is television. Fred W. Friendly, one of America's most influential television producers, has observed that "no mighty king, no ambitious emperor, no pope or prophet, even dreamt of

[22] Ronnie Dugger, *The Politician: The Life and Times of Lyndon Johnson* (New York: Norton, 1982), pp. 21–24.

Technology in Its Infancy. *The technology of communications was in its infancy during the term of President Franklin D. Roosevelt. Still, he was the first president to use the radio to communicate directly with "my fellow Americans." Americans were fearful of the consequences of the Great Depression. Roosevelt used his "Fireside Chats" to reassure people, even when the economic conditions seemed scarcely to improve. When World War II neared, he again used the radio. Here is his broadcast of a 1940 speech proclaiming that the United States would be an "arsenal of democracy" for Britain in its resistance to Nazi aggression.*

such an awesome pulpit, so potent a magic wand . . . . The president, in his ability to command the national attention, has diminished the power of all other politicians." [23]

The sheer visibility of the president overshadows those popes, emperors, and prophets of whom Friendly spoke. Bruce Miroff examined two years of *Time* and *Newsweek* coverage. He found that more than half of the lead stories dealt with the American president and his activities. [24] Presidents, of course, have a **press secretary,** the White House official responsible for sharing the president's perspective on the news with reporters. But presidents have more than a mere press secretary to handle their public's perceptions. President Reagan relied upon Michael Deaver to manage every aspect of scheduling, public appearances, and public images for the president. Deaver could even tell the president when the presidential helicopters were, and were not, close enough for the noise to drown out reporters' questions. Presidents are whisked here and there by those helicopters. A veritable armada of them, plus armored cars and airplanes, are at the president's immediate disposal. (Once, when President Johnson was visiting a war zone in Vietnam, he wandered back to a helicopter to depart. A young officer respectfully pointed to another helicopter, saying "Excuse me, Mr. President, that's your helicopter over there." The imperious President Johnson replied, "Son, they're all my helicopters.") Among all the citizens of the world, only the president of the United States can directly dial the Kremlin.

The president of the United States does not merely watch the news; he *is* the news. Doris Kearns reports that President Johnson liked to watch the news on all three networks at once and thus installed a special television in the Oval Office; it received all three networks at once. Near the oversized set stood news tickers from AP, UPI, and Reuters. They brought the White House instant news. "Those tickers," said Lyndon Johnson, "were like friends tapping at my door for attention. I loved having them around. They kept me in touch with the outside world. They made me feel that I was truly in the center of things. I could stand beside the tickers for hours on end and never be lonely." [25]

Among recent presidents, only Lyndon Johnson could be so honest about the exhilaration of being at "the center of things." But all of them are, and it is hard to imagine any president who would not be exhilarated by it. No one could help but be flattered—just a bit at least—by being at center stage of the entire world. Technology helps put the president at the center of things. Well-managed technology can keep him there, especially in the hearts and minds of the American public.

Power from the People: The President's Popularity. The most powerful office in the Western world, the presidency is often called a popularly

[23] Foreward to Newton W. Minow, John Bartlow Martin, and Lee M. Mitchell, *Political Television* (New York: Basic Books, 1973), pp. vii–viii. Cited in Bruce Miroff, "Monopolizing the Public Space," in Cronin (ed.), *Rethinking the Presidency*, p. 219.

[24] Miroff, "Monopolizing the Public Space," p. 219.

[25] Doris Kearns, *Lyndon Johnson and the American Dream* (New York: Harper & Row, 1976), p. 7.

The President, Technology, and the Public. *Technology has reshaped the president's ability to communicate directly with the people. Presidents have ready access to the media, with all the power that entails. But this "personalized presidency" has its costs: It means that people are likely to hold the president directly responsible for the country's problems.*

elected office, with much of its power derived from the American people. Strictly speaking, it is not a popularly elected position, the incumbent securing his post through the complex procedures of the electoral college, which we examined in Chapter 9. Yet the president is very close to the people. He enters their living rooms almost every evening at the dinner hour (though people may choose not to invite him in through their own one-screen sets); he shapes their history and their recollection of it; he affects, as much as any other person, their jobs, their taxes, and their inflation rates. Presidents pay ample attention to the people. They put him into office, and they can brush him out of office in four years.

President-watching is one of our favorite American pastimes. Historians rate presidents, and so do the people. For years, even back to the time of Franklin D. Roosevelt, the Gallup Organization has asked Americans this question: "Do you approve of the way (John Kennedy, or Ronald Reagan, or whoever) is handling his job as president?" These polls give us, and presidents as well, a monthly barometer of presidential popularity. You can examine the trends in presidential popularity from Truman to Reagan in ⑤. If you look carefully at the trends shown there, you will quickly detect a "roller coaster" effect. There are ups and downs in presidential popularity, and they come in predictable cycles. Any president's popularity is high just after he moves into 1600 Pennsylvania Avenue, then steadily erodes. The only recent exception was in Dwight

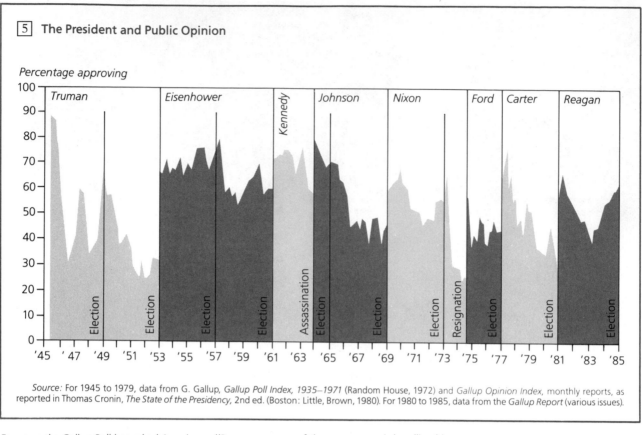

Percentage approving

Source: For 1945 to 1979, data from G. Gallup, *Gallup Poll Index, 1935–1971* (Random House, 1972) and *Gallup Opinion Index*, monthly reports, as reported in Thomas Cronin, *The State of the Presidency*, 2nd ed. (Boston: Little, Brown, 1980). For 1980 to 1985, data from the *Gallup Report* (various issues).

For years the Gallup Poll has asked Americans, "Do you approve of the way _____ is handling his job as president?" Here you can track the percentage approving presidential performance from Truman to Reagan. Notice that all presidents seem to be most popular when they first enter office; later on, their popularity eroded.

Eisenhower's first term, when his popularity stayed relatively stable. Taking office, the president can usually expect a "honeymoon" period during which his popularity is better than it will ever be again. Presidents sensibly try to take advantage of this period and push policies on Congress at a furious pace. Few have made better use of this honeymoon period in recent years than Ronald Reagan. His first year was marked by tax cuts, spending limitations, arms buildups, and other policies promised during his campaign. Things got tougher for him in his second year.

What accounts for the erosion of presidential popularity over a term? In part, argues John Mueller, it occurs because presidents must inevitably alienate part of their electoral constituency.[26] Countless people supported a president for countless reasons, each no doubt believing that the new president would right whatever wrong had brought them to the coalition. But presidents cannot do everything. They put some issues on the back burner of their agenda and lose the support of those who think their issue—abortion, unemployment, busing, whatever—should be the president's main concern. For his first election, a solid phalanx of rock-

[26] John E. Mueller, *War, Presidents, and Public Opinion* (New York: Wiley, 1973). For a useful review of the evidence on presidential popularity, see Stephen J. Wayne, "Great Expectations," in Cronin (ed.), *Rethinking the Presidency*, Chap. 15.

hard conservatives voted for Ronald Reagan, certain that he would devote his first year to their policy agendas. When he did much about economic policy and little initially about banning abortions or bringing back school prayer, Reagan's support among "moral majoritarians" wavered.

A president begins his term with high expectations. Once and for all, his most optimistic supporters hope, peace will be at hand, unemployment will be reduced, inflation slowed, crime controlled, taxes pared, and other promises turned into performance. But great expectations can be dashed on the hard rocks of political and economic reality. For that reason, argues James Stimson, time itself is an important predictor of popularity decline. [27]

George C. Edwards, III, has conducted a careful and statistical study of presidential popularity and its connection with many factors. [28] One of these is the state of the economy. Somewhat surprisingly, people's personal economic circumstances—whether they are unemployed or feel the pinches of inflation—make little difference in their assessment of the president. But people do seem to look at the broader picture: how well people see the president's management of the economy is a significant factor in their evaluation of him.

From time to time, public opinion polls show an upward "spike" in presidential popularity, sometimes associated with some major crisis. The deaths of American troops in some strife-torn area, a sudden worsening of Soviet-American relations, or a crisis somewhere can rally people around the president for a time. But, as Edwards explains, these are rare and isolated events. They leave little lingering impact on any president's popularity.

Presidential Power and the "Two Presidencies"

One reason people exaggerate presidential power, despite all its varied sources and trappings, is that the presidency is in fact a two-sided office. Aaron Wildavsky put it like this: "The United States has one president, but it has two presidencies: one for domestic affairs and the other for defense and foreign policy." [29] One presidency looks ever outward, dealing with problems of the global connection; the other deals with internal domestic policies that concern equality, the economy, energy and the environment, and other issues. Wildavsky goes on to make an important point about presidential power. "Presidents," he emphasizes, "have had much greater success in controlling the [global connection] than in dominating domestic policies." In the foreign policy presidency, the president is usually powerful enough to get things done his way, while in the domestic presidency he is rarely king of the policymaking mountain.

[27] James Stimson, "Public Support for American Presidents: A Cyclical Model," *Public Opinion Quarterly* 40 (Spring 1976): 1–21.

[28] George C. Edwards, III, *The Public Presidency: The Pursuit of Popular Support* (New York: St. Martin's, 1983), Chap. 6.

[29] Aaron Wildavsky, "The Two Presidencies," in Aaron Wildavsky (ed.), *Perspectives on the Presidency* (Boston: Little, Brown, 1975), p. 448.

If this thesis about the two presidencies is correct, it follows that presidents should be more successful in getting their way in foreign than in domestic policy arenas. There is some evidence from recent presidencies that this is indeed the case. Even presidents who came to office with little experience in foreign affairs often scored their major successes there. Former Georgia Governor Jimmy Carter, never really able to dominate our economic or energy policies at home, nonetheless secured a Panama Canal treaty, got a nuclear arms limitation treaty signed, and presided over dramatic Middle Eastern peace negotiations between Israel and Egypt, resulting in the Camp David accords.

The President and the Global Connection

Why the President Dominates Global Policymaking. Presidential powers to shape our foreign and military policy, including the ultimate power of nuclear war, are awesome. So great are presidential military powers that our last two wars, in Korea and in Vietnam, have been fought on the president's initiative, ignoring the plain words of the Constitution that "the Congress shall have power . . . to declare war." His constitutional powers regarding the global connection—making treaties, recognizing governments, being commander in chief—are ample, but not by themselves sufficient to explain why presidents call the tune and orchestrate it in foreign policy.

One reason is that the larger the global connection looms, the more dominant becomes the president's voice. After World War II, both parties supported the idea of a "bipartisan foreign policy," believing that the nation could not stand divisiveness about such vital matters as defense and foreign policy in such dangerous times. In practice, the bipartisan foreign policy meant, until the Vietnam War, that whatever presidents did, Congress supported. Nuclear weapons, large standing armies, and today's international economy all combine to favor centralization of power in the presidency.

Presidents, of course, capitalize on the feeling that we need a strong president in global policy. Assembling an elite team of advisors, they made foreign policy personally, secretly, and decisively—at least until the Vietnam War. Even now the global president overshadows both the domestic president and Congress itself. Two cases will explain what we mean.

Kennedy and the Cuban Missile Crisis. For thirteen days in October 1962, the United States and the Soviet Union came as close as ever before or since to nuclear war. [30] The cause was the Soviet government's decision to locate offensive missiles in Cuba, ninety miles from the American shore. Missiles launched from Cuba could reach and destroy American targets within minutes.

[30] This account of the Cuban missile crisis relies on Graham T. Allison, *Essence of Decision: Explaining the Cuban Missile Crisis* (Boston: Little, Brown, 1971), and on Irving L. Janis, *Victims of Groupthink* (Boston: Houghton Mifflin, 1972), Chap. 6.

On October 14, 1962, an American U-2 plane photographed a missile site being built in Cuba. At 11:45 A.M., the Executive Committee of the National Security Council met to discuss the missiles and stayed in almost continuous session for the next five days. Its members were President Kennedy, Secretary of State Dean Rusk, Secretary of Defense Robert McNamara, Secretary of the Treasury Douglas Dillon, and White House Foreign Policy Advisor McGeorge Bundy. The Attorney General, Robert Kennedy, was a frequent participant. At the first meeting, President Kennedy announced that "acquiescence was impossible." He ordered the group to find a way of getting the missiles out of Cuba before they became operational. After several days of meetings, Kennedy and his advisors decided to set up a military blockade of Cuba. The navy was ordered to surround the island.

On October 22, Kennedy made a dramatic, even frightening, television address announcing the presence of the missiles and the military blockade. He hinted that more drastic measures could follow if the Soviet Union made the missile facility operational. On October 23 and 24, several Soviet vessels, apparently carrying warheads, appeared in Cuban waters. But on October 25 they turned around. On October 28, the Soviet Union announced that it would withdraw its Cuban missile operations in exchange for an American guarantee not to invade the island.

It was the president's show all the way. Operating in strict secrecy until the speech on October 22, Kennedy and a handful of top aides decided the American response—unencumbered by Congress, the press, interest groups, or public opinion. It was a close call, in retrospect, but it proved to be a presidential success.

Lyndon Johnson and the Vietnam War. Lyndon Johnson did not start the Vietnam War.[31] He inherited it. The inheritance was small—a financial commitment to help the South Vietnamese government and provide some American "advisors" to the South Vietnamese army—but the commitment grew under his stewardship. At one time, America had more than 600,000 men in Vietnam; we dropped more bombs on Vietnam than on Germany in all of World War II.

Johnson had no tolerance for opponents of his Vietnam policy. He assembled a small group of advisors for lunch each Tuesday, a group devoted to prosecuting the war. National Security Advisor McGeorge Bundy (later replaced by Walt Rostow), Secretary of Defense Robert McNamara (later replaced by Clark Clifford), Secretary of State Dean Rusk, and a few others were regulars. These were men of a single mind, unified by a belief in the rightness of American involvement and the probability of ultimate success. As the war grew more intractable and as Congress and public opinion became more hostile, they listened less and less to outsiders. Advisors who dissented from their views (such as George Ball, undersecretary of state and from the start a dissenter from Johnson's policy of escalating American involvement) were gradually left out of the meetings.

[31] The literature on Johnson and Vietnam is voluminous. Some useful references include Kearns, *American Dream*, Chaps. 9–11; Janis, *Groupthink*, Chap. 5; and Schandler, *Unmaking of a President*.

During the meetings, Johnson vacillated between depression and enthusiasm. As the war worsened, he launched long monologues:

> Once Johnson started one of his monologues, it was difficult to stop him. If one of his listeners interrupted, trying to pull him back to the business at hand, he would become enraged. Yet if the listeners acquiesced by a smile or a sympathetic nodding of the head, Johnson would feel encouraged and continue on. In such moods, Johnson's vanity proved unappeasable. [32]

The reaction of the participants was, said Irving Janis, a case of "groupthink," in which members of a closeknit group come to think like one another and to see outsiders as hostile or ill-informed. [33] Johnson ran the meetings, and his ideas became everyone's ideas. They soon came to follow a dictum of George Reedy about the presidency: "The first strong observations to attract the favor of the President become subconsciously the thoughts of everyone in the room." [34] When members left the group, they were seen almost as traitors to a cause.

What the Two Cases and Other Global Decisions Have in Common. In both the Cuban missile crisis and the Johnson decisions on Vietnam, the president was the main policymaker. Surrounded by a small group of aides, he could make decisions in virtual secrecy. Decisions, once made, were implemented by the foreign and military policy bureaucracies. When Kennedy ordered a blockade, the navy went full-steam to Cuba. When Johnson ordered bombings of Vietnam, planes took off. The president's authority was unquestioned, his powers were unambiguous, and his capacity to get his policies implemented was great. It was (to turn Harry Truman's observation about Eisenhower on its head) just like the army.

Congress, the President, and the Global Connection. Though charged by the Constitution with declaring war and voting the military budget, Congress long ago became accustomed to short-run commitments of troops or naval vessels by the president. Recently, though, presidents have paid even less attention to constitutional details. Congress never declared war in either Korea or Vietnam. Johnson used a purported attack on two United States destroyers, the *C. Turner Joy* and the *Maddox*, by the North Vietnamese to justify sending American troops to Vietnam. As a result of the attack, the "Gulf of Tonkin resolution" was hastily passed by Congress and then used by Johnson as a virtual blank check to increase American involvement. (Johnson later conceded that "it might have been a whale" attacking the destroyers, for all he knew. [35])

Upset as the Vietnam War dragged on, and eager to reassert its constitutional powers, Congress passed (over Nixon's veto) the **War Powers Act** in 1973. It emphasized the right of Congress to declare war, spelling out

---

[32] Kearns, *American Dream*, p. 377.
[33] Janis, *Groupthink*.
[34] Reedy, *Twilight*, p. 25.
[35] Barber, *Presidential Character*, p. 37.

conditions under which the president could commit American troops without congressional approval. It required that

1. Within forty-eight hours after committing United States troops abroad, the president must report and explain his decision to Congress.
2. Such a commitment could extend only sixty to ninety days unless Congress authorized an extension.
3. Within that period, Congress could end the American combat commitment by passing a resolution not subject to presidential veto.

It may not have been quite what the Founding Fathers had in mind when they said that only Congress could declare wars, but it was an honest attempt to rein in a war-minded president. It was going to be difficult, critics maintained, for Congress to resist a presidential *fait accompli*. Indeed, twice in 1975 Gerald Ford sent troops on a short-term basis to southeast Asia, arguing that the War Powers Act did not apply to those cases.

The President and the Domestic Agenda

If the global presidency is largely a one-man show, with bit parts for other players and an occasional critical review thereafter, the domestic president shares center stage with a cast of thousands. If the foreign-policy presidency is mostly a command performance, the domestic one is the bargaining presidency.

In domestic affairs, the president rarely commands obedience. He shares the policymaking stage with too many other actors to dominate it absolutely. In *Presidential Power*, perhaps the most influential book ever written on the American presidency, Richard E. Neustadt emphasized that presidential power is the power to persuade rather than the power to command, especially on domestic matters.[36] The president need not resort to wheedling to persuade, for his political resources are impressive. But, emphasizes Neustadt, he must persuade other powerholders that it is in *their* interest to do what is in *his* interest. Neustadt's book was a sort of bible for the newly elected John F. Kennedy. (Neustadt himself, a Harvard political scientist, advised Kennedy during the transition period.) Neustadt urged presidents on, wrote a manual on how to use power in the White House, and insisted that many things were possible with wisely used presidential power.

Some years later, reviews of the domestic presidency sang a different tune. Paul Light interviewed 126 key presidential staff members from five administrations (Kennedy through Carter).[37] Many found that presidential leadership was under constant challenge—threatened by Congress, by the bureaucracies, and by powerful interest groups. One Carter aide

---

[36] Neustadt, *Presidential Power*.
[37] Paul C. Light, "Presidents as Domestic Policymakers," in Cronin (ed.), *Rethinking the Presidency*, p. 352.

From HERBLOCK THROUGH THE LOOKING GLASS (Simon and Schuster, 1984).

©1983 HERBLOCK

"THE BUTLER DID IT"

told Light, "This has become a 'no win' job. It involves a series of obstacles; one hurdle after another. Each problem is followed by a second, more difficult problem." [38] What is possible and even essential for the president is to pull together his own policy agenda, push it in Congress, and hope that Congress will support it.

Light outlined the strategies and problems in presidential agenda building. Issues come from many places, but the president takes only a few as his own. Some of these are shaped by his campaign and its promises, by his party and its platform. Ronald Reagan's agenda was filled with promises to cut taxes, slow the growth of federal spending, hike defense spending, and reduce the regulation of business and the environment. All of these were fully congruent with the Republican party's 1980 platform, and as we saw in Chapter 8, parties usually do what they say they will do. Behind these commitments usually stands the president's own ideology, whether Reagan's conservatism or Johnson's populist liberalism. No recent presidents have had more success in their first years in making their agenda the nation's agenda—and the Congress' agenda—than Lyndon B. Johnson and Ronald Reagan.

Whatever the agenda, it is important to start early. The honeymoon period is short, certainly not lasting beyond a year. Bills must flow to Congress, and in press conferences and speeches the president must stress the critical character of each presidential initiative. Few presi-

[38] Ibid., p. 368.

dents started faster than Ronald Reagan. David Stockman, the new director of the Office of Management and Budget, put together an alternative to Jimmy Carter's budget—a process that normally covers a full year of activity—in only six weeks. Speed and persuasion are of the essence.

President Reagan's first term amounted to a whirlwind of legislative successes for his budget policy. But it was followed by halting efforts in his second. When Reagan was inaugurated a second time in 1985, the nation faced a $200 billion budget deficit. During his 1984 campaign, he had promised never to raise taxes. His initial legislative proposals to Congress included no new taxes and proposals for $50 billion in savings through program cuts. Even in the Republican-controlled Senate, though, it was hard for the President to push increased defense spending and domestic spending reductions

The Domestic Presidency and Congress. Much of the president's effort as chief legislator is devoted to shaping the congressional agenda. The State of the Union message itself is delivered just as the new Congress is

The Domestic Presidency. *Unlike the foreign policy presidency, the domestic presidency reflects pluralism in American politics. Bargaining and persuasion characterize presidential leadership in domestic policymaking. Nothing so symbolizes the need for coalition-building strategies as the ritual of signing a key bill with numerous pens and handing them out to the bill's assembled supporters and sponsors. LBJ did just that when he called together mayors and congressional leaders to watch him ink his name on an urban renewal bill in 1965. Mayor Robert Wagner of New York has just gotten his pen; Mayor Richard J. Daley is shown getting his.*

beginning its business. Similarly, the Economic Report of the President is delivered early in the session. Dozens of bills appear in the hopper as presidential priorities. The congressional agenda is largely the one the president sets for it.

The president may set the agenda for Congress, but it seems clear that his influence on congressional voting decisions is weaker than in the foreign-policy presidency. Aage Clausen's analysis of congressional roll-call behavior found presidential influence strong on foreign policy issues, weaker on domestic ones. [39]

No tradition of bipartisan policy can help the president deal with Congress on domestic affairs. So, like relations between siblings, lovers, or spouses, those between president and Congress are likely to wax and wane. When the president's party is the majority party in Congress, especially when it is a decisive majority (as with Lyndon Johnson and the 1965-67 Congress or Ronald Reagan and the 1981 Senate), relations are likely to be cozy. It could have been said from 1965 to 1967 that "whatever Lyndon wants, Lyndon gets."

Relations become more strained when the president and majorities in Congress are from different parties. Richard Nixon, never one to doubt that his opponents were out to get him, saw the Democratic Congress as his natural enemy. An *impoundment* controversy resulted. When Congress appropriated funds over his veto, he impounded them—refused to spend them. Cities, states, and members of Congress objected, and took Nixon to court over the impoundment issue. In *Train* v. *City of New York* (1975), the Supreme Court unanimously ruled that the president's obligation to "take care that the laws be faithfully executed" included his obligation to spend money Congress appropriated. Congress itself, writing a new Congressional Budget Act in 1974, required the president to spend appropriated funds.

This sort of conflict sorely tests the relationship between presidents and the Congress. The occasional outburst of conflict, though, is less important than the steady oscillation of presidential and congressional power. The power to determine the nation's agenda has tended to gravitate toward the presidential end of Pennsylvania Avenue. A president who can virtually declare war, who sets out the preliminary budget for Congress, and who sends down most of the important legislative initiatives, has become a chief legislator. Every so often, Congress chafes at the restraints of its lessened role. In foreign policy, it passes a War Powers Act. For domestic policy, it passes its own budget act and sets up its own budget office. It awaits presidential initiatives eagerly, but deplores its own lack of initiative. The drift of power to the presidency is sorely regretted in Congress. Yet of the president's power to set the congressional agenda, even the nation's agenda, few on Capitol Hill have doubts.

Not only members of the Congress but scholars of the presidency as well ask these days whether the presidency has become too powerful for our own good.

[39] Aage Clausen, *How Congressmen Decide: A Policy Approach* (New York: St. Martin's, 1973), Chap. 8.

UNDERSTANDING THE AMERICAN PRESIDENCY

During the 1950s and 1960s, it was fashionable for political scientists, historians, and commentators to favor a powerful presidency. Historians rated presidents from strong to weak, there being no question that "strong" meant good and "weak" meant bad. Political scientists waxed eloquent about the role of the presidency as the epitome of democratic government. [40]

By the 1970s, no one was quite so sure. The Vietnam War was unpopular. Lyndon Johnson and his war made people rethink presidential power, but Richard Nixon and his Watergate redoubled their thinking. Duplicity by several presidents was revealed in the Pentagon Papers, a series of secret documents slipped to the press by Daniel Ellsberg. Nixon's "enemies list," his avowed goal to "screw our enemies" by illegally auditing their taxes, tapping their phones, and using "surreptitious entry" (a euphemism for burglary), asserted that presidents are above the law. His lawyers argued solemnly to the Supreme Court and Congress that the presidency has "inherent powers" permitting presidents to order acts that otherwise would be illegal. He protected himself with an umbrella defense of executive privilege, claiming that he need not provide evidence to Congress or the courts.

Early defenders of a strong presidency made sharp turnabouts in their position. Historian Arthur Schlesinger, an aide of John Kennedy's, wrote *The Imperial Presidency*, arguing that the presidency had become too powerful for the nation's own good. [41] (Critics pointed out that he did not seem to feel that way when he worked in the White House.) An older generation of scholars had written glowing accounts of the presidency. A newer generation wrote about "The Swelling of the Presidency" and "Making the Presidency Safe for Democracy." [42]

THE PRESIDENCY SUMMARIZED

The presidency is an office with high expectations: more democratic than the Founding Fathers planned it to be, it is also less powerful than we expect it to be—especially on the domestic side. Presidents have mainly the "power to persuade" in setting the domestic policy side of the agenda. On the foreign side, though, presidents are king of the hill. But the awesome nature of the president's power gives it an inherent limitation.

In this chapter, we have looked at the presidents and the presidency. Two myths—one of the overworked president and the other of the president as powerhouse—cloud our image of presidential reality. Presidents

[40] A good example is Clinton Rossiter, *The American Presidency*, rev. ed. (New York: Harcourt Brace Jovanovich, 1960).

[41] Arthur Schlesinger, *The Imperial Presidency* (Boston: Houghton Mifflin, 1973).

[42] The titles of Chaps. 5 and 11 in Cronin, *State of the Presidency*.

play many roles, including head of state, commander in chief, foreign-policy maker, agenda builder, chief executive, chief legislator, party leader, crisis manager, and above all, politician.

Presidents, however, do not work alone: The Cabinet, the Executive Office of the President, and the White House staff all assist the president. Gone are the days when the presidency meant the man in the White House plus an aide or two.

We can rightly speak of "two presidencies." The one is the global presidency, powerful and in virtual mastery of the global agenda. The other is the domestic presidency. On the domestic front, the president is, of course, our main agenda builder, but he shares power with many other political forces.

Key Terms

Watergate
Twenty-second Amendment
impeachment
Twenty-fifth Amendment

veto
pocket veto
crisis
cabinet
National Security Council (NSC)

Council of Economic Advisors (CEA)
Office of Management and Budget (OMB)
press secretary
War Powers Act

For Further Reading

Cronin, Thomas E. *The State of the Presidency*, 2nd ed. (1980). Textbook on the presidency with a provocative concluding chapter on "Making the Presidency Safe for Democracy."

———, ed. *Rethinking the Presidency* (1983). Excellent collection of articles on the president and the presidency.

Edwards, George. *The Public Presidency* (1983). The relationship between the president and public opinion.

Hess, Stephen. *Organizing the Presidency* (1976). Examines how different presidents approached the problem of staffing the White House.

Light, Paul. *The President's Agenda* (1983). The presidential role in setting the Washington issue agenda.

Neustadt, Richard E. *Presidential Power*, rev. ed. (1976). The most important piece of scholarship on the American presidency; argues that presidential power is "the power to persuade."

Page, Benjamin I., and Mark P. Petracca. *The American Presidency* (1983). A very good textbook on the presidency.

Shogan, Robert. *None of the Above* (1982). A journalist's account of "why presidents fail."

The Bureaucracies

MEMO

Pity the poor bureaucrat. Unsung, taunted by cartoonists, maligned by columnists, the bureaucrat is the whipping boy of American politics. Presidents we may call great, members of Congress we at least repeatedly reelect, but almost no one loves the bureaucrats.

There are lots of myths about bureaucracy, but the most common one is that it is ineffective and inefficient. We identify bureaucracy with "red tape." To me, inefficiency is not the main problem with the governmental bureaucracy. I've never seen any reason to believe that public bureaucracies are any more inefficient or ineffective than private bureaucracies. If you have ever tried to deal with a credit card company's computer, you'll know what I mean.

My view is that the important problem for a democratic government is *controlling* bureaucracies. They are so powerful that our elected policy-makers constantly find it difficult to control them. But before we can analyze this problem, we need to see what the bureaucracies are and how they make policy. So I will examine the following:

■ Who the bureaucrats are, how they got there, and what they do.
■ How the bureaucracy is organized.
■ How bureaucracies function as makers, implementers, administrators, and regulators of public policy.

GARY MILLER AND TERRY MOE rightly observe that "public bureaucracy has never been especially popular, but in recent years its image has gone from bad to worse."[1] Every recent president has railed against the very agencies he hoped to administer. President Reagan suggested as a part of his 1985 deficit reduction package that federal workers could pitch in by taking a 5 percent pay cut.

Nothing better illustrates the complexity of modern government than its massive bureaucracies. The *Federal Register* lists all the government regulations issued annually by Washington bureaucracies; it now hovers at an annual size of 60,000 pages. Americans are required to submit more than 2 billion forms and documents (mostly about taxes) to the government each year. One plant with seventy-five employees kept two people working half-time writing reports required by the federal government.[2]

Bureaucratic power extends to every corner of American economic and social life. Yet bureaucracies are scarcely hinted at in the Constitution. Each bureaucratic agency was created by Congress, which sets its budget and writes the policies it administers. Most agencies are responsible to the president, whose constitutional responsibility to "take care that the laws shall be faithfully executed" sheds only a dim light on the problems of managing so large a government. How to manage and control bureaucracies is, in this bureaucratic age, a central problem of democratic government.

THE BUREAUCRATS

Some Bureaucratic Myths and Bureaucratic Realities

Bureaucrat-baiting is a popular American pastime. George Wallace, former Alabama governor and frequent presidential hopeful, warmed up his crowds with a line about "pointy-headed Washington bureaucrats who can't even park their bicycles straight." Even successful presidential candidates climbed aboard the antibureaucracy bandwagon. Jimmy Carter complained about our "complicated and confused and overlapping and wasteful" bureaucracies; Gerald Ford complained about the "dead-weight" of bureaucracies; Ronald Reagan insisted that bureaucrats "overregulated" the American economy, causing a decline in productivity.

Any object of such unpopularity will spawn plenty of myths. Four of the most prevalent follow:

1. *Americans dislike their bureaucrats.* Despite the rhetoric about bureaucracies, Americans are generally satisfied with bureaucrats and the treatment they get from them. Daniel Katz and his associates studied the relationship between citizens and bureaucrats. Americans may dislike bureaucracies, but they like bureaucrats.

[1] Gary J. Miller and Terry M. Moe, "Bureaucrats, Legislators, and the Size of Government," *American Political Science Review* 77 (June 1983):297.
[2] These and other tidbits about the federal paperwork burden are described in Herbert Kaufman, *Red Tape* (Washington, D.C.: The Brookings Institution, 1977), pp. 5–6.

Controlling the Bureaucracy. *Here is one image of the uncontrollable bureaucracy, made up of paperwork and red tape, let loose on Washington.*

Katz et al. found a "relative high degree of satisfaction" with bureaucratic encounters. [3] Some 57 percent thought that the bureaucrats they dealt with did the "right amount" to help them; another 16 percent thought the bureaucrats did "more than they had to."

2. *Most federal bureaucrats work in Washington, D.C.* Only about 350,000 of 2.9 million federal employees work in Washington. California leads the nation in federal employees, with 300,000. New York and Texas have more than 150,000 each, and another 120,000 work in foreign countries and American territories.

3. *Bureaucracies are growing bigger and bigger each year.* This myth is half true and half false. The number of *government* employees *has* been expanding, but not the number of *federal* employees. Almost all the growth in the number of public employees has occurred in state and local governments. The 11 million state and local public employees dwarf the 2.9 million civilian federal government employees. As a percentage of our total work force, *federal* govern-

[3] Daniel Katz et al., *Bureaucratic Encounters: A Pilot Study in the Evaluation of Government Services* (Ann Arbor: Survey Research Center, University of Michigan, 1975), p. 184.

ment employment has been shrinking, not growing. Of course, many of these state and local employees work on programs that are federally funded. □1

4. *Bureaucracies are ineffective, inefficient, always mired in red tape.* This image of bureaucracies dies hard. Newspapers provide plenty of grist for the mill that grinds out the myth of bureaucratic inefficiency. No words describing bureaucratic behavior are better known than "red tape." Yet bureaucracy is no more and no less than a way of organizing people to perform work. General Motors, your college or university, the United States Army, the Department of Health and Human Services, and the Roman Catholic Church are all bureaucracies. Bureaucracies are a little like pro football referees: When they work well, no one gives them much credit, but when they do not, everyone calls them unfair or incompetent or inefficient. Bureaucracies may be inefficient at times, but no one has found a substitute for them. And no one has yet demonstrated that government bureaucracies are more or less inefficient, ineffective, or mired in red tape than private bureaucracies.

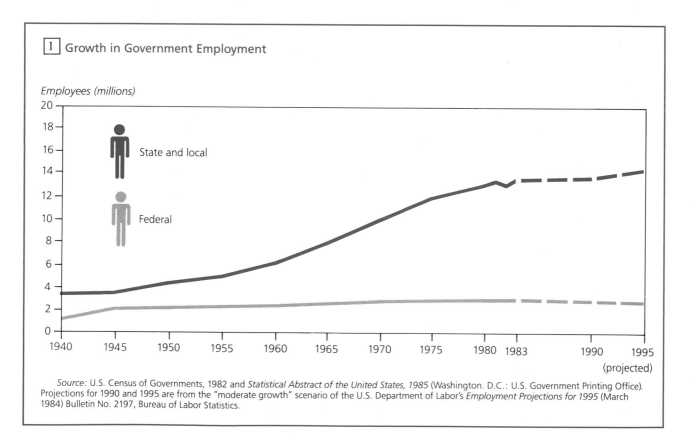

□1 Growth in Government Employment

Employees (millions)

Source: U.S. Census of Governments, 1982 and *Statistical Abstract of the United States, 1985* (Washington. D.C.: U.S. Government Printing Office). Projections for 1990 and 1995 are from the "moderate growth" scenario of the U.S. Department of Labor's *Employment Projections for 1995* (March 1984) Bulletin No. 2197, Bureau of Labor Statistics.

The number of government employees has grown rapidly since 1950. However, the real growth has been the state and local sector, with its millions of teachers, police officers, and other service deliverers. Many state and local employees and programs, though, are supported by federal grants in aid. (Note that the figures for federal employment do not include military personnel.)

Anyone who looks with disdain on our bureaucracies should contemplate life without them. Despite all the carping about bureaucracies, the vast majority of tasks carried out by governments at all levels are noncontroversial. Bureaucrats deliver our mail, test our milk, clean our streets, issue our social security and student loan checks, run our national parks, and perform other perfectly acceptable governmental tasks. Most of the folks who work for cities, states, and the national government are ordinary people, the sort who are likely to be your neighbors or mine.

The diversity of bureaucratic jobs mirrors the diversity of private sector jobs, including occupations literally ranging from *A* to *Z*. Working for government are accountants, bakers, census analysts, defense procurement specialists, electricians, foreign service officers, guards in federal prisons, home economists, Indian affairs agents, judges, kitchen workers, lawyers, missile technologists, narcotics agents, ophthalmologists, postal carriers, quarantine specialists, radiologists, stenographers, truck drivers, underwater demolition experts, virologists, wardens, X-ray technicians, youth counselors, and zoologists.

A plurality of all federal civilian employees work for just a few agencies. The Department of Defense employs about 36 percent of federal workers: San Antonio depends heavily upon the defense department for its economic base; San Jose depends upon the defense contracts provided by DOD, Washington's abbreviation for the Department of Defense. The postal service accounts for another quarter, and the various health professions account for nearly 10 percent (one in three doctors, for example, works for the government).

Who They Are and How They Got There

There are 2.9 million bureaucrats (14 million if we add state and local public employees), so it is hard to imagine a statistically typical bureaucrat. They are male and female, black and white, well paid and not so well paid. Like other institutions, the federal government has been under pressure to expand its hiring of women and minorities. Congress has ordered federal agencies to make special efforts to recruit and promote previously disadvantaged groups, but women and nonwhites still cluster at the lower ranks. (Congress has exempted itself from these rules.)

Almost all federal employees obtain their jobs through one of two routes. The great majority enter through the Civil Service system; a few at the very top, though, are appointed by the president.

Civil Service: From Patronage to Protection to (Critics Say) Overprotection. Until roughly a hundred years ago, you got a job with the government through the patronage system. **Patronage** is a hiring and promotion system based on knowing the right people. Working in a congressional campaign, making large donations, and having the right connections helped win jobs with the government. Nineteenth-century presidents staffed the government with their friends and allies. Scores of officeseekers would swarm over the White House after Inauguration Day.

THE CIVIL SERVICE AS IT IS.

Hon. Member of Congress presenting a Few of his Constituents for Office.

The Patronage System. *Before passage of the Pendleton Act in 1883, appointments to government offices were made on the basis of patronage. Members of Congress might make their recommendations to the president, who passed out federal jobs. It was the assassination of President James A. Garfield by a frustrated office-seeker that opened the way to the federal civil service system. Garfield's successor, Chester A. Arthur—himself once the recipient of plum patronage positions—signed the act into law.*

It is said that during a bout with malaria, Lincoln told an aide to "send in the officeseekers" because he finally had something to give them all.

It was a disappointed officeseeker named Charles Guiteau who helped end this "spoils system" of federal appointments in 1881. Frustrated because President James A. Garfield would not give him a job, he shot Garfield. It was the Prince of Patronage himself, Vice-president Chester A. Arthur, who stepped into Garfield's shoes. Arthur had been collector of the customs for New York, a patronage-rich post. But Arthur surprised his critics by pushing for passage of the **Pendleton Act** (1883), which created a federal Civil Service. At first, only about 10 percent of federal employees were covered by Civil Service. Today, only 15 percent are *exempt* from it, and most agencies not covered by Civil Service have developed their own merit hiring systems to prevent patronage.

The rationale for all **civil service** systems rests on the idea of merit and the desire to create a nonpartisan government service. The **merit principle**—using entrance exams and promotion ratings—is intended to produce administration by people with talent and skill. Creating a nonpartisan civil service means insulating government workers from the risk of being fired because a new party comes to power.

The Office of Personnel Management (OPM) is in charge of hiring for most agencies of the federal government. Its members are appointed by the president and confirmed by the Senate. The OPM has elaborate rules about hiring, promotion, working conditions, and firing. To get a Civil Service job, normally you must first take a test. If you pass, you will be sent to agencies when jobs requiring your skills open up. For each position that is open, the OPM will send three names to the agency. Except under unusual circumstances, the agency must hire someone on this list of three eligibles. (This process is called the "rule of three.") Once hired, you are assigned a **G.S. (General Schedule) rating**, ranging from G.S.1 to G.S. 18. Salaries are keyed to rating and experience. In 1983, a lowly G.S. 1 (a messenger, for example) got a paltry $8,676 in his or her first year. A G.S. 13 (an accountant, say) earned $34,930, and a G.S. 17 (supervisor or director of a bureau) earned about $57,000 as a starting salary. At the very top of the civil service system is the *Senior Executive Service*, the "cream of the crop" of the federal employees. These executives earn high salaries and may be moved from one agency to another as leadership needs change.

Once hired, and after a probationary period, civil servants are protected—overprotected, claim critics—by the Civil Service system. Ensuring a nonpartisan civil service requires that workers have protection from dismissals that are really politically motivated. But protecting all workers against political firings may also protect the few from dismissal for good cause. Firing incompetents is hard work. In one recent year, the government managed to fire only 236 employees for incompetence, a fraction of a percent of the 2.9 million federal workers. According to Civil Service regulations, the right of appeal must be exhausted before one's paycheck stops. Appeals can consume weeks, months, or even years. More than one agency has decided to tolerate incompetents, assigning them trivial or no duties, rather than invest its resources in the nearly hopeless task of discharging them. Firing female, minority, or older workers may be even more difficult than dislodging young or middle-aged white males. These minority groups not only have the usual Civil Service protections but also can resort to antidiscrimination statutes to appeal their firings. When one agency tried to fire a forty-eight year old messenger for abusive behavior, he sued, charging age discrimination. He lost, but the case dragged on more than three years. [4]

The rise of public service unions has also made it more difficult to remove federal employees. Not all federal employees are unionized, but almost all employees in the postal service and in some other agencies are. Federal employees are forbidden by law to strike. Government unionization became a prominent issue in 1981 when the Professional Air Traffic Controllers Organization (PATCO), the men and women who monitor and direct take-offs and landings at airports, went on strike for higher pay and better working conditions. The strike was in violation of federal law and an oath they had signed. President Reagan and his secretary of transportation, Drew Lewis, responded after only two days by firing the

[4] *Chicago Tribune*, May 28, 1978, p. 6.

controllers who refused to report to work. New controllers were hired, and federal unionization suffered a severe blow.

President Carter tried to make it easier to fire nonperformers. In 1978, he pushed through Congress legislation that reformed the firing system. Procedures for firing unproductive civil servants are still elaborate, however. After receiving a notice of termination, an employee has thirty days to appeal to a Merit Systems Protection Board; the agency must present evidence of his or her incompetence to the board. If the board orders the discharge, the employee can still appeal to federal courts.

The courts have been very protective of the right to keep a federal job. In 1974, in *Arnett* v. *Kennedy*, the Supreme Court held that federal employees could not be fired without "due process of law," a provision of the Fifth Amendment applying to property. In layman's terms, the Supreme Court in effect held that federal jobs are private property, in the same way that your furniture or house is private property. Workers willing to take the federal government to court have a very good chance of keeping their jobs.[5]

The Other Route to Federal Jobs: Recruiting from the Plum Book. As an incoming administration celebrates its victory and prepares to take control of the government, Congress publishes the **plum book.** It lists top federal jobs (that is, "plums") available for direct presidential appointment, often with Senate confirmation. Hugh Heclo has estimated that there are about 300 of these top policymaking posts, mostly cabinet secretaries, undersecretaries, assistant secretaries, bureau chiefs, and a couple of thousand lesser ones.[6] Every incoming president launches a nationwide talent search to fill them. His aides write scholars, influential members of Congress, state officials, interest group leaders, and others seeking advice on who to appoint to key posts. He seeks individuals who combine executive talent, political skills, and sympathy for his positions. He often tries to include men and women, blacks and whites, people from different regions, and people representing different interests within his party (although few recent presidents have appointed so high a percentage of middle-aged white males as did Ronald Reagan). A few of these top-flight appointees will be civil servants, temporarily elevated to a "supergrade" status on the General Schedule. Most, though, are political appointees, "in-and-outers" who stay for a while and then leave.

Once in office, these administrative policymakers constitute what Heclo has called a "government of strangers." Their most important trait is their transience. The average assistant secretary or undersecretary lasts about twenty-two months.[7] Few top officials stay long enough to know their own subordinates well, much less people in other agencies. Administrative routines, budget cycles, and legal complexities are often new to them. To these new political executives, the possibilities of power may seem endless. They soon learn, however, that senior civil servants

[5] Robert M. Kaus, "How the Supreme Court Sabotaged Civil Service Reform," *Washington Monthly* 10 (December 1978): 38–44.

[6] Hugh M. Heclo, *A Government of Strangers: Executive Politics in Washington* (Washington, D.C.: The Brookings Institution, 1977), p. 94.

[7] Ibid., p. 103.

know more, have been there longer, and will outlast them. One newly appointed political executive told of his experience:

> I spent the first days up with [the secretary], and it was marvelous all the plans we were making—the executive suites, limousines, and all that. Then I went down to the catacombs and there were all these gray men, you know—GS 15s, 16s, and I understood what they were saying to me. "Here we are. You may try to run us around. You may even run over us and pick a few of our boys off, but we'll stay and you won't. Now what's in it for us, sonny boy?" [8]

The security of the civil servants' jobs, the transience and even ignorance of their superiors, all contribute to the bureaucracy's resistance to change. Plum-book appointees may have the outward signs of power, but most find it very difficult to exercise real control over what their subordinates do.

What They Do: Some Theories of Bureaucracy

Bureaucracies govern modern states. They enshrine the technology of administration. But governmental bureaucracies are not our only bureaucracies. (Perhaps the oldest is the hierarchical governance of the Roman Catholic Church.) Bureaucracies run our armies, our corporations, our schools, and almost every other social, political, and economic institution. Following are three theories of bureaucracy which you should think about.

The Weberian Model. Most of us have confronted a bureaucracy only to be told: "Perhaps Mrs. Smith could help you; your problem is really under her jurisdiction" or "you'll have to talk to the supervisor, because I am only enforcing our rules."

The classic conception of bureaucracy was advanced by the German sociologist Max Weber. He stressed that the bureaucracy was a "rational" way for a modern society to conduct its business. [9] To Weber, a **bureaucracy** depends upon certain elements: It has a *hierarchical authority structure*, in which power flows from the top down and responsibility from the bottom up; it uses *task specialization* so that experts instead of amateurs are performing technical jobs; it develops extensive *rules*, which may seem nit-picking at times but which allow similar cases to be handled similarly instead of capriciously. Bureaucracies work on the *merit principle*, in which entrance and promotion are on the basis of demonstrated abilities rather than on "who you know." Bureaucracies behave with *impersonality* so that all of their clients are treated impartially. Weber's classic prototype of the bureaucratic organization depicts the bureaucracy as a well-organized machine with plenty of working, but hierarchical, parts.

Another View: The Acquisitive, Monopolistic Bureaucracy. The agency head sits before the congressional committee. The subject is her

[8] Ibid., pp. 194–95.
[9] H. H. Gerth and C. Wright Mills, *From Max Weber: Essays in Sociology* (New York: Oxford University Press, 1958), Chap. 8.

budget for next year. Rarely will she, or any other agency head (unless under overwhelming pressure from the White House), testify that the agency needs a *lower* budget next year.

The neat, Weberian model is only one way of thinking about bureaucracy. Other, more contemporary writers have seen bureaucracies as essentially "acquisitive," busily maximizing their budgets and expanding their powers. Conservative economist William Niskanen, now a member of President Reagan's Council of Economic Advisors, believes that bureaucracies are like private corporations in seeking goals,[10] except that private corporations seek to maximize their *profits* while governmental bureaucracies seek to maximize their *budgets*. Bureaucratic administrators are committed to the "products" they "sell" —national security, schooling, public health, higher education, police protection—and their piece of the government's total budget pie is a good measure of how highly their product is valued. Moreover, all administrators take more professional pride in running a large, well-staffed agency than a puny one. For these reasons, insists Niskanen, bureaucracies are themselves largely responsible for the growth of modern governments.[11] Bureaucracies may even couple with Congress in an unholy alliance to expand big government. (See the discussion of Fiorina's theory in Chapter 12, pages 371–372).

Not only can bureaucracies be acquisitive, they can also be monopolistic. In the private sector, a monopoly, being the sole supplier of some key good, is free from competition. It can afford to exact high prices and behave inefficiently. Public bureaucracies are typically monopolies, too. As a general rule (unless you're well off) there is no alternative to the local school system, the fire department, or the water supply system; certainly, there is no alternative to the national defense system. Only well-to-do people really have an alternative to the social security system or government-run medicare for the elderly. Some of our complaints about bureaucracies really are complaints about bureaucratic monopoly. No matter how the bureaucracies behave, they won't lose their clients. There's no competitive pressure to force them to improve service. Many conservative, and even liberal, critics of bureaucracy have favored *privatizing* some bureaucratic services to cut back on their monolithic and monopolistic power.[12] For example, local garbage collection or fire protection could be contracted out to private companies. Governments might thus accept the best service at the lowest price.

One More Perspective: Garbage Cans and Bureaucracies. One Washington official, trying to peddle some policy changes in the hyper-

---

[10] William Niskanen, *Bureaucracy and Representative Government* (Chicago: Aldine-Atherton, 1971).

[11] For some critiques of the Niskanen perspective, see Miller and Moe, "Bureaucrats, Legislators, and the Size of Government"; David Lowery and William D. Berry, "The Growth of Government in the United States: An Empirical Assessment of Competing Explanations," *American Journal of Political Science* 27 (November 1983):665–95.

[12] See, e.g., E. S. Savas, *Privatizing the Public Sector* (Chatham, N.J.: Chatham House, 1982).

pluralistic climate of our nation's capital, told John Kingdon: [13]

> I can trace the path of ideas. But my personal theory is that people plant seeds every day. There are a lot of ideas around. . . . The real question is, which of these ideas will catch hold? When you plant a seed, you need rain, soil, and luck.

Both the Weberian model and the model of the acquisitive, monopolistic bureaucracy make bureaucracies sound calculating and purposive. Another view of bureaucracy, though, makes them sound ambling and groping, affected by chance and happenstance. Cohen, March, and Olsen suggest that the typical organization is a "loose collection of ideas, [rather than] a coherent structure." [14] Likely as not, they say, organizations operate by trial and error. Far from being tightly controlled, they are typically loosely run. For most organizations, technological certainty is low. It is rarely clear that one policy will work and another fail. Lots of ideas may be floating around any organization. Faced with a particular problem, members of the organization may pull one of them from the "garbage can" of ideas and latch onto it. Organizations are not necessarily trying to find solutions to problems; just as often, solutions are in search of problems. The police department gets a new computer and then discovers how many tasks it has that need computerizing. Kingdon's careful study of governmental agenda building found much to recommend the "garbage can" model of policymaking. [15]

Each of these bureaucratic perspectives offers a different view of our administrative state. None of them is completely right. Consider each of them as you examine the organization and functions of bureaucracies in the modern state.

HOW THE BUREAUCRACIES ARE ORGANIZED

A complete organization chart of the American federal government would be big enough to occupy a large wall. You could pore over this chart, trace the lines of responsibility and authority, and see how government is organized—at least on paper. You can see a very simplified organizational chart at 2. A much easier way to look at how the federal executive branch is organized is to group agencies into four basic types: the cabinet departments, the regulatory agencies, the independent agencies, and the government corporations.

The Cabinet Departments

Each of the thirteen cabinet departments is headed by a secretary (with the exception of the Department of Justice, headed by the Attorney

[13] John Kingdon, *Agendas, Alternatives and Public Policies* (Boston: Little, Brown, 1984), p. 81.

[14] Michael Cohen, James March, and Johan Olsen, "A Garbage Can Model of Organizational Choice," *Administrative Science Quarterly* 17(March 1972):1.

[15] Kingdon, *Agendas, Alternatives and Public Policies*, pp. 88–94.

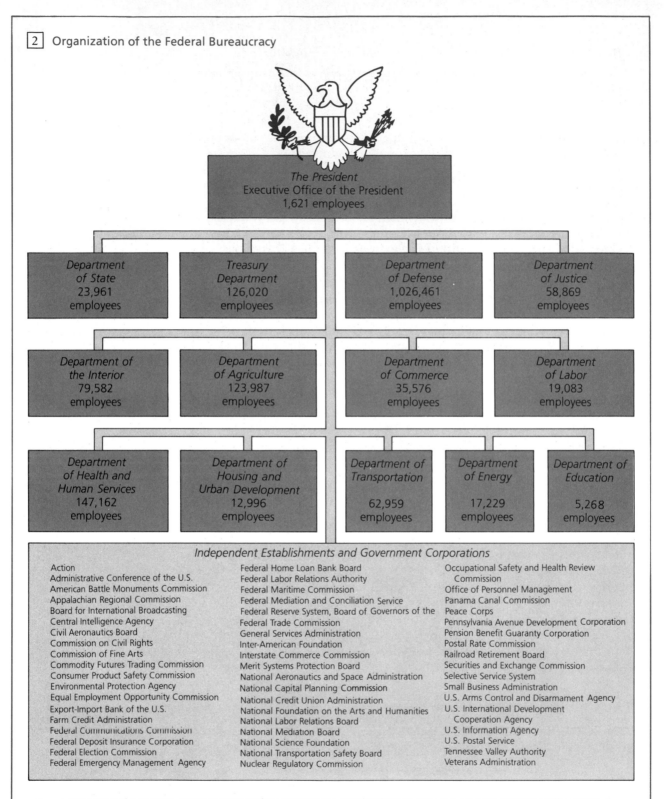

The President
Executive Office of the President
1,621 employees

| *Department of State* 23,961 employees | *Treasury Department* 126,020 employees | *Department of Defense* 1,026,461 employees | *Department of Justice* 58,869 employees |

| *Department of the Interior* 79,582 employees | *Department of Agriculture* 123,987 employees | *Department of Commerce* 35,576 employees | *Department of Labor* 19,083 employees |

| *Department of Health and Human Services* 147,162 employees | *Department of Housing and Urban Development* 12,996 employees | *Department of Transportation* 62,959 employees | *Department of Energy* 17,229 employees | *Department of Education* 5,268 employees |

Independent Establishments and Government Corporations

Action
Administrative Conference of the U.S.
American Battle Monuments Commission
Appalachian Regional Commission
Board for International Broadcasting
Central Intelligence Agency
Civil Aeronautics Board
Commission on Civil Rights
Commission of Fine Arts
Commodity Futures Trading Commission
Consumer Product Safety Commission
Environmental Protection Agency
Equal Employment Opportunity Commission
Export-Import Bank of the U.S.
Farm Credit Administration
Federal Communications Commission
Federal Deposit Insurance Corporation
Federal Election Commission
Federal Emergency Management Agency

Federal Home Loan Bank Board
Federal Labor Relations Authority
Federal Maritime Commission
Federal Mediation and Conciliation Service
Federal Reserve System, Board of Governors of the
Federal Trade Commission
General Services Administration
Inter-American Foundation
Interstate Commerce Commission
Merit Systems Protection Board
National Aeronautics and Space Administration
National Capital Planning Commission
National Credit Union Administration
National Foundation on the Arts and Humanities
National Labor Relations Board
National Mediation Board
National Science Foundation
National Transportation Safety Board
Nuclear Regulatory Commission

Occupational Safety and Health Review Commission
Office of Personnel Management
Panama Canal Commission
Peace Corps
Pennsylvania Avenue Development Corporation
Pension Benefit Guaranty Corporation
Postal Rate Commission
Railroad Retirement Board
Securities and Exchange Commission
Selective Service System
Small Business Administration
U.S. Arms Control and Disarmament Agency
U.S. International Development Cooperation Agency
U.S. Information Agency
U.S. Postal Service
Tennessee Valley Authority
Veterans Administration

Source: Department of Commerce, *Statistical Abstract of the United States, 1985* (Washington, D.C.: U.S. Government Printing Office, 1984), pp. 300, 325.

General) chosen by the president and approved by the Senate. Beneath the secretary are a slew of undersecretaries, deputy undersecretaries, and assistant secretaries. Each department manages some specific policy areas (see the list on page 422). Each has its own budget and its own staff.

Until the 1970s, the largest of the cabinet departments was the Department of Defense. Today the Department of Health and Human Services is the biggest federal department in dollars spent (although the Department of Defense still has more employees). Spending a third of the federal budget, HHS runs such massive programs as social security, medicare, medicaid, welfare, and health. In Washington, it is known as the most unwieldy government agency.

The Regulatory Agencies

Each **independent regulatory agency** has responsibility for some sector of the economy, making rules supposedly to protect the public interest. So far-reaching are their powers that they are sometimes called "the fourth branch of government."[16] They are also sometimes called the alphabet soup of governments, because most such agencies are known in Washington by their initials. Here is a sampling of these independent regulatory agencies:

— *ICC* (the Interstate Commerce Commission), the oldest of the regulatory agencies, founded in 1887 to regulate railroads and, later, other interstate commerce, specifically trucking.
— *FRB* (the Federal Reserve Board), charged with governing banks and —even more important—regulating the supply of money.
— *NLRB* (the National Labor Relations Board), created to regulate labor-management relations.
— *FCC* (the Federal Communications Commission), charged with licensing radio and TV stations and regulating their programming in the public interest, and with regulating interstate long-distance telephone rates.
— *FTC* (the Federal Trade Commission), intended to regulate business practices and control monopolistic behavior, now involved extensively in policing the accuracy of advertising.
— *SEC* (the Securities and Exchange Commission), created to police the stock market.

[16] On the independent regulatory agencies, the classic work in Marver Bernstein, *Regulating Business by Independent Commission* (Princeton, N.J.: Princeton University Press, 1955). See also on regulation, James Q. Wilson (ed.), *The Politics of Regulation* (New York: Basic Books, 1980); A. Lee Fritschler and Bernard H. Ross, *Business Regulation and Government Decision-Making* (Cambridge, Mass.: Winthrop, 1980); and the February, 1982 issue of the *Policy Studies Review.*

◄ *This very simplified organization chart of the United States government focuses on the cabinet departments and the independent agencies. You can see the relative sizes of the thirteen cabinet departments by looking at the number of employees in each (the figures are from 1984). In 1979, Congress reorganized the Department of Health, Education, and Welfare, moving its education functions to a new Department of Education, and changing HEW's name to Health and Human Services.*

Each of these independent regulatory agencies is governed by a small commission, usually with five to ten members appointed by the president and confirmed by the Senate, who serve fixed terms. Unlike cabinet officers or members of the president's staff, regulatory commission members cannot be fired by the president. So said the Supreme Court when President Franklin Roosevelt fired a man named Humphrey from the Federal Trade Commission. Poor Humphrey died shortly afterward, but his angry executors sued for back pay, getting the Court to hold that presidents could not fire members of regulatory agencies whenever they wanted (*Humphrey's Executor* v. *United States*, 1935).

To say that interest groups consider the rule-making by independent regulatory agencies—and, of course, their membership—important is a little like saying that engines are important to cars. The FCC can deny a multimillion-dollar TV station a license renewal, a power that certainly sparks the interest of the National Association of Broadcasters. The Federal Trade Commission regulates business practices, especially advertising, a power prompting both business and consumers to pay careful attention to its activities and membership.

So interested are the interest groups in the regulatory bodies that critics often point to the "capture" of the regulators by the regulatees.[17] It is not uncommon for members of commissions to be drawn from the ranks of the regulated. Sometimes, too, members of commissions or staffs of these agencies move on to jobs in the very industries they were regulating. Some lawyers among them can use contacts and information gleaned at the agency later, when they represent clients before their former employers at the agency.

The Government Corporations

The federal government also has a handful of **government corporations.** These are not exactly like private corporations in which you can buy stock and collect dividends. But they *are* like private corporations—and different from other parts of the government—in two ways. First, they provide a service that *could be* handled by the private sector. Second, they typically charge for their services, though often at cheaper rates than the consumer would pay a private-sector producer.

The granddaddy of the government corporations is the Tennessee Valley Authority (TVA), which provides inexpensive electricity to millions of Americans in Tennessee, Kentucky, Alabama, and neighboring states. Comsat is a modern-day government corporation that sells time-sharing on NASA satellites. Through Comsat you can rent time on a space satellite for radio communications. Even the post office, one of the original cabinet departments (first headed by Benjamin Franklin), has become a government corporation: the United States Postal Service. Once in a while, the government has taken over some "sick industry" and

---

[17] Bernstein, *Regulating Business*, p. 90. For a partial test of the capture theory, which finds it not altogether accurate, see John P. Plumlee and Kenneth J. Meier, "Capture and Rigidity in Regulatory Administration," in Judith May and Aaron Wildavsky (eds.), *The Policy Cycle* (Beverly Hills, Calif.: Sage, 1978). Another critique of the capture theory is Paul J. Quirk, *Industry Influence in Federal Regulatory Agencies* (Princeton, N.J.: Princeton University Press, 1981).

made it into a government corporation. Amtrak, the railroad passenger service, is one example. Riders may complain that "it's a hell of a way to run a railroad." Congress grumbles about Amtrak's multibillion-dollar subsidy (although some critics point out that billions of dollars in federal highway funds also constitute something of a subsidy for the auto industry). But members of Congress have only reluctantly agreed to let Amtrak shed its most unprofitable runs.

The Independent Executive Agencies

The **independent executive agencies** are essentially all the rest of the government—not cabinet departments, not regulatory commissions, and not government corporations. Their administrators are typically appointed by the president and serve at his pleasure. To list and describe these scores of bureaus would consume the rest of this chapter, but you can track them down by checking the current issue of the *United States Government Organization Manual*. A few of the biggest (in size of budget) are

— *General Services Administration* (GSA), the government's landlord, which handles buildings, supplies, and purchasing.
— *National Science Foundation* (NSF), which supports scientific research.
— *National Aeronautics and Space Administration* (NASA), the agency that brings us landings on the moon, Mars, and points beyond.
— *Veterans Administration* (VA), which pays billions in benefits to millions of veterans.

BUREAUCRACIES AS POLICYMAKERS

In modern governments, ours included, bureaucracies have three main functions:

— Bureaucrats are *implementors* of policy. They take congressional and presidential policy pronouncements and develop procedures and rules for implementing policy goals.
— Bureaucrats are *administrators* of policy. They manage the routines of government, from delivering mail to collecting taxes to policing the neighborhoods.
— Bureaucrats are *regulators*. This is the most controversial role of the bureaucracies. Yet Congress gives them broad mandates to regulate activities as diverse as interest rates, the location of nuclear power plants, and food additives.

Let us now focus on each of these bureaucratic functions.

Bureaucracies as Implementers

What Implementation Means. Public policies are sometimes self-executing; that is, they are carried out almost automatically. President Kennedy announced a military blockade of Cuba, and the navy was almost instantly on the move. Congress passed the revenue-sharing program and, shortly after developing a computer program, the Treasury Department was rushing checks to waiting state and local officials.

Most policies, though, are not self-executing. Congress typically announces the goals of a policy in broad terms, sets up an administrative apparatus, and leaves to the bureaucracy the task of working out the details of the program, of implementing it. Donald Van Meter and Carl Van Horn defined implementation like this: "Policy **implementation** encompasses those actions by public and private individuals (and groups) that are directed at the achievement of goals and objectives set forth in prior policy decisions."[18] Two different authors, writing in the same year, cribbed and paraphrased a famous line from German General Karl von Clausewitz about war, and applied it to the implementation process: "Implementation is the continuation of policymaking by other means."[19] At a minimum, implementation includes three elements:

1. Creation of a new agency or assignment of responsibility to an old one.
2. Translation of legislative goals into operational rules of thumb; development of guidelines for the program or policy.
3. Coordination of agency resources and personnel to achieve the intended goals.[20]

Why the Best-Laid Plans Sometimes Flunk the Implementation Test.
There is a famous line from the Scottish poet Robert Burns: "The best laid schemes o' mice and men/Gang aft a-gley [often go awry]." So, too, with the best-intended public policies. Policies that people expect to work often fail. Martha Derthick told the sad tale of a "new towns in-town" program in which the government was to sell surplus property to groups helping to expand urban housing. In fact, little property was sold and few houses were built.[21] High expectations followed by dashed hopes is the all-too-common fate of well-intended public policies.

Implementation can break down and produce nothing when something was promised for several reasons. One is faulty program design. "It is impossible," said Eugene Bardach, "to implement well a policy or program that is defective in its basic theoretical conception." Consider, he suggested, the following hypothetical example:

> If Congress were to establish an agency charged with squaring the circle with compass and straight edge—a task mathematicians have long ago shown is impossible—we could envision an agency coming into being, hiring a vast number of consultants, commissioning studies, reporting that progress was being made, while at the same time urging in their appropriations request for the coming year that the Congress augment the agency's budget.[22]

[18] Donald S. Van Meter and Carl E. Van Horn, "The Policy Implementation Process," *Administration and Society* 6 (February 1975): 447.

[19] Eugene Bardach, *The Implementation Game* (Cambridge, Mass.: The MIT Press, 1977), p. 85; Robert L. Lineberry, *American Public Policy: What Government Does and What Difference It Makes* (New York: Harper & Row, 1977), p. 71. Clausewitz called war "the continuation of politics by other means."

[20] Lineberry, *American Public Policy*, pp. 70–71.

[21] Martha Derthick, *New Towns In-Town* (Washington, D.C.: The Urban Institute Press, 1972).

[22] Bardach, *The Implementation Game*, pp. 250–51.

One Washington bureaucrat, tired of hearing complaints about the federal bureaucracy, put the blame for bureaucratic failure on the poor design of programs by Congress: "Consider, if you will, the mass of poorly designed, ill-focused legislation the bureaucrat has to administer. Think of the Internal Revenue code, the Guaranteed Student Loan Program, Medicare and Medicaid, and so on. No band of angels, much less mere human beings, could cope with the complexities or the schizophrenic nature of these programs."[23] If faulty policymaking is the problem, the blame lies with policymakers in Congress, not with the bureaucracies.

A second enemy of program implementation is hyperpluralism. If every group affected by a policy has the power to veto or delay it, policies will not get implemented—as the fate of the Oakland jobs program illustrated (page 62).

[23] Edward P. Snyder, "Letter to the Editor," *New York Times*, June 13, 1978, p. 34. Copyright © 1978 by the New York Times Company. Reprinted by permission.

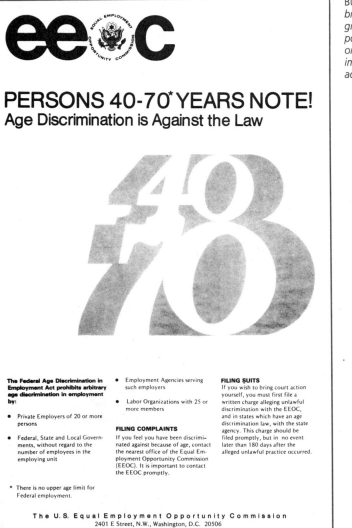

Bureaucrats Implement. *They take broad policy goals established by Congress and turn them into operating policies. Equal opportunity policies are one example. Bureaucrats have to implement policies before they can administer and regulate.*

Implementing the Voting Rights Act of 1965. *Policy implementation does not always work. But even when the goals are controversial, implementation can be effective if goals are clear and means to achieve the goals are unambiguous. The Voting Rights Act of 1965 had a simple goal: register black Americans to vote in southern counties where few blacks had ever been permitted to vote. This federal registrar in Lowndes County, Alabama, like hundreds of other registrars, worked for the Department of Justice. With support from the Department, and the U.S. marshalls if necessary, they registered black voters throughout southern states and counties.*

Some case studies can give you a better idea of the implementation process in action.

Case 1: Successfully Implementing the Voting Rights Act of 1965. In 1965, Congress, reacting to generations of discrimination against prospective black voters in the South, passed the Voting Rights Act. It singled out six states in the Deep South where the number of black registrants was minuscule. Congress ordered the Justice Department to send federal registrars to each county in those states to register qualified voters. Congress outlawed literacy tests and other tests previously used to discriminate against black registrants. Stiff penalties were provided for those who interfered with the work of federal registrars.

Congress charged the Attorney General with implementing the Voting Rights Act. He acted quickly, dispatching hundreds of registrars, some protected by United States marshals, to southern counties. Within seven and a half months after passage of the act, more than 300,000 new black voters were on the rolls. The proportion of the southern black population registered to vote increased from 43 percent in 1964 to 66 percent in 1970, partly (though certainly not entirely) because of the Voting Rights Act. [24]

The Voting Rights Act was, by any reasonable standard, a successful case of implementation, but not because it was popular with everyone. Southern representatives and senators were outraged by it and a filibuster delayed its passage in the Senate. It was successful because its goal was clear (register large numbers of black voters), its implementation was straightforward (send out people to register them), and the authority of the implementers was plain (they had the support of the Attorney General and even United States marshals).

Case 2: Implementing Equal Opportunity in College Athletics. Congress is fond of stating a broad policy goal in legislation and then leaving implementation up to the bureaucracies. Then, messy details need not bother busy members of Congress; moreover, blame for the implementation decisions can be placed elsewhere.

One such policy was the controversial "Title IX" of the Education Amendments of 1972, [25] which said: "No person in the United States shall, on the basis of sex, be excluded from participation in, be denied the benefits of, or be subjected to discrimination under any education program or activity receiving federal financial assistance." Because almost every college and university receives some federal financial assistance, almost all were thus forbidden to discriminate by sex. Interest groups supporting women's athletics had convinced Congress to include a provision about college athletics as well. So Section 844 read: "The Secretary [of HEW then, today of Education] shall prepare and publish . . . pro-

---

[24] On the implementation and impact of the Voting Rights Act, see Charles S. Bullock, III and Harrell R. Rodgers, Jr., *Law and Social Change: Civil Rights Laws and Their Consequences* (New York: McGraw-Hill, 1972), Chap. 2; Richard Scher and James Button, "Voting Rights Act: Implementation and Impact," in C. S. Bullock and C. M. Lamb (eds.), *Implementation of Civil Rights Policy* (Monterey, Calif.: Brooks/Cole, 1984), Chap. 2.

[25] The implementation of the athletics policy is well documented in two articles by Cheryl M. Fields in the *Chronicle of Higher Education*, December 11 and 18, 1978, on which this account relies.

posed regulations implementing the provisions of Title IX . . . relating to prohibition of sex discrimination in Federally assisted education programs *which shall include with respect to intercollegiate athletic activities reasonable provisions considering the nature of the particular sports."*

Now what exactly was that supposed to mean? Supporters of women's athletics thought it meant that discrimination against women's sports was also prohibited. Some looked forward to seeing women's sports on an equal footing with football. They had reason to think so. One member of the House-Senate Conference Committee had proposed language specifically exempting "revenue-producing athletics" (read "football and basketball") from the prohibition. The Conference Committee rejected this suggestion, but to colleges and universities with big-time athletic programs, and to some alumni, the vague Section 844 called for equality in golf and swimming—not men's football and basketball programs, which could continue to have the lion's share of athletic budgets.

Joseph Califano, President Carter's secretary of HEW, was the man in the middle on this tricky problem. His staff developed a "policy interpretation" of the legislation, which he announced in December 1978. HEW's interpretation of the hundred or so words of Section 844 of Title IX took thirty pages. It recognized that football was "unique" among college sports. If football was unique, the interpretation implied (but did not directly say) male-dominated football programs could continue to outspend women's athletic programs.

Supporters of equal budgets for male and female athletics were outraged. Charlotte West of the Association for Intercollegiate Athletics for Women called it "a multitude of imprecise and confusing explanations, exceptions, and caveats." Even the football-oriented National Collegiate Athletic Association was wary of the new rules. One of its lawyers allowed, "They are trying to be fair. The question is how successful they are." A one-hundred-word section in a congressional statute, which prompted a thirty-page interpretation by the bureaucracy, in turn prompted scores of court suits. The courts have had to rule on such matters as whether or not Title IX requires that exactly equivalent dollar amounts be spent on women's and men's athletics.

The complex case of implementing Title IX for intercollegiate athletics contains an important lesson: Policy problems that Congress cannot resolve are not likely to be resolved easily by bureaucracies.

Case 3: Implementing Policies on Biotechnology. External elements can often influence the implementation of a policy. One such case involves the bureaucracies' efforts to make policy for biotechnological research on genetic engineering.

In May 1984, Judge John Sirica (already famous as the judge who tried the participants in the Watergate escapade and contributed to the downfall of President Nixon) issued an injunction. It had been demanded by a Washington lawyer named Jeremy Rifkin, the nation's leading opponent of biotechnological research, especially genetic engineering experiments. What happened follows: A University of California scientist named Steven E. Lindow planned to spray genetically altered bacteria on some Oregon potato fields. The new bacteria would, Lindow hoped, reduce the possibility of frost damage. But Jeremy Rifkin is an opponent of any and all genetic engineering, believing it could be dangerous. Considering the splitting of genes as serious an affront to human life as the splitting of the atom, he uses the courts to prevent such experimentation.

Judge Sirica's injunction forbade the University of California experiment and directed the National Institutes of Health (NIH) to develop guidelines for such research. Consequently, NIH rushed to approve new rules for genetic experiments. Taking advantage of a loophole in Sirica's decision—which had barred the University of California and its employees from the potato experiment—NIH's Recombinant DNA Advisory Committee agreed to permit a private company (Advanced Genetic Sciences of Greenwich, Connecticut) to conduct the same experiment. Rifkin, of course, was furious at this backdoor maneuver. NIH unwittingly helped hasten a White House-level review of policies governing genetic research. In January 1985, representatives of seventeen federal agencies, which regulated genetic research, published their new policies in the *Federal Register*. Each agency would be directed to publish specifically its rules on how and whether people could experiment with nature's genetic makeup. [26]

What do these cases tell us about policy implementation? First, they suggest that it is a complex process, typically involving not only the bureaucracy but courts, interest groups, and other agencies. Second, it seems that bureaucracies can probably implement legislation only about as well as Congress can write it. When legislative intent is crisp—as in the Voting Rights Act—a bureaucracy can do a snappy job of implementing the legislation. But sometimes Congress does a poor job of providing policy design and guidance to the agencies. In the new area of biotechnology, for example, Congress is almost silent, leaving the agencies to wrestle directly with the interest groups and the courts. When legislative intent is murky—as in the case of college athletics—bureaucrats have a hard time implementing policy. Third, the cases point out that conflict over a policy does not necessarily mean it will be poorly implemented. The Voting Rights Act was a very controversial policy, but it was swiftly and deftly implemented. Clarity of Congress' intent may be more important than consensus in getting a policy implemented.

Bureaucracies as Administrators

Policy implementation includes all that goes on between the pronouncement of a policy and the time it becomes a matter of routine administration. The average American deals regularly with federal bureaucrats performing their administrative roles. Not even counting the one federal bureaucrat who daily drops by your doorstep (but never on Sunday), you meet dozens of others in person, by phone, or by mail.

---

[26] Information on the biotech implementation comes from David Remnick, "One Man's Crusade to Save Us from the 'Ultimate Disaster,'" *Washington Post National Weekly Edition*, June 4, 1984, p. 29; *Chronicle of Higher Education*, June 13, 1984; and Michael Schrage, "Biotechnology Passes a Test," *Washington Post National Weekly Edition*, January 14, 1985, p. 33.

Park rangers, IRS agents, passport clerks, agricultural agents, and FBI agents have scores of encounters with citizens every day. To understand their behavior as administrators, two concepts are useful: *routine* and *discretion*.

Administrative Routine. For most bureaucrats, most of the time, administration is a routine matter. By **administrative routine** we mean that repetitive tasks are performed and similar cases are handled in roughly similar ways. [27] Rules help make routine easier and more likely. Almost every bureaucrat works with one or more volumes of agency rules. The Internal Revenue Code is the bible of the IRS agent; the customs agent has binders filled with rules and regulations about what can be brought to the United States free of duty. Routine behavior is also encouraged by a similarity of cases and problems. Almost every request for a grant received by the National Science Foundation, whether to study high-speed particle physics or the sociology of racism, can be handled the same way. When problems recur, agencies develop rules and routines to deal with them.

Administrative Discretion. Paradoxically, bureaucrats operate not only within the confines of routines but often with considerable discretion to behave in this way or that. **Administrative discretion** is the authority of administrative actors to select among various responses to a given problem. Discretion is greatest when rules do not fit a case; but even in agencies with elaborate rules and regulations, especially when more than one rule fits, there is still room for discretion. The IRS code is massive—seventy-nine volumes—but the IRS wields vast discretion even if it tries to follow the code to the letter. The IRS agent must be "armed against the machinations, not of the average citizen, but of the cleverest adversary the best law schools can produce." [28] A couple of examples:

— Congress and the IRS code say that medical expenses above a certain percentage of income are deductible. But how about the expenses of a vasectomy? (The IRS said yes.)
— A girl ordered to take strenuous exercise under the supervision of a doctor was enrolled by her father in $8,436 worth of ballet lessons. Was it deductible? (The IRS said no.)
— Congress and the IRS code say that business expenses are deductible. But can an airline flight attendant deduct the cost of clothes? (The IRS said yes.)
— Are taxi expenses incurred in visiting your stockbroker a deductible expense? (The IRS said yes.)

Some administrators exercise more discretion than others. Michael Lipsky coined the term **street-level bureaucrats** to refer to those bureaucrats who are in constant contact with the public (often a hostile one) and have considerable discretion, including police officers, welfare

Bureaucrats Administer. *Two key notions—bureaucratic routine and bureaucratic discretion—characterize the administrative process. Customs officers handle the routine task of applying thousands of pages of rules to millions of passengers. But there is discretion in the job, too. Choosing who to search carefully and who to let by with a quick check requires judgment and the exercise of discretionary authority.*

[27] On routines of administration, see Ira Sharkansky, *The Routines of Politics* (New York: Van Nostrand Reinhold, 1970).
[28] Gerald Carson, *The Golden Egg* (Boston: Houghton Mifflin, 1977), p. 10. The examples given in this paragraph are from Carson.

Bureaucrats as Administrators.
*Although bureaucrats are regulators
and implementors, an overwhelming
proportion of bureaucratic endeavors
is devoted to administering the laws.
Although bureaucracies are often controversial, most of their administration
is actually quite straightforward. One
of the many tasks of federal civil
servants is to administer drug laws.
These agents of the federal government are charged with enforcing drug
laws. To be sure, this is not a completely noncontroversial activity. The
laws, and their interpretations,
though, are not made by these "street
level bureaucrats." They confront a
sometimes hostile public and are
charged with application of volumes
of rules.*

workers, and lower court judges.[29] No amount of rules, not even the seventy-nine volumes of the IRS code and the thousands of pages of IRS rules, will eliminate the need for bureaucratic discretion on some policies.

Bureaucracies as Regulators

Government **regulation** is the use of governmental authority to control or change some practice in the private sector. All sorts of things are subject to government regulation. Regulations by government pervade our everyday lives and the lives of businesses, universities, hospitals, and other institutions.

Regulation in the Economy and in Everyday Life. The notion that our economy is largely a "free enterprise" one, unfettered by government intervention, is about as up-to-date as a shiny new Model T Ford. Just as you could get a glimpse of the way our economy works by examining the way an automaker produces cars, you can see how sweeping the scope of governmental regulation is by thinking about how that car is regulated. Buying and selling stock in the automobile corporation is regulated by the Securities and Exchange Commission; relations between the workers and managers of the auto company come under the scrutiny of the National Labor Relations Board; because automakers are major government contractors, affirmative action in hiring workers is mandated and administered by the Department of Labor and the Equal Employment Opportunity Commission; pollution-control, energy-saving, and safety devices are required by the Environmental Protection Agency, the National Highway Traffic Safety Administration, and the Department of Transportation; unfair advertising and deceptive consumer practices in marketing the car come under the watchful eye of the Federal Trade Commission.

Everyday life itself is the subject of bureaucratic regulation. ③ Almost all bureaucratic agencies—not merely the ones called independent regulatory agencies—are in the regulatory business.

Regulation: How It Grew, How It Works. From the beginnings of the American Republic until 1887, the federal government made almost no regulatory policies. The little regulation produced was handled by state and local authorities. Even the minimum regulatory powers of state and local governments were then much disputed. In 1877, the United States Supreme Court upheld the right of government to regulate the business operations of a firm in a case called *Munn* v. *Illinois*. The case involved the right of the state of Illinois to regulate the charges and services of a Chicago warehouse. During this time, farmers were seething about alleged overcharging by railroads, grain elevator companies, and other business firms. In 1887—a decade after *Munn*—Congress created the first

---

[29] Michael Lipsky, "Toward a Theory of Street-Level Bureaucracy," in Willis D. Hawley et al., *Theoretical Perspectives in Urban Politics* (Englewood Cliffs, N.J.: Prentice-Hall, 1976), Chap. 8.

regulatory agency, the Interstate Commerce Commission (ICC). It was created to regulate the railroads, their prices, and their services to farmers; and it set the precedent for regulatory policymaking.

As regulators, bureaucratic agencies typically operate with a large grant of power from Congress, which may detail goals to be achieved but permits the agencies to sketch out the regulatory means. In 1935, for example, Congress created the National Labor Relations Board to control "unfair labor practices," but the NLRB had to play a major role in defining *fair* and *unfair*. Most agencies charged with regulation first have to develop a set of rules, often called *guidelines*. The appropriate agency may specify how much food coloring it will permit in a wiener, how many contaminants it will permit an industry to dump into a stream, how much radiation from a nuclear reactor is too much, and so forth.

---

3 A Full Day of Regulation

Factory worker John Glasswich (not his real name) works in the city of Chicago and lives with his wife and three young children in suburban Mount Prospect, Illinois. Both at work and at home, his day is filled with the impact of federal regulations. He is awakened at 5:30 A.M. by his clock radio, set to a country music station licensed to operate by the Federal Communications Commission. For breakfast he has cereal, whose content is passed upon by the Food and Drug Administration, as is the lunch his wife packs for him. The processed meat in his sandwich is packed under the careful supervision of the Food Safety and Quality Service of the U.S. Department of Agriculture.

John takes the train to work, buying a quick cup of coffee before the journey. The caffeine in his coffee, the FDA has warned, has caused birth defects in laboratory animals, and there is discussion in Washington about regulating it. Paying his fare (regulated by the government), he hops aboard and shortly arrives at work, a small firm making refrigeration equipment for the food industry.

At home, Mrs. Glasswich is preparing breakfast for the children. The price of the milk she serves is affected by the dairy price supports regulated by the Agricultural Stabilization and Conservation Service. As the children play, she takes note of the toys they use, wanting to avoid any that could be dangerous. A Washington agency, the Consumer Product Safety Commission, also takes note of children's toys, regulating their manufacture and sale. The lawn mower, the appliances, the microwave oven, and numerous other items around the Glasswich house are also regulated by the Consumer Product Safety Commission. Setting out for the grocery store and the bank, Mrs. Glasswich encounters even more government regulations. The car has seat belts mandated by the

National Highway Traffic Safety Administration and gets gas mileage certified by the Department of Transportation. It happens that its pollution-control devices are now in need of service, because they do not meet the requirements of the Environmental Protection Agency. The bank at which Mrs. Glasswich deposits money and writes a check is among the most heavily regulated institutions she encounters in her daily life. Her passbook savings rate is regulated by the Depository Institutions Deregulation Committee.

Meanwhile, John Glasswich is working assembling food-processing machinery. He and his fellow workers are members of the International Association of Machinists. Their negotiations with the firm are held under rules laid down by the National Labor Relations Board. One day not too long ago, the firm was visited by inspectors from the Occupational Safety and Health Administration, a federal agency charged with ensuring worker safety. OSHA inspectors noted several violations and forwarded a letter recommending safety changes to the head of the firm. Getting home, Glasswich has a beer before dinner. It was made in a brewery carefully supervised by the Bureau of Alcohol, Tobacco, and Firearms, and when it is sold, federal and state taxes are collected.

After dinner (almost all the food served has been transported by a heavily regulated trucking industry), the children are sent to bed. An hour or so of television, broadcast on regulated airwaves, is followed by lights-out for the Glasswiches. A switch will turn off the electric lights, whose rates are regulated by the Illinois Commerce Commission and the Federal Regulatory Commission.

Source: Based on a more elaborate account by James Worsham, "A Typical Day Is Full of Rules," *Chicago Tribune,* July 12, 1981, pp. 1 ff.

Bureaucrats Regulate. *Regulation is often controversial. But much bureaucratic regulation is non-controversial and, by almost everyone's standards, in the public interest. The U.S. Department of Agriculture is charged with regulating the quality of meat products, a task it was given after novelist Upton Sinclair wrote about the unsanitary state of meat-packing at the turn of the century.*

Guidelines are developed in consultation with, and sometimes with the agreement of, the objects of regulation.

Next, the agency must apply and enforce its rules and guidelines, either in court or through its own administrative procedures. Sometimes it waits for complaints to come to it, as the Equal Employment Opportunity Commission does. Sometimes it sends inspectors into the field, as the Occupational Safety and Health Administration does. Sometimes it requires applicants for a permit or license to demonstrate performance consistent with congressional goals and agency rules, as the Federal Communications Commission does. Often government agencies take violators to court, hoping to secure a judgment and fine against an offender. Whatever strategy Congress permits a regulating agency to use, all regulation contains these elements: (1) a *grant of power and set of directions* from Congress, (2) a *set of rules and guidelines* by the regulatory agency itself, and (3) some *means of enforcing compliance* with congressional goals and agency regulations.

Government regulation of our economy and our lives, of course, has grown in recent decades. The budgets of regulatory agencies, their level of employment, and the number of rules they issue are all increasing—even during the Reagan administration. As the "full day of regulation" ③ showed, there are few niches of our lives in which regulation is not a reality. Not surprisingly, this has led to charges that government is overdoing it.

Is There Too Much Regulation? Almost every regulatory policy was created to achieve some desirable social goal. Who would disagree with the goal of a safer workplace, when more than 10,000 people are killed annually in industrial accidents? Who would dissent from greater highway safety when more than 50,000 die each year in automobile accidents? Who would disagree with policies to promote equality in hiring, when the history of opportunities for women and minorities is one of discrimination? Who would disagree with policies to reduce industrial pollution, when pollution threatens health and lives?

To be sure, regulations are rarely popular with the regulated. Automobile manufacturers do not appreciate regulations to install expensive pollution-control equipment; business managers would feel little regret if the Occupational Safety and Health Administration disappeared tomorrow. Aside from the expected opposition from the objects of regulation, though, it is still possible to pose the question, How much regulation is enough?

Critics are fond of stressing that we rarely evaluate the costs of regulation in relation to its benefits. Suppose, for example, that some particular condition of working in the chemical industry is associated with four deaths and several hundred injuries annually. If hundreds of millions of dollars must be spent to improve or eliminate such a condition, the cost per life saved may be prohibitively high. John Morrall has drawn attention to the peculiar differences in the valuation of human life imposed by different regulatory agencies.[30] The Occupational Health and Safety

[30] John Morall, III, "OSHA and U.S. Industry," in Robert F. Lanzilotti (ed.), *Economic Effects of Government-Mandated Costs* (Gainesville: University of Florida Press, 1979), Chap. 5.

Administration insisted that the steel industry improve the safety of its coke ovens, estimated to be responsible for twenty-seven deaths annually among steelworkers. But the cost of saving lives by making the improvements (perhaps $1.3 billion) is high indeed, ranging from $9 to $48 million per life saved. In another agency, the National Highway Traffic Safety Administration, proposed regulations requiring air bags in cars could have a cost-to-life-saved ratio of less than $120,000.

Critics also point out that regulation is often confusing, contradictory, and inefficient. Sometimes regulation itself seems hazardous to your health. One case involved children's sleepwear. In 1972, the Consumer Product Safety Commission required that children's sleepwear be treated with a flame-retardant chemical. A chemical called Tris was used, and prices jumped 20 percent. Five years later, though, the same Consumer Product Safety Commission banned Tris as a cancer-causer. As Margorie Boyd remarked, "Parents were understandably shocked to learn that they had been paying a higher price in order to expose their children to a cancer-causing agent." [31]

Few government regulations have been as controversial as those in the area of worker safety and health. The Occupational Safety and Health Administration (OSHA) has become the favorite whipping boy of regulatory critics. But government has been in the business of regulating worker safety for a long time. The evidence on the success of such efforts is mixed, as you will see at 4 .

[31] Margorie Boyd, "The Protection Consumers Don't Want," *Washington Monthly* 9 (September 1977): 32.

Regulating the Environment. Environmental regulations have increased in number in the past decade. Automobile exhausts, toxic waste dumps, and the dumping of wastes into lakes and rivers have all been regulated by the federal government. Some contend that the regulations are too extreme and stifle economic growth and the creation of jobs. President Reagan has taken just that position. Others believe that environmental legislation and regulation are essential to protect the nation's air, land, and water.

ANTI-POLLUTION TEST VEHICLE
operating on natural gas

Is There a Better Way? Charles L. Schultze, chairman of President Carter's Council of Economic Advisors, was—like Murray L. Weidenbaum, who once had the same position under President Reagan—a critic of the current state of federal regulation. Schultze reviewed the regulatory activities of the Environmental Protection Agency and the Occupational Safety and Health Administration. Neither, he concluded, has worked very well.[32] The existing system he described as a **command-and-control policy:** The government tells business how to reach certain goals, checks that these commands are followed, and punishes offenders. Schultze prefers an **incentive system.** Instead of telling businesses how their ladders must be constructed, measuring the ladders, and charging a small fine for violators, Schultze has argued that it would be more efficient and effective to levy a high tax on firms with excessive worker injuries. Instead of trying to develop standards for 62,000 pollution sources, as EPA now does, it would be easier and more effective to levy a

[32] Charles L. Schultze, *The Public Use of the Private Interest* (Washington, D.C.: The Brookings Institution, 1977).

| 4 | Regulating Worker Health and Safety: Two Views |

It was Republican President Richard Nixon who first put the issue of worker safety on the national agenda. Unions had long sought a bill to protect workers, and Nixon's Vietnam policies had received solid support from "hard hats." So, in 1969, President Nixon proposed to Congress a bill to involve the federal government in regulating conditions in the workplace. Over the last several years, the president argued, there had been more injuries from industrial hazards and more deaths from industrial accidents than from the Vietnam War. (This was true, although the number of job-related deaths and injuries had peaked in 1937 and declined steadily since then.)

In December 1970, the Occupational Safety and Health Administration was created by Congress to "assure" for "every working man and woman … safe and healthful working conditions." It was a noble goal. More than 10,000 workers are killed annually in industrial accidents. OSHA went to work implementing its authority and writing regulations to ensure a safe working environment.

The small business owners, looking for ways to comply with OSHA, might write for a copy of its requirements. OSHA would send a copy of its forty-one page book, *OSHA Handbook for Small Businesses,* but it only scratches the surface. OSHA regulations are found in the Code of Federal Regulations, Title 29, Part 1910. There are 455 pages of small print, legalese, and equations. If our small business owner was concerned about the safety of the ladder he had around the shop, here is what he would find:

A ladder is an appliance usually consisting of two side rails joined at regular intervals by crosspieces called steps, rungs, or cleats, on which a person may step in ascending or descending.

He can then read several length columns of fine print detailing the design of extension ladders, sectional ladders, trestle ladders, and several others, and also defining the term *wood.* If he wants to find out whether his ladders are strong enough to hold his employees, he is given the following equation:

The angle (*a*) between the loaded and unloaded rails and the horizontals is to be calculated from the trigonometric equation:

$$\text{Sine } a = \frac{\text{Difference in deflection}}{\text{Ladder width}}$$

There were plenty of other requirements for a safe workplace (such as the shape of toilet seats), all detailed carefully in the Code of Federal Regulations. Our small businesses may protest loudly this taxing of their brains and their pocketbooks, but they need not fear the powers of OSHA. It has only 800 inspectors to handle 5 million businesses, and chances are they will get to you but once every sixty-six years. OSHA violations only cost an average of a $25 fine, and only two companies were convicted of criminal violations during OSHA's first three years.

The Carter administration pruned some of the OSHA regulations, and OSHA was high on the list of agencies that President Ronald Reagan wanted to pare. He

high tax on those who cause pollution. We could even provide incentives as rewards for such socially valuable behavior as developing technology to reduce pollution. Incentives, Schultze has argued, use marketlike strategies to manage the market. They are, he claims, more effective and efficient than command-and-control regulation.

Not everyone is as keen on the use of incentives as Schultze. Defenders of the command-and-control system of regulation might compare our present system to preventive medicine; it is designed to minimize pollution or workplace accidents before they become too severe. They might argue, too, that penalties for excessive pollution or excessive workplace accidents take place only after substantial damage has been done. And, they might go on, if taxes on pollution or unsafe work environments are merely externalized (that is, passed along to the consumer as higher prices), they are not much of a deterrent.

Toward Deregulation. These days, *deregulation* is a fashionable term in Washington. The idea behind deregulation is that the number and com-

---

4   Regulating Worker Health and Safety: Two Views (continued)

appointed a Florida construction executive, Thorne G. Auchter, to head the agency. Auchter promised to cut back on "excessive, unnecessary, and unfounded regulation."

Regulation of the workplace to ensure worker safety did not begin in general until the passage of the OSHA legislation in 1970. There is one American industry, however, where occupational safety has long been on the legislative agenda—coal mining, one of the nation's most demanding and dangerous occupations. Since 1900, more than 100,000 coal miners have met death on the job. Thousands more have died an agonizing death from black lung disease, caused by prolonged exposure to coal dust.

Crises, as we argued in Chapter 11 (pages 348–349), are one way a policy proposal can get on the political agenda. Mine disasters have put mine safety on the congressional agenda. The first coal mine safety legislation was passed in 1941, following the deaths of ninety-one miners at Bartley, West Virginia, and of seventy-three miners at Neffs, Ohio, in the preceding year. Historian Edward Wieck remarked somewhat grimly that "Dead miners have always been the most powerful influence in securing passage of mining legislation." Later mine disasters led to stronger legislation in 1952 and 1969.

Most of these regulations required companies to spend money to adopt safer conditions. Companies usually opposed these regulations. In debate on the 1969 legislation, a lobbyist for the Bituminous Coal Association insisted that "I don't think you can legislate safety."

The real question is whether a generation of public policy changes made an important impact on worker safety. Michael Lewis-Beck and John Alford employed data on injuries and deaths since 1932 to determine whether safety improvements could be linked to federal regulation. Fatalities over the period were reduced significantly, and the legislation was directly responsible for much of this improvement. As they concluded: "A 1976 coal miner was over four times less likely to be killed while working than a 1932 coal miner, a fact attributable in no small way to federal safety legislation."

Should the successful regulation of coal mining be generalized to all other industries? It does seem to show that careful, vigorously enforced federal legislation can improve occupational safety. But coal mining is an unusual, high-risk occupation. There are only a small number of mines, making inspection and enforcement easier. Certainly the example suggests that regulation *can* produce effective results. It does not, however, demonstrate that regulation *always* produces those results.

Source: For more information on OSHA, see the sources from which this discussion is derived: Murray L. Weidenbaum, *Business, Government, and the Public* (Englewood Cliffs, N.J.: Prentice-Hall, 1977), pp. 62–65; and Michael Levin, "Politics and Polarity: The Limits of OSHA Reform," *Regulation* (November–December 1979): 33–39. On the coal mining regulation and its success, see Michael S. Lewis-Beck and John R. Alford, "Can Government Regulate Safety? The Coal Mine Example," *American Political Science Review* 74 (1980): 745–56. The quotation from Wieck is cited by Lewis-Beck and Alford at p. 746.

plexity of regulatory policies has made regulation too much of a good thing. To critics, the problem with regulation is that regulation raises prices, distorts market forces and—worst of all—does not work. Specifically, here are some of the accusations against the regulatory system:

— It raises prices. If the producer is faced with expensive regulations, their cost inevitably will be borne by the consumer in the form of higher prices.
— It hurts our competitive position abroad. Other nations may have fewer regulations on pollution, worker safety, and other business practices than we do. Thus, American products may simply cost more in the international marketplace, hurting our sales in other countries.
— It does not always work well. Tales of woe abound about regulation. Regulatory policies may be difficult or cumbersome to enforce. Critics charge that regulations sometimes just do not achieve the results that Congress intended—and that they simply create massive regulatory bureaucracies.

Not surprisingly, President Reagan's conservative political philosophy is not suited to much government regulation. But even before the Reagan administration, sentiment toward deregulation was building in the Washington community. Even liberals sometimes joined the chorus of anti-regulation. Among them was Senator Edward Kennedy of Massachusetts, who pushed for airline deregulation. Indeed, deregulation was pressed by the airline industry, too. In 1978, the Civil Aeronautics Board (the CAB) began to deregulate airline prices and airline routes. Today, competitive airline fares, including inexpensive "no-frills" flights, are the result of Congress's and the bureaucracy's decisions to dismantle the regulation of airlines. In 1984, the Civil Aeronautics Board formally disbanded itself, even bringing in a military bugler to play taps at its last meeting. Not everyone, though, believes that deregulation is in the nation's best interest. [5]

UNDERSTANDING BUREAUCRACIES

Bureaucracy and Democracy

Bureaucracies constitute one of our two unelected policymaking institutions (courts being the other). In democratic theory, popular control of government depends on elections. We could not possibly elect the 2.9 million federal civil servants, or even the few thousand top men and women, though they spend almost a trillion dollars of our GNP. Nevertheless, the fact that we do not elect civil servants does not mean that bureaucracies cannot respond to and represent the public's interests. Much depends on whether bureaucracies are effectively controlled by people we do elect—the president and Congress.

Presidents Try to Control the Bureaucracy. In Chapter 13, we took a look at some of the frustrations presidents endure in trying to control the government they are elected to run. Presidents try hard—not always with success—to impose their policy preferences on the agencies. Here are some of their methods:

— *Appoint the right people to head the agency.* Normally, presidents control the appointments of agency heads and subheads. Putting his people in charge is one good way for a president to influence agency policy; yet even this has its problems. President Reagan's efforts to whittle the powers of the Environmental Protection Agency resulted in his appointment of controversial Anne Gorsuch to head that agency. Gorsuch had previously supported policies opposite to the goals of the EPA. Legal squabbles with Congress and political controversy ensued when Gorsuch attempted to implement her policies, which ultimately led to her resignation. To patch up the damage Gorsuch had done to his reputation, Reagan named a moderate and seasoned administrator, William Ruckelshaus to run the agency. Ironically, Ruckelshaus demanded, and got, more freedom from the White House than Gorsuch had sought.

— *Issue orders.* Presidents can issue **executive orders** to agencies. More typically, presidential aides pass the word that "the President was wondering if. . . . " That usually suffices, although agency heads are reluctant to run afoul of Congress or the press on the basis of a broad presidential hint.

---

5 Deregulation: A Dissenting View

Surveys about deregulation are pretty clear on one point: most Americans do favor less government regulation in general, although they approve of almost every specific area of regulation, for example, worker safety, pollution, and consumer product controls. These days, most conservatives and many liberals believe that governmental regulation has simply gone too far. It is time, they insist, to start deregulating the economy, permitting the market to work in its own way.

Of course, every regulation was once put into effect for some specific purpose or in response to a specific group demand. Two dissenters to the whole idea of deregulation are Susan J. Tolchin and Martin Tolchin. In their book *Dismantling America*, they make a case that the rush to deregulate is a poor idea. "Regulatory reform," they say, "has turned out to be an exercise in national self-deception because of the singularity of its dominant goal: short-term relief for business." Far from costing money, they argue, government regulation has saved lives and money. Crib safety standards have reduced infant injuries by 44 percent since 1964; air pollution regulations may have saved between $5 and $58 billion a year in health and other costs; automobile safety standards have probably saved over 28,000 lives in an eight-year period, with seat belt requirements alone responsible for a 20 percent reduction in automobile deaths.

Businesses, say Tolchin and Tolchin, favor deregulation because it saves them money. Pesky pollution controls, bothersome worker safety regulations, and obnoxious noise abatements may cost billions to corporations. But they may save lives and money, too. There is, at least, some support for the idea that regulation is not too much of a good thing.

Source: Susan J. Tolchin and Martin Tolchin, *Dismantling America: The Rush to Deregulate* (New York: Oxford University Press, 1983).

— *Tinker with an agency's budget.* The Office of Management and Budget is the president's own final authority on any agency's budget. OMB's threats to cut here or add there will usually get an agency's attention. However, each agency has its constituents in and outside Congress, and Congress, not the president, does the appropriating.

— *Reorganizing an agency.* President Reagan promised, proposed, and pressured to abolish the Department of Energy and Department of Education. He never succeeded, largely because each was in the hands of an entrenched bureaucracy, backed by elements in Congress and strong constituent groups. Reorganizing an agency is hard to do—if it is a large and strong one—and often not worth the trouble if it is a small and weak one.

Congress Tries to Control the Bureaucracy. Congress exhibits a paradoxical relationship with the bureaucracies. On the one hand (as Morris Fiorina has shown), members of Congress often find a big bureaucracy congenial.[33] Big government provides services to constituents. Moreover, when Congress lacks the answers to policy problems, it hopes the bureaucracies will find them. Unable itself, for example, to resolve the touchy issue of equality in intercollegiate athletics, it passed the ball to HEW. Unable to decide how to make a workplace safer, it produced OSHA. As we saw in Chapter 12, Congress is increasingly the problem-identifying branch of government, setting the bureaucratic agenda but letting the agencies decide how to implement the goals it sets.

On the other hand, Congress has found it hard to control this Frankenstein's monster it helped create. There are several measures Congress can take to oversee the bureaucracy:

— *Influence the appointment of agency heads.* Even when senatorial approval of a presidential appointment is not required, members of Congress are not shy in putting forward their ideas about who should and should not be running the agencies. When congressional approval is required, members are doubly influential. Committee hearings on proposed appointments are almost guaranteed to bring ulcers if some members find the nominee's likely orientations unpalatable. University of Chicago Law School Dean Norval Morris, nominated by President Carter to head the Law Enforcement Assistance Administration, was shot down by antigun-control senators who found his writings about gun control objectionable.

— *Tinker with an agency's budget.* With the congressional power of the purse comes a mighty weapon for controlling bureaucratic behavior. At the same time, Congress knows that agencies perform services that its constituents demand. Too much budget cutting may make an agency more responsive at the price of losing an interest group's support for a reelection campaign.

— *Hold hearings.* Committees and subcommittees can hold periodic hearings as part of their oversight job. Flagrant agency abuses of congressional intent can be paraded in front of the press. But

[33] Morris Fiorina, *Congress: Keystone of the Washington Establishment* (New Haven, Conn.: Yale University Press, 1977).

J. Edgar Hoover, Powerful Bureaucrat (right). *Few agencies in the American government possess the reputation of the Federal Bureau of Investigation. The image of the F.B.I. is a result of the careful cultivation and almost autocratic control of one man, J. Edgar Hoover, its first director.*

Hoover first took over the fledgling agency in the 1920s, when prohibition-era gangsterism made headlines. After World War II, he consolidated control over the agency, and began collecting information on presidents, members of Congress, and later, liberal groups and civil rights leaders like Martin Luther King, Jr., whose phone he tapped.

Partly because otherwise powerful people never knew what Hoover might have in his files, dislodging him—even when near retirement age—was all but impossible. Hoover's career shows how one powerful bureaucrat can shape an entire agency in his image.

responsibility for oversight typically goes to the very committee that created a program; the committee thus has some stake in showing the agency in a favorable light.

— *Rewrite the legislation or make it more detailed.* Every statute is filled with instructions to its administrators. To limit bureaucratic discretion and make its instructions clearer, Congress can write new or more detailed legislation. Still, even voluminous detail (as we saw in the case of the IRS) can never eliminate discretion.

Through these and other devices, Congress tries to keep bureaucracies under its thumb. Never entirely successful, Congress faces a constant battle to limit and channel the vast powers that it delegated to the bureaucracy in the first place.

Bureaucracies, Pluralism, and Hyperpluralism: The Iron Triangles

There is one other crucial explanation for the difficulty presidents and Congress face in controlling bureaucracies: Agencies have strong ties to interest groups on the one hand and to congressional committees and subcommittees on the other. Here we confront pluralism again shaping the policy process. To the degree that these tight alliances resist control by the president and the whole Congress, we confront hyperpluralism.

We learned in Chapter 10 that bureaucracies often enjoy cozy relationships with interest groups and with committees or subcommittees of Congress. When agencies, groups, and committees all depend on one another and are in close, frequent contact, they form what are sometimes called *iron triangles* or *subgovernments.* [34] These triads have advantages on all sides. [6] There are plenty of examples of the subgovernments at work. A subcommittee on aging (especially one including Florida's forceful policy entrepreneur for the aged, Representative Claude Pepper), senior citizens' interest groups, and the Social Security Administration are likely to agree on the need for more social security benefits. Robert Rettig has recounted how an alliance slowly jelled around the issue of fighting cancer. It rested on three pillars: cancer researchers, agencies within the National Institutes of Health, and members of congressional health subcommittees. [35]

These iron triangles can foster hyperpluralism. When they shape policies for senior citizens, or cancer, or tobacco, or anything else, each policy is made independently of the others, sometimes even in contradiction to other policies. Moreover, their decisions tend to bind larger institutions, like Congress and the White House. Congress willingly lets its committees and subcommittees make decisions. The White House may be too busy wrestling with the global connection to fret over agricultural issues, older Americans, or cancer. If so, these subgovernments add a strong decentralizing and fragmenting element to the policymaking process.

The explosion of legislative subcommittees has greatly increased Congress' oversight activities. Numerous subcommittees may look over the shoulder of and review the actions of a single agency. More subcommittees have meant more oversight: A half-dozen or more subcommittees may review the activities of the Department of Energy, the Department of Agriculture, or the Department of Commerce. But different committees may send different signals to the same agency. One may press for sterner enforcement, another for more exemptions. As the oversight process has become more vigorous, it has also become more fragmented, thus limiting the effectiveness of the bureaucracies.

BUREAUCRACIES SUMMARIZED

Bureaucracies shape policy as administrators, as implementers, and as regulators. In this chapter, we examined who the bureaucrats are, how they got there, and what they do. Today, most bureaucrats working for the federal government got there through the Civil Service system, although a few at the very top are appointed by the president.

Generally we can divide the bureaucratic apparatus into four types: the cabinet departments, the regulatory agencies, the government corporations, and the independent agencies.

[34] On the role of subgovernments and iron triangles, see Randall Ripley and Grace Franklin, *Congress, Bureaucracy and Public Policy,* 3rd ed. (Homewood, Ill.: Dorsey Press, 1984), pp. 8–12.

[35] Robert Rettig, *Cancer Crusade* (Princeton, N.J.: Princeton University Press, 1977).

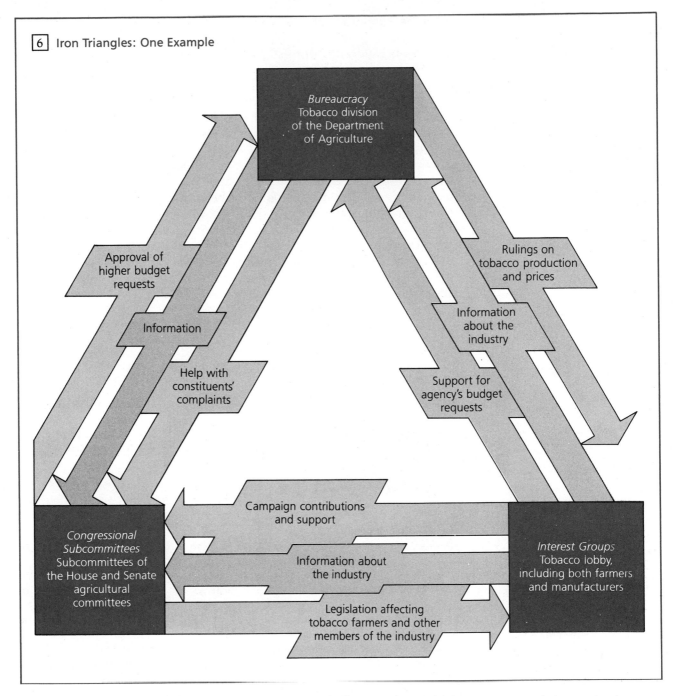

Bureaucracy
Tobacco division
of the Department
of Agriculture

Approval of
higher budget
requests

Information

Help with
constituents'
complaints

Rulings on
tobacco production
and prices

Information
about the
industry

Support for
agency's budget
requests

**Congressional
Subcommittees**
Subcommittees of
the House and Senate
agricultural
committees

Campaign contributions
and support

Information about
the industry

Legislation affecting
tobacco farmers and other
members of the industry

Interest Groups
Tobacco lobby,
including both farmers
and manufacturers

Iron triangles—composed of bureaucratic agencies, interest groups, and a congressional committee or subcommittee—dominate much domestic policymaking by combining internal consensus with a virtual monopoly on information in their area. The tobacco triangle is one example; there are dozens more. Iron triangles are characterized by mutual dependency, in which each element provides key services, information, or policy for the others. The arrows indicate some of these mutually helpful relationships.

As policymakers, bureaucrats play three key roles. First, they are policy implementers, translating legislative policy goals into programs. Policy implementation does not always work well, and when it does not, bureaucrats usually take the blame, whether they deserve it or not.

473

Second, bureaucrats administer public policy. Much of administration involves routine, but almost all bureaucrats still have some discretion. Third, bureaucracies are regulators. Congress increasingly delegates large grants of power to bureaucratic agencies and expects them to develop rules and regulations. Scarcely a nook or cranny of American society or the American economy escapes the long outreach of bureaucratic regulation.

Trying to understand bureaucracies, we saw that although bureaucrats are not elected, bureaucracies are not necessarily undemocratic. But it is essential that bureaucracies be controlled by elected decision makers. Presidential or congressional control over bureaucracies is difficult, however. One reason is that bureaus have strong support from interest groups. This contributes to pluralism, because interest groups try to forge common links with bureaucracies and congressional committees. These "iron triangles" tend to decentralize policymaking, contributing to hyperpluralism.

Key Terms

patronage
Pendleton Act
civil service
merit principle
Office of Personnel
  Management (OPM)
G.S. (General Schedule)
  rating
plum book

bureaucracy
independent regulatory
  agency
government
  corporations
independent executive
  agency
implementation
administrative routine

administrative
  discretion
street-level bureaucrats
regulation
command-and-control
  policy
incentive system
executive orders

For Further Reading

Edwards, George C., III. *Implementing Public Policy* (1980). A good review of the issues involved in implementation.

Fritschler, A. Lee, and Bernard H. Ross. *Business Regulation and Government Decision-Making* (1980). Focuses on the impact of regulations on business.

Heclo, Hugh. *A Government of Strangers* (1977). A study of the top executives of the federal government, who constitute (says the author) a "government of strangers."

Pressman, Jeffrey, and Aaron Wildavsky. *Implementation*, 3rd ed. (1984). The classic—and often witty—study of implementation.

Quirk, Paul J. *Industry Influence in Federal Regulatory Agencies* (1981). Casts doubt on the belief that regulatory agencies often become captives of regulated industries.

Ripley, Randall, and Grace Franklin. *Congress, Bureaucracy and Public Policy*, 3rd ed. (1984). A very solid introduction to the connections between the burcaucracy and congress.

Savas, E. S. *Privatizing the Public Sector* (1982). A conservative economist's argument that many public services performed by bureaucracies would be better handled by the private sector.

Tolchin, Susan J. and Martin Tolchin. *Dismantling America* (1983). A powerful critique of deregulation philosophy, politics, and practice.

Weiss, Leonard W., and Michael W. Klass, eds. *Case Studies in Regulation* (1981). Articles on regulatory policy in eight policy areas.

Wilson, James Q., ed. *The Politics of Regulation* (1980). Excellent essays on regulation and deregulation.

15

The Courts

MEMO

In the 1830s, the great French traveller and observer of American politics, Alexis de Tocqueville, wrote that all political questions in America eventually become judicial questions. His words apply today, even more than yesterday, for sooner or later almost all Americans end up in court, even if only for jury duty. The policymaking role of the courts is great and has been ever since the days of the arch-Federalist John Marshall. Still, myths about the courts abound. Here, we will try to set some of them straight. These are the main topics we will address:

- Judges are wrapped not only in black robes, but in the mystery and majesty of the law. Yet they are hardly above politics, and appointments to the courts help ensure that judges follow the tunes played by the presidents who appoint them.
- Next we examine how the courts are organized. We distinguish between state and federal courts. Some are courts of original jurisdiction, some are appellate courts.
- The highest appellate court is the United States Supreme Court. But even our Supreme Court rarely settles an issue once and for all. Judicial implementation depends on many players in our pluralist system.
- How well the court system dovetails with democracy is an old question, one we address at a time when many think that a litigation explosion is upon us.

I F YOU HAPPEN TO VISIT the Supreme Court, you will first be impressed by the marble Supreme Court building, with the motto "Equal Justice under Law" engraved over its imposing columns. The Court's surroundings and procedures suggest the nineteenth century. The justices, clothed in black robes, take their seats at the bench in front of a red velvet curtain. Behind the bench there are still spitoons, one for each justice. (Today they are used as wastebaskets.) The few cases the Court selects for oral arguments are scheduled for about an hour each. Lawyers arguing before the Court often wear frock coats and striped trousers. They find a goose quill pen on their desk, bought by the Court from a Virginia supplier. (They may take it with them as a momento of their day in Court.) Each side is normally allotted thirty minutes to present its case. The justices may, and do, interrupt the lawyers with questions. When the time is up, a discreet red light goes on at the lawyer's lectern.

However impressive the Supreme Court may be, only the tiniest fraction of American judicial policy is made there. To be sure, the Court decides a handful of key issues each year. Some will shape our lives, even deciding issues of life and death. In recent years, the Court has authorized abortions, upheld busing to end school segregation, vacillated about capital punishment, upheld some forms of affirmative action programs while rejecting others, and ordered President Nixon to release secret White House tapes during the Watergate affair. In addition to the Supreme Court, there are twelve federal circuit courts of appeal, ninety-four federal district courts, and thousands of state and local courts. It is in these less noticed courts that the great bulk of our legal business is transacted.

Our court system is complex, just as our federal system itself is complex. There are state court systems and a federal court system. Most cases start and end in one or the other, usually, of course, in the state courts. Sometimes judges' and juries' decisions are appealed to a higher court, but no one has any constitutional right to take a case to the Supreme Court. The Supreme Court hears only a very small percentage of all cases brought to court in America. In this chapter, we will be dealing with all sorts of courts, both state and federal. And we will be dealing with all sorts of judges, the men and women in black robes who are important judicial policymakers.

THE JUDGES

Who They Are

Once they arrive on the bench, judges and justices (only members of the Supreme Court are called justices; all others are called judges) must draw on their backgrounds and beliefs to guide their decision making. Some, for example, will be more supportive of abortion, or of prayer in the public schools, than others. Presidents and others involved in the appointment process know perfectly well that judges are not neutral automatons who methodically and literally interpret the law.

The number of judges and the number of courts are set by Congress. The Constitution simply says: "The judicial Power of the United States, shall be invested in one supreme Court, and in such inferior Courts as the Congress may from time to time ordain and establish." On the Supreme Court today, there are nine justices—the chief justice and eight associate justices. The federal circuit courts of appeal have 132 judges. Another 485 serve as federal district judges. Still others serve on a handful of special federal courts, such as the United States Court of International Trade and the United States Claims Court. Thousands more serve on state and local courts.

The Constitution lists no special requirements for judges. John Schmidhauser's collective portrait of the federal judiciary, though, shows that federal judges seem to qualify as an American elite. Said Schmidhauser: "The typical Supreme Court justice has generally been white, Protestant (with a penchant for a high social status denomination), usually of ethnic stock originating in the British Isles, and born in comfortable circumstances in an urban or small-town environment."[1] The Supreme Court has been virtually closed to minority groups. Associate Justice Thurgood Marshall is the only black ever to don a Court robe, and the first woman, Sandra Day O'Connor, was seated on the Court in 1981.

Thurgood Marshall. *Marshall was chief attorney for the NAACP in* Brown v. Board of Education *(1954). Named by Lyndon Johnson in the 1960s, he became the first black American appointed to the U.S. Supreme Court.*

Scholars have examined the connection between background characteristics of Supreme Court justices and their voting choices. Justices who were Democrats, for example, tended to be more liberal than those who were Republicans. Even the previous jobholding experiences of the high court justices were connected to their voting: Former prosecutors serving on the Supreme Court were likely to be less sympathetic toward defendants' rights than other justices.[2] It is precisely because judges' interpretations of the law vary that the appointment process is so important.

How They Got There

Getting on the Supreme Court. The Constitution specifies that the president, with the agreement of the Senate, shall appoint members of the Supreme Court. Exactly 102 people have served on the Supreme Court since its creation. Guaranteed by the Constitution the right to serve "during good behavior," they are, for all practical purposes, in for life. Constitutionally, only impeachment can remove them. Thus, appointing a Supreme Court justice is a president's chance to leave his enduring mark on the American legal system.

Ronald Reagan had that chance in 1981. After twenty-three years on the bench, Justice Potter Stewart delivered a letter of resignation to the president. Stewart said he was "a firm believer that it's better to go too soon than stay too long." Since candidate Reagan had promised to name a woman to the Supreme Court, speculation on and suggestions of female nominees were amply supplied after Stewart's resignation. At the urging of Arizona's Senator Barry Goldwater, among others, the president

[1] John Schmidhauser, *Judges and Justices: The Federal Appellate Judiciary* (Boston: Little, Brown, 1978), p. 96.
[2] C. Neal Tate, "Personal Attribute Models of the Voting Behavior of United States Supreme Court Justices: Liberalism in Civil Liberties and Economics Decisions, 1946–78," *American Political Science Review* 75 (1981): 355–67.

selected Arizona Court of Appeals Judge Sandra Day O'Connor. Conservative groups opposed her alleged support of abortion and the Equal Rights Amendment. But after going through an elaborate confirmation process she was appointed as the first female Supreme Court justice and sworn in for the term beginning in October 1981.

After the president has settled on a name and the FBI has checked on that person's background, the president sends the nomination to the Senate.[3] The Senate Judiciary Committee holds hearings, reviews the nominee's record, and recommends approval or rejection by the Senate. The president's nominees usually, but not always, win Senate approval easily. Two of Richard Nixon's nominees, Clement Haynsworth and G. Harrold Carswell, were rejected by the Senate. This was the first time a nominee had been rejected since 1930, and the first time two had been rejected consecutively since the days of Grover Cleveland, at the end of the nineteenth century. Both of Nixon's nominees were southerners, and both agreed with the president's conservative philosophy. Haynsworth, though, was a federal appeals court judge who had voted in cases involving corporations in which he held stock. Carswell, another federal judge, was said to be hostile to civil rights litigants, to have made racist speeches in a political campaign, and, as U.S. attorney, to have helped a public golf course turn private to avoid having to desegregate. His overall record as a federal judge was, several senators remarked, "mediocre." Nebraska Senator Roman Hruska grumbled, supposedly in Carswell's defense, that "mediocre people need representation, too," a remark that

[3] A good review of this nomination process is in Schmidhauser, *Judges and Justices*, Chap. 3.

Sandra Day O'Connor. *Arizona state jurist Sandra Day O'Connor was nominated to the Supreme Court in 1981 by President Ronald Reagan and became the first female member of the Court. Here, Chief Justice Burger accompanies her to her swearing-in ceremonies.*

hardly helped Carswell's chances. After lengthy debate, the Senate refused to confirm either nomination.

Judicial nominees are almost always from the president's party. Most judges and justices have been active in politics before their appointment. Thus, partisanship as well as ideology is an important ingredient in appointment to the high Court. This is no less the case for the president's appointments to other federal courts.

Appointment to the Lower Federal Courts. The United States Supreme Court is at the top of the federal court hierarchy; in addition, there are two other layers of federal courts. At the bottom rung of the judicial ladder are the **federal district courts.** Today there are ninety-four federal district courts, distributed geographically around the country. Each will have one or (typically) more federal judges. The **courts of appeal** are the intermediate federal courts. Cases may be appealed from the district courts to them; the only recourse above them is the Supreme Court itself. There are twelve courts of appeal, each with a panel of judges.

Even though public scrutiny is lavished on Supreme Court appointments, the fact is that appointments to the courts of appeal and the district courts are almost as important. The nation's "second most important court," for example, is the District of Columbia Court of Appeals, sitting just a few hundred yards from the Supreme Court itself. Because of its location, suits by and against government agencies are often filed there. Two judges—liberal, activist former Chief Judge David Bazelon, and former judge, now Chief Justice Warren Burger—were arch-rivals on the D.C. Court of Appeals. (When Burger was appointed chief justice, Bazelon was said to be "sick and speechless for a week.") Until recently, a liberal majority dominated the D.C. Court, embarking on new judicial paths to protect the environment, the rights of the mentally ill, and criminal defendants. The Supreme Court under Chief Justice Burger reversed decisions of the other appeals courts 63.4 percent of the time; it reversed the D.C. Court in 73.3 percent of its cases.[4]

As with appointments to the Supreme Court, presidents nominate and the Senate must confirm appointees to the courts of appeal and the district courts. Two leading students of the lower federal courts, Carp and Rowland, emphasize that "despite the popular myth that judges are 'nonpolitical,' the evidence is overwhelming that American presidents have not shared in this belief."[5] For that reason, they work hard to ensure that their appointees are partisan and ideological supporters. More than 90 percent of appointees, for example, come from the president's own party.

Appointments to the courts of appeal are handled much like appointments to the Supreme Court. Many of these nominations come from the federal district courts. More than two-fifths of appellate judges are, in effect, "promoted" from the lower federal courts. Jimmy Carter insisted

[4]Harold Spaeth, "Supreme Court Dispositions of Federal Circuit Court Decisions," *Judicature* 68 (December 1984–January 1985), pp. 245–50.
[5] Robert A. Carp and C. K. Rowland, *Policymaking and Politics in the Federal District Courts* (Knoxville, Tenn.: University of Tennessee Press, 1983), p. 51.

that he wanted judicial court appointments made on the merit principle. He therefore created panels of citizens in each appeals circuit to advise him on meritorious appointments. Nonetheless, the vast majority came from his own party. President Reagan put the judicial nominating boards in mothballs.

Appointments to the federal district courts work differently. A quaint practice called **senatorial courtesy** is an important constraint on the president's freedom to appoint his choice. Under the senatorial courtesy rule, the Senate permits a senator of the president's party to veto a judicial appointment in his state. In one celebrated case, President Kennedy had to pay a political price for the appointment of black, liberal Thurgood Marshall to the Court of Appeals: He had to agree to the appointment of Mississippi Senator James O. Eastland's old college roommate—and a racial reactionary—to the federal bench there. Despite having to play politics with the Senate, presidential appointments have generally turned out the way presidents had hoped. Federal judges appointed by Democrats have tended to be liberal on the bench, those appointed by Republicans conservative. [6]

What They Do

The Courts at Work. On a hot day in September 1984, both state and federal courts were in session in San Antonio. In the Bexar County Court House, two full floors of courtrooms were busy. Like all American courts, the task of their judges is to apply and interpret the law in a particular **case.** Every case has a **plaintiff** and a **defendant,** the former bringing some charge against the latter. Sometimes the plaintiff is the government itself, which may bring a charge against an individual or a corporation. The government may charge the defendant with the brutal murder of Jones; or the XYZ Corporation with illegal trade practices. All cases are identified with the name of the plaintiff first and the defendant second, for example, *State* v. *Smith* or *Anderson* v. *Baker.* The task of the judge or judges is to apply the law to the case, determining whether the plaintiff or the defendant is legally correct. In many (but not all) cases, a **jury** is responsible for the determination of guilt.

Two kinds of cases were being heard in the Bexar County Court House: *criminal law* and *civil law.* In **criminal law** cases, an individual is charged with violating a specific law, the punishment for which may be jail or a fine. In San Antonio, you often see criminal defendants brought from the county jail to court in groups, chained together, awaiting their time before the court.

In Judge Raymond Wietzel's court, Mr. Hernandez was unlocked from his fellow prisoners. A deputy sheriff escorted him to where his lawyer stood, in front of the judge's bench. Judge Wietzel asked if he understood his rights and the bargain he was about to make, and a district attorney announced the plea bargain (see page 158) agreed upon by the state and the defendant. The judge accepted it and formally handed Mr. Hernandez over to the custody of state corrections officers. Down the hall, Judge

[6] Ibid., p. 81.

Bexar County Courthouse. *Although most of our judicial attention is paid to the Supreme Court, most of the cases begin and end in a state court. At the Bexar County Courthouse, in San Antonio, two floors of courtrooms hear civil and criminal cases.*

Rickhoff was presiding over a jury trial. Four beefy defendants were accused of knifing and beating up two men at Big J's Lounge.

Civil law involves no charge of criminality, no charge that a law has been violated. It concerns a dispute between two parties (one of whom, of course, may be the government itself). In the 225th District Court, for example, Judge Chapa was hearing the case of *Chavez* v. *Edgewood School District*. Ms. Chavez was suing the school district over a workman's compensation issue. An employee of the district, she had lifted a box and claimed to have injured herself.

Across town in Hemisfair Plaza, the Federal Court of the Western District of Texas was in session that afternoon. A Mr. Gonzales was suing the San Antonio Police Department. His rights under federal civil rights laws were violated because, he claimed, police used excessive force to subdue him when he was arrested in July 1979. A police officer was testifying that ample force had been required to arrest Gonzales, who had even bit one officer.

Just as it is important not to confuse state and federal courts, it is equally important not to confuse criminal and civil law. The vast majority of all civil and criminal cases involve state law and are tried in state courts. Civil cases such as divorce and criminal cases such as burglary normally begin and end in the state, not the federal, courts.

Policymaking and Policy Application. It is easy to think that the legislative and executive branches are our only policymaking institutions. After all, they spend the money and write the laws. However, courts are constantly making policy, too. They decide important national policies, determining which schools our children will attend, whether a woman may have an abortion, or whether we can buy a pornographic magazine at the corner food store. Judges may prefer to define their roles more narrowly, but we often give them no alternative to a policymaking role.

There are strong disagreements concerning the appropriateness of a policymaking role in the courts. Many scholars and judges favor a policy of **judicial restraint,** in which judges play minimal policymaking roles, leaving that strictly to legislatures. Other judges and scholars support **judicial activism,** in which judges make bolder policy decisions, even charting new constitutional ground with a particular decision. Proponents of judicial restraint become dismayed when judges make decisions on social issues (like abortion and school prayer) which, they think, are best left to legislatures.

Actually, courts more often apply policy than chart new policy directions. The vast majority of cases reaching the courts are settled on the principle of ***stare decisis*** (a Latin phrase which means, "let the decision

Judicial Activism and Restraint. *No issue in the judiciary is as disputed as the proper role of the courts in a democratic government. Some judges and legal scholars favor a policy of judicial activism, where judges may use the law to achieve broader ends. The late Supreme Court Justice William O. Douglas (left) was a leading proponent of judicial activism. Other judges, like Supreme Court Justice William Rehnquist (right), are noted for their policy of judicial restraint. The justification for judicial restraint is that it leaves power over society and the economy to the democratically elected legislatures. Opponents of judicial restraint, though, suspect that it is merely a cover for judicial conservatism.*

stand"), that is, an earlier decision should hold for the case being considered. All courts rely heavily on **precedent**—the way similar cases were handled in the past—as a guide to current decisions. Lower courts, of course, are expected to follow the precedents of higher courts in their decision making. For example, if the Supreme Court rules in favor of abortions in certain cases, it has established precedent and lower courts are expected to follow that precedent.

HOW THE COURTS ARE ORGANIZED

Participants in the Judicial System

Judges are the policymakers of the American judicial system, but they are not the only participants. In judicial policymaking, only a small part of the action takes place in the courtroom, and there are only a few participants: the judge, the **litigants** (the plaintiff and the defendant) nervously watching a process they do not always understand, the ever-present lawyers, and sometimes a jury trying very hard to pay attention.

Litigants end up in court for a variety of reasons. Some are very reluctant participants—the defendant in a criminal case, for example. Others are eager for their day in court. For some, the courts can be a potent weapon in the search for a preferred policy. Atheist Madlyn Murray O'Hair was an enthusiastic litigant, always ready to haul the government into court for (as she saw it) promoting religion.

Because they know well the power of the courts to shape policy, interest groups often seek out litigants whose cases seem particularly strong. Few groups have been more successful in finding good cases and good litigants than the National Association for the Advancement of Colored People. It selected the school board of Topeka, Kansas, and a young schoolgirl named Linda Brown as the litigants in *Brown* v. *Board of Education*. NAACP legal counsel Thurgood Marshall (later a Supreme Court justice) believed that Topeka presented a stronger case than other school districts in the United States. The American Civil Liberties Union, an ardent defender of individual liberties, is another interest group that is always seeking good cases and good litigants. One ACLU attorney, stressing that principle took priority over a particular client, even admitted that the ACLU's clients are often "pretty scurvy little creatures. . . . It's the principle that we're going to be able to use these people for that's important." [7] (For an example, see the case of the Nazis who tried to march in Skokie, Illinois, on page 149.)

Lawyers have become another indispensable actor in the judicial system. Law is the nation's fastest growing profession. [8] The United States counted about 100,000 lawyers in 1960 but over 600,000 in 1984. Lawyers busily translate policies into legal language and then enforce them, or challenge them. Jimmy Carter's secretary of labor, Ray Marshall

[7] Quoted in Lawrence C. Baum, *The Supreme Court*, 2nd. ed. (Washington, D.C.: Congressional Quarterly Press, 1981), p. 72.

[8] Tom Goldstein, "Law, the Fastest Growing Profession, May Find Prosperity Precarious," *New York Times*, May 16, 1977, p. 1.

—a mere economics professor by trade—told of his problems with his department's lawyers when he was trying to understand one regulation:

> I remember that I called in one of our lawyers—and I've since learned that we have 400 of them—and asked him to bring me the law and let me read it.
>
> He said, "It wouldn't do you any good. You couldn't understand it." I said, "Well, I'm not illiterate, why can't I understand it?" He just said flatly, "Well, you just can't." So I said, "Well, do you understand it?" And he replied, "Yes, but I'm a lawyer."
>
> That stopped me for a moment. So I tried another tack. "Well, can you write it so that I can understand it?" He agreed that he could write it so I could understand it. But, he said, "We wouldn't be able to enforce it, then." [9]

Lawyers create the need for more lawyers.

Once lawyers were mostly available for the rich. Today public interest law firms can sometimes handle legal problems of the poor and middle classes. A federally funded Legal Service Corporation employs lawyers to serve the legal needs of the poor, though the Reagan administration has made drastic cuts in legal aid. Some employers and unions now provide legal insurance, which works like medical insurance. Members with legal needs—for a divorce, a consumer complaint, or whatever—can secure legal aid through prepaid plans. As a result, more people than ever before can take their problems to the courts.

The audience for this judicial drama is a large and attentive one that includes interest groups, the press (a close observer of the judicial process, especially of its more sensational aspects), and the public, who often have very strong opinions about how the process works. All these participants—plaintiffs, defendants, lawyers, interest groups, and others—play a role in the judicial drama, even though many of their activities take place outside the courtroom. How they arrive in the courtroom and which court they go to reflects the structure of the court system.

Structure of the Courts

Our court system is complex. The august serenity and majesty of the United States Supreme Court is a far cry from the grimy urban court where strings of defendants are bused from the local jail for their day—often only a few minutes—in court. ☐1 One important distinction among our courts comes in the matter of jurisdiction. Courts with **original jurisdiction** are those in which a case is heard first, usually in a trial. These are the courts that determine the facts about a case. The great majority of our judicial business is transacted in courts of original jurisdiction—the county or municipal courts that first hear a traffic charge, a divorce case, or a criminal charge. Most of our judicial business also ends in these courts. More than 90 percent of court cases begin and end in the court of original jurisdiction.

Lawyers can sometimes appeal an adverse decision to a higher court

[9] Quoted in *Current Public Policy Research* (May 1977): 8.

Our impression of the judicial system is often shaped by our perceptions of the Supreme Court or by television coverage of some major trial. We expect our judicial system to be fair, impartial, consistent, and evenhanded. Most of our judicial business is handled by local courts, however, and many studies have indicated that great differences in procedure and punishment exist from place to place at the local level.

Political scientist Malcolm Feeley looked carefully at local courts in New Haven, Connecticut. The courts he studied handled misdemeanor cases, that is, such minor offenses as drunk driving, speeding, and assault. He called his book on New Haven courts *The Process is the Punishment.* Feeley found that in New Haven defendants, innocent and guilty alike, were punished by the very process of getting justice. They were arrested, had to hire a lawyer, make bail, and go on trial. The problems and psychological burdens of defending oneself made the experience of the judicial process a grinding ordeal. The guilty got formal punishment as well, although Feeley discovered that few defendants were convicted and that fines rarely totaled more than $50.

John Ryan examined the way local justice is dispensed in the misdemeanor courts of Columbus, Ohio. In Columbus, Ryan found, the outcome of a trial is the punishment. An extensive system of public defenders reduces the costs an individual must bear for his or her own defense, unlike what Feeley found in New Haven. But justice is swifter and more severe than in New Haven —few defendants are acquitted, and most face substantial fines or even jail terms.

Other assessments of local courts have confirmed the existence of disparities in procedure and punishment throughout the United States. Baltimore's sanctions, for example, are more severe than the sanctions for comparable offenses in Chicago or Detroit. Since most justice is and always has been handled at the local level, our concept of "Equal Justice under Law" is not an accurate portrayal of a major part of our judicial system.

Sources: On New Haven, see Malcolm Feeley, *The Process is the Punishment* (New York: Russell Sage, 1979). On Columbus, see John Ryan, "Adjudication and Sentencing in a Misdemeanor Court: The Outcome Is the Punishment," *Law and Society Review* 15 (1980–81): 79–108. On Baltimore and two other cities, see James Eisenstein and Herbert Jacob, *Felony Justice* (Boston: Little, Brown, 1977).

for another decision. Courts with **appellate jurisdiction** hear cases brought to them on appeal from a lower court. Appellate courts do not review the factual record, only the legal issues involved. At the state level, the appellate process normally ends with the state's highest court of appeal, usually called the state supreme court. Appeals from a state high court can be taken only to the United States Supreme Court.

Most of the business of the United States Supreme Court comes from the appellate process. You can see in 2 that the United States Supreme Court has appellate jurisdiction over both state and federal cases. Plainly, the court cannot hear every case that plaintiffs or defendants would like reviewed. In the 1983–84 term, 5,099 cases were filed before the Court. Like all political institutions, the Court must control its own agenda.

Traditionally, the Supreme Court uses the "rule of four" to decide whether it will hear a case: Four of the justices must agree that a case deserves the Court's attention. In one common way to put a case on its docket, the Supreme Court issues a **writ of certiorari,** a formal document that calls up the case. Most writs of certiorari involve cases that were tried in federal courts. The Court may also agree to hear a case based on a defendant's constitutional right of appeal. The Court will hear such a case, however, only if it involves federal statutes or treaties or the Constitution. A defendant convicted in a state court might demonstrate, for example, that his or her trial was not fair as required by the Bill of Rights, which was extended to cover state court proceedings by the due process clause of the Fourteenth Amendment.

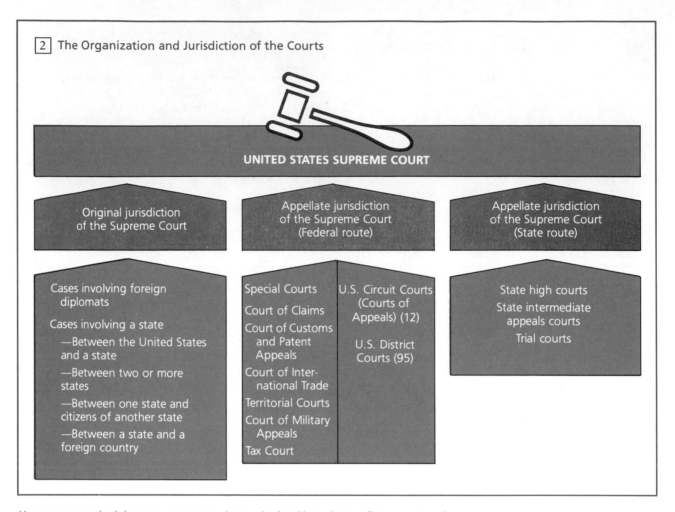

UNITED STATES SUPREME COURT

Original jurisdiction of the Supreme Court	Appellate jurisdiction of the Supreme Court (Federal route)	Appellate jurisdiction of the Supreme Court (State route)
Cases involving foreign diplomats Cases involving a state —Between the United States and a state —Between two or more states —Between one state and citizens of another state —Between a state and a foreign country	Special Courts Court of Claims Court of Customs and Patent Appeals Court of International Trade Territorial Courts Court of Military Appeals Tax Court U.S. Circuit Courts (Courts of Appeals) (12) U.S. District Courts (95)	State high courts State intermediate appeals courts Trial courts

Here you can see both how our court system is organized and how the appellate process works. There are three roads to the Supreme Court. Very few cases get to the Supreme Court through its original jurisdiction: most come by the federal appeals route or through an appeal from a state high court. Remember that the vast majority of cases are handled at the lowest judicial level, especially by city, county, or state trial courts.

THE COURTS AS POLICYMAKERS

"Judicial decision making," a former Supreme Court law clerk wrote in the *Harvard Law Review*, "involves, at bottom, a choice between competing values by fallible, pragmatic, and at times nonrational men [and women, he could have added] in a highly complex process in a very human setting."[10] This is an apt description of policymaking on the Supreme Court, and on other courts, too. Let us look, then, at how courts make policy. We pay particular attention to the role of the United States Supreme Court. It is not the only court involved in policymaking and policy interpretation, but its decisions have the widest implications for policy.

[10] Quoted in Nina Totenberg, "Behind the Marble, Beneath the Robes," *New York Times Magazine*, March 16, 1975, p. 37.

The Courts Decide

Deciding what to decide about is the first step in all policymaking. Courts of original jurisdiction cannot very easily decide not to consider a case. Appeals courts, including the United States Supreme Court, have much more control over their agendas. The 5,100 cases submitted annually to the United States Supreme Court must be read, culled, and sifted. Every Wednesday afternoon and every Friday morning the nine justices meet in conference. Alongside them in the conference room sit some twenty-five or so carts, each wheeled in from the office of one of the nine, and each filled with petitions, briefs, memoranda, and every item the justices are likely to need during their discussions. These meetings operate under the strictest secrecy; only the justices themselves attend.

At these weekly conferences, two important matters are hammered out. First is an agenda: The justices consider the chief justice's "discuss list" and decide which cases they want to discuss. Few of the justices can take the time to read materials on every case coming to the Court. Most rely heavily on their law clerks (each now has four) to screen them. If four justices agree to take on a case, it can be scheduled for oral argument or decided on the basis of the written record already on file with the Court.

The second task of the weekly conference is to discuss cases actually accepted and argued before the Court. The chief justice, who presides, raises the case of *Smith* v. *Jones* and invites discussion, turning first to the senior associate justice. Discussion can range, it is said, from perfunctory to profound and from brotherly to bitter. If the votes are not clear from the individual discussions, the chief justice may ask each justice to vote. Once a tentative vote has been reached, it is necessary to write an **opinion,** a statement of the legal reasoning behind the decision.

Opinion writing is not a mere formality. In fact, the content of an opinion may be as important as the decision itself. Broad and bold opinions have far-reaching implications for future cases; narrowly drawn opinions may have little impact beyond the case being decided. Tradition in the Supreme Court requires that the chief justice, if he is in the majority, assign the writing of the opinion to himself or to some other justice in the majority. If the chief justice is part of the minority, the opinion is assigned by the senior associate justice in the majority. (Opponents of Chief Justice Burger have charged that he has manipulated this assigning role, sometimes unilaterally assigning the writing of the majority opinion even when he was in the minority.) Drafts are then circulated among the majority and suggestions are made. Votes can be gained or lost by the content of the opinion. An opinion that proves unacceptable to a clear majority is reworked and redrafted.

Justices are free to write their own opinions, to join in other opinions, or to associate themselves with part of one opinion and part of another. *Dissenting opinions* are those written by justices opposed to all or part of the majority's decision. *Concurring opinions* are those written to support a majority decision, but to stress a different constitutional or legal basis for the judgment. When the opinions are written and the final vote taken, the decision is announced.

Once announced, a decision is conveyed to the press in mimeo form as it is being formally announced in open court. But media coverage of the court remains primitive. Graber reports that "much court reporting, even at the Supreme Court level, is imprecise and sometimes wrong."[11] More importantly in the legal community, the decisions are bound weekly and made available to every law library and lawyer in the United States. There is, of course, an air of finality to the public announcement of a decision: A felon is freed; another one is executed; a massive corporation is split up in an antitrust case. But in fact, court decisions are not self-implementing.

Implementing Court Decisions

Reacting bitterly to one of Chief Justice Marshall's decisions, President Jackson is said to have grumbled: "John Marshall has made his decision; now let him enforce it." Court decisions carry legal, even moral, authority; but courts do not possess a staff of police officers to enforce their decisions. They must rely upon other units of government to carry out their enforcement. **Judicial implementation** refers to how and whether court decisions are translated into actual policy, affecting the behavior of others.

You should think of any judicial decision as the end of one process—the litigation process—and the beginning of another process—the process of judicial implementation. Sometimes delay and footdragging follow upon even decisive court decisions. There is, for example, the story of the tortured efforts of a young black man named Virgil Hawkins to get himself admitted to the University of Florida Law School.[12] Hawkins's efforts began in 1949, when he first applied for admission, and ended unsuccessfully in 1958, after a decade of court decisions. Despite a 1956 order from the United States Supreme Court to admit Hawkins, continued legal skirmishing produced a 1958 decision by the United States District Court in Florida ordering the admission of nonwhites, but upholding the denial of admission to Hawkins himself. Both other courts and other institutions of government can be roadblocks in the way of judicial implementation.

Johnson and Canon suggest that implementation of court decisions involves several elements.[13] First, there is an *interpreting population*, heavily composed of lawyers and other judges. They must correctly sense the intent of the original decision in their subsequent actions. Second, there is an *implementing population*. Say that the Supreme Court (as it did) held that prayers in the public schools are unconstitutional. Then the implementing population (school boards and school administrators) must actually abandon prayers. Police departments, hospitals, corporations, government agencies—all may be a part of the implementing population. Third, every decision involves a *consumer population*. The potential "consumers" of an abortion decision are those who want abortions; the consumers of the *Miranda* decision (see page 156) are criminal

Virgil Hawkins. *The caption on this 1956 Associated Press photograph of Virgil Hawkins reads: "Admittance Ordered: Virgil Hawkins, Negro Student, has been ordered admittance to the University of Florida by the United States Supreme Court. The ruling to be put into affect [sic.] immediately." Unfortunately, it was not to be. Judicial implementation is a complex matter; while Virgil Hawkins' long and persistent legal battle helped integrate the University of Florida Law School, he himself was never admitted. A final district court decision ordered the desegregation of the law school, but refused to require the University to admit Hawkins himself.*

[11] Doris Graber, *Mass Media and American Politics*, 2nd ed. (Washington, D.C.: Congressional Quarterly Press, 1984), p. 249.

[12] Baum, *The Supreme Court*, pp. 181–182.

[13] Charles Johnson and Bradley C. Canon, *Judicial Policies: Implementation and Impact* (Washington, D.C.: Congressional Quarterly Press, 1984), Chap. 1.

defendants and their attorneys. The consumer population must be aware of their newfound rights and stand up for them.

Congress and presidents can also help or hinder judicial implementation. In 1954, the Supreme Court held that segregated schools were "inherently unconstitutional" and ordered public schools desegregated with "all deliberate speed." President Eisenhower, though, was strongly opposed to this famous decision in *Brown* v. *Board of Education*, but once sent federal troops to Little Rock, Arkansas, to help enforce it. Nor was Congress much more helpful; only a decade later did Congress pass legislation denying federal aid to segregated schools. Different presidents have differing commitments to a particular judicial implementation. After years of court and presidential decisions supporting busing to end racial segregation, the Reagan administration in December 1984 went before the Supreme Court and argued against a school busing case in Norfolk, Virginia. Presidents and Congresses can be supporters of, or opponents of, policies of courts.

Implementing a Court Decision: The Case of Abortions. In 1971 the Supreme Court heard oral argument on a thorny constitutional question: Does a woman have a right to an abortion, or does a state have the constitutional power to regulate, limit, or even forbid abortions? The case involved a plaintiff from Texas who remained technically anonymous (hence the name of the case, *"Roe"* v. *Wade*). Texas lawyer Sarah Weddington urged the Court to declare unconstitutional a Texas statute limiting the right of abortion. Weddington argued that numerous constitutional provisions forbade state intervention in an abortion decision. Justice Byron White pressed her on the difficult subject of when during the course of a pregnancy a state law might limit abortion. Weddington insisted that "the Constitution, as I see it, gives protection to people only after birth." In defense of the Texas statute, the state's Assistant Attorney General Jay Floyd faced spirited questioning by Justice Thurgood Marshall. If Texas contended that an unborn fetus had constitutional rights, Marshall wanted to know, then when did those rights begin? "There is life," Floyd contended, "from the moment of impregnation." Pressed by Justice Marshall on the constitutional protection of a newly conceived embryo, Floyd finally admitted that "there are unanswerable questions in this field." [14]

Announced in 1973, the Court's opinion turned on its insistence that the right of privacy "is broad enough to encompass a woman's decision whether or not to terminate her pregnancy." At the same time, the Court held, this right was not absolute. During the first three months of pregnancy a state could not regulate abortions; during the second trimester a state could regulate abortions to insure the health of the mother; and in the third trimester a state could regulate and even forbid abortions to protect the life of the fetus.

Response to the Court's decisions was sharply divided. While some felt it was a wise compromise, it was strongly opposed by anti-abortion

[14] The account of the oral argument before the Court relies on Bob Woodward and Scott Armstrong, *The Brethren* (New York: Avon, 1979), pp. 193–96. On the implementation of the *"Roe"* v. *Wade* case, see also Johnson and Canon, *Judicial Policies*, Chap. 1.

groups. Chief among these were the National Right to Life Committee and the Ad Hoc Committee in Defense of Life. These and other groups took their case to Congress. They unsuccessfully pressed for an amendment to the Constitution that would forbid abortions altogether. They had more success in promoting legislation sponsored by Representative Henry Hyde (R.—Ill.) which forbade the use of federal medicaid funds to pay for poor women's abortions. Also active in the states, anti-abortion groups urged state legislatures to restrict the use of public funds for abortions. A few radical anti-abortionists have picketed and even bombed abortion clinics.

More than a decade of spirited, often bitter, public debate has followed the *"Roe"* v. *Wade* decision. Abortion was an annual issue in Congress and the legislatures; courts considered hundreds of additional cases after *"Roe"*; presidential campaigns and presidential nominating conventions included heated abortion debates. What, then, has been the impact of the Supreme Court's decision? Has the number of abortions increased significantly since the decision? The number of abortions *did* increase after the 1973 decision. An estimated 740,000 legal abortions were performed in 1973. Gradually increasing each year, by 1982 an estimated 1.6 million legal abortions were performed. Susan Hansen, though, concluded that *"Roe"* v. *Wade* was only one of many factors associated with the increase in abortions after *"Roe,"* and perhaps a minor one at that. Abortions had been increasing at a faster rate before the 1973 decision, and many factors, including the increasing public acceptance of abortion, were associated with the increase.[15]

As the abortion case suggests, the fate and effect of a Supreme Court decision are complex and unpredictable. The implementation of any court decision involves many actors besides the judges, and the judges have no way to ensure that their decisions and policies will be implemented. Courts have made major changes in our public policies not because their decisions are automatically implemented, but because the courts both reflect and help to determine our national policy agenda.

THE COURTS AND THE POLICY AGENDA

As judicial scholar Jonathan Casper once remarked, "The Court functions as a kind of access point and agenda-setter, not a final decision maker."[16] Even though our courts and judges work largely alone and in isolation from daily contact with other political institutions, we have seen that they do play a key role in shaping our policy agenda. Like all policymakers, however, the courts are choice-takers. Confronted with controversial policies, they make controversial decisions that leave some people winners and others losers. They have made policy about slavery and segregation, about corporate power and capital punishment, and

[15] Susan B. Hansen, "State Implementation of Supreme Court Decisions: Abortion Rates Since *'Roe'* v. *Wade*," *Journal of Politics* 42 (1980): 372–95.

[16] Jonathan D. Casper, *Lawyers before the Warren Court* (Urbana: University of Illinois Press, 1972), p. 160.

about dozens of other controversial matters. Few played a more important role in making the Court an important national agenda-setter than John Marshall, chief justice from 1801 to 1834. But his successors have continued not only to respond to the political agenda but also to shape discussion and debate about it.

Courts and the Policy Agenda: A Historical Review

John Marshall and the Growth of Judicial Review. Scarcely was the government housed in its new capital when Federalists and Democrats clashed over the courts. In the election of 1800, Democrat Jefferson had beaten Federalist John Adams. Determined to leave at least the judiciary in trusted hands, John Adams tried to fill it with Federalists. He allegedly stayed up all night signing commissions on his last day in the White House.

In the midst of this flurry, Adams appointed William Marbury to the minor post of justice of the peace in the District of Columbia. But in the rush, Marbury's commission was not delivered. When the omission was discovered, Jefferson's new secretary of state, James Madison, refused to deliver it, thereby depriving the Federalists of a judicial post. Marbury sued Madison. He took his case directly to the Supreme Court under the Judiciary Act of 1789, which gave the Supreme Court original jurisdiction in such matters.

The chief justice of the Federalist-infested Supreme Court was John Marshall, himself one of Adams's "midnight appointments." Marshall and his Federalist colleagues were in a spot. Threats of impeachment came from Jeffersonians fearful that the Court would vote for Marbury. But to deny Marbury's claim was to concede the issue to the Jeffersonians.

Marshall devised a shrewd solution to the case of *Marbury* v. *Madison*. In February 1803, he delivered the opinion of the Court. Marshall and his colleagues held that the Judiciary Act of 1789, under which Marbury had brought suit, contradicted the plain words of the Constitution about the Court's original jurisdiction. Marshall dismissed Marbury's claim, saying that the Court, according to the Constitution, had no power to require the commission to be delivered. But Marshall thereby asserted a greater power for the Court—that of **judicial review,** the power of the courts to hold acts of Congress and the executive in violation of the Constitution. Conceding a small battle over Marbury's commission (he did not get it), Marshall won a much larger war, asserting for the courts the power to determine what is and is not constitutional.

More than any other power of the courts, judicial review has embroiled them in policy controversy. Before the Civil War, the Supreme Court, headed by Chief Justice Roger Taney, held the Missouri Compromise unconstitutional because it restricted slavery in the territories. The decision was one of many steps along the road to the Civil War. After the Civil War, the Court was again active, this time using judicial review to strike down dozens of state and federal laws curbing the growing might of business corporations.

The Nine Old Men. Never was the Court so controversial as during the New Deal of Franklin D. Roosevelt. At Roosevelt's urging, Congress passed dozens of laws designed to end the Depression. The Court, though, was dominated by conservative justices, most appointed by Republican presidents, who viewed federal intervention in the economy as unconstitutional and tantamount to socialism.

The Supreme Court began to dismantle New Deal policies one by one. One of the string of antidepression measures was the National Recovery Act. It was never particularly popular, but the Court sealed its doom in *Schechter Poultry Corporation* v. *United States* (1935), declaring the Act unconstitutional because it regulated purely local business that did not affect interstate commerce. Incensed, Roosevelt in 1937 proposed what critics called a "court-packing plan." Noting that the average age of the Court was over seventy, he railed against those "nine old men." Since Congress can set the number of justices, he proposed that Congress expand the size of the Court, a move that would have allowed him to appoint additional justices sympathetic to the New Deal. Congress objected and never passed the plan. Indeed, it became irrelevant when two Supreme Court justices, Chief Justice Charles Evans Hughes and Associate Justice Owen Roberts, began switching their votes, in favor of

The "Court-packing" Plan. *During the New Deal, the Supreme Court struck down many of President Roosevelt's policies as unconstitutional. Roosevelt proposed to "pack" the Court by adding one new member for each member over seventy years old. This step would have created a Court in FDR's image, but the idea was opposed even by many New Deal proponents.*

The Courts and Democracy. *Federal judges are among our unelected policymakers, and critics have often claimed that their decisions have contradicted the public's preferences. Unable to vote judges out of office, their critics look for other ways to influence the courts. So bold and liberal were the Warren Court's decisions that calls for Warren's impeachment sprang up. In the halls of Congress, Representative (later President) Gerald R. Ford led the unsuccessful drive to impeach Justice William O. Douglas, with whom Ford strongly disagreed.*

New Deal legislation. (One wit called it the "switch in time that saved nine.") Shortly thereafter, Associate Justice William Van Devanter retired, and Roosevelt got to make the first of his many appointments to the Court.

The Warren Court. Few eras of the Supreme Court have been as active in shaping public policy as that of the Warren Court, presided over by Chief Justice Earl Warren (1953–69). Scarcely had President Eisenhower appointed Warren when the Court faced the issue of school segregation. In 1954 it held that laws requiring segregation of the public schools were unconstitutional. Later it expanded the rights of criminal defendants, extending the right to counsel and protections against unreasonable search and seizure and self-incrimination (see pages 155–156). It ordered states to reapportion their legislatures according to the principle of one person, one vote. So active was the Warren Court that right-wing groups, fearing that it was remaking the country, posted billboards all over the United States, urging "Impeach Earl Warren." [17]

The Burger Court. Warren's retirement in 1969 gave President Richard Nixon his hoped-for opportunity to appoint a "strict constructionist"— that is, one who interprets the Constitution narrowly—as chief justice.

[17] An excellent overview of the Warren period is by former Watergate special prosecutor and Harvard law professor Archibald Cox, *The Warren Court* (Cambridge, Mass.: Harvard University Press, 1968).

He chose Minnesotan Warren E. Burger, then a conservative judge on the District of Columbia Court of Appeals. As Nixon hoped, the Burger Court turned out to be more conservative than the liberal Warren Court. It narrowed defendants' rights, though it did not overturn the fundamental contours of the *Miranda* decision. The conservative Burger Court, however, also wrote the abortion decision in *"Roe"* v. *Wade* (see pages 489–490), required school busing in certain cases to eliminate historic segregation, and upheld affirmative action programs in the *Weber* case (see pages 496–497). One of the most notable decisions of the Burger Court weighed against Burger's appointor, Richard Nixon. At the height of the Watergate scandal (pages 407–409), the Supreme Court was called upon to rule on whether Nixon's White House tapes must be turned over to Congress. It ordered him unanimously to do so, and thus sealed his presidential doom (***United States* v. *Nixon,*** 1974).

By the mid-1980s, Ford, Nixon, and Reagan appointees composed a clear Supreme Court majority. Its two most liberal members, Marshall and Brennan, were two of the oldest justices, and five of the nine justices were over 75. One justice, Harry A. Blackmun, even took the extraordinary step of speaking out publicly at the Cosmos Club in Washington. The Supreme Court, he said, "was moving to the right . . . where it wants to go, by hook or by crook." It had become, he remarked sadly, "a rotten way to earn a living." [18] Like other justices, including its Chief, he complained about the growing agenda of the Court. Now, as in times past, issues of equality and the economy are prominent on that agenda; now, too, courts deal more and more with questions of energy and environment.

The Supreme Court and Equality

From Slavery to "Separate but Equal." In an era of slavery, the Supreme Court, like other American institutions, consistently upheld the slave system. The boldest—and by contemporary standards, the most inegalitarian and outrageous—decision in defense of slavery was ***Dred Scott* v. *Sandford*** (1857). The case involved the claim by the slave Dred Scott that he should be declared a free man. His owner had taken him to several states and territories where slavery was illegal. He sued to have the Court declare that his residence in a free territory made him free. Chief Justice Taney, in a far-reaching decision, bluntly announced that slaves were not citizens and therefore were not entitled to sue. Further, he said, Congress had no authority to ban slavery in the territories.

A trilogy of post-Civil War amendments shaped subsequent policy regarding the equality of black Americans. The Thirteenth abolished slavery. The Fourteenth forbade any state to deny its citizens "equal protection of the laws." The Fifteenth guaranteed the right to vote, regardless of race. Sadly, an era of segregation followed the era of slavery.

The Court provided a constitutional justification for segregation in the 1896 case of ***Plessy* v. *Ferguson.*** The case came to the Court on appeal from Louisiana, whose legislature had required "equal but separate accommodations for the white and colored races" in railroad transportation. Plessy, himself seven-eights white, had been arrested for refusing to

[18] *Washington Post Weekly Review,* October 1, 1984, p. 33.

leave a railway car reserved for white persons. The Supreme Court upheld the Louisiana statute. Segregation was not unconstitutional, the Court said, if facilities were separated but substantially equal. In subsequent decisions, though, the Court paid more attention to the separate than to the equal part of this dictum. Southern states were permitted, for example, to maintain high schools and professional schools for whites, even if there were none for blacks.

Ending Segregation. In the late 1940s, a new era began to dawn. The Court inched toward the end of its separate-but-equal doctrine. The first cracks came in decisions regarding admission to professional schools. In an Oklahoma case, *McLaurin* v. *Oklahoma Board of Regents* (1950), a black man had been admitted to law school but was required to sit in separate areas, even to eat at a segregated cafeteria table. The Court ordered the full integration of the law school, so long as the state had no law school for blacks. Texas had a different strategy. It bought an old house not far from the University of Texas campus, put a few library books in it, hired a few black lawyers to teach there, and called it a black law school. In *Sweatt* v. *Painter* (1950) the Court rejected the notion that the hastily built law school could be substantially equal.

The end of legal segregation came in 1954. In **Brown v. Board of Education,** the Supreme Court set aside its earlier precedent in *Plessy* and held legally enforced school segregation inherently unconstitutional. (For more on *Brown*, see 3 .) Outraged southerners threatened to close their public schools, and a few counties did.

Throughout the South, the response to *Brown* was delay followed by more delay. But with a push from Congress in the Civil Rights Act of 1964, which cut off federal aid to segregated southern schools, desegregation progressed steadily in the South. Several federal courts ordered the busing of school children to achieve racially balanced schools, a practice upheld by the Burger Court in *Swann* v. *Charlotte-Mecklenberg County Schools* (1971). Issues of school desegregation moved north in the 1960s and 1970s, as northern federal courts found that school districts had used a variety of policies to promote segregation. School busing was ordered by courts in northern cities like Boston, Detroit, Denver, and Cleveland.

Affirmative Action. The 1960s and 1970s were an era of far-reaching policies, advocated by both Congress and the courts, to expand black equality. Many of these innovations used affirmative action programs (which we discuss at some length in Chapter 18). One such program was at the University of California at Davis. Eager to produce more minority physicians for California, the medical school set aside sixteen of a hundred places in the entering class for "disadvantaged groups." One white applicant who did not make the freshman class was Allan Paul Bakke. After he received his rejection letter from Davis, he decided to sue, claiming that he had been denied equal protection of the laws. The result was an important Supreme Court decision called **Regents of the University of California v. Bakke.** [19] 3

---

[19] For a thorough discussion of the affirmative action issues raised by the *Bakke* case, see Allan P. Sindler, *Bakke, De Funis, and Minority Admissions* (New York: Longman, 1978).

Bakke ended up in medical school, but Brian Weber, whom we met earlier (page 29), did not get into an apprenticeship program he wanted in Louisiana. In **Weber v. Kaiser Aluminum Company** (1979), the Court found that Kaiser's special training program was intended to rectify years of past employment discrimination at Kaiser. Thus, it said, a union-management sponsored program to take more blacks than whites did not discriminate against Weber. Emphasizing strongly the "narrowness of our inquiry," Justice Brennan's majority opinion was carefully couched to avoid a blanket endorsement of affirmative action programs.

The Burger Court did not go as far as most proponents of affirmative action would have preferred. The majority of the Court insisted in case after case that judicial remedies could not be applied unless an *intent* to discriminate could be shown. Lawyers for black police officers in Washington, D.C., for example, argued that a civil service test for police

---

3 | *Brown* and *Bakke:* Two Cases on Equality

BROWN v. BOARD OF EDUCATION (1954)

After searching carefully for the perfect case to challenge legal school segregation, the National Association for the Advancement of Colored People selected the case of Linda Brown. A black student in Topeka, Kansas, she was required by Kansas law to attend a segregated school. In Topeka, the visible signs of education—teacher quality, facilities, and so on—were substantially equal between black and white. Thus the NAACP chose the case in order to test the *Plessy* v. *Ferguson* doctrine of "separate but equal." The Court would be forced to rule directly on whether school segregation was *inherently* unequal and thus violated the Fourteenth Amendment's requirement that states guarantee "equal protection of the laws." Decisions in several recent cases (*Sweatt* and *McLaurin,* for example) had hinted that the Supreme Court was ready to overturn the *Plessy* precedent. The NAACP's general counsel, Thurgood Marshall, argued Linda Brown's case before the Supreme Court.

Chief Justice Earl Warren had just been appointed by President Eisenhower. So important was *Brown* that the Court had already heard one round of arguments before Warren joined the Court. The justices, after hearing the oral arguments, met in the Supreme Court Room. As is traditional, the chief justice summarized the case to his colleagues briefly and then turned to the most senior associate justice to present his views. Each, from the most senior to the newest member of the Court, spoke. Believing that a unanimous decision, with the opinion itself written by the chief justice, would have the most impact, the justices agreed that Warren himself should write the opinion.

Shortly before the decision was to be announced,

President Eisenhower invited the Warrens to dinner at the White House. Pointedly seating the chief justice near John W. Davis, the lawyer arguing the southern states' case in *Brown,* the president went out of his way to tell Warren what an able man Davis was. Taking Warren by the arm on the way to after-dinner coffee and drinks, Eisenhower put in his word against school integration. After Warren announced the *Brown* decision, he was never again invited to the White House by the man who appointed him. Although Eisenhower objected strongly to the decision, he later sent federal troops to Central High School in Little Rock, Arkansas, in 1958 to enforce its desegregation.

The Warren Court that decided Brown v. Board of Education *in 1954. From left to right, the justices are (front) Felix Frankfurter, Hugo Black, Earl Warren, Stanley Reed, William O. Douglas, (back) Tom Clark, Robert Jackson, Harold Burton, and Sherman Minton.*

All nine justices joined in making Brown *a unanimous decision.*

officers seeking promotions should be held unconstitutional by the Supreme Court. The effect of the test, they argued, was discriminatory because proportionally more whites than black officers passed the tests. But the Supreme Court held in *Washington* v. *Davis* (1976) that the intent and not the effect of a policy made it discriminatory. Showing an intent to discriminate, of course, was not always easy. Affirmative action was thus constitutionally circumscribed.

The Courts and the Economy

Class and elite theorists maintain that our economics and our politics are closely linked. Our political system, they say, depends upon and nurtures an economy of property, where divisions of wealth are preserved. The courts may play a key role in economic decisions; they may

---

3 *Brown* and *Bakke:* Two Cases on Equality (continued)

REGENTS OF THE UNIVERSITY OF CALIFORNIA v. BAKKE (1978)

Allan Bakke, a thirty-two-year-old white male, applied to the medical school of the University of California at Davis. For two straight years, 1973 and 1974, he was rejected. UC-Davis operated a Special Admissions program, however, to facilitate a larger enrollment of "disadvantaged" students. Sixteen of the hundred entering slots were reserved for students applying under the Special Admissions Program. The mean scores of students admitted under this program were the forty-sixth percentile on verbal tests and the thirty-fifth on science tests. (These scores were from the MCAT—Medical College Admissions Test.) Bakke's scores on the same tests were at the ninety-sixth percentile on the verbal test and at the ninety-seventh on the science test. Bakke sued UC-Davis, claiming that it denied him equal protection of the law by discriminating against him because of his race.

The California Supreme Court agreed almost entirely with Bakke. It ordered UC-Davis to admit him to its freshman class. It also forbade UC-Davis to use race in any way as an admission standard. "No applicant," it said, "may be rejected because of his race, in favor of another who is less qualified." Losing in California's courts, UC-Davis took its case to the United States Supreme Court.

On June 28, 1978, the Court announced its decision. Unlike *Brown*, this case found the justices badly split. There were six separate opinions written by the justices. Justice Powell wrote the majority opinion. Joining him were Chief Justice Burger and Justices Stewart, Rehnquist, and Stevens. The Court ordered Bakke admitted, holding that the Davis Special Admissions Program did discriminate against him because of his race. But it

refused to order Davis never to use race as a criterion for admission. A university *could*, it said, adopt an "admissions program where race or ethnic background is simply one element—to be weighed fairly against other elements—in the selection process." It could *not*, as UC-Davis' Special Admissions Program did, set aside a quota of spots for particular groups.

Bakke graduated from the UC-Davis Medical School in 1982 and began his internship at the Mayo Clinic in Rochester, Minnesota.

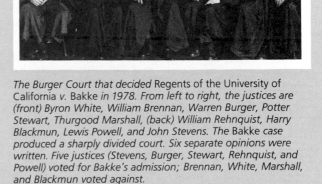

The Burger Court that decided Regents of the University of California v. Bakke in 1978. From left to right, the justices are (front) Byron White, William Brennan, Warren Burger, Potter Stewart, Thurgood Marshall, (back) William Rehnquist, Harry Blackmun, Lewis Powell, and John Stevens. The Bakke case produced a sharply divided court. Six separate opinions were written. Five justices (Stevens, Burger, Stewart, Rehnquist, and Powell) voted for Bakke's admission; Brennan, White, Marshall, and Blackmun voted against.

buttress—or weaken—the underpinnings of the capitalist economy. For most of our history, the courts have stood foursquare behind the capitalist system. In one of its early but important decisions, the Supreme Court faced a seemingly insignificant issue involving tiny Dartmouth College. Dartmouth, it seemed, faced a battle with the New Hampshire legislature, bent on revoking its charter granted by the king in colonial days. The Supreme Court, in ***Dartmouth College v. Woodward*** (1819) held that a charter of a corporation, such as Dartmouth's, is a legal contract and cannot be tampered with by a government. This was a momentous decision in favor of private property. Today, courts even consider corporations as "legal persons" for some purposes. Like you and me, a corporation enjoys constitutional protections.

Legal historian Morton Horwitz, carefully tracing the development of American law from 1780 through 1860, showed how it came to support a capitalist system. "By the middle of the nineteenth century," he concluded, "the legal system had been reshaped to the advantage of men of commerce and industry at the expense of farmers, workers, consumers, and other less powerful groups within society." [20] It protected corporations against public regulation, supported creditors against debtors, and guaranteed the sanctity of private property.

After the Civil War, the Supreme Court continued to protect business interests. In case after case the Court struck down state efforts to regulate business. It frequently used the Fourteenth Amendment's "due process" clause as the basis for these decisions. Congressional efforts to rein in the massive trusts of the era were also blunted by the Court. In 1895 the Court held (in *United States* v. *E. C. Knight Company*) that antitrust laws did not apply to firms engaged in manufacturing, which was, of course, where most of the trusts were. For years, this decision thwarted the government's power to control monopolies.

Well into the 1930s, when the Depression raged, the Court held firmly to its probusiness philosophy. It was President Calvin Coolidge who said, "The business of America is business," but the words could have come from the Court. Most efforts by Roosevelt and the Congress to use federal policy to stimulate the economy met opposition from the "nine old men" of the Court. Only the "switch in time that saved nine" headed off a constitutional collision between Roosevelt and the Court.

Today, about two-fifths of all Supreme Court cases involve economic issues. [21] Mighty AT&T, "Ma Bell," was broken up into one large and seven small telephone companies (the "Baby Bells") because of a court decision that the telephone company could not have a monopoly. That you can now own your phone and have a choice of long-distance companies is a result of a court-ordered breakup of the multibillion-dollar Bell System.

---

[20] Morton J. Horwitz, *The Transformation of American Law, 1780–1860* (Cambridge, Mass.: Harvard University Press, 1977), pp. 253–54.

[21] Craig R. Ducat and Robert L. Dudley, "Supreme Court Economic Decisions," paper presented at the Annual Meeting of the Midwest Political Science Association, Chicago, Illinois, April 11–15, 1984, p. 2.

The Courts and Economic Policy. *Court decisions have a great impact on the American economy. For years, the United States Department of Justice (including these staff members) battled the giant communications monopoly, AT&T. Finally, they reached an out-of-court agreement to break AT&T up into smaller companies. The agreement, which would raise long distance telephone rates considerably, had to be approved by a federal district court judge. Judge Harold Greene ordered the parties to modify the agreement so the new local phone companies and their customers would get a fairer shake.*

The Courts, Energy, and Environment

For most of our nation's two centuries, issues of environment and energy were not on our policy agenda, and certainly not on the judicial agenda. Still, technological changes put them high on the country's list of worries and thus—as de Tocqueville predicted—in the courtroom. Environmentalists have enjoyed more success than perhaps any other group in using the courts to accomplish policy ends.[22] An endangered species, a proposed nuclear plant, a leasing of federal lands to oil seekers —all will bring instant suit from an environmental legal action group.

The environmentalists' legal salvation has been the National Environmental Protection Act, called NEPA for short.[23] Passed during the Nixon administration, it requires all governmental and most private units undertaking a project that might affect the environment to issue an "environmental impact statement." Technically, even if an environmental impact statement filed with the Environmental Protection Agency asserted that the sky would fall if such-and-such were built, no one can forbid its construction on that ground alone. However, environmental lawyers have become specialists at "analysis paralysis." They can often persuade judges to hold that environmental impact statements were improperly prepared and thus delay projects year after unprofitable year.

[22] On group use of the litigation process, see Karen Orren, "Standing to Sue: Interest Group Conflict in the Federal Courts," *American Political Science Review* 70 (September 1976): 723–42.
[23] On NEPA in the courts, see Richard Liroff, *A National Policy for the Environment: NEPA and Its Aftermath* (Bloomington: Indiana University Press, 1976).

Because challenges to regulatory commissions (such as the Nuclear Regulatory Commission, which licences nuclear plants) must come to the District of Columbia Court of Appeals, that liberal tribunal has done much to support environmental policies. In one notable clash between courts, the D.C. Circuit in 1978 decided a case called *Vermont Yankee Nuclear Power Plant* v. *Natural Resources Defense Council*. Environmentalists had sued the utility constructing a plant called Vermont Yankee, charging that the environmental protection statements were in error. The D.C. Court ordered construction halted, thus driving up the cost even if the plant was subsequently built. Later the Burger Court wrote a blistering decision overturning the D.C. appeals court. Unanimously, the Supreme Court held that the decision was "judicial intervention run riot." Vermont Yankee was back in business, but only after years of delay.

UNDERSTANDING THE COURTS

The Courts and Democracy

Announcing his retirement, Justice Potter Stewart made a few remarks to the handful of reporters present. Embedded in his brief statement was this observation: "It seems to me that there's nothing more antithetical to the idea of what a good judge should be than to think it has something to do with representative democracy." He meant that judges should not be subject to the whims of popular majorities. In a nation that insists so strongly that it is democratic, where do the courts fit in?

In some ways, the courts are not a very democratic institution. Federal judges are not elected and are almost impossible to remove. Indeed, their social backgrounds probably make the courts the most elite-dominated policymaking instituion. If democracy requires that key policymakers always be elected or be continually responsible to those who are, then the courts diverge sharply from the requirements of democratic government.

Yet the courts are not entirely independent of popular preferences. Turn-of-the-century Chicago humorist Finley Peter Dunne had his Irish saloonkeeper character "Mr. Dooley" quip that "th' Supreme Coort follows th' iliction returns." Many years later, political scientist Richard Funston analyzed the Supreme Court decisions in critical election periods. He found that "the Court is normally in line with popular . . . majorities." [24] Even when the Court seems out of step with other policymakers, it eventually swings around to join the policy consensus, as it did in the New Deal.

Courts can also promote pluralism. When groups go to court, they use litigation to achieve their policy objectives. We have seen that both civil rights groups and environmentalists have blazed a path to the courts. The legal wizard of the NAACP's litigation strategy, Thurgood Marshall, not only won most of his cases, but won for himself a seat on the Supreme

[24] Richard Funston, "The Supreme Court and Critical Elections," *American Political Science Review* 69 (1975): 810.

Court. Be aware that where there is pluralism, hyperpluralism may not be far behind. Almost every major policy decision these days ends up in court. Chances are good that some judge can be found who will see things your way. Agencies and businesses commonly find themselves ordered by different courts to do opposite things. The habit of always turning to the courts as a last resort can add to delay, deadlock, and inconsistency—the hallmarks of hyperpluralism.

Too Strong, Too Weak, or About Right? The Issue of Judicial Power

The courts, Alexander Hamilton wrote in the Federalist Papers, "will be least in capacity to annoy or injure" the people and their liberties. Throughout our history, critics of judicial power have disagreed. They see the courts as too powerful for their own—or the nation's—good. Yesterday's critics focused on John Marshall's "usurpations" of power, on the proslavery decision in *Dred Scott*, or on the efforts of the "nine old men" to kill off Franklin Roosevelt's New Deal legislation. Today's critics are never short of ammunition to show that courts go too far in making policy.

Courts make policy on both large and small issues. In recent years, courts have made policies on major issues involving school busing, abor-

The Courts and Social Policy: Bilingual Education. *These days, more and more crucial social policies are examined by the courts. One of these is bilingual education. The hispanic population of the United States is increasing, both in cities like San Antonio and in rural areas as well. Some hispanic parents have sued their local school district to compel the use of bilingual instruction in the schools. The courts have had to ask whether a citizen has a constitutional right to be instructed in his native language. Frequently, the courts have answered in the affirmative. They have also insisted that states with high levels of Spanish-speaking voters must print bilingual ballots.*

tions, affirmative action, nuclear power, and other key issues. In other cases around the country, courts have done the following:

— Ordered the city of Mobile, Alabama, to change its form of government because it allegedly discriminated against minorities (the Supreme Court overturned this decision).
— Closed some prisons and ordered other states to expand their prison size.
— Eliminated high school diplomas as a requirement for a fireman's job.
— Decided that Mexican-American children have a constitutional right to a bilingual education. [25]

Critics of judicial activism stress that the courts, as unelected policymakers, are the least democratic branch of government. They believe that such decisions go well beyond the "referee" role of the courts in a democracy. Defenders of judicial activism weigh in with the argument that the courts are protectors of the Constitution, whether or not we agree with every judicial decision. Today, we expect the courts to right many wrongs. Some believe there is a "litigation explosion" in America.

"Hyperlexis": Is There a Litigation Explosion?

Michael Chow runs a Chinese restaurant in Manhattan. After a restaurant review in the *Guide Gault-Millau* that panned his pancakes, he sued the reviewers, winning $20,000. One federal court found that the Fourteenth Amendment's equal protection clause entitled a young female plaintiff the right to play Little League baseball. A San Jose man suffered the indignities of a broken date and sued, winning a court award of $38. A popular television show pits battlers in small claims court against one another and competes well with soap operas. At the end its announcer solemnly warns: "Don't take the law into your own hands, take 'em to court." To Chief Justice Burger and other observers of the American court system, more and more Americans are doing just that. We face, they say, a judicial gridlock from "hyperlexis" (a trumped-up Latin word from hyper = too much, and lexis = law).

Chief Justice Burger makes an annual State of the Judiciary speech. In recent years, his theme has been our growing litigiousness and the consequent judicial burden. The judicial system is so burdened, he remarked in 1983, that it "may literally break down before the end of this century." [26] Here are some bits of evidence for our "hyperlexis":

— Between 1960 and 1982, the number of civil suits filed in federal courts grew three and a half times.
— Federal court appeals grew sevenfold in the same periods.
— In state courts, which hear 98 percent of the civil cases, the number of civil suits increased by 22 percent in a recent five-year period.

[25] These and other examples of judicial activism are reported in a critical assessment of judicial intervention by Donald Horowitz, *The Courts and Social Policy* (Washington: The Brookings Institution, 1977), pp. 4–5.

[26] The quotation from the chief justice, together with the statistics on litigiousness, are from the *New York Times*, June 1, 1983, p. A17.

— The number of $1 million or larger verdicts in damage suits grew from one in 1962 to 239 twenty years later.

To many observers, America is turning into a nation of plaintiffs. There are several reasons, the first being *big government* itself. Regulations breed challenges to regulation. Individuals and groups sue the government to block unwanted regulation; the government in turn sues to enforce its regulations. Second is the phenomenal *growth of the legal profession.* The number of lawyers in America has doubled since 1960 to more than 600,000, with 35,000 new lawyers spewing from our law schools annually. One in every 400 Americans is a lawyer, compared with fewer than one in a thousand in England. Crèvecoeur's *Letters of an American Farmer* (1787) remarked that lawyers "promote litigiousness and amass more wealth than the most opulent farmer with all his toil." [27]

Not every scholar agrees that we are in the midst of a litigation explosion. The most important work undertaken on the topic is by Marc Galanter and David Trubek. [28] Most disputes, they found, never come to court. In five judicial districts, they conducted surveys to determine the

[27] Ibid.
[28] Marc Galanter, "Reading the Landscape of Disputes: What We Know and Don't Know (and Think we Know) about out Allegedly Contentious and Litigious Society," *UCLA Law Review* 31 (October 1983): 4–71; David M. Trubek, et al., "The Costs of Ordinary Litigation," *UCLA Law Review,* 31 (November 1983): 72–127.

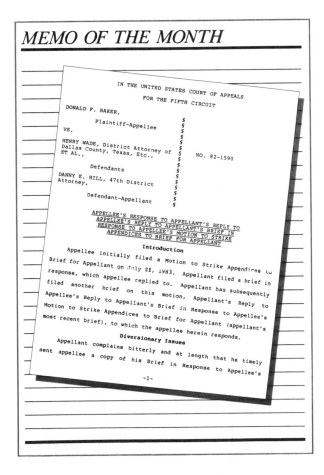

MEMO OF THE MONTH

IN THE UNITED STATES COURT OF APPEALS
FOR THE FIFTH CIRCUIT

DONALD F. BAKER,

    Plaintiff-Appellee

VS.

HENRY WADE, District Attorney of
Dallas County, Texas, Etc.,
ET AL.,

               NO. 82-1590

    Defendants

DANNY E. HILL, 47th District
Attorney,

    Defendant-Appellant

APPELLEE'S RESPONSE TO APPELLANT'S REPLY TO
APPELLEE'S REPLY TO APPELLANT'S BRIEF IN
RESPONSE TO APPELLEE'S MOTION TO STRIKE
APPENDICES TO BRIEF FOR APPELLANT

Introduction

Appellee initially filed a Motion to Strike Appendices to Brief for Appellant on July 11, 1983. Appellant filed a brief in response, which appellee replied to. Appellant has subsequently filed another brief on this motion, Appellant's Reply to Appellee's Reply to Appellant's Brief in Response to Appellee's Motion to Strike Appendices to Brief for Appellant (appellant's most recent brief), to which the appellee herein responds.

Diversionary Issues

Appellant complains bitterly and at length that he timely sent appellee a copy of his Brief in Response to Appellee's

-1-

Litigation. Sometimes litigation can get out of hand. This memo is a rather silly and perhaps innocuous example of the extremes to which lawyers can be carried. However, some are concerned that the level of litigation in the United States has reached ominous proportions. The memo was cited in the Washington Monthly of June 1985 as the Memo of the Month.

dispute resolution process. These included business disputes, neighborly (or unneighborly) disputes, and other sorts of conflicts among people. Just over 11 percent eventually led to litigation. Of those disputes taken to court, the vast majority were settled before they came to trial, abandoned, or withdrawn. Trials are a relatively rare event in American life. Overall, 9 percent of Americans have had experience with a major civil court and 14 percent with a minor one, sometimes merely as a juror.

Even though disputes that go to court are relatively rare, Galanter and Trubek found that litigation was increasing. They reported a "dramatic rise" in the number of cases filed in federal courts in recent years and a significant increase in the number of appeals from state to federal courts. One reason is that, as a rule, "litigation pays." In the typical court case that actually came to trial, the plaintiffs recovered more than they spent on the cost of the trial. And, of course, it pays for attorneys, too. The typical attorney in Trubek's study made $45,000 a year. Five percent made more than $100,000. Where there is money to be made in litigation, attorneys will be there to help people make it.

Those who fear the litigation explosion argue that it not only overburdens the courts, but also puts policymaking into the hands of inexpert individuals (judges). Ours is a technologically complex society. Judges, says Horowitz, are generalists, the least likely among national policymakers to be informed fully about complex issues. "That judges are generalists," he adds, "means, above all that they lack information and may also lack experience and skill to interpret such information as they may receive."[29] Nevertheless, judges must decide on issues ranging from

[29] Horowitz, *The Courts and Social Policy*, p. 31.

"*If I make you drink your milk you'll sue me?*"

Drawing by W. Miller; © 1978 The New Yorker Magazine, Inc.

ethical and biomedical problems of abortions to engineering problems of a nuclear power plant's environmental impact statement. Congress and the president solve their information problems by relying on specialized bureaucracies and staffs. But judgeships are typically one-person operations. Even the Supreme Court justices have only four clerks apiece, each juggling scores of cases at any one time.

As long as Americans insist on taking their grievances to court, and as long as congress and the bureaucracy adopt thousands of regulations and laws annually, the Courts will be expected to intervene. Our age is hardly the first in which the policymaking role of the courts has been under attack.

THE COURTS SUMMARIZED

Ours is a complex system of justice. Sitting at the pinnacle of the judicial system is the Supreme Court, but its importance is often exaggerated. Most judicial policymaking and norm enforcement take place in the state courts and the lower federal courts.

Throughout our political history, courts have shaped public policy about the economy, equality, and, most recently, energy and the environment. In the economic arena, courts traditionally favored corporations, especially when government tried to regulate them. Since the New Deal, though, the courts have been more tolerant of government regulation of business, shifting much of their policymaking attention to issues of equality. From *Dred Scott* to *Plessy* to *Brown*, the Court has moved from a role of reinforcing discriminatory policy toward racial minorities to a role of shaping new policies. Today, it confronts in cases like *Bakke* and *Weber* the complex issue of affirmative action. Most recently, environmental groups have used the courts to achieve environmental goals.

The courts have exhibited democratic, elitist, pluralist, and hyperpluralist tendencies. A critical view of the courts claims that they are too powerful for the nation's own good and rather ineffective policymakers besides. Throughout our history, however, judges have been important agenda-setters in our political system, particularly in the policy arena of equality and minority rights.

Key Terms

federal district courts	precedent	*Brown* v. *Board of*
courts of appeal	litigants	*Education*
senatorial courtesy	original jurisdiction	*Regents of the*
case	appellate jurisdiction	*University of*
plaintiff	writ of certiorari	*California* v. *Bakke*
defendant	opinion	*Weber* v. *Kaiser*
jury	judicial	*Aluminum*
criminal law	implementation	*Company*
civil law	judicial review	*Dartmouth College* v.
judicial restraint	*United States* v. *Nixon*	*Woodward*
judicial activism	*Dred Scott* v. *Sanford*	
stare decisis	*Plessy* v. *Ferguson*	

For Further Reading

Baum, Lawrence. *The Supreme Court*, 2nd ed. (1985). A brief, excellent work on the operations and impact of the Court.

Carp, Robert A., and C. K. Rowland. *Policymaking and Politics in the Federal District Courts* (1983). The best work on the operations of the lower federal courts.

Cox, Archibald. *The Warren Court* (1968). A generally sympathetic view of the Warren period.

Feeley, Malcolm. *The Process is the Punishment* (1979). A study of local courts in New Haven, showing that justice at the local level departs significantly from our norms of equal justice under law.

Horowitz, Donald. *The Courts and Social Policy* (1977). Critical assessment of the courts' role in social issues.

Johnson, Charles A., and Bradley C. Canon. *Judicial Policies: Implementation and Impact* (1984). One of the best overviews of judicial policy implementation.

Wasby, Stephen. *The Supreme Court in the Federal Judicial System*, 2nd ed. (1984). A standard text on the Supreme Court.

Woodward, Bob, and Scott Armstrong. *The Brethren* (1979). A gossipy, "insider's" portrayal of the Supreme Court.

Budgeting: Taxing, Spending, and Public Policy

MEMO

The rise of public spending is one of the most universal characteristics of modern government. In our four communities, and everywhere else, the government's budget touches the lives of families and firms.

There are two keys to understanding government budgets: the budgetary *process* and the budget's *content,* both of which we examine in this chapter. Congress, the bureaucracies, the president, and the interest groups are actively involved in the budget process. The content of the budget refers to its sources and to the items it supports. Thus "where it comes from" and "where it goes" are two important budget issues.

Today our government in Washington spends about $1,000,000,000,000 a year—$1 trillion. Its use—and, some people think, misuse—is one of the most hotly contested issues in national politics.

When President Reagan was first elected in 1980, he promised to pare the federal budget. It was, he claimed, too large and thus required too much of our hard-earned dollars in taxes. In his 1984 campaign, he reiterated his call for major reductions in the government's budget without a tax increase. By then, it was more than a matter of philosophy. Government was running $200 billion in the red by the first year of Reagan's second term. Yet, well into the president's second term, government had not stemmed the tide of rising budgets. Even an influential president like Ronald Reagan has not been able to pare the size of government. It is worth trying to figure out why.

IN SAN ANTONIO, federal dollars had funded most of the construction of highway I-35. It linked San Antonians with high-tech industries in and around nearby Austin. In San Jose, federal defense contracts keep high-tech industries going, even at a time when families and firms buy less hardware and software. Of course, Smyrna could never have put together a package to attract the Nissan plant without federal dollars. U.S. government moneys helped train workers, build new utilities, and inspect the occupational safety of the Nissan plant. And no community is more in need of federal aid than Bethlehem. Governmental benefits have helped keep the wolf from the door of many an unemployed steel worker's family.

Let us be honest: Few people enjoy budgeting and even fewer enjoy reading about budgets, for they seem forbidding and complicated. President Reagan's proposed 1986 budget, the one he submitted to Congress in February 1985, was a massive document. But packed into its pages were public policies, the decisions of government on thousands of issues. Our job in this chapter is not only to show what government does with its $1 trillion annual budget, but also to connect that budget to the lives of people. One way of doing so is shown in ①.

---

① People, Policies, and Budgets: Reagan's Hit List

As President Reagan began his second term, the government was awash in an ocean of red ink. Forecasters predicted at least a $200 billion annual shortfall between revenues and expenditures every year for the rest of the 1980s. Against these dire projections, Reagan proposed to Congress an austere budget for domestic programs in 1985. The cuts, he insisted, were necessary to reduce the deficit and fund a 13 percent increase in the defense budget.

Where angels fear to tread, budget directors may have to wade in. The president's budget director, David Stockman, waded in hip-deep. Reagan's budget, he said, would end a "twenty-year binge" of aid to college students. It would cut out the Job Corps. The cost of each Job Corps training slot, he stressed, was $15,200, which "nearly equals the annual cost of sending a student to Harvard or Stanford." Military retirement benefits drew his ire. "It's a scandal," he said, that "institutional forces in the military are more concerned about protecting their retirement benefits than they are about protecting the security of the American people." It was a long hit list, this detailing of the various government budgets which Reagan proposed to cut. Together, they would save $55 billion a year.

Here is a short listing of some of the programs that Reagan's 1986 budget would reduce and the estimated two-year savings from each item:

— Cut back drastically, and eventually eliminate, subsidies to farmers.
— Reduce general revenue sharing for localities by $12.6 billion. This would, for example, eliminate support in some communities for local police and fire departments and other services. There would be fewer police and fire personnel hired and trained and fewer on the streets.
— Reduce college student loan obligations by $700 million. Only families making less than $32,000 would be eligible for student loans, which would be limited to $4,000 a year. Students at more expensive and private schools would lose their aid altogether; those from upper middle-class families would be on their own in paying for books and tuition.
— Eliminate the Job Corps, providing job training for 80,000 young men and women, but costing $100 million a year.
— Confine all Veterans Administration medical care to the disabled, the poor, and those with war-related injuries at a savings of a $1 billion.

These are but a few of the proposals to reduce government expenditures outlined in the president's budget message. Chances are that one or more of them has some effect on you or someone you know.

James C. Miller III, Director of the OMB. *When David Stockman, President Reagan's first director of the Office of Management and Budget, left Washington for Wall Street, he was succeeded by James C. Miller III. Miller had been chairman of the Federal Trade Commission. He promised to be less outspoken and a more team-oriented budget director than his predecessor had been.*

One reason for these reductions in spending in Reagan's 1986 budget was that government was short of money under the Reagan administration. The national debt was rising sharply. By the end of December 1984, the total federal debt was $1.663 trillion, growing to an expected $1.9 trillion by the end of 1985, and more than $2 trillion in 1986. If these estimates are correct, it will have balooned from less than $1 trillion to more than $2 trillion in just five years. About 15 percent of all current budget expenditures go to paying just the *interest* on this debt.

A budget **deficit** occurs when federal **expenditures** exceed federal **revenues.** The purpose of this chapter is to examine how those expenditures, revenues, and deficits come about. In a word, we look at how government manages its money—really, of course, *our* money.

BIG GOVERNMENT, BIG BUDGETS

Among the most important changes of the twentieth century is the rise of large governments.[1] The phenomenon of government growth is not unique to the United States. Large as it is, our government is small relative to other nations. Among western nations, we have one of the *smallest* public sectors relative to the size of our GNP. The explanations for the universal growth of government cannot, therefore, be unique to the United States.

[1] For some perspectives on the rise of government expenditures, see Daviel Tarschys, "The Growth of Public Expenditures: Nine Modes of Explanation." *Scandanavian Political Studies* 10 (1975):9–31; David Cameron, "The Expansion of the Public Economy: A Comparative Analysis," *American Political Science Review* 72 (December, 1978):1243–61; David Lowery and William D. Berry, "The Growth of Government in the United States: An Empirical Assessment of Competing Explanations," *American Journal of Political Science* 27 (November 1983):665–94.

As with other western democracies, the growth of government in the United States has been dramatic. Political scientist E.E. Schattschneider took a long look backward at government growth:

> The beginnings were almost unbelievably small. In 1792, the federal government was about as large as that of Poughkeepsie or Green Bay today. It resembled the present government in about the way Henry Ford's old bicycle shop resembles the modern Ford Motor Company. President Washington made his budget on a single sheet of paper. Jefferson ran his Department of Foreign Affairs with a staff of six writing clerks. The government issued three patents in 1790. As late as 1822 the government spent $1000 for the improvement of rivers and harbors and President Monroe vetoed a $9000 appropriation for the repair of the Cumberland Road. [2]

This was, said Schattschneider, the "grain of mustard seed" from which our government has grown. Today, our governments—national, state, and local—spend a third of the Gross National Product. The national government alone spends about 23 percent of the GNP.

No one, of course, knows exactly why government has grown so rapidly in all the western democracies. Lowery and Berry launched a major assault on the question but came up with no strong support for any particular theory of government growth. [3] This we know for sure: The rise of big government has been strongly resistant to reversal. Even Ronald Reagan, popular and personally persuasive, has succeeded in slowing the *growth* of government, but not in actually trimming its size.

Two conditions associated with government growth in America are the rise of the social service state and the rise of the national security state. Let us examine them briefly.

The Rise of the Social Service State

In 1935, during the depths of the Great Depression and the administration of President Franklin D. Roosevelt, the **Social Security Act** was passed by Congress. It was intended to provide a minimal level of sustenance to older Americans and thus to save them from poverty.

In January 1940, the treasurer of the United States sent the nation's first social security check to Mrs. Ida Fuller of Brattleboro, Vermont. The check was for the sum of $22.54. An early entrant into the then fledgling social security program, Mrs. Fuller had contributed less than the amount of her first check to the system. But by the time she died in December 1974, at the age of 100, she had collected $20,944.42 from the Social Security Administration. These days, nearly 40 million Americans receive checks (now coming in a rainbow of colors and without the familiar punched holes) from the social security system. Each check is mailed dutifully on the third day of each month from Washington. In the 1950s, disability insurance was included in the social security program. Thus, workers who had not retired but who were disabled could also

Social Security Retirement Benefits. *Ida Fuller was the first recipient of a social security check. She had paid a total of $22 in social security taxes, and she received more than $20,000 in benefits from the Social Security Administration between 1940 and her death in 1975 at age 100.*

[2] E. E. Schattschneider, *Two Hundred Million Americans in Search of a Government* (New York: Holt, Rinehart and Winston, 1969), pp. 29–30.
[3] Lowery and Berry, "Growth of Government."

collect benefits. In 1965, added to the system was **medicare,** which provides both hospital and physician coverage to retired and to some poor persons. Today, barely half the social security checks go to retired workers—people who are today's equivalents of Mrs. Fuller. Others go to the disabled, to Medicare patients, and others who qualify. Social Security has become the most expensive public policy in the world.

Social security is less than an insurance program than a sort of intergenerational contract. [2] Money is essentially taken from the working members of the population and spent on the retired members. Today, demographic and economic realities threaten to dilute this intergenerational bargain. In 1940 the entire social security system was financed with a 3 percent tax on payrolls; by the 1980s, the tax was about 14 percent, and it was to go higher. Economist Eli Ginzberg calculated that in 1945 fifty workers paid taxes to support each social security beneficiary. In 1980 each beneficiary was supported by about three workers. By 2035, when you will presumably be waiting for your social security check, fewer than two workers will be supporting each beneficiary.[4]

Not surprisingly, the social security program faced a problem as the 1980s dawned. As Paul Light candidly described the problem: "It was going broke fast. More money was going out in benefits than was coming in. . . . At the height of the crisis, social security was spending about

[4] Eli Ginzberg, "The Social Security System," *Scientific American* (January 1982):55. See also Alicia H. Munnell, *The Future of Social Security* (Washington, D.C.: The Brookings Institution, 1977).

---

[2] Is There Justice Between Generations? The Dilemma of Social Security

Phillip Longman retells an old thirteenth-century folktale about justice between generations. It is called "The Tale of the Ungrateful Son." An old man, it seems, has finally decided that he is unable to take care of himself and asks his adult son if he can move in with him and his family at their country farm. Promising to hand over his modest wealth when he dies, the old man moves in. But he becomes a greater and greater burden. Finally, the son decides to move his father to the barn where he can die quietly. Too embarrassed to tell his father directly, he asks his own son to take the grandfather to the barn and wrap him in their best horseblanket. The grandson sorrowfully does as he is told, but tears the blanket in half, giving the old man only one half of it. Yet the father is angry upon hearing that the child has used only half the blanket to wrap the grandfather and curses the grandson. "But father," the child replies, "I am saving the other half for you."

What, one should ask, does one generation owe to another? In the United States today, the Social Security system represents our major intergenerational commitment. It is a major commitment indeed. We spend more on older people at all levels of government than we do

on persons seventeen and younger by more than three to one. Not all of these older people, of course, are poor. Though there are poor people among the aged, older people's actual after-tax per capita income is higher than that of the rest of the population.

One thing which all older Americans have in common is a strong belief that they are entitled to benefits from the Social Security system, a program into which they paid for their working lives. Yet the Social Security system itself is troubled, and likely to become more so. The Social Security Administration's most optimistic predictions nonetheless contain gloomy scenarios. By 2055 the cost of disability benefits, pension benefits, and Medicare (Social security's three main programs) will be equivalent to 42 percent of *all* taxable payrolls in the United States. At the present, it consumes only 14 percent of all payrolls.

Like the farmer in the old folktale, we must ask, as a matter of public policy, what one generation owes to another.

Source: Phillip Longman, "Justice Between Generations," *Atlantic Monthly,* June, 1985, pp. 73–81.

$3000 more per minute than it was taking in." [5] Worse, that was only the short-term problem. Over the longer run, an aging population added more people to the social security rolls annually; once there, people tended to stay on the rolls because life expectancies are increasing. Said Light: "Diseases that once were life-threatening had been rendered harmless. If longevity continued to grow, most retirees could expect to live past ninety by the turn of the century." [6] Building automatic escalators for taxes has become a congressional necessity.

Social security, of course, is not the only social policy of the federal government that costs money. In health, education, job training, and scores of other areas, the rise of the social service state has contributed to our growing budget. No brief list could do justice to the range of social programs of the government, which provides moneys to assist the aged, businesses run by minority entrepreneurs, consumer education, drug rehabilitation, environmental education, food subsidies for the poor, guaranteed loans to college students, housing allowances for the poor, inspections of hospitals, and so on, running the alphabetical gamut. Liberals often favor these programs to assist individuals and groups in society; conservatives see them as a drain on the federal treasury. In any event, put them all together and they spell money.

The Rise of the National Security State

A generation ago, the most expensive part of the federal budget was not its social services, but its military budget. It was President Eisenhower—not some liberal antimilitary activist—who coined the term **military industrial complex** to characterize the close correspondence between military brass and the corporations who supply their hardware needs.

Before World War II, the United States largely disbanded its military forces at the end of a war. Since World War II, a "cold war" with the Soviet Union has resulted in a permanent military establishment and expensive military technology. Fueling the military machine has greatly increased the cost of government.

While President Reagan proposed scrapping scores of domestic programs in his 1986 budget request, he also urged Congress to increase the defense budget by 13 percent, but Congress balked. About $100 billion of his proposed $287.5 billion military budget would be spent on **procurement,** the purchase of military hardware. The costs of military procurement are high, even though total military expenditures have been declining as a percentage of our GNP since the end of World War II. The cost of technology, though, makes any weapon, fighter plane, or component more expensive than its predecessors. Critics single out particularly outrageous Pentagon expenditures as examples of military extravagance. One $436 hammer supplied by a defense contractor called Gould, Inc., could have been duplicated at your local hardware store for $10. Cost overruns are common. The Pentagon signs a contract for, say, a fighter-

[5] Paul Light, *Artful Work: The Politics of Social Security Reform* (New York: Random House, 1985), p. 89.
[6] Ibid., p. 95.

A Trident Submarine. *This is a Trident submarine, one of the jewels in the crown of the United States Navy and General Dynamics, whose Electric Boat Division built it. This one, in Florida, was christened by Marcia Meyers Carlucci, wife of the Deputy Secretary of Defense Frank Carlucci, in November 1981. The Trident can launch nuclear missiles and, because of its relative invisibility, is considered less vulnerable to Soviet attack than conventional land-based nuclear missiles. But it was an expensive piece of weaponry, a textbook example of the problem of cost-overruns in the Pentagon.*

bomber to be produced for $20 million per unit, but delays, unpredicted costs, and (some say) sheer profiteering raise the cost at delivery time. In 1984 and 1985, congressional hearings zeroed in on the most extreme of these abuses, particularly entertainment expenses, golf club memberships, and travel by executives of the defense contractors. Yet typically, the Pentagon has little option but to pay or reject the fighter-bomber it had wanted for its arsenal. Defense Secretary Weinberger claimed to have launched major reforms in procurement, even going so far as to cancel contracts temporarily with mighty General Dynamics. ☐3

Even without Pentagon extravagance, today's era of technological warfare is expensive. James Fallows remarks that "in nearly every weapons system, designers have pushed technology as the solution to American military problems, without distinguishing between the innovations that simply breed extra layers of complexity and those . . . that represent dramatic steps toward simplicity, flexibility, and effectiveness."[7] Payrolls for military personnel and pensions for its retirees add to an already high defense budget.

The rise of the social service state and the national security state together are linked with much of our governmental growth since the end of World War II. In the United States, although our social services have expanded less than they have in Western European nations, our military expenditures have expanded more rapidly. Together, they help explain why the watchword of governmental budgeting these days is growth.

---

[7] James Fallows, *National Defense* (New York: Vintage Books, 1981), p. 49.

One of the nation's largest defense contractors, General Dynamics, does $7 billion of business annually with the Defense Department. One of our largest (and in some years *the* largest) Pentagon contractors, General Dynamics alone could equip a mighty military with its Trident Submarines, Abrams Tanks, F-16 Fighters, and a host of other weaponry. Over the years, General Dynamics has run up millions, even billions, in cost overruns.

The Trident submarine was built by General Dynamics's Electric Boat Division in Groton, Connecticut. It cost nearly $1 billion more than the Navy contract specified. Congressional investigators discovered that mismanagement, poor morale, failure to order parts on time, and perhaps even fraudulent claims ran up the bills, which were paid by the Navy. General Dynamics billed the government for 90 percent of its $22 million in air travel costs, including ninety flights from headquarters in St. Louis to Albany, Georgia, where its president, David Lewis, owned a weekend retreat. (Lewis later allowed that "because of the horrible image we're getting out of this ... we have written the government and withdrawn our request for payment on all of those flights, period.")

More was to come. Company records indicated that General Dynamics billed the government for country club membership fees totalling $18,000 and even for kennel charges for an executive's dog. A Pentagon spokesman called the congressional testimony of two company executives "nauseating." Under pressure from Congress, Defense Secretary Weinberger in March 1985, suspended payments to General Dynamics for at least thirty days and ordered other changes in Pentagon procurement.

In May, 1985, the Defense Department went further. It cancelled two major contracts with General Dynamics and fined it $676,000 for giving gifts to Admiral Hyman Rickover, father of the Navy's nuclear submarine program. General Dynamics Chairman, David Lewis, announced his retirement no later than January 1, 1986. It was, said Admiral Stuart Pratt, "a horn to be heard all across the industry" of defense contractors. Critics thought it was more a beep than a foghorn.

Source: On the General Dynamics case, see *Newsweek*, February 11, 1985, pp. 24–25.

BUDGETING: THE PROCESS

Everyone has a basic understanding of budgeting. Public budgets are superficially like people's budgets. Aaron Wildavsky has remarked, "[A public budget] is a document, containing words and figures, which proposes expenditures for certain items and purposes." But there is more here than bookkeeping, because a **budget** is a policy document allocating burdens (taxes) and benefits (expenditures). Thus, budgeting is "concerned with the translation of financial resources into human purposes. A budget, therefore, may be characterized as a series of goals with price tags attached." [8]

You can get a quick overview of the federal budget if you examine the graph in 4 . It shows the two sides of the budgetary coin: revenues and expenditures. But the distribution of the government's $973.7 billion budget for fiscal year 1986 is the outcome of a very complex budgetary process. Nestled inside those tax and expenditure figures were thousands of policy choices, prompting plenty of politics.

Budgetary Politics

Public budgets are the supreme example of Harold Lasswell's definition of politics as "who gets what, when, and how." Budget battles are

[8] Aaron Wildavsky, *The Politics of the Budgetary Process*, 3rd ed. (Boston: Little, Brown, 1979), pp. 1–2. See also Robert D. Lee, Jr., and Ronald W. Johnson, *Public Budgeting Systems*, 2nd ed. (Baltimore: University Park Press, 1977), pp. 11–15.

fought over contending interests and ideologies. And everyone in Washington gets into the budgetary act.

Stakes and Strategies. Every political actor has a stake in the budget. Mayors want to keep federal grants-in-aid flowing in; defense contractors like a big defense budget; scientists like to see the National Science Foundation given a large budget. Not only groups outside the government but also agencies within it work to protect their interests. Individual members of Congress act as policy entrepreneurs for new ideas—which cost money—and support constituent benefits, which also do not come free. Presidents try to use budgets to manage the economy and leave their imprint on Congress' policy agenda.

You can think of budgetary politics as resembling a game in which players choose among strategies.[9] Agencies pushing their budgetary

[9] A good description of budgetary strategies is in Wildavsky, *The Politics of the Budgetary Process*, Chap. 3.

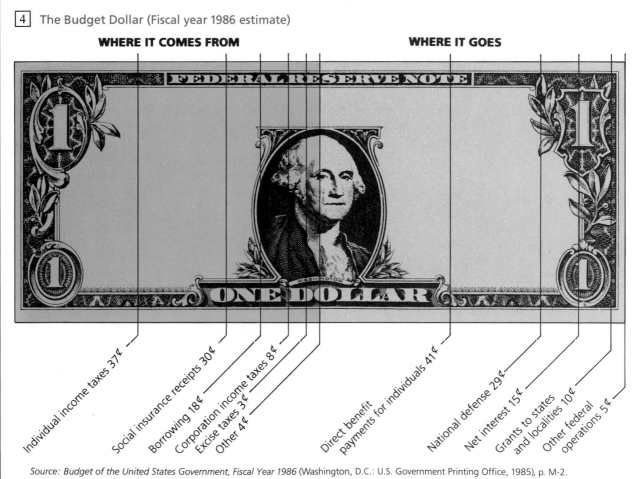

4 The Budget Dollar (Fiscal year 1986 estimate)

WHERE IT COMES FROM

WHERE IT GOES

Individual income taxes 37¢
Social insurance receipts 30¢
Borrowing 18¢
Corporation income taxes 8¢
Excise taxes 3¢
Other 4¢

Direct benefit payments for individuals 41¢
National defense 29¢
Net interest 15¢
Grants to states and localities 10¢
Other federal operations 5¢

Source: Budget of the United States Government, Fiscal Year 1986 (Washington, D.C.: U.S. Government Printing Office, 1985), p. M-2.

Farm Protests. *In 1985, the plight of the American farmer became a serious political issue. Bankruptcies among farmers were at high levels; prices for their products were not. The Reagan administration proposed reducing farm subsidies and returning agriculture to a "free market." These farmers came to Capitol Hill to protest this idea.*

needs to the president and Congress, for instance, try to link the benefits of their program to a senator's or representative's electoral needs.[10] Almost invariably, agencies pad their requests a bit, hoping that the almost inevitable cuts will be bearable. (President John Adams justified this now-common budgetary gambit by saying to his cabinet, "If some superfluity not be given [Congress] to lop off, they will cut into the very flesh of the public necessities.") Interest groups try to identify their favorite programs with the national interest. Mayors tell Congress, not how much they like to have federal aid flowing, but how crucial cities are to our national survival. Farmers do not stress that they like federal aid but that feeding a hungry nation and world is the main task of American agriculture. And so on. All the players have their own strategies in the game of budgetary politics. And in the pluralistic politics of budget-making, there are plenty of players.

The Players. Deciding how to carve up almost a quarter of the GNP is a process likely to attract plenty of interest, from those formally required to participate in the budgeting process as well as from those whose stakes are too big to ignore it. Here are the dramatis personae:

— *Interest groups.* No lobbyist worth his or her pay would ignore the budget. Lobbying for your group's needs takes place in the agencies, with the president (if you have access to him), and before congressional committees. The smart agency head will be sure to involve interest groups in defending his or her budget request.
— *The agencies.* Convinced of the importance of their mission, the heads of agencies almost always push for higher budget requests.

[10] For a discussion of the ways bureaucracies manipulate benefits to gain advantage with members of Congress, see Douglas Arnold, *Congress and the Bureaucracy* (New Haven, Conn.: Yale University Press, 1979), and the articles in Barry S. Rundquist (ed.), *Political Benefits* (Lexington, Mass.: D. C. Heath, 1980).

They send their requests to the Office of Management and Budget, but later they get a chance to go before congressional committees as well.

— *The Office of Management and Budget (OMB)*. OMB is responsible to the president, its boss. But no president has the time to understand and make decisions about the billions of dollars in the budget, parceled out to hundreds of agencies, some of which he never heard of. The director and staff of OMB have considerable independence from the president, making them major actors in the annual budget process.

— *The president*. The final decisions on what to propose to Congress are the president's. In early January, after the Congress has convened, the president gives a budget address and unveils the proposed budget, then spends many a day trying to make sure that Congress sticks close to his recommendations.

— *The tax committees in Congress*. You cannot spend money you do not have. The **House Ways and Means Committee** and the **Senate Finance Committee** write the tax codes, subject to the approval of Congress as a whole.

— *The Budget Committees and the CBO*. The Congressional Budget Office, the congressional equivalent of the OMB, and its parent committees, the Senate and House budget committees, are supposed to monitor the congressional budget process and keep it on schedule.

— *The subject-matter committees*. Committees of Congress write new laws, which require new expenditures. Committee members may use hearings to publicize the accomplishments of their pet agencies, thus supporting larger budgets for them, or to needle agency heads about waste or overspending.

— *The appropriations committees and their subcommittees*. The appropriations committee in each house decides who gets what. These committees take new or old policies coming from the subject-matter committees and decide how much to spend. Their subcommittees hold hearings on specific agency requests.

— *Congress as a whole*. The Constitution requires that Congress as a whole approve taxes and appropriations. Senators and representatives have a strong interest in delivering federal dollars to the folks back home. A dam here, a military base there, a new post office somewhere else—these are the items members look for in the budget.

— *The General Accounting Office (GAO)*. Congress' role does not end when it has passed the budget. The GAO works as Congress' eyes and ears, auditing, monitoring, and evaluating what agencies are doing with their budgets.

Budgeting involves a cast of thousands. But their roles are carefully scripted, their time on stage limited. This is because budget-making is both repetitive—the same things must be done each year—and cyclical—they must be done in the proper order and, more or less, on time. The budget cycle begins in the executive branch a full nineteen months before the fiscal year begins.

The Budget: Congress, the President and Public Opinion. *The Reagan administration sought numerous ways to reduce federal expenditures and also reduce the number of government-enforced regulations. One such reduction was a major political embarrassment. The Department of Agriculture, which supports and regulates the nutritional standards of school lunch programs, issued new rules which counted the ketchup on a hamburger as a vegetable. To dramatize the impact of the new rule and embarrass the administration, several members of the Senate ate an officially approved school lunch, complete with ketchup, in the Senate dining room. For this display, the press was more welcome than it usually is in the Senate dining room.*

The President's Budget

Until 1921, the various agencies of the executive branch sent their budget requests to the secretary of the treasury, who in turn forwarded them to the Congress. Presidents played a limited role in proposing the budget, or sometimes no role at all. Agencies basically peddled their own budget requests to Congress. But in 1921 Congress passed the Budget and Accounting Act. It required the president to propose an executive budget to Congress and created the Bureau of the Budget to help him. President Nixon reorganized the Bureau of the Budget and gave it a new name—the Office of Management and Budget (OMB). Its director is a presidential appointee requiring Senate approval. It now supervises preparation of the federal budget and advises the president on budgetary matters.

It takes a long time to prepare a presidential budget.[11] By law, the president must submit his budget on the fifteenth day of the new congressional session in January. Almost a year before, the process begins. [5] OMB communicates with each agency, sounding out its requests and tentatively issuing guidelines. By the summer, the president has decided

[11] One good review of the formation of the executive budget is in Dennis S. Ippolito, *The Budget and National Politics* (San Francisco: W. H. Freeman, 1978), Chap. 2.

on his overall policies and priorities and has established general targets for the budget. These are communicated to the agencies.

The budget-makers now get down to details. During the fall, the agencies submit formal, detailed estimates for their budgets, zealously pushing their needs to OMB. Budget analysts at OMB pare, investigate, weigh, and meet on agency requests. Typically, agency heads are asking for hefty increases. Sometimes they threaten to go directly to the president if their priorities are not met by OMB. As the Washington winter is setting in, the budget document is readied for final presidential approval. There is some last-minute juggling. Agencies may be asked to change their estimates to conform to the president's decisions. Cabinet members may make a last-ditch effort to bypass OMB and convince the president to increase their funds. With only days—or hours—left before the submission deadline, the budget document is rushed to the printers. The next steps are up to Congress.

---

5 | The President's Budget: An Approximate Schedule

SPRING

Budget policy developed

OMB presents an analysis of the economic situation to the president and discusses with him the budgetary outlook and policies. OMB then gives guidelines to the agencies, who review current programs and submit their projections of budgetary needs for the coming year to OMB. OMB goes over these projections and prepares recommendations to the president on final policy, programs, and budget levels. The president establishes guidelines and targets.

SUMMER

Agency estimates submitted

OMB conveys the president's decisions to the agencies and advises and assists them in preparing their budgets.

FALL

Estimates reviewed

The agencies submit to OMB formal budget estimates for the coming fiscal year, along with projections for future years. OMB holds hearings, reviews its assessment of the economy, and prepares budget recommendations for the president. The president reviews these recommendations and decides on the agencies' budgets and overall budgetary policy. OMB advises the agencies of these decisions.

WINTER

President's budget determined and submitted

The agencies revise their estimates to conform with the president's decisions. OMB once again reviews the economy. It drafts the president's budget message and prepares the budget document. The president revises and approves the budget message and transmits the budget document to Congress within fifteen days after it convenes.

Congress Gets into the Budget Act

According to the Constitution, all federal appropriations must be authorized by Congress. Thus, Congress always holds one trump card in national policymaking, the power of the purse.[12] No money is spent and no taxes are collected in direct response to the president's budget. He proposes, but Congress disposes. By law, Congress must figure out between January, when the president submits his proposed budget, and October 1, when the fiscal year begins, how to spend a trillion dollars.

For years, Congress budgeted in a piecemeal fashion. Each agency request was handled by a subcommittee of the House and Senate appropriations committees; then all these appropriations were added up to make a total budget. People never quite knew what the budget's "bottom line" would be until all the individual bills were totaled up. What Congress spent had little to do with any overall judgment of how much it should spend.

The **Congressional Budget and Impoundment Control Act of 1974** was designed to streamline the congressional budgetary process. Its supporters hoped that it would also make Congress less dependent on the president's budget and more able to set and meet its own budgetary goals. Here is what it established.

— *A fixed budget calendar.* For each step in the budgetary process there is an established completion date. In the past, Congress sometimes failed to appropriate money to agencies until after the fiscal year was over, leaving agencies drifting for months with no firm budget. Now there is a firm timetable mandated by law. ⬚6⬚
— *A committee on the budget in each house.* These two supercommittees must recommend to Congress target figures for the *total* budget size by April 15. By May 15, Congress must agree on the total size of the budget, which guides the appropriations committees in juggling figures for individual agencies.
— *A congressional budget office.* The new **Congressional Budget Office (CBO)** advises Congress on the likely consequences of its budget decisions; it forecasts revenues; and it is a counterweight to the president's OMB.

The new budgeting system was supposed to force Congress to consider the budget (both projected expenditures and projected revenues) as a whole, rather than in bits and pieces as it had before. An important part of the process of establishing a budget is setting limits on expenditures based on revenue projections. This is supposed to be done through a **reconciliation resolution.** Thus, in April, both Houses are expected to agree upon a reconciliation resolution, which binds Congress to a total expenditure level. This should be the bottom line of all federal spending for all programs. Only then is Congress supposed to begin acting on the individual appropriations. Later, it is supposed to pull these individual items together into a second reconciliation resolution.

[12] One important work on congressional budget-making is Richard Fenno, *The Power of the Purse* (Boston: Little, Brown, 1966). See also Allen Schick, *Congress and Money* (Washington, D.C.: The Brookings Institution, 1980).

Look at it like this. Family A might decide to budget by adding up all its needs and wants and calling that its budget. Such strategies almost guarantee overspending one's income. Family B, though, might begin by looking first at its revenue and then trying to bring its total expenditures into line with its revenue before dealing with its individual expenditure decisions. With its 1974 reforms, Congress was trying to force itself to behave more like Family B than Family A.

Have these reforms worked? If "worked" means whether Congress has brought its spending into line with its revenues, then the reforms are almost a total failure. Congressional budgets have been in the red every year since the 1974 amendments. Worse, the red ink has grown from a puddle to an ocean. The appropriations committees and their subcommittees still retain ample power to boost the budget recommendations beyond the reconciliation resolution. On the other hand, the 1974 reforms have helped to bring the big picture as well as the little ones to the

---

6 | **The Congressional Budget: Targets and Timetables**

JANUARY—APRIL 15 Information gathering and analysis		Congress receives the president's budget within fifteen days after it convenes. Committees and subcommittees hold hearings.
	March 15	Committees submit reports on outlays and revenues to the budget committees in each house.
	April 1	CBO submits a budget report to the budget committees, including an analysis of the president's budget.
APRIL 15—MAY 15 Debate and adoption of a congressional budget; establishment of spending priorities	April 15	The budget committees report their First Concurrent Resolution, which sets a total for budget outlays, an estimate of expenditures for major budget categories, and the recommended level of revenues. This resolution acts as an agenda for the remainder of the budgetary process.
	May 15	Committees report new proposed legislation authorizing expenditures. Both houses adopt the First Budget Resolution.
MAY 15—EARLY SEPTEMBER Enactment of spending bills	Seventh day after labor Day	Appropriations bills are passed and sent to the president. Congress completes action on all bills providing authority for the fiscal year beginning October 1. Budget committees prepare and report a Second Concurrent Resolution, which sets spending, revenue, and other ceilings for the coming fiscal year.
SEPTEMBER 15—SEPTEMBER 25 House and Senate actions reconciled; final budget determined	September 15	Congress adopts a Second Concurrent Resolution on the budget, which reaffirms or revises the first resolution.
	September 25	Congress completes action on any bills so budget totals for enacted legislation conform with the ceilings established in the Second Concurrent Resolution on the budget.
	October 1	The new fiscal year begins.

Source: Derived from Aaron Wildavsky, *The Politics of the Budgetary Process*, 3rd ed. (Boston: Little, Brown, 1979).

attention of the whole Congress, early in the process. Now Congress can at least see the forest as well as the trees.

The budgetary forest essentially consists of two major questions: Where does government's money come from, and where does it go?

THE CONTENT: WHERE IT COMES FROM AND WHERE IT GOES

Where It Comes From

"Taxes," said the late Supreme Court Justice Oliver Wendell Holmes, Jr., "are what we pay for civilization." Despite his assertion, "I like to pay taxes," most taxpayers throughout history have not agreed. The art of taxation, said Louis XIV's finance minister Jean-Baptiste Colbert, is in "so plucking the goose as to procure the largest quantity of feathers with the least possible amount of squealing." [13] You can see in ⑦ where the

[13] Quoted in Gerald Carson, *The Golden Egg: The Personal Income Tax, Where It Came From, How It Grew* (Boston: Houghton Mifflin, 1977), p. 12.

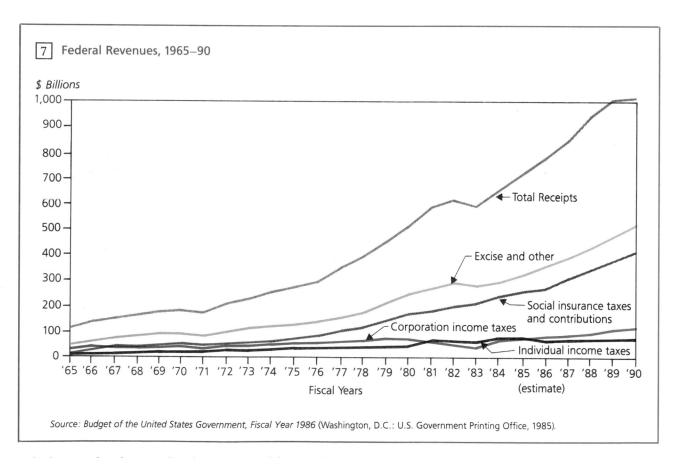

⑦ Federal Revenues, 1965–90

Source: Budget of the United States Government, Fiscal Year 1986 (Washington, D.C.: U.S. Government Printing Office, 1985).

Federal revenues have been growing. Their major growth has come from two sources: the individual income tax and the social insurance tax (usually called social security). Social security taxes are predicted to grow as America grows older.

federal government has been getting its feathers. Only a small share comes from excise taxes (for example, those on gasoline) and other sources; the three major sources of federal revenues are (1) the personal and corporate income tax, (2) social insurance taxes, and (3) borrowing and deficit spending.

Income Tax: The Government's Golden Egg? Bleary-eyed, millions of American taxpayers struggle to the post office before midnight every April 15 to mail their income tax forms. **Income taxes** take a share of wages earned. Although the government briefly adopted an income tax during the Civil War, the first peacetime income tax was enacted in 1894. Though the tax was only 2 percent of income earned beyond the then-magnificent sum of $4000, a lawyer opposing it called the tax the first step of a "communist march." The Supreme Court wasted little time in declaring the tax unconstitutional (*Pollock* v. *Farmer's Loan and Trust Co.*, 1895).

In 1915, the **Sixteenth Amendment** was added to the Constitution, explicitly permitting Congress to levy an income tax. Congress had already started one before the amendment was ratified. The **Internal Revenue Service** (first called the Bureau of Internal Revenue) was established to collect it. Today, the IRS receives about 128 million tax returns each year, subjecting every one to some scrutiny by people or computer. It audits in more detail about 2.6 million, investigates thousands of suspected criminal violations of the tax laws, and annually gets over a thousand guilty pleas or convictions of errant taxpayers (or non-payers). [14]

Corporations, like individuals, pay income taxes. Once corporate taxes yielded more revenues than individual income taxes, but no longer. Today, corporate taxes yield about 13 cents of every federal revenue dollar, compared with 43 cents coming from individual income taxes.

Social Insurance Taxes. Social Security taxes come from both employers and employees. Money is deducted from employees' paychecks and matched by their employers. Unlike other taxes, these payments do not go into the government's general money fund. They are already earmarked for a specific purpose: the Social Security Fund, to pay benefits to the old, the disabled, and the widowed.

Social Security taxes have grown faster than any other source of federal revenue and they will surely grow even more. In 1957, they were a mere 12 percent of federal revenues; today they are about a third. In 1985, the government in Washington collected $208 billion in Social Security taxes out of $647 billion it collected in taxes altogether. To keep the Social Security system solvent, Congress has scheduled a series of increases in Social Security taxes throughout the 1980s.

The Never-Ending Quest for Tax Reform. Gripes about taxes are at least as old in our country as the Boston Tea Party. "Loopholes" given to one special interest in return for its political support are hard to deny to

[14] On the number of returns and audits, U.S. Department of Commerce, *Statistical Abstract of the United States, 1985*.

the next one that comes along. During his 1984 campaign, President Reagan solemnly promised that he would not raise anyone's taxes. Nonetheless, quests for tax reform had been brewing in the Congress for years. Democratic members like Senator Bill Bradley of New Jersey and Representative Richard Gephardt of Missouri, as well as Republicans like Senator Bob Kasten of Wisconsin, had tossed tax reform bills into the congressional hopper. The president's Treasury Department worked on a reform plan late in 1984. It came to be called "Treasury I," the first version of a massive tax simplification scheme that offended nearly every interest in Washington. Treasury I, for example, proposed to tax the fringe benefits employers set aside for employees. This included life and health insurance benefits. It prompted a $6 million advertising campaign by the insurance industry. When Treasury I proposed to tax charitable contributions, foundations and private universities called for their lobbyists. By the time President Reagan unveiled "Treasury II" in May, 1985, two-thirds of the tax breaks eliminated by Treasury I had been restored.

Reagan's tax reforms proposed to eliminate some tax deductions and tax expenditures (for example, business meals costing more than $15 per person for lunch and interest deductions on second homes), enabling the government to reduce its overall tax rates. Three rates (35 percent, 25 percent, and 15 percent) would replace the multi-step graduated tax system, now topped off at 50 percent. It would, observers predicted, produce yet another battle between tax reformers and interest groups braced to hold onto their own little part of tax benefits.

Borrowing. Like families and firms, the federal government may borrow money to make ends meet. When families and firms need money, they go to their neighborhood bank, savings and loan association, or their friendly neighborhood money lender. When the federal government wants to borrow money, the Treasury Department sells bonds, guaranteeing to pay interest to the bondholder. You can buy these government bonds; so can corporations, mutual funds, and other financial institutions. There is a lively market in government bonds.

Today, the **federal debt**—all of the money borrowed over the years and still outstanding—approaches $2 trillion. (To give you an idea of how fast it is increasing, the second edition of *Government in America*, published just three years before this third edition, said "Today, [the federal debt] exceeds $1 trillion.") When President Reagan took office in 1981, the debt was about 35.5 percent of the gross national product. By early 1985, it had risen to about 44 percent of the GNP. (Actually it was even more—two-thirds of the GNP—in 1956.) Both President Reagan and the Congress worked to pare about $50 billion from the budget in early 1985. Still, about half of that $50 billion—not easy to whittle away in any case—would go simply to paying increased interest rates on the government's borrowed money.[15] Government borrowing, too, invariably crowds out private borrowers from the loan marketplace. (After all, your local bank may know that you are a fine credit risk, but it thinks the federal government is an even better one.) In 1984, more than a quarter of all money available for borrowing went to the federal government.

Aside from its impact on private borrowing (and, some economists believe, on interest rates), there are other concerns about the federal debt. Given current interest rates, every dollar that the government borrows today will cost taxpayers $24 in interest over the next 30 years. Government is not so much borrowing for its capital needs, as individuals and firms do when they buy a house or build a factory, as for its day-to-day expenses. Your family wisely does not borrow money for its food and clothing; yet the government is largely borrowing money for its farm subsidies, its military pensions, and its aid to states and cities.

The perceived perils of gigantic deficits have led to calls for a **balanced budget amendment.** Now passed in somewhat varied forms by the legislatures of 35 states, the proposed amendment to the Constitution would instruct Congress to hold a national convention for the purpose of proposing to the states a requirement that peacetime federal budgets be balanced. Only a three-fifths vote in both houses of Congress could authorize a specific expenditure beyond government's expected revenues.[16]

However large government's borrowing, most of its income still comes from taxes. Few government policies provoke more heated discussion than taxation.

Taxes and Public Policy

Probably no government policy affects as many of us as that of tax policy. Government can use taxes to make our incomes more or less equal, to encourage or discourage growth in the economy, and to promote

[15] John M. Berry, "Buddy, Can You Spare $2 Trillion," *Washington Post Weekly Edition*, February 18, 1985, pp. 6–7.

[16] On the proposed balanced budget amendment, see Aaron Wildavsky, *How to Control Government Spending* (Berkeley: University of California Press, 1980); William R. Keech, "A Theoretical Analysis of the Case for a Balanced Budget Amendment," paper presented at the Annual Meeting of the American Political Science Association, Washington, D.C., August 30–September 2, 1984.

specific interests. In Chapters 17 and 18 we will see how taxes affect the economy and equality arenas. Here, we zero in on how tax policies can promote the interests of particular groups or encourage specific activities.

Tax Loopholes. No discussion of taxes goes very far before the subject of tax loopholes comes up. Hard to define, a tax loophole presumably is some "tax break" or "tax benefit" that the critic of the particular loophole thinks is unfair. The Internal Revenue Code, which specifies what income is subject to taxation, is riddled with exemptions, deductions, and special cases. Jimmy Carter, campaigning for the presidency, called our tax system a "national disgrace" because of its special treatment for favored taxpayers. Some taxpayers, he stressed, get advantages from the tax code that not everyone else can use. Businessmen, he complained, can deduct as business expenses costly "three-martini lunches" (a phrase coined by Florida governor Reuben Askew in his keynote address to the 1972 Democratic National Convention). Ordinary workers, carrying a sandwich and coffee in a thermos to work, cannot write off their expenses for lunch.

Tax-writing is done by the House Ways and Means Committee and the Senate Finance Committee. Their periodic revisions of the tax codes (sometimes called "tax reforms") almost invariably add another string of exemptions and special considerations. Cutting through the jargon may reveal that only a handful of individuals can benefit from an exemption. In November 1975, Texas computer magnate H. Ross Perot benefited from an obscure change in the tax code to the tune of about $15 million. Perot's legal advisor was a former Internal Revenue Service commissioner and Perot was reported to be a generous contributor to the campaign chests of several members of congressional tax-writing committees.[17] One clause in the 1978 tax reform amendment was designed to benefit the heirs of Ernest and Julio Gallo, the California winemakers. Permitting them to pay inheritance taxes over a period of years instead of all at once, the bill saved the Gallo heirs a tidy sum. Despite President Carter's urging to clean up tax loopholes, the 1978 Congress added dozens of exemptions to the already exemption-ridden tax code.

However outraged people may be by such stories, the fact is that very little federal money is lost through these and other "raids on the federal treasury." They may offend our sense of fair play, but they cost the federal budget very little. "Loopholes" are really only especially objectionable tax expenditures.

Tax Expenditures. What does cost the federal budget a substantial sum is the system of tax expenditures. **Tax expenditures** are defined by the 1974 Budget Act as "revenue losses attributable to provisions of the federal tax laws which allow a special exemption, exclusion, or deduction." They represent the difference between what the government actually collects in taxes and what it would have collected without special exemptions. Tax expenditures thus amount to subsidies for some activity.

[17] Carson, *The Golden Egg*, pp. 181–82.

Some examples will clarify the idea:

— If it wanted to, government could send checks for billions of dollars to charities. Instead, it permits taxpayers to deduct their contributions to charities from their income, thus encouraging charitable contributions.
— If it wanted to, government could give cash to families wise enough or rich enough to buy a home. Instead, it permits homeowners to deduct from their income the billions of dollars they annually pay in mortgage interest.
— If it wanted to, government could write a check to all those Americans who happened to get their income from interest on stocks and bonds instead of from wages and salaries. It does not, but it does tax income from increases in the value of stocks and bonds (*capital gains*) at lower rates than it taxes ordinary income. Holders of stocks and bonds get, in effect, a subsidy unavailable to other taxpayers.

Tax expenditures are among the most obscure aspects of the generally obscure budgetary process. Few ordinary citizens seem to realize their scope. You can see their magnitude in 8.

On the whole, tax expenditures benefit middle- and upper-income taxpayers and corporations. Poorer people, who tend not to own homes, can take little advantage of provisions that permit home-buyers to deduct mortgage interest payments. Poorer people, who tend to make fewer and smaller expenditures, can take less advantage of a deduction for charitable expenses.

To some, business-related deductions, tuition tax credits, capital gains tax rates, and the like are loopholes. To others, they are public policy choices supporting a social activity worth subsidizing. Loopholes or tax expenditures, they amount to the same thing: revenues that the government loses because certain items are exempted from normal taxation or are taxed at lower rates.

The Never-Ending Quest for Tax Cutting. The annual rite of spring—the preparation of individual tax returns—is invariably accompanied by calls for tax reform and, more and more frequently these days, tax reduction. The tax reduction movement began at the grassroots level in 1978. In California, a policy entrepreneur named Howard Jarvis gathered a strong following and pressed for reduction in local property taxes. Jarvis and his followers collected the thousands of signatures needed to put the question on the ballot, and on June 6, 1978, California voters went to the polls and did what millions of Americans wished they could do: They cut their own property taxes. The vehicle was **Proposition 13,** which called for a cut in property taxes by limiting tax rates on houses and other property to 1 percent of market value. Tax revolt fever quickly spread to other states. In the November 1978 elections, twelve other states passed some form of tax or spending limitation. In 1980 Massachusetts voters, determined to shed their state's reputation as "Taxachusetts," passed their version of Proposition 13, called Proposition 2 ½, because it limited local property taxes to 2 ½ percent of assessed value each year.

8 Tax Subsidies: The Money Government Doesn't Collect

Tax expenditures are essentially moneys that government could collect, but does not because they are exempted from taxation. The Office of Management and Budget and the Joint Committee on Taxation of the Congress estimated that the total tax expenditures in 1985 would equal $353 billion. This amounted to about a third of the total federal appropriations. Individuals received $226.9 billion in tax expenditures; investors got $37.5 billion; and corporations got $86.4 billion. Here are some of the largest tax expenditures and their cost to the Treasury:

Tax Expenditure	Main beneficiary	Cost
Company contributions to pension funds	Families	$56 billion
Investment tax credit	Corporations	$26 billion
Mortgage interest on owner-occupied houses	Families	$25 billion
Accelerated depreciation	Corporations	$24 billion
Deductions for state and local taxes	Families	$22 billion
Company-paid benefits	Families	$22 billion
Social Security benefits	Families	$17 billion
Special treatment on capital gains	Investors	$16 billion

In other words, government could easily close its $200 billion budget deficit by taxing things it does not now tax, such as Social Security benefits, pension fund contributions, charitable contributions, and the like. You can easily figure out, though, that those are not popular items to tax and would evoke strong opposition from powerful interest groups.

Source: The source of the data above is the OMB and the Joint Committee on Taxation, reported in the *U.S. News and World Report*, March 12, 1984, p. 77.

Tax Revolt. *California, Massachusetts, and other states have seen voters take action against taxes at the ballot box. California's Proposition 13 was followed by Massachusetts's Proposition 2½, so called because it limited total local property taxes to 2½ percent of the assessed value of each city's taxable property. Passage of Proposition 2½ led to reductions in state and local services, including the renovation of this police precinct station.*

Ronald Reagan, a Californian himself, carried tax revolt fever into the White House. During the Carter administration, Senator William Roth (R.—Del.) and Representative Jack Kemp (R.—N.Y.) had written the Kemp-Roth bill, a plan to cut federal income taxes in stages. The 1980 Republican platform enthusiastically endorsed Kemp-Roth and promised tax cuts if Republicans were returned to power in Washington. They were, and Reagan and his administration set about cutting federal taxes.

Early in his administration, President Reagan proposed a massive tax-cut bill, essentially a slightly modified version of the original Kemp-Roth proposal. Kemp and Roth had proposed a three-year period of reductions, with a 10 percent cut in tax rates each year. The Republican administration and the Democratic congressional leadership parried over the terms. House Ways and Means Committee Chairman Dan Rostenkowski (D.—Ill.) proposed a one-year reduction, but this was rejected by Reagan's aides. Standing in the way of tax cuts is never easy, and late in July Reagan's tax-cutting proposal passed the House by a vote of 238–195. The margin in the Republican-dominated Senate was even larger. Over a three-year period, Americans would have their federal tax bills reduced by 25 percent—for a total reduction of $754.4 billion. Here are some of the provisions of that tax legislation:

— Over a thirty-three-month period beginning in October 1981, individuals would receive tax reductions amounting to 5 percent in 1981, 10 percent in 1982, and another 10 percent in 1983.
— Corporate taxes would also be reduced in 1982 and 1983.
— New tax incentives would be provided for savings, both to stimulate savings and to help bail out the financially troubled savings and loan industry.
— Taxes would be *indexed* to the cost of living beginning in 1985. Government would no longer get a larger share of income when inflation pushed incomes into higher brackets while the tax rates stayed the same. (This is important because people who have high incomes also pay a higher *percentage* of their incomes in taxes.)

Jack Kemp. *Congressman Jack Kemp, a New York Republican, has been a major policy entrepreneur on budgetary issues. The author with Senator William Roth of a supply-side tax reduction scheme, Kemp has become a vicar of tax-cutting movements. His efforts have led him to a leadership position among conservative Republicans. Here Kemp hosts an autograph party to peddle his book,* The American Idea.

President Reagan and his aides celebrated the 1981 tax reductions with champagne toasts. Workers, generally blessed with an additional $3 to $7 in their weekly paychecks, may have done the same. Actually, what President Reagan expected them to do was save and invest. He hoped that people would put their savings into investments that might create jobs, rather than frittering it away on "consumables."

The tax cuts did not fall evenly on all Americans. In April 1984, the Congressional Budget Office released a report on the impact of the new tax cuts. About 80 percent of tax reductions went to families earning between $20,000 and $80,000 annually, that is, families making more than the median family income. Only 7 percent of tax cuts went to those families earning less than $20,000. Because many social service programs were curtailed, benefits to poorer families were often lost. Thus, when the net losses in benefits were figured in, families below the median income fared even more poorly. The family earning $10,000 to $20,000 came out only $30 ahead. One earning less than $10,000 gained $20 in tax cuts, but lost $410 in benefits. [18]

Where It Goes: Federal Expenditures

In 1932, when President Franklin D. Roosevelt took office in the midst of the Great Depression, the federal government was spending just over $3 billion a year. Today, that sum would get the federal government only through a day. Programs once measured in the millions are now measured in the billions. Comparisons over time are, of course, a little misleading, because they do not take account of changes in the value of the dollar. You can see in 9 how the federal budget has grown in actual dollars.

The Big Change: Declining Defense Budgets and Growing Social Budgets. In the 1950s and early 1960s, spending for past, present, and future wars amounted to over half the federal budget. The Department of Defense got the lion's share of the federal dollar. Liberals complained that government was short-changing the poor while lining the pockets of defense contractors. Neither liberals waiting for the pro-poor revolution in public expenditures nor conservatives fearing it seemed to notice when it came. So, as Aaron Wildavsky remarked, "people are still waiting for this revolution in public policy to come when it has already been." [19] Over a decade and a half, from the mid-1960s to the early 1980s, defense expenditures crept downward in real dollars; social welfare expenditures more than doubled.

The biggest slice of the budget pie, once reserved for defense, now belongs to "income security" expenditures, a bundle of policies extending direct and indirect aid to the old, the poor, and the needy. These were the expenditures whose rate of growth in the first year of the Reagan era was pared substantially. The Reagan budget also devoted a larger share to military spending. (We will review the defense budget and the issue of

[18] Congressional Budget Office, reported in *Time.* April 16, 1984, p. 23.
[19] Aaron Wildavsky, *Speaking Truth to Power* (Boston: Little, Brown, 1979), p. 86.

defense spending in Chapter 20, on pages 616–622.) Even so, income security expenditures continued, even in the more austere Reagan years, to make up the largest share of the federal budget.

Other social service expenditures paralleled the upward growth of income security. In the past fifteen years, health expenditures have grown to support medicaid, medical education, and research. Education aid, worker training programs, and urban aid grew, too. Together they total a burgeoning budget for social expenditures.

Incrementalism. Sometimes political scientists use the term *incrementalism* to describe the spending and appropriations process. **Incrementalism** means simply that the best predictor of this year's budget is last year's budget, plus a little bit more (an increment). According to Aaron Wildavsky, "the largest determining factor of the size and content

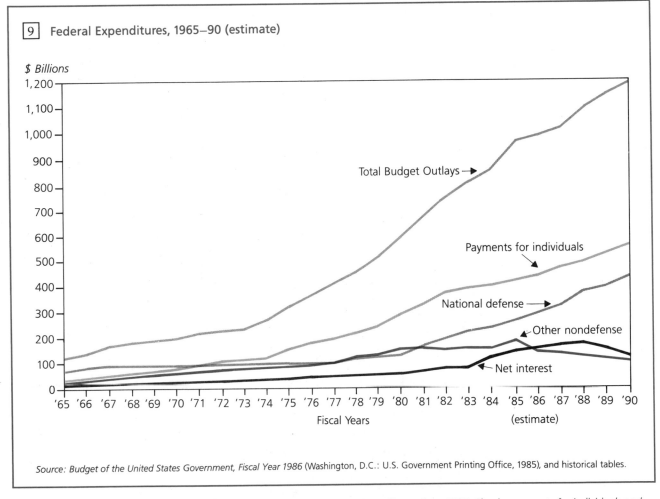

9 Federal Expenditures, 1965–90 (estimate)

$ Billions

Total Budget Outlays →

Payments for individuals

National defense →

→ Other nondefense

← Net interest

Fiscal Years   (estimate)

Source: Budget of the United States Government, Fiscal Year 1986 (Washington, D.C.: U.S. Government Printing Office, 1985), and historical tables.

Here is the distribution of federal expenditures since 1965. Clearly, payments for individuals and national defense are the two largest items in the budget. Note, though, that interest payments on the federal debt have been going up recently. (Also note how optimistic the government's projections are about future interest payments.)

of this year's budget is last year's budget. Most of the budget is a product of previous decisions." [20] According to Wildavsky, incremental budgeting has several features:

— Very little attention is focused on the budgetary *base*, the amounts agencies have had over the last couple of years. Most of the time, agencies can safely assume that they will get at least what they had last year.
— Most debate and attention is focused on the proposed increment.
— The budget for any given agency therefore tends to grow by a little bit every year.

This picture of the federal budget is one of constant slow growth. Wildavsky and his colleagues devised a very simple mathematical model of the incremental process; it predicted federal budgets with remarkable accuracy. [21] Other students of the budget suggest that the incremental theory leaves something to be desired. John Gist, for example, showed that although expenditures mandated by an existing law or obligation (such as social security) followed a neat pattern of increase, other parts of the budget did not. [22] Paul Schulman showed that budgets for the National Aeronautics and Space Administration were hardly incremental: They first rose as fast as a NASA rocket but later plummeted to a fraction of their former size. [23] Incrementalism may be a *general* tendency of the budget, but it does not fully describe all budgetary politics.

Precisely because so much of the budgetary process looks incremental —as well as poorly thought out, ill-informed, and irrational—there is a never-ending quest for the Holy Grail of budgetary reform. The idea is always to make it easier to compare programs, so that the "most deserving" ones can be supported and the "wasteful" ones cut. Lyndon Johnson tried to impose *PPBSs, Program-Planning-Budgeting-Systems,* on the whole government. According to this system, agencies must budget by programs and show explicitly the goals being achieved. The congressional reforms of 1974 were Congress' effort to make budgeting more rational. Jimmy Carter brought *zero-base budgeting* (ZBB) ideas that he had practiced as the governor of Georgia to Washington. ZBB requires agencies making up budget requests to pretend that their base is zero and then justify everything above zero, a virtually hopeless task. When the Department of Agriculture experimented with ZBB, it found a big increase in its budgetary workload, with little change in the results. [24]

Incrementalism makes it hard to pare the budget. The budget is too big to review each year, even for the most systematic and conscientious members of Congress. But there is another reason federal spending is hard to control. More and more of it has become uncontrollable. "The

[20] Wildavsky, *The Politics of the Budgetary Process,* p. 13.
[21] Otto Davis, M. A. H. Dempster, and Aaron Wildavsky, "A Theory of the Budgetary Process," *American Political Science Review* 60 (September 1966):529–47.
[22] John R. Gist, *Mandatory Expenditures and the Defense Sector* (Beverly Hills, Calif.: Sage, 1974).
[23] Paul R. Schulman, "Nonincremental Policymaking: Notes toward an Alternative Paradigm," *American Political Science Review* 69 (December 1975):1354–70.
[24] Wildavsky, *The Politics of the Budgetary Process,* pp. 207–09.

growth in federal spending," insists Lance LeLoup, "is almost completely attributable to growth in uncontrollable items."[25]

The "Allowance Theory" and "Uncontrollable Expenditures." At first glance it is hard to see how we could call the federal budget uncontrollable. After all, Congress has the constitutional authority to budget, to add or subtract money from an agency. And indeed, President Reagan has proposed and Congress has adopted some of his proposals to cut the growth of government spending. How, then, can we speak of an uncontrollable budget?

Consider for a moment what we might call the "allowance theory" of the budget. In this theory, a governmental budget works rather like an allowance. Mom and Dad hand over to Mary Jean and Tommy a monthly allowance, say $10 each, with the stern admonition: "Make that last till the end of the month because that is all we are giving you until then." In the allowance model of the budget, Congress plays this parental role, the agencies the role of Mary Jean and Tommy. Congress thus allocates a lump sum, say, $5.2 billion, and instructs the agency to meet its payrolls and other expenses throughout the fiscal year. When most of us think of the government's budget, we think of the budget as something of an allowance to the agencies.

Yet about three quarters of the government's budget does not really work this way at all. Vast expenditures are determined not by how much Congress appropriates to an agency, but by *how many eligible beneficiaries* there are for some particular program. **Uncontrollable expenditures** result from policies that make some group automatically eligible for some benefit. Thus, an expenditure is classified as uncontrollable "if it is mandated under current law or by a previous obligation."[26] Congress writes the eligibility rules; the number of people eligible and their level of guaranteed benefits determine how much Congress must spend. The Social Security Administration, for example, does not merely provide benefits on a first-come-first-served basis until the money runs out. Many expenditures are uncontrollable because Congress has in effect obligated itself to pay X level of benefits to Y number of recipients. Each year, Congress' bill is a straightforward function of the X level of benefits times the Y beneficiaries. A look at two major uncontrollables will help you understand the concept:

— The biggest uncontrollable of all, of course, is the social security system, costing $202 billion in fiscal year 1986, up from $33.8 billion as recently as 1970. Men who are over sixty-five and women who are over sixty-two get automatic social security payments. Of course, Congress can, if it desires, cut the benefits or tighten eligibility restrictions. Doing so, though, would provoke a monumental outcry from millions of older voters.

— Similarly, most federal grants-in-aid to states and localities are determined by automatic formulas written by Congress. The total

[25] Lance LeLoup, *Budgetary Politics: Dollars, Deficits, Decisions* (Brunswick, Ohio: King's Court, 1977) p. 62.

[26] Ibid.

grants-in-aid package now approaches $100 billion. So large and complex is this expenditure that the federal government has trouble figuring out where all its money is going. Three different estimates of how much federal education aid Michigan received *differed by a quarter of a billion dollars.* [27]

Other items—veterans aid, military pensions, civil service workers' retirement benefits, interest on the national debt—fit the uncontrollable label, too. Government cannot decide this year, for example, that it will not pay the interest on the federal debt, or chop in half the pensions earned by former military personnel.

Altogether, the federal budget document itself estimates that *fully three quarters of the federal budget is uncontrollable*—meaning that Congress *can* control them, but only by changing a law or existing benefit levels. To control the uncontrollables, Congress can either (1) cut the benefits, or (2) cut down on the beneficiaries. You can see why this is not a popular strategy for an elected Congress.

UNDERSTANDING BIG GOVERNMENT AND ITS BIG BUDGET

Citizens and politicians alike fret about whether government is too big. President Reagan sailed to reelection by stressing that government has too many hands in our pockets. But is the government too big? The answer, of course, depends upon your standards of the ideal-sized government. In comparison with other western nations, ours is a small public sector. Compared to what it once was, government is certainly larger than ever. Political scientists and economists have tried for years to nail down some precise explanations for government growth.

You will have to make your own assessment of whether or not the government's taxing and spending are too large. Our four theories of American government will help you to understand big government and its big budgets.

Democracy and Big Government

Almost all democracies have seen a substantial growth in government in the twentieth century. One explanation for this growth is that politicians spend money to "buy" votes. They don't buy votes in the sense that a corrupt political machine pays off voters to vote for its candidates. Rather, policymakers spend public money on things voters will like—and remember on election day. As we saw in Chapter 12, members of Congress have incentives to make government grow: They use both constituency services and pork-barrel policies to deliver benefits to the folks back home.

Economists Allen Meltzer and Scott Richard argued that government grows in a democracy because of the equality of suffrage. In the private sector, they argue, people's incomes are unequal; but in the political

[27] Thomas J. Anton, "Data Systems for Urban Fiscal Policy: Toward Reconstruction," paper presented at the Conference on Comparative Urban Research, University of Chicago, April 26–27, 1979, p. 20.

arena, power is much more equally distributed. Each voter has one vote. Parties must appeal to a majority of the voters. Hence, they claim, poorer voters will always use their votes to support public policies redistributing benefits from rich to poor. Even if they cannot win more equality in the marketplace, they can use the electoral process to secure more equality. As Meltzer and Richard put it, "Government continues to grow because there is a decisive difference between the political process and the market process. The market process produces a distribution of income that is less equal than the distribution of votes. Consequently, those with the lowest income use the political process to increase their income."[28] Many politicians willingly cooperate with the desire of working-class voters to expand their benefits because voters return the favor at election time. As we would expect from this reasoning, the rapidly growing uncontrollable expenditures are items like social security, medicaid, medicare, and social welfare programs, which benefit the poor more than the rich.

Poor and rich voters alike have voted for parties and politicians who promised them benefits. When the air is foul, we expect government to help clean it up. When we get old, we expect a social security check. In a democracy, what people want has some link to what government does. Citizens are not unwilling victims of big government and its big taxes. They are at least co-conspirators.

Big Government and Elite and Class Theory

Often we think of elites, particularly corporate elites, as being opposed to big government. Yet we have also seen Lockheed and Chyrsler Corporation appeal to big government for large bailouts when times got rough. Corporations have hardly bitten the hand that fed them with contracts, subsidies, and other benefits. A $100 billion procurement budget at the Department of Defense benefits defense contractors, their workers, and their shareholders.

Many class theorists believe that large government spending is necessary for the maintenance of a capitalist system. Capitalists take profits

[28] Allen Meltzer and Scott F. Richard, "Why the Government Grows (and Grows) in a Democracy," *The Public Interest* 52 (Summer 1978): 117.

Government-supported Infrastructure. One of the costs of doing business that government often winds up paying for is the cleanup of pollution. Mostly through federal funds, a massive cleanup of chemical pollution was launched at Love Canal in Niagara Falls, New York. Homes, schools, stores, and streets were systematically torn up and the contaminated debris cleared away. All this happened because the Hooker Chemical Company dumped barrels of dangerous chemicals onto vacant land it owned next to Love Canal—and then donated the area to the community.

The Nixon administration began a plan to shift the costs of chemical cleanups to a "Superfund," supported by the chemical industry.

for themselves, but expect government to provide an infrastructure of services—roads, fire protection, utilities, and the like—essential to the capitalist system. Government is also expected to handle the untidy byproducts of capitalism. A factory pollutes, capitalists take the profits, and government is expected to handle the cleanup. [29]

Sometimes government social services are needed to placate the underclasses in a capitalist system. Government may help the poor not in response to the troubles they have, but in response to the troubles they cause. In one forceful argument, Piven and Cloward suggest that governmental welfare expenditures rise in response to protests of the poor, not in response to their numbers or their needs. [30] High crime rates and urban racial disorders of the 1960s were followed, they show, by massive government poverty expenditures. This occurred even though the actual rate of poverty was declining. In the view of many class and elite theorists, government grows to protect the capitalist system from challenges to it.

Pluralism, Hyperpluralism, and Big Government

Government also grows by responding to groups and their demands. The parade of PACs is one example of groups asking government for assistance. From agricultural lobbies supporting loans, to farmers, to zoologists pressing for aid from the National Science Foundation, groups seek to expand their favorite part of the budget. In Chapter 14 we met the "iron triangles" which epitomize hyperpluralism. They are the beehives of government, working within it and outside it for budgetary support of their projects and priorities.

TAXES, SPENDING, AND BUDGETS SUMMARIZED

When the government budget consumes a third of our gross national product, it demands our close attention. In all western democracies, government budgets have grown during the twentieth century. In the

---

[29] A much more sophisticated argument along these lines is in James O'Connor, *The Fiscal Crisis of the State* (New York: St. Martins, 1973).

[30] Francis Fox Piven and Richard Cloward, *Regulating the Poor* (New York: Vintage, 1971) and *Poor People's Movements* (New York: Pantheon, 1977). For some evidence on behalf of the Piven and Cloward thesis, see Alexander Hicks and Duane Swank, "Civil Disorder, Relief Mobilization, and AFDC Caseloads: A Reexamination of the Piven and Cloward Thesis," *American Journal of Political Science* 27 (November 1983): 695–716.

United States, the rise of the social service state and the national security state have been closely linked with this growth.

Budget-making is complex, with many actors playing many roles. The president sets the budgetary agenda, while congress and its committees approve the budget itself.

We examined carefully where our government's money comes from and where it goes. The biggest revenue source, of course, remains the income tax. Lately, more and more of the government's budget has been financed through borrowing. Annual deficits of around $200 billion have boosted our federal debt to about $2 trillion.

On the spending side, the big change is from a government dominated by defense spending during the 1950s to one dominated by social services spending in the 1980s. President Reagan, for one, wants to reverse this balance by increasing military expenditures and cutting domestic ones. Nonetheless, much of our budget consists of "uncontrollable" expenditures, which are extremely difficult to pare. Many of these are associated with social security payments and with grants-in-aid.

There is no easy answer to the question of "How big is too big?" Invoking our four theories of American government—democracy, class and elite theory, pluralism, and hyperpluralism—helped us to understand why our government has grown larger.

Key Terms

deficit
expenditures
revenues
Social Security Act
medicare
military industrial
   complex
procurement
budget
House Ways and Means
   Committee

Senate Finance
   Committee
Congressional Budget
   and Impoundment
   Control Act of 1974
Congressional Budget
   Office (CBO)
reconciliation
   resolution
income taxes
Sixteenth Amendment

Internal Revenue
   Service
federal debt
balanced budget
   amendment
tax expenditures
Proposition 13
incrementalism
uncontrollable
   expenditures

For Further Reading

Congressional Quarterly, Inc. *Budgeting for America* (1982). A very useful overview of the federal budgetary process.

Light, Paul. *Artful Work: The Politics of Social Security Reform* (1985). A study of the perennial crisis of social security and what has been done about it.

Piven, Francis Fox, and Richard Cloward. *Regulating the Poor* (1971). Argues that government budgets increase in response to the troubles the poor cause, not the troubles the poor have.

Rose, Richard, and B. Guy Peters. *Can Governments Go Bankrupt?* (1978). The answer is not clear from the book, but it is a useful discussion of the crisis of finance in modern democracies.

Schick, Allen. *Congress and Money* (1980). A readable review of Congress' role in the budgetary process.

Wildavsky, Aaron. *The Politics of the Budgetary Process*, 4th ed. (1984). The standard work on budgetary politics; weak, though, on the rise of the uncontrollable budget.

_____ . *How to Limit Government Spending* (1980). A forceful, but balanced plea for a constitutional amendment to control government spending.

POLICIES

Throughout *Government in America* we have focused on three policy areas: our political economy, equality, and energy and environment. These do not cover, of course, every possible issue on our crowded national policy agenda. Still, many of the oldest debates in American politics are about these issues. In Part V, we meet these policy arenas head on.

Chapter 17 describes today's political economy, specifically the ways in which our economic life is determined by policy decisions. Politicians have every reason to be interested in managing the economy since the evidence is clear that elections are partly (though only partly) won on the basis of economic conditions. Through taxing, subsidizing, and regulating, government controls the contours of economic activities.

Chapter 18 returns to an old issue in American politics and *Government in America,* the politics of equality. Whatever equality means—and definitions vary widely—Americans seem to support the notion of equality. Not all Americans, however, support all politics carried under the broad banner of equality.

In Chapter 19 we address another familiar issue: energy and the environment. Now that the fear associated with gas lines and OPEC power are abating, it should be possible to take a careful, dispassionate look at our energy and environmental policies.

Each policy arena, we have suggested, has two faces: one facing inward, the other toward a global connection. Issues of economics, equality, and energy and the environment are not issues of domestic policy alone. Our foreign and military policies confront them, too, as we will see in Chapter 20.

Political Economy
and Public Policy

MEMO

Not too many years ago, the American economy, with its high per capita incomes, growth rates, and vast industrial capacity, was the envy of the world. Something happened, though, during the 1970s. Our growth rates declined, our per capita incomes slipped, and our vast industrial base faced stern competition from abroad.

Government has never been an innocent bystander in our economic system, which is why ours is called a *mixed economy.* This chapter is about the links between the economy and government and its policies. States, cities, and even the national government have tried to revitalize the American economy, partly by moving to a "high-tech" economic system. Yet the challenges to our economic lifeblood remain.

In this chapter, I will try to do the following:

■ Show why economic conditions, particularly inflation and unemployment, are high priority items on political agendas;

■ Describe the instruments which political leaders use to affect the state of the economy; and

■ Review the ABCs of economic policy, showing how policies have shaped the areas of agriculture, business, consumer, and labor policy.

As you read this chapter, remember that the decisions government makes are likely to shape your own economic fortunes as we enter the third American century.

THERE ARE FEW policy issues that evoke stronger disagreements than policies about the economy.

Policymakers worry a lot about the state of the economy, and today, there is a lot to worry about, as you can see in ⬚1⬚. Compared to the economy of the 1960s, the economy of the 1980s has not been robust, but sluggish. Lately, says Robert Kuttner, "events have been unkind to the economy, and unkinder still to economists."[1] Professional economists have been busy diagnosing, prescribing, and postulating about the state of the American economy for a generation. Yet their advice to policymakers has been a cacaphony, not a chorus. Today, all sorts of descriptions of the American economy are available; being so diverse, not all of them can be correct. This chapter explores our economy and public policies dealing with it.

POLITICS AND ECONOMICS

We are accustomed to seeing politics and economics as two quite different subjects. In contrast, Robert Reich remarks that:[2]

> Americans tend to divide the dimensions of our national life into two broad realms. The first is the realm of government and politics. The second is the realm of business and economics. . . . The choice is falsely posed. In advanced industrial nations like the United States, drawing such sharp distinctions between government and the market has ceased to be useful.

To Reich, the view that politics and economics are closely linked is neither new nor unique. At first glance, James Madison, the architect of our Constitution, and Karl Marx, the founder of communist theory, seem to have little in common. Yet each argued strongly that economic conflict was at the root of politics. Both argued for a *class-based* interpretation of political life. The viewpoint we take in this chapter is that politics and

[1] Robert Kuttner, "The Poverty of Economics," *Atlantic* (February 1985):74.
[2] Robert B. Reich, *The Next American Frontier* (New York: Penguin Books, 1983), pp. 4–5.

⬚1⬚ The State of the Economy: Some Comparisons over Time

Indicator	Averages					
	1960–67	1968–72	1973–80	1981	1982	1983
Inflation	1.6	4.6	8.9	10.4	6.2	4.5
Unemployment	5.1	4.7	6.6	7.6	9.6	9.6
Rate of growth of GNP	4.3	3.3	2.8	2.0	−1.8	5.5
Rate of growth of productivity	3.8	3.3	1.1	1.8	.4	4.5

Sources: *Economic Report of the President 1983*, Table B41 and Kenneth Dolbeare, *Democracy at Risk* (Chatham, N.J.: Chatham House, 1984), p. 60.

economics are powerful, intertwined forces shaping our public policies—and our private lives. Bethlehem's steel industry did not decline because of market forces alone. You can see in ② some public policy choices that affect steel, the lifeblood of Bethlehem.

Policymakers argue endlessly about economic policy. *Liberals* have tended to favor a government active in economic policy, smoothing out the rough edges of capitalism. *Conservatives* have sought an unfettered capitalist system, one only minimally regulated by governmental policy.

---

② Public Policy, Steel, and Life in Bethlehem

Congressman Don Ritter, whom we met in Chapter 12, is an unlikely incumbent in the Bethlehem-Allentown area. In a unionized, blue-collar, working-class area, it is unusal to find a conservative Republican representing folks in Washington. Don Ritter does, though, and has for some years. One reason is his eagerness to speak up for the steel industry; for like much of older, industrial America, Bethlehem needed all the help it could get. Import quotas, air pollution policies, policies to reduce gasoline consumption, labor regulation, and a host of other governmental policies affect the steel industry—and what affects the steel industry affects neighborhoods and families in Bethlehem.

By 1985, the steel industry, once one of America's strongest, operated at only 42 percent of capacity. Some 200,000 jobs had disappeared in the industry since 1965. Bethlehem Steel, among others, was busy selling off even its profitable plants to find capital for other nonsteel ventures. Part of Big Steel's problems stemmed from Japanese competition. Cheaper labor costs and more advanced technology permitted Japanese companies to sell their steel cheaper than American steel. This led to Congressman Ritter's efforts to persuade President Reagan to cut imports from Japan. Counting Japan as a valued ally, and suspecting that the Japanese would retaliate against other American products, Reagan refused. Japan, though, continued to cooperate with voluntary quotas and Prime Minister Nakasone even urged a "buy American" program in his country.

Other government policies affect profits and jobs in Bethlehem. Take the case of energy policies. Short of oil, Congress and the Department of Transportation adopted policies to reduce energy consumption in cars. Automobile manufacturers were ordered to produce cars lighter in weight to consume less fuel. Heavy steel was the loser to lighter aluminum and plastics. A 1977 Ford car contained 2,344 pounds of steel; a 1985 Ford car contained 1,520 pounds. In 1976, the steel industry sent 25 percent of its total output to the automobile industry.

A Highly Technological Japanese Steel Plant. *This is the nerve center of a Japanese steel plant. These computers and their technicians monitor the heat and waste recycling of the plant. A dominant problem in the American steel industry has been the increased productivity and lower wages of foreign steel production. United States Steel, one of Bethlehem's chief competitors, has responded by diversifying, buying up non-steel enterprises.*

Five years later—after environmental and energy regulations on the auto industry—only 15 percent of Big Steel's output went to the automobile industry.

As one business journal bluntly put it:

Congress, in legislating fuel-consumption standards for American cars, committed itself to a radically different industrial structure. You downsized American cars to save gas, and you wound up downsizing not only the U.S. auto industry itself but a substantial part of the industrial base that supported it. You saved gasoline. And you destroyed blue-collar jobs.

Source: The story of steel, autos, and government regulation is taken from Kenneth Dolbeare, *Democracy at Risk* (Chatham, N.J.: Chatham House, 1984), pp. 70–71. The quotation from *Forbes* is from the November 22, 1982 issue, p. 161.

Our policymakers have confronted a jangle of economic advice. Economic philosophies like *Keynesianism*, *post-Keynesianism*, *monetarism*, *rational expectations*, and *supply-side economics* are sure to glaze over the eyes of the most attentive politician (these terms will be explained later in the chapter). They, of course, are eager to keep the economy humming. Politicians believe—and some political scientists agree—that the most sensitive part of the voter's anatomy (his or her pocketbook) affects the most sensitive part of the politician (his or her reelection).

Why Policymakers Try Hard to Control the Economy

It was President Harry Truman who coined the line about pocketbooks and the voter anatomy. Political leaders before and since Truman have believed that voters take out their economic grievances on incumbents at the polls. Some political scientists believe that the politicians are right. Gerald Kramer, for example, studied the connections between economic conditions and the congressional vote from 1896 through 1964. When people's real incomes declined, incumbent members of the House lost votes. Good times in the economy produced good times for the incumbents. [3]

No one has argued more strongly for the link between economic conditions and political outcomes than Edward Tufte. He says, "When you think economics, think elections; when you think elections, think economics." [4] His reasoning is, he says, "obvious enough . . . Incumbent politicians desire reelection and they believe that a booming pre-election economy will help to achieve it." [5] His evidence suggests that the difference between a bouyant and a sluggish economy at election time means a difference of 3 to 4 percent in the congressional or presidential vote, enough to swing twenty-five to forty-five House seats. [6] And, he claims, policymakers go to great pains to insure that the economy is robust rather than wheezing at election time. Tufte's evidence suggests that real (after-tax and after-inflation) income grows faster in even-numbered than odd-numbered years, coinciding exactly with the congressional election cycle. Unemployment, on the other hand, goes down in the months just before a presidential election.

A neat trick if you can do it, one might say about the ability of politicians to control so precisely our economic conditions at election time. Yet there are some missing links in the argument. Controlling income and unemployment with such precision is like stopping on an economic dime. A careful analysis by David Cameron finds the view that

---

[3] Gerald H. Kramer, "Short-term Fluctuations in U.S. Voting Behavior, 1896–1964," *American Political Science Review* 65 (March 1971):131–43. See also Edward Tufte, "Determinants of the Outcome of Midterm Congressional Elections," *American Political Science Review* 69 (September 1975):812–26.

[4] Edward R. Tufte, *Political Control of the Economy* (Princeton, N.J.: Princeton University Press, 1978), p. 65.

[5] Ibid., p. 5.

[6] Ibid., p. 119.

politicians perform economic magic at election time to be greatly over-blown. He examined national elections between 1948 and 1984. Looking at changes in unemployment, real disposable income, and inflation, he found that their ups and downs were largely unsynchronized with election cycles. Cameron found only scanty "traces of evidence" that politicians can fiddle with the economy for their own electoral ends. [7]

To say that politicians are none too successful in manipulating the economy at election time does not prove that politicians do not *believe* that economic conditions help determine elections. They may even *behave* in accordance with that belief. Indeed, the two parties have long offered different economic alternatives.

The Parties, the Voters, and the Twin Economic Evils

Unemployment and Inflation. Unemployment and inflation trouble families, pinch paychecks, and create severe social problems. They are also political evils. Unemployment and inflation do no good for a family's bank balance or peace of mind. Neither do they do much good for the politician's political credit or peace of mind. Too much unemployment or inflation can increase unemployment among politicians.

Defining and measuring unemployment is one task of the Bureau of Labor Statistics (BLS) in the Department of Labor. Traditionally, the BLS has measured the **unemployment rate** as the proportion of the labor force

---

[7] David Cameron, "Elections and the Economy," paper presented at the annual meeting of the American Political Science Association, September, 1984. p. 33.

Texas Unemployment. *The Sunbelt has been a lure for those throughout the country who expect their hopes and dreams to be fulfilled by migration. Texas may conjure up the "Dallas" of television fame, but it is also a state that has attracted thousands of Americans looking for their big chance. Some make it; some do not. So far at least, these new Texans have not.*

actively seeking work but unable to find jobs. If we change the definition even slightly, however, we drastically change the unemployment rate. The BLS, for example, does not count people sixty-five or older as part of the labor force. If the BLS changed the cutoff to age seventy, the "labor force" would expand. Nor has the BLS counted as part of the labor force what it calls "discouraged workers," people who have become so frustrated that they have stopped actively seeking employment. If we count them, we would increase the unemployment rate. If we counted only those people who are unemployed long enough to cause them severe hardship, we would cut the unemployment rate. All this may not prove the old adage, "There are liars, damn liars, and statisticians," but it does show that unemployment—like any other measure of a policy problem—is partly a matter of definition.

One careful analysis of the consequences of unemployment was completed by M. Harvey Brenner. He conducted a complex statistical analysis of the effects of unemployment from 1940 to 1973. He found that a 1 percent increase in the unemployment rate was associated with

— An increase of 4.1 percent in the suicide rate.
— A 3.4 percent increase in admissions to state mental hospitals.
— A 1.9 percent increase in deaths from cirrhosis of the liver (usually associated with alcoholism).
— A 5.7 percent increase in the homicide rate. [8]

The effects of unemployment, of course, are probably more subtle than statistical analyses suggest. It is unlikely that people who lose their jobs suddenly become alcoholics or murderers. But it is likely that economic conditions are associated in a very significant—though very complex—way with social problems.

The problem of inflation is the other half of the dilemma. For years, the government has kept tabs on the **Consumer Price Index (CPI)**, our key inflation measure. In recent years, it was based on the average prices in 1967. Prices in that year were figured as 100, and annual cost-of-living changes were measured from that base. It had to happen sometime, and in November 1978, the consumer price index topped 200: What cost $1 in 1967 cost $2 in 1978. (In 1982, the CPI base year was changed from 1967 to 1977.) Throughout the late 1970s, the cost of medical care, housing, energy, and almost everything else was soaring. Prices were escalating so fast that the average family's real income (its income after the effects of inflation had been discounted) was actually going down. Inflation was low in the 1980s, though, permitting real wages to catch up with their former levels.

Like unemployment, inflation exacts a social price as well as an economic one. Its effects on mental and physical health, crime rates, and other social problems are less dramatic than the effects of unemployment [9]; they are more general, because inflation affects everyone. Some

[8] M. Harvey Brenner, *Estimating the Social Costs of National Economic Policy: Implications for Mental and Physical Health, and Criminal Aggression* (Washington, D.C.: U.S. Government Printing Office, 1976).
[9] Ibid.

groups, though, are hit especially hard by inflation. Persons living on fixed incomes, as senior citizens often are, can be prime victims. Small wonder, then, that politicians worry about inflation and unemployment.

Voters, Unemployment, and Inflation. People who are unemployed, worrying over the prospect of unemployment, or struggling with a racing inflation rate have at least one thing in common: They are (or can be) voters. Ample evidence indicates that voters pay attention to economic conditions in making up their minds on election day: not only to their own personal circumstances—whether they are employed or how secure their job is—but also to national economic circumstances.

Roderick Kiewiet has studied the connection between unemployment, inflation, and voting behavior. He analyzed survey studies of the American electorate in nineteen presidential and congressional elections between 1956 and 1978. Generally, voters who had experienced some unemployment in their family were more likely to support Democratic candidates for president and for Congress. While Democratic candidates enjoyed only a modest advantage, it was a consistent one, present in eighteen of the nineteen elections Kiewiet studied. It was not only the personal experience with unemployment that gave the Democratic party an edge. Voters who felt that unemployment was a serious national problem (whether or not they were personally affected by it) leaned strongly to the Democratic party. There is, concludes Kiewiet, "a mass of evidence showing voters reacting to their concern over unemployment by voting more Democratic." [10] Concern over inflation, on the other hand, had no particular connection to voters' choices. Thus, politicians and political scientists seem to agree on the connection between economic conditions and voting. As Kiewiet's review of nineteen elections discovered, and as a Reagan administration official remarked in February 1982, "You don't lose elections because of inflation. You do lose elections because of unemployment." [11]

The Parties, Unemployment, and Inflation. Since voters are sensitive to economic conditions, the parties must pay close attention to them when making up their platforms and selecting their policies. In the United States and around the world, different parties choose different economic policies, and many of those choices affect unemployment and inflation.

Some years ago, economist Paul Samuelson articulated a not-uncommon belief about the two parties in the United States. "We tend to get our recessions during Republican administrations," he remarked. "The Democrats," he continued, "are willing to run with some inflation; the Republicans are not." [12] This leads us to an interesting hypothesis about party behavior: Republicans are willing to risk higher unemployment

[10] D. Roderick Kiewiet, "Policy-oriented Voting Response to Economic Issues," *American Political Science Review* 75 (June 1981):459.

[11] *Time*, February 8, 1982, p. 22.

[12] Quoted in Douglas Hibbs, "Political Parties and Macroeconomic Policy," *American Political Science Review* 71 (December 1977):1467.

and recession, while Democrats will tolerate more inflation. Douglas Hibbs investigated this hypothesis, looking systematically at differences in the inflation and unemployment rates during Democratic and Republican administrations.[13] He found that when the Republican party has been in power, there has been a significantly higher unemployment rate.

Parties, then, behave very much the way voters expect them to. As we saw in Chapter 7, the Democratic coalition is made up heavily of groups—union people, minorities, and the poor—who worry about unemployment. The Democratic party has usually behaved as its coalition expected it to, pursuing policies designed to lower unemployment. Similarly, the Republican coalition rests more heavily on a base of people wrestling with the ravages of inflation—business owners and managers, professional people—those who worry less about unemployment. Trying to hold down inflation, Republican administrations have endured somewhat more unemployment.

The efforts of politicians and parties to control the economy are not as easy as they might seem to be. The American economy is a complex system; indeed, the impact of government on it is significant. Let us see how government policy affects that economy.

GOVERNMENT'S INSTRUMENTS FOR CONTROLLING THE ECONOMY

The time has long passed—if it ever really existed—when government could ignore such economic troubles as unemployment and inflation, confidently asserting that the private marketplace could handle them. Especially since the Great Depression and the New Deal, government has been actively involved in the economy. When the stock market crash of 1929 sent unemployment soaring, President Herbert Hoover clung to the **laissez-faire** principle that government should not meddle in the economy. In the next presidential election he was handed a crushing defeat by Franklin D. Roosevelt, whose New Deal experimented with dozens of new policies to turn the tide of the depression.

At least since the New Deal, policymakers have made every effort to control the economy. They cannot do it by magic or prayers (when George Bush was campaigning against Ronald Reagan in 1980, he called Reagan's economic policy "voodoo economics"). They need policy tools, and the American political economy offers four main ones: subsidies and benefits, tax benefits, monetary policy, and fiscal policy.

Subsidies and Benefits

Government provides billions of dollars in benefits to individuals, state and local governments, and businesses. Even in the austere Reagan budget of 1986, nearly $500 billion is transferred from Washington to individuals, families, firms, and other institutions. To control various

[13] Ibid.

aspects of our national economy, government can increase or lower benefits any time it wants. Maximum political benefit can be gained, though, if benefits are increased just before an election. In fact, Edward Tufte even contends that in election years government benefits reach their peak in October or early November, just before the November elections. In nonelection years, benefits tend to peak in December.[14] Social security increases tend to come in checks delivered in October or early November, just before voters go to the polls. (Increases in social security *taxes*, in contrast, almost always take effect on January 1—after an election in November.) A similar pattern characterizes veterans' benefits. Payments to veterans are almost always greatest in the fourth quarter of election years. The effect of these increases at election time is to put more dollars in people's pockets just before they go to the polls.

Tax Benefits

Tax benefits can be specific or general. Specific tax breaks can be given to specific groups whose support parties or politicians like to maintain or secure. Avocado growers, airlines, and people who are paying interest on loans, among others, benefit from specific tax breaks. Or taxes can be reduced in general, as they were in 1981 when Ronald Reagan and Congress agreed on a major three-year reduction in federal income taxes.

Both subsidies and tax breaks can be short-run, "quick fix" solutions to a party in need of votes and an economy in need of stimulation. Two other policies to control the economy—monetary and fiscal—have slower but more enduring economic impacts. They are also subject to fiercer debate between conservative and liberal economists, and between Republican and Democratic politicians.

Monetary Policy and the Fed

Government can also control the economy through **monetary policy,** that is, the manipulation of the supply of money in private hands. An economic theory called **monetarism** holds that the supply of money is the key to a nation's economic health. Monetarists believe that too much cash and credit in circulation produces inflation. Essentially, they seek to hold the growth in money supply to growth in the real (that is, after inflation) gross national product. Politicians worry constantly about the money supply because of its close connection with inflation, mortgage rates, and other tracers of economic well-being.

The main instrument for making monetary policy is called "the Fed." Its formal title is the Board of Governors of the **Federal Reserve System.** It was created by Congress in 1913 to regulate the lending practices of banks and thus, (as we will see) the money supply. The Fed was intended to be formally beyond the control of the president and Congress. The seven-member Board of Governors is supposed to stand above partisan politics. Its members are appointed by the president, with the consent of

---

[14] Tufte, *Political Control of the Economy,* p. 39.

the Senate. They serve fourteen-year terms designed to insulate them from politics. The most powerful member of the Fed is the chairman, who is appointed from among the members for a four-year, renewable term.

Here is how the Fed makes monetary policy. Say the Smiths in San Jose put their savings in the First National Bank of San Jose. Everyone knows that the bank is not going to keep that money locked up in a safe for them, but will loan it out to the Joneses, or to Hewlett-Packard, or to some enterprising young computer whiz who thinks he has the next Apple on his hands. But the bank must keep *some* of its money on deposit, in case the Smiths want it back. It is the Fed that regulates the amount of money that the bank must keep on deposit. If the money supply is too tight and recession may be on the horizon, the Fed lowers the amount the bank must retain. When the supply of money and credit is swelling too fast, it sells government securities and requires the bank to buy them. This "tightens" the amount the bank has to loan to the Joneses, Hewlett-Packard, or the computer entrepreneur.

These complicated financial dealings have a single purpose: to expand or contract the amount of money and credit in the economy. Too much, economists believe, leads to inflation. Too little leads to economic belt-tightening, perhaps even recession. This economic tightrope walking is bound to attract the attention of politicians.

Presidents especially worry over the Fed's policies. Beck, for example, has shown that these policies often change with a new administration.[15] Few presidents have fretted over the Fed as much as Richard Nixon. John Ehrlichman reports that "Nixon was determined to control the Fed while maintaining the image of its independence from all politicians, including himself." He appointed conservative, pipe-smoking Arthur Burns as chairman of the Fed. But "he went about as far as he could, lecturing—even scolding—Burns about what the Fed must do to free up the money supply."[16] In the second half of his term, when he needed the confidence of the financial community, Jimmy Carter brought in towering, cigar-smoking Paul Volcker, a self-made member of America's banking elite. A graduate of Princeton, Harvard, and the London School of Economics, Volcker spent all his adult life jockeying between government jobs in Washington and private banking in Manhattan. Reappointed by President Reagan, he pursued a generally tight money course.

Elite and class theorists, of course, would find the Fed valuable ammunition for their view that elites control public policy. Staffed by and sensitive to the banking community, the Federal Reserve Board is a vintage example of elite control of a key policy arena—our money supply. Voters and their democratically elected representatives might prefer easing access to credit and low interest rates. But bankers—with inflation eroding their billions of dollars in loans—have a strong interest in tight money.

---

[15] Nathaniel Beck, "Presidential Influence on the Federal Reserve in the 1970s," *American Journal of Political Science* 26 (August 1982):415–45.

[16] John Ehrlichman, *Witness to Power* (New York: Pocket Books, 1982), p. 217.

Manager of the Money Supply: Paul Volcker. *Few people in the United States wield more economic and political power than the chairman of the Federal Reserve Board. The "Fed" essentially controls the supply of money available to businesses and consumers. It permits banks to use more or less of their money for loans, making the money supply "tight" or not. The chairman of the Fed thus plays a central role in determining the cost of money, the interest rate, and the inflation rate. President Jimmy Carter's appointee to this post was Paul Volcker. Volcker had worked for the Chase Manhattan Bank in New York until Lyndon Johnson made him deputy undersecretary of Treasury for Monetary Affairs. He then became chairman of the regional branch of the Fed in New York. When President Carter was searching for a new chairman of the Federal Reserve Board in Washington, he sought someone with Democratic ties, but one who supported "tight" money. Volcker's tight money policies aggravated businesses and consumers who sought low interest rates, but they delighted both Carter and Reagan, advocates of a tight-fisted monetary policy.*

Fiscal Policy: Deficits, Government Spending, and the Economy

Whether the government is in the red or the black is one factor determining whether citizens and corporations are in the pink economically. **Fiscal policy** describes the impact of the federal budget—taxes, spending, and borrowing—on the economy. Unlike monetary policy, which is mostly controlled by the Fed, fiscal policy is almost entirely determined by Congress and the president, who are our budgetmakers. Some economists have emphasized that government spending and deficits can help the economy weather its normal ups and downs. **Keynesian economic theory,** named after English economist John Maynard Keynes, has long been in favor with mainstream economists and liberal politicians.

Keynesianism has been our dominant economic philosophy since the end of World War II. Its proponents have tried to use the power of government to stimulate the economy when it is lagging—when, for example, unemployment is high and plants lie idle. When these conditions exist, Keynesians argue, government should pursue policies to whet consumer spending, which in turn should spur hiring and production. Taxes, for example, can be cut to put more money into consumers' hands,

Taxes and the Economy. *President Reagan came to office committed to a major tax cut. His belief in "supply-side economics" suggested that more money in consumers' hands would spur economic growth. He used television effectively to push his tax reduction plan and compare it to a Democratic alternative.*

as they were during the Kennedy administration. Federal government aids to state and local governments or to individuals can be increased to produce more spending and more jobs. Conversely, when things in the economy are humming along, it is wise, Keynesians say, to cut back on such government efforts, even to run a little black ink against a rainy day.

So dominant was Keynesian thinking in government policymaking that Democrats and Republicans alike adhered to its basic tenets—until Ronald Reagan. A theory popularized by President Reagan and his economic gurus, called **supply-side economics,** also proposed using government policy to boost the private economy.[17] Though faddish within the economics profession, supply-side economics attracted its share of adherents among conservatives. To supply-siders, government taxes soak up too much of our gross national product. By taxing too heavily and regulating too much, government curtails economic growth. Supply-siders feel that cutting back the scope and expenditures of government and, of course, its taxes will bring incentives to save, work harder, and create more jobs. University of Southern California economist Arthur Laffer proposed (legend says on the back of a cocktail napkin) a curve, called by his disciples a "Laffer curve." It suggested that the more government taxes, the less people work, and thus, the smaller the government's tax revenues. Cut the taxes, Laffer reasoned, and people would work harder and thereby stimulate the economy. Congressman Jack Kemp (R—N.Y.) was an early convert to supply-side economics in general and the Laffer curve in particular.

Supply-side economics was partly rhetoric and partly a realistic philosophical underpinning of Reagan's economic policies. During his first administration, President Reagan fought for, and won, massive tax cuts, mostly for the well-to-do. But his inability to restrain spending led to huge deficits to match the huge tax cuts. Some members of the Reagan

[17] One supply-side theory can be found in George Gilder, *Wealth and Poverty* (New York: Basic Books, 1981).

administration, including Budget Director David Stockman and former Chairman of the Council of Economic Advisors Martin Feldstein, stressed the need for balanced budgets. But other supply-siders touted the virtues of the tax cuts even without the spending reductions. Thus, massive tax cuts, coupled with still-growing federal expenditures, produced massive deficits. To finance its $200 billion deficit, the government was borrowing one in four dollars borrowed in 1985.

THE ABCs OF ECONOMIC POLICY

When governments spend a third of the gross national product and regulate much of the other two thirds, you can be sure that its policies will provoke debate. Interest groups may seek benefits, protection from unemployment, or protection from some allegedly hurtful business practice. Agriculture, business, consumers, and a host of other groups are actors in, and objects of, government economic policy.

Agriculture and Public Policy: The Bitter Harvest

President Reagan's budget director, David Stockman, was testifying before a Senate Budget Committee hearing in February 1985. Pressed by farm-state senators on why the president's budget proposed drastic cuts in aid to beleaguered farmers, Stockman mused, "For the life of me, I cannot figure out why the taxpayers of this country have the responsibility to go in and refinance bad debt that was willingly incurred by consenting adults who went out and bought farmland when the price was going up and thought that they could get rich, or who went out and bought machinery and production assets because they made a business

American Agriculture: A Victim of Its Own Success. *American agriculture has been enormously successful in getting more production out of the land—so successful that most commodities constantly have surpluses. One aim of governmental policy has been to control production to reduce surpluses. This is done by contracting with a farmer to plant only so many acres in return for government guarantees ("price supports") to purchase the production at a fixed price.*

judgment that they could make some money." [18] Farm-state senators and representatives were incensed. Said House Agriculture Committee chairman Kika de la Garza: (D—Tex.): "Let's cut off the arms and legs of the patient. Then he'll be thirty pounds lighter and less of a burden." [19] The administration, undeterred, proposed to reduce federal farm subsidies so much that a free market would once again dominate agriculture.

Ever since the Agricultural Adjustment Act of 1933, the government has subsidized farmers. Through **price supports,** the government guarantees the prices of certain commodities, regularly buying surplus crops in order to keep prices high. In return, farmers agree to limit their planting in a given year. The government also purchases food directly and stores it, thus pushing prices up by cutting supplies to consumers. In 1983, for example, the government bought 12 percent of all dairy products and stored away (presumably for a rainy, cheeseless, day) some 17 billion pounds of butter, cheese, and dried milk. Dairy supports cost the government $2 billion in 1983. (Said one critic of the program, Senate Majority Leader Robert Dole, "this program is so bad, even the cows are laughing.")

American agriculture policies have been designed to reduce production (thereby giving farmers a more reasonable price for their product), but the side-effects of those policies have been significant. A technological revolution in agriculture has reduced the need for labor while increasing the prices of farm inputs, such as tractors and other machinery. Family farms have been squeezed out. In the decade between 1960 and 1970, the farm population of the United States dropped by a third, from about 15 million to about 10 million people. Farmers often bought land at low interest rates, expecting to see its value continue to grow. During the 1980s, though, the value of farm property declined in many counties. Farm debts soared from $50 million in 1970 to more than

[18] Quoted in *Time,* February 18, 1985, p. 24.
[19] Ibid.

$200 billion in 1984. Exports were down and bankruptcies rivalled depression-era rates.

Hence, in 1985, the Reagan administration proposed a new course. Believing in the free market in agriculture as well as in other segments of society, it proposed essentially to let farmers plant what they wanted and sell what they could. Over a five-year period, President Reagan proposed to Congress, federal agricultural subsidies would be reduced from $15 billion to less than $5 billion. Coming as they did at a time of farm depression, these proposals got a chilly reception in Congress.

Business and Public Policy: Subsidies Amidst Regulations

At the center of the American economy stands the corporation. Ever since the Supreme Court in *Dartmouth College* v. *Woodward* (1819) upheld the rights of a corporation against the government, the corporation has been the bastion of the capitalist system. Certainly we have limited the corporation's rights since then—to pay any wage it wanted, to pollute the air wantonly, to endanger worker safety, and the like.

But to class and elite theorists, corporations and their leaders are at the pinnacle of power in American politics. *Fortune* magazine publishes an annual listing of the *Fortune 500*, the 500 largest corporations in the United States. (One recent listing of their top 25 is in ⬚3.) Their leaders are the giants of American business, controlling assets larger than the governmental budgets of most of the world's nations. They represent, to some elite and class theorists, "monopoly capital," a concentration of wealth sufficient to shape both this nation's and the world's economy. [20] Corporate giants have also internationalized. Some **multinational corporations** (MNCs), large businesses with vast holdings in many countries, are larger than most governments. Jobs and capital have flowed to other countries, since higher profits can often be earned abroad. [21]

Multinationals. *Multinational corporations are not restricted to American labor markets, American environmental regulations, and American taxes. Their inherent mobility permits them to seek cheaper labor costs elsewhere. Moving "offshore" can enhance profit margins by lowering wage costs and the expense of environmental protection. Many multinational companies locate in rural undeveloped areas. Here is one multinational factory in the province of Tabasco, Mexico.*

Challenges to Corporate Capitalism. As on the farm, lately things have not gone so well in the boardroom. Robert Reich points out one set of problems. We have entered, he says, a time of "paper entrepreneurialism." Even though critics claim that our economy is short of the capital needed for investment, corporations now spend scarce capital buying one another up. Instead of investing in new steel production in Pennsylvania, for example, United States Steel bought Marathon Oil Company for $3 billion, earning $1 billion in tax advantages. Billions are spent by conglomerates buying up and buying out other companies. Millions, even hundreds of millions, in profit can be made merely by threatening to buy another company. "Greenmailers," as they are called, buy some stock in Corporation X, make public their desire to secure

---

[20] The argument that the American economy is dominated by "monopoly capital" is a common one among Marxist economists. See, for example, James O'Connor, *The Fiscal Crisis of the State* (New York: St. Martin's, 1973).

[21] See, for example, Raymond Vernon, *Storm over the Multinationals* (Cambridge, Mass.: Harvard University Press, 1977); Richard Barnet and Ronald Müller, *Global Reach* (New York: Simon and Schuster, 1974).

3	America's Twenty-five Largest Industrial Corporations	
Rank (in 1983)	Company	Sales (in $ thousands)
1	Exxon (New York)	88,561,134
2	General Motors (Detroit)	74,581,600
3	Mobil (New York)	54,607,000
4	Ford Motor (Dearborn, MI)	44,454,600
5	International Business Machines (Armonk, NY)	40,180,000
6	Texaco (Harrison, NY)	40,068,000
7	E.I. du Pont de Nemeurs (Wilmington, DE)	35,378,000
8	Standard Oil (Indiana) (Chicago)	27,635,000
9	Standard Oil of California (San Francisco)	27,342,000
10	General Electric (Fairfield, CT)	26,797,000
11	Gulf Oil (Pittsburgh)	26,581,000
12	Atlantic Richfield (Los Angeles)	25,147,036
13	Shell Oil (Houston)	19,678,000
14	Occidental Petroleum (Los Angeles)	19,115,700
15	U.S. Steel (Pittsburgh)	16,869,000
16	Phillips Petroleum (Bartlesville, OK)	15,249,000
17	Sun (Radnor, PA)	14,730,000
18	United Technologies (Hartford)	14,669,265
19	Tenneco (Houston)	14,353,000
20	ITT (New York)	14,155,408
21	Chrysler (Highland Park, MI)	13,240,399
22	Procter & Gamble (Cincinnati)	12,452,000
23	R.J. Reynolds Industries (Winston-Salem, NC)	11,957,000
24	Getty Oil (Los Angeles)	11,600,024
25	Standard Oil (Ohio) (Cleveland)	11,599,000

Source: *Fortune*, April 30, 1984. Corporations are ranked by sales in dollars.

controlling interest in the company, watch their stock values suddenly soar, and take millions or tens of millions in profit. The massive Phillips Petroleum Corporation in tiny Bartlesville, Oklahoma, was the green-mailers' plaything in 1984. Unluckily, paper entrepreneurialism produces no products and no new jobs. "Paper entrepreneurs," Reich insists, "provide nothing of tangible use. . . . [R]esources circulate endlessly among giant corporations, investment bankers, and their lawyers, but little new is produced."[22]

Foreign competition has not helped the American corporation either. Foreign products account for about a fifth of all American consumption, and Bethlehem and other similar communities have suffered from this foreign competition. Not even high technology is monopolized by American industries. By the 1980s, there were 36,000 industrial robots working in Japan, but only 6,500 in the United States.[23] Some advisors have peddled American high technology as a solution to the corporation's—

[22] Reich, *The Next American Frontier*, p. 57.
[23] *Time*, May 30, 1983.

and the nation's—economic problems. Take a look at [4] for one perspective on the economics and politics of high technology.

Government has not been a silent partner in the American corporation. In a few cases, namely, Lockheed Corporation, Chrysler, and the nation's railroads, government loans or buyouts have made government a very real partner or owner in corporate America. Corporate leaders may feel that they are underappreciated and over-regulated, but in fact, government has provided not only regulation, but also subsidies to American business.

Regulating Business. Government regulation of business is at least as old as the first antitrust act, the Sherman Act, passed in 1890. The purpose of **antitrust policy** is to ensure competition and prevent monopoly (control of a market by one company). Huge trusts or monopolies are able to drive competitors out because of their ability to undersell them; then, when they are the only supplier left, the monopoly can command high prices. Antitrust legislation permits the Justice Department to sue in federal court to break up companies controlling too large a share of the market. Enforcement of antitrust legislation, however, has varied. Some presidents have prided themselves on being "trustbusters," while others, like Ronald Reagan, have made antitrust enforcement a low priority.

Antitrust suits are usually lengthy and always expensive; some last decades and cost millions of corporate and federal dollars. The recently settled suits against AT&T and IBM (leaders in the communication and computer industries respectively) were no exception. Both companies were the target of justice department antitrust charges. After seven years, an out-of-court settlement with AT&T resulted in its agreement to sell twenty-two local operating companies. A thirteen-year effort to break up IBM was deemed without merit by the Attorney General's office and the case was dropped. In the AT&T case the government achieved what it set

---

[4]   Why Are People Saying Such Nice Things About "High Tech"?

Why are states and cities scrambling for this thing called "high tech"? It promised a new generation of jobs, the remaking of the American economy—a virtual rerun of the industrial revolution. When a group of computer companies put together $100 million for a proposed research and development center, twenty-seven states lined up eagerly to offer their reasons for locating it in their backyards. (Austin, Texas, won, and San Antonio hoped to profit from being almost literally in its backyard.) State governments have used their public policies to promote high tech within their borders. Whether they have kept business away from Japan or merely pirated it from one another has never been clear.

What economic benefits does the new technology bring? Donald Tomaskovic-Devey and S. M. Miller used several definitions of high-tech industries and looked at their growth potential. They report that "the record of high-technology firms in generating jobs is not reassuring." In recent years, job growth in the high-technology industries accounted for only 5 percent of our total employment growth. (The use of high-technology products in other industries may also displace workers there.) High-tech firms are less likely than other firms to employ women and minorities. Generally, job projections show that the highest growth rates are in the service industries (nurses, janitors, sales clerks, and so on).

Source: For information on economic development and high-tech industries, see Donald Tomaskovic-Devey and S. M. Miller, "Recapitalization: The Basic U.S. Urban Policy of the 1980s," in Norman I. Fainstein and Susan S. Fainstein (eds.), *Urban Policy Under Capitalism* (Beverly Hills, Calif.: Sage, 1982), Chap. 2.

Government Aids Business. *Corporate chairman and folk hero Lee Iacocca put Chrysler back on its feet. Pulled from the jaws of bankruptcy, Chrysler made $701 million in net earnings in 1983, its best year ever. But it could not have been done if the federal government had not given the third-ranked automobile manufacturer a massive loan guarantee. Chrysler paid its loans off early.*

out to do. Due to the upheaval of the two industries, however, the eventual result of both suits may be increased competition, a consequence that is consistent with President Reagan's policy toward United States business. It is unlikely that his administration will launch antitrust suits of the same scale as those against AT&T and IBM, for to some they mark the end of an era in antitrust litigation.

Antitrust issues become even more complex when international competition is involved. The existence of powerful multinational corporations, especially in the oil industry, has raised new debates about regulating big business. Some critics of the oil companies, for example, have called on government to force a breakup of the largest companies. The industry has responded by arguing that the oil industry is less concentrated than other industries and that only big oil companies can successfully confront competition from the OPEC countries and the high cost of exploring for oil.

Antitrust policy is hardly the only way business is regulated. We reviewed in Chapter 14 a variety of regulatory policies affecting businesses (pages 462–468). Business owners and managers, especially in small businesses, constantly complain about regulation. Indeed, before they complain too much, they should remember some of the benefits they get from government.

Benefiting Business. Although there are many programs to aid business, none tops in size the purchases of governments. Governments in 1984 purchased $748 billion in goods and services from private businesses. The army bought shoelaces, guns, butter, and countless other items. State and local governments are big buyers themselves, purchasing police cars, snow removal equipment, school lunch food, office furniture, and tens of thousands of other items. For most of these purchases, competitive bidding is required: Several companies submit bids and the agency selects the lowest one. At the federal level, the General Services Administration is the government's main buyer, spending billions to buy everything from paper clips to paper shredders.

The Department of Commerce is a veritable storehouse of aids for business. It collects data on products and markets through the Bureau of the Census, helps businesses export their wares, and protects patents through the Patent Office. The Small Business Administration is the government's counselor, advisor, and loan maker to small businesses.

One of the reasons official Washington is so hospitable to business interests is that industry lobbyists in Washington are well organized and sophisticated. They meet regularly, plan strategy, and maintain close ties with members of the House and Senate. Businesses organized for lobbying have been around for years. On the other hand, consumer groups are a very new entry onto the economic policy stage.

Consumer Policy: Ralph Nader and the Rise of the Consumer Lobby

Years ago, consumers were about as potent politically as bird watchers. The governing economic principle of consumerism was *caveat emptor*, a Latin phrase meaning "Let the buyer beware." With a few exceptions, public policy ignored consumers and their interests. One major exception, and the first major consumer protection policy in the United States, was the Food and Drug Act of 1906. It prohibited the interstate transportation of dangerous or adulterated food and drugs. Today the Food and Drug Administration in the Department of Health and Human Services has broad regulatory powers over the contents, marketing, and labeling of food and drugs. It must approve all drugs marketed in the United States. Its refusal to approve the use of a drug called laetrile, claimed by its promoters to cure cancer, has involved the FDA in dozens of lawsuits with cancer patients.

Consumerism, though, was a sleeping political giant until the 1960s. It was awakened by a gaunt Connecticut lawyer named Ralph Nader, whose book, *Unsafe at Any Speed*, claimed that the automobile industry was producing cars dangerous to their drivers. (The unsuccessful efforts of

The Government and Product Safety. *One of the many regulatory tasks of the government is consumer product safety, a job of the Consumer Product Safety Commission. Lawn mowers, appliances, teddy bears, dolls, and other items used around the house are subject to safety testing in the CPSC's laboratories.*

the automobile industry to dig up some dirt on Nader's private life only added to his stature as a consumer policy entrepreneur.[24] The 1960s and 1970s saw a new flood of consumer protection policies, sparked in large part by Nader-inspired consumer interest groups. Today, the Consumer Product Safety Commission (CPSC) regulates the safety of items ranging from toys to lawn mowers. Created in 1972 by the Product Safety Act, CPSC has broad powers to ban from the market products it considers hazardous to your health.

Not only do new agencies and policies promote consumer interests; old ones have gotten into the act of late. The **Federal Trade Commission (FTC)** traditionally has been responsible for regulating false and misleading trade practices. In the 1960s and 1970s, they became zealous defenders of consumer interests in truth in advertising. They ordered Carter's Little Liver Pills to drop "liver" from their name because the pills have no medical effect on the liver. They made new rules about the use of celebrities in advertising, about product labeling, and about exaggerated claims for products. In 1968, Congress made the FTC the administrator of the new Consumer Credit Protection Act. Whenever you borrow money, even if only by using a credit card, you will receive a form stating the exact amount of interest you must pay. Through these forms, and through other means, the FTC enforces truth in lending.

Labor and Government

Regulations and Benefits. Public policy toward labor unions has made something close to a 180-degree turn in the last century. Throughout most of the nineteenth century and well into the twentieth, the federal government allied with business elites to squelch labor unions. The courts interpreted the antitrust laws to apply to unions. Until the Clayton Antitrust Act of 1914 exempted unions from antitrust laws, the mighty arm of the federal government was busier busting unions than trusts. Government lent its hand to enforcing the hated "yellow dog contracts," which forced workers to agree not to join a union as a condition of employment.

The 1930s and the administration of Franklin D. Roosevelt marked a turnabout in public policy toward labor. In 1935, Congress passed the **National Labor Relations Act,** often called the Wagner Act after its sponsor, Senator Robert Wagner of New York. It guaranteed workers the right of **collective bargaining,** that is, the right to have representatives of their labor unions negotiate with management to determine working conditions. It also set rules to protect unions and organizers. An employer cannot, for example, fire a worker who talks up the possibility of unionizing around the shop. It also created the **National Labor Relations Board,** which regulates labor-management relations and negotiations.

After World War II, a series of strikes and a new Republican majority in Congress made it easy to tilt the labor-management balance a little more

---

[24] On the emergence of the consumerism movement and its policy consequences, see Mark V. Nadel, *The Politics of Consumer Protection* (Indianapolis: Bobbs-Merrill, 1971).

Nissan, Smyrna, and the Unions. *Tennessee is a "right to work" state—that is, workers are not required to join the union—and union leaders claimed that this was one reason mighty Nissan picked Tennessee for their new plant. When the Smyrna plant opened, union members demonstrated at the gates to protest the new location.*

toward management. The Taft-Hartley Act of 1947 continued to guarantee unions the right to collective bargaining. But it also included Section 14B, which permitted states to adopt what union opponents called a **right-to-work law,** forbidding requirements that workers join a union to hold their jobs. The effect of right-to-work laws is to subject unions to the free-rider problem (pages 304–306). Unions complained that the Taft-Hartley Act was a "slave labor law." Repeal of Section 14B has long been one of their key legislative goals. Taft-Hartley also allowed the president to halt major strikes by seeking a court injunction for an eighty-day "cooling off" period.

Later public policies focused on union corruption. In 1959, Congress tried to crack down by passing the Labor-Management Reporting and Disclosure Act, called the Landrum-Griffin Act. Stirred by revelations of mismanagement of funds, racketeering, and violence by some unions, Congress required that members control their officials more tightly and forbade ex-convicts from serving as union officials for five years after their release.

Partly as a result of successful lobbying by unions, government offers other benefits to workers: It guarantees a minimum wage, setting a floor on the hourly wages that employers may pay; it furnishes job-training programs—with disputable results. Government also provides unemployment compensation, paid for by workers and employers, to cushion the blows of unemployment.

POLITICS, POLICY, AND POLITICAL ECONOMY SUMMARIZED

It is an error to draw a sharp distinction between government on the one hand and the private sector on the other. Rather, the political and economic sectors are closely intermingled in the United States; their

561

linkage is called *political economy*. Politicians feel strongly about the economy and pay close attention to it. Only scattered evidence indicates that politicians may try to manipulate the economic situation at election time. The two parties do have different economic policies, particularly with respect to unemployment and inflation. Democrats try to curb unemployment more than Republicans do, though they risk inflation in doing so.

Four major instruments are available to government for managing the economy. *Subsidies* and *benefits* add moneys to the pockets of voters and consumers. *Monetary policy* and *fiscal policies*, while fiercely debated by economists, are both used by government to control the economy.

Through public policy, government also regulates sectors of the economy. We reviewed policies directed toward agriculture, business, consumers, and labor.

Key Terms

unemployment rate
Consumer Price Index (CPI)
laissez-faire
monetary policy
monetarism
Federal Reserve System

fiscal policy
Keynesian economic theory
supply-side economics
price supports
multinational corporations
antitrust policy

Federal Trade Commission (FTC)
National Labor Relations Act
collective bargaining
National Labor Relations Board
right-to-work law

For Further Reading

Barnet, Richard J., and Ronald Müller. *Global Reach* (1974). The definitive work on the multinational corporation.

Dolbeare, Kenneth M. *Democracy at Risk* (1984). A perspective from the left on the politics of economic renewal.

Gilder, George. *Wealth and Poverty* (1981). A supply-sider's bible.

Reich, Robert. *The Next American Frontier* (1983). Argues that "paper entrepreneurs" are loose in the economy, to no good end.

Rousseas, Stephen. *The Political Economy of Reaganomics* (1982). On Reagan's economic policies and philosophy.

Tufte, Edward R. *Political Control of the Economy* (1978). Argues that politicians manipulate the economy to their electoral advantage.

Public Policy and Equality

MEMO

Americans have always wrestled with the problem of equality. These days, almost no one opposes it directly, but we do not always agree on its meaning. Is equality best achieved by letting our economy operate freely without governmental intervention? Or, do we need special policies to give advantage to the previously disadvantaged? Issues such as these divide conservatives from liberals.

Disputes over equality normally center around three major dimensions of inequality: race, sex, and income. As Americans, we have inherited a long legacy of discrimination on the basis of race and sex. Even when we agree that such discrimination is wrong, we cannot easily agree on the direction of our policy courses. We talk less about discrimination on the basis of income, but the realities of poverty amidst wealth are everpresent. Numerous public policies have tried to do something about it.

In this chapter, we will do the following:

■ Examine how equality has been defined and show how different conceptions of equality lead to different policy choices.
■ Describe the principal dimensions of inequality, specifically related to race, sex, and income.
■ Show what policies government has pursued to deal with inequality.

Martin Luther King, Jr. *As leader of the American civil rights movement, King earned a Nobel Peace Prize. But his work also led to his assassination in Memphis in 1968.*

JUSTICE JOSEPH P. BRADLEY said in an 1873 decision, "The paramount destiny and mission of women are to fulfill the noble and benign offices of wife and mother. This is the law of the Creator." So said the Supreme Court when an Illinois woman, Myra Bradwell, wanted it to declare unconstitutional an Illinois law forbidding women to practice law. Times have changed since then. Eleven decades later, the Supreme Court unanimously held that a law partnership in Atlanta discriminated against women when it kept Ms. Elizabeth Hishon on the staff but denied her right to become a full-fledged partner in the firm (*Hishon* v. *King and Spalding*, 1984).

Few issues have so dominated American political life as equality. Rufus Browning and his colleagues remark that "the idea of political equality has exerted extraordinary force in human history."[1] More is involved that just political equality, for individuals want and expect equalities of all kinds, including economic. Our Founding Fathers addressed the issue when they decided that slavery would not be forbidden in the Constitution (though the importation of slaves could be regulated); a civil war was fought, in part, over issues of equality. A hundred years later in 1964, President Lyndon Johnson also confronted inequality and declared a "war on poverty." Critics charge that President Reagan's budget and tax cuts have helped the rich and harmed the poor, thus exacerbating inequality.

Whatever equality is, most Americans believe in it but do not agree on what it means or on how our public policies should achieve it. Minority group leaders such as Martin Luther King, Jr., and women's leaders such as Elizabeth Cady Stanton have attacked discrimination and championed equal rights. The landscape of public policies is covered with rules to end discrimination and promote equality.

INEQUALITY IN AMERICA

Despite two centuries of attention, many problems related to inequality continue to exist today. We may agree in theory with the ringing words of the Declaration of Independence that "all men are created equal"; but in the concrete world of reality, the words are often obscured by conflicts.

The language of politics can at times be circuitous and even confusing. Almost all of us—from the president to the representatives of minority groups—can deplore inequality. Groups advocating more rights for women may invoke the principle of equality. Yet other groups, even other women's groups, can and have argued that equality for women should be tempered by protection for women.

Where does one start describing, defining, and deploring the countless inequalities in American life? Let us begin with poverty, one form of inequality.

[1] Rufus P. Browning, et al., *Protest is Not Enough* (Berkeley: University of California Press, 1984), p. 1.

San Antonio, Texas, is the poorest of our large cities. Immigrants, both legal and illegal, swell the city's population. The north side of San Antonio is generally prosperous, the south and west sides generally are not. Although San Antonio's poor, like the poor everywhere, are the least able and likely to vote, they turned out in great numbers to vote for Henry Cisneros, the first successful Mexican-American candidate for mayor. In his reelection in 1983, Cisneros received 75 percent of the popular vote.

The struggle to beat poverty is a long and hard one; sometimes government and its policies assist and sometimes they do not. A few years back, San Antonio confronted a policy issue concerning its school financing, which led to a major Supreme Court decision. Children in one school district, Edgewood, were at a financial disadvantage. Their poor district, heavily populated by Mexican-American families, had little valuable property to tax for its schools, and students received only the bare necessities for education. In contrast, students in suburban Alamo Heights benefited from a generous property tax base and enjoyed much greater educational advantages. The Supreme Court in *Rodriguez* v. *San Antonio Independent School District* (1973) declined to rule that these inequalities in school finance violated the Constitution. Today, the Texas legislature has improved state aid to poor districts such as those where Mr. Rodriguez's children went to school. Still, poverty is grinding in San Antonio.

The poor in American cities—like our communities of San Antonio, San Jose, Bethlehem, and Smyrna—have a harder life that most of us. A few of them are the "new poor," once comfortable middle-class Americans, now almost permanently laid off in communities like Bethlehem, left behind in the wake of technological change. Many are members of minority groups. Many of the poor are illiterate. Jonathan Kozol estimates that one in five Americans is marginally illiterate, one of the reasons that the United States ranks 49th in literacy rates among the world's 158 nations. [2] The poor are more likely than most to be victims of crime and are less healthy than the rest of us. Males in the lowest family incomes have a 49 percent higher mortality rate than the general male population. [3] Increases in energy prices affect the poor seven times more than they affect the rich. [4]

Women are more likely to land in the ranks of the poor than men. Most poverty in the United States occurs in households headed by single women. Worse, the ranks of the poor in the last three or four years, have begun to grow again. Recent cutbacks in federal social expenditures have reduced the benefits of the poor more than the rich. About 45 percent of the reductions in federal spending will fall upon the households in the under $10,000 income class; less than 1 percent will strike those in the $80,000 and greater income class. [5]

[2] Jonathan Kozol, *Illiterate America* (Garden City, N.Y.: Anchor Press/Doubleday, 1985).

[3] Carroll Estes, et al., *Political Economy, Health and Aging* (Boston: Little, Brown, 1984), p. 77.

[4] Lester Thurow, *The Zero-Sum Society* (New York: Bantam Books, 1981), p. 29.

[5] United States Congressional Budget Office, *Effects of Tax and Benefit Reductions Enacted in 1981 for Households in Different Income Categories* (Washington, D.C.: Congressional Budget Office, 1982).

Hard to define, and harder still to remedy, almost no one advocates that we eliminate all income differences to address poverty. Almost all questions of equality break down to this: How much inequality and what kinds are we willing to tolerate?

Here, for example, are goals that nearly all Americans can support:

— Equal rights to speak out about our political views.
— Equal education for children regardless of race.
— Equal access to a home you can afford.
— Equal pay for the same job, regardless of whether you are male or female, black or white.

However, there are sharp differences of opinion about *how* to achieve equality. Here are some policies many Americans support but which others would oppose vigorously:

— "Comparable worth," in which equivalent work—say a female secretary who works as hard and has as much experience as a male foreman—is paid the same.
— "Job quotas," in which a certain percentage of women or minority applicants would be hired to compensate for past discrimination against women and minorities.
— School busing to achieve racial balance, sometimes imposed by federal courts to remedy a legacy of racial segregation in the schools.

Few people today would disagree that it is wrong, utterly wrong, to deny women or minority groups the right to vote. But what about the legacy of past discrimination, which prevented minority groups or women from making it to the polling places, or from getting to first base on the job, or from getting that college degree which was the first step on the way to a good job?

How Shall We Define Equality?

Surely, supporting equality as a policy does not mean treating everyone exactly the same. We do not seriously believe that both an aging, disabled person and a fit young one should receive social security benefits. What do we mean by equality when we say that public policy should promote equality of persons? The simplest form of public policy promoting equality is **equal opportunity,** meaning essentially that the rules of the game should be the same for everyone. Segregation and discrimination are clearly at odds with this concept of equality. **Segregation** exists when social customs or public policies require the separation of specific groups in schools, housing, or other activities. **Discrimination** exists when individuals are treated differently solely because of some trait: race, sex, or class.

Countless public policies have been designed to promote equal opportunity, to curb discrimination and segregation. Making the rules fair for all, though, does not reverse the legacy of past discrimination. Removing the barriers to a group's chances for advancement would not ensure that all members of the group suddenly become full competitors in the American way.

Segregation. *In the era of segregation, blacks and whites were separated from the cradle to the grave. The most important things of life—housing, schools, jobs—and the lesser things—drinking fountains, rest rooms—were all classified "White" or "Colored."*

Thus, equal opportunity does not necessarily produce **equal results.** Another view of the role of public policy in promoting equality, then, is that it should be affirmative, not merely neutral, in opening the doors of opportunity.

The Politics of Affirmative Action

Affirmative action means that people responsible for allocating some value—jobs, college admissions, promotions, and so on—give some form of special consideration to members of groups that have been traditionally disadvantaged.[6] "Special consideration" may mean many things. In its weaker version, it may mean only that jobs, for instance, are widely advertised so that many applicants from different groups hear about them. Or, in its strongest version, affirmative action may mean that quotas are established requiring that a specific percentage of jobs or school admissions be set aside for previously underrepresented groups.

Affirmative action programs began when black interest groups (and later women's groups) prevailed on Congress to write into most federal legislation a *nondiscrimination* clause. This clause states that no federal contracts, grants, or aid can go to recipients (whether federal contractors, cities, or states) who discriminate against people because of their race or sex. Few American institutions could claim to be utterly blameless of discrimination. Cabinet departments and other bureaucratic agencies developed guidelines for implementing these new congressional policies (Title IX, which concerned discrimination and led to heated disputes about men's and women's athletic programs, is one example). Meeting the guidelines often required affirmative action programs.

On bureaucratic and judicial battlefields, the war over affirmative action has raged. Revenue-sharing funds were withheld from Chicago because plaintiffs demonstrated in court that the city had practiced racial discrimination in hiring police officers. The University of California, as well as other colleges and universities, nearly lost federal aid because only a few blacks and women were members of the faculty. Only after elaborate negotiations with several federal agencies was a bargain struck, permitting the university to retain its grants and contracts. In return, the University of California agreed to a hiring program to rectify racial and sexual imbalances in its past hiring.[7]

A young man named Allan Paul Bakke came to symbolize this conflict over affirmative action. Son of a mailman, devoted to jogging, and the father of three, Bakke was an engineer intent upon going to medical school. In 1973, at the age of thirty-three, he applied to a dozen medical schools; all turned him down. A letter of rejection from the University of California at Davis particularly angered him. Bakke had discovered that Davis was using a quota system, setting aside sixteen of its hundred

[6] On affirmative action, see the guardedly favorable assessment in Allan P. Sindler, *Bakke, DeFunis, and Minority Admissions* (New York: Longman, 1978), and the sharply critical assessment in Nathan Glazer, *Affirmative Discrimination* (New York: Basic Books, 1975).

[7] Sheila K. Johnson, "It's Action, but Is It Affirmative?" *New York Times Magazine*, May 11, 1975, pp. 18 ff.

Allan Bakke. *Denied admission to the University of California's medical school at Davis, Allan Bakke took the university to court. He claimed unconstitutional discrimination because of a school policy to set aside sixteen of its one hundred places for disadvantaged applicants. The Supreme Court ordered him admitted to the medical school. In June 1982, he graduated from UC-Davis at the age of 42.*

places for minority students. Bakke's test scores were higher by far than students admitted under this special program (though lower than other applicants also denied admission). To Dr. George Lowery, chairman of the Davis admissions committee, he wrote: "I am convinced that a significant fraction [of medical school applicants to Davis] is judged by a separate criteria. I am referring to quotas, open or covert, for racial minorities. I realize that the rationale for these quotas is that they attempt to atone for past racial discrimination, but insisting on a new racial bias in favor of minorities is not a just situation." [8] Bakke sued UC-Davis and eventually won a Supreme Court decision admitting him to the Davis medical school. (See ③ in Chapter 15, page 497.)

In 1979 the Court again wrestled with the difficult question of affirmative action when aluminum worker Brian Weber sued his employer, Kaiser Aluminum. Kaiser had set up a training program with an equal number of slots for black and white trainees. When Weber applied for the program, he was rejected, but two black workers with less seniority were accepted. Weber charged that the company was discriminating against white employees, in violation of the 1964 Civil Rights Act. In *Weber* v. *Kaiser Aluminum Company* (1979), the Supreme Court came down on the side of affirmative action. It ruled that because Kaiser's program was a temporary effort to correct a massive imbalance in previous employment practices and because the program did not prohibit the hiring or advancement of whites, it did not violate the intent of the Civil Rights Act. Moreover, because Kaiser's program was a voluntary agreement between private parties—the company and the United Steelworkers union—the court held that it did not involve the constitutional question of equal protection of the laws. Thus Weber could not claim that he had been unconstitutionally discriminated against.

To advocates of affirmative action, past policies have produced equal opportunity, at least in principle, but not equal results from group to group. Advantages enjoyed by dominant groups for 200 years do not disappear with a new pronouncement that discrimination in hiring and housing opportunities is now to end. More than equal opportunity is needed to produce a similar distribution of values from one group to another.

To opponents, affirmative action has three undesirable features. First, it is "reverse discrimination": Members of one group suffer discrimination to compensate for past discrimination against another group. Second, the most advantaged members of a disadvantaged group (say, children of a black physician) are likely to benefit at the expense of the least advantaged members of the advantaged group (say, children of a poor white coal miner). Third, groups who are economically disadvantaged today, like blacks and women, are given special considerations that other groups (like Irish and Jews) never had.

To evaluate the politics of affirmative action, it will be useful to understand the major dimensions of inequality in America and to see what public policy has done to promote more equality. Only then can we decide whether policy should do even more.

---

[8] The Bakke letter is quoted in J. Harvie Wilkinson, III, *From Brown to Bakke: The Supreme Court and School Integration, 1954–78* (New York: Oxford University Press, 1979), pp. 254–55.

RACE AND PUBLIC POLICY

Era of Slavery

As involuntary immigrants, blacks spent the first two-and-a-half centuries of their American experience in slavery. Despite Jefferson's stirring words about equality in the Declaration of Independence, he and many of his fellow Founding Fathers were slaveowners. In the era of slavery, public policy was aimed at perpetuating the slave system. [1] When the slave Dred Scott escaped to a territory prohibiting slavery, the Supreme Court ordered him returned to his owner. *Dred Scott* v. *Sandford* (1857) firmly upheld the constitutionality of slavery. Public policy promoted racial inequality quite successfully. Only after the Civil War was the idea of racial equality taken seriously even by a few.

Era of Segregation

The **Thirteenth Amendment,** passed after the Civil War, forbade slavery and involuntary servitude. But the Civil War was succeeded not by a time of racial equality but by a period of segregation lasting nearly a century. From the constitutional end of slavery until the 1950s and 1960s, segregation was required by law in the South and by practice in the

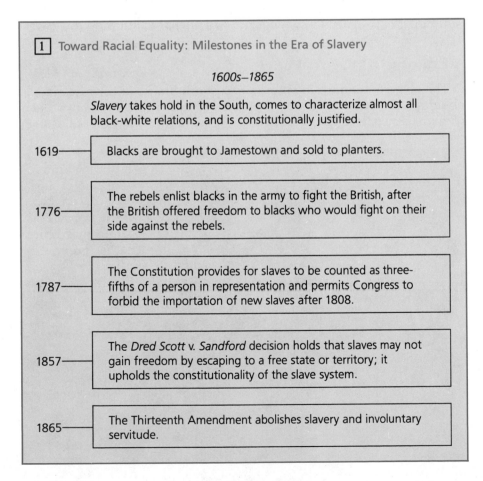

[1] Toward Racial Equality: Milestones in the Era of Slavery

1600s–1865

Slavery takes hold in the South, comes to characterize almost all black-white relations, and is constitutionally justified.

1619 — Blacks are brought to Jamestown and sold to planters.

1776 — The rebels enlist blacks in the army to fight the British, after the British offered freedom to blacks who would fight on their side against the rebels.

1787 — The Constitution provides for slaves to be counted as three-fifths of a person in representation and permits Congress to forbid the importation of new slaves after 1808.

1857 — The *Dred Scott* v. *Sandford* decision holds that slaves may not gain freedom by escaping to a free state or territory; it upholds the constitutionality of the slave system.

1865 — The Thirteenth Amendment abolishes slavery and involuntary servitude.

North. It was even justified by the Supreme Court. In the case of *Plessy* v. *Ferguson* (1896), the Supreme Court approved the principle of "separate but equal," according to which facilities for blacks and whites could be separate so long as they were equal. For over fifty years, segregated schools, public facilities, and housing were justified under this principle —even though, in fact, facilities were usually very unequal.

In the post-Civil War era, however, steps were taken toward political equality. 2 The Fifteenth Amendment guaranteed suffrage to blacks. Adopted in 1870, it said, "The right of citizens to vote shall not be abridged by the United States or by any state on account of race, color, or previous condition of servitude." But the gap between these constitutional words and their implementation remained wide for a full century. Only the Supreme Court took the Fifteenth Amendment even half-seriously. States seemed to outdo one another in imaginative policies to thwart Negro voting. Grandfather clauses, white primaries, literacy tests, poll taxes, and plain intimidation were some of the strategies to keep blacks from voting. From the cradle to the grave, southern life was segregated. Blacks were born in black hospitals and buried in black cemeteries. They attended black schools and, if they were available, black colleges.

It is hard to mark a date when the era of segregation finally began to end. But the years 1954–55 are perhaps best, containing as they did two momentous events: a bus boycott in Montgomery, Alabama, and a Supreme Court decision involving a black girl named Linda Brown.

Era of Civil Rights Policy

The **civil rights movement** organized both blacks and whites to end policies and practices of segregation. The day in 1955 when a black woman named Rosa Parks refused to give up her seat in the front of a bus

Rosa Parks. *Tired after a long day at work, Rosa Parks refused to give her seat to a white man on a segregated Montgomery, Alabama bus in 1955. A black boycott of the municipal bus line started, spearheaded by local minister Martin Luther King, Jr. If any event marked the beginning of the civil rights movement and the end of legally enforced segregation, it was Ms. Parks's action on the bus. Later, she moved to Detroit. Here, she is surrounded by students at the Rosa Parks Arts Center in Detroit.*

Toward Racial Equality: Milestones in the Era of Segregation

1865–1954

Segregation is legally required in the South and sanctioned in the North. Lynchings of blacks occur in the South. Beginning of civil rights policy.

1870 — The Fifteenth Amendment forbids racial discrimination in voting, although many states find ways to prevent or discourage blacks from voting.

1877 — End of Reconstruction. Black gains made in the South (such as antidiscrimination laws) will be reversed as former Confederates return to power. Jim Crow laws flourish, making segregation legal.

1883 — In the *Civil Rights Cases,* the Supreme Court rules that the Fourteenth Amendment does *not* prohibit discrimination by private businesses and individuals.

1896 — The *Plessy* v. *Ferguson* decision permits "separate but equal" public facilities, providing a constitutional justification for segregation.

1910 — The National Association for the Advancement of Colored People (NAACP) is founded by blacks and whites.

1915 — *Guinn* v. *United States* bans the grandfather clause that had been used to prevent blacks from voting.

1941 — Executive order forbids racial discrimination in defense industries.

1944 — The *Smith* v. *Allwright* decision bans all-white primaries.

1948 — Truman orders the armed forces desegregated.

1950 — *Sweatt* v. *Painter* finds the "separate but equal" formula generally unacceptable in professional schools.

---

to a white man was one of the first milestones. This incident prompted a bus boycott led by a local minister, Martin Luther King, Jr. He became the best-known policy entrepreneur (see Chapter 11) in the civil rights arena until he was assassinated in 1968.

Registration and the Civil Rights Movement. *The civil rights movement stirred an impulse to vote among southern blacks. Before, those who had tried were often prevented by legal means or economic pressures. Sometimes, the pressures were more physical than economic. The civil rights movement, plus the Voting Rights Act of 1965, produced a major expansion of the number of blacks in the southern electorate. Black elected officials are found in many towns and some larger cities. Atlanta's mayor and former United Nations Ambassador Andrew Young is among them.*

Sit-ins, marches, and civil disobedience were key strategies of the civil rights movement. It sought to establish equal opportunities in the political and economic sectors and to end policies that put up barriers against people because of race. Its trail was long and sometimes bloody. Its nonviolent marchers were set upon by police dogs in Birmingham, Alabama. Others were murdered in Meridian, Mississippi, and Selma, Alabama. Fortunately, the goals of the civil rights movement appealed to the national conscience. By the 1970s, overwhelming majorities of white Americans supported the goals of integration advocated by the civil rights movement. [9]

It was the courts, as much as the national conscience, that put civil rights goals on the nation's policy agenda. The 1954 *Brown* v. *Board of Education* (page 496) case was only the beginning of a string of Supreme Court decisions holding various forms of discrimination unconstitutional. *Brown* and these other decisions gave a great boost to the civil rights movement that would begin and grow in the years that followed.

As a result of conscience, the courts, the civil rights movement, and the increased importance of black voters, the 1950s and 1960s saw a marked increase in public policies to foster racial equality. Often passed only after filibusters in the United States Senate and southern delay in the House Rules Committee, congressional innovations included policies to promote voting rights, access to public accommodations, open housing, and nondiscrimination in other areas of social and economic life. The **Civil Rights Act of 1964** made racial discrimination against any group in hotels, motels, and restaurants illegal. It also forbade many kinds of job discrimination. The Voting Rights Act of 1965 (extended in 1982) was the most extensive federal effort to crack century-old barriers to black voting in southern counties. It sent federal registrars to certain states and counties to prevent actions against blacks seeking to vote. [10] (For a fuller discussion of this policy, see Chapter 8.) An Open Housing Act of 1968 took steps to forbid discrimination in the sale or rental of housing.

The *Brown* decision applied to only seventeen states, mostly southern ones, which required school segregation by law. In northern school districts, segregation was just as real, but it resulted from the fact that blacks and whites were residentially segregated and went to their own neighborhood schools. Federal courts later began to extend the *Brown* ruling to northern districts. In both North and South, they ordered school busing to achieve integration. In **Swann v. *Charlotte-Mecklenburg County Schools*** (1971), the Supreme Court upheld the right of judges to order school busing. In both North and South, it was met by resistance, sometimes even violence.

So many congressional and judicial policies came down from 1954 on that scarcely any way of denying equal opportunity escaped some legislative or judicial policy. By the 1980s, there were few, if any, forms of discrimination left to forbid by law. ③

---

[9] D. Garth Taylor, Paul B. Sheatsley, and Andrew M. Greeley, "Attitudes toward Racial Integration," *Scientific American* 238 (June 1978):42–49.

[10] On the implementation of the Voting Rights Act, see Richard Scher and James Button, "Voting Rights Act: Implementation and Impact," in Charles S. Bullock, III and Charles M. Lamb, (eds.), *Implementation of Civil Rights Policy* (Monterey, Calif.: Brooks Cole, 1984), Chap. 2.

Toward Racial Equality: Milestones in the Era of Integration

1954–1968

Integration becomes a widely accepted goal; civil rights movement grows, followed by urban racial disorders in the 1960s; black voting increases; attention shifts to equal results and affirmative action.

1954 — *Brown* v. *Board of Education of Topeka* holds that segregated schools are inherently unequal and violate the Fourteenth Amendment's equal protection clause.

1955 — Martin Luther King, Jr., leads a bus boycott in Montgomery, Alabama.

1957 — Federal troops enforce desegregation of a Little Rock, Arkansas, high school.

1963 — Civil rights demonstrators numbering 250,000 march on Washington, D.C.

1964 — Title VI of the Civil Rights Act forbids discrimination in public accommodations and provides that federal grants and contracts may be withheld from violators.
Title VII of the Civil Rights Act forbids discrimination by employers and empowers the Justice Department to sue violators. The Twenty-fourth Amendment ends the poll tax in federal elections.

1965 — The Voting Rights Act sends federal registrars to southern states and counties to protect blacks' right to vote and gives registrars the power to impound ballots in order to enforce the Act. Executive order requires companies with federal contracts to take affirmative action to ensure equal opportunity. Riots occur in Watts, California, and other cities; they will reappear in various cities every summer for five years.

1966 — The *Harper* v. *Virginia* decision holds that the Fourteenth Amendment forbids making a tax a condition of voting in any election.

1967 — Cleveland becomes the first major city to to elect a black mayor (Carl Stokes).

1968 — The *Jones* v. *Mayer* decision finds all discrimination in the sale or rental of housing to be illegal.

(box continues on next page)

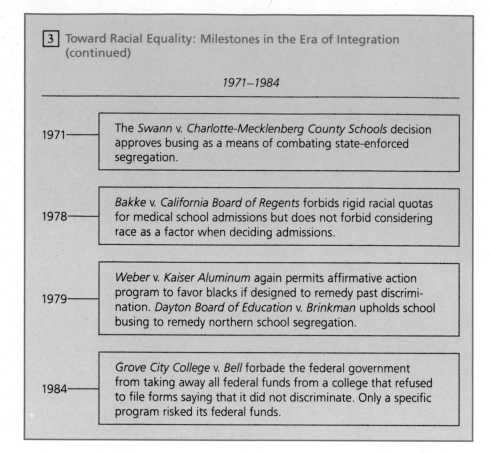

3 Toward Racial Equality: Milestones in the Era of Integration (continued)

1971–1984

1971 — The *Swann* v. *Charlotte-Mecklenburg County Schools* decision approves busing as a means of combating state-enforced segregation.

1978 — *Bakke* v. *California Board of Regents* forbids rigid racial quotas for medical school admissions but does not forbid considering race as a factor when deciding admissions.

1979 — *Weber* v. *Kaiser Aluminum* again permits affirmative action program to favor blacks if designed to remedy past discrimination. *Dayton Board of Education* v. *Brinkman* upholds school busing to remedy northern school segregation.

1984 — *Grove City College* v. *Bell* forbade the federal government from taking away all federal funds from a college that refused to file forms saying that it did not discriminate. Only a specific program risked its federal funds.

SEX DISCRIMINATION AND PUBLIC POLICY

For women, as for blacks, the first steps toward equality led through the ballot box (see pages 275–277). Winning the right to vote, however, did not automatically win equal status. In fact, the movement for women's equality seemed to lose instead of gain momentum after the suffragists' victory. An initial campaign to pass an Equal Rights Amendment failed in the 1920s, and fewer women than men even bothered to vote.

Public policy toward women continued to be dominated not by the principle of equality but by protectionism. Laws protected working women from the burdens of overtime work, night work, and heavy lifting. Public policy assumed that women were overwhelmingly at home, not in the labor force, and most state laws concentrated on keeping them at home. Fathers were breadwinners and wives were bread bakers, and state laws intended to perpetuate these roles. In most states, husbands were legally required to support their families, even after a divorce. Custody of children was almost automatically awarded to mothers after a marriage ended. Fathers were supposed to pay child support (and alimony in some states—although in many cases, neither was actually paid). Thus, public policy both reflected and reinforced prevailing views of the family. It aimed to preserve and protect the role of motherhood and hence, supporters claimed, to protect the family and the country's moral fabric. But the real result, feminists claimed, was to perpetuate sexual inequality.

The family pattern that protectionists sought to preserve—father working, mother staying at home and looking after the children—is becoming a passing lifestyle. In 1984, the female civilian labor force amounted to about 50 million (as compared to 64 million males). Of these, 27 million were married and 18 million had children under the age of eighteen.[11] As conditions have changed, demands for public policies have changed, too. The era of protectionism is not over, but the policy issue of equality keeps nudging protectionist policies to the background. In the courts, in Congress, and in the states, women's groups have battled for equality instead of protection. The National Women's Political Caucus and the National Organization for Women (NOW) have been especially influential in this fight, demanding a place for women's issues in party platforms, in political campaigns, and in political office.

The campaign has been a slow one. Not until 1971 did the Supreme Court hold that a state sex-related law violated the equal protection clause of the Fourteenth Amendment *(Reed* v. *Reed)*. As recently as 1961, the Court in *Hoyt* v. *Florida* had firmly announced, "It is still true that a woman's place is in the home." Not everyone agreed. Women who did not share that view lobbied in the states and Congress for guarantees of equal pay and promotion and for other policies for equal rights. Many policies

[11] *Statistical Abstract 1985* (Washington, D.C.: U.S. Government Printing Office, 1984).

Women in Congress. *Only two women sit in the Senate and both are Republicans. One is Kansas's respected Nancy Landon Kassebaum (left). So invincible is Senator Kassebaum that it was almost impossible to track down her opponent's campaign headquarters during her last campaign. All members of Congress are still officially called "Congressmen," but the number of women in Congress is increasing. Even so, there is a long way to go before women make up half of the Congress. Many women have earned their positions of influence through sheer tenacity and hard work. One is Representative Patricia Schroeder of Colorado (right). Women in Congress are found in both parties and are no more conservative or liberal than other Americans. Schroeder does what most successful members of Congress do: She maintains close constituency relations, selects a few issues on which to become an acknowledged expert, and juggles a busy schedule in Washington and at home.*

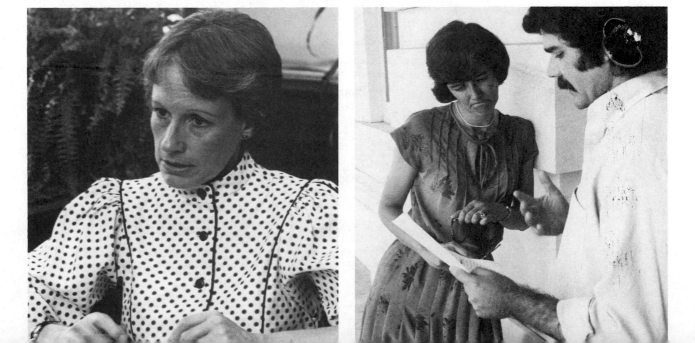

forbidding discrimination by sex and calling for affirmative action were passed. 4

Often, feminists supported changes in the laws that sought to protect women. It was this willingness to abandon protective legislation that led to sharp conflict over the **Equal Rights Amendment.** Simply worded (the amendment read "Equality of rights under the law shall not be denied or abridged by the United States or by any state on account of sex") but

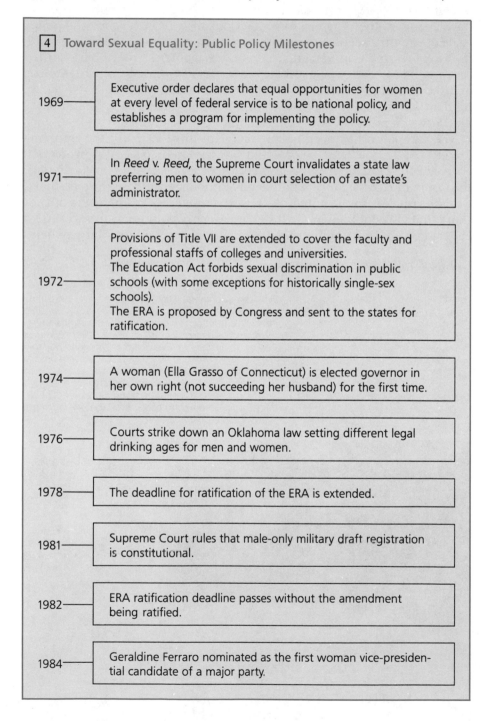

4 Toward Sexual Equality: Public Policy Milestones

1969 — Executive order declares that equal opportunities for women at every level of federal service is to be national policy, and establishes a program for implementing the policy.

1971 — In *Reed* v. *Reed,* the Supreme Court invalidates a state law preferring men to women in court selection of an estate's administrator.

1972 — Provisions of Title VII are extended to cover the faculty and professional staffs of colleges and universities.
The Education Act forbids sexual discrimination in public schools (with some exceptions for historically single-sex schools).
The ERA is proposed by Congress and sent to the states for ratification.

1974 — A woman (Ella Grasso of Connecticut) is elected governor in her own right (not succeeding her husband) for the first time.

1976 — Courts strike down an Oklahoma law setting different legal drinking ages for men and women.

1978 — The deadline for ratification of the ERA is extended.

1981 — Supreme Court rules that male-only military draft registration is constitutional.

1982 — ERA ratification deadline passes without the amendment being ratified.

1984 — Geraldine Ferraro nominated as the first woman vice-presidential candidate of a major party.

HEY, I'VE GOT NOTHING WHATEVER AGAINST THEM

THEY LIVE IN MY NEIGHBORHOOD

MY KIDS WENT TO SCHOOL WITH THEIR KIDS

WE EVEN EAT IN THE SAME RESTAURANTS

SO IT HURTS WHEN THEY SAY I DISCRIMINATE

WHY, SOME OF MY BEST FRIENDS ARE WOMEN!

YEAH, BUT WOULD YOU WANT YOUR DAUGHTER TO MARRY ONE?

holding the potential to bring sweeping changes, the ERA was proposed by Congress in 1972. It was bitterly opposed by some women's groups. In 1978, pro-ERA groups won an extension of the deadline for passage, hoping that an additional three years would give them time to persuade three more states to ratify, pushing the number to the constitutionally required thirty-eight. But no state budged, and the ERA became a constitutional dead letter in 1982. ERA proponents vowed to reintroduce the amendment in Congress and pressed hard for state-level action on women's rights.

Members of Congress did reintroduce the ERA, but the House defeated it in late 1983. Women's groups, never really giving up on the ERA, nonetheless turned their attention to other issues. One of the most controversial was **comparable worth.** According to this view, women were often stuck in "women's work," paid less than men for jobs of comparable skill. A female secretary and a male account clerk might be far apart in wages after years of similar work. The Washington State Supreme Court ruled in 1983 that its state government had for years discriminated against women by denying them "comparable worth." The United States Supreme Court, thus far at least, has been silent on the issue. Clarence Pendleton, the conservative head of the United States Civil Rights Commission, called comparable worth "the craziest idea since Looney Tunes," and argued that it would reduce incentives for women to get into higher-paying, previously male jobs. It would be, in any event, an issue that would surface again.

THE NEW CHALLENGES TO AFFIRMATIVE ACTION

Between the 1960s and the 1970s, the government in Washington seemed clearly embarked on a policy to promote advancement of minorities and women through governmental action. Republican and Democratic administrations alike filed suit against thousands of businesses,

Governor Tony Anaya. *Hispanic officials are still rare in American politics and still come mainly from the American southwest, where Hispanics are often majorities or near-majorities of the population. New Mexico's Governor Tony Anaya is one southwestern Hispanic official. Hispanics remain deeply committed to the Democratic party, despite the fact that President Reagan has made significant overtures to the Hispanic community, appearing in San Antonio on a Cinco de Mayo celebration.*

school districts, colleges, and municipalities, seeking court-ordered elimination of barriers to minority groups and women.

By the 1980s those efforts seemed to be in reverse. The Reagan administration had very different views of civil rights from earlier administrations. Its appointees to the United States Civil Rights Commission carped about burdensome federal regulations. They thought any hint of "quotas" in hiring was demeaning to minority groups and women. Opportunities for the advancement of the previously disadvantaged, they insisted, would be found in a generally expanding economy, and not in special programs targeted to minority groups and women.

Both the Reagan administration and the Supreme Court backed cautiously away from a strong commitment to affirmative action. In one notable case, **Grove City College v. Bell** (1984), issues of affirmative action came to a head in the Supreme Court. Grove City College was a small Philadelphia college that wanted federal financial aid money for its students. Because it did not want other forms of federal aid, the college refused to file papers confirming antidiscriminatory policies regarding other programs. The college felt that only its student loan program should be investigated because it was the only program that fell under the federal government's civil rights statutes. The Department of Education, however, sought to make a test case of Grove City College, and argued that it should lose its student aid because it was not willing to guarantee nondiscrimination *throughout* the college. Eventually, the Supreme Court held that only the particular program receiving federal aid, rather than the whole school, could be deprived of aid for discrimination. The implications were significant. Presumably, a school could discriminate in its athletic program and retain student aid funds if its student aid programs were nondiscriminatory. Civil rights groups vowed to seek legislation reversing the *Grove City* decision.

On December 6, 1984, civil rights leaders found more worries. For the first time, the federal government argued that a local school board should be permitted to abandon school busing even if it would increase racial segregation in neighborhood schools. The case involved Norfolk, Virginia schools. Years before, federal courts had ordered busing to achieve racial balance there. However, the Reagan administration strongly argued that mandatory busing worsened racial segregation. Administration lawyers insisted that it encouraged whites to flee to the suburbs. Again, civil rights leaders saw an effort to reverse a generation of commitment to racial equality in the public schools.

INCOME AND PUBLIC POLICY

With a median family income of about $24,580 Americans are among the richest people on earth (no longer the richest, as Arab oil skeikdoms and several western European countries have inched ahead of us). Still, we are an affluent society, a "people of plenty." Within our affluence, sadly, there is also poverty. Government is not a neutral party in affecting who gets what. Through public policy, governments help shape the distribution of income within the nation.

Who's Getting What?

Income Distribution. F. Scott Fitzgerald once wrote to his friend Ernest Hemingway, "The rich are different from you and me." "Yes," wrote back Hemingway, "they have more money." Some Americans, of course, have a *lot* more money than others. Pen's parade (page 28) illustrated how unequal is the distribution of income in America. (**Income distribution** refers to the "shares" of the national income earned by various groups.) People at the beginning of the income parade are dwarfs; by comparison, the very rich are as tall as skyscrapers.

The range of American income is truly enormous. But the old saying, "the rich get richer and the poor get poorer," does *not* apply to the United States in recent years. There has, in fact, been *practically no change whatever* in the distribution of income in the United States since 1950. [12] The rich get almost exactly the same share of today's income that they got then; the poor also get the same share. Changes have been minuscule. [5] In 1950 and now, the top 20 percent of earners collect over 40 percent of the income earned. The bottom 20 percent get about 5 percent of all income. The well off, in other words, get twice their "share" of all the income. The bottom fifth get only about a quarter of their "share."

[12] U.S. Department of Commerce, *Social Indicators 1976* (Washington, D.C.: U.S. Government Printing Office, 1977), pp. 458–59, Table 9/7.

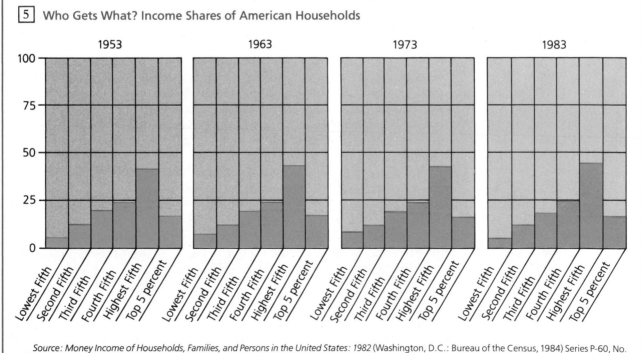

5 Who Gets What? Income Shares of American Households

Source: Money Income of Households, Families, and Persons in the United States: 1982 (Washington, D.C.: Bureau of the Census, 1984) Series P-60, No. 142, Table 17 and *Statistical Abstract of the United States, 1985* (Washington, D.C.: U.S. Government Printing Office, 1984).

Wealth. Income and wealth, however, are not the same thing, even though they may be related to one another. **Income** is the amount of funds collected between any two points in time (weeks, months, or years). **Wealth** is the amount already owned. It includes bank accounts, stocks, bonds, and property and it is used to produce income. Wealth is distributed much less evenly than income. Economists James D. Smith and Stephen D. Franklin traced the share of wealth held by the top 1 percent of wealth holders from 1953 to the 1970s. These wealthy Americans held about 25 percent of all the wealth in the United States. Their share in the 1970s was only a fraction less than their share in the 1950s. [13]

Who's Getting the Least? Poverty in America

To count the poor, we have to define *poverty.* But defining it is not easy. Poverty is meaningful only by comparison to something else. When we compare our poor to people in India, our poor families look well off. When we compare them to our rich families, they look very poor. Deciding where to draw the line between poor and nonpoor is difficult.

Often, we rely on the Bureau of the Census's **poverty line,** which takes into account what a family would need to spend for "austere" but minimally adequate amounts of nutrition, housing, and other needs. According to the bureau's poverty line, the percentage of Americans who were poor plummeted in the 1960s. But as stagflation set in during the 1970s, the decline in the poverty population leveled off. In the 1980s, it increased. By 1983, about 35.3 million people—15.2 percent of the population—were poor.

A careful, decade-long study of 5,000 American families showed that poverty may be even more extensive than the poverty line suggests. [14] In this representative sample of American families, almost a third were below the poverty level at least once during the decade, suggesting that as many as 70 million Americans live close enough to the poverty line that some crisis can push them into poverty. About a fifth of the poor were poor in nine of the ten years studied; thus, about 4 to 5 million Americans were in the throes of permanent poverty. No distinctive set of attitudes—no "culture of poverty"—distinguished the poor from the nonpoor. Instead, it was more commonly some crisis or opportunity—losing a job, getting a divorce, working longer hours, "moonlighting," having a new mouth to feed—that accounted for movement into or out of the poverty class.

Although the poor are a varied group, poverty is more common among some groups—blacks, young Americans, female-headed families, and rural residents—than among others. [6] Lots of factors—the state of the economy, what people do for themselves, plus a large measure of luck—determine who gets what in the American scramble for income and wealth. Government and its policies are also crucial factors in determining who's poor and who's not.

[13] James D. Smith and Stephen D. Franklin, "The Concentration of Personal Wealth," *American Economic Review.* Cited in Department of Commerce, *Social Indicators 1976,* p. 466, Table 9/15.

[14] Greg J. Duncan and James N. Morgan (eds.), *Five Thousand American Families* (Ann Arbor: University of Michigan Institute for Social Research, 1977).

6 Who Are the Poor? Characteristics of Persons Below the Poverty Line		
Group	Percentage of All Poor People	Percentage of This Group Who Are Poor
White	68	12
Black	28	36
Spanish origin	12	28
Married couple families	50	8
Families with male head, no wife present	3	13
Families with female head, no husband present	47	36
Under 15	33	23
65 or older	11	14
Metropolitan residents	62	14
Nonmetropolitan residents	38	18
Northeast	19	13
South	38	17
Midwest	24	15
West	19	15

Source: U.S. Bureau of the Census, "Characteristics of the Population below the Poverty Level: 1983," *Current Population Reports,* Series P-60 (1985).

How Public Policy Affects Income

Incomes are affected by many ingredients. Some people work hard; others are lazy. Some are born into opportunities galore; others must make their own. Some persons are harbingers of good fortune; others have seemingly endless bad fortune. Government, which spends one in three dollars in the U.S. economy, can have a major impact on both wealth and income. There are two principal ways in which government can affect your income:

— Government can manipulate incomes through its taxing powers.
— Government can affect income through its expenditure policies.

Taxation. "Nothing," said Benjamin Franklin, "is certain in life but death and taxes." (Many Americans believe that death is more even-handed.) Although recently there have been calls for tax simplification and tax reform, the question here is how taxes affect our income *equality.* And clearly they do.

Taxes can impact on your income in three ways. First, if the government takes a bigger bite from the income of a rich family than from the income of a poor family, we have a **progressive tax.** Thus, we would charge the millionaires 50 percent of their income and the poor 5 percent of theirs. Second, if the government takes the same shares from everyone, rich and poor alike, we have a **proportional tax**—for example, when Alice Rich and Anthony Poor both pay 20 percent of their incomes in taxes.

581

Third, we can also have a **regressive tax,** where the share of the poor is greater than the share of the rich. If a poor family pays 50 percent of its income in taxes and a rich one 5 percent, this is regressive taxation.

Rarely are taxes obviously regressive. No state really charges a higher rate of taxes for poor families and a lower rate for rich ones. It is the *effect* that counts. Poor families typically spend a larger proportion of their income on things subject to state sales taxes, while rich families spend money on stocks, bonds, or tax shelters. This means that poor families are subject to higher levels of taxation at the state level than are well-to-do families.

Taxes, therefore, can impact on the distribution of income in three ways:

1. Progressive taxes can make the poor richer and the rich poorer.
2. Proportional taxes can have no net effect on income.
3. Regressive taxes can make the rich richer and the poor poorer.

Class and elite theorists emphasize the disproportionate burden of taxes in a capitalist society which falls upon those least able to pay. This is only partly true. In fact, the best evidence indicates that the overall incidence of taxes in America is proportional, not regressive or progressive. Regressive state and local taxes counterbalance more progressive federal taxes. Benjamin Page has collected some good evidence about the burden of taxes in America. Overall, he concludes, "The U.S. tax system is virtually proportional for the vast majority of American families." [15]

There is little likelihood that this would be changed, and it could possibly be worsened, by the introduction of a *flat tax* proposed by some members of Congress and of the Reagan administration. A flat tax would enshrine the proportional principle in the federal tax structure. Its proponents claim that many exemptions would be eliminated with a flat tax, thus making it fairer to all. Upper income groups, though, would surely press for any and all tax advantages they now have.

There is one more important way in which government can affect your income, that is, through its spending and benefits.

Government Expenditures and Income Distribution. Government can affect the income you receive by a simple act: It can write you a check. Literally billions of government checks are written every year, mostly to social security beneficiaries and retired government employees. Government, too, can give you an "in-kind payment," something with cash value, even if it is not cash itself (food stamps are one example; a low-interest loan for your college education is another). All these benefits from government are called **transfer payments.** Both cash transfers and in-kind transfers are a rapidly growing part of the federal budget. In 1983, *cash* transfers amounted to $27.6 billion, while the market value of *in-kind* transfers was estimated at $49.8 billion. [16]

[15] Benjamin Page, *Who Gets What from Government* (Berkeley: University of California Press, 1983), p. 41.

[16] *Characteristics of Households and Persons Receiving Noncash Benefits, 1983* (Census, 1984, Series P-60. No. 148).

No one has done a more careful job of assessing the impact of government expenditures on the distribution of income than Benjamin Page. In *Who Gets What from Government*, he meticulously unravels the maze of government benefits. Equally important, he links them to beneficiaries among the various income classes. [17] One point is clear in program after program: Policies thought to benefit mainly the poor do not always do so. Unemployment compensation is one example. Only a fifth of the benefits of unemployment compensation go to poor families. [18] Public housing is another example. It seems to benefit contractors about as much as it benefits poor families needing subsidized housing.

Elite and class theorists believe that a few have held tightly to the reins of power and have used government to preserve and protect existing inequalities. Clearly, government could do a great deal to manipulate the distribution of income. Conservatives, even President Reagan, sometimes believe that government has done too much to help the poor. The facts seem to be otherwise. Despite a generation of wars on poverty, of expanded government spending, and of policies to promote more equality, the distribution of income is much the same as it was before government started.

The most careful (and complicated) study of government's impact on income has been conducted by Morgan Reynolds and Eugene Smolensky. They estimated the effect of government expenditures in various categories (schooling, highways, defense, policing, and so on) on individual incomes. Looking at three points in time, 1950, 1960, and 1970, they concluded that government spending had done little to make incomes more equal. Despite massive government commitments to social programs during this thirty-year period, income inequality has hardly been touched by public policy. [19] Clearly, income inequality is a common feature of life in technological societies, and one that has not been easily reversed in the United States.

EQUALITY AND POLICY SUMMARIZED

Equality in America is one of our oldest policy dilemmas. Almost all Americans believe in equality. But in practice, they disagree sharply about both the ends and the means of it. Once, those disagreements focused on issues such as slavery and segregation. Today, they are more likely to center on issues like affirmative action and comparable worth.

Most of the key conflicts about equality concern race, sex, and income. Government policies did much to promote legal equality between the races after the civil rights movement of the 1950s and 1960s. The impact of these policies was important, but equal opportunity did not really produce equal results.

Equality between men and women is also a source of policy debate. Today's labor market has a higher percentage of women in it than ever

[17] Page, *Who Gets What from Government*.
[18] Ibid., p. 184.
[19] Morgan Reynolds and Eugene Smolensky, *Public Expenditures, Taxes, and the Distribution of Income* (New York: Academic Press, 1977).

before. Efforts by groups to add the Equal Rights Amendment to the Constitution ended in failure in 1982, though many people today focus on the issue of comparable worth, that is, the notion that equivalent but not identical jobs should be paid the same.

Affirmative action, those policies designed to promote the advancement of women and minority groups, is being challenged in new ways. Many of these challenges are on the judicial policy agenda. In *Grove City College* v. *Bell,* for example, the Supreme Court held that federal aid could not be withheld from all programs in a college even if there was possible discrimination in one of them. This reduced the ability of federal policies to promote affirmative action.

Income and wealth differences also produce conflict. Income policies are seldom directly on the policy agenda, but numerous policies that affect them are. Taxes are one way in which the government can affect income. Taking more from the rich or the poor affects the ultimate incomes they enjoy. Overall, there is little evidence that governmental policies have produced major changes in the distribution of income in America.

Key Terms

equal opportunity	*Swann* v. *Charlotte-*	income distribution
segregation	*Mecklenburg*	income
discrimination	*County Schools*	wealth
equal results	Equal Rights	poverty line
affirmative action	Amendment	progressive tax
Thirteenth Amendment	comparable worth	proportional tax
civil rights movement	*Grove City College* v.	regressive tax
Civil Rights Act of 1964	*Bell*	transfer payments

For Further Reading

Browning, Rufus P., Dale Rogers Marshall, and David H. Tabb. *Protest is Not Enough* (1984). The efforts of poor groups, aided by federal antipoverty programs, to increase their political power in California cities, including San Jose.

Hochschild, Jennifer L. *What's Fair?* (1981). A study of people's attitudes toward income and income distribution.

McGlen, Nancy, and Karen O'Conner. *Women's Rights: The Struggle for Equality in the Nineteenth and Twentieth Centuries* (1983). A good account of the struggle for equal rights for women.

Okun, Arthur. *Equality and Efficiency* (1977). Okun is an economist who believes we could stand a good deal more equality without adversely affecting our economic efficiency.

Page, Benjamin. *Who Gets What from Government* (1983). The most thorough analysis available of the impact of government on individual incomes.

Wilkinson, J. Harvie, III. *From Brown to Bakke: The Supreme Court and School Desegregation* (1979). An excellent account of the politics of equal education in the public schools.

Wilson, William J. *The Declining Significance of Race* (1978). Argues that the problems of race are gradually being displaced by the problems of class and income.

Energy, Environment, and Public Policy

19

MEMO

Throughout *Government in America,* I have emphasized that policymaking is choice-taking. True, there are policy goals we all share. Surely one is clean air and water; another is the achievement of low-cost energy resources without having to strip-mine the Rockies to get them. In the politics of energy and environmental policy, as elsewhere, it is easy to achieve consensus on abstractions, harder to guarantee unanimity on actual policies.

We begin with a parable and a law. Both are part of the bible of the environmental movement. One tells us that, in the quaint language of the economist, we overconsume collective goods. The second tells us that resource exploitation and environmental despoliation are two sides of the same coin.

Issues of energy and environment are new on our policy agenda. Though conservation is a hallowed American value, the rough-and-tumble politics of energy and environment are recent products of the 1970s. They continue today, as one administration's approach to policy implementation differs dramatically from another's. I will also show you that environmental policy can become entangled in the regional political conflicts between Sunbelt and Frostbelt states (defined in Chapter 4).

Throughout this chapter, keep in mind that righteous abstractions must translate into hard political realities. Remember that individuals whose lives are affected by environmental and energy issues—the people at Love Canal, for example—are very real.

FOR MOST OF OUR NATION's first two centuries, there were few issues on the policy agenda concerning energy and the environment; now there are many. Our policy agenda includes concerns about oil supplies, acid rain, toxic waste dumps, dioxin, water pollution, sinking water tables, and energy costs. None of our four communities and our four states have escaped these and related issues on their political agendas.

Water is a policy issue in California. After World War II, the water table in California's fertile but dry central valley was 50 to 100 feet below the surface of the land. By the 1980s, it had dropped to 217 feet. Dry southern California has been trying to get wetter northern California to join in building a huge canal (to be called the Peripheral Canal) to bring more water to the south. In 1982, California voters debated a measure to move ahead on the canal. Farmers thought the probable cost too high and environmentalists opposed it because of its potential hazards to the land. Because "environmentalists provided the rhetoric and farmers supplied the clout," the canal was defeated.[1] Still, water, air pollution, toxic wastes, oceanside oil leaks, and others are still very important environmental issues in California.

Tennessee, with almost luxurious water resources insured by the federal government's Tennessee Valley Authority (TVA), faces few water problems. Since the middle of the 1970s, though, under the careful prodding and pressuring of former Senate Majority Leader Howard Baker, the federal government has poured hundreds of millions into a project called the Clinch River breeder reactor.

Tennessee has long been a leader in nuclear power. The present Senator Gore's father, Senator Albert Gore, sponsored legislation as early as 1956 to permit the federal government to build experimental nuclear power plants. The Oak Ridge National Laboratories, in the eastern part of the

[1] Terry Christensen and Larry N. Gerston, *The California Connection* (Boston: Little, Brown, 1984), Chap. 11; the quotation is at p. 263.

Clinch River. *It would have been the most expensive experiment in history. This is an architect's rendering of the Clinch River Breeder Reactor Plant. Senator Howard Baker of Tennessee, powerful partly because he was the Senate Majority Leader, pressed for funds to build the Clinch River facility. A breeder reactor "breeds" energy, using plutonium as its base fuel. The Soviet Union now has the largest breeder reactor in the world, but the French are completing a larger "Super Phoenix" breeder. With Senator Baker's departure from the Senate, congressional enthusiasm for the breeder project waned.*

Environmental Control, Smokestacks, and Acid Rain. *The burning of coal to produce energy, steel, and other industrial products is a major source of pollution in the United States. Our most abundant fuel, coal, is also our most polluting fuel, and a dangerous one besides. There is more radioactivity at the top of a coal-powered energy plant than atop a nuclear-powered one. Coal is a solid. When burned, it generates solid particles which we call pollution—the coal-blackened sides of buildings, the coal-blackened insides of miners' lungs, and the coal-blackened wastes that fall on forests and lakes. The Environmental Protection Agency adopted policies to reduce coal particles over cities. Among them was a policy to require tall smokestacks in such places as Bethlehem, Pennsylvania. The idea was that taller smokestacks would put noxious SO_x and NO_x waste particles further up into the atmosphere away from the lungs of the urban populations. The problem, though, was that these particles in the atmosphere drop on land and lakes as "acid rain." Canadian and United States' inspectors regularly test lakes in the eastern continental area for acid rain. On the basis of these inspections, Canadian officials maintain that more than 2,000 lakes have suffered "eutrification," that is, the death of plants and fish that live in them. Forests, as well as lakes, suffer from acid rain. The issue of acid rain involves domestic environmental politics as well as the global connection.*

state, are a national center for nuclear research. The Clinch River plant would be built near them.

A breeder reactor is different from a conventional nuclear reactor in that it "breeds" the rare plutonium from a more abundant form of uranium. Plutonium is a lethal, highly radioactive substance, and because it has a half-life of 24,000 years, the waste from these plants remains toxic and must be disposed of carefully. Those problems aside, the costs of Clinch River have mushroomed like the splitting of atoms. The Department of Energy estimates final costs of $3.6 billion; the General Accounting Office tallies them at $8.5 billion. Even the former chairman of the TVA called Clinch River a "technological turkey."[2]

In Bethlehem, water supply is less of a problem than the need for clean water and air. Back in 1970, the Environmental Protection Agency, trying to reduce urban air pollution from industrial sources, ordered industrial plants to increase the height of their smokestacks, thus throwing pollutants higher into the sky. Industrial plants in and around Bethlehem met these mandates and began spewing SO_x and NO_x (sulfur and nitrous oxides) high into the sky. Now, these pollutants fall on farms, forests, rivers, and lakes as "acid rain." Increases in the use of coal are particularly associated with acid rain in the atmosphere. Lakes in the eastern United States and Canada are major victims of this poisonous

[2] The story of the Clinch River reactor is told in William Lanouette, "Dream Machine," *Atlantic* (April 1983):35 ff.

byproduct of contemporary industrial technology.[3] Canadian officials have pressed for American legislation to reduce acid rain, which they estimate has already ended life in 2000 to 4000 Ontario lakes. The Reagan administration has promised to study the problem.

In few states are environmental and energy issues more fundamental than Texas. Texas's political leaders, with rare exceptions, have promoted the interests of oil. None excelled at it better than Congressmen, then Senator, then President Lyndon B. Johnson. Congressman Johnson was first sent to Washington in the depression-ridden 1930s. Even then, oil flowed relentlessly from east Texas oil fields. By the 1940 congressional campaign, Johnson was the "conduit for [the] cash" of "the newly rich Texas independent oilmen."[4] Never would oil slip far from the front of the agenda of Texas politics. Lyndon Johnson, among others, would not let it.

These days, oil even in Texas is dwindling. The days of seemingly abundant, cheap energy are over. More and more, we face trade-offs in making energy and environmental policy. The paradox is that more energy can be found, but often at the cost of environmental degradation; the environment can be cleaner, but at the cost of more expensive energy.

THE ECOLOGICAL VIEW: A PARABLE AND A LAW

The Greek philosopher Aristotle long ago noted, "What is common to the greatest number gets the least amount of care." The things we all enjoy will thus be taken for granted and often used neither wisely nor well. More recently, the distinguished biologist Garrett Hardin sketched a parable, which he called the **tragedy of the commons.** [5] Suppose, he said, some farmers graze their sheep on a common meadow. They sell the sheep or use them for their families' food. Each farmer, of course, has an incentive to raise as many sheep as he can. Each sheep is worth money, so it is better to increase your flock as much as possible. The inevitable result is that the commons becomes overgrazed, useless to all the farmers, finally sustaining no sheep at all. Each farmer contributed only a little to the destruction of the commons—one, two, or even three extra sheep could, after all, not matter much. But all suffer alike when the commons becomes worn out.

Surely, Hardin and his fellow ecologists say, the parallels to our use of the environment are obvious. One person's contribution to overconsumption is extremely small and hard to notice: If you sold all your worldly goods, moved into a pioneer cabin, and never used another drop of oil, no one would even notice, much less thank you. But the effects of collective consumption are enormous. This is true for each resource. No individual

Texas Oil. *Oil in Texas made Lyndon Johnson presidential material, the University of Texas one of the best-endowed institutions in the country, and the state of Texas dominated by oil interests for five decades. Oil is a finite, nonrenewable resource. Only so much is available under the Texas earth, and only so much can contribute to the power of oil interests. Even Texas will run dry. Many Texas political and business leaders—technologist H. Ross Perot is one—insist that Texas will have to prepare for a post-petroleum economy. Texas has chosen to invest more heavily in education and research. The politics of high technology are almost certain to be different than the politics of wild-catting.*

---

[3] *The Global 2000 Report to the President* (New York: Penguin Books, 1982), pp. 335–36.

[4] Robert A. Caro, *The Path to Power: The Years of Lyndon Johnson* (New York: Knopf, 1982), pp. 636–37.

[5] Garrett Hardin, "The Tragedy of the Commons," in Garrett Hardin and John Baden (eds.), *Managing the Commons* (San Francisco: Freeman, 1977), Chap. 3.

is personally responsible for exhausting the supplies of oil, tin, copper, and so on. Each person's consumption is a tiny portion of the total. There is little incentive for any user to reduce his or her consumption, because no one else is likely to follow suit. Self-denial may be good for the soul, but noble souls must watch others behave "rationally" and selfishly.

The same somber logic applies to pollution resulting from the use of resources. The resources of the natural environment—minerals, air, land, water—constitute the raw materials for modern life. The natural environment is also the garbage heap for all of life's wastes. The **law of materials balance** states that the total weight of materials taken from nature will equal the total weight of wastes discharged into the environment plus the total weight of any materials recycled.[6] In other words, what goes in must come out. Oil makes gas that runs cars; but gas also makes pollution. Nuclear fuel runs power plants, and it becomes radioactive waste. Each use of a material results in a form of waste. Just as there are billions of people consuming the earth's bounty, there are billions of people polluting it. And just as one person's use of resources goes virtually unnoticed, one person's pollution goes virtually unnoticed. ☐1

Together, the parable of the commons and the law of materials balance present the basic problem of environmental and energy politics. Because everyone contributes to the problem, no one has a strong incentive to cut back on his or her resource exploitation or environmental despoliation. As William Ophuls put it, "The essence of the tragedy of the commons is that one's own contribution to the problem (assuming that one is even aware of it), seems infinitesimally small, while the disadvantages of self-

---

[6] Allen V. Kneese, Robert O. Ayres, and Ralph C. d'Arge, *Economics and the Environment: A Materials Balance Approach* (Baltimore: Johns Hopkins Press, 1971).

☐1 What Goes In Must Come Out: The Law of Materials Balance

The law of materials balance links what we take from nature—exploitation—with what we return to the natural environment in the form of waste and pollution—despoliation. The more we consume, the more we also pollute. For example:

One American baby born in 1973 will require	*In his or her lifetime he or she will discard*
26 million gallons of water	10,000 no-return bottles
52 tons of iron and steel	17,500 cans
1,200 barrels of petroleum	27,000 bottle caps
13,000 pounds of paper	2.3 automobiles
21,000 gallons of gasoline	126 tons of garbage
50 tons of food	9.8 tons of particulate air pollution
10,000 pounds of fertilizer	

Source: From G. Tyler Miller, Jr., *Living in the Environment: Concepts, Problems, and Alternatives* (Belmont, Calif.: Wadsworth, 1975), p. 15. © 1975 by Wadsworth Publishing Company. By permission.

denial loom very large." [7] California farmers, who almost certainly never heard of the "tragedy of the commons," behaved in accord with it. Because California has no policies forbidding them from taking all the water they needed from beneath the ground, California "farmers have pumped water from the ground under the assumption that if they don't, others will." [8]

Americans have sometimes sorely tested the law of materials balance. Growth has always been a major American preoccupation. Virtually every American city and state values growth. An expanding population, people often believe, brings jobs to the community and new dollars to the tax base. These days, communities search for the Holy Grail of the "high tech" growth company. Each one hopes that it can entice new industry, grow in size, and expand its economy. Growth, though, has its costs. Local water supplies, as in California, may be strained. Local pollution levels may escalate. Often, environmental losses occur at the expense of economic gains. ☐2

[7] William Ophuls, *Ecology and the Politics of Scarcity* (San Francisco: Freeman, 1977), p. 150.
[8] Christenson and Gerston, *The California Connection*, p. 272.

☐2 The Growth-Environment Trade-off: The Case of San Antonio

Sociologist Harvey Molotch once wrote that "the city is, for those who count, a growth machine." By this he meant that community elites have a strong, consensual commitment to growth. The newspaper editor wants to sell more papers; the real estate broker wants to sell more homes; and the banker seeks more depositers. Politicians and public officials, too, share a common interest in local growth—they prefer to preside over a thriving place rather than a static one. It is rare to find an anti-growth ideology in a local community, especially because Americans almost always link more growth to more jobs. (Molotch showed, incidentally, that slow- and fast-growing communities have about the same unemployment problem.)

San Antonio, now the nation's tenth largest city, was no exception to this pro-growth mentality. For those who counted in the 1940s through the 1970s, growth was the touchstone of effective local government. Beginning in the 1940s, San Antonio's elite started a major drive to legally annex to the city any areas outside the city likely to be developed for residential and commercial use. Mayor after mayor supported this drive. In 1972, for example, the massive annexation of 63 miles of unincorporated land led to a major legal case (which the city finally lost). Throughout the post-war period, local

Chamber of Commerce leaders, newspaper editors, and business people supported efforts to attract new industry to the city.

But growth policies can easily collide with the law of materials balance, specifically with environmental quality. One casualty of rapid growth in the Austin-San Antonio corridor was a degradation of water quality in the massive Edwards Aquifer. This huge underground lake was the source of San Antonio's water supply. Water quality in the aquifer declined as residential and industrial growth continued unabated. (At one point, nearby Austin's Barton Springs pool, which is fed by cold springs from the Edwards Aquifer, turned green with algae and was closed.) The issue crystallized in 1976 after the San Antonio City Council re-zoned an area for a shopping mall above the Edwards Aquifer. Environmental and neighborhood groups mobilized, demanded a referendum, and defeated the mall re-zoning by a four-to-one margin. That issue also helped to seal the fate of the long-time elite who ran San Antonio, and to bring new leaders such as Henry Cisneros to power.

Source: Harvey Molotch, "The City as a Growth Machine," *American Journal of Sociology*, 82 (September, 1976): 309–22; Arnold Fleischman, "Sunbelt Boosterism: The Politics of Postwar Growth and Annexation in San Antonio," in David C. Perry and Alfred Watkins, eds., *The Rise of the Sunbelt Cities* (Beverly Hills, Calif.: Sage, 1977), Chap. 6.

The Modern Commons. *The tragedy of the commons is a parable about sheep overgrazing a common meadow. Yet it has modern parallels. California's San Joaquin Valley is an irrigated agricultural region, producing an annual $5 billion in crops. Farmers import nearly 60 percent of the water through irrigation systems. Irrigation water inevitably carries salt. And high salt concentrations in the valley threaten to render hundreds of thousands of acres unusable. The parable of the commons tells us that people naturally tend to overconsume nature's bounty. Water is one of the resources now in diminishing supply in California and all over the American Southwest.*

ENERGY POLITICS AND POLICY

Once we used wood power, people power, and horse power. Today, 95 percent of our energy consumption comes from oil, coal, and natural gas. Hydroelectric and nuclear power account for only a small portion.

Oil itself accounts for half the energy Americans use. Oil is one of nature's **nonrenewable resources,** that is, resources that nature does not replace when consumed. A single nation, Saudi Arabia, may sit astride 152 billion of the 658 billion barrels of oil in the noncommunist world.[9] Less than 5 percent of the world's proven reserves are in the United States.[10] For this reason, the United States now imports about a third of its petroleum, sending billions of dollars to oil-producing nations in return for millions of barrels of petroleum. Natural gas, our cleanest and scarcest energy source, is often found near petroleum.

Coal, not oil, is America's most abundant fuel. An estimated 90 percent of our energy resources are in coal deposits. Coal, however, accounts for only a fifth of the energy we use. Our dirtiest fuel, it is responsible for the black lungs of coal miners and the blackened cities of the coal-dependent northeast. Places like Bethlehem still have coal-blackened buildings.

Most controversial among our energy sources is nuclear power. It accounts for a minuscule share of America's energy profile. At Seabrook,

[9] Andrew Flowers, "World Oil Production," *Scientific American* 238 (March 1978):43. For a more elaborate assessment of energy supplies, see *The Global 2000 Report*, pp. 189–191.
[10] *The Global 2000 Report*, p. 191.

New Hampshire, Diablo Canyon, California (just down the road from a fault), and other nuclear plants, protesters demonstrated while environmental lawyers delayed the projects. The environmental movement fears nuclear power both because of the possibility of a radiation leak at a plant, and because of the enormous difficulty of disposing of nuclear waste safely. Despite considerable media attention to newer fuels—solar energy, windmills, geothermal power, and the like—their contribution to our energy supply is negligible.

The Department of the Interior and the Department of Energy are two principal federal agencies responsible for energy policy. James Watt, President Reagan's first secretary of the interior, was fond of telling environmental groups to "watch my record, not my rhetoric." They watched, listened, and were horrified. In the trade-offs between environmental goals and energy production, Watt made no secret of where he stood: on the side of energy developers. He embarked on a major federal program to sell off, frequently at bargain prices, federal lands for energy exploitation. After leasing reserves estimated at 1.6 billion tons of coal in Wyoming's Powder River Basin to coal companies, the General Accounting Office estimated that Watt's deal netted the taxpayers $100 million less than the market value.

Through its ownership of land (about half the land in the state of California is government-owned) and its regulatory policies, the government in Washington shapes our energy policies. David Davis, a political scientist who has examined our energy policy, believes it to be fragmented. Energy policy is "multifaceted. Coal politics is independent of

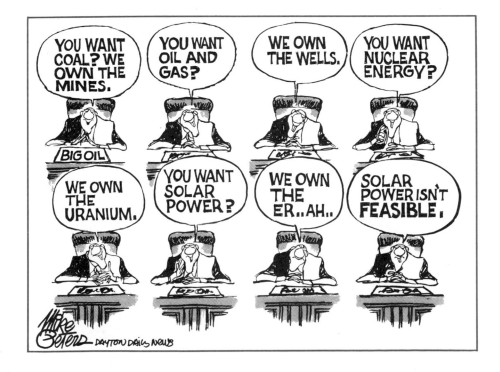

oil politics, which is independent of nuclear politics."[11] Even though oil and natural gas are found side-by-side in the same underground reservoirs, the public policies that control them are different. Some energy sources such as coal have always been left mostly to the free market, relatively free of regulation. At the other extreme, nuclear energy is rigidly regulated.

Oil stands in the middle on this regulatory continuum. Given the power of the oil industry, it is not easy to bring government's regulatory power to bear. By almost any measure, oil is the world's biggest business. Seven worldwide oil companies, called the "Seven Sisters" (Exxon, Texaco, Gulf, Standard Oil of California, Mobil, Royal Dutch Shell, and British Petroleum), are among the largest corporations in the world. Companies with enough private capital to build the $7.7 billion Alaskan pipeline are large indeed.[12] And, companies with that much capital often have much clout in Washington politics. Elite and class theorists make much of the potent political impact of "Big Oil." For years, oil-state senators and representatives were able to write into tax legislation an **oil depletion allowance,** a massive tax credit which oil investors received. Oil companies had gotten Congress to define oil as their "capital," and were thus permitted to "depreciate" it as it was drilled. Whittled back over the years, the oil depletion allowance for decades was the symbol of the incredible power of petroleum in politics. Even with this setback, major oil corporations still wield considerable influence in American politics. President Jimmy Carter's halting hints to split up "big oil" got an unsympathetic reception with Congress.

ENVIRONMENTAL POLITICS AND POLICIES

Even environmental groups might admit that few people in the 1980s have done more to spur interest in environmental issues than Coloradans James Watt, President Reagan's first secretary of the interior, and Anne Burford Gorsuch, his first Environmental Protection Agency administrator. They had a knack for painting themselves into corners, and as a result, dramatizing environmental causes. Neither had much sympathy with a generation of environmental legislation; neither lasted until the end of the first Reagan term. Their goal in office was to "deregulate" the environment. The tactless Watt impaled himself on countless policy conflicts with environmentalists, the last straw being a quip about appointing "a cripple" to an important commission. Burford came to the end of her tether after refusing to release information, despite a congressional subpoena. Needless to say, environmental groups were not sorry to see them go.

One might think that such cherished handiwork as our natural environment would almost be above politics. After all, public opinion

[11] David Davis, *Energy Politics*, 2nd ed. (New York: St. Martins, 1977), p. 12.
[12] On the power of big oil and the Seven Sisters, see Robert Engler, *The Brotherhood of Oil* (Chicago: University of Chicago Press, 1977).

analyst Louis Harris reported in the early 1980s that "the American people's desire to battle pollution is one of the most overwhelming and clearest we have ever recorded in our twenty-five years of surveying public opinion."[13] Yet, as we have learned throughout *Government in America*, politics infuses itself into all public decisions, even measures to control air and water pollution.

Environmental controls figure prominently in the debate about local and state economic development. As we saw in Chapter 5, the federal system is a competition for economic advantage. Millions of dollars are spent by states and cities pushing for a billion-dollar GM Saturn plant. New business is a boon to the local and state economies—and the political fortunes of their politicians. Thus, business elites can often argue that stringent pollution control laws will drive businesses away by driving up their costs. Firms may be reluctant to locate themselves in a heavily unionized state, when wages are lower in less unionized states. The same is true for pollution control. Why should a firm build in a state with strong pollution control laws, when costs may be lower in a state with weak laws?

Inevitably, business and government battle over the impact of pollution control on economic development. This is one of the *trade-offs* policymakers often face: will tougher pollution legislation drive away commerce and industry? No one, of course, knows for sure. The New York Department of Environmental Conservation, charged with enforcing New York state's tough environmental legislation, came up with some statistics to defend the state against such opposition. It showed that the private and public sectors in New York spent about $3.5 billion for pollution abatement in 1980 or about 1.9 percent of its state personal income. (But, the country as a whole spent about 2.4 percent of the national personal income on pollution abatement.) Those expenditures, it concluded, produced net benefits of $21.4 billion (mostly in improved health) in cleaner air alone.[14] Whatever the facts from state to state, there will still be arguments about the impact of tough pollution legislation on state and local economic development. Politicians have not been slow to figure out that pollution regulations can have an impact on economic development. ☐3

Policies and Their Implementation

A long history of American conservationism predated the environmental movement, which came into being during the 1960s.[15] During the 1960s and 1970s, Congress passed one law after another designed to clean up the nation's air and water.

[13] Lou Harris, The *Washington Post,* January 15, 1982.
[14] Policy Planning Unit, New York State Department of Environmental Conservation, *Pollution Abatement: Costs and Benefits,* February, 1985.
[15] For a recent restatement of the conservationist view, see Helen M. Ingram and R. Kenneth Godwin, "Conservation and the Forces of Change," paper delivered at the annual meeting of the American Political Science Association, Chicago, Ill., September 1–4, 1983.

The centerpiece of federal environmental policy was the **National Environmental Policy Act (NEPA),** passed in 1969.[16] It requires **environmental impact statements:** Every time a government agency proposes to undertake a policy potentially disruptive of the natural environment, it must file a statement with the Environmental Protection Agency that specifies what environmental effects the policy would have. Big dams and small post offices, major port construction and minor road widening, are all covered.

Strictly speaking, an environmental impact statement is merely a procedural requirement. "In theory," said William Ophuls, "an agency can report that a proposed activity will cause the sky to fall . . . and still proceed with the project once it has satisfied the procedural requirements of the act."[17] In practice, filing impact statements alerts environmentalists to proposed projects. Environmentalists can then take agencies to court for violating the Act's procedural requirements by filing incomplete or inaccurate impact statements. Time and again, agencies have abandoned proposed projects to avoid prolonged court battles with environmental action groups. Chances are that many of the great public works projects of the last century—the Hoover Dam, Kennedy Airport, Cape Canaveral's space facility, the TVA, and others—would not have survived the environmental scrutiny available today under NEPA. To

[16] For a legislative and administrative discussion and evaluation of NEPA, see Richard A. Liroff, *A National Policy for the Environment: NEPA and Its Aftermath* (Bloomington: Indiana University Press, 1976).

[17] Ophuls, *Ecology and the Politics of Scarcity,* p. 177.

---

3 "Nondegradation" and the Sunbelt–Frostbelt Conflict: A Case Study of Environmental Politics

The fledgling Environmental Protection Agency (EPA), created in 1970, had to deal with industrial pollution, among other things. Not surprisingly, the dirtiest air is in the northeastern quadrant of our country, with places like Bethlehem, Pennsylvania, at its hub. Congress required that the EPA set standards for "ambient air"—standards about how clean air had to be. States and localities were required to take policy actions to bring air up to standards set by the EPA. Naturally, environmentalists insisted that *higher* standards be adopted for those areas with *cleaner* air. Logical enough, you may say, for it would be silly to set standards low enough in clean-air San Antonio so that industries and autos might pollute it to the level of dirty-air Bethlehem.

Sure enough, in 1977 Congress wrote some amendments to the Clean Air Act, formally requiring the "nondegradaiton" standard. A community could not, the policy insisted, permit "degradation" of its air quality, whether it started out with pristine air or the foulest air in the country. Let us say you wanted to locate a new

plant in a community with little pollution. You could not, the law said, worsen air quality there, even if it might still be better than the air in 99 percent of the rest of the country. So you would have to install expensive "scrubbers," if you used coal, or other expensive pollution abatement techniques if you did not.

The results were predictable. Industries were discouraged from relocating in clean-air environments, mostly in the Sunbelt, because of the cost of doing so. Robert Crandall did a careful analysis of the supporters of this clean-air amendment. Not surprisingly, they hailed mostly from urban, industrialized areas of the northeast— the areas likely, without a nondegradation policy, to lose industry to the Sunbelt. No doubt each vote was motivated by a sincere environmental concern. Still, environmental concern can often be mixed with an equal measure of regional self-interest.

Source: Robert Crandall, *Controlling Industrial Pollution* (Washington: The Brookings Institution, 1983).

environmentalists, though, NEPA has been a significant policy, preventing further environmental despoliation.

Automotive pollution got policy attention, too. The **Clean Air Act** of 1970 charged the Department of Transportation (DOT) with the responsibility of reducing automobile emissions. For years thereafter, fierce battles raged between the automobile makers and DOT about how stringent the requirements had to be. Automakers claimed it was impossible to meet DOT standards; DOT claimed that automakers were deliberately dragging their feet in hopes that Congress would delay or weaken the requirements. In fact, Congress did, again and again.

The **Water Pollution Control Act** of 1972 was intended to clean up the nation's rivers and lakes. Municipal, industrial, and other polluters had to secure permits for discharging waste products into waters. The Environmental Protection Agency had to issue these licenses to pollute. Polluters were supposed to use "the best practicable [pollution] control technology."

Implementing Clean Air and Water Policies

After policies are passed, the complex process of implementation starts. Environmental legislation has involved implementing thousands of regulations applicable to hundreds of thousands of polluters. Much of the responsibility for implementing environmental policies falls to the **Environmental Protection Agency (EPA),** created in 1970. It supports research on environmental quality, but its main job is regulating pollution to promote cleaner air and water. It is the biggest single independent regulatory agency. Given the scope of its responsibilities, we can see why.

Take, for example, EPA's responsibility for regulating water pollution under the Water Pollution Control Act. All polluters—whether cities, industries, or big farmers—dumping pollutants into a waterway need a permit. Yet there are 62,000 "point sources"—places where substantial discharges are dumped into waterways—in the United States. The EPA had to assess each one, making judgments about how much discharge was justified and trying to monitor compliance as best it could. By 1976 it had developed some 492 guidelines and issued 45,000 permits.[18] Constantly in court over one permit or another, EPA was sued by environmentalists who claimed that it was too permissive and by industries and cities who thought that it was too restrictive.

It was no easier to clean up the air. The Clean Air Act of 1972 saddled EPA with the job of developing and enforcing "ambient air standards" for polluted air. In thirty-seven especially dirty areas, Congress gave the EPA wide discretion to secure cleaner air. Different areas had different problems, so the EPA tried to tailor its requirements to the unique aspects of each area. In Boston, at one point, it tried to get local authorities to cut a quarter of the downtown parking spaces to reduce car travel and the accompanying pollution. Almost everywhere, the jumble of EPA require-

[18] These data and a critique of the pollution control program are in Charles Schultze, *The Public Use of the Private Interest* (Washington, D.C.: The Brookings Institution, 1977), pp. 52–53.

ments aggravated local officials seeking new industry, plagued industries that had to install expensive pollution-control equipment, and worried workers fearful that cleaner air could cost them jobs.

Nowhere was the task of regulating environmental hazards tougher than in the area of toxic or chemical wastes. The most widely publicized case to haunt citizens and the government was on the shores of Love Canal, near Niagara Falls, New York. During the 1940s and 1950s, the Hooker Chemical Company used it as a dumping ground for toxic wastes. Then, in 1953, the company generously donated to the city of Niagara Falls a sixteen-acre plot next to the canal to build a school. A suburban development was built directly over the site. Years later, the land began to crumble. Tons of chemicals, some in rotting barrels, were discovered. Sludge crept into basements, shrubbery died, and pools of chemicals formed in yards. Children and adults developed kidney, liver, and other medical problems. Taxpayers—local, state, and national—have spent some $100 million on cleanup and medical costs at Love Canal; lawsuits total billions of dollars.

The Love Canal saga is an extreme example of the problem of chemical waste dumps. Yet, an estimated 80,000 chemical waste disposal sites containing a range of chemicals exist today. More than 55,000 man-made substances have been put into the environment during the past few decades. While most are perfectly safe, the EPA has listed some 2000 chemicals as suspect, meaning that they may—or may not—pose health hazards to humans.

In the late 1970s, Congress had created a $1.6 billion **superfund** to clean up toxic waste sites by charging taxes and fees to chemical companies. The EPA would administer the fund, identifying particularly dangerous sites and ordering restoration, which would be funded from the superfund. Gorsuch, who believed that her agency could be twice as effective with half the staff, proposed to reduce the personnel enforcing toxic waste disposal regulations to forty-six and to rely heavily on voluntary compliance by industry.[19] Gorsuch's superfund administrator, Rita Levelle, went to jail in 1985 for lying to Congress about the agency's activities.

Clearly, policies to clean up the environment involve bureaucracy, legislation, and law. As with other policies, bureaucracies play a key role in implementing congressional intent, for as we have learned time and again, policies are not self-executing.

ENERGY AND ENVIRONMENT SUMMARIZED

Issues about energy and environment are relatively new on our policy agenda. They are two faces of the same policy problem. The *tragedy of the commons* suggests that we often overconsume public goods. The *law of materials balance* holds that the amount of resource exploitation will be linked with the amount of environmental despoliation.

[19] David Osborne, "Environmental Deregulation," in Bruce Stinebrickner (ed.), *American Government* (Guilford, Conn., 1983), p. 240.

American energy profiles are changing, although we still rely heavily upon oil as our main fuel source. Coal, more available, also pollutes more. Nuclear power mired in litigation and regulation is the most controversial energy source. Politics in each energy domain is relatively independent of policies in other domains.

There is no shortage of policies affecting the environment. Most of these began during the 1970s, though there is a long history of American conservationism. Various water and air pollution laws entrusted bureaucratic agencies, particularly the Environmental Protection Agency, with developing regulations for a cleaner environment. These policies have hardly been politically neutral. We may all, in theory, support a cleaner environment, but in reality, the political conflicts surrounding environmental protection divide the parties and the Washington community.

Key Terms

tragedy of the
   commons
law of materials
   balance
nonrenewable
   resources
oil depletion allowance

National
   Environmental
   Policy Act (NEPA)
environmental impact
   statements
Clean Air Act

Water Pollution
   Control Act
Environmental
   Protection Agency
   (EPA)
superfund

For Further Reading

Ackerman, Bruce, and William T. Hassler. *Clean Coal, Dirty Air* (1980). Excellent account of the politics of energy regulation and legislation.

Council on Environmental Quality and the Department of State. *The Global 2000 Report to the President* (1980). Massive report on global issues of energy and environment.

Crandall, Robert W. *Controlling Industrial Pollution* (1983). An account of the politics and economics of air pollution policies.

Davis, David. *Energy Politics*, 3rd ed. (1982). A fuel-by-fuel description of our energy policies.

Kash, Don E., and Robert W. Rycroft. *U.S. Energy Policy: Crisis and Complacency* (1984). A review of energy politics and policy.

Ophuls, William. *Ecology and the Politics of Scarcity* (1977). An ecologist's pessimistic account of the environmental future.

Simon, Julien. *The Ultimate Resource* (1981). Simon, no environmentalist, takes a dim view of doomsayers among the ecologists.

The Global Connection

MEMO

Nowhere has the technological revolution made more difference than in our foreign and military policy. The technology of warfare produces an immense defense budget and the capacity to obliterate the earth. Our capacity to make war depends upon sophisticated and incredibly expensive technology. Just as there is an arms race, there is also a technology race. How both affect our lives will be discussed in this chapter.

Specifically, we will examine the following issues:

■ War and peace in their most up-to-date, nuclear version.
■ How American foreign policy is made, and the many actors who are involved in shaping it.
■ The politics of military spending and President Reagan's efforts to increase the defense budget.
■ Why the "American Gulliver" has troubles around the world despite his economic and military power.
■ Why issues of the world economy, inequalities among and within nations, and energy and the environment loom large, even beside problems of war and peace.

COMMUNITIES AND CITIZENS in every corner of the country are linked into the global connection. Only minutes are required to send American missiles to Moscow, the same time it would take to send Soviet missiles here. The globe is connected by the currents of missile routings. But these are not the only global connections. Today, an interdependent economy connects all nations. Each is part of the web we call the global connection. However unsettled and difficult our domestic issues appear, they seem tame by comparison with global ones: terrorism, cocaine trafficking, trade balances, nuclear proliferation, world poverty, arms races, Central American revolution, to name just a handful. Handled well, these problems become crises avoided; handled badly, most run the risk of escalating into war.

A MACABRE SCENARIO FOR NUCLEAR WAR

There are two kinds of war in the modern world. Conventional war, fought without nuclear weapons, was the only sort of war we knew before 1945. Since the first use of nuclear weapons against Japan in 1945, nuclear war has been an awesome possibility.

Contrary to our popular imagery, nuclear wars are not started by pushing a button, but by turning a key. Sitting underneath the earth in large egg-shaped containers in the North Dakota wheat fields are numerous pairs of young Air Force officers. These are our "missile men," the lieutenants, captains, and majors whose job it would be to launch our nuclear arsenal toward the Soviet Union or other targets. Each officer sits at a separate console and carries only a revolver for protection. The console contains a computer terminal, a video display screen, collections of codes, and failsafe procedures. The consoles are so placed that one officer cannot reach two keyboards. If the order to launch came, each pair of officers would have to insert their keys and turn them almost simultaneously. That is how it would begin. Here is what would happen under one scenario.

If all goes according to plan, missiles would be launched from thousands of silos in the Dakotas and other plains and southern states. Aging B-52 bombers would also take off, flying only a few hundred feet above the ground (to avoid Soviet radar detection), winging their way to Moscow and other strike sites. No doubt missiles and bombers would be flying from the other direction as well. Showers of nuclear bombs would rain on the earth. Cities would disintegrate; radiation would stick to the skins of the survivors; forests would be in flames. According to American war plans, Moscow would be hit with 60 nuclear warheads, Leningrad with more than 40, and the next largest forty Soviet cities with an average of 14.4 warheads each. Eighty percent of all Soviet cities with a population greater than 25,000 would be hit. Each would be in flames. Presumably, American cities would suffer similar fates. [1]

The effects of this nuclear outburst are not entirely clear, but very likely, a "nuclear winter" would follow within hours or days. If only 40

[1] Thomas Powers, "Nuclear Winter and Nuclear Strategy," *Atlantic* (November 1984):63.

percent of the superpowers' warheads struck, igniting forests, cities, people, farms—literally everything—the total smoke emission would exceed 100 million metric tons. And "one hundred million tons of smoke, if it were distributed as a uniform cloud over the entire globe, could reduce the intensity of sunlight reaching the ground by as much as 95 percent."[2] Probably, the smoke would be concentrated mainly in the northern hemisphere, reaching perhaps to the tropics. In the northern hemisphere, "local freezing could occur within two or three days." Over a longer period, "practically no area of the globe, north or south, would be safe from nuclear winter."[3]

We do not know for certain all the effects of nuclear war. The Pentagon, however, maintains the Defense Nuclear Agency (DNA), headquartered next to a golf course in northern Virginia. It spends about $400 million annually to assess the effects of nuclear weapons on military capacity. It conducts research and publishes military manuals on the effects of radiation on soldiering. As a result of DNA studies of radiation after-effects, the combat commander now confidently knows that tank loaders exposed to 1000 "rads" of radiation (about 1000 times as much as a chest X-ray) will remain "combat effective" for about 100 minutes. Within a day, they will be "combat ineffective"; within about a month, they will die. DNA also maintains a massive underground explosive unit in White Oak, Maryland, where virtually every military weapon is exposed to

[2] Richard P. Turco, et al., "The Climatic Effects of Nuclear War," *Scientific American* (August 1984):37.
[3] Ibid., p. 42. See also Paul R. Ehrlich, et al., *The Cold and the Dark: The World after Nuclear War* (New York: W.W. Norton, 1985).

Nuclear War: Real and Imagined. *This church scene, from the popular television movie* The Day After, *shows the results of imagined nuclear war. In the movie, the people tried to rebuild their lives and their farms. In real life, a nuclear winter may preclude any rebuilding. Real nuclear war begins with the turn of a key. The keys are turned by young officers in midwestern missile bases only after an order from the president is relayed through the Strategic Air Command headquarters in Omaha. Two missile men in the same launch capsule must each turn a key simultaneously.*

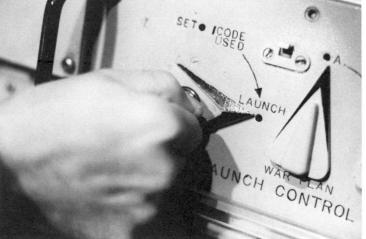

simulated nuclear explosions—10 million volts of gamma rays—to see how it performs after irradiation. [4] Someone, after all, has to find out whether those B-52 pilots could keep flying to Moscow after they and their planes have been radiated.

Planning for nuclear war is but one part of the United States' overall planning for war. The president as commander in chief is responsible for all war plans and preparations. Typically, the president will sign a short document, perhaps ten pages in length, which will outline military goals and strategies in case of a war. (President Reagan's was called National Security Decision Directive 13.) The Pentagon will elaborate it further. The Strategic Air Command (SAC) in Omaha, Nebraska, is responsible for the nuclear component of the strategy. It is SAC which aims the missiles and orders the specific bombing routes. [5] The Pentagon made public the broad outlines (not, of course, specific details) of its war plan in May 1982. The 125-page document would be the basis for its congressional budget requests in the coming years. The document itself sketched the broad picture of United States strategy in a nuclear war. [6] First, emphasized the Department of Defense (DOD), the United States should be prepared for what the document called a "protracted" conflict, that is, a war that could go on for days, weeks, or months beyond an initial nuclear exchange. Here are some principles DOD spelled out for such a war:

— An American nuclear attack on the Soviet Union would target key political and military leadership and communication lines.
— The conventional (nonnuclear) strategy would allocate military forces in priority order, first to the defense of the United States homeland, next to the defense of Western Europe, and then to protecting oil resources in the Persian Gulf; Asia, the Pacific, and Latin America would have low priority.
— Some military assistance would go to the People's Republic of China, hoping that a Chinese-Soviet conflict would reduce Soviet abilities to fight elsewhere.

The plan outlined in the document depends on the critical assumption that nuclear war can begin and then go on. The beginnings, though, are the easy part. The Congressional Office of Technology Assessment reviewed a scenario for the beginnings of a "limited nuclear war," that is, one devoted only to strikes at missile sites. [7] A limited attack, confined only to key missile sites, could kill from 2 million to 20 million people.

War and peace are serious business. Much of the energy of our foreign-policy makers is devoted to pursuing peace and planning for war, and such plans and pursuits have become ever more important in the interdependent world we live in. Military policy is the making and implementing of policies devoted to war. Foreign policy is the making and implementing of policies devoted—we hope—to peace.

[4] Rick Atkinson, "Rehearsing for Nuclear War: How Long Could an Irradiated Pilot Keep Flying?," *Washington Post Weekly Edition*, June 18, 1984, pp. 6–8.
[5] Powers, "Nuclear Winter and Nuclear Strategy," p. 64.
[6] Richard Halloran, "Pentagon Draws up First Strategy for Fighting a Long Nuclear War," *New York Times*, May 30, 1982, pp. 1ff.
[7] Cited in *Newsweek*, October 5, 1981, p. 37.

AMERICAN FOREIGN POLICY: METHODS AND ACTORS

Foreign policy is like domestic policy—it involves choice-taking—but it involves choices about relations with the rest of the world. The president of the United States is our chief foreign-policy maker. At 9:30 every morning, the president receives a highly confidential intelligence briefing. It may cover Soviet naval movements, or last night's events in some trouble spot on the globe, or Fidel Castro's health. It is part of the massive informational arsenal the president uses to manage American foreign policy. In the middle of March 1985, for example, President Reagan faced these developments on the global stage:

— The aging Soviet leader, Konstatin Chernenko, died and a younger Soviet leader, Mikhail Gorbachev, was immediately announced as his successor. The president thought about, but quickly decided against, attending the funeral and meeting the new Soviet leader.

— The situation in war-torn Lebanon continued to deteriorate as Christian troops began a revolt against the nation's Catholic President. Having lost hundreds of American marines to a terrorist attack in Lebanon a year before, there was little the White House felt inclined to do besides evacuating the American embassy in Beirut.

— Japanese officials were unhappy about American criticisms of their trade policies. President Reagan had refused to limit imports of Japanese cars (thereby worsening the plight of steelworkers in Bethlehem), but his administration was pressuring the Japanese to open their markets to more American trade.

— Central American conflict raged there and in Congress, too. The president's pleas for Congressional appropriations for antigovernment forces in Nicaragua were falling on unsympathetic ears in Congress. But when Nicaraguan president Ortega went to Moscow seeking aid, Congress relented.

Elite Succession in the Soviet Union. *The Soviet Union does not rely on elections, but rather on death, to trigger leadership change. The most recent case was the passing of President and General Secretary Konstantin Chernenko. After a series of aging leaders, the Soviet leadership chose Mikhail S. Gorbachev (next to guard) as General Secretary of the Communist Party. He, in turn, elevated former Foreign Minister Gromyko to the position of president and named his own foreign minister.*

In making decisions about these problems, Reagan faced a task with some similarities to domestic policymaking. In both foreign and domestic affairs, policymakers select goals, adopt policies in order to achieve them, and then try to implement these policies.

There are also differences between the instruments of domestic and foreign policy. All foreign policies depend ultimately on three types of tools: military, economic, and diplomatic. *War* and the threat of war are the oldest instruments of foreign policy. German General Karl von Clausewitz once called war a "continuation of politics by other means." Today, though, *economic* instruments are becoming almost as potent weapons as those of war. The control of oil can be as important as the control of guns. Trade regulations, tariff policies, and monetary policies are other economic instruments of foreign policy. *Diplomacy* is the quietest instrument. It often evokes images of ambassadors at chic cocktail parties, but the diplomatic game is played for high stakes. Sometimes national leaders meet in *summit* talks. More often, less prominent negotiators work out treaties handling all kinds of national contracts, from economic relations to stranded tourists.

Actors on the World Stage

If all the world's a stage, there are more actors on it than ever. Once foreign relations were almost exclusively transactions between nations, using military, economic, or diplomatic methods to achieve foreign policy goals. Today's world stage is more crowded.

International organizations act as both a player and a stage for international conflict. Best known of these is the **United Nations (UN).** Now housed in a magnificent skyscraper in New York City, it was created in 1945. Its members agree to renounce war and respect certain human and economic freedoms. The UN General Assembly is composed of all member nations, today numbering 157. Each has one vote. The Security Council, though, is the seat of real power in the UN. Five of its eleven members (the United States, Great Britain, China, France, and the Soviet Union) are permanent members. The others are chosen from session to session by the General Assembly. Each permanent member has a veto over Security Council decisions, including any that would commit the UN to a military, peacekeeping operation. The Secretariat directs the administration of UN programs; its head, the secretary general, usually comes from a neutral or nonaligned nation.

The UN is only one of many international organizations. The International Monetary Fund, for example, helps regulate the chaotic world of international finance. The World Bank finances development projects in new nations. The International Postal Union helps get the mail from here to there.

Regional organizations have proliferated in the post-World War II era. These are organizations of several nations bound by a treaty, often for military reasons. **NATO, the North Atlantic Treaty Organization,** was created in 1949. Its members—the United States, Canada, most western European nations, and Turkey—agreed to combine military forces and to treat a war against one as a war against all. Today, more than a million NATO troops are spread from West Germany to Portugal. They face 1.25

million troops from the **Warsaw Pact,** a regional security community of the Soviet Union and its eastern European allies.

Regional organizations can be economic rather than military. The **EEC, European Economic Community,** is an economic alliance of the major western European nations, often called the Common Market. The EEC coordinates monetary, trade, immigration, and labor policies, so EEC members have become one economic unit, just as the fifty United States are an economic unit. Other economic federations exist in Latin America and Africa, but they are not as unified as the EEC.

We have already discussed the newest entrants on the world stage, the potent *multinational corporations* or MNCs. (See page 555.) Today, a third of the world's industrial output comes from these corporations. [8] Sometimes more powerful (and often much wealthier) than the government under which they operate, MNCs have voiced strong opinions about governments, taxes, and business regulations. They have even linked forces with the CIA to overturn governments they disliked. In the 1970s, for example, several of these corporations worked with the CIA to "destabilize" the Marxist government in Chile; Chile's military overthrew the government in 1973. Even when they are not so heavy-handed, MNCs are forces to be reckoned with in almost all nations.

Groups are also actors on the global stage. Churches and labor unions have long had international interests and activities. Today, environmental and wildlife groups have also proliferated. Save-the-whales, save-the-oceans, save-the-seals, and other ecological interests are active in international, as well as national politics. Groups that are interested in protecting human rights, such as Amnesty International, have also grown. Not all groups are committed to saving whales or oceans. Some are committed to the overthrow of particular governments, and operate as terrorists around the world. Airplane hijacking, assassinations, bombings, and similar terrorist attacks have made the world a more unsettled place. Conflicts within a nation or region thus spill over into world politics.

Finally, *individuals* are international actors. The tourist explosion sends Americans everywhere and brings floods of Japanese, European, and Third World tourists to America. Tourism creates its own costs and benefits. It always affects the international economic system. Tourists may create more friendship and understanding among nations, but if more of *us* go to see *them* than the other way around, tourism can also worsen problems with our balance of payments. Growing numbers of students going to and coming from other nations are also carriers of ideas and ideologies.

Just as there are more actors on the global stage than in the past, there are also more American decision makers involved in foreign policy problems.

The Foreign-policy Makers

The president, as we saw in Chapter 13, is our chief foreign-policy maker. His power as commander in chief makes him our master of the

---

[8] Raymond Vernon, *Storm over the Multinationals: The Real Issues* (Cambridge, Mass.: Harvard University Press, 1977), p. 15.

military machine; his power to make treaties makes him our chief diplomat. But, as Page and Petracca say, "the president, of course, does not act alone in foreign policy; he is aided (and sometimes thwarted) by a huge national security bureaucracy."[9] Let us look at the diplomatic and the defense sides of that vast foreign policy and national security bureaucracy.

The Diplomats. The Department of State is the foreign policy arm of the U.S. government. The **Secretary of State** (Thomas Jefferson was our first) has traditionally been the key advisor to the president on foreign policy matters. The State Department now staffs more than 250 overseas posts and employs 24,000 people, of whom 8,000 are foreign service officers. The department itself is organized into area specialties. There is

[9] Benjamin Page and Mark P. Petracca, *The American Presidency* (New York: McGraw-Hill, 1983), p. 347.

The Secretaries of State. *While the position of secretary of state remains the key diplomatic post, it has not recently been "the vicar of American foreign policy," as Reagan's first secretary of state, Alexander Haig (right), called the post. The Secretary presides over a global bureaucracy of diplomats. No recent secretary of state has had the charisma of Henry Kissinger (below), Nixon's second secretary. He smoothed relations with China and played "shuttle diplomacy" in the Middle East. President Reagan's first secretary of state was Kissinger's former aide and NATO Commander Alexander Haig. But his swashbuckling style ran afoul of Reagan's aides and Reagan informed him that his resignation was accepted. Haig's successor was former economics professor and Bechtel chief George Schultz. Schultz (lower right) brought more stability to the post.*

a section on Middle Eastern affairs, one on European affairs, and so on. Each country is handled by a "country desk." American ambassadors represent our country in 132 embassies and nine international organizations. Once mostly a dignified and genteel profession, diplomacy is increasingly a dangerous game. The seizure of the American embassy in Tehran is a most extreme example of the hostilities that diplomats can face.

Most recent presidents have found the State Department over-bureaucratized and intransigent. Even its colloquial name, "Foggy Bottom," taken from the part of Washington where it is located, conjures up a less-than-crisp image. Many recent presidents have tended to rely more and more on their special assistant to the president for national security affairs, a role vastly expanded by flamboyant, globe-trotting Henry Kissinger, Nixon's first national security advisor. More than most recent presidents, President Reagan has relied on his secretaries of state. The short and unhappy reign of Alexander Haig has been followed by a longer and happier one of George Schultz.

The National Security Establishment. These days, foreign and military policy are closely linked. Thus, the Department of Defense is a key foreign policy actor. Often called "the Pentagon" after the five-sided building in which it is located, the Defense Department was created after World War II. It unified the Army, Navy, and Air Force departments into one giant department. The **Secretary of Defense** manages a budget larger than most nations and is the president's main military advisor.

The top brass of each of the services constitute the **Joint Chiefs of Staff,** which includes each of the commanding officers of the services. American military leaders are sometimes portrayed as gung-ho "hawks" in foreign-policy making, presumably eager to crush some small nation with a show of American force. This view is simply wrong. Richard Betts carefully examined the advice given to the president by the joint chiefs in many crises, and found the joint chiefs only slightly more likely than civilian advisors to push an aggressive military policy. (The most hawkish advice, incidentally, came from the admirals. Curiously, the most dovish advice came from the army generals and—of all places—the Marine Corps. [10]) Steeped in stereotypes of Generals George Patton and Curtis Lemay, many Americans would be surprised at the cautious attitudes of America's top military leaders. [1]

American foreign and military policy are supposed to be coordinated. To do this, an organization called the National Security Council was created in 1947. The NSC is composed of the president, the vice-president, the secretary of defense, the secretary of state, and the president's national security advisor, who is the council's chief administrator. This last position first gained public prominence when it was occupied by Henry Kissinger in President Nixon's first term. Despite the coordinating role assigned to the National Security Council, conflict within the foreign policy establishment remains common. One casualty was Secretary of State Alexander Haig, who resigned in June 1982 over personal and

[10] Richard Betts, *Soldiers, Statesmen, and Cold War Crises* (Cambridge, Mass.: Harvard University Press, 1977), p. 216, Table A.

policy differences with National Security Advisor William Clark and other members of President Reagan's White House staff.

No discussion of the institutional structures of foreign policy would be complete without mentioning the **Central Intelligence Agency (CIA).** It was created after World War II to coordinate American intelligence activities abroad. But the CIA quickly became involved in intrigue, conspiracy, and meddling, as well as intelligence-gathering. Technically, its budget and staff are secret; estimates put them about $750 million and 16,500 people. [11]

The CIA has a long history of involvement in other nations' internal affairs. After the end of World War II, when eastern European nations had fallen under Moscow's shadow and western European nations were teetering, the CIA provided aid to anti-communist parties in Italy and West Germany. It was no less busy in the Third World, where it nurtured coups in Iran in 1953 and in Guatemala in 1954, for example. It has also trained and supported armies. The most notable, of course, was in Vietnam. It has subsidized communist defectors, often in a style to which we would all love to become accustomed. The most recent worries about CIA activity have been in Central America. A group called the Sandanistas overthrew Nicaraguan dictator Anastasio Samoza in 1979. Acceptance of this new regime by the Carter administration turned to cold hatred by the Reagan administration. Congressional inquiries suggested that the CIA was quietly aiding a group of old Samoza allies called the "contras." President Reagan pushed for formal aid to the contras in 1985, and

---

[11] The best source of material on the CIA is a popular volume by two of its former employees, Victor Marchetti and John D. Marks, *The CIA and the Cult of Intelligence* (New York: Dell, 1974), a book the CIA tried unsuccessfully to suppress. Data on the size of the CIA are at pp. 74–77.

---

1 | The Generals and the Admirals: What Do They Think?

Andrew Kohut and Nicholas Horrock report on a Gallup survey, sponsored by *Newsweek,* of 257 generals and admirals, the top brass of the Army, Navy, Air Force, and Marine Corps. The American military is almost completely dominated by veterans of the Vietnam War. Nearly nine in ten had served there. As one might expect, their attitudes toward the press are mostly negative.

On the average, the generals and admirals were a moderately conservative group which expressed temperate political attitudes and cautious, even moderate, views on military policy. Support for the women's movement (42 percent were sympathetic) gleaned more enthusiasm than support for the Moral Majority (31 percent). On military matters, a clear majority (58 percent) thought America's goal should be parity with the Soviets, not superiority (35 percent). Three quarters believed that there could be no winner in a nuclear war. Two thirds could not imagine a circumstance in which they could justify a first strike against the Soviets.

The Gallup Organization divided the top brass' attitudes toward nuclear war into two types, called "scary" and "wary." Scary attitudes were held by those who thought there could be a winner in a nuclear war or who thought that circumstances might justify America firing the first missile. Wary attitudes included skepticism that any side could win a nuclear conflict and a refusal to justify a first strike. A majority of the nation's top brass held wary, not scary, attitudes toward nuclear war.

You are unlikely to find a two-star general or admiral leading your local nuclear freeze movement. Nevertheless, even a majority of our nation's military leaders thought that the nuclear freeze movement did not exaggerate the horrors of nuclear war.

Source: Andrew Kohut and Nicholas Horrock, "Generally Speaking: Surveying the Military's Top Brass," *Public Opinion,* November, 1984, pp. 42–49.

Nicaragua at the United Nations. *By the 1980s, the former stronghold of Anastasio Samoza, the nation of Nicaragua, was controlled by a group called the Sandinistas. Their leader was Daniel Ortega, who spoke at the United Nations in 1983. The Carter administration tolerated the leftist Sandinistas' regime; the Reagan administration deplored it, and tried to undermine it. The Sandinistas represented an effort to overturn an old economic order, where a handful of elite families owned and controlled an entire Central American country. They did so by increasing their contacts with Cuba and the Soviet Union. It was Ortega's trip to Moscow in search of aid that finally pried loose congressional support for aid to Ortega's opponents, the "contras."*

Congress eventually provided it. The CIA, though, did not abandon its interest in Central America.

The years after World War II saw a steady growth of all these military and foreign-policy making institutions. As the American role on the world stage grew, so did the importance of these institutions as foreign policy instruments.

BEYOND THE COLD WAR? AMERICAN FOREIGN POLICY AFTER WORLD WAR II

The Waning of American Isolationism

Throughout most of its history, the United States followed a foreign policy course called **isolationism.** It tried to stay out of other nations' conflicts, particularly European wars. The famous Monroe Doctrine, enunciated by President James Monroe, reaffirmed our inattention to Europe's problems. It warned European nations to stay out of Latin America. The United States saw Central and South America as its own political backyard. It did not hesitate to send Marines or gunboats or both to intervene in South American and Carribean affairs. However, when European nations were at war, Americans relished their ocean-width distance from the conflicts. So it was until World War I (1914–18).

In the wake of World War I, President Woodrow Wilson urged the United States to join the League of Nations. The United States Senate refused to ratify the League of Nations treaty, for the Senate was not ready to abandon the long-standing American habit of isolationism. It was Pearl Harbor that dealt a death-blow to American isolationism. At a conference in San Francisco in 1945, a charter for the United Nations was signed. The United States was an original signatory and soon donated land to house the United Nations permanently in New York City.

609

The Cold War

Containment and Korea. At the end of World War II, Germany and Japan were vanquished and much of Europe was strewn with rubble. The United States was unquestionably the dominant world power, both economically and militarily. It had not only helped to bring the war to an end but also inaugurated a new era in warfare by dropping the first atomic bombs on Japan in August 1945. Since only the United States possessed nuclear weapons, Americans looked forward to an era of peace secured by their nuclear umbrella.

After World War II, the United States forged strong alliances with the nations of western Europe. It poured billions of dollars into war-ravaged European nations to help them rebuild their economies. This aid package was called the Marshall Plan, after its architect, Secretary of State George C. Marshall. A military alliance was also forged. The creation of NATO in 1949 affirmed the mutual military interests of the United States and western Europe. Ever since, the Atlantic alliance has been a cornerstone of American foreign and defense policy.

Many Americans also expected cooperative relations with their wartime ally, the Soviet Union. These hopes were soon abandoned.

There is still much dispute about how the cold war between the United States and the Soviet Union started.[12] Yet even before World War II ended, some American policymakers feared that their Soviet allies were intent on spreading communism not only to their neighbors but everywhere. All of eastern Europe fell under Russian domination as World War II ended. Soviet support of a revolt in Greece in 1946 and their 1948 blockade of Berlin added to fears of Soviet aggression. In 1946 Winston Churchill warned that the Russians had sealed off eastern Europe with an "iron curtain." Writing in *Foreign Affairs* in 1947, foreign-policy strategist George F. Kennan proposed a policy of "containment."[13] His **containment doctrine** called for the United States to isolate the Soviet Union, "contain" its advances, and resist its encroachments—by peaceful means if possible, but with force if necessary.

The fall of China to Mao Zedong's communist-led forces in 1949 seemed to confirm American fears that communism was a cancer spreading over the "free world." In the same year, the Soviet Union exploded its first atomic bomb. The invasion of pro-American South Korea by communist North Korea in 1950 fueled American fears further. Believing the Korean invasion was linked with Soviet imperialism, President Truman said bluntly, "We've got to stop the Russians now," and sent American troops to Korea under United Nations auspices. The Korean War was a chance to put containment into practice. Until July 23, 1953, it dragged on, involving China as well as North Korea.

The 1950s were the decade of the **cold war:** Never quite erupting into armed battle, the United States and the Soviet Union were often on the brink of war. John Foster Dulles, secretary of state under Eisenhower,

---

[12] One excellent treatment of the origins of the cold war is Daniel Yergin, *Shattered Peace: The Origins of the Cold War and the National Security State* (Boston: Houghton Mifflin, 1977).

[13] The article was titled "Sources of Soviet Conduct" and appeared in *Foreign Affairs* (July 1947), under the pseudonym *X*.

Kennedy Goes to Berlin. *President John F. Kennedy went to Berlin on June 26, 1963 as a gesture of American support for Berlin, the old German capital nestled deep in the heart of East Germany. In one cold war maneuver, the Soviet Union built a meandering wall dividing the eastern Soviet area from western sectors of the city. Kennedy reviewed the wall and declared in a speech from the city hall that "Ich bin ein Berliner" (I am a citizen of Berlin).*

even proclaimed a policy of "brinksmanship." He felt the United States should be prepared to use nuclear weapons in order to influence the actions of the Soviet Union and of communist China. Fear of communism affected domestic as well as foreign policy. **McCarthyism** at home assumed that international communism was conspiratorial, insidious, bent on world domination, and infiltrating American government and cultural institutions. Named after Senator Joseph McCarthy, who with flimsy evidence fingered scores of prominent Americans as communists, McCarthyism flowered during the Korean War. Domestic policy generally was deeply affected by the cold war abroad and anticommunist fears at home. A burgeoning budget for defense during the Korean War and then later in the 1950s, was another result.

The Swelling of the Pentagon. The cold war transformed the American economy into a permanent war machine. As early as 1947, aircraft manufacturers were noting that the decline of military needs after World War II would injure the industry. To avert dislocation, they launched a campaign to sell planes to the Air Force.[14] Thus were forged some of the first links between policymakers' perceptions of the Soviet threat and corporations' awareness of profits to be made from military hardware. Generals and admirals felt they needed weapons systems. Private industry was happy to supply them for a profit. Defense expenditures grew to be the largest component of the federal budget in the 1950s, consuming $13 of every $100 of the GNP by 1954. Large parts of this defense budget were spent on weapons supplied by giant companies like Westinghouse, RCA, Western Electric, and General Motors.

[14] Yergin, *Shattered Peace*, p. 268.

611

The interests shared by the armed services and the defense contractors produced what some call a military-industrial complex. The term was coined not by a left-wing critic of the military but by President Dwight D. Eisenhower, himself a former general. Elite theorists especially pointed to this tight alliance between business and government. Economist Seymour Melman wrote about *Pentagon Capitalism,* linking the military's drive to expand with the profit motives of private industry.[15] As the defense budget grew, so did the profits of aircraft producers and other defense contractors.

Some writers have argued that we face a trade-off between defense spending and social spending. A nation, so this argument goes, must choose between guns and butter, and more guns means less butter. There is very little evidence, though, to support the existence of such a trade-off. Russett, for example, looked at federal domestic and military expenditures over 39 years and found that mostly they went up or down together rather than one going up when the other went down.[16] Examining four countries since 1948, Domke and his colleagues found much the same thing: Defense and welfare expenditures seem to be independent of one another.[17] Ronald Reagan's efforts to increase military expenditures while cutting back civilian expenditures seem to stem more from his own ideology than from any inevitable choice between the two. ☐2

[15] Seymour Melman, *Pentagon Capitalism: The Political Economy of War* (New York: McGraw-Hill, 1970).

[16] Bruce Russett, "Defense Expenditures and National Well-Being," *American Political Science Review* 76 (December 1982):767–77.

[17] William K. Domke, Richard C. Eichenberg, and Catherine M. Kelleher, "The Illusion of Choice: Defense and Welfare in Advanced Industrial Democracies, 1948–78," *American Political Science Review* 77 (March 1983):19–35.

---

2 Guns and Butter

Political scientists have unearthed little evidence that there is an aggregate trade-off between "guns" and "butter," that is, that more money for defense necessarily means less for social programs. In fact, the two tend to rise and fall together. There is no doubt, though, that individual defense expenditures compete with individual domestic expenditures. Seymour Melman, a long-time critic of military spending, compiled for the *New York Times* a list of some of the costs of defense-related items and what a comparable amount would buy in domestic programs. Here is a sampling of his listing:

Estimated cost of cleaning up 10,000 toxic-waste dumps	= $100 billion	= Navy's Trident II submarine and F-19 jet fighter programs
Proposed 1986 cuts in guaranteed student loan program and other student aid	= $2.3 billion	= 1986 budget for the M1 Abrams tank
460 meals for the homeless	= $439	= one 155-mm shell

Source: Seymour Melman, "The Butter That's Traded Off for Guns," *New York Times,* April 22, 1985, p. A19.

Nonetheless, beginning in the 1950s, an **arms race** between the Soviet Union and the United States began. One side's weaponry became the other side's goad to procure more weaponry. And so on and on, with one missile leading to another. Shortly, we will examine efforts to control this arms race.

The Vietnam War. Even though they reached their peak during the 1960s, American efforts in Vietnam did not begin then. The Korean War and the 1949 victory of Mao Zedong's communist forces in China fixed the government's attention on Asian communism. In 1950, while the Korean war raged and just after the fall of Chiang Kai-shek in China, President Truman decided to aid the French effort to retain their colonial possessions in southeast Asia.[18] (French efforts to control Vietnam dated back at least to 1787, when King Louis XVI sent 1,650 French officers to subdue the Vietnamese.[19])

During the early 1950s, the Viet Minh, the Vietnamese Communist forces, began to receive military aid from the new communist government in China. In 1954, the French were defeated in a battle at Dien Bien Phu by the Viet Minh, led by Ho Chi Minh. U.S. Defense Department officials seriously considered using atomic weapons to aid the French cause at Dien Bien Phu, but decided against it. On May 7, 1954, the Viet Minh raised their flag at Dien Bien Phu. The next morning, peace talks, including the participants and other major powers, began in Geneva, Switzerland. Though a party to the agreements, the United States never accepted the Geneva agreement to hold national elections in Vietnam in 1956. Instead, it began supporting one leader after another in South Vietnam, each seemingly more committed than the last to defeating Ho Chi Minh's forces in the north. Vietnam first became an election year issue in 1964. President Lyndon B. Johnson, who had succeeded the assassinated John F. Kennedy, was seeking his first full term. His Republican opponent, Arizona Senator Barry Goldwater, was a foreign policy hardliner. Since Truman's time, the United States had sent military "advisors" to South Vietnam, which was suffering the military uprising of the Viet Cong, who sought reunification of South Vietnam with communist North Vietnam. During the 1964 campaign, Johnson promised that he would not "send American boys to do an Asian boy's job" of defending the pro-American regime in South Vietnam. Goldwater advocated tough action in Vietnam; he would send American troops if necessary and even defoliate the jungles with chemicals so that the Viet Cong guerrillas would have no place to hide.

There was a standing joke after Johnson's victory in 1964: "They told me that if I voted for Goldwater, we'd have half a million American troops in Vietnam in two years. I did, and we do." Unable to contain the guerrilla forces of the Viet Cong (also known as the National Liberation Front) with United States advisors, Johnson sent in American troops—more than 500,000 at the peak of the undeclared war. And he dropped more bombs

[18] Stanley Karnow, *Vietnam: A History* (New York: Penguin Books, 1983), p. 43. Karnow's book is one of the best of many excellent books on Vietnam. See also Frances FitzGerald, *Fire in the Lake* (Boston: Little, Brown, 1972) and David Halberstam, *The Best and the Brightest* (New York: Random House, 1972).

[19] Karnow, *Vietnam: A History*, p. 63.

Decision-Making in the Vietnam War. *Many decisions about the war were made at weekly Tuesday luncheons in the White House, where Lyndon Johnson assembled his top foreign-policy advisors. Decisions about the war were implemented in the villages and cities of Vietnam.*

on communist North Vietnam than we had dropped on Germany in all of World War II. President Johnson and his secretaries of defense and state deluded both themselves and many of the American people into believing that the war was winnable and victory was around the corner. But massive firepower failed to contain the Viet Cong. Widespread protests at home against the war contributed to Johnson's decision not to run for reelection in 1968, and his decision to begin peace negotiations.

The new Nixon administration prosecuted the war vigorously, in Cambodia as well as in Vietnam, but also worked to negotiate a peace treaty with the Viet Cong and North Vietnam. At last a peace treaty was signed in 1973, but no one really expected it to hold. South Vietnam's capital, Saigon, finally fell to the Viet Cong in 1975. South and North Vietnam were reunited into a single nation. Saigon was renamed Ho Chi Minh City, in honor of the late leader of communist North Vietnam.

Looking back on the Vietnam War, few Americans think it was worthwhile. The only war the United States ever lost, it divided the nation, caused us to be painfully aware of the ability of our government to lie to its citizens—and perhaps worse, to itself—and reminded us that military might is not effective in guerrilla wars.

From One Republican to Another: Nixon to Reagan

Even while the Vietnam War was being waged, Richard Nixon—an old cold-war fighter—supported a new policy that came to be called détente. The term was popularized by Nixon's national security advisor, later secretary of state, Henry Kissinger.

Détente represented a slow transformation from conflict thinking to cooperative thinking in foreign policy strategy. It sought a relaxation of tensions between the superpowers, coupled with firm guarantees of mutual security. The policy assumed that the United States and the Soviet Union had no long-range and irrevocable sources of conflict; that both had an interest in peace and world stability; and that a nuclear war was—and should be—unthinkable. Thus, foreign policy battles between the United States and USSR were to be waged with diplomatic, economic, and propaganda weapons; the threat of force was played down.

One major initiative coming out of détente was the **Strategic Arms Limitation Talks,** known as **SALT.** They represented an effort by the United States and the Soviet Union to agree to scale down their nuclear capabilities, with each maintaining sufficient power to deter a surprise attack by the other. The first SALT treaty was signed by Nixon in 1972 and was followed by negotiations for a second SALT treaty. SALT II was laboriously negotiated for six years and finally signed and sent to the Senate by President Carter in 1979. The United States Senate never approved the SALT II treaty, although both Jimmy Carter and Ronald Reagan insisted that they would be committed to its limitations. SALT II would have limited the United States and the Soviet Union to no more than 2,250 strategic nuclear missile launchers and would have made other nuclear weaponry limitations on both sides.

The philosophy of détente was applied to the People's Republic of China as well as to the Soviet Union. After the fall of pro-American Chiang Kai-shek in 1949, the United States had refused to extend diplomatic recognition to the world's most populous nation, recognizing instead Kai-shek's government-in-exile on the nearby island called Taiwan. As a senator in the early 1950s, Richard Nixon was an implacable foe of "Red China," even suggesting that the Democratic administration had traitorously "lost" China. However, it was the same Richard Nixon (some called him a "New Nixon") who, as president two decades later, first visited the People's Republic and sent an American mission there. President Jimmy Carter extended formal diplomatic recognition in November 1978. Since then, cultural and economic ties between the

Nixon Goes to China. *President Richard Nixon, an early foe of the Communist government in Beijing (Peking), opened the way to normal diplomatic relations between the United States and the People's Republic of China by visiting Peking in February 1972. Here he is shown reviewing Chinese troops with Prime Minister Chou Enlai.*

United States and China have increased greatly. Hardly an American state fails to claim a "sister province" relationship with one of the provinces in China.

Throughout the cold war years, the potential for conflict between the United States and the USSR was great. Few saw more threats from the "evil empire," as he called the Soviet Union, than Ronald Reagan. He viewed the Soviet invasion of Afghanistan in 1979 as typical Russian aggression, which, if unchecked, could only grow more common. He hailed "anticommunist" governments everywhere and pledged to increase American defense spending.

THE DEFENSE OF THE REALM: THE POLITICS OF MILITARY SPENDING

Reversing the Decline: The Reagan Rearmament

From the middle of the 1950s to 1981, the defense budget had been declining as a percentage of both the total federal budget and the gross national product. In 1955, during the administration of President Eisenhower, the government was spending 61 percent of its budget for defense purposes. This amounted to about 10 percent of our GNP, the total value of all the goods and services produced in the United States that year. By 1984, less than 27 percent of the federal budget and 6.4 percent of our GNP were devoted to paying for past, present, and future wars. This was a substantial cut indeed, though it came about more because levels of social spending increased than because military spending declined. Republican Richard Nixon used to boast that he was the first president in recent history who committed more of our national budget to social services than the military services.

President Ronald Reagan was determined to reverse this historic diminishing of defense spending. Telling Congress that American military power was growing obsolete and was dangerously behind the growth of Soviet military power, Reagan proposed to embark on a five-year defense buildup. The cost he proposed was $1.5 trillion. In December 1981, Congress passed, and President Reagan signed, a record defense spending authorization. Just shy of $200 billion, the defense budget for fiscal year 1982 was substantially larger than that of any recent year.

During his campaign for the presidency, Ronald Reagan had argued that "We cannot negotiate arms control agreements that will slow down the Soviet military buildup as long as we let the Soviets move ahead of us in every category of armaments." By 1980, the Soviet Union was spending nearly $175 billion for defense; the United States was spending about $125 billion. The United States faced, Reagan said, a "window of vulnerability" because the Soviet Union was galloping ahead of the United States in military spending.

Sometimes charts and graphs are published to show comparisons between land-based and submarine-based missiles, bombers, and other offensive weapons. ③ Yet these can be misleading. Dollar-for-dollar comparisons merely reflect what the Soviet Union would have spent if it had bought weapons systems at American prices. Moreover, such com-

Political leaders frequently brandish estimates showing that the United States and the Soviet Union are closely competitive in the weapons race, or worse, that the Soviet Union is well ahead. These estimates should be viewed with considerable caution. They depend on many factors—accuracy and quality of weapons systems, for example—that are not reflected in the numbers. Here is one of those estimates of the strategic balance.

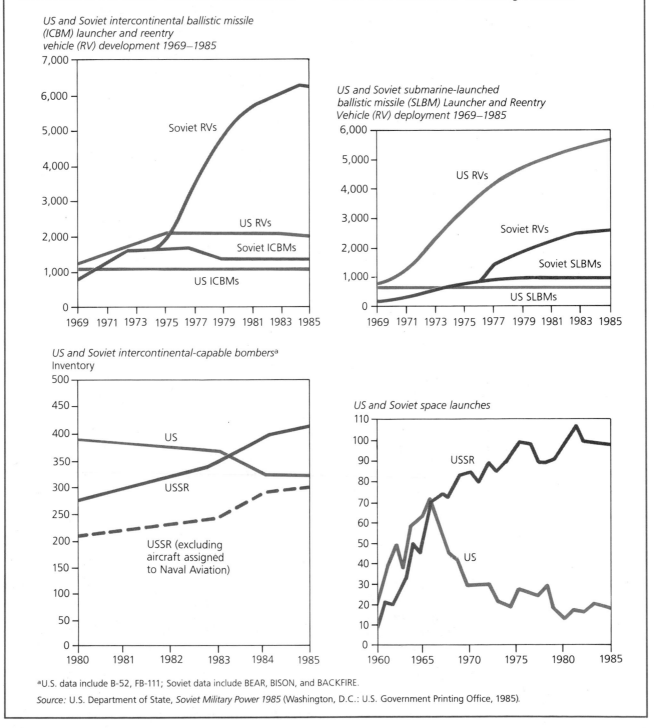

US and Soviet intercontinental ballistic missile (ICBM) launcher and reentry vehicle (RV) development 1969–1985

US and Soviet submarine-launched ballistic missile (SLBM) Launcher and Reentry Vehicle (RV) deployment 1969–1985

US and Soviet intercontinental-capable bombers[a]
Inventory

US and Soviet space launches

[a]U.S. data include B-52, FB-111; Soviet data include BEAR, BISON, and BACKFIRE.

Source: U.S. Department of State, *Soviet Military Power 1985* (Washington, D.C.: U.S. Government Printing Office, 1985).

parisons ignore quality factors completely. American Vietnam-era M-16 rifles frequently jammed; Soviet tanks are subject to frequent breakdowns. Comparisons of missiles are even riskier. The number of missiles may be less important than their accuracy, their ability to withstand a first strike, and the computer programs that support them. In the last analysis, of course, missile systems represent the largest investment the world has ever seen in a system that has never been tried.

Since the Reagan administration took office, the Soviet Union increased its lead in ICBM (intercontinental ballistic missile) warheads by about 1000, but mostly because the United States was retiring old missiles. In submarine-based missiles, where the United States has the strongest advantage over the Soviets, the United States added 400 warheads and the Soviets added 644. [20]

Critics of defense spending see excessive investment in weapons as bordering on scandalous. Vast sums of money are involved. On a single day in March 1982, two ships launched for the Navy cost a total of $1.63 billion. Few critics of defense spending have compiled a more careful set of charges than James Fallows, once Jimmy Carter's chief speechwriter. Each side, he says, has become committed to increasing technology in warfare. Thus, each weapons system becomes more complex and also more expensive. "Running through all the arguments in favor of high technology," he says, "is the idea that the United States really has no choice." He quotes former Secretary of Defense Harold Brown: "Our technology is what will save us." [21] Yet technology can be cumbersome, unworkable, untested, and, of course, expensive.

The early days of the Reagan administration were the most critical in building up defense spending. The news came down to the Pentagon rank-and-file quickly: President Carter's last budget had proposed a big defense spending increase. The Reagan administration would add $32 billion on top of that. Nicholas Lemann described it like this: [22]

> Now in the first week in February [1981], they were asked to come up with more programs, to meet the new Administration's numbers. Here is the way one former Pentagon budget officer recalls that period: "It was a kind of unique situation. I was working for the Navy, and there was a numbers drill that said, If you had half a billion or a billion more, what would you do with it? My stuff was only five billion total. We put in a minesweeper that had been on the books for years, for example."
>
> Another account, from a different budget officer: "I was in the Office of the Secretary, working for the readiness accounts. Carter had given us a lot. The Weinberger team came in and said, 'Add more. Find room to add. Find places to put more money.' "

Defense spending is a thorny political issue. Ideological issues are entangled in issues of military spending. Liberals think that the Pentagon wastes our money and that we buy too many guns and too little butter. Conservatives point to Soviet military buildups and insist that we

[20] Walter Pincus and Don Oberdorfer, "The Nuclear Balance Has Changed Little Under Reagan," *Washington Post National Weekly*, December 31, 1984, p. 15.
[21] James Fallows, *National Defense* (New York: Random House, 1981), pp. 59–60.
[22] Nicholas Lemann, "The Peacetime War," *Atlantic*, October, 1984, p. 72.

need to match them. In January 1985, President Reagan proposed a 13 percent increase in the defense budget. One big item in his budget proposal was the purchase of some MX missiles.

The MX: From the Racetrack to the Bargaining Table

In June 1979, the Carter administration announced plans to build the largest missile in the United States arsenal, called the *MX* (which stands for *experimental missile*). Every missile would be seventy feet long and weigh 192,000 pounds. Each would contain ten warheads, any one of which could be aimed at a different site. Each warhead would possess more destructive force than thirty of the original atomic bombs dropped at Hiroshima and Nagasaki and would be accurate to within 600 feet (about a city block), even when fired from 6,000 miles away.[23]

Debate ensued about where to house the MX missiles. They would fit in existing silos for Minuteman missiles. The problem was that if American missiles could land on a dime and knock out Soviet missiles, there was every reason to assume that Soviet missiles were as accurate. Department of Defense planners came up with the idea of creating a mobile missile system. SLBMs (submarine-launched ballistic missiles) were already mobile and hidden beneath the sea. If the MX missiles could be moved about on land—hidden in a nuclear shell game—an attacker would waste missiles trying to locate them and knock them out. Thus emerged a variety of plans for what Herbert Scoville, Jr., called "the classical shell game with the Soviet Union in which the MX missile was a 190,000 pound pea and heavy concrete shelters were the shells."[24] Toying with a variety of options—putting the missiles in dirigibles, building a

[23] Herbert Scoville, Jr., *MX* (Cambridge, Mass.: MIT Press, 1981), pp. 12–14.
[24] Ibid., p. 18.

The MX Missile. *Here is a prototype of the "missile without a home," the MX. The Air Force displayed the missile and its "transporter emplacer" in the Nevada desert. The emplacer weighs 1.4 million pounds with its missile cargo aboard and travels at a speed of thirteen miles per hour.*

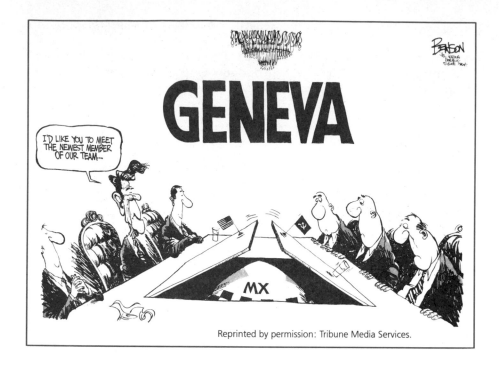

GENEVA

I'D LIKE YOU TO MEET THE NEWEST MEMBER OF OUR TEAM...

MX

Reprinted by permission: Tribune Media Services.

9,100-mile-long covered trench, placing the missiles on hovercraft—the Department of Defense finally settled on the idea of housing them in silos somewhere in the American West. The plan finally adopted by the Ford administration, and then the Carter administration, would build 4,600 silos to house 200 missiles. Pentagon planners devised a scheme to build 40,000 miles of roads—a sort of racetrack around which the MXs would travel. Trucks could convey each missile from one silo to another around an area about the size of New Jersey. One version of the plan even proposed to create public parks and recreational areas along the roads. The official estimate of the cost was $35 billion, an estimate almost everyone thought was too low. The Air Force even suggested a site, the Great Basin region of Utah and Nevada.

In those states, even people strongly and ideologically committed to nuclear superiority over the Soviet Union did not want the missiles in their backyards. Utah Senator Jake Garn, a Reagan Republican, and Nevada Senator Paul Laxalt, one of Ronald Reagan's strongest legislative supporters, found the MX idea appealing but the location wanting. So did the Mormon church, not only a religious but also a political power in the region. Environmentalists were no happier. As with every other public project that would disturb nature, the MX project had to have an Environmental Impact Statement (EIS) prepared. (We examined the EIS in Chapter 19, on page 595.) The EIS for MX was massive, running 1,900 pages in nine volumes. MX construction, the Air Force claimed, would create 60,000 jobs in the region; but boom times would be followed by bust times, as workers drawn to the construction would encounter joblessness after its completion. More than 160,000 acres of land would have to be cleared for MX, some of which would permanently lose its native vegetation. Water for construction would have to be diverted from the Colorado River, the source of water for millions in Arizona and

California. The problems, the Air Force said, were "manageable." To environmentalists, they were catastrophic.

The Reagan administration reviewed the options. Locating the missiles proved harder than building them. President Reagan appointed a commission, headed by former National Security Advisor Brent Scowcroft, to review the MX, which the President then started calling the "Peacekeeper" missile. The Scowcroft commission decided that it might not be important after all to make the MX a mobile missile. Even an existing missile silo would do. No longer did the MX need to be a flying Dutchman among missile systems. It would, the President insisted, be an important bargaining chip with the Russians. How, he asked, could they believe that we meant business at the arms reduction talks if we were already throwing in the towel on the MX?

Angry over an American decision to deploy Pershing missiles in Europe, the Soviet Union walked out of arms control talks in Geneva in December 1983. On March 13, 1984, the MX again appeared as a bargaining chip in negotiations with the Soviets, as Secretary of Defense Caspar Weinberger went to Congress again to urge MX production. Linking the missile with restarting the **START (Strategic Arms Reduction Talks)** talks, the defense secretary brought along Paul Nitze, the Reagan administration arms control advisor. Together they stressed the importance of having the MX funding as a bargaining tool to pressure the Soviet Union to return to the START talks. The next month, the presidential commission recommended basing 100 MX missiles in existing silos. Finally, in July 1984, Congress approved funds for twenty-one of the MX missiles. Again in 1985, there were MX debates in the House and Senate. And again, Congress approved more funding for the missiles, although capping the number at forty, about half of what President Reagan had requested.

It had been a long, ironic story. The world's most powerful missile, pushed by the world's most powerful office-holder, had nothing but trouble finding a home. A Flying Dutchman among weapons systems, the MX finally came about because President Reagan persuaded Congress that more military hardware was important to persuade the Soviets to help reduce military hardware. Arms control seems to work that way.

Restarting START and the Star Wars Gambit

In 1983, President Reagan unveiled a new plan for defense against missiles. He called it the Strategic Defense Initiative (SDI). Critics quickly renamed it "Star Wars." The 1972 Strategic Arms Limitations Talks had prohibited the development of antiballistic missiles (ABMs), defensive weapons that would supposedly knock out missiles before they could strike. Reagan's Star Wars proposals would have created a global umbrella in space, where "fifth generation" computers would scan the skies and use various high-tech devices to destroy invading missiles. Because President Reagan was not very specific about the system he had in mind, all sorts of speculation flooded Washington and the scientific community. The administration proposed a research program costing $26 billion in fiscal years 1985 through 1990. The Pentagon's Strategic

Defense Initiative Organization (SDIO) had the task of sorting out science from science fiction.

All proposals for a space-based defense had to consider certain facts. A missile's trip from the Soviet Union to a silo in Montana (or to the White House) would take about thirty minutes. It would go through several stages: lift-off, entry into space, mid-course, and re-entry. Presumably, a missile—or thousands of missiles—could be intercepted at any point on its trajectory. Detection would be crucial. Missiles generate heat and light and radar images, but so do thousands of other items in the sky. A system would have to distinguish between missiles and airplanes, satellites, space junk, and, of course, decoys. Chemical and X-ray lasers were proposed. Each would be based in space, presumably in some sort of space station. Eventually, the SDIO researchers decided to settle on a "first generation" capacity that emphasized weapons that rely upon kinetic energy. These included "smart rocks" (anti-missile missiles that respond to heat generated by warheads) and "railguns" (devices that use electromagnets to accelerate a projectile along a rail to high speeds before launching).

Any Star Wars system, though, would require the perfection of computers vastly more powerful than any currently produced. Because the system would have to be fully computerized, it is unlikely that human decisions could interfere. Only seconds or minutes would be allowed for crucial decisions. Automatic decisions would have to be made. Thus, computers using artificial intelligence would be expected to perform tasks that only the President could perform before. The first head of the Defense Department's DDI study estimated that any program for the SDI would have to be put through 50 million debugging runs before it would be battle-ready. But, critics asked, would even this be enough? Computers not only make errors on their own, but are dependent upon the errors humans build into their programs. During the Falklands War, the highly sophisticated British destroyer *Sheffield* was destroyed by an Argentine missile that its high-tech radar recognized as an Exocet missile. But because the *Sheffield* was programmed to fight the Russians, its computers failed to see the French-made Exocet missile as a hostile one. In any event, deployment of any system would violate the 1972 SALT agreements, which prohibited defensive missile systems.[25]

The Soviet Union, partly eager to present a new face of peace under its new administration and partly concerned about the implications of Star Wars, returned to the START talks in Geneva in the spring of 1985. Ronald Reagan promised he would work there to secure a lasting reduction of nuclear capacity.

Today, though, awesome as nuclear weapons are, there are more issues on the world stage than nuclear weaponry. Mighty powers such as the United States and the Soviet Union are mired in smaller, but intractible issues. The Soviets wrestle with dissent at home and in eastern Europe, with declining productivity at home, and with corruption. The United States, too, wrestles with issues across the globe, issues that the mighty Gulliver of international politics feels it should not have to face.

[25] Our discussion of "Star Wars" relies on "Exploring the High Tech Frontier," *Time*, March 11, 1985; and Johnathan Jocky, "The 'Star Wars' Defense Won't Compute," *Atlantic*, June, 1985, pp. 18–30.

GULLIVER'S TROUBLES AND THE NEW GLOBAL AGENDA

By whatever standards we use, the United States is surely the world's mightiest power. Yet its very strength seems to belie an essential weakness. Events on the world stage often appear to run counter to the American script. In the long and controversial Vietnam War, 500,000 American troops could not defeat the Viet Cong. Economic vulnerability increased. Oil supply lines depend on a precarious Middle Eastern peace and safe passage of huge tankers through a sliver of water called the Strait of Hormuz. In Asia, Africa, and Latin America, movements of national liberation are often opposed by the United States, but they topple pro-American (and often right-wing) governments anyway, as the Sandinistas did in Nicaragua. In Iran, the United States for years supported the pro-American but brutally repressive regime of the Shah. His oil riches and military power inspired a 1976 best-seller, *The Crash of '79*, which spun a scenario about how the Shah could dominate, even annihilate, the world. Yet power—even power backed by American weapons—is fragile. What really happened in 1979 was not conquest by the Shah but his overthrow by Islamic revolutionaries and a new government run by mullahs and ayatollahs.

Harvard political scientist Stanley Hoffman likened the United States' plight to that of Jonathan Swift's Gulliver, the human-sized traveler seized and bound by the tiny Lilliputians.[26] For us, as for Gulliver, merely being big and powerful is no guarantee of dominance. Time after time and place after place, so it seems, the American Gulliver loses to the Lilliputians. Nowhere does Gulliver confront more problems than in the troubled Middle East.

A Case in Point: The Middle East

The Middle East is a great triangle of civilization, roughly bounded by Iran on the east, Egypt on the south, and Turkey on the north. It has been a place of turbulence for at least a millennium. Until recently, the United States could safely ignore it. In 1948, after World War II, the victorious Western powers created the state of Israel, intended as a homeland for Jews surviving the scourge of fascism. Returning the Jews to their historic homeland, though, involved displacing Palestinians from theirs. Millions of homeless Palestinians live today in camps near Israeli borders. Spawning dozens of organizations committed to the destruction of Israel—the Palestinian Liberation Organization (PLO) is merely the best known—the Palestinians have created a major hurdle for Middle Eastern peace. Six times since its founding, Israel has gone to war with its Arab neighbors. Each time, the United States has been Israel's key supporter and arms supplier.

The American commitment to Israel, long supported by the American Jewish community, later had to confront the new reality of Arab oil.

---

[26] Stanley Hoffman, *Gulliver's Troubles, or the Setting of American Foreign Policy* (New York: McGraw-Hill, 1968).

Though bested repeatedly by Israeli military power, Arab nations had an economic weapon Israel could not match, one on which American dependence grew annually. An oil boycott by the Arab members of **OPEC (the Organization of Petroleum Exporting Countries)** in the winter of 1973–74 brought home to the United States the reality of economic power in world politics. If it did nothing else, it persuaded Washington that peace between Israel and her Arab neighbors would have to be the primary foreign policy goal of the United States.

The United States finally succeeded in persuading Egypt and Israel to sign a peace treaty in 1979, largely through the efforts of President Carter, who arranged a week of meetings at Camp David with Egyptian President Anwar el Sadat and Israeli Prime Minister Menachem Begin. Henry Kissinger, to whom President Sadat gave the pen he had used in signing the Camp David accords, remarked, "It is a new world now." But euphoria and exuberance in Washington, Cairo, and Jerusalem only temporarily overshadowed backlash in the Arab world. Sadat was praised in Washington and Jerusalem, but scorned in Arab capitals. Even the more moderate Arab nations cut off diplomatic relations and aid to Egypt. OPEC quickly announced a series of staggering increases in oil prices. Significantly, President Carter, immediately after bidding farewell to President Sadat and Prime Minister Begin, went to work on the task of finding a new energy policy. And two years after signing the treaty, Anwar Sadat was assassinated in Egypt by a band of militant Moslem fundamentalists.

Israel, in fact, was never fully supportive of the framework of the 1979 treaty. To protect its borders from the PLO, it invaded Lebanon in the summer of 1982, leading to bloody attacks on refugee camps in Beirut.

Beirut, 1983. *The role of Middle Eastern policemen was not an easy one for the Reagan administration. A decision to locate American marines in Beirut as "peacekeepers" resulted in a car bombing of the garrison there in 1983. The U.S. Embassy was then destroyed by a bomb. American Marines withdrew and troubles in Lebanon went from bad to worse. In June of 1985, American passengers on a TWA flight were hijacked and held for seventeen days by Lebanese military units.*

The United States, Britain, and Italy agreed to send troops to Lebanon to separate the warring factions there. In a terrorist attack, hundreds of American marines were killed a year later. President Reagan moved the remaining troops offshore and later eliminated almost completely an American presence in Lebanon.

Energy, religion, and politics are the volatile ingredients of Middle Eastern politics. Israeli nationalism now confronts resurgent Islamic fundamentalism, particularly in Iran, home of vast oil fields and a government of ayatollahs.

Why Gulliver Has Troubles: New Issues

One explanation for Gulliver's tribulations is that his supposed strong suit—military might—is no longer the primary instrument of foreign policy. Robert Keohane and Joseph Nye have described the minor role of military force in contemporary international politics. Among the developed nations, they said, "the perceived margin of safety has widened: Fears of attack in general have declined, and fears of attacks by one another are virtually nonexistent." [27] Even between the old cold warriors, the United States and the Soviet Union, military might is so balanced that both willingly entered into strategic arms limitation talks.

Today, military power is utterly useless in resolving many international issues. "Force," argued Keohane and Nye, "is often not an appropriate way of achieving other goals (such as economic and ecological welfare) that are becoming more important [in world affairs]." [28] Economic conflicts do not readily yield to nuclear weapons. We cannot persuade Arab nations to sell us cheap oil by bombing them; nor can we prop up the lagging steel industry's position in world trade by military might. Gulliver is long on firepower at the very time firepower is no longer the major instrument of foreign policy.

Big-power conflict, the threat of nuclear war, the "balance of terror," and the possibility of conventional war certainly have not disappeared. But grafted onto them are new issues. Former Secretary of State Henry Kissinger described the new era eloquently:

> The traditional agenda of international affairs—the balance among major powers, the security of nations—no longer defines our perils or our possibilities. Now we are entering a new era. Old international patterns are crumbling; old slogans are uninstructive. The world has become interdependent in economics, in communications, in human aspirations.[29]

It is time to examine the new international patterns directly. Like our American domestic politics and policy, they revolve around three issues: equality, economics, and energy and the environment. The domestic and international aspects of these issues are becoming as closely linked as the strands of the DNA double helix.

---

[27] Robert O. Keohane and Joseph S. Nye, *Power and Interdependence: World Politics in Transition* (Boston: Little, Brown, 1977), p. 77.

[28] Ibid., pp. 27–28.

[29] Quoted in Keohane and Nye, *Power and Interdependence*, p. 3.

THE CHANGING GLOBAL AGENDA

Inequality and World Politics

Rich and Poor. One major transformation in the international system is the change from the East-West conflict of the cold war to today's North-South conflict. The cold war meant continuous conflict between the Soviet Union and the West. World politics today supplements this East-West conflict with a growing conflict between rich and poor nations. Rich nations are mostly concentrated in the northern hemisphere; poor nations are mostly in the southern hemisphere. ☐4

The old expression, "The rich get richer and the poor get poorer," describes fairly accurately the inequalities among nations today. The income gap between rich, industrialized nations and poor, under-developed ones widens instead of narrows. One reason for the widening gap is suggested by a modern-day twist on the old line about rich and poor: "The rich get richer and the poor get children." While birth rates in the developed nations are leveling off, birth rates in the poorer nations skyrocket, outpacing any increases in their gross national products. If a nation's gross national product increases by 3 percent but its birth rate is 5 percent, you have to divide 3 percent more money among 5 percent more people.

Less developed countries responded to their poverty by borrowing

☐4 Rich Nations, Poor Nations

	Population (millions)	Population Growth (percent)	Life Expectancy at Birth (years)	Gross National Product (per capita)
SOME LOW-INCOME NATIONS				
Zimbabwe	8.1	2.9	52	670
Bangladesh	96.5	3.1	48	160
Indonesia	165.8	2.2	46	600
Pakistan	94.1	2.9	48	380
China	1,020.9	1.3	63	335
SOME MIDDLE-INCOME NATIONS				
Algeria	20.7	3.1	55	2,290
Malaysia	15.0	2.3	60	2,030
Colombia	28.3	2.1	59	1,280
SOME HIGH-INCOME NATIONS				
United States	233.9	.9	73	14,120
Japan	119.3	.7	75	9,700
Qatar	.3	3.4	NA	27,000
France	54.7	.5	74	9,410

Source: Central Intelligence Agency, *Handbook of Economic Statistics,* September, 1984, Tables 2–5. NA = not available.

money. International banks were willing participants in this debt dependency. Nations unable to pay the installments could simply refinance their debt, though naturally at ever-higher interest rates. Viewed from any perspective, the foreign debts of Third World governments are truly staggering, amounting to from a tenth to a third to half *or more* of their gross national products.

There is another complication to the international inequality issue. Not only are there wide gaps between rich and poor nations (international inequality); there are also big gaps between the rich and poor within developing countries (intranational inequality). Every nation has income inequality. ⑤ The poorer the nation, though, the wider the gaps between rich and poor. [30] The poor in a poor country are doubly disadvantaged. Not only does their economic system produce little wealth, but a handful of rich families often hoard the wealth of the country. Moreover, many people feel that economic aid from other nations has further enriched the few without helping the many.

American Policy and International Inequality. Much of the world's inequality is economic, dividing rich from poor between and within nations. Some of it is racial, with one racial group dominating another. Whatever their form, inequalities are a thorny thicket for foreign policy.

If American policy has done little to alter income distribution at home, it would be surprising to discover that American foreign policy had attempted to eliminate international inequalities. At various conferences underdeveloped nations, claiming that the developed nations have exploited their resources, pass resolutions calling for a redistribution of the world's wealth. These requests have never gotten a sympathetic hearing in Washington.

Several American policy initiatives, however, have been directed at the problem of world poverty. Foreign aid programs have aided agricultural modernization, irrigation, and population control programs. Food for Peace programs have subsidized the sale of American agricultural products to poor countries (which also gives an economic boost to American farmers). Peace Corps volunteers have fanned out over the globe to provide medical care and other services in less developed nations. Yet foreign aid has never been very popular with Americans. Lacking a constituency, it is easy to cut in Congress. Today the United States devotes a smaller share of its GNP to foreign economic development than any other developed nation.

Yet in an increasingly interdependent economic system it will be harder to ignore claims of poor nations. Nations Lilliputian in size have discovered that possessing significant economic resources adds to their stature. Natural gas in Mexico, like copper in Chile and oil in Iran, supplies American needs. Inequalities become harder to ignore when the poor control resources that the rich need. Following the OPEC lead, poor countries now try to obtain higher prices for products they produce.

[30] Michael Don Ward, *The Political Economy of Distribution: Equality versus Inequality* (New York: Elsevier, 1978), p. 44.

All nations exhibit inequalities between the rich and the poor, the powerful and the powerless. Nowhere, though, are the inequalities as visible as in the Republic of South Africa. The white-run government of South Africa is one of the last vestiges of the colonial era, which sent European colonizers to Asia, Africa, and Latin America to exploit native resources and extend western European empires. The years after World War II witnessed both quiet revolutions and bloody ones that swept away remnants of colonialism everywhere in Africa except South Africa and its neighbor, Rhodesia. White rule in Rhodesia began to crumble under a worldwide economic boycott.

South Africa's 18.5 million blacks and coloreds are ruled with an iron fist by 4.2 million whites, mostly a mixture of descendants of Dutch and British settlers. The policy tool by which the white minority governs the black majority is *apartheid,* a rigid system of racial segregation that strictly confines blacks to menial jobs, the poorer countryside, and starkly subordinate social conditions. Armed with vast powers under the Suppression of Communism Act, the government can silence even white opponents of apartheid.

It is obvious that the South African regime conflicts with key American beliefs about majority rule, minority rights, civil liberties, and equality. But the United States refused to join an effort to pressure South Africa through a boycott sponsored by black African nations. The South African government argues that blacks living there have higher incomes and better nutrition than in any African country with black rule. South Africa is also a storehouse of some of the world's key raw materials, which the United States needs.

American policy options are numerous. The United States could:

— Refuse to involve itself at all in the internal problems of South Africa, invoking the familiar argument that intervening in the internal affairs of other nations may not achieve any goals and may even create more problems.
— Join the black African boycott of South Africa, even though South Africa is a major source of several key resources.
— Support South African guerrilla movements with indirect or direct aid, even though a successful revolution in South Africa might produce a government hostile to the United States.

Student and other protestors have recently argued for a complete "divestiture" of American investments in South Africa. If American corporations doing business with South Africa pull out, they suggest, the regime will collapse and oppressive apartheid can be ended. Nobel Peace Prize winner Bishop Desmond Tutu supported a phased withdrawal of American investments. To these alternatives, the Reagan administration was staunchly opposed. More could be gained, it insisted, by quiet diplomacy. In the mid-1980s, the South African government did soften some of the harshest edges of apartheid, permitting, for example, intermarriage among the races. But racial riots there, and harsh police responses, suggested that the battle over the heart of South Africa would be a long and bloody one.

The International Economy

A Tangled Web of Interdependency. Once upon a time, nations took pains to wall themselves off from the world. They erected high tariff barriers to fend off foreign products; they amassed large armies to defend their borders against intruders. Times have changed. One key word keeps cropping up to describe today's international economy: interdependency. When two people are independent, they can go about their business without fearing that the actions of one will affect the actions of the other. In a time of **mutual dependency,** our actions reverberate and affect each other's economic lifelines.

Nothing so clearly illustrates our deep involvement in the international economic web than the high-tech industry. Americans believe that our high-tech industries in San Jose, Austin-San Antonio, and elsewhere are sunrise industries, growing in sharp contrast to the sunset industries surrounding Bethlehem. However, in 1984, the United States accumulated a $6.8 billion trade deficit in the nation's electronics sector. [31] We imported, in other words, nearly $7 billion more in electronics (computers, silicon chips, consumer electronic goods, and so on) than we sold abroad. Said *Business Week* about the problem: "America's vaunted leadership in high technology, the wellspring of innovation for the entire industrial sector, is eroding rapidly in every major electronics market." [32] The flagship of the American computer industry, the **IBM PC,** costs $860 to manufacture, but $625 worth of its parts are not even made in the United States. [6]

Moreover, foreign products are not free. When we pay for them, we send dollars out of the country. When an oil tanker arrives in Houston, dollars travel to Saudi Arabia. If other nations do not buy as many of our products as we do of theirs, we are paying out more than we are taking in. And if American tourists spend their dollars abroad, they, too, carry American dollars away. If we put military bases in Germany, the money soldiers spend for a night on the town goes into German pockets. All these combine to upset the **balance of payments,** the ratio of what we pay for imports to what we earn from exports. When we import more than we export, we have a balance of payments *deficit*. Year after recent year, the United States balance of payments has been preceded by a minus sign. A poor balance of payments causes us to pay more for foreign products and use less of them, and exacerbates unemployment in Bethlehem and elsewhere. Though not the only culprit, the excess of our imports over our exports decreases the dollar's buying power against marks, yens, pounds, and other currencies, making us pay more for goods we buy from other nations.

Not only dollars but also jobs are flowing abroad. Labor is cheaper in Mexico, Taiwan, South Korea, and Japan, so products made there can be priced lower than American-made products. Sometimes American firms have shut down their domestic operations and relocated in countries with lower labor costs. The AFL-CIO claims that 1 million American jobs have been lost to foreign competition. Under a special act guaranteeing compensation to American workers who lose their jobs to foreign competition, the Department of Labor has aided 318,000 workers. However, short-run aid, they would be the first to note, is no substitute for a long-run job.

Making United States International Economic Policy: Hyperpluralism at Work. Coping with foreign economic issues is becoming just as difficult, and increasingly as important, as coping with domestic ones. In a simpler time, the main instrument of international economic policy was the **tariff,** a special tax added to the cost of imported goods. It is intended to raise the price of those goods and thereby protect American businesses and workers from foreign competition. Tariff making, though, is a game everyone can play. High United States tariffs encourage other nations to respond with high tariffs on American products. In the twentieth century, the world economy has moved from a period of high tariffs

[31] "America's High Tech Crisis: Why Silicon Valley Is Losing Its Edge," *Business Week*, March 11, 1985, p. 56.
[32] Ibid.

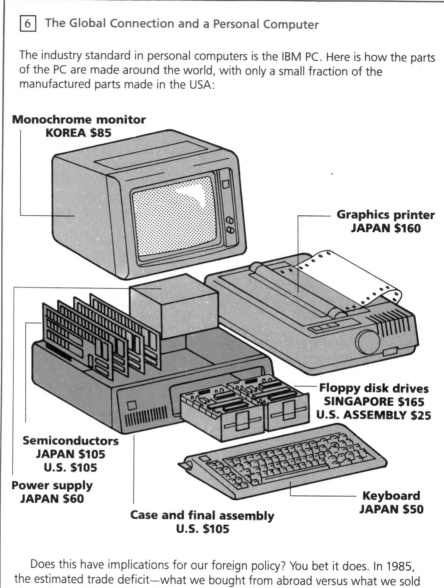

6　The Global Connection and a Personal Computer

The industry standard in personal computers is the IBM PC. Here is how the parts of the PC are made around the world, with only a small fraction of the manufactured parts made in the USA:

Monochrome monitor
KOREA $85

Graphics printer
JAPAN $160

Floppy disk drives
SINGAPORE $165
U.S. ASSEMBLY $25

Semiconductors
JAPAN $105
U.S. $105

Power supply
JAPAN $60

Case and final assembly
U.S. $105

Keyboard
JAPAN $50

Does this have implications for our foreign policy? You bet it does. In 1985, the estimated trade deficit—what we bought from abroad versus what we sold abroad—was $150 billion, about three quarters as large as the federal budget deficit. Foreign economic policies must try to cope with this problem by making American products more saleable abroad.

Source: Reprinted from the March 11, 1985 issue of *Business Week* by special permission. © 1985 by McGraw-Hill, Inc.

and protectionism to one of lower tariffs and freer trade. The high tariffs that we enacted just before (and some say helped cause) the Great Depression were the last of their kind. But growing interdependence has posed new challenges to American foreign economic policy.

Our international economic policies are dominated by a multiplicity of decision makers and interests. Presidents may dominate military and diplomatic policymaking, but pluralism pervades the tangled politics of foreign economic policy. Stephen D. Cohen examined our system for international economic policymaking, and found dozens of agencies and actors making pieces of foreign economic policy. All in all, he concluded, "the society of the United States is hopelessly pluralistic. Government in general and international economic policy in particular reflects this situation." [33] Texas Senator Lloyd Bentsen said that our foreign economic policy is shaped "almost by accident . . . a kind of guerrilla warfare among the Departments of State, Treasury, Agriculture, the Federal Reserve Board [and others]." [34] Agencies and their constituents each pursue their own policy goals. The Department of Agriculture and Commerce and their constituencies, farmers and businessmen, want to peddle American products abroad. The Department of Labor and the unions worry that we may export not only products but jobs to other countries where labor costs are cheap. The Treasury Department and the Federal Reserve Board worry about our negative balance of payments, while the Department of Defense spends billions in other countries to maintain American troops abroad.

On some issues of foreign policy, particularly those involving military and diplomatic decisions, presidential dominance gives American policy a centralized character. But issues of economic policy, where fragmented policymaking is characteristic, are increasingly sharing center stage with military and diplomatic issues. And so, too, are issues of energy and the international environment.

The Global Connection, Energy, and the Environment

Nothing so symbolizes the global connection of energy and the environment as the massive oceangoing oil tankers. In 1946, the largest oil tanker was a mere 18,000 tons. Today the biggest are 326,000 tons, and bigger ones are planned. They have made several men very rich; they have made it possible to import a third of the oil we now use; and they have also despoiled fisheries and beaches when they have split apart and spilled their contents.

Growing Energy Dependency. Most, though not all, of those tankers are sailing from nations of OPEC. OPEC first made headlines in 1973 when it responded to American support of Israel in the short Yom Kippur War by embargoing oil shipments to the United States and western European nations.

Energy transfers show convincingly that world politics is a politics of growing dependency. The less-developed nations have long depended on more industrialized nations. Recently, the industrialized nations have discovered the meaning of dependency, especially because of their growing need for imported energy sources. But we are less dependent on imported oil than most nations. The European Economic Community imports almost 100 percent of its oil. Japan does not produce a barrel of its own. Most of the less-developed nations also depend on oil imports,

[33] Stephen D. Cohen, *The Making of United States International Economic Policy* (New York: Praeger, 1977), p. 103.
[34] Ibid.

but they have fewer resources to pay the new oil barons than the United States, the EEC, or Japan.

With some flair, and perhaps some oversimplification as well, three University of California political scientists captured our new worries about oil and energy dependence:

> Oil is energy; energy is money; money is control; control is power. Oil in the wrong hands is money misspent and control corrupted; control corrupted is power abused; power abused is force misused; with oil out of control, force follows. With force out of control, so may be the world. [35]

This is a grim view. Perhaps it assumes too much about the importance of oil as a resource of control. In fact, food is also a resource that everybody needs, and the United States is to food what OPEC is to oil. Nonetheless, the new era of oil scarcity and dependence has ushered in a new challenge to American foreign policy.

The era of oil dependency has meant many things. It has worsened our balance of payments, as dollars flow backward along the same routes tankers follow. It has required adjustments in our support for Israel against her oil-rich Arab neighbors. It has forced us to seek alternative energy sources, pay higher prices for oil, and worry more than ever about American vulnerability.

Environment and the World Commons. The oceans traveled by the supertankers are an important part of the world's commons (recall the "tragedy of the commons" discussed on pages 588–589). When a super-tanker cracks up and spills its oil on the beaches, it makes environmental headlines. But supertankers are hardly the only ecological problem in the world commons.

---

[35] Edward Friedland, Paul Seabury, and Aaron Wildavsky, "Oil and the Decline of Western Power," *Political Science Quarterly* 90 (Fall 1975):437.

Bhopal. *Environmental tragedies do not stop at Canadian acid rain and Love Canal. Here, families of survivors identify victims of the Union Carbide chemical plant explosion in Bhopal, India. The Union Carbide Company, a multinational corporation, made fertilizers there. Industrializing nations, such as India, often welcome industrial development there, even though the factories may not be governed by strict environmental regulation.*

Almost every nation faces environmental problems at least as severe as our own. A nation's political ideology seems unrelated to its level of environmental despoliation. The Soviet Union certainly ranks among the worst offenders. [36] West Germany has poured as many chemicals into the Rhine as Americans have poured into our rivers. Underdeveloped nations almost always trade off ecological sensitivity for economic growth. Environmentalists have preached at less developed nations to think ecologically, but in places where economic development means the difference between starvation and salvation, most ecological pleas go unheard.

Global issues of environment and energy have crept slowly onto our nation's policy agenda. We have bargained with other nations to restrict overfishing of some of the world's fishing areas; we have pressured (successfully) the Japanese to eliminate whaling; we have shown our concern about pollution in the Rhine and the deforestation of the tropical rain forests. Issues closer to home, though, are often harder to preach about. The Canadian government has become gravely concerned about acid rain, which afflicts the eastern half of their country and ours, too. Rain more than 10 times the normal acidity falls on lakes in the northeastern United States and Canada. On the Ph scale, a measure of acidity where 7 is neutral, the Adirondack Lakes in the northeast consistently measure 5 (vinegar measures 3, for example). Acid rain has soured some good will with our Canadian neighbors, but global issues of the world commons have yet to become a major issue of American foreign policy.

THE GLOBAL CONNECTION SUMMARIZED

The world—its politics and its economics—intrudes on us more each year. In this chapter, we looked at America's global connection and the contours of our foreign policy.

The cold war began shortly after World War II, when the containment doctrine was made the basis of American foreign policy. Cold war gave way to hot wars in Korea and Vietnam, when the United States tried to contain communist advances. With containment came a massive buildup of our military apparatus, resulting in what some people called a "military-industrial complex." Gradually, containment has been balanced by détente, although we still maintain an enormous military apparatus.

For many years, the share of our national budget spent on defense declined. Advocates of a stronger military posture argued that the Soviet Union was becoming militarily superior to the United States. Ronald Reagan was one of those advocates of expanded defense spending, and his budget priorities reflected a greater commitment to the Department of Defense. Like presidents before him, Reagan grappled with the content as well as the amount of defense spending. The tangled decision making about the MX missile, for example, has extended over the administrations of three American presidents.

[36] Marshall L. Goldman, *The Spoils of Progress: Environmental Pollution in the Soviet Union* (Cambridge, Mass.: MIT Press, 1972).

The American Gulliver has been strong in military power, but many of the world's issues today are not military ones. Interconnected issues of equality, economics, and energy and the environment have become important. As the inequalities between rich and poor nations widen, the North-South cleavage has become more important. The international economic system pulls the United States deeper and deeper into the world's problems as our own interdependence and vulnerability become more apparent. Also on the global policy agenda are issues of energy and the environment.

The world today is a world of new issues, where military power does not automatically bring success in foreign policy. In an era of a tight global connection, problems of equality, the economy, and energy and the environment do not merely parallel their domestic manifestations; the way foreign policy confronts the international face of these key issue areas shapes what we can do about them at home.

Key Terms

foreign policy
United Nations (UN)
North Atlantic Treaty
　　Organization
　　(NATO)
Warsaw Pact
European Economic
　　Community (EEC)
Secretary of State
Secretary of Defense
Joint Chiefs of Staff

Central Intelligence
　　Agency (CIA)
isolationism
containment doctrine
cold war
McCarthyism
arms race
détente
Strategic Arms
　　Limitation Talks
　　(SALT)

START (Strategic Arms
　　Reduction Talks)
Organization of
　　Petroleum
　　Exporting Countries
　　(OPEC)
mutual dependency
balance of payments
tariff

For Further Reading

Destler, I.M. *Making Foreign Economic Policy* (1980). Perhaps the most useful work on the politics of foreign economic policy.

Ehrlich, Paul R., et al. *The Cold and the Dark: The World After Nuclear War* (1985). A study of the "nuclear winter" phenomenon.

Fallows, James. *National Defense* (1981). A very critical look at American defense policy, contending that too much money is spent on technologically sophisticated materials that are simply ineffective.

Fitzgerald, Frances. *Fire in the Lake: The Vietnamese and the Americans in Vietnam* (1972). A Pulitzer-prize-winning study of the Vietnam War.

Karnow, Stanley. *Vietnam: A History* (1983). A major history of Vietnam, with specific attention to the Vietnam War.

Oye, Kenneth, et al., eds. *Eagle Defiant: United States Foreign Policy in the 1980s* (1983). An excellent collection of articles on U.S. foreign policy.

Scoville, Herbert. *MX* (1981). A critical account of the origins of the MX missile.

Sick, Gary. *All Fall Down* (1985). A chronicle of the U.S. bureaucracy and the Iranian hostage crisis.

Yergin, Daniel. *Shattered Peace: The Origins of the Cold War and the National Security State* (1977). An excellent political history of the early years of the cold war and containment.

The Declaration of Independence*

IN CONGRESS, JULY 4, 1776

The unanimous Declaration of the thirteen united States of America

When in the Course of human events it becomes necessary for one people to dissolve the political bands which have connected them with another, and to assume among the Powers of the earth, the separate and equal station to which the Laws of Nature and of Nature's God entitle them, a decent respect to the opinions of mankind requires that they should declare the causes which impel them to the separation.

We hold these truths to be self-evident, that all men are created equal, that they are endowed by their Creator with certain unalienable Rights, that among these are Life, Liberty and the pursuit of Happiness. That to secure these rights, Governments are instituted among Men, deriving their just powers from the consent of the governed, That whenever any Form of Government becomes destructive of these ends, it is the Right of the People to alter or to abolish it, and to institute new Government, laying its foundation on such principles and organizing its powers in such form, as to them shall seem most likely to effect their Safety and Happiness. Prudence, indeed, will dictate that Governments long established should not be changed for light and transient causes; and accordingly all experience hath shown, that mankind are more disposed to suffer, while evils are sufferable, than to right themselves by abolishing the forms to which they are accustomed. But when a long train of abuses and usurpations, pursuing invariably the same Object evinces a design to reduce them under absolute Despotism, it is their right, it is their duty, to throw off such Government, and to provide new Guards for their future security.—Such has been the patient sufferance of these Colonies; and such is now the necessity which constrains them to alter their former Systems of Government. The history of the present King of Great Britain is a history of repeated injuries and usurpations, all having in direct object the establishment of an absolute Tyranny over these States. To prove this, let Facts be submitted to a candid world.

He has refused his Assent to Laws, the most wholesome and necessary for the public good.

He has forbidden his Governors to pass Laws of immediate and pressing importance, unless suspended in their operation till his Assent should be obtained; and when so suspended, he has utterly neglected to attend to them.

* This text retains the spelling, capitalization, and punctuation of the original.

He has refused to pass other Laws for the accommodation of large districts of people, unless those people would relinquish the right of Representation in the Legislature, a right inestimable to them and formidable to tyrants only.

He has called together legislative bodies at places unusual, uncomfortable, and distant from the depository of their Public Records, for the sole purpose of fatiguing them into compliance with his measures.

He has dissolved Representative Houses repeatedly, for opposing with manly firmness his invasions on the rights of the people.

He has refused for a long time, after such dissolutions, to cause others to be elected; whereby the Legislative Powers, incapable of Annihilation, have returned to the People at large for their exercise; the State remaining in the mean time exposed to all the dangers of invasion from without, and convulsions within.

He has endeavored to prevent the population of these States; for that purpose obstructing the Laws for Naturalization of Foreigners; refusing to pass others to encourage their migration hither, and raising the conditions of new Appropriations of Lands.

He has obstructed the Administration of Justice, by refusing his Assent to Laws for establishing Judiciary Powers.

He has made Judges dependent on his Will alone, for the tenure of their offices, and the amount and payment of their salaries.

He has erected a multitude of New Offices, and sent hither swarms of Officers to harass our People, and eat out their substance.

He has kept among us, in times of peace, Standing Armies without the Consent of our Legislature.

He has affected to render the Military independent of and superior to the Civil Power.

He has combined with others to subject us to a jurisdiction foreign to our constitution, and unacknowledged by our laws; giving his Assent to their acts of pretended Legislation:

For quartering large bodies of armed troops among us:

For protecting them, by a mock Trial, from Punishment for any Murders which they should commit on the Inhabitants of these States:

For cutting off our Trade with all parts of the world:

For imposing taxes on us without our Consent:

For depriving us in many cases, of the benefits of Trial by Jury:

For transporting us beyond Seas to be tried for pretended offenses:

For abolishing the free System of English Laws in a neighboring Province, establishing therein an Arbitrary government, and enlarging its Boundaries so as to render it at once an example and fit instrument for introducing the same absolute rule into these Colonies:

For taking away our Charters, abolishing our most valuable Laws, and altering fundamentally the Forms of our Government:

For suspending our own Legislature, and declaring themselves invested with Power to legislate for us in all cases whatsoever.

He has abdicated Government here, by declaring us out of his Protection and waging War against us.

He has plundered our seas, ravaged our Coasts, burnt our towns, and destroyed the lives of our people.

He is at this time transporting large armies of foreign mercenaries to compleat the works of death, desolation and tyranny, already begun with circumstances of Cruelty & perfidy scarcely paralleled in the most barbarous ages, and totally unworthy the Head of a civilized nation.

He has constrained our fellow Citizens taken Captive on the high Seas to bear Arms against their Country, to become the executioners of their friends and Brethren, or to fall themselves by their Hands.

He has excited domestic insurrections amongst us, and has endeavored to bring on the inhabitants of our frontiers, the merciless Indian Savages, whose known rule of warfare, is an undistinguished destruction of all ages, sexes and conditions.

In every stage of these Oppressions We have Petitioned for Redress in the most humble terms: Our repeated Petitions have been answered only by repeated injury. A Prince, whose character is thus marked by every act which may define a Tyrant, is unfit to be the ruler of a free People.

Nor have We been wanting in attention to our British brethren. We have warned them from time to time of attempts by their legislature to extend an unwarrantable jurisdiction over us. We have reminded them of the circumstances of our emigration and settlement here. We have appealed to their native justice and magnanimity, and we have conjured them by the ties of our common kindred to disavow these usurpations, which, would inevitably interrupt our connections and correspondence. They too have been deaf to the voice of justice and consanguinity. We must, therefore, acquiesce in the necessity, which denounces our Separation, and hold them, as we hold the rest of mankind, Enemies in War, in Peace Friends.

We, therefore, the Representatives of the united States of America, in General Congress, Assembled, appealing to the Supreme Judge of the world for the rectitude of our intentions, do, in the Name, and by Authority of the good People of these Colonies, solemnly publish and declare, That these United Colonies are, and of Right ought to be Free and Independent States; that they are Absolved from all Allegiance to the British Crown, and that all political connection between them and the State of Great Britain, is and ought to be totally dissolved; and that as Free and Independent States, they have full Power to levy War, conclude Peace, contract Alliances, establish Commerce, and to do all other Acts and Things which Independent States may of right do. And for the support of this Declaration, with a firm reliance on the Protection of Divine Providence, we mutually pledge to each other our Lives, our Fortunes and our sacred Honor.

JOHN HANCOCK

New Hampshire

JOSIAH BARTLETT,   MATTHEW THORNTON.
WM. WHIPPLE,

Massachusetts Bay

SAML. ADAMS,   ROBT. TREAT PAINE,
JOHN ADAMS,   ELBRIDGE GERRY.

Rhode Island

STEP. HOPKINS,   WILLIAM ELLERY.

Connecticut

ROGER SHERMAN,   WM. WILLIAMS,
SAM'EL HUNTINGTON,   OLIVER WOLCOTT.

New York

WM. FLOYD,   FRANS. LEWIS,
PHIL. LIVINGSTON,   LEWIS MORRIS.

New Jersey

RICHD. STOCKTON,   JOHN HART,
JNO. WITHERSPOON,   ABRA. CLARK.
FRAS. HOPKINSON,

Pennsylvania

ROBT. MORRIS,   JAS. SMITH,
BENJAMIN RUSH,   GEO. TAYLOR,
BENJA. FRANKLIN,   JAMES WILSON,
JOHN MORTON,   GEO. ROSS.
GEO. CLYMER,

Delaware

CAESAR RODNEY,   THO. M'KEAN.
GEO. READ,

Maryland

SAMUEL CHASE,   THOS. STONE,
WM. PACA,   CHARLES CAROLL
                                          of Carrollton.

Virginia

GEORGE WYTHE,   THOS. NELSON, jr.,
RICHARD HENRY LEE,   FRANCIS LIGHTFOOT
TH. JEFFERSON,   LEE,
BENJA. HARRISON,   CARTER BRAXTON.

North Carolina

WM. HOOPER,   JOHN PENN.
JOSEPH HEWES,

South Carolina

EDWARD RUTLEDGE,   THOMAS LYNCH, jnr.,
THOS. HEYWARD, Junr,.   ARTHUR MIDDLETON.

Georgia

BUTTON GWINNETT,   GEO. WALTON.
LYMAN HALL,

The Constitution of the United States of America*

(Preamble)

We the people of the United States, in Order to form a more perfect Union, establish Justice, insure domestic Tranquility, provide for the common defence, promote the general Welfare, and secure the Blessings of Liberty to ourselves and our posterity, do ordain and establish this Constitution for the United States of America.

ARTICLE I.

(The Legislature)

SECTION 1. All legislative Powers herein granted shall be vested in a Congress of the United States, which shall consist of a Senate and House of Representatives.

SECTION 2. The House of Representatives shall be composed of Members chosen every second Year by the People of the several States, and the Electors in each State shall have the Qualifications requisite for Electors of the most numerous Branch of the State Legislature.

No person shall be a Representative who shall not have attained to the Age of twenty five Years, and been seven Years a Citizen of the United States, and who shall not, when elected, be an Inhabitant of that State in which he shall be chosen.

Representatives and direct [Taxes] [1] shall be apportioned among the several States which may be included within this Union, according to their respective Numbers [which shall be determined by adding to the whole Number of free Persons, including those bound to Service for a Term of Years, and excluding Indians not taxed, three fifths of all other Persons]. [2] The actual Enumeration shall be made within three Years after the first Meeting of the Congress of the United States, and within every subsequent Term of ten Years, in such Manner as they shall by Law direct. The Number of Representatives shall not exceed one for every thirty Thousand, but each State shall have at Least one Representative; and until such enumeration shall be made, the State of New Hampshire shall be entitled to chuse three, Massachusetts eight, Rhode-Island and Providence Plantations one, Connecticut five, New-York six, New Jersey four, Pennsylvania eight, Delaware one, Maryland six, Virginia ten, North Carolina five, South Carolina five, and Georgia three.

* This text retains the spelling, capitalization, and punctuation of the original. Brackets indicate passages that have been altered by amendments.

[1] See Amendment XVI.
[2] See Amendment XIV.

When vacancies happen in the Representation from any State, the Executive Authority thereof shall issue Writs of Election to fill such Vacancies.

The House of Representatives shall chuse their Speaker and other Officers; and shall have the sole Power of Impeachment.

SECTION 3. The Senate of the United States shall be composed of two Senators from each State [chosen by the Legislature thereof], [3] for six Years; and each Senator shall have one Vote.

Immediately after they shall be assembled in Consequence of the first Election, they shall be divided as equally as may be into three Classes. The Seats of the Senators of the first Class shall be vacated at the Expiration of the second year, of the second Class at the Expiration of the fourth Year, and of the third Class at the Expiration of the sixth Year, so that one third may be chosen every second Year [and if Vacancies happen by Resignation, or otherwise, during the Recess of the Legislature of any State, the Executive thereof may make temporary Appointments until the next Meeting of the Legislature, which shall then fill such Vacancies]. [4]

No Person shall be a Senator who shall not have attained to the Age of thirty Years, and been nine Years a Citizen of the United States, and who shall not, when elected, be an Inhabitant of that State for which he shall be chosen.

The Vice President of the United States shall be President of the Senate, but shall have no Vote, unless they be equally divided.

The Senate shall chuse their other Officers, and also a President pro tempore, in the Absence of the Vice President, or when he shall exercise the Office of President of the United States.

The Senate shall have the sole Power to try all Impeachments. When sitting for that Purpose, they shall be on Oath or Affirmation. When the President of the United States is tried, the Chief Justice shall preside: And no Person shall be convicted without the Concurrence of two thirds of the Members present.

Judgment in Cases of Impeachment shall not extend further than to removal from Office, and disqualification to hold and enjoy any Office of honor, Trust or Profit under the United States; but the Party convicted shall nevertheless be liable and subject to Indictment, Trial, Judgment and Punishment, according to Law.

SECTION 4. The Times, Places and Manner of holding Elections for Senators and Representatives, shall be prescribed in each State by the Legislature thereof; but the Congress may at any time by Law make or alter such Regulations, except as to the Places of chusing Senators.

[The Congress shall assemble at least once in every Year, and such Meeting shall be on the first Monday in December, unless they shall by Law appoint a different Day.] [5]

SECTION 5. Each House shall be the Judge of the Elections, Returns and Qualifications of its own Members, and a Majority of each shall constitute a Quorum to do Business; but a smaller Number may adjourn from day to day, and may be authorized to compel the Attendance of absent Members, in such Manner, and under such Penalties as each House may provide.

Each House may determine the Rules of its Proceedings, punish its Members for disorderly Behaviour, and, with the Concurrence of two thirds, expel a Member.

[3] See Amendment XVII.
[4] Ibid.
[5] See Amendment XX.

Each House shall keep a Journal of its Proceedings, and from time to time publish the same, excepting such Parts as may in their Judgment require Secrecy; and the Yeas and Nays of the Members of either House on any question shall, at the Desire of one fifth of those present, be entered on the Journal.

Neither House, during the Session of Congress, shall, without the Consent of the other, adjourn for more than three days, nor to any other Place than that in which the two Houses shall be sitting.

SECTION 6. The Senators and Representatives shall receive a Compensation for their Services, to be ascertained by Law, and paid out of the Treasury of the United States. They shall in all Cases, except Treason, Felony and Breach of the Peace, be privileged from Arrest during their Attendance at the Session of their respective Houses, and in going to and returning from the same; and for any Speech or Debate in either House, they shall not be questioned in any other Place.

No Senator or Representative shall, during the Time for which he was elected, be appointed to any civil Office under the Authority of the United States, which shall have been created, or the Emoluments whereof shall have been encreased during such time; and no Person holding any Office under the United States, shall be a Member of either House during his Continuance in Office.

SECTION 7. All Bills for raising Revenue shall originate in the House of Representatives; but the Senate may propose or concur with Amendments as on other Bills.

Every Bill which shall have passed the House of Representatives and the Senate, shall, before it become a Law, be presented to the President of the United States; If he approves he shall sign it, but if not he shall return it, with his Objections to that House in which it shall have originated, who shall enter the Objections at large on their Journal, and proceed to reconsider it. If after such Reconsideration two thirds of that House shall agree to pass the Bill, it shall be sent, together with the Objections, to the other House, by which it shall likewise be reconsidered, and if approved by two thirds of that House, it shall become a Law. But in all such Cases the Votes of both Houses shall be determined by yeas and Nays, and the Names of the Persons voting for and against the Bill shall be entered on the Journal of each House respectively. If any Bill shall not be returned by the President within ten Days (Sundays excepted) after it shall have been presented to him, the Same shall be a Law, in like Manner as if he had signed it, unless the Congress by their Adjournment prevent its Return, in which Case it shall not be a Law.

Every Order, Resolution, or Vote to which the Concurrence of the Senate and House of Representatives may be necessary (except on a question of Adjournment) shall be presented to the President of the United States; and before the Same shall take Effect, shall be approved by him, or being disapproved by him, shall be repassed by two thirds of the Senate and House of Representatives, according to the Rules and Limitations prescribed in the Case of a Bill.

SECTION 8. The Congress shall have Power To lay and collect Taxes, Duties, Imposts and Excises, to pay the Debts and provide for the common Defence and general Welfare of the United States; but all Duties, Imposts and Excises shall be uniform throughout the United States;

To borrow Money on the credit of the United States;

To regulate Commerce with foreign Nations, and among the several States, and with the Indian Tribes;

To establish a uniform Rule of Naturalization, and uniform Laws on the subject of Bankruptcies throughout the United States;

To coin Money, regulate the Value thereof, and of foreign Coin, and fix the Standard of Weights and Measures;

To provide for the Punishment of counterfeiting the Securities and current Coin of the United States;

To establish Post Offices and post Roads;

To promote the Progress of Science and useful Arts, by securing for limited Times to Authors and Inventors the exclusive Right to their respective Writings and Discoveries;

To constitute Tribunals inferior to the supreme Court;

To define and punish Piracies and Felonies committed on the high Seas, and Offences against the Law of Nations;

To declare War, grant Letters of Marque and Reprisal, and make Rules concerning Captures on Land and Water;

To raise and support Armies, but no Appropriation of Money to that Use shall be for a longer Term than two Years;

To provide and maintain a Navy;

To make Rules for the Government and Regulation of the land and naval Forces;

To provide for calling forth the Militia to execute the Laws of the Union, suppress Insurrections and repel Invasions;

To provide for organizing, arming, and disciplining, the Militia, and for governing such Part of them as may be employed in the Service of the United States, reserving to the States respectively, the Appointment of the Officers, and the Authority of training the Militia according to the discipline prescribed by Congress;

To exercise exclusive Legislation in all Cases whatsoever, over such District (not exceeding ten Miles square) as may, by Cession of particular States, and the Acceptance of Congress, become the Seat of the Government of the United States, and to exercise like Authority over all Places purchased by the Consent of the Legislature of the State in which the Same shall be, for the Erection of Forts, Magazines, Arsenals, dock-Yards, and other needful Buildings;–And

To make all Laws which shall be necessary and proper for carrying into Execution the foregoing Powers, and all other Powers vested by this Constitution in the Government of the United States, or in any Department or Officer thereof.

Section 9. The Migration or Importation of such Persons as any of the States now existing shall think proper to admit, shall not be prohibited by the Congress prior to the Year one thousand eight hundred and eight, but a Tax or duty may be imposed on such Importation, not exceeding ten dollars for each Person.

The Privilege of the Writ of Habeas Corpus shall not be suspended, unless when in Cases of Rebellion or Invasion the public Safety may require it.

No Bill of Attainder or ex post facto Law shall be passed.

[No Capitation, or other direct, Tax shall be laid, unless in Proportion to the Census or Enumeration herein before directed to be taken.] [6]

No Tax or Duty shall be laid on Articles exported from any State.

No Preference shall be given by any Regulation of Commerce or Revenue to the Ports of one State over those of another; not shall Vessels bound to, or from, one State, be obliged to enter, clear, or pay Duties in another.

No Money shall be drawn from the Treasury, but in Consequence of Appropriations made by Law; and a regular Statement and Account of the Receipts and Expenditures of all public Money shall be published from time to time.

No Title of Nobility shall be granted by the United States; And no Person holding any Office of Profit or Trust under them, shall, without the Consent of the

[6] See Amendment XVI.

Congress, accept of any present, Emolument, Office, or Title, of any kind whatever, from any King, Prince, or foreign State.

SECTION 10. No state shall enter into any Treaty, Alliance, or Confederation; grant Letters of Marque and Reprisal; coin Money; emit Bills of Credit; make any Thing but gold and silver Coin a Tender in Payment of Debts; pass any Bill of Attainder, ex post facto Law, or Law impairing the Obligation of Contracts, or grant any Title of Nobility.

No State shall, without the Consent of the Congress, lay any Imposts or Duties on Imports or Exports, except what may be absolutely necessary for executing its inspection Laws; and the net Produce of all Duties and Imposts, laid by any State on Imports or Exports, shall be for the Use of the Treasury of the United States; and all such Laws shall be subject to the Revision and Controul of the Congress.

No State shall, without the Consent of Congress, lay any Duty of Tonnage, keep Troops, or Ships of War in time of Peace, enter into any Agreement or Compact with another State, or with a foreign Power, or engage in War, unless actually invaded, or in such imminent Danger as will not admit of delay.

ARTICLE II.

(The Executive)

SECTION 1. The executive Power shall be vested in a President of the United States of America. He shall hold his Office during the Term of four Years, and, together with the Vice President, chosen for the Same Term, be elected, as follows.

Each State shall appoint, in such Manner as the Legislature thereof may direct, a Number of Electors, equal to the whole Number of Senators and Representatives to which the State may be entitled in the Congress; but no Senator or Representative, or Person holding an Office of Trust or Profit under the United States, shall be appointed an Elector.

[The Electors shall meet in their respective States, and vote by Ballot for two Persons of whom one at least shall not be an Inhabitant of the same State with themselves. And they shall make a List of all the Persons voted for, and of the Number of Votes for each; which List they shall sign and certify, and transmit sealed to the Seat of the Government of the United States, directed to the President of the Senate. The President of the Senate shall, in the Presence of the Senate and House of Representatives, open all the Certificates, and the Votes shall then be counted. The Person having the greatest Number of Votes shall be the President, if such Number be a Majority of the whole Number of Electors appointed; and if there be more than one who have such Majority, and have an equal Number of Votes, then the House of Representatives shall immediately chuse by Ballot one of them for President; and if no Person have a Majority, than from the five highest on the List the said House shall in like Manner chuse the President. But in chusing the President, the Votes shall be taken by States, the Representation from each State having one Vote; A quorum for this Purpose shall consist of a Member or Members from two thirds of the States, and a Majority of all the States shall be necessary to a Choice. In every Case, after the Choice of the President, the Person having the greatest Number of Votes of the Electors shall be the Vice President. But if there should remain two or more who have equal Votes, the Senate shall chuse from them by Ballot the Vice President.] [7]

The Congress may determine the Time of chusing the Electors, and the Day on which they shall give their Votes; which Day shall be the same throughout the United States.

---

[7] See Amendment XII.

No Person except a natural born Citizen, or a Citizen of the United States, at the time of the Adoption of this Constitution, shall be eligible to the Office of President; neither shall any Person be eligible to that Office who shall not have attained to the Age of thirty five Years, and been fourteen Years a Resident within the United States.

[In Case of the Removal of the President from Office, or of his Death, Resignation, or Inability to discharge the Powers and Duties of the said Office, the same shall devolve on the Vice President, and the Congress may by Law provide for the Case of Removal, Death, Resignation or Inability, both of the President and Vice President, declaring what Officer shall then act as President, and such Officer shall act accordingly, until the Disability be removed, or a President shall be elected.] [8]

The President shall, at stated Times, receive for his Services, a Compensation, which shall neither be encreased nor diminished during the Period for which he shall have been elected, and he shall not receive within that Period any other Emolument from the United States, or any of them.

Before he enter on the Execution of his Office, he shall take the following Oath or Affirmation:—"I do solemnly swear (or affirm) that I will faithfully execute the Office of President of the United States, and will to the best of my Ability, preserve, protect and defend the Constitution of the United States."

SECTION 2. The President shall be Commander in Chief of the Army and Navy of the United States, and of the Militia of the several States, when called into the actual Service of the United States; he may require the Opinion, in writing, of the principal Officer in each of the executive Departments, upon any Subject relating to the Duties of their respective Offices, and he shall have Power to grant Reprieves and Pardons for Offences against the United States, except in Cases of Impeachment.

He shall have Power, by and with the Advice and Consent of the Senate, to make Treaties, provided two thirds of the Senators present concur; and he shall nominate, and by and with the Advice and Consent of the Senate, shall appoint Ambassadors, other public Ministers and Consuls, Judges of the supreme Court, and all other Officers of the United States, whose Appointments are not herein otherwise provided for, and which shall be established by Law; but the Congress may by Law vest the Appointment of such inferior Officers, as they think proper, in the President alone, in the Courts of Law, or in the Heads of Departments.

The President shall have Power to fill up all Vacancies that may happen during the Recess of the Senate, by granting Commissions which shall expire at the end of their next Session.

SECTION 3. He shall from time to time give to the Congress Information of the State of the Union, and recommend to their Consideration such Measures as he shall judge necessary and expedient; he may, on extraordinary Occasions, convene both Houses, or either of them, and in Case of Disagreement between them, with Respect to the Time of Adjournment, he may adjourn them to such Time as he shall think proper; he shall receive Ambassadors and other public Ministers; he shall take Care that the Laws be faithfully executed, and shall Commission all the Officers of the United States.

SECTION 4. The President, Vice President and all civil Officers of the United States, shall be removed from Office on Impeachment for, and Conviction of, Treason, Bribery, or other high Crimes and Misdemeanors.

[8] See Amendment XXV.

ARTICLE III.

(The Judiciary)

SECTION 1. The judicial Power of the United States, shall be vested in one supreme Court, and in such inferior Courts as the Congress may from time to time ordain and establish. The Judges, both of the supreme and inferior Courts, shall hold their Offices during good Behaviour, and shall, at stated Times, receive for their Services, a Compensation, which shall not be diminished during their Continuance in Office.

SECTION 2. The judicial Power shall extend to all Cases, in Law and Equity, arising under this Constitution, the Laws of the United States, and Treaties made, or which shall be made, under their Authority;—to all Cases affecting Ambassadors, other public Ministers and Consuls;—to all Cases of admiralty and maritime Jurisdiction;—to Controversies to which the United States shall be a Party; —to Controversies between two or more States; [—between a State and Citizens of another State;—] [9] between Citizens of different States,—between Citizens of the same State claiming Lands under Grants of different States, [and between a state, or the Citizens thereof, and foreign States, Citizens or Subjects.] [10]   In all Cases affecting Ambassadors, other public Ministers and Consuls, and those in which a State shall be Party, the supreme Court shall have original Jurisdiction. In all the other Cases before mentioned, the supreme Court shall have appellate Jurisdiction, both as to Law and Fact, with such Exceptions, and under such Regulations as the Congress shall make.

The Trial of all Crimes, except in Cases of Impeachment, shall be by Jury; and such Trial shall be held in the State where the said Crimes shall have been committed; but when not committed within any State, the Trial shall be at such Place or Places as the Congress may by Law have directed.

SECTION 3. Treason against the United States, shall consist only in levying War against them, or in adhering to their Enemies, giving them Aid and Comfort. No Person shall be convicted of Treason unless on the Testimony of two Witnesses to the same overt Act, or on Confession in open Court.

The Congress shall have Power to declare the Punishment of Treason, but no Attainder of Treason shall work Corruption of Blood, or Forfeiture except during the Life of the Person attainted.

ARTICLE IV.

(Interstate Relations)

SECTION 1. Full Faith and Credit shall be given in each State to the public Acts, Records, and judicial Proceedings of every other State. And the Congress may by general Laws prescribe the Manner in which such Acts, Records and Proceedings shall be proved, and the Effect thereof.

SECTION 2. The Citizens of each State shall be entitled to all Privileges and Immunities of Citizens in the several States.

A Person charged in any State with Treason, Felony, or other Crime, who shall flee from Justice, and be found in another State, shall on Demand of the executive Authority of the State from which he fled, be delivered up, to be removed to the State having Jurisdiction of the Crime.

[9] See Amendment XI.
[10] Ibid.

[No Person held to Service or Labour in one State under the Laws thereof, escaping into another, shall, in Consequence of any Law or Regulation therein, be discharged from such Service or Labour, but shall be delivered up on Claim of the Party to whom such Service or Labour may be due.] [11]

SECTION 3. New States may be admitted by the Congress into this Union; but no new State shall be formed or erected within the Jurisdiction of any other State; nor any State be formed by the Junction of two or more States, or Parts of States, without the Consent of the Legislatures of the States concerned as well as of the Congress.

The Congress shall have Power to dispose of and make all needful Rules and Regulations respecting the Territory or other Property belonging to the United States; and nothing in this Constitution shall be so construed as to Prejudice any Claims of the United States, or of any particular State.

SECTION 4. The United States shall guarantee to every State in this Union a Republican Form of Government, and shall protect each of them against Invasion, and on Application of the Legislature, or of the Executive (when the Legislature cannot be convened) against domestic Violence.

ARTICLE V.

(Amending the Constitution)

The Congress, whenever two thirds of both Houses shall deem it necessary, shall propose Amendments to this Constitution, or on the Application of the Legislatures of two thirds of the several States, shall call a Convention for proposing Amendments, which, in either Case, shall be valid to all Intents and Purposes, as Part of this Constitution, when ratified by the Legislatures of three fourths of the several States, or by Conventions in three fourths thereof, as the one or the other Mode of Ratification may be proposed by the Congress; Provided that no Amendment which may be made prior to the Year One thousand eight hundred and eight shall in any Manner affect the first and fourth Clauses in the Ninth Section of the first Article; and that no State, without its Consent, shall be deprived of its equal Suffrage in the Senate.

ARTICLE VI.

(Debts, Supremacy, Oaths)

All Debts contracted and Engagements entered into, before the Adoption of this Constitution, shall be as valid against the United States under this Constitution, as under the Confederation.

This Constitution, and the laws of the United States which shall be made in Pursuance thereof; and all Treaties made, or which shall be made, under the Authority of the United States, shall be the supreme Law of the Land; and the Judges in every State shall be bound thereby, any Thing in the Constitution or Laws of any State to the Contrary notwithstanding.

The Senators and Representatives before mentioned, and the Members of the several State Legislatures, and all executive and judicial Officers, both of the United States and of the several States, shall be bound by Oath or Affirmation, to support this Constitution: but no religious Test shall ever be required as a Qualification to any Office or public Trust under the United States.

[11] See Amendment XIII.

ARTICLE VII.

(Ratifying the Constitution)

The Ratification of the Conventions of nine States, shall be sufficient for the Establishment of this Constitution between the States so ratifying the Same.

Done in Convention by the Unanimous Consent of the States present the Seventeenth Day of September in the Year of our Lord one thousand seven hundred and Eighty seven and of the Independence of the United States of America the Twelfth. IN WITNESS whereof we have hereunto subscribed our Names,

Go. WASHINGTON
Presid't. and deputy from Virginia

Attest
WILLIAM JACKSON
Secretary

DELAWARE
Geo. Read
Gunning Bedford jun
John Dickinson
Richard Basset
Jaco. Broom
MASSACHUSETTS
Nathaniel Gorham
Rufus King
CONNECTICUT
Wm. Saml. Johnson
Roger Sherman
NEW YORK
Alexander Hamilton
NEW JERSEY
Wh. Livingston
David Brearley.
Wm. Paterson.
Jona. Dayton

PENNSYLVANIA
B. Franklin
Thomas Mifflin
Robt. Morris
Geo. Clymer
Thos. FitzSimons
Jared Ingersoll
James Wilson.
Gouv. Morris
NEW HAMPSHIRE
John Langdon
Nicholas Gilman
MARYLAND
James McHenry
Dan of St. Thos. Jenifer
Danl. Carroll.

VIRGINIA
John Blair
James Madison Jr.
NORTH CAROLINA
Wm. Blount
Richd. Dobbs Spaight.
Hu. Williamson
SOUTH CAROLINA
J. Rutledge
Charles Cotesworth Pinckney
Charles Pinckney
Pierce Butler.
GEORGIA
William Few
Abr. Baldwin

Articles in addition to, and amendment of the Constitution of the United States of America, proposed by Congress and ratified by the Legislatures of the several states, pursuant to the Fifth Article of the original Constitution.

(The first ten amendments were passed by Congress on September 25, 1789, and were ratified on December 15, 1791.)

Amendment I–Religion, Speech, Assembly, Petition

Congress shall make no law respecting an establishment of religion, or prohibiting the free exercise thereof; or abridging the freedom of speech, or of the press; or the right of the people peaceably to assemble, and to petition the Government for a redress of grievances.

Amendment II—Right to Bear Arms

A well regulated militia, being necessary to the security of a free State, the right of the people to keep and bear arms, shall not be infringed.

Amendment III—Quartering of Soldiers

No Soldier shall, in time of peace be quartered in any house, without the consent of the owner, nor in time of war, but in a manner to be prescribed by law.

Amendment IV—Searches and Seizures

The right of the people to be secure in their persons, houses, papers, and effects, against unreasonable searches and seizures, shall not be violated, and no warrants shall issue, but upon probable cause, supported by oath or affirmation, and particularly describing the place to be searched, and the persons or things to be seized.

Amendment V—Grand Juries, Double Jeopardy, Self-incrimination, Due Process, Eminent Domain

No person shall be held to answer for a capital, or otherwise infamous crime, unless on a presentment or indictment of a Grand Jury, except in cases arising in the land or naval forces, or in the militia, when in actual service in time of war or public danger; nor shall any person be subject for the same offence to be twice put in jeopardy of life or limb; nor shall be compelled in any criminal case to be a witness against himself, nor be deprived of life, liberty, or property, without due process of law; nor shall private property be taken for public use, without just compensation.

Amendment VI—Criminal Court Procedures

In all criminal prosecutions, the accused shall enjoy the right to a speedy and public trial, by an impartial jury of the State and district wherein the crime shall have been committed, which district shall have been previously ascertained by law, and to be informed of the nature and cause of the accusation; to be confronted with the witnesses against him; to have compulsory process for obtaining witnesses in his favor, and to have the assistance of counsel for his defense.

Amendment VII—Trial by Jury in Common-law Cases

In Suits at common law, where the value in controversy shall exceed twenty dollars, the right of trial by jury shall be preserved, and no fact tried by a jury, shall be otherwise reexamined in any Court of the United States, than according to the rules of the common law.

Amendment VIII—Bails, Fines, and Punishment

Excessive bail shall not be required, nor excessive fines imposed, nor cruel and unusual punishments inflicted.

Amendment IX—Rights Retained by the People

The enumeration in the Constitution, of certain rights, shall not be construed to deny or disparage others retained by the people.

Amendment X—Rights Reserved to the States

The powers not delegated to the United States by the Constitution, nor prohibited by it to the States, are reserved to the States respectively, or to the people.

Amendment XI—Suits against the States (Ratified February 7, 1795)

The Judicial power of the United States shall not be construed to extend to any suit in law or equity, commenced or prosecuted against one of the United States by Citizens of another State, or by Citizens or Subjects of any Foreign State.

Amendment XII—Election of the President and Vice President (Ratified June 15, 1804)

The Electors shall meet in their respective states, and vote by ballot for President and Vice-President, one of whom, at least, shall not be an inhabitant of the same state with themselves; they shall name in their ballots the person voted for as President, and in distinct ballots the person voted for as Vice-President, and they shall make distinct lists of all persons voted for as President, and of all persons voted for as Vice-President, and of the number of votes for each, which lists they shall sign and certify, and transmit sealed to the seat of the government of the United States, directed to the President of the Senate;—The President of the Senate shall, in the presence of the Senate and House of Representatives, open all the certificates and the votes shall then be counted;—The person having the greatest number of votes for President, shall be the President, if such number be a majority of the whole number of Electors appointed; and if no person have such majority, then from the persons having the highest numbers not exceeding three on the list of those voted for as President, the House of Representatives shall choose immediately, by ballot, the President. But in choosing the President, the votes shall be taken by states, the representation from each state having one vote; a quorum for this purpose shall consist of a member or members from two-thirds of the states, and a majority of all the states shall be necessary to a choice. [And if the House of Representatives shall not choose a President whenever the right of choice shall devolve upon them, before the fourth day of March next following, then the Vice-President shall act as President, as in the case of the death or other constitutional disability of the President.] [12]—The person having the greatest number of votes as Vice-President, shall be the Vice-President, if such number be a majority of the whole number of Electors appointed, and if no person have a majority, then from the two highest numbers on the list, the Senate shall choose the Vice-President; a quorum for the purpose shall consist of two-thirds of the whole number of Senators, and a majority of the whole number shall be necessary to a choice. But no person constitutionally ineligible to the office of President shall be eligible to that of Vice-President of the United States.

Amendment XIII—Slavery (Ratified on December 6, 1865)

SECTION 1. Neither slavery nor involuntary servitude, except as a punishment for crime whereof the party shall have been duly convicted, shall exist within the United States, or any place subject to their jurisdiction.

SECTION 2. Congress shall have power to enforce this article by appropriate legislation.

Amendment XIV—Citizenship, Due Process, and Equal Protection of the Laws (Ratified on July 9, 1868)

SECTION 1. All persons born or naturalized in the United States, and subject to the jurisdiction thereof, are citizens of the United States and of the State wherein

[12] Amendment XX.

they reside. No State shall make or enforce any law which shall abridge the privileges or immunities of citizens of the United States; nor shall any State deprive any person of life, liberty, or property, without due process of law; nor deny to any person within its jurisdiction the equal protection of the laws.

SECTION 2. Representatives shall be apportioned among the several States according to their respective numbers, counting the whole number of persons in each State, excluding Indians not taxed. But when the right to vote at any election for the choice of electors for President and Vice President of the United States, Representatives in Congress, the Executive and Judicial officers of a State, or the members of the Legislature thereof, is denied to any of the male inhabitants of such State, being twenty-one years of age, and citizens of the United States, or in any way abridged, except for participation in rebellion, or other crime, the basis of representation therein shall be reduced in the proportion which the number of such male citizens shall bear to the whole number of male citizens twenty-one years of age in such State.

SECTION 3. No person shall be a Senator or Representative in Congress, or elector of President and Vice President, or hold any office, civil or military, under the United States, or under any State, who, having previously taken an oath, as a member of Congress, or as an officer of the United States, or as a member of any State legislature, or as an executive or judicial officer of any State, to support the Constitution of the United States, shall have engaged in insurrection or rebellion against the same, or given aid or comfort to the enemies thereof. But Congress may by a vote of two-thirds of each House, remove such disability.

SECTION 4. The validity of the public debt of the United States, authorized by law, including debts incurred for payment of pensions and bounties for services in suppressing insurrection or rebellion, shall not be questioned. But neither the United States nor any State shall assume or pay any debt or obligation incurred in aid of insurrection or rebellion against the United States, or any claim for the loss or emancipation of any slave, but all such debts, obligations and claims shall be held illegal and void.

SECTION 5. The Congress shall have power to enforce, by appropriate legislation, the provisions of this article.

Amendment XV—The Right to Vote (Ratified on February 3, 1870)

SECTION 1. The right of citizens of the United States to vote shall not be denied or abridged by the United States or by any State on account of race, color, or previous condition of servitude.

SECTION 2. The Congress shall have power to enforce this article by appropriate legislation.

Amendment XVI—Income Taxes (Ratified on February 3, 1913)

The Congress shall have power to lay and collect taxes on incomes, from whatever source derived, without apportionment among the several States, and without regard to any census or enumeration.

Amendment XVII—Election of Senators (Ratified on April 8, 1913)

The Senate of the United States shall be composed of two Senators from each State, elected by the people thereof, for six years; and each Senator shall have one vote. The electors in each State shall have the qualifications requisite for electors of the most numerous branch of the State legislatures.

When vacancies happen in the representation of any State in the Senate, the executive authority of such State shall issue writs of election to fill such vacancies: *Provided*, That the legislature of any State may empower the executive thereof to make temporary appointments until the people fill the vacancies by election as the legislature may direct.

This amendment shall not be so construed as to affect the election or term of any Senator chosen before it becomes valid as part of the Constitution.

Amendment XVIII—Prohibition (Ratified on January 16, 1919)

SECTION 1. After one year from the ratification of this article the manufacture, sale, or transportation of intoxicating liquors within, the importation thereof into, or the exportation thereof from the United States and all territory subject to the jurisdiction thereof for beverage purposes is hereby prohibited.

SECTION 2. The Congress and the several States shall have concurrent power to enforce this article by appropriate legislation.

SECTION 3. This article shall be inoperative unless it shall have been ratified as an amendment to the Constitution by the legislatures of the several States, as provided in the Constitution, within seven years from the date of the submission hereof to the States by the Congress. [13]

Amendment XIX— Women's Right to Vote (Ratified on August 18, 1920)

The right of citizens of the United States to vote shall not be denied or abridged by the United States or by any State on account of sex.

Congress shall have power to enforce this article by appropriate legislation.

Amendment XX—Terms of Office, Convening of Congress, and Succession

SECTION 1. The terms of the President and Vice President shall end at noon on the 20th day of January, and the terms of Senators and Representatives at noon on the 3d day of January, of the years in which such terms would have ended if this article had not been ratified, and the terms of their successors shall then begin.

SECTION 2. The Congress shall assemble at least once in every year, and such meeting shall begin at noon on the 3d day of January, unless they shall by law appoint a different day.

SECTION 3. If, at the time fixed for the beginning of the term of the President, the President elect shall have died, the Vice President elect shall become President. If a President shall not have been chosen before the time fixed for the beginning of his term, or if the President elect shall have failed to qualify, then the Vice President elect shall act as President until a President shall have qualified; and the Congress may by law provide for the case wherein neither a President elect nor a Vice President elect shall have qualified, declaring who shall then act as President, or the manner in which one who is to act shall be selected, and such person shall act accordingly until a President or Vice President shall have qualified.

[13] See Amendment XXI.

SECTION 4. The Congress may by law provide for the case of the death of any of the persons from whom the House of Representatives may choose a President whenever the rights of choice shall have devolved upon them, and for the case of the death of any of the persons from whom the Senate may choose a Vice President whenever the right of choice shall have devolved upon them.

SECTION 5. Sections 1 and 2 shall take effect on the 15th day of October following the ratification of this article.

SECTION 6. This article shall be inoperative unless it shall have been ratified as an amendment to the Constitution by the legislatures of three-fourths of the several States within seven years from the date of its submission.

Amendment XXI—Repeal of Prohibition (Ratified on December 5, 1933)

SECTION 1. The eighteenth article of amendment to the Constitution of the United States is hereby repealed.

SECTION 2. The transportation or importation into any State, Territory, or possession of the United States for delivery or use therein of intoxicating liquors, in violation of the laws thereof, is hereby prohibited.

SECTION 3. This article shall be inoperative unless it shall have been ratified as an amendment to the Constitution by conventions in the several States, as provided in the Constitution, within seven years from the date of the submission hereof to the States by the Congress.

Amendment XXII—Number of Presidential Terms (Ratified on February 27, 1951)

No person shall be elected to the office of the President more than twice, and no person who has held the office of President, or acted as President, for more than two years of a term to which some other person was elected President shall be elected to the office of the President more than once. But this Article shall not apply to any person holding the office of President when this Article was proposed by the Congress, and shall not prevent any person who may be holding the office of President, or acting as President, during the term within which this Article becomes operative from holding the office of President or acting as President during the remainder of such term.

Amendment XXIII—Presidential Electors for the District of Columbia (Ratified on March 29, 1961)

SECTION 1. The District constituting the seat of Government of the United States shall appoint in such manner as the Congress may direct:

A number of electors of President and Vice President equal to the whole number of Senators and Representatives in Congress to which the District would be entitled if it were a State, but in no event more than the least populous State; they shall be in addition to those appointed by the States, but they shall be considered, for the purposes of the election of President and Vice President, to be electors appointed by a State; and they shall meet in the District and perform such duties as provided by the twelfth article of amendment.

SECTION 2. The Congress shall have power to enforce this article by appropriate legislation.

Amendment XXIV—Poll Tax (Ratified on January 23, 1964)

SECTION 1. The right of citizens of the United States to vote in any primary or other election for President or Vice President, for electors for President or Vice President, or for Senator or Representative in Congress, shall not be denied or abridged by the United States or any State by reason of failure to pay any poll tax or other tax.

SECTION 2. The Congress shall have power to enforce this article by appropriate legislation.

Amendment XXV—Presidential Disability and Vice Presidential Vacancies (Ratified on February 10, 1967)

SECTION 1. In case of the removal of the President from office or of his death or resignation, the Vice President shall become President.

SECTION 2. Whenever there is a vacancy in the office of the Vice President, the President shall nominate a Vice President who shall take office upon confirmation by a majority vote of both Houses of Congress.

SECTION 3. Whenever the President transmits to the President pro tempore of the Senate and the Speaker of the House of Representatives his written declaration that he is unable to discharge the powers and duties of his office, and until he transmits to them a written declaration to the contrary, such powers and duties shall be discharged by the Vice President as Acting President.

SECTION 4. Whenever the Vice President and a majority of either the principal officers of the executive departments or of such other body as Congress may by law provide, transmit to the President pro tempore of the Senate and the Speaker of the House of Representatives their written declaration that the President is unable to discharge the powers and duties of his office, the Vice President shall immediately assume the powers and duties of the office as Acting President.

Thereafter, when the President transmits to the President pro tempore of the Senate and the Speaker of the House of Representatives his written declaration that no inability exists, he shall resume the powers and duties of his office unless the Vice President and a majority of either the principal officers of the executive department or of such other body as Congress may by law provide, transmit within four days to the President pro tempore of the Senate and the Speaker of the House of Representatives their written declaration that the President is unable to discharge the powers and duties of his office. Thereupon Congress shall decide the issue, assembling within forty-eight hours for that purpose if not in session. If the Congress, within twenty-one days after receipt of the latter written declaration, or, if Congress is not in session, within twenty-one days after Congress is required to assemble, determines by two-thirds vote of both Houses that the President is unable to discharge the powers and duties of his office, the Vice President shall continue to discharge the same as Acting President; otherwise, the President shall resume the powers and duties of his office.

Amendment XXVI—Eighteen-year-old Vote (Ratified on July 1, 1971)

SECTION 1. The right of citizens of the United States, who are eighteen years of age or older, to vote shall not be denied or abridged by the United States or by any State on account of age.

SECTION 2. The Congress shall have power to enforce this article by appropriate legislation.

Beyond the Call of Duty: Data and Documents

Listed by chapter below are some primary source materials on the topics covered in *Government in America*. We hope that you will find them useful as you undertake additional work on the important subject of American government and politics.

Chapter 1 Politics and Government in the Third American Century

This is a chapter for which there are no obvious data or documentary sources. So instead, let us suggest some things you could profitably follow while you are reading *Government in America* this term. First, you will probably want to read a good newspaper regularly. With all due respect to local papers, you might prefer to keep up with the *New York Times* or the *Washington Post*. The *Times* is probably better on foreign news than the *Post*, but the *Post*, for obvious reasons, covers a lot of goings-on in the nation's capital. The *Times* has a particularly good "News of the Week in Review" section in each Sunday edition. You should also read a weekly newsmagazine like *Time* or *Newsweek*. There are, though, two other weekly publications that may be even more valuable than the newsmagazines. One is the *Congressional Quarterly Weekly Report*, which has excellent coverage of Congress and elections. The other is the *National Journal*, which covers the administrative branch of government and the policy issues addressed there. And there are, of course, lots of journals of commentary and opinion of all political persuasions. Some very good ones are *The Public Interest, The Nation*, the *National Review, Commentary*, and *The New Republic*. The American Enterprise Institute publishes a very informative magazine called *Public Opinion*, which contains political analysis and useful summaries of what people are thinking.

Chapter 2 Understanding American Government

Nothing will give you a better idea of the complexity of American government than the *U.S. Government Organization Manual*, published annually by the Government Printing Office. The *Federal Register*, also published annually, is a compilation of all government regulations; the *U. S. Code Annotated* is a compilation of the laws passed by Congress and their key judicial interpretations.

Chapter 3 The First American Century: The Constitution

Obviously, there is not much "data" in the form of figures, numbers, public polls, and the like on the period of nation building. Richard Merritt, in his *Symbols of the American Community, 1735–1775*, rev. ed. (1976) provides a thorough analysis of colonial newspapers and their role in the nation-building process. The members of the Philadelphia convention kept no official records, but there is an extensive collection of records and documents compiled by historian Max Ferrand, *The Records of the Federal Convention of 1787*, 4 vols., rev. ed. (1966).

Chapter 4 The American Governments: Federalism

The frequent reports of the Advisory Commission on Intergovernmental Relations are an excellent source of data on federalism in operation. The commission is composed of representatives from the national, state, and local governments. Its regular publication, *Significant Features of Fiscal Federalism*, printed by the U.S. Government Printing Office, is a good source of data on the fiscal side of federalism. The Bureau of the Census also does a *Census of Governments*. It is conducted every five years (in years ending in a 2 or a 7), but publication is often delayed. The Bureau of the Census also publishes annual information on government employment, expenditures, revenues, and debt.

Chapter 5 Civil Liberties and Public Policy

Cases involving civil liberties all appear in official court reports. The Data and Documents section for Chapter 15 tells how to identify a particular case in the official reports of the Supreme Court or other courts. If you want to know something about crime rates, the most important source is the Federal Bureau of Investigation's annual *Uniform Crime Reports*, which compile data on crime and arrests by city, state, and population group. Their validity is, however, much disputed by criminologists, because not all crimes are reported to the police.

Chapter 6 The American People: Public Opinion and Political Action

The explosion of survey research and opinion polling now makes it easy to find out what people are thinking. Major newspapers regularly publish Gallup and Harris Polls. Gallup publishes the *Gallup Report* every month. Each issue is devoted to the latest results of polls on three or four subjects, ranging from evaluations of presidential performance to attitudes toward gun control. Most public and university libraries subscribe to Gallup's monthly report. Harder to obtain are the high-quality surveys done since 1952 by the Survey Research Center of the University of Michigan. Many questions have been repeated in their surveys, giving political scientists the chance to monitor trends in opinion and behavior for almost three decades. Many universities have banded together to form the Inter-University Consortium for Political and Social Research with headquarters in Ann Arbor, Michigan. Membership in the ICPSR gives individual universities and their political science departments fairly easy access to the Michigan surveys and other important data on public opinion and political behavior. The American Enterprise Institute's *Public Opinion* magazine is a monthly collection of timely articles and survey results. The Bureau of the Census periodically publishes a fascinating volume called *Social Indicators*. The latest is the third edition, dated November, 1980. It relies on both census and non-census materials to present a useful statistical overview of the American people, their leisure and work habits, incomes, education, and the like. A drier but more extensive compilation of information from the Bureau of the Census is the annual *Statistical Abstract*.

Chapter 7 The Political Parties

The Gallup and Harris Polls and the University of Michigan's Survey Research Center regularly collect data on the party identifications of Americans. Party platforms are published by the parties themselves, of course. But they are also available in the Congressional Quarterly publication *Congressional Quarterly Almanac*, for the appropriate year. Donald B. Johnson has assembled the texts of all the platforms for a 136-year period in his two volume *National Party Platforms, 1840–1976* (Urbana: University of Illinois Press, 1978). This source is continually revised as well; a 1982 supplemental volume contains the 1980 platforms.

Chapter 8 Running for Office: Nominations and Campaigns

The *Congressional Quarterly* remains the outstanding source of information on American nominations and campaigns, past and present. The Congressional Quarterly Press' *Guide to U.S. Elections*, with an introduction by Nelson Polsby, contains an excellent statistical and textual history of nominations, elections, and campaigns. Each election year CQ publishes an overview of the election, including background on the primary and caucus dates, campaign finances, and regional and historical patterns. One increasingly important issue in campaigns and nominations is money. The Federal Election Commission publishes a monthly update, *Report*, which provides up-to-date information on technicalities of the law and candidate and PAC expenditures. A new source on PACs is Larry J. Sabato's *PAC Power: Inside the World of Political Action Committees* (New York: W. W. Norton, 1984). Before the FEC came into being, data on campaign finances were almost single-handedly collected by Professor Herbert Alexander, now of the University of Southern California. Most of his books contain extensive documentation of past and recent patterns of expenditures and revenues of campaigns.

Chapter 9 Elections: The Voters Decide

Of course, some of the materials listed for Chapter 8 are relevant here, particularly the various publications of the Congressional Quarterly Press. For many years, Richard Scammon has edited a post-election volume called *America Votes* (Washington, D.C.: Governmental Affairs Institute), which contains detailed information on county, state, and national patterns in the preceding election. The Inter-University Consortium on Political and Social Research at the University of Michigan also maintains an extensive historical file on elections. Election information for state—and especially local—races is harder to find. The official repository in most states is the Secretary of State or a state election commissioner. On the local level, check with your city clerk or county board of elections.

Chapter 10 Interest Groups

The *Encyclopedia of Associations* (annual) offers the closest approximation to a census of groups, although it depends on the reliability of groups' own reports about membership totals, staff, and programs. Because the Federal Regulation of Lobbying Act is full of loopholes, the registration data on lobbying groups is even more suspect. The various publications of the Congressional Quarterly, especially the annual *Congressional Quarterly Almanac*, do list official registrations, however, and review their congressional activities.

Chapter 11   Politics and Policy in Washington

Keeping tabs on the public agenda is not as hard as knowing what is on the government's agenda. Most of the major polls like Gallup and Harris report regular soundings on a question like "What's the most important problem facing the country today?" You can find these polls published in many newspapers—the *New York Times* or the *Washington Post* are particularly good. These organizations also publish regular reports. The journals *Public Opinion* and the *Gallup Report* often report up-to-date data on current policy issues. To find out about the government's agenda, the *New York Times*, the *Washington Post*, or other good newspapers can be helpful. The *Times* also has a useful index.

Chapter 12   Congress

The *Congressional Quarterly Weekly Report* and other publications of Congressional Quarterly Press are filled with key roll-call votes, information on committee and leadership activities, and election information. The CQ is indispensable for a serious study of Congress. Fortunately, it is available in almost all college and university libraries. The *Congressional Record* is published by the Congress and purports to be a record of everything said and done by the House and Senate. So it is, more or less, but members can take considerable liberties with the record of their speeches and statements. Still, it is informative and sometimes even entertaining reading, especially when members print trivia to please constituents, duly sending along a copy to the people whose names are in that issue of the *Congressional Record*. The reports of congressional committees are all available in a "repository" library, one that collects all government documents. They can be ordered from the Government Printing Office (which takes forever to send out its mail). The best way to get committee reports and hearings is to write your congressman and request very specifically what you need. Another source of information on Congress, particularly on members and their districts, is the *Almanac of American Politics*. For data on the characteristics of congressional districts, see the Bureau of the Census's *Congressional District Data Book*.

Chapter 13   The President

Because much of the presidency operates behind closed doors (only Richard Nixon was foolhardy enough to tape the Oval Office), we lack direct data on presidential decision making. However, we do have a documentary source on the results of decision making. Called *Public Papers of the President*, it is issued annually by the U.S. Government Printing Office and easily located in most public and university libraries. Presidents have traditionally donated their papers to the public, and several recent presidents have presidential libraries housing their papers. Kennedy's, for example, is in Boston and Johnson's is in Austin. The Congressional Quarterly's publications provide information and data on presidential activities that involve Congress.

Chapter 14   The Bureaucracies

The most important record of bureaucratic decision making is the *Federal Register*. No one has ever claimed that it is entertaining reading, but it contains the rules and regulations of all the administrative agencies of the U.S. government. Almost every agency of government also publishes an annual report, available by writing to the agency itself, contacting your Senator or Representative, or checking a repository library. The *Annual Report* of the U.S. Civil Service Commission (now the Office of Personnel Management), for example, will tell you about government employment, coverage of the Civil Service System, and information about pay and job ratings.

Chapter 15   The Courts

It is not difficult to track down decisions of the Supreme Court and other federal courts. The Supreme Court decisions are bound annually and published in *U.S. Reports*. Each volume is numbered. To find a given case, you need to know how it is "styled"—for example, *Smith* v. *Jones* or *U.S.* v. *Brown*. Knowing the right year of the case, you can track it down in the appropriate volume of the *U.S. Reports*. Technically, cases are coded as, for example, 411 U.S. 105, meaning that it appears on page 105 of volume 411 of the *U.S. Reports*. More immediately available is the *U.S. Law Week*, which publishes Supreme Court decisions on a weekly basis. Almost all college, university, and major public libraries subscribe to the *U.S. Reports*. Many will also subscribe to *U.S. Law Week*. Not so many will have the *Federal Reporter* or the *Federal Supplement*, the reports of cases decided by the circuit courts of appeal and the federal district courts. You may have to go to a law school library or the county bar association library to find these.

Chapter 16   Budgeting: Taxing, Spending, and Public Policy

The president's proposed budget to Congress is published annually under the title, *Budget of the United States Government for Fiscal 19—*. It is a weighty document, listing past budget trends, budget projections, and current expenditures. A much more useful source, though, is *The Budget in Brief*, a shorter version of the large budget document, containing much of the key information. A variety of projections and analyses of the budget are published by the Congressional Budget Office. All of these publications are available in a government documents section of a college or university library and in most larger public libraries.

Chapter 17   The Political Economy and Public Policy

The best source of up-to-date information about the American economy is the *Annual Report* of the Council of Economic Advisors. Filled with tables on employment, inflation, spending habits, and other economic indicators, the CEA's *Annual Report* is published in January of each year and accompanies the president's annual economic message to Congress. The *Monthly Labor Review*, a publication of the Department of Labor, also has extensive data on various indicators of the economy's health. The annual reports of various federal departments and agencies regulating the economy also give you an idea of their policy activities.

Interest groups like the AFL-CIO and the Chamber of Commerce also prepare reports and gather data on important economic issues. Their publications are, of course, favorable to the cause they represent, but many are of very high quality, reflecting the work of large, sophisticated research staffs.

Chapter 18 Public Policy and Equality

The source of most data on American equality and inequality is the United States Bureau of the Census. Its *Statistical Abstract* (annual) is the handiest compilation of data on income, race, earnings, and other conditions described in this chapter. An informative source, with graphs, charts, and tables is *Social Indicators* (Government Printing Office, 1980), located in most college and public libraries. Especially useful are the sections on income and wealth, the family, and social mobility. If you need to track down laws dealing with equality policy, you need the *United States Code,* the compilation of all laws passed by Congress.

Chapter 19 Energy, Environment, and Public Policy

Two of the best sources of information on public policy regarding energy and environment are the annual reports of the Council on Environmental Quality and various reports of the Department of Energy. The CEQ is charged with monitoring air and water quality, as well as with advising the president on environmental issues. Useful, too, are the reports of the Environmental Protection Agency. Although they are obviously slanted in favor of the oil industry, several publications of the American Petroleum Institute, such as its *Oil and Gas Journal,* are very informative.

Chapter 20 The Global Connection

The quality of data available about the global connection and foreign policies varies greatly. It is difficult to find reliable data about the military and the economy of other nations. Not surprisingly, nations try to keep military information secret. The United States Arms Control and Disarmament Agency, though, publishes good estimates of military strength and expenditures. The United Nations' *Statistical Yearbook* provides much economic and social data on member nations. One useful place to look for international political and governmental data is *Political Handbook of the World,* a regularly updated publication of the Center for Political Analysis at SUNY-Binghamton under the editorship of Arthur S. Banks.

Glossary

Note: Numbers in parentheses indicate the chapter where the term is discussed.

activation. A consequence of political campaigns for voters in which the voter is prompted to contribute money or ring doorbells for a candidate in addition to voting. See also **conversion** and **reinforcement.** (8)

actual group. That part of the **potential group** who actually join. (10)

administrative discretion. The authority of administrative actors to select among various responses to a given problem. It is greatest when rules do not fit a case. Compare with **administrative routine.** (14)

administrative routine. When repetitive tasks are performed and similar cases are handled in roughly similar ways by administrative actors. Compare with **administrative discretion.** (14)

affirmative action. Policies that give special consideration or compensatory treatment to members of traditionally disadvantaged groups in an effort to promote more **equal results** in such areas as education and employment. Compare with **equal opportunity.** (1, 18)

agenda. See **governmental agenda, policy agenda, public agenda.**

agents of socialization. Families, schools, television, peer groups, and other influences that contribute to **political socialization** by shaping formal and especially informal learning about politics. (6)

Antifederalists. Opponents of the Constitution at the time when the states were contemplating its adoption. They argued that the Constitution was an aristocratic document, that it would create an overpowering central government, and that it would weaken the power of the states. See also **Federalists.** (3)

antitrust policy. A policy designed to ensure competition and prevent monopoly, which is the control of a market by one company. (17)

appellate jurisdiction. The authority of courts in cases that are brought on appeal from a lower court. Most of the business brought to the United States Supreme Court comes from the appellate process. Compare with **original jurisdiction.** (15)

arms race. Military build up by the United States and the Soviet Union in which one side's weaponry becomes the other side's goad to procure more weaponry. (20)

Articles of Confederation. The articles that established a United States government dominated by the states and created a national legislature, the Continental Congress. The Articles were adopted by the Congress in 1777 and put into effect in 1781. (3)

balance of payments. The ratio of what is paid for imports to what is earned from exports. (20)

Barron v. Baltimore. The 1833 Supreme Court decision that the **Bill of Rights** restrained only the national government, not the states and cities. Compare with ***Gitlow v. New York.*** (5)

bicameral legislature. A legislature that is divided into two separate houses. The House of Representatives and the Senate are the two bodies of the national bicameral legislature in the United States. Of the fifty states, Nebraska has the only unicameral legislature. (12)

bill. A proposed law drafted in precise, legal language. Anyone can draft a bill but only members of the House of Representatives or the Senate can formally submit a bill for consideration. (12)

Bill of Rights. The first ten amendments to the Constitution, which came in response to some of the

661

Antifederalist concerns. These amendments emphasize the protection of individual liberties. (3, 5)

block grants. A form of federal aid to states and cities that is given more or less automatically to support broad programs in areas such as community development, health services, and social services. Compare with **categorical grants** and **revenue sharing.** (4)

Brown v. *Board of Education of Topeka.* The landmark 1954 decision in which the Supreme Court ruled that legally enforced school **segregation** was inherently unconstitutional. (15)

budget. A policy document which allocates burdens (taxes) and benefits (expenditures). (16)

bureaucracy. An organization that depends on a hierarchical authority structure, uses task specialization, and develops extensive rules. (14)

cabinet. The group of presidential advisors consisting of twelve secretaries and the attorney general who head executive departments. (13)

capitalism. An economic system in which individuals and corporations, not the government, own the principal means of production and seek profits. Pure capitalism means the strict noninterference of the government in business affairs. Compare with **mixed economy.** (1, 3)

case (court). A dispute between two parties (the government, corporations, or individuals) that comes to a court for settlement. The case is the basic unit of a court's activities. See also **defendant** and **plaintiff.** (15)

casework. When a member of Congress helps constituents as individuals, cutting through some bureaucratic red tape in order to get people what they think they have a right to get. It is a means of "servicing the constituency." See also **pork barrel.** (12)

categorical grants. A form of federal aid to states and cities that can be used only for specific purposes and only if certain standards are met. These grants are designed to encourage governments to alter their policy agendas but tend to burden applicants with large amounts of paperwork. Compare with **block grants** and **revenue sharing.** (4)

caucus (congressional). A group of members of Congress based on some shared interest or characteristic. (12)

caucus (state party). A meeting of state party leaders in which the delegates to the **national party convention** are selected. It is an institution that is fading as **presidential primaries** are being more frequently used. (8)

census. The enumeration of a population. In the United States, the Bureau of the Census conducts a census every ten years and also collects a variety of data on characteristics of the population. (6)

Central Intelligence Agency (CIA). The federal agency created after World War II to coordinate American intelligence activities abroad. It has become a major national security establishment, although its involvement in clandestine activities and coups abroad have made the CIA a subject of controversy as well. (20)

chairmen (committee). The most important influencers of the congressional agenda. They play a dominant role in scheduling hearings, hiring staff, appointing subcommittees, and managing committee bills when they are brought before the full house. Rule changes in the 1970s allow committee members of the majority party to select their chairman, although **seniority** continues to play a role in these decisions. (12)

change (in public opinion). A dimension of public opinion that refers to the way opinions differ over time. (6)

checks and balances. An important part of the **Madisonian model** which required that power be balanced among the different governmental institutions and that these institutions should continually check each other's activities. Through such a system, Madison believed that no single institution could dominate. See also **separation of powers.** (3)

civil disobedience. A form of **political participation** in which people consciously choose to disobey a law and announce a willingness to accept the legal consequences. (6)

civil law. The body of law that involves no transgression of **criminal law** but a dispute between two parties (the government, corporations, or individuals). Compare with **criminal law.** (5)

civil liberties. Legal and constitutional protections of individuals against government. Civil liberties issues often come to our attention in the form of a court **case.** (5)

Civil Rights Act of 1964. The law that made illegal discrimination against any group in public facilities and in many areas of employment. See also **civil rights movement.** (18)

civil rights movement. A movement that began in the 1950s and organized both blacks and whites to end policies and practices of **segregation.** See also **Civil Rights Act of 1964.** (18)

civil service. The system of government hiring and promotion that rests on the **merit principle** in order to create a nonpartisan government service and prevent **patronage.** (14)

Clean Air Act of 1970. The law that charged the Department of Transportation (DOT) with the responsibility of reducing auto emissions. (19)

clear and present danger. The test proposed by Justice Holmes for determining when government may restrict free speech. Restrictions are permissible, he argued, only when speech provokes a "clear and present danger" to people. See also *Schenck v. United States*. (5)

coalition.   A group of individuals (or a group of groups) that join together for the purpose of winning an election. See also **minimum winning coalition.** (7)

cold war.   The period of the 1950s during which relations between the United States and the Soviet Union never erupted into armed opposition but remained on the brink of war. (20)

collective bargaining.   Negotiations between representatives of labor unions and management to determine acceptable working conditions. (17)

collective good.   Something of value that cannot be withheld from a group member. See also **free-rider problem** and **Olson's law of large groups.** (10)

command-and-control policy.   The existing regulatory system in the United States in which the government tells business how to reach certain goals, checks that these commands are followed, and punishes offenders. Compare with **incentive system.** (14)

committees (congressional).   See **conference committees, joint committees, select committees, standing committees.**

comparable worth.   View that women are discriminated against since traditionally female jobs are lower-paying than male-dominated jobs, even when they require similar skills. (18)

conference committees.   Formed when the House of Representatives and the Senate pass a particular bill in different forms. Party leaders appoint members from each house to a conference committee to iron out the differences and report back a single bill. (12)

conflict (in public opinion).   A dimension of public opinion where the pros and the antis are sharply divided. Compare with **consensus.** (6)

Congressional Budget and Impoundment Control Act of 1974.   The law designed to streamline the congressional budgetary process and make Congress less dependent on the president's budget and more able to set and meet its own budgetary goals. It established a fixed budget calendar and created a budget committee in each house as well as the **Congressional Budget Office (CBO).** (16)

Congressional Budget Office (CBO).   The office that advises Congress on the likely consequences of its budget decisions and forecasts revenues. It is a counterweight to the president's **Office of Management and Budget (OMB).** (16)

Connecticut Compromise.   The compromise reached at the Constitutional Convention that established two houses of Congress: the House of Representatives, in which **representation** is based on a state's share of the United States population, and the Senate, in which each state has two representatives. Compare with **New Jersey Plan** and **Virginia Plan.** (3)

consensus (in public opinion).   A dimension of public opinion where there is agreement. Compare with **conflict.** (6)

consent of the governed.   According to John Locke, the required basis for government. The **Declaration of Independence** reflected Locke's view that governments derive their authority from the consent of the governed. (3)

Constitution.   The document written in 1787 and ratified in 1788 that sets forth the institutional structure of the United States government and the tasks that these institutions perform. It replaced the **Articles of Confederation.** See also **unwritten constitution.** (1, 3)

Consumer Price Index (CPI).   The key measure of inflation which relates prices in one year to prices for a base year. The base year prices are figured as 100 and annual cost of living changes are measured from that base. (17)

containment doctrine.   Foreign-policy strategist George Kennan's call for the United States to isolate the Soviet Union, "contain" its advances, and resist its encroachments—by peaceful means if possible but with force if necessary. (20)

convention.   See **national party convention.**

conversion.   A consequence of political campaigns for voters in which some voters will convert or change their mind about who to vote for. See also **activation** and **reinforcement.** (8)

cooperative federalism.   A system of government in which powers and policy assignments are shared between states and the national government. Costs, administration, and even blame are shared among the different governmental units. Compare with **dual federalism.** (4)

Council of Economic Advisors (CEA).   Part of the **Executive Office of the President** consisting of three members appointed by the president to advise him on economic policy matters. (13)

counties.   Subdivisions of states that are the least numerous of four major types of local government. (4)

courts of appeal.   Intermediate level federal courts (the only recourse above them is the Supreme Court); judges are nominated by the president and must be confirmed by the Senate. (15)

crime rate.   An annual report of the number of serious personal crimes (e.g., homicide and rape) and property crimes (e.g., burglary and auto theft) in the United States. (5)

criminal law.   The body of law in which an individual is charged with violating a specific statute of government and conviction typically results in a fine or imprisonment. Compare with **civil law.** (15)

crisis. An abrupt and often unexpected event that threatens grave danger unless it is resolved. Crises often bypass **linkage institutions** and go directly to policymakers. (11, 13)

critical election period. A time period usually lasting over several elections during which the majority party is displaced by the other major party as a result of **party realignment.** (7)

cruel and unusual punishment. Court sentences prohibited by the **Eighth Amendment.** The most controversial punishment today is the death penalty. While the Supreme Court has held that mandatory death sentences for certain offenses are unconstitutional, it has not held that the death penalty itself constitutes cruel and unusual punishment. (5)

Dartmouth College v. Woodward. The 1819 Supreme Court decision that held that Dartmouth's charter, as well as the charter of any corporation, is a legal contract that cannot be tampered with by a government. (15)

debt. See **federal debt.**

Declaration of Independence. The document approved by representatives of the American colonies in 1776 that stated their grievances against the British monarch and declared their independence. (3)

defendant. The party (government, corporation, or individual) that is charged with committing a transgression by a **plaintiff** in a court **case.** (15)

deficit (in the federal budget). An excess of federal expenditures over federal revenues. (16)

democracy. A means of selecting policymakers and organizing government to ensure that policy represents and responds to the public's preferences. See also **traditional democratic theory.** (2)

democratic theory. See **traditional democratic theory.**

demography. The science of population that includes the study of population changes: births, deaths, residential movements; the racial, sexual, and social composition of the population; and its age structure. (6)

Dennis v. United States. The 1951 Supreme Court decision that permitted the government to jail several American communist party leaders under the Smith Act, a law which forbids the advocacy of the violent overthrow of the United States government. (5)

dependency. See **mutual dependency.**

deregulation. A reduction in the number and scope of rules affecting the private economy. (14, 19)

detente. A slow transformation from conflict thinking to cooperative thinking in foreign-policy strategy. In American politics, the term was first used

during the Nixon administration in reference to the intent to relax the tension between the United States and the Soviet Union, coupled with firm guarantees of mutual security. (20)

direct primaries (in state elections). Used to select candidates for the United States Senate, the House of Representatives, governors, and other state offices. (9)

discrimination. When individuals are treated differently solely because they are members of a particular group—a race, a sex, a religion, or a class. Compare with **segregation.** (18)

Dred Scott v. Sandford. The 1857 case in which the Supreme Court held that a slave was not a citizen and therefore was not entitled to sue for his freedom. It further held that Congress had no authority to ban slavery in the territories. (15, 18)

dual federalism. A system of government in which states and the national government each remain supreme within their own spheres. The powers and policy assignments of the layers of government are distinct; the states are responsible for some policies, the federal government for others. Compare with **cooperative federalism.** (4)

due process clause. The part of the **Fourteenth Amendment** ensuring that the United States government and the state governments may not impair rights of individuals guaranteed by the Constitution without due process of law. See also *Gitlow v. New York.* (5)

Eighth Amendment. The constitutional amendment that forbids excessive bail and court sentences and anything else constituting **cruel and unusual punishment.** (5)

electioneering. The direct involvement of **interest groups** in the electoral process. They aid candidates financially, urge the adoption of their policies by the parties, mobilize members to support a favored candidate, and provide campaign assistance, including speech writing and doorbell ringing. (10)

electoral accountability. The ability of the electorate to vote out of office anyone who has not accurately or honestly represented the majority's policy goals. (2)

electoral college. Under this system, each state has as many electoral votes as it has United States senators and representatives. State electors are chosen by the state parties and vote in a block for the popular winner in the state. Their votes are then forwarded to the president of the Senate. (9)

elites. The few who govern the many, according to the **elite and class theory** of politics. These few occupy positions of power and control, not only by holding public office but by holding key posts in the private sector. Elite roles are often interlocking roles. (2)

elite and class theory. The theory of politics that

holds that the few will rule and the many will be ruled, regardless of how a government is arranged. Elite and class theorists believe that **elites** control policymaking and government. Compare with **hyperpluralism, pluralist theory,** and **traditional democratic theory.** (2)

empirical theory. A theory based on observations or data that can be verified with evidence. Its purpose is to explain observable phenomena with accuracy and precision. Compare with **normative theory.** (2)

Engel* v. *Vitale. The 1962 Supreme Court decision that state officials violated the **First Amendment** when they wrote a prayer to be recited by New York's schoolchildren. (5)

entrepreneur. See **policy entrepreneur.**

enumerated powers. Powers of the federal government that are specifically addressed in the Constitution; for Congress, these powers are itemized in Article I of the Constitution. Compare with **implied powers.** (4)

environmental impact statement. A report filed with the **Environmental Protection Agency (EPA)** that specifies what environmental effects a proposed policy would have. The **National Environmental Policy Act** of 1969 requires that whenever a governmental agency proposes to undertake a policy potentially disruptive of the environment, it must file a statement with the EPA. (19)

Environmental Protection Agency (EPA). An **independent regulatory agency** of the federal government created in 1970 to support research on environmental quality and whose primary purpose is to regulate polluters in order to promote cleaner air and water. (19)

equal opportunity. Policies designed to try to give everyone a fair chance for opportunities in such areas as education, housing, and employment without discriminating on the basis of sex, skin color, religion, or some other characteristic. **Segregation** and **discrimination** deny people equal opportunities. Compare with **affirmative action.** (1, 16, 18)

equal results. A concept of equality that emphasizes the outcome of policies in this area. Because **equal opportunity** does not necessarily produce equal results, some have advocated policies of **affirmative action.** (1, 18)

Equal Rights Amendment. A constitutional amendment proposed by Congress in 1972 and sent to the state legislatures for ratification that would prohibit discrimination on the basis of sex. It was approved by only thirty-five of the thirty-eight states required and did not, despite an extension, meet its ratification deadline. (18)

establishment clause. The part of the **First Amendment** prohibiting the establishment of a church officially supported by the national government. (5)

European Economic Community (EEC). A regional economic alliance of the major western European nations, often called the Common Market. (20)

exclusionary rule. The rule that evidence, no matter how incriminating, cannot be used against a **defendant** in a criminal trial unless it was lawfully obtained. It prohibits the use of evidence obtained through **unreasonable search and seizure.** (5)

executive order. Direct means by which the president imposes policy preferences on bureaucratic agencies. (14)

exit polls. Surveys taken at polling places by television networks and other media representatives to predict the winner of an election before all the votes have been tallied. (9)

expenditures. Federal spending of revenues; major areas of spending are social services and the military. (16)

factions. Interests arising from the unequal distribution of property or wealth that James Madison attacked in the **Federalist papers** No. 10. The parties or interest groups of today are what Madison had in mind when he warned of the instability in government caused by factions. (3)

federal debt. The total amount of money the federal government has borrowed. Today it is almost $2 trillion. (16)

federal district courts. Lower-level federal court system (below the Supreme Court and the courts of appeal); judges are appointed by the president but choices may be vetoed by a senator of the president's party. See **senatorial courtesy.** (15)

Federal Election Campaign Act. A law passed in 1974 that created the **Federal Election Commission (FEC),** set limits for contributions, provided some public financing for **presidential primaries** and general elections, set limits for presidential campaign spending, and required disclosure to the FEC on sources and uses of funds. (8)

Federal Election Commission (FEC). A bipartisan, six-member body established by the 1974 **Federal Election Campaign Act** to administer campaign finance laws and enforce compliance with their requirements. (8)

federalism. A way of organizing a nation so that two levels of government have formal authority over the same area and people. In any **federal system** of government, each level of government must have some domain in which its policies are dominant and have some genuine political or constitutional guarantee of its authority. Compare with **unitary government.** (4)

Federalist papers. A collection of eighty-five articles written by Alexander Hamilton, John Jay, and James Madison under the name of "Publius" to defend the Constitution in detail. Collectively, these papers are second only to the Constitution in characterizing what the framers had in mind. (3)

Federalists. Supporters of the Constitution at the time when the states were contemplating its adoption. See also **Antifederalist** and **Federalist papers.** (3)

Federal Regulation of Lobbying Act. The 1964 law requiring lobbyists to register and state their policy goals. The Supreme Court held that only groups whose "principal" purpose is lobbying are legally required to register. (10)

Federal Reserve System. A body created by Congress in 1913 to regulate the lending practices of banks and, therefore, a key actor in making **monetary policy.** The seven members of its Board of Governors are appointed to fourteen-year terms by the president with the advice and consent of the Senate. (17)

Federal Trade Commission (FTC). The **independent regulatory agency** traditionally responsible for regulating false and misleading trade practices. The FTC has recently become active in defending consumer interests through truth in advertising rules and in administering the Consumer Credit Protection Act. (17)

Fifteenth Amendment. The constitutional amendment adopted in 1870 to extend **suffrage** to blacks. (9, 18)

Fifth Amendment. The constitutional amendment designed to protect the rights of persons accused of crimes, including protection against double jeopardy, **self-incrimination,** and punishment without due process of law. (5)

filibuster. A method used in the United States Senate whereby a senator or senators tie up the legislative agenda by holding the floor and continuing to speak indefinitely. Unlike the House of Representatives, there is no time limit on debate in the Senate. (12)

First Amendment. The constitutional amendment that established the principles of free speech and press, religious tolerance, and freedom of assembly, and prohibits the United States Congress from infringing these rights. (5)

fiscal federalism. The patterns of spending, taxing, and grants between governmental units where the federal government has become increasingly supreme. (4)

fiscal policy. The use of the federal budget—taxes, spending, and borrowing—to stimulate the economy. It is based on **Keynesian economic theory.** Compare with **monetary policy.** (17)

foreign policy. Like domestic policy, it involves choice-taking, but it is choice-taking about relations with the rest of the world. (20)

Fourteenth Amendment. The constitutional amendment adopted after the Civil War that forbids states to make laws that interfere with individual rights guaranteed under the Constitution or infringe on these rights without due process of law. It also ensures equal protection of the laws to all persons. (5)

free-rider problem. When potential members share in the **collective goods** and policy gains that the **actual group** secures. It is the basic problem leading to **Olson's law of large groups.** (10)

Frostbelt. States and cities of the northern regions of the United States that have experienced a general decline in population and jobs as people move to the **Sunbelt.** (4)

Furman **v.** *Georgia.* The 1972 Supreme Court decision that overturned Georgia's death penalty law but did not declare the death penalty itself unconstitutional. The majority of the court found that the imposition of the death sentence was often "freakish" and "random" and that blacks were disproportionately sentenced to death. (5)

gatekeeping. Mechanisms created by all policymaking institutions to regulate their agendas by filtering the increasing demands placed on them. (11)

general elections. Elections in which voters select officeholders from those candidates nominated by the parties. (9)

General Schedule rating. See **G.S. (General Schedule) rating.**

Gideon **v.** *Wainwright.* The 1963 Supreme Court decision that anyone accused of a felony, where imprisonment may be imposed, has a right to a lawyer, thus extending the **right to counsel** provision of the **Sixth Amendment.** (5)

Gitlow **v.** *New York.* The 1925 Supreme Court decision that the **due process clause** of the **Fourteenth Amendment** protected the freedoms of press and speech from impairment by the states as well as the federal government. Compare with *Barron* **v.** *Baltimore.* (5)

government. The institutions and processes through which **public policies** are made for a society. (1)

governmental agenda. Consists of those issues policymakers actually consider. Compare with **policy agenda** and **public agenda.** (11)

government corporations. Organizations within the federal government which provide a service that could be handled by the private sector and which typically charge for their services, though at cheaper rates than a private firm would charge. The United States Postal Service and the Tennessee Valley Authority are examples. (5)

Gregg **v.** *Georgia.* The 1976 Supreme Court decision that upheld the constitutionality of the death penalty, stating that, "It is an extreme sanction, suitable to the most extreme of crimes." The court did not, therefore, believe that the death sentence constitutes **cruel and unusual punishment.** (5)

gross national product (GNP). The total dollar value of all goods and services produced in a nation in a year. (1, 17)

Grove City College v. *Bell.* The 1984 decision in which the Supreme Court ruled that in order to be eligible for federal aid, the college was required to guarantee antidiscriminatory policies only in the particular program for which students had applied for assistance. (18)

G.S. (General Schedule) rating. Salary ratings of **civil service** employees, ranging from GS 1 to GS 18. Salaries are keyed to rating and experience. (14)

high-tech politics. Politics in which the behavior of citizens and policymakers, and the political agenda itself, are increasingly shaped by technological change. (1)

House Ways and Means Committee. The House of Representatives committee responsible for writing tax codes that are subject to the approval of Congress as a whole. (16)

House Rules Committee. Agenda-setting committee in the House of Representatives that reviews and schedules debates for all proposed bills before they go to the full House. (11)

hyperpluralism. An exaggerated or perverted form of **pluralism.** Due to the proliferation of demanding groups, government is so decentralized and pluralistic that it has trouble getting anything done and, as a consequence, performs poorly and ineffectively. Compare with **elite and class theory** and **traditional democratic theory.** (2)

ideology. See **political ideology.**

impacts. See **policy impacts.**

impeachment. The constitutional provision for removing an unwanted president from office that is roughly equivalent to a criminal indictment. A president may be impeached by a majority vote in the House of Representatives, after which he is tried in the Senate. A two-thirds vote in the Senate results in conviction and removal from office. (13)

implementation. The private and public activities involved in translating the goals and objectives of a policy into an operating, ongoing program. All policies require implementation before than can work and have results, or **policy impacts.** (1, 2, 14)

implied powers. Powers of the federal government that go beyond those enumerated in the Constitution. The Constitution states that Congress has the power to "make all laws necessary and proper for carrying into execution" the powers enumerated in Article

I. The exercise of implied powers was first acknowledged in the Supreme Court decision in *McCulloch* v. *Maryland.* Compare with **enumerated powers.** (4)

incentive system. Providing inducements to businesses to comply with certain standards instead of imposing elaborate regulatory rules, as in **command-and-control policy.** Providing tax incentives is a method that has been proposed to encourage firms, for example, to make conditions safe for workers and to stop polluting. (14)

income. The amount of funds collected between any two times (weeks, months, or years). Compare with **wealth.** (18)

income distribution. The shares of the national income earned by various groups. Income distribution in the United States is unequal, where relatively few people receive a disproportionately large share of income, and many people receive far less; it has changed little since 1950. (18)

income taxes. Shares of individual wages and corporate revenues collected by the government. The first income tax was declared unconstitutional by the Supreme Court in 1895, but the **Sixteenth Amendment** explicitly authorized Congress to levy a tax on income. (16)

incrementalism. When the best predictor of this year's budget is last year's budget plus a little bit more (an increment). According to Aaron Wildavsky, "Most of the budget is a product of previous decisions." (16)

incumbent. An elected official presently holding office. In running for reelection, incumbents generally have an advantage over challengers. (12)

independent executive agencies. Federal agencies that are neither **cabinet** departments, **independent regulatory agencies,** nor **government corporations.** The Veterans Administration and the National Aeronautics and Space Administration are examples. (14)

independent regulatory agencies. Federal agencies, each of which is responsible for some sector of the economy. Their influence is so extensive that these agencies alone are sometimes referred to as a fourth branch of government. The Interstate Commerce Commission and the **Environmental Protection Agency** are examples. (14)

industrial revenue bonds. Bonds that make government credit available to industries for building or modernization of plants. (4)

information gap. The inequality between classes in the amount and variety of available information. (6)

initiative. Petition that permits a certain percentage of the state's voters to put a proposed law directly on the ballot. If a majority of the voters vote in favor of this law, it becomes state policy even if the legislature does not act. (9)

interest group. An organization of people with

policy goals that enter the policy process at several points to try to achieve these goals. (10)

interest group liberalism. Where groups are powerful but government is fragmented and its authority weak. According to Theodore Lowi, in this situation **interest groups** can work so that policies may never be instituted or, if instituted, never implemented. (2, 10)

intergovernmental relations. The workings of the federal system, which means the entire set of interactions among the various units of government and their officials. It describes how governments interact. (4)

Internal Revenue Service (IRS). The office established to collect federal income taxes, investigate violations of the tax laws, and prosecute tax criminals. (16)

isolationism. Foreign policy that stressed avoidance of other nations' conflicts, particularly European wars. (20)

Joint Chiefs of Staff. Consists of the senior officers of the United States Army, Navy, and Air Force who advise the secretary of defense and the president on military issues. (20)

joint committees. The few congressional subject-matter committees consisting of members from both the House of Representatives and the Senate. (12)

judicial activism. Policy that supports an active role for judges in policymaking decisions (e.g., decisions on social issues like abortion and school prayer). (15)

judicial implementation. The process by which court decisions are translated into actual policy. (15)

judicial restraint. Policy that favors a minimal role for judges in policymaking decisions, leaving that function strictly to legislatures. (15)

judicial review. The authority of the Supreme Court to decide whether laws and executive actions of the federal government and the states square with or are in violation of the Constitution. This power was first asserted by Chief Justice John Marshall and his associates in the case of *Marbury* v. *Madison.* (3, 15)

jury. A committee of legally selected individuals who are responsible for the determination of guilt in a legal case. (15)

Keynesian economic theory. The theory that government spending can help the economy weather economic downturns. It is the basis for **fiscal policy,** where government spending is increased to stimulate a lagging economy. (17)

laissez-faire. The principle that government should not meddle in the economy. See also **capitalism.** (17)

law of materials balance. The natural law that

states that the total weight of materials taken from nature will equal the total weight of wastes discharged into the environment plus the total weight of any materials recycled. (19)

libel. The publication of knowingly false or malicious statements that damage someone's reputation. (5)

limited government. The idea that certain things are out of bounds for government because of certain **natural rights** of citizens. A call for limited government was part of John Locke's philosophy, and it contrasted sharply with the prevailing view of the divine right of monarchs. (3)

linkage institutions. The channels or access points through which issues are put on the policy agenda; a means of getting government to listen to and to act on popular preferences. Parties, elections, and interest groups are the three big linkage institutions between people and politics in the United States. (1, 7)

litigants. **Plaintiffs** and **defendants** in a court case. (15)

lobbying. According to Lester Milbrath, a "communication, by someone other than a citizen acting on his own behalf, directed to a governmental decision-maker with the hope of influencing his decision." (10)

McCarthyism. The assumption that international communism was conspiratorial, insidious, bent on world domination, and infiltrating American governmental and cultural institutions. It is named for the actions of Senator Joseph McCarthy who, with flimsy evidence, fingered scores of prominent Americans as communists at the time of the Korean War. (20)

McCulloch* v. *Maryland. An 1819 Supreme Court decision that established the supremacy of the national government over state governments. In deciding the case, the Court also held that Congress had certain **implied powers** in addition to the **enumerated powers** found in the Constitution. (4)

McGovern-Fraser Commission. Commission appointed by delegates at the 1968 Democratic convention to propose reforms that would make the party more representative of the electorate. (7)

machine. According to Danfield and Wilson, "a party organization that depends crucially on inducements that are both specific and material." A specific inducement can be given or withheld from someone; a material inducement is monetary or has a monetary value. See also **patronage.** (7)

Madisonian model. James Madison's blueprint for government that emphasized placing as much of the government as possible beyond the direct control of a majority, separating the powers of different institutions, and creating a system of **checks and balances.** The Madisonian model continues to shape the policymaking process in the United States today. See also **separation of powers.** (3)

majority leader. Selected by the majority party, the member of the House of Representatives and the member of the Senate who schedules floor activities, rounds up votes on bills the party favors, and influences committee assignments. (12)

majority rule. The "rule" that prescribes that in choosing among alternatives, the alternative preferred by the greater number is to be selected. Majority rule is one of the basic principles of **traditional democratic theory.** (2)

Mapp v. *Ohio.* The 1961 Supreme Court decision that extended the **exclusionary rule** to illegally seized evidence used in state trials, in addition to federal trials. (5)

Marbury v. *Madison.* The 1803 case in which Chief Justice John Marshall and his associates first asserted the Supreme Court's right to determine what the Constitution means. The decision established the Court's power of **judicial review** over acts of Congress, in this case the Judiciary Act of 1789. (3, 15)

medicare. Added to the social security program in 1965, it provides both hospital and physician coverage to social security recipients and to some other poor people. (16)

merit principle. The use of entrance exams and promotion ratings, intended to produce government administration by people with talent and skill. The merit principle is the basis for the **civil service** system. Compare with **patronage.** (14)

military industrial complex. A tight alliance between business and government produced by the interests shared by the armed services and defense contractors. This term was first used by President Eisenhower. (20)

Miller v. *California.* The 1973 Supreme Court decision that avoided defining obscenity by holding that community standards should be used to determine whether material is obscene in terms of appealing to a "prurient interest." (5)

minority leader. Selected by the minority party, the member of the House of Representatives and the member of the Senate who shares power with various minority party committees and leaders. (12)

minority rights. The guarantee of the right to participate in government; minority rights are one of the basic principles of **traditional democratic theory.** (2)

Miranda v. *Arizona.* The 1966 Supreme Court decision that sets guidelines for police questioning of accused persons in order to protect their **right to counsel** and their protection against **self-incrimination.** (5)

mixed economy. Where the government is a leading economic actor and deeply involved in decisions that affect the economy. The United States can be called a mixed economy. Compare with **capitalism.** (1)

monetarism. An economic theory associated with Milton Friedman that identifies the supply of money as the major determinant of a nation's economic health. Conservative economists generally insist that a swollen supply of money and credit is the main cause of inflation. See also **monetary policy.** (17)

monetary policy. Based on **monetarism,** the manipulation of the supply of money and credit by which the government can control the economy. The **Federal Reserve System** is crucial in making monetary policy. Compare with **fiscal policy.** (17)

multinational corporations. Large businesses with operations in several countries. Many of these companies are larger than most governments. (17)

municipalities. City governments, which are one of four major types of local government. (4)

mutual dependency. When one nation's behavior profoundly affects another nation. (20)

national chairperson. An individual, usually selected by a party's presidential candidate who, along with the **national committee,** is responsible for managing the affairs of the party, organizing the **national party convention,** raising funds, and acting as a liaison among different elements of the party. (7)

national committee. A formal institution of the national parties composed of representatives from the states and territories who, with the **national chairperson,** have the purpose of organizing the **national party convention** as well as keeping the party operating between conventions. (7)

National Environmental Policy Act (NEPA). The centerpiece of federal environmental policy passed in 1969 that established the requirements for **environmental impact statements.** (19)

National Labor Relations Act. A 1935 law, also known as the Wagner Act, that guaranteed workers the right of **collective bargaining,** set down rules to protect unions and organizers, and created the **National Labor Relations Board** to oversee relations between labor and management. (17)

National Labor Relations Board. The body established by the **National Labor Relations Act** in 1935 to regulate labor-management negotiations. (17)

national party convention. The supreme institution of the **political party** that meets every four years primarily for the **nomination** of candidates for president and vice-president and for writing the party's **platform.** (7, 8)

National Security Council (NSC). Part of the **Executive Office of the President** that links the president's key foreign and military advisors. The Council formally consists of the president, vice-president, secretaries of state and defense, and informally includes the president's Special Assistant for National Security Affairs. (13)

NATO. See **North Atlantic Treaty Organization.**

natural rights. Rights held to be inherent in human beings, not dependent on governments. John Locke asserted that natural law, which is superior to human law, specifies certain rights of "life, liberty, and property." This sentiment is reflected in the **Declaration of Independence.** (3)

Near v. Minnesota. The 1931 Supreme Court decision that the **First Amendment** protects newspapers from **prior restraint.** (5)

New Deal coalition. Coalition of voters aligned with the Democratic party due to President Roosevelt's New Deal policies. (7)

New Jersey Plan. The proposal at the Constitutional Convention that called for equal **representation** of each state in Congress regardless of the state's population. Compare with **Virginia Plan** and **Connecticut Compromise.** (3)

New York Times v. Sullivan. The 1964 Supreme Court decision in favor of the *Times* that held that public officials have the right to sue for **libel** only when malice is shown. The Court reasoned that a free press requires that criticism of public officeholders be allowed. (5)

Nineteenth Amendment. The constitutional amendment adopted in 1920 to extend **suffrage** to women. (9, 17)

nomination. A **political party's** endorsement of a candidate for office which is made at the **national party convention.** Winning the nomination game gives a candidate a chance to play for even higher stakes in the election game. (8)

nonrenewable resources. Minerals and other resources that are not readily replenished by nature once consumed. Many commonly used energy resources, such as oil and coal, are nonrenewable. (1, 19)

normative theory. A theory that evaluates rather than merely explains. Normative theories label things good or bad and deal with questions of "should" or "ought to." Normative theories of politics offer judgments about government. Compare with **empirical theory.** (2)

North Atlantic Treaty Organization (NATO). An organization established by a treaty in 1949 between the United States, Canada, most of the western European nations, and Turkey. The members agreed to combine military forces and to treat a war against one as a war against all. (20)

Office of Management and Budget (OMB). Part of the **Executive Office of the President** that, after a reorganization, replaced the Bureau of the Budget, created in 1921. The OMB supervises the preparation of the federal budget and advises the president on budgetary matters. (13, 16)

Office of Personnel Management (OPM). The office in charge of hiring for most agencies in the federal government. The OPM established elaborate rules for hiring, promotions, working conditions, and firing, functions previously performed by the Civil Service Commission. Its members are appointed by the president and confirmed by the Senate. (14)

oil depletion allowance. A tax law that permits oil companies to take a tax deduction for the depletion of their oil supplies. Oil lobbies and members of Congress from oil-producing states have long succeeded in getting this tax advantage. (19)

Olson's law of large groups. According to Mancur Olson, "The larger the group, the further it will fall short of providing an optimal amount of a collective good." In other words, the larger the group, the more serious is the **free-rider problem,** where individuals can partake in a collective good without joining a group. (10)

OPEC. See **Organization of Petroleum Exporting Countries.**

opinion. A statement of legal reasoning behind a decision of a court. (15)

Organization of Petroleum Exporting Countries (OPEC). An economic organization, consisting primarily of Arab nations, that controls the price and amount of oil its members produce and sell to other nations. The United States has become increasingly dependent on foreign oil, such as that provided by OPEC, and this has affected United States **foreign policy** toward the Arab states. (20)

original jurisdiction. The authority of courts where cases are first heard, typically at the trial court level. Compare with **appellate jurisdiction.** (15)

oversight. The process of monitoring the **bureaucracy** and its administration of policy. The legislative oversight role is handled mainly through committee hearings and in reviewing agency budgets. (12)

PAC. See **political action committee.**

party. See **political party.**

party competition. The battle of the parties for control of public office. (7)

party dealignment. A steady decline in the influence of the **political parties** on the voters and the government. (7)

party desertion. A voter's abandonment of either party for a nonparty attachment. (7)

party era.　Long periods of time in which one or the other **political party** claims a consistent majority of the people. (7)

party identification.　The self-classified preference of an individual for one of the **political parties.** (7)

party image.　The general ideology associated with each political party that gives the electorate cues for voting. (7)

party realignment.　The process by which the majority **political party** is displaced by the other major party over a series of elections that constitute a **critical election period.** (7)

patronage.　A key form of inducement that a political **machine** uses to gain support, including providing jobs or contracts to secure an individual's support. Patronage is a hiring and promotion system based on knowing the right people. (7, 14)

Pendleton Act.　A law passed in 1883 that created a federal **civil service** in order to prevent **patronage.** (14)

plaintiff.　The party (government, corporation, or individual) who charges a **defendant** in a court **case** with committing a transgression. (15)

plea-bargaining.　A negotiation between a prosecutor and a **defendant** when the defendant agrees to plead guilty to a lesser charge if the prosecutor agrees to drop the more serious ones. (5)

Plessy v. Ferguson.　An 1896 Supreme Court decision where Louisiana's "equal but separate accommodations for the white and colored races" **segregation,** was not held to be unconstitutional. (15)

plum book.　Published by Congress, it lists top federal jobs, the "plums," available for direct presidential appointment, often with Senate confirmation. (14)

pluralist theory.　A theory which contends that the American **political system** is made up of competition among groups, each vying for policies to foster its own interest. Compare with **elite and class theory, hyperpluralism,** and **traditional democratic theory.** (2)

pocket veto.　When Congress adjourns within ten days after submitting a bill to the president, who simply allows it to die by neither signing nor vetoing it. See also **veto.** (13)

policy.　See **public policy.**

policy agenda.　A set of policy issues that people and policymakers think are important at a given time and demand government action. Agenda refers to priorities. Compare with **public agenda** and **governmental agenda.** (1, 11)

policy communities.　Informally organized groups of policy specialists who research and promote particular policy areas (e.g., drugs, aging, water pollution control). (11)

policy entrepreneur.　One who invests his or her political "capital" in a policy issue. Policy entrepreneurs may be public officials, aspiring officials, or private individuals. (11)

policy impacts.　The effects a **public policy** has on people and problems. Analyzing impacts means assessing how well a policy has met its goal and at what cost. (1)

policy implementation.　See **implementation.**

policy voting.　When the policy positions of a **political party** or candidate influence how a person votes. (9)

policy window.　An opportunity for advocates of a particular policy area to draw attention to their special interests and proposed solutions. (11)

political action committee (PAC).　A corporation, union, or interest group that is specifically permitted to put its money directly into political campaigns. PACs have proliferated in recent years. (8)

political consultant.　A campaign professional who is engaged primarily to give advice and services (such as polling, media creation and production, and direct mail fund-raising) to candidates, their campaigns, and other political groups. (11)

political economy.　The ways economic factors influence political and governmental decision-making, and vice versa. (1)

political efficacy.　The belief that one's **political participation** really matters, that one's vote, for example, can make a difference. (9)

political ideology.　A coherent set of beliefs about politics and public policy. (6)

political issue.　An issue over which people disagree, and at least some of them want government to enact a policy about it. (1)

political participation.　Includes all activities by citizens aimed at influencing the selection of political officeholders or the public policies they pursue. Participation is one of the basic principles of **traditional democratic theory.** (6)

political party.　According to Anthony Downs, a "team of men [and women] seeking to control the governing apparatus by gaining office in a duly constituted election." See also **national party convention** and **nomination.** (7)

political socialization.　The process by which an individual acquires a political orientation, including learning about **politics** and **public policy.** See also **agents of socialization.** (6)

political system.　A set of institutions and activities that link people, **politics,** and **public policy.** (1)

politics.　According to Harold Lasswell, "who gets what, when, and how." Politics involves conflict over what **governments** should do. (1)

pork barrel.　The list of federal projects, grants,

and contracts available to cities, businesses, colleges, and institutions in a district. For members of Congress, these provide a means of "servicing the constituency." See also **casework.** (12)

potential group.   Composed of all people who might be group members because they share some common interest. Potential groups are almost always larger than **actual groups.** (10)

poverty line.   According to the Bureau of the Census, this line is drawn at a sum of money that takes into account what a family would need to spend for "austere" but minimally adequate amounts of nutrition, housing, and other needs. (18)

power.   According to Robert Dahl, the capacity to get others to do something they would not otherwise do. The desire for power is one reason why people play the **politics** game. (1)

precedent.   The way similar **cases** were settled in the past that proves to be important in later decisions. (15)

presidential primary.   An election in which party voters in a state vote for a candidate (or a slate of delegates committed to the candidate) as their choice for the party's **nomination.** (8)

press secretary.   The White House official responsible for sharing the president's perspective on the news with reporters. (13)

price supports.   Mechanisms through which the federal government guarantees the prices of certain agricultural commodities, often by buying surplus crops to keep prices high. In return for this, farmers must accept some government **regulation.** (17)

primary.   See **presidential primary.**

prior restraint.   Governmental approval of newspaper articles before they are published. This is a common method of limiting the press in some nations but is unconstitutional in the United States, according to the **First Amendment** and confirmed in the 1931 Supreme Court case of *Near v. Minnesota.* (5)

probable cause.   When the police have reason to believe that a person should be arrested. In making the arrest, they are allowed legally to search for and seize incriminating evidence. Compare with **unreasonable search and seizure.** (5)

procurement.   The purchase of military hardware. (16)

progressive tax.   A tax that takes a bigger share of a rich family's income than of a poor family's income. Compare with **proportional tax** and **regressive tax.** (18)

proportional tax.   A tax that takes the same share, or portion, of income from everyone, rich and poor. Compare with **progressive tax** and **regressive tax.** (18)

Proposition 13.   A 1978 proposition on the California ballot that called for a cut in property taxes by limiting tax rates on houses and property to 1 percent of market value; marked the beginning of the tax revolt movement in the United States. (16)

protest.   A form of **political participation** in which people try to achieve policy change through dramatic and unconventional tactics that are also meant to attract the attention of the media. (6)

public agenda.   The set of issues the public as a whole considers important. Compare with **governmental agenda** and **policy agenda.** (11)

public interest.   A collective good; interests superior to the private interests of groups and individuals. (10)

public interest lobbies.   According to Jeffrey Berry, organizations that seek "a collective good, the achievement of which will not selectively and materially benefit the membership or activists of the organization." They lobby, in other words, on behalf of the public interest. (10)

public opinion.   The distribution of the population's beliefs about politics and policy issues. (6)

public policy.   The course of action **government** takes in response to some **political issue.** When government acts, in one way or another or not at all, public policy results. (1)

reconciliation resolution.   An important part of establishing a **budget** that requires both houses of Congress to agree on the bottom-line spending limit for all programs before they begin to appropriate funds for individual programs. (16)

referendum.   Form of direct legislation in which voters are given the chance to approve or disapprove a law passed by the legislature or a proposed constitutional amendment. (9)

Regents of the University of California v. Bakke.   A 1978 Supreme Court decision that a state university could not admit less qualified individuals solely because of their race. The Court did not, however, rule that such **affirmative action** policies and the use of race as a criterion for admission were unconstitutional, only that they had to be formulated differently. (15)

registration.   A system that began in the 1890s in the United States requiring voters to meet certain conditions, such as length of residency in an area, and register in advance of the election day in order to be allowed to vote. (9)

regressive tax.   A tax which takes a bigger share of a poor family's income than of a rich family's income. Compare with **progressive tax** and **proportional tax.** (18)

regulation.   The use of governmental authority to control or change some practice in the private sector. (14)

regulatory agency. See **independent regulatory agency.**

reinforcement. A consequence of political campaigns for voters in which the voter's preference for his or her candidate is reinforced. See also **activation** and **conversion.** (8)

representation. The relationship between the few leaders and the many followers. Representation is one of the basic principles of **traditional democratic theory.** (2)

responsible party model. A model proposed by the American Political Science Association calling for parties and voters to meet certain criteria in order to become more effective. The parties, according to the model, must have an **ideology,** offer clear alternatives to voters, and carry out their promises once elected; the voters must examine the party's promises and its ideology and vote accordingly. (7)

revenue sharing. A program in which the federal government allocates funds to states and cities with virtually no strings attached. Compare with **block grants** and **categorical grants.** (4)

revenues. The financial resources of the federal government; the individual income tax and social insurance tax are two major sources of income. (16)

right to counsel. The right of the accused to have a lawyer defend his or her case in court. This right is protected by the **Sixth Amendment** and has been extended to apply to all felony cases where imprisonment may be imposed when the **defendant** cannot afford to hire a lawyer. See also *Gideon v. Wainwright* and *Miranda v. Arizona.* (5)

right to privacy. Prohibits some intrusions by the government into private decisions, such as those about sex and the conception of life. The right to privacy is implicitly protected by the **First,** Third, Fourth, **Fifth,** and Ninth **Amendments.** (5)

right-to-work law. A state law that forbids requirements that workers must join a union to hold their jobs. State right-to-work laws were specifically permitted by the Taft-Hartley Act of 1947. (17)

Roe v. *Wade.* A 1973 Supreme Court decision that a state ban on all abortions was an unconstitutional infringement on a woman's personal privacy. It laid down the rule that a state cannot forbid abortions during the first trimester of pregnancy. (5)

Roth v. *United States.* A 1957 Supreme Court decision that obscenity was not within the area of constitutionally protected speech or press. (5)

SALT. See **Strategic Arms Limitation Talks.**

Schenck v. *United States.* The 1919 Supreme Court decision in which Justice Holmes argued that government can restrain free speech only when speech provokes a **clear and present danger** to people. (5)

school districts. One of the four major types of local government that are distinct from both city and county governments and are responsible for elementary and secondary education. (4)

search warrant. A written authorization from a judge that specifies what the police are looking for and why they believe incriminating evidence will be found. It must be obtained in advance in order to make a legal search of a person's home or other premises. (5)

Secretary of Defense. The president's main military advisor and head of the Department of Defense. (20)

Secretary of State. The key advisor to the president on foreign-policy matters and head of the Department of State. (20)

segregation. When social customs or public policies require the separation of specific groups in schools, housing, or other public or private activities. See also **discrimination.** (18)

select committees. Congressional committees in either the House of Representatives or the Senate that are appointed for a specific purpose, such as to investigate an event or problem. (12)

self-incrimination. When an individual accused of a crime is compelled to be a witness against himself or herself in court. The **Fifth Amendment** forbids self-incrimination. See also *Miranda v. Arizona.* (5)

Senate Finance Committee. The Senate committee responsible for writing tax codes that are subject to the approval of the Congress as a whole. (16)

senatorial courtesy. A tradition in the Senate that a senator of the president's party can veto a federal judicial appointment in his state by stating that the appointment is "personally obnoxious." The Senate may then reject the nomination. (15)

seniority system. The method of selecting committee **chairmen,** exclusively used until the 1970s, where the longest serving committee member whose party controlled Congress automatically became the chairman, regardless of his or her loyalty to the party, mental state, or competence. It still plays an important role in the selection process. (12)

separation of powers. An important part of the **Madisonian model** that required each of the three branches of government—executive, legislative, and judicial—to be relatively independent of one another so one could not control the others. Power is shared among these three institutions. See also **checks and balances.** (3)

severance taxes. Means used by several states to enhance their revenue bases; these taxes are most often levied on minerals (oil, coal, and gas) exported to other states. (4)

Shays's Rebellion. A series of attacks on court-houses by a small band of farmers led by Revolutionary

War Captain Daniel Shays, to block foreclosure proceedings. (3)

single issue groups. Groups that are characterized by their narrow interest, their tendency to dislike compromise, and their practice of often drawing membership from people new to politics. See also **single issue politics.** (2)

single issue politics. Politics where **single issue groups** are fixed on one interest and are often unwilling to compromise. Abortion, nuclear power, and gun control are examples of issues where single issue groups and politics have emerged in recent years. (2)

Sixteenth Amendment. The constitutional amendment adopted in 1915 that explicitly permitted Congress to levy an income tax. (16)

Sixth Amendment. The constitutional amendment designed to protect individuals accused of crimes, including the **right to counsel,** the right to confront witnesses, and the right to a speedy and public trial. (5)

Social Security Act. A 1935 law passed during the Roosevelt administration that was intended to provide a minimal level of sustenance to older Americans. (16)

Speaker of the House. The legislative leader of the House of Representatives chosen by the majority party and second in line (behind the vice-president) to succeed a deceased or removed president. (12)

special districts. The most numerous of the four major types of local government that handle such policy responsibilities as airport operation, mosquito abatement, and health care. (4)

standing committees. Congressional subject-matter committees that handle bills in different policy areas. Both the House of Representatives and the Senate have their own standing committees. (12)

stare decisis. Latin for "let the decision stand," a principle on which American courts heavily rely in enforcing norms. (15)

Strategic Arms Limitation Talks (SALT). A major initiative coming out of **détente** that represented an effort by the United States and the Soviet Union to agree to scale down their nuclear capabilities while each maintaining sufficient power to prevent a surprise attack by the other. Two SALT agreements were signed by the two nations, one in 1972 and one in 1979, although the latter was never approved by the Senate. See also **Strategic Arms Reduction Talks.** (20)

Strategic Arms Reduction Talks (START). Begun in Geneva by President Reagan to follow up on the **Strategic Arms Limitation Talks (SALT)** between the United States and the Soviet Union. (20)

street-level bureaucrat. According to Michael Lipsky, those bureaucrats, or government services employees, who are in constant contact with the public (often a hostile public) and who have considerable discretion. Police officers, welfare workers, and lower court judges are examples. (14)

subgovernments. The network of interest group leaders, an administering agency, and members of congressional committees and subcommittees, all concerned with the same policy. These relationships are also known as iron triangles. (10)

suffrage. The legal right to vote, extended to blacks by the **Fifteenth Amendment,** to women by the **Nineteenth Amendment,** and to people over the age of eighteen by the **Twenty-sixth Amendment.** (9)

Sunbelt. States and cities of the southern regions of the United States that have experienced growth in population and jobs as people move there from the **Frostbelt.** (4)

superfund. A $1.6 billion fund created by Congress in the late 1970s to clean up toxic waste sites. Money comes from taxes and fees charged to chemical companies. (19)

supply-side economics. The theory, advocated by President Reagan, that the economy can be restimulated by increasing the supply of resources in the private sector while reducing the size of the public sector. Tax reductions are a key part of supply-side economics. (1, 16, 17)

Swann v. *Charlotte-Mecklenburg County Schools.* A 1951 Supreme Court decision that upheld the right of judges to order school busing, although this policy continued to be met with resistance in many areas. (15)

tariff. A special tax added to the cost of imported goods. (20)

tax expenditure. Defined by the 1974 Budget Act as "revenue losses attributable to provisions of the federal tax laws which allow a special exemption, exclusion, or deduction." Tax exemptions amount to subsidies for some activities. (16)

Tenth Amendment. The constitutional amendment that holds that the states or the people are supreme over all activities that are not delegated to the national government or prohibited by the Constitution. (4)

third parties. Electoral contenders other than those of the two major parties. (7)

Thirteenth Amendment. A constitutional amendment passed after the Civil War that forbade slavery and involuntary servitude. (18)

Three-fifths Compromise. The decision reached at the Constitutional Convention that representatives in Congress would be based on the number of "free persons" plus three-fifths of "all other persons." Each slave, then, would be counted as three-fifths of a person. (3)

ticket splitting. Not voting the "straight ticket" in an election, which would be voting for every candidate affiliated with one of the political parties. Instead, the voter picks candidates from different parties, thereby "splitting" his or her vote. (7)

trade-offs. When some of one goal may have to be sacrificed in order to achieve another goal. Public policymaking as choice-taking usually involves making trade-offs. (1)

traditional democratic theory. A theory of **democracy** based on several principles: that people are equal, that information must be full and free, that participation should be high, that "the rule" of the majority is preferred, and that the leaders should represent the followers. See also **actual representation, majority rule,** and **political participation.** (2)

tragedy of the commons. Garrett Hardin's parable, illustrating that even though individual overconsumption may seem inconsequential, collective overconsumption of a common resource can eventually deplete the resource altogether to the detriment of all. (19)

transfer payments. Government payments in cash or things of cash value to individuals, increasing their **income.** Welfare benefits are an example of a cash transfer payments; food stamps are an example of a noncash, "in-kind" transfer. (18)

Twenty-fifth Amendment. A constitutional amendment adopted in 1967 that permits the vice-president to become acting president if both he and the president's **cabinet** determine the president is disabled. It also outlines how a recuperated president can reclaim his office. (13)

Twenty-second Amendment. A constitutional amendment adopted in 1951 that limits presidents to two four-year terms of office. (13)

Twenty-sixth Amendment. A constitutional amendment adopted in 1971 to extend **suffrage** to everyone over the age of eighteen. (9)

Twenty-third Amendment. A constitutional amendment adopted in 1961 that gave residents of the District of Columbia the right to select presidential electors, just as residents of the states do. (9)

uncontrollable expenditures. A result from policies that make some group of people (or governments) automatically eligible for some benefit. Social security and grants-in-aid are the two biggest uncontrollable items for the federal government. (16)

unemployment rate. As measured by the Bureau of Labor Statistics (BLS), the proportion of the labor force actively seeking work but unable to find jobs. (17)

unitary government. Exists when all formal authority rests with a central government. Geographical subdivisions, when they exist, are only administrative outposts of the central government. Compare with **federalism.** (4)

United Nations (UN). An international organization created in 1945 and headquartered in New York City, whose members, now representing 157 nations, agree to renounce war and respect certain human and economic freedoms. (20)

United States v. *Nixon.* The 1974 decision in which the Supreme Court unanimously held that the doctrine of executive privilege was implicit in the Constitution but could not be extended to protect documents relevant to criminal prosecutions. (15)

unreasonable search and seizure. Obtaining evidence in a haphazard or random manner, a practice prohibited by the **Fourteenth Amendment.** Both **probable cause** and a **search warrant** are required for a legal and proper search for and seizure of incriminating evidence. (5)

unwritten constitution. The body of tradition, practice, and procedure that is as important as the written **Constitution.** Changes in the unwritten constitution can change the spirit of the Constitution. **Political parties** and **national party conventions** are a part of the unwritten constitution in the United States. (3)

veto. The rejection of a congressional bill by the president. If a president vetoes a bill, it is sent back to Congress, where it can be overridden and made into law with a two-thirds vote in each house. See also **pocket veto.** (13)

Virginia Plan. The proposal at the Constitutional Convention that called for **representation** of each state in Congress in proportion to each state's share of the United States population. Compare with **New Jersey Plan** and **Connecticut Compromise.** (3)

Voting Rights Act of 1965. A law designed to help put an end to formal and informal barriers to black **suffrage.** Under this law, federal registrars went to many southern states and counties to register blacks, many of whom had never voted before. In 1982, the Voting Rights Act was extended for another twenty-five years. (9, 17)

War Powers Act. A law passed in 1973 that emphasized the right of Congress to declare war but also spelled out the conditions under which the president could commit American troops without congressional approval. (13)

Warsaw Pact. A regional security community of the Soviet Union and its eastern European allies. (20)

Watergate. The events and scandal surrounding a break-in at the Democratic National Committee headquarters in 1972 and the subsequent cover-up of White House involvement, leading to the eventual resignation of President Nixon under the threat of **impeachment.** (13)

Water Pollution Control Act. A 1972 law intended to clean up the nation's lakes and rivers. It requires polluters to obtain licenses to pollute from the **Environmental Protection Agency** so that discharges of waste can be monitored and controlled. (19)

wealth. The amount of funds already owned. Compare with **income.** (18)

Weber v. *Kaiser Aluminum Company.* A 1979 Supreme Court decision that Kaiser's union-management sponsored training program was intended to rectify years of past employment **discrimination** by the company and was not, therefore, unconstitutional. (1, 15)

whips. Party leadership positions in the House of Representatives and the Senate. Whips work with the **majority leaders** by carrying the word to party troops, counting votes beforehand, and leaning on waverers whose votes are crucial to a bill. (12)

writ of certiorari. A formal document issued by the Supreme Court by which it puts a case on its docket. The "rule of four" means that at least four Supreme Court justices must agree that a case merits the Court's attention before it is called up for review. (15)

Zurcher v. *Stanford Daily.* A 1978 Supreme Court decision that a proper **search warrant** can be applied to a newspaper just as it is applied to anyone else without necessarily violating the **First Amendment** right to freedom of the press. (5)

Index

The pages on which definitions appear are given in italics. See also the Glossary (pages 661–676).

679